Nili Shupak

Where can Wisdom be found?

ORBIS BIBLICUS ET ORIENTALIS

Published by the Biblical Institute of the University
of Fribourg Switzerland
the Seminar für Biblische Zeitgeschichte
of the University of Münster i.W. Federal Republic of Germany
and the Schweizerische Gesellschaft
für orientalische Altertumswissenschaft
Editor: Othmar Keel
Coeditors: Erich Zenger and Albert de Pury

The Author:

Nili Shupak, born in Haifa, studied Old Testament, Egyptology and Archaeology at the Hebrew University in Jerusalem (1967ff.). She spent two years at the Egyptological Institute of the University of Tübingen as a research fellow of DAAD (1978-1979). Dr. Shupak obtained her Ph. D. in Biblical Studies at the Hebrew University (1984). She worked as an Assistant in the Biblical Studies Department at Ben-Gurion University in Beer-Sheba as well as in the Israel Museum in Jerusalem (1968-1973). Since 1975 she teaches at the University of Haifa where she is a Senior Lecturer in the Departments of Biblical Studies and the History of Israel. As a visiting Assistant Professor she taught at the Jewish Theological Seminary of America in New York (1989). Her research interests lie in the field of the linguistic, cultural and historical contacts between Ancient Egypt and Israel, on which she has published numerous articles in various periodicals and encyclopaedias. She published as well an *Introduction to the Old Testament Wisdom Literature* in the series «The Open University» (Hebrew) (1990). At present she is engaged in preparing the publication of a Corpus of Egyptian Wisdom texts.

Orbis Biblicus et Orientalis 130

Nili Shupak

Where can Wisdom be found?

The Sage's Language in the Bible and in Ancient Egyptian Literature

University Press Fribourg Switzerland
Vandenhoeck & Ruprecht Göttingen

Die Deutsche Bibliothek – CIP-Einheitsaufnahme

Shupak, Nili: Where can wisdom be found?: the sage's language in the Bible and in ancient Egyptian literature / Nili Shupak. - Freiburg/Schweiz: Univ.-Verl.; Göttingen: Vandenhoeck und Ruprecht, 1993
(Orbis biblicus et orientalis; 130)
ISBN 3-525-53765-4 (Vandenhoeck und Ruprecht)
ISBN 3-7278-0899-3 (Univ.-Verl.)
NE: GT

Die Druckvorlagen wurden von der Verfasserin als reprofertige Dokumente zur Verfügung gestellt

Paulusdruckerei Freiburg Schweiz

ISBN 3-7278-0899-3 (University Press)
ISBN 3-525-53765-4 (Vandenhoeck & Ruprecht)

In memory of

my beloved aunt

Rena Nuss-Talmor

CONTENTS

LIST OF TABLES

ACKNOWLEDGEMENTS

This book began as a doctoral thesis submitted to the Hebrew University of Jerusalem in 1984. Since then many studies have been published on Biblical wisdom literature and relevant Egyptian literature, as have new Egyptian texts belonging to the wisdom cycle. In light of these, and my own subsequent work, my views have changed on a number of matters. The present book is the result of this ongoing research. As far as possible, I have tried to take account of the pertinent literature as available up to 1990.

To collect the Egyptian material, I received a grant from the Deutscher Akademischer Austauschdient for a stay at the Egyptological Institute of Tübingen University in 1978-1980. Similarly, I received awards from the Memorial Foundation for Jewish Culture and from the Peri foundation of the Hebrew University. For these I am indeed grateful.

I owe a personal debt of thanks to several people. My supervisors in the doctoral research were Professor M. Haran and the late Professor J. Polotsky, whose guidance also exerted an effect on the present work. Special thanks go to Professor H. Brunner, who during my years in Tübingen acquainted me with the secrets of Egyptian wisdom. I am indebted to him not only for his incisive comments and advice while the thesis was in progress but also for making me feel so welcome on my frequent subsequent visits to Germany. Professor Brunner also kindly gave of his time to write the *Geleitwort* to this book.

Thanks are also due to my friend and colleague Dr. B. Ockinga, who read parts of the book and made helpful suggestions for improving the English style. Likewise I thank my colleagues at the University of Haifa Dr. T. Fenton and Professor B. Kedar, with whom I held discussions on various problems regarding the book; and also my friends Eng. G. Landau and S. Nathan for help in reading proofs.

M. Raveh worked with me on the translation and contributed greatly to improving the English style. D. Bruggeman applied his consistent efficiency to editing the book and preparing it for print. H. Kernoff typeset the first part of it and G. Breitstein the remainder, expertly and with rare devotion. I am indebted to them all.

The Faculty of Humanities of the University of Haifa gave financial support toward the printing costs of this research, for which I am deeply grateful.

Particular thanks are owed to the Research Authority of the University of Haifa, which financed the preparation of the book for printing, and above all to Professor O. Keel, who has honored me by publishing the book in the OBO series.

Haifa, November 1991 Nili Shupak

ABBREVIATIONS AND SYMBOLS

AA	*Alttestamentliche Abhandlungen* (Münster)
AAA	*Annals of Archaeology and Anthropology* (Liverpool)
ÄAT	*Ägypten und Altes Testament*, ed. M. Görg (Wiesbaden)
AB	*The Anchor Bible* (New York)
AEA	M. Lichtheim, *Ancient Egyptian Autobiographies Chiefly of the Middle Kingdom: A Study and an Anthology, OBO* 84, (Freiburg-Göttingen 1988)
ÄgHWb	A. Erman and H. Grapow, *Ägyptisches Handwörterbuch* (Hildesheim 1961)
ÄHG	J. Assmann, *Ägyptische Hymnen und Gebete* (Zurich-Munich 1975)
AJSL	*American Journal of Semitic Languages and Literatures* (Chicago)
Akka.	Akkadian
ANET	*Ancient Near Eastern Texts Relating to the Old Testament*, ed. J.B. Pritchard (Princeton 1955)
ANOR	*Analecta Orientalia*
Arab.	Arabic
Aram.	Aramaic
AW	H. Brunner, *Altägyptische Weisheit* (Zurich-Munich 1988)
BDB	F. Brown, S.R. Driver, C.A. Briggs, *A Hebrew-English Lexicon of the O.T.* (Oxford 1966^{6})
BIFAO	*Bulletin de l'Institut Français d'Archéologie Orientale* (Cairo)
Blumenthal	E. Blumenthal, *Untersuchungen zum ägyptischen Königtum des Mittleren Reiches* I. *Die Phraseologie, Abhandlungen der sächsischen Akademie der Wissenschaften zu Leipzig* 61/1 (Berlin 1970)
BM	British Museum

BN	*Biblische Notizen* (Bamberg)
BS	*The Book Ben Sira, Text, Concordance and an Analysis of the Vocabulary*, the Academy of the Hebrew Language and the Shrine of the Book (Jerusalem 1973)
BZAW	*Beihefte zur Zeitschrift für die alttestamentlichen Wissenschaft* (Berlin)
Calice	F. Calice, *Grundlagen der ägyptisch-semitischen Wortvergleichung*; *Beihefte zur Wiener Zeitschrift für die Kunde des Morgenlandes* 1 (Wien 1936)
CB	*Cambridge Bible for Schools and Colleges* (Cambridge)
CBQ	*Catholic Biblical Quarterly* (Washington)
Černý	J. Černý, *Coptic Etymological Dictionary* (Cambridge 1976)
Copt.[SABF]	Coptic dialects: Sa'idic, Achmimic, Bohairic, Fayyumic
Crum	W.E. Crum, *A Coptic Dictionary* (Oxford 1962)
DE	*Discussions in Egyptology* (Oxford)
Dem.	Demotic
Dyn.	Dynasty
Eg.	Egyptian
EMiqr	*Encyclopaedia Biblica* (Jerusalem 1965-1982) (Hebrew)
Erichsen	W. Erichsen, *Demotisches Glossar* (Copenhagen 1954)
FaL	*Fragen an die altägyptische Literature, Studien zum Gedenken an E. Otto*, eds. J. Assmann, E. Feucht, R. Grieshammer (Wiesbaden 1977)
Faulkner	R.O. Faulkner, *A Concise Dictionary of Middle Egyptian* (Oxford 1964)
GM	*Göttinger Miszellen* (Bamberg-Munich)
Gr	A. Gardiner, *Egyptian Grammar* (London 1966[3])
Gr.	Greek
Griffith Studies	*Studies presented to F. Ll. Griffith* (London 1932)
Hamito-Semitica	*Hamito-Semitica: Proceedings of Colloquium Held by the Historical Section of the Linguistics Association at the School of Oriental and African Studies, University of London, on the 18th, 19th, 20th March 1970*, eds. J. and T. Bynon (The Hague-Paris 1975)

HAT	*Handbuch zum Alten Testament* (Tübingen)
Heb.	Hebrew
HH	H. Brunner, *Das hörende Herz, Kleine Schriften zur Religions- und Geistesgeschichte Ägyptens,* ed. W. Röllig, *OBO* (Freiburg 1988)
Hier. Ostr.	*Hieratic Ostraca* I, J. Černý and A.H. Gardiner (Oxford 1957)
HO	*Handbuch der Orientalistik*, ed. B. Spuler, I/2 *Ägyptologie: Literatur* (Leiden 1952)
HTR	*Harvard Theological Review* (Cambridge)
HUCA	*Hebrew Union College Annual* (Cincinnati)
ICC	*The International Critical Commentary* (Edinburgh)
Isr. Wisd.	*Israelite Wisdom, Theological and Literary Essays in Honor of S. Terrien*, ed. J.G. Gammie et al. (New York 1978)
JAC	*Jahrbuch für Antike und Christentum* (Münster-Westfalen)
Janssen	J. Janssen, *De Traditioneele Egyptische Autobiografie vóór Het Nieuwe Rijk* — I *Teksten*; II *Vertaling en Commentaar* (Leiden 1946)
Jansen-Winkeln	K. Jansen-Winkeln, *Ägyptische Biographien der 22. und 23 Dynastie*, Teil I: *Übersetzung und Kommentar*, Teil II: *Phraseologie*, Teil III: *Texte* (Wiesbaden 1985)
JAOS	*Journal of the American Oriental Society* (New Haven)
JARCE	*Journal of the American Research Center in Egypt* (Cambridge, Mass.)
JBL	*Journal of Biblical Literature* (New York - New Haven - Philadelphia)
JBR	*Journal of Bible and Religion* (Boston)
JEA	*Journal of Egyptian Archeology* (London)
JEOL	*Jaarbericht van het Vooraziatisch — Egyptisch Gezelschap Ex Oriente Lux* (Leiden)
JNES	*Journal of Near Eastern Studies* (Chicago)
JNSL	*Journal of Northwest Semitic Languages* (Stellenbosch, South Africa)

JSOR	*Journal of the Society of Oriental Research* (Toronto)
JSS	*Journal of Semitic Studies* (Manchester)
JSSEA	*Journal of the Society for the Study of Egyptian Antiquities*
JTS	*Journal of Theological Studies* (Oxford)
JQR	*Jewish Quarterly Review* (Philadelphia)
KAT	*Kommentar zum Alten Testament* (Leipzig)
KBL	L. Koehler and W. Baumgartner, *Lexicon in Veteris Testamenti Libros* (Leiden 1985 [1958]).
KBL[3]	W. Baumgartner, *Hebräisches und aramäisches Lexikon zum Alten Testament* (Leiden 1967-1990)
KCG	*Kairo Catalogue General* (Cairo 1914)
LÄ	*Lexikon der Ägyptologie*, eds. W. Helck and W. Westendorf (Wiesbaden 1972-1989)
LEM	*Late Egyptian Miscellanies*, A.H. Gardiner, *Bibliotheca Aegyptica* VII (Brussels 1937); translation and Commentary: B.A. Caminos, *Brown Egyptological Studies* I (London 1954)
Les.	K. Sethe, *Ägyptische Lesestücke, Texte des Mittleren Reiches* (Hildesheim 1959)
Lesko	L.H. Lesko, *A Dictionary of Late Egyptian*, vols. I-IV (Providence 1982-1989)
LEWL	M. Lichtheim, *Late Egyptian Wisdom Literature in the International Context; A Study of Demotic Instructions*, *OBO* 52 (1983)
MDAIK	*Mitteilungen des Deutschen Archäologischen Instituts* (Cairo)
Meeks	D. Meeks, *Anneé Lexicographique*: I (1977), II (1978), III (1979) (Paris 1980-82)
Mél. Masp.	*Mélanges Maspero*, vol. I, *Orient Ancien* (Cairo 1935-38)
OBO	*Orbis Biblicus et Orientalis* (Freiburg/Schweiz - Göttingen)
OLZ	*Orientalistische Literaturzeitung* (Leipzig - Berlin)
OTL	*The Old Testament Library* (London)
Otto	E. Otto, *Die biographischen Inschriften der ägyptischen*

	Spätzeit, Ihre Geisgesteschichte und literarische Bedeutung (Leiden 1954)
Pap.	Papyrus
Polotsky	H.J. Polotsky, *Zu den Inschriften der 11. Dynastie* (Hildesheim 1964)
PSBA	*Proceedings of the Society of Biblical Archaeology* (Bloomsbury-London)
PWM	W. McKane, *Prophets and Wise Men, Studies in Biblical Theology* 44 (London 1965)
RÄR	H. Bonnet, *Reallexikon der ägyptischen Religiongeschichte* (Berlin-New York 1971[2])
RB	*Revue Biblique* (Paris)
Rd'E	*Revue d'Egyptologie* (Cairo)
Rössler	O. Rössler, *Das Ägyptische als semitische Sprache, Christentum am Roten Meer* I, eds. F. Altheim, and R. Steehl (Berlin-New York 1971), 263-326
SAIW	*Studies in Ancient Israelite Wisdom*, ed. J.L. Crenshaw (New York 1976)
SAK	*Studien zur altägyptischen Kultur* (Hamburg)
SAL	*Studien zu altägyptischen Lebenslehren*, eds. E. Hornung and O. Keel, *OBO* 28 (1979)
Sandman	H.M. Sandman, *Texts from the Time of Akhenaten* (Brussells 1938)
SAT	*La Sagesse de l'Ancien Testament*, ed. M. Gilbert (Louvain 1979).
SBL	*Society of Biblical Literature*
SIANE	*The Sage in Israel and the Ancient Near East*, eds. J.G. Gammie and L.G. Perdue (Winona Lake 1990).
SPOA	*Les Sagesses du Proche-Orient Ancien. Colloque de Strasbourg, 17-19 Mai 1962* (Paris 1963)
SVT	*Supplements to Vetus Testamentum* (Leiden)
Syr.	Syriac
TDOT	*Theological Dictionary of the Old Testament*, eds. G.J. Botterweck and H. Ringgren, trans. J.T. Willis, vols. I-VI (Michigan 1977ff.)

Thesaurus	S.E. Loewenstamm and J. Blau, *Thesaurus of the Language of the Bible* (Jerusalem 1957), vols. I-III
ThLZ	*Theologische Literaturzeitung* (Leipzig-Berlin)
TWAT	*Theologisches Wörterbuch zum Alten Testament*, eds. G.J. Botterweck, H. Ringgren and H.J. Fabry (Stuttgart-Berlin- Cologne- Mainz 1973ff.) vols. IV, V, VI
Ugar.	Ugaritic
Urk. IV	K. Sethe, *Urkunden der 18 Dynastie*, 4 vols. (Leipzig 1927-1930[2]); W. Helck, Heft 17-22 (Berlin 1955-1958)
VT	*Vetus Testamentum* (Leiden)
Wb.	*Wörterbuch der ägyptischen Sprache*, eds. A. Erman and H.Grapow, 7 vols. (Berlin-Leipzig 1926-1963)
WC	*Westminster Commentaries* (London)
WdO	*Die Welt des Orients*, eds. W. Röllig and W. von Soden (Göttingen)
Westendorf	W. Westendorf, *Koptisches Handwörterbuch* (Heidelberg 1965-1967)
WZKM	*Wiener Zeitschrift für die Kunde des Morgenlandes* (Vienna)
ZÄS	*Zeitschrift für ägyptische Sprache und Altertumskunde* (Leipzig-Berlin)
ZAW	*Zeitschrift für die alttestamentliche Wissenschaft* (Berlin)
ZDMG	*Zeitschrift der Deutschen Morgenländischen Gesellschaft* (Leipzig-Wiesbaden)
‖	Synonymous parallelism
#	Antithetic parallelism
( )	Parentheses, enclose additions in the English translation
[ ]	Square brackets, enclose restorations
...	Row of dots, ellipsis in the English translation

GLOSSARY

analogous	similar to.
cognate	a word in one language that has the same root and similar meaning as one in another language.
collocation	a combination of words which "naturally" go together.
conjunction	a word or preposition that characteristically links words or sentences (the commonest conjunction in Biblical Hebrew is w^e ["and"]).
equivalent	a word equal in meaning, a precise semantic parallel.
expression	a word or group of words.
idiom	an expression peculiar to a language; usually a fixed group of words with a special meaning which is different from the meaning of the individual words.
lexeme	a dictionary item.
parallel	a word that is clearly similar or comparable to another word.
phrase	a group of words forming a unit.
Psalm with wisdom features	a Psalm where wisdom ideas or terms, or both, may be found but which is not commonly regarded as wisdom Psalm.

GELEITWORT

Es hat im Abendland Zeiten gegeben, in denen die Weisheit der Bibel, voran das Buch der Sprichwörter (Proverbien), eine dominante Rolle im Geistesleben, nicht nur in der Erziehung, gespielt hat. In der altorientalischen Weisheit, die damals in Europa nur durch die im Alten Testament erhaltenen Beispiele bekannt war, bestimmt ein klares, elementares Menschenbild auch die Erziehung: Der junge Mann soll selbstbeherrscht, fleißig, fromm, dem Staate (=König) loyal ergeben sein, sich allen Menschen höflich und gerecht zuwenden.

Mit dem Aufkommen der Individualpsychologie im 19.Jahdt. trat diese Art der Betrachtung des Menschen und seiner Bewährung in Staat und Gesellschaft zurück — andere Bücher der Bibel fanden in Kirche und Theologie, im allgemeinen Geistesleben und auch in der Wissenschaft stärkere Beachtung. Das ist weitgehend bis heute so geblieben; lediglich die Bibelwissenschaft schenkte den M^{e}šalim und einigen ihnen in Haltung und Form nahestehenden Teilen der Bibel, vor allem gewissen Partien des Buches Hiob, vermehrtes Interesse, seit eine ägyptische "Quelle" einiger Teile der "Sprüche Salomos" entdeckt worden war.

Ist es wirklich nur jene kleine Schrift des deutschen Ägyptologen Adolf Erman aus dem Jahre 1923 gewesen, die bei den Theologen, und nicht nur bei diesen, den Blick erneut auf die biblische Weisheit lenkte? Ob sich nun diese philologische Entdeckung mit einer geänderten geistigen Verfassung traf oder nicht, jedenfalls verlangte sie eine neue Sicht der Beziehungen zwischen Israel und Ägypten. Die Besetzung Palästinas durch Ägyptische Truppen (etwa 1500 bis 1200) hatte mehr als nur militärische und wirtschaftliche Bedeutung, wurde doch damals der Grund gelegt für Anerkennung der Überlegenheit der Niltalkultur, die noch jahrhundertelang in Palästina-Syrien ihren Ausdruck u.a. in der

Übernahme zahlloser ägyptischer Motive in Kunst und Kleinkunst (Skarabäen!) finden sollte. Als dann Salomo das Davidische Großreich mit einer soliden Verwaltung auszustatten hatte, nahm er sich Ägypten, den Beamtenstaat, zum Vorbild, und das wiederum hatte, wenn nicht geradezu eine Übernahme, so doch eine starke Beeinflussung des Schulsystems zur Folge, hatte doch die "Schule" als wichtigsten, vielleicht sogar einzigen Zweck die Ausbildung von Verwaltungsbeamten vor Augen — in Ägypten wie in Israel-Juda.

Nun fanden sich damals, zu Beginn des 1.Jahrtausends v.Chr., ausgebildete Schulsysteme nur am Nil und in Mesopotamien, so daß der Blick der Herrscher, die ein israelitisches Reich gründeten, sich notwendig dorthin wandte. In beiden Flußtalreichen lagen umfangreiche Schulbücher vor, und wen sollte es wundern, wenn diese auch der frühen Königszeit als Vorbilder dienten, ja, wie oben gesagt, teilweise einfach übersetzt wurden, wenn auch nicht ohne Anpassung an den anderen Gottesglauben und die andere Gesellschaftsform. Die Bibel selbst verweist auf "die Weisheit aller Söhne des Ostens (dazu paßt die Angabe Prov. 30 und 31, daß diese Teile der Bibel von einem arabischen Stamm übernommen sind) und alle Weisheit Ägyptens" (1 Kön. 5,9). Sollte nicht auch aus dem Nilland, wo die Weisheit schon seit mehr als tausend Jahren eine leitende Rolle im Geistesleben einnahm, so mancher Gedanke, ja sogar so manche Formulierung übernommen worden sein, auch wenn das nicht ausdrücklich gesagt war? Sollte sich nicht außer der oben genannten Übersetzung aus der Lehre des Amenemope noch weiteres Weisheits – und Spruchgut Ägyptens in den Weisheitsbüchern der Bibel finden?

Diese Frage mußte bisher offen bleiben. Zwar waren die ägyptischen Weisheitslehren (es sind der bekannten und hinreichend gut erhaltenen etwa 17) bekannt, ohne daß sich weitere wörtliche Entlehnungen fanden. So ließ sich bisher die Frage des ägyptischen Einflusses zwar stellen, auch mit Vermutungen, ja mit Wahrscheinlichkeit bejahend beantworten, doch nicht nachweisen.

Das vorliegende Buch betritt hier neue Wege, die eine saubere Antwort erlauben: Ja, auch ohne daß wir einem hebräischen einen ägyptischen Text gegenüberstellen können (was sich aber bei

Papyrus-Neufunden in ägyptischem Boden oder in Museen jederzeit ändern kann), läßt sich der ägyptische Einfluß auf die israelitische Weisheit exakt nachweisen.

Frau Nili Shupak hat eine neue Methode entwickelt und in diesem Buch überzeugend durchgeführt: Sie sammelt auf beiden Seiten, in Ägypten wie in Israel, die spezifisch weisheitlichen Fachausdrücke, nachdem sie die einschlägigen Texte sorgfältig gegen die übrige Literatur abgegrenzt hat. Die beiden Lexika werden dann gewissenhaft verglichen, und es ergibt sich klar, daß ein Großteil hebräischer Fachausdrücke, die ausschließlich oder doch weit überwiegend nur in den Weisheitsbüchern vorkommen, ihre genauen Entsprechungen in den weit älteren ägyptischen Lehren haben. Einzelne Beispiele wären nicht beweiskräftig, doch wenn nach gewissenhafter Untersuchung jedes einzelnen Terminus eine erkleckliche Anzahl solcher Begriffs– (nicht Wort!–) Übernahmen zusammenkommen, wird man dem Schluß nicht ausweichen können, daß ägyptische Lehren, auch solche, die uns verloren sind, als Vorbilder gedient haben, wahrscheinlich damals, als Salomo für den Aufbau seines Großreiches eine schreibkundige Beamtenschaft in kurzer Zeit heranzubilden hatte. Daß das aus dieser Notwendigkeit entstandene Corpus später umgebaut, vor allem erweitert worden ist, versteht sich. Die Bibel nennt als Sammler die Gelehrten aus der Zeit des Königs Hiskia. Aber daß der Grund zur biblischen Weisheit nicht ohne starken Einfluß Ägyptens gelegt wurde und daß das damals geschaffene Fachvokabular auch weiterhin wirkte, das kann nicht bezweifelt werden.

Doch geht der Ertrag dieser neuen Methode noch weiter. Es stellt sich heraus, daß bestimmte Vokabeln (und damit bestimmte Auffassungen vom Wesen des Menschen und den Erziehungszielen) nicht übernommen werden, obwohl sie in Ägypten zentral sind, z.B. das Idealbild des "wahren Schweigers", also des Menschen, der in Selbstzucht nicht nur bei Streitereien oder gegenüber Vorgesetzten still ist, sondern der auch bei dem, was Gott schickt, stillhält, nicht wider den Stachel löckt, der sich fügt, der also nicht mit dem Schicksal hadert. Gewiß, manche dieser Züge sind in Israel bekannt und werden bei der Erziehung der jungen Beamten angestrebt, doch spielen sie keine derart zentrale Rolle wie in Ägypten. Es versteht sich, daß andererseits in Israel Züge des Menschenbildes hervorgehoben werden, die in Ägypten fehlen oder nur am Rande erwähnt werden. Kurz, die Eigenheiten beider Völker mit ihrem Menschenbild treten durch die Shupaksche Methode deutlich hervor.

Man mag einwenden, daß die Vergleichsbasis, als der Umfang der Texte auf beiden Seiten doch recht beschränkt ist, enger noch in Israel als in Ägypten. Besonders die Annahme, daß eine Vokabel im Sprachschatz nicht vorhanden sei, wenn sie in den Weisheitsbüchern nicht vorkommt, ist nicht zwingend. Wenn etwa neue hebräische Teile des Sirach-Buches auftauchen, könnte dort dennoch das eine oder andere, jetzt vermißte Wort belegt sein. Doch wird sich, das läßt sich mit Gewißheit sagen, am Gesamtergebnis und an der Gesundheit der angewandten Methode nichts ändern, dazu ist das vorliegende Material an Übereinstimmung zu umfangreich. Details können diskutiert werden, aber der neue Weg führt zu neuen gesicherten Erkenntnissen.

Zwei weitere Gesichtspunkte seien angefügt. Die Nähe der biblischen Weisheit zur ägyptischen wird erneut deutlich werden, wenn eine entsprechende Vokabel-Untersuchung für die babylonischen Belege dieser Literaturgattung durchgeführt sein wird: Dort wird sich eine ähnliche Nähe, ja Übernahme von Begriffen nicht erweisen lassen. Und dann: Sind schon die Herkunftsangaben einiger Teile der Proverbia sichere Belege für die Internationalität der Weisheit schon zu Beginn des 1. Jahrtausends (also nicht erst im Hellenismus), so fügt das vorliegende Buch einen weiteren Beleg hinzu. Zur Zeit Salomos traten die zwischenstaatlichen Beziehungen, die sich bis dahin weitgehend auf Warentausch und diplomatische Beziehungen der Fürsten sowie auf Kriege beschränkt hatten, in eine neue Phase ein: Auch geistige Güter wanderten von einem Volk zum anderen. In dieser Frühheit, als das Gebiet des östlichen Mittelmeeres begann, ein melting pot zu werden, wußte man noch um die Herkunft der einzelnen Sprichwörter, Zitate und Textteile und überlieferte solche "Quellen" sogar gelegentlich. In den letzten Jahrhunderten v. Chr. dagegen waren gerade solche prägnanten Weisheitsformulierungen Allgemeingut, deren Ursprung weder die Zeitgenossen kannten, die sie in ihre jeweilige Muttersprache faßten, noch der heutige Gelehrte festzustellen vermag. Diese Ubiquität orientalischer Weisheit in der zweiten Hälfte des letzten Jahrtausends hat Miriam Lichtheim in ihrer gründlichen Untersuchung (Late Egyptian Wisdom in the International Context, 1983) überzeugend nachgewiesen. Frau Shupaks Buch erhellt die Anfänge dieser großen und fruchtbaren Bewegung geistigen Austauschs im östlichen Mittelmeergebiet.

Tübingen, Januar 1991 Hellmut Brunner

INTRODUCTION

The publication of *The Instruction of Amenemope* in 1923 initiated intensive and ongoing comparative research of the ancient Egyptian and Biblical writings as a whole and of the wisdom literature contained in them in particular. The main concern of the present study is the semantic determination of terms in the Biblical wisdom literature as compared with the Egyptian wisdom literature. It covers a narrow and circumscribed area, as yet to some extent neglected, within the broad sphere of the cultural contacts between Egypt and the world of the Bible.

An investigation of this sort must obviously be based on earlier studies that laid the foundations for comparative research on these two cultures. The following brief review of key works in the field, therefore, is meant to introduce the reader to the principal publications in the field of comparative investigation of Egyptian and Biblical wisdom writings, particularly to those studies which have contributed and are related to my own research.

A. Erman initiated the comparative study of Egyptian and Biblical wisdom with the publication in 1924 of his pioneering study, "Eine ägyptische Quelle der Sprüche Salomos," in which he showed a direct contact between *The Instruction of Amenemope* and Proverbs 22,17-23,11.

Erman was followed in the same year by H. Gressmann (1924), who identified other passages in Proverbs that could be linked with that recently discovered Egyptian work, and also pointed out the affinities between Chapter 4 of the Egyptian composition and both Jeremiah 17,5-8 and Psalm 1. Gressmann was the first to consider the literary form of Hebrew wisdom compositions in connection with the wisdom writings of ancient Egypt. However, it was P. Humbert's *Recherches sur les sources égyptiennes de la littérature sapientale d'Israël* (1929) which laid the foundations, still applicable today, of comparative scholarship in Egyptian and Biblical wisdom. Humbert greatly expanded the scope of inquiry by considering not only *The Instruction of Amenemope* but the entire corpus of Egyptian wisdom compositions known in his time. He compared these Egyptian works with the wisdom books of the Bible, as well as Ben Sira, from three aspects: content, form and terminology.

Like Erman and Gressmann, W.O.E. Oesterley (1930) focused on *The Instruction of Amenemope*, extending his investigation of its links with the Old Testament to include Deuteronomy and Psalms. Oesterley distinguished between two varieties of contact — one being direct parallelism between *Amenemope* and Proverbs 22-23, the other indirect parallelisms deriving from a store of wisdom legacy shared by both compositions.

P. Montet in *L'Egypt et la Bible* (1959) traced Egyptian influences in the Old Testament from the time of the stories of the Patriarchs, the slavery in Egypt and the Exodus to the period of the Jewish exile in Egypt at the time of Jeremiah. Montet pursues Egyptian motifs, customs, and names embedded in Biblical writings, and concludes with a comparison of *The Instruction of Amenemope* with Proverbs and of *The Words of Petosiris* with Psalms. His study complements W. Spiegelberg's *Aegyptologische Randglossen zum Alten Testament* written some fifty years earlier.

In his comprehensive study, W. Helck (2nd ed., 1971) examines the contacts between Egypt and Asia from the third millennium B.C. to the period of the Israelite Monarchy. He investigated the entire range of ties — historical, cultural, commercial, religious, and linguistic — on the basis of epigraphic and archaeological evidence.

The connection between the Hebrew Psalms and Egyptian religious writings in form of expression and thought was studied by A. Barucq in his *L'expression de la louange divine et de la prière dans la Bible et en Egypte* (1962). Barucq's meticulous analysis reveals the extent to which the two are close in form and content.

After an interval of several decades, when the study of the relation between Hebrew and Egyptian wisdom literature all but ceased, G.E. Bryce (1979) took up the premise that the wisdom of the Old Testament was influenced by that of Egypt. Bryce's innovation lies in his efforts to determine the types of contact between the two literatures. He proposes three stages — the adaptive, assimilative, and integrative — at which this contact took place.[1] In his view the social and political setting of Biblical wisdom literature was the court of the Israelite kings, which was influenced by the Egyptian royal establishment.

The forms of the instruction genre in the ancient Near East are the special subject of two studies by K.A. Kitchen (1977, 1979). This scholar's work has refreshed the entire field of comparative research into Egyptian and Hebrew wisdom, as well as the study of Biblical wisdom in its own right. Kitchen's thesis that Egyptian and Hebrew wisdom writings are similar owing to their common use of literary patterns characteristic of the ancient Near East rather than to Hebrew borrowing from Egyptian casts new light on the connections between the two wisdom literatures. Moreover, Kitchen's conclusions raise questions about the accepted view of the construction of the book of Proverbs, and contradict the doubts of scholars concerning the traditional attribution of the book to Solomon.

Of primary interest for our investigation is M. Lichtheim's book (1983) demonstrating the contact of Demotic wisdom with international wisdom. The first to draw up a glossary of subjects and words typical of *The Instruction of Ankhsheshonqy* and *Papyrus Insinger*, Lichtheim discusses thoroughly the key terms and concepts which dominate these compositions (e.g., "wise-fool," "character," "wisdom") and thus makes a special contribution to the linguistic-conceptual study of late Egyptian wisdom literature.

Turning to a review of the study of lexical and etymological connections between Egyptian and Hebrew — that is, of Semitic words occurring in the former and Egyptian loan words in the latter — one must begin by noting the instructive article published by T.O. Lambdin in *JOAS* (1953) which elucidates the Egyptian roots of a number of Old Testament terms. A similar though less reliable study was made nearly twenty years earlier by P. Calice (1936), who claimed to have identified

948 Semitic words in Egyptian. He divided these into four groups on the basis of their proximity to the Semitic. In determining Semitic origin he used two criteria — phonetics and meaning — which were later also applied by his critic W. Vycichl (1958-59), who concluded that Calice had identified correctly only 200 of the total number of words he proposed. Recently, interest in the comparative lexical study of Egyptian and the Semitic language has risen, with the emphasis on phonetics. Two prominent scholars in this field are D. Rössler (1971) and C.T. Hodge (1981).

Finally, a succinct and thorough summary of the present state of comparative research on ancient Egypt and Israel may be found in two articles by R.J. Williams (*Theologische Realenzyclopädie* I; *SVT* 1975), which offer examples from a variety of spheres of contact as well as an exhaustive bibliography. Williams' studies were lately completed by the brief review of the interrelationships between the two cultures during the first millennium B.C., presented by K.A. Kitchen (*SVT* 1988).

The foregoing review, though not, of course, exhaustive, demonstrates that the comparative study of ancient Egyptian and Hebrew literature has tended to focus on content and ideas rather than style and terminology. The reason is, simply, that Biblical scholars have generally preferred to investigate Canaanite and Akkadian sources, languages which belong to the same family as Hebrew, rather than texts in Egyptian, which do not. Hence, secondary sources were used for the study of Egyptian texts, which inevitably narrowed the scope of research. The areas of style and vocabulary therefore have been investigated to date by only a handful of scholars. Apart from Humbert's study mentioned above, the second decade of this century saw the publication of the work of A.S. Yahuda (1929; English edition 1934), who compared the language of the Pentateuch with that of ancient Egyptian sources. Yahuda, however, went to extremes in trying to establish Egyptian influence on the Hebrew text and claimed to find Egyptian traces in the most unlikely places. On the other hand, the studies by Père B. Couroyer, published in *RB* (1949 ff.), significantly advanced our knowledge of idioms common to the Bible and ancient Egyptian writings. More recently M. Görg has joined the scholars inquiring into the formulas shared by the two languages; his findings have been set out in his *Gott-König Reden in Israel und Ägypten* (1975) and in a number of articles that appeared in *BN* beginning in 1974. The articles of J. Zandee (1979) also deserve mention, although the author is sometimes over-zealous in identifying Egyptianisms in Old Testament Hebrew. Much the same can be said of the work of I.M. Grintz (1979).

However, none of the preceding studies is devoted exclusively to examining the terminology of Biblical wisdom compositions in relation to Egyptian literature. While Barucq, Bryce, and Humbert[2] have dealt with this question, the issue on the whole has been used as a secondary research tool, to be used with other criteria, such as content and form, in determining whether the Biblical author borrowed from the Egyptian sources (this is particularly true of Humbert). In this connection, the studies of L. Kaligula and H. Brunner deserve special consideration.

Kaligula's *The Wise King* (1980) is partly concerned with defining the semantic field of Biblical and extra-Biblical wisdom, but the contribution of this study to our subject is limited since the author's terminological analysis treats each cultural sphere (Egypt, Mesopotamia, Israel, etc.) separately rather than comparatively. Kaligula's semantic discussion, moreover, is subordinate to the main theme of his research, and as a result he deals with a relatively small number of terms pertaining to the language of wisdom literature.

Brunner's pioneering work "Zentralbegriffe ägyptischer und israelitischer Weisheitslehren" (1984), in which he gives a thorough analysis of central concepts in the Egyptian sapiential literature in comparison with their Biblical equivalents (e.g., *mꜣʿ.t* and *ṣᵉdāqâ*, *ṣaddîq* — *rāšāʿ*, *ḥākām* — *ʾewîl* and the "silent" and "heated man"), is most important to our research. Brunner is the first to have emphasized the importance of the comparative terminological study of both cultures, although his article focuses on the conceptual aspect and not upon the semantic determination of the terms he discusses.

The present study thus deals with an area of comparative research of Biblical and Egyptian writings that so far has received only slight attention. Its goal is to add the analysis of Hebrew and Egyptian terminology to existing scholarship on the relations between these two literatures.

Every new idea or even theory arises out of earlier views and assumptions. The findings and hypothesis of previous scholars thus serve as points of departure for my own approach, and accordingly three principal issues underlie the present study:

(1) Scholars today generally agree that cultural and intellectual contact existed between ancient Israel and Egypt, and the evidence for this, among other things, is furnished by the wisdom writings of both civilizations.[3] We can therefore legitimately ask if the wisdom literature of the Old Testament contains terms, phrases, and idioms that are close to or analogous with and perhaps influenced by those found in the same class of Egyptian compositions.

(2) In both Israel and Egypt, wisdom writings formed a distinct genre, set apart from other varieties of literary compositions not only by style and content, but apparently by terminology too. The latter has been studied in regard to Biblical wisdom,[4] but has still to be investigated in corresponding Egyptian works.

(3) One of the characteristic features of wisdom writings in both literatures is that they tend to preserve the traditions of the past. In Egyptian works of the instruction type we find citations from earlier compositions written in the same vein; in the speculative wisdom writings of the Old Testament (i.e., Job and Qoheleth) the themes and literary forms of the conventional wisdom are taken up in an effort to reinforce or sometimes even to refute them.[5] Presumably, therefore, at least part of the vocabulary of earlier wisdom compositions in both literatures will reappear in later writings of this genre.

Before turning to the objectives, method, and content of the present study, it should be noted that the terminology, or list of terms, characteristic of Biblical wisdom was established by R.N. Whybray in his *The Intellectual Tradition in the Old Testament* (1974).[6] Whybray's findings have since been contested. The controversy between Whybray and his critics, led by Crenshaw, turns on the question of whether the occurrence in non-wisdom texts of the vocabulary characteristic of Biblical wisdom books — which Whybray calls the "terminology of the intellectual tradition" — indicates the influence of a wisdom tradition.[7] While this question hardly concerns the immediate aim of our own research, the following argument recently raised against Whybray's philological method deserves our consideration: The Biblical wisdom vocabulary demarcated by Whybray consists of words only, while close scrutiny shows that the Hebrew sapiential phraseology also makes use of collocations and special word combinations.[8]

The present study has three primary objectives, which may be summarized as follows: First, to draw up a glossary of Egyptian wisdom terms, a task as yet not undertaken elsewhere. Second, to elucidate the semantics of these terms. Third — and this is my main purpose — to clarify the wisdom vocabulary of the Hebrew sages in relation to the corresponding Egyptian terminology.

This means that the aim of this study is not a monolingual analysis of the Egyptian wisdom terminology, and certainly not of the Hebrew. Primary concern is with the clarification of terms which are commonly used in Hebrew wisdom writings but do not conform to ordinary Biblical usage. The question is whether these exceptional instances of usage are evidence of foreign influence.

The secondary objectives of this study are to shed light on some of the general questions concerning Old Testament wisdom writings, which may be achieved through a fresh comparative inquiry into Hebrew and Egyptian wisdom vocabulary: Did Hebrew wisdom evolve from a secular to a religious stage? Does the Hebrew *ḥākām* ("sage") signify a function or a quality, a class or a title? Did Hebrew wisdom develop independently or did it derive from an Egyptian tradition which was assimilated by way of the Israelite royal court and/or an educational institution modeled on the Egyptian school? Our attempt to answer the last question involved another line of inquiry, i.e., whether there existed analogies in the vocabularies of the Biblical and Egyptian wisdom literatures. If we find that there were, we shall be adding support to the long accepted view of the existing relationship between the civilizations of Israel and Egypt. But if such analogies are found to be absent, we shall be obliged to conclude that we are dealing with two distinct literatures, with no direct connections in thought and world view. Either conclusion, of course, depends on the extent to which a vocabulary reflects the world of its users.[9]

In terms of methodology, a comparative semantic study of two closed literary corpora is difficult, particularly when these are written in dead languages. The problems to be addressed, and the methods used to solve them, are the following:

(1) As noted, the first problematic area is the establishment of a glossary of Egyptian wisdom terms along Whybray's lines with corresponding material in the Old Testament.[10] The corpus of Egyptian writings selected for this study reveals two categories of terms that are relevant: (a) terms that recur frequently some even exclusively,[11] and (b) terms that appear less frequently but are of major significance for wisdom ideology (e.g., *sbꜣy.t*). Consequently, a twofold criterion was used in determining whether a term was to be included in an Egyptian wisdom glossary — frequency of occurrence and ideological significance. Not all the terms characteristically employed by the Hebrew sage and his Egyptian counterpart are discussed. The ones chosen for consideration are principally those relevant to a bilingual semantic comparison. But we shall also have occasion to discuss terms that are unique to either Biblical or Egyptian wisdom and without analogy in the other language; while it is important to determine the semantic contact between parallel terms in the wisdom texts of the two civilizations, it is no less important to discern that some terms in one of the languages have no parallel in the other, and to discover why.

(2) A further difficulty is how to determine the meaning of words in the two dead languages, Egyptian and Biblical Hebrew. Linguists have devised a number of tools that can be usefully applied:[12]

(a) *Synchronic analysis of paradigmatic and syntagmatic relations.* Paradigmatic relation is established by the lexical value of a term, or of the place of a word in the linguistic system as a whole. This is done by examining the collocations in which the word occurs and determining the synonyms, antonyms, and like characteristics. For this purpose dictionaries of Biblical Hebrew and ancient Egyptian have been used. Syntagmatic relation refers to the status of a word within its context. In the framework of the present study particular attention had to be paid to the type of literature with which a word is connected. For example, in the Old Testament we need to know whether the composition is prose narrative or verse; in the Egyptian sources we must determine whether it belongs to the genre of instruction, whether it is an instance of speculative literature, or whether it is an example of royal court phraseology, and so on.

(b) *Diachronic analysis.* This is twofold: The study of a word's change of meaning as the language develops, and the study of a word's etymology, i.e., determining its meaning on the basis of its origin. The latter should be pursued carefully, for the meaning of a root need not be the same in later periods.[13] Etymological analysis is commonly used in Biblical scholarship, since Hebrew shares a large number of roots with other languages of the same Semitic family. For Egyptian, if a word has survived long enough to be retained by the language in the later phases of its development, then its meaning in the Demotic or Coptic can be useful. But here too care must be taken through the complementary application of the synchronic to the diachronic analysis.[14]

(3) Synchronic and diachronic analyses are among the principles of the semantic field theory, first put forward by J. Trier (1931) under the name of "lexical field" theory.[15] This theory has been used in the present study with certain restrictions. Semantic principles are applied only when they can determine the sense of a given word. Greater consideration has been given to syntagmatic than to paradigmatic analysis, since our interest is the semantic investigation of a particular literary genre rather than an entire language system. For the same reason, in certain cases a discussion of synonymous terms that are not part of wisdom terminology is omitted. Semantics in general and semantic field theory in particular have only recently been applied to Biblical research, among others by J.F.A. Sawyer and J. Barr, whose pioneering works have been used as a guide in this study. Research on

the classification of the vocabulary of wisdom literature in Hebrew is ahead of that in Egyptian, on which very few monographs have been published.[16] Nor has any effort been made as yet to apply the general principles of semantics to the Egyptian sphere. This study, though only a beginning, is the first to employ semantics in the field of Egyptian studies — any future research along these lines would certainly be welcome.

In the context of our study over 120 terms were examined. As the research does not deal with either Egyptian language or Biblical Hebrew alone, the discussion centers on terms that lend themselves to comparative study. The terms chosen have been arranged in thematically ordered chapters. Thus, Chapters one to eight treat terms and phrases reflecting various aspects of the world of wisdom: expressions concerning teaching and instruction, phrases defining positive and negative human types, the wise man and the fool, expressions of various kinds of wise sayings, and the parts of the body that serve to acquire wisdom and knowledge.

The corpus of this research taken from the Biblical wisdom literature consists of Proverbs, Job, Qoheleth and "wisdom Psalms" and, from the apocryphal wisdom literature, the book of Ben Sira. The corpus coming from the Egyptian sources includes not only wisdom compositions proper — instructions, school writings, and speculative literature — but also compositions showing an indirect contact with the wisdom circle — royal inscriptions, autobiographies, and religious literature. For the non-specialist in wisdom literature, a list has been included of the sources on which this study is based and of the manuscript publications we have used, as well as of the main scholarly works in the field, highlighting the details that are most important for semantic determination, namely, literary genres, distinction between original stratum and additions, date of composition, etc.[17]

A comparative study of this kind is of necessity bound by certain objective limitations. First, a scholar who turns to the Old Testament after having been deeply immersed in the language and literature of ancient Egypt may find it hard to resist the temptation of "discovering"

Egyptianisms everywhere in the Hebrew text. Second, in making a comparative analysis of languages and literatures of a period so remote from our own we face the problem of how to distinguish between the source and the borrower — a certain degree of doubt must always accompany our conclusions. Third, the general uncertainty noted in the preceding point applies particularly to semantics: a precise understanding of a linguistic form depends on perfect familiarity with the speaker's world.[18] Plainly, such a level of knowledge of the cultures of ancient Egypt and Israel is beyond our reach.

Another limitation — this one subjective — is that, while one of the principles of this research has been to use throughout the original Egyptian texts, this was not possible for the Demotic compositions, where translations had to be used.[19]

Finally, this research touches on three areas — Biblical studies, Egyptology, and linguistics — but it does not claim to treat any of these exhaustively. Nor does it offer any new discoveries on the semantic rules of Biblical Hebrew and Egyptian. Its intention has been primarily to determine the presence or absence of contact between the vocabularies of Biblical and Egyptian wisdom literature, and to fix the semantic boundaries of selected Hebrew wisdom terms in comparison with the same genre in Egyptian literature. Should this endeavor within the modest scope it has set itself have succeeded, the author will have been amply rewarded.[20]

CORPUS[1]

I. THE HEBREW SOURCES — BIBLICAL AND JEWISH WISDOM LITERATURE[2]

The term "Biblical wisdom literature" in the present study is applied primarily to the books of Proverbs, Job and Qoheleth. Two forms of wisdom may be discerned in the wisdom literature of the ancient Near East, namely, didactic and speculative. The former is practical and aimed at educating and providing guidance in everyday life. In contrast to the abundant optimism of didactic wisdom, speculative wisdom consists of speculations and reflections on man's destiny, criticizes the contradictions between conventional dogmas and actual reality and ponders the problems of retribution and divine theodicy. The book of Proverbs is an outstanding example of ancient didactic wisdom, while Job belongs to speculative wisdom. Qoheleth, like Job, belongs to speculative wisdom, but it does contain didactic wisdom as well. Some of the Psalms (called "wisdom Psalms") are an inseparable part of Biblical wisdom and, like Qoheleth, contain a mixture of practical, didactic wisdom alongside speculative, critical wisdom.

A. The Book of Proverbs

This book comprises nine collections of sayings, distinguished from each other by title, content and literary form. The first collection (1-9) entitled "The Proverbs of Solomon," is set within the framework of a father addressing his son. This literary form parallels the Egyptian "instruction" genre. Two subjects appear repeatedly: a warning to shun "a strange woman" and an appeal to avoid the company of the evil murderers. These fatherly moral admonitions are interspersed with poetical stanzas in which the personified Wisdom takes the form of a woman speaking of her singularity and good qualities (1,20 ff.; 8;9).

The second collection (10-22,16), whose title is "The Proverbs of Solomon," is composed of proverbs in parallelism of members. The topics of the proverbs vary and they are not arranged according to a uniform theme.

The third collection (22,17-24,22), entitled "The Sayings of the Wise," may be subdivided into two units: The first is 22,17-23,11 which contains literal parallels to *The Instruction of Amenemope*; the sentence beginning "Have I not written to you *šālišôm* (*Qᵉrî*: *šālîšîm*) sayings of counsel and knowledge," undoubtedly refers to the thirty chapters of the Egyptian instruction.[3] The second unit is 23,12-24,22, whose literary form is a combination of the first and second collections, i.e., a father's words to his son as in the first collection, interspersed with proverbs written in the pattern of parallelism as in the second.

The fourth collection (24,23-34), entitled "These are also the Sayings of the Wise," is an appendix to the preceding collection.

The fifth collection (25-29) bearing the title "These also are proverbs of Solomon which the men of Hezekiah, King of Judah, copied out," resembles the second, being composed mainly of proverbs arranged in a short, impersonal form without consistency and continuity of subject matter. Two sub-groups of proverbs may be discerned: 25-27, which tends toward rational rather than moral wisdom, and 28-29 which is kept in a more theological vein.

While the first five collections include didactic ideas and admonitions and are directly or indirectly ascribed to Solomon, those that follow differ in their speculative spirit, in the foreign color of their language and in their attribution to the "Sons of Qedem" (*bᵉnê Qedem*).

The writer of the sixth collection (30, 1-14), entitled "The words of Agur the son of Jakeh of Massa," belongs to the Arab tribe of Massa. His words convey a recognition of human ignorance and an admonition directed to his generation.

The collection that follows (30, 15-33), known as "To *'Ălûkâ*," contains five numerical sayings based on the observation of the world of nature and human customs.[4]

The eighth collection (31, 1-9) "The words of King Lemuel of Massa," resembles the first collection in its literary genre. But in this case the instruction is not made by a father-teacher but by a mother, and includes, *inter alia*, warnings against women. Other details such as taking the side of the poor, etc., are in the spirit of speculative wisdom.

The ninth collection (31, 10-31) is an alphabetical poem eulogizing the ideal woman to whom are attributed all the qualities praised by the wise in the first five collections.[5]

Thus, Proverbs was not written by one single person but is a compilation of collections of sayings. Recent research on the content and literary forms of Proverbs in the light of extra-Biblical sources refutes most of the arguments of 19th- and early 20th-century scholarship which dated the book in the exilic and post-exilic eras.[6]

At present the tendency is increasingly to assume that the transmission of material began in Solomon's time and continued in that of Hezekiah, when it was edited by his men during the 7th century B.C. (Prov. 25,1). The book contains ancient material belonging to the pre-exilic period, with no Aramisms or Greek words to indicate a later period.[7]

B. The Book of Job

The book in which Hebrew speculative wisdom literature appears in its full stature is also not a homogeneous unit. Job comprises two parts, original separate entities, that differ in form and content: the prosaic framework (1,1-2,13; 42,7-17), in which Job is described as a righteous man unjustly punished as a test; and the poetic dialogue (3,1-42,6), which presents Job as a wise man and contains a cycle of discussions between Job and his friends, the words of Elihu (32-37) and the speeches of God (38,1-42,6) combined with Job's answers.

Most scholars believe that the text we now have was not written as a unit but contains later additions. However, it is usually agreed that Job was composed at some time during the post-exilic period (between the 5th and 4th centuries). The arguments for this view are the foreign tone in the language of Job[8] and the doctrine of personal retribution presented by his friends, but these arguments for a late dating of the book are contestable.[9] Similarly, there is no clear proof that the book was written before the exile. But there is a resemblance in form and content between Job and the Mesopotamian wisdom texts from *The Sumerian Job* up to *I Will Praise the Lord of Wisdom*, *A Dialogue about Human Misery* and *The Dialogue between Master and Servant*, as well as with the Egyptian text, *The Man Who Was Tired of Life*.[10] Therefore, even if the book was edited later, as indicated by its language, its content is evidently ancient, going back to the First Temple period.

To sum up, the book was certainly composed later than the crystallization of the traditional wisdom concepts expressed by the friends of Job, but any attempt at an exact chronological dating must remain speculative.[11]

C. Qoheleth

Qoheleth stands midway between traditional wisdom on the one hand and sceptical wisdom on the other, for although he repeats the conventional dogmas, he confronts and denies them as well. The book comprises independent units, unconnected in content; it lacks uniformity and contains contradictions. It is the result of the special personality of the author, who was probably reared on traditional ancient wisdom but finally broke away from it. This is evident from the text, which weaves statements from traditional wisdom literature together with negations of them.[12]

The book is the work of one man. The sole addition which should be attributed to the compiler is the title in 1,1 and the section in 12,9-14 which reflects theological wisdom.

The prevailing 19th century opinion that Qoheleth was strongly influenced by Greek philosophy has long been rejected; most of the "Grecisms" can be explained in the light of contact with ancient Near Eastern wisdom.[13]

In terms of language and content Qoheleth belongs to the

transitional period between Biblical and Jewish literature. The language is pre-Mishnaic Hebrew,[14] and the book's exceptional conceptual position finds its expression in the spiritual vacuum posited by Qoheleth who argues the "vanity" of life and the worthlessness of man's actions. This argument originates in an awareness of Yahweh's inconceivable omnipotence, which produces a sense of distance and indifference.[15]

The latest possible dating for Qoheleth is fixed by the book of Ben Sira, written about 180 B.C., whose author was familiar with the book of Qoheleth, and by fragments of the book found in Qumran (from 150 B.C.). It was probably composed in the 3rd century B.C., although its sources were ancient, rooted in the Hebrew wisdom of the First Temple period and in the tradition of ancient Near Eastern wisdom.

D. Wisdom Psalms

Research has conferred this title on several psalms within the book of Psalms since they have an affinity, in form, style or content, with the wisdom literature. Several attempts have been made to determine criteria for the identification of these psalms. Murphy (1963) was the first to establish two such criteria for defining them: by their formal and stylistic resemblance to, and conceptual affinity with, wisdom literature. He was followed by Kuntz (1974), who not only tried to reinforce and broaden these criteria but who also added another — wisdom vocabulary — the limitations of which he acknowledged. The importance of vocabulary as a means of defining wisdom Psalms was recently emphasized by A. Hurvitz's article (1988), and his thorough study *Wisdom Language in Biblical Psalmody* (1991).[16] In spite of these efforts to find a single tested definition for the *Gattung* of wisdom Psalms, there is still no agreement among scholars as to their identification.[17] In the present study the problem is solved by including all psalms to be among the wisdom Psalms which (1) the majority of scholars (at least three) have included in the wisdom circle; and which (2) satisfy the Murphy-Kuntz criteria mentioned above. The distinctive features of the wisdom Psalm are accordingly: (a) rhetorical and formal elements: the *'ăšrê* formula, the address to "sons," admonition and warning, the "better" saying (*ṭôb-Spruch*), alphabetical structure (acrostic), simile and comparison, numerical saying and rhetorical question; (b) subjects and motifs: the contrast between righteous and wicked, traditional doctrine of retribution, the two ways of life (good and bad), identification of the Torah with Wisdom, praise and thanksgiving to God, fear of God and advice on everyday conduct.

The wisdom Psalms are therefore: 1, 19(8-15), 32, 34, 37, 49, 73, 78, 105, 106, 111, 112, 119, 127, 128, 133. Like the other wisdom texts, the wisdom Psalms were the work of the sages, in this instance probably connected with the temple singers. It is difficult to define their *Sitz im Leben*: Were they meant for instruction of pupils or for use in the temple cult? The former seems more likely, since the discourses of Ben Sira, who was a teacher in his *bêt midrāš* (school), are interspersed with poems and hymns. The writings of the Egyptian school also contain hymns of praise and prayers to god.

The wisdom Psalms belong to the late stage of development of Hebrew wisdom. The book of Psalms was compiled at the beginning of the Second Temple period, but it is difficult to determine the dates of the individual psalms; at least some of them are pre-exilic.

E. Wisdom in the Apocrypha — Ben Sira

For hundreds of years after the Biblical era the wisdom tradition continued, leaving its mark on apocryphal writings which were regarded sacred by the Egyptian Jews. The following apocryphal books belong to wisdom literature: Ben Sira, the Wisdom of Solomon, Tobit, 1 Edras and Baruch, all of which contain elements of wisdom and were written between the 2nd century B.C. and the 1st century A.D. Of the apocryphal books, only the book of Ben Sira is discussed in this study. The fact that original parts of its Hebrew text have survived makes it most valuable for our purposes.[18]

The Book of Shimon ben Joshua ben Elazar ben Sira who was a sage, a scribe, and a teacher, was written originally in Hebrew about 180 B.C.

It was translated into Greek by the author's grandson in 130 B.C. and parts of it, ascribed to the 1st century B.C., were discovered in the Qumran caves and at Masada. The book of Ben Sira may be regarded as a continuation of Biblical wisdom in form and in content, but it differs from the latter in its varied use of literary models and in its nationalistic Yahwistic motifs. It identifies wisdom with the Torah of Yahweh, praises God the Creator, eulogizes the Patriarchs, and so on.[19] Ben Sira is located on the border between the world of the Bible and the world of Hellenism.[20] His book, the language of which is clearly post-Biblical Hebrew (but which the author took pains to embellish with literary devices in the classical style) nevertheless reflects the Hellenistic world.

II. THE EGYPTIAN SOURCES

The Egyptian corpus includes: (1) works which belong to or are clearly connected with the wisdom tradition: the instructions (*Lebenslehren*), speculative-pessimistic compositions and school texts; (2) works indirectly connected with the wisdom sphere — the royal inscriptions, autobiographies and religious literature.[21]

A. Wisdom Literature

It is surprising that the Egyptians, whose wisdom had become a symbol and a model in the ancient world (cf. 1 Kgs. 5,10), had no specific term for "wisdom literature." In the absence of any other suitable expression, this term, adapted from Biblical studies, is commonly used to denote the texts which cover an area in Egyptian literature corresponding to Biblical wisdom. These may be divided into two groups: (1) didactic wisdom; (2) speculative-pessimistic wisdom or "Egyptian prophecy."

First and foremost in Egyptian wisdom literature are the instructions (*sbꜣy.t*), which are highly reminiscent in form and content of the book of Proverbs, and to a lesser degree of Qoheleth. The literary pattern of a father speaking to his son is characteristic of these texts.

This genre has a long tradition in Egypt, and there are instructions on record dating back to the 25th century B.C. (the 4th-5th Dynasties) up to the 1st century B.C. The two "loyalist" instructions ascribed to the early Middle Kingdom (19th century B.C.) constitute a separate section within this group. These works, like the other instructions, are didactic, but their main purpose is propaganda and support for the reigning monarch.

The second group is made up of works that are close both to Biblical speculative wisdom literature and to Biblical prophecy. Their gloomy, pessimistic atmosphere reminds us of Job and Qoheleth while the repeated motifs of distress, social-moral admonitions and a coming salvation evoke the world of the Hebrew prophets. Scholars are divided as to whether the theme of distress and national disorder treated in these compositions is rooted in a historical event, namely, the breakdown of central government during the First Intermediate Period (2180-2130 B.C.),[22] in which case they may be dated to that time, or whether this is only a literary topic, in which case the work may be dated to the flourishing period of the Middle Kingdom (2130-1780 B.C.).[23]

B. School Texts

These texts do not belong directly to wisdom literature but are still an inseparable part of the creative circle of Egyptian wisdom, since the wisdom instructions were copied, taught and sometimes written in schools for scribes.[24] The recurrent themes in this corpus — admonitions to students, adulation of teachers, praises for the scribal profession and prayers to Thoth, the god of the scribes — reflect the ambience of the Egyptian school.

C. Royal Inscriptions and Autobiographies

This group contains: (1) inscriptions emanating from the setting of the royal court, including historical and official documents, royal stele, and biographies of monarchs and high officials. The sources presented are from the 11th up to the 18th Dynasties (21st to approximately the 13th century B.C.); (2) later autobiographies, taken from tombstones and coffins of senior officials in the administration of the Ptolemies.

E. Otto, in his study *Die biographischen Inschriften* (1954) clearly demonstrated the affinity of the royal inscriptions and the autobiographies to wisdom literature. He showed that the entire range of ideas in the autobiography of the Late Period — including the relation to god, the conception of death, the human image, the familial and social relationships and moral values — are identical to those present in the instructions. Otto's conclusions were later confirmed by the investigations of H. Brunner and M. Lichtheim. Brunner points to quotations from the instructions in the royal inscriptions and autobiographies. The same phenomenon appears in the anthology of autobiographies published by Lichtheim.[25]

D. Religious Literature

J. Assmann has pointed out the connection between the religious concept of the wisdom tradition and the literature of "personal piety" (*persönliche Frömmigkeit*) in the New Kingdom.[26] Accordingly, a selection of Egyptian hymns and prayers from different periods is included.

EDITIONS OF THE EGYPTIAN SOURCES

Listed below are the Egyptian sources in chronological order as well as the publications of those manuscripts used; the names of selected studies and monographs have also been given. A list of the other references relating to these texts is included in the general bibliography.[27]

A. Wisdom Literature

Didactic Wisdom — Instructions

1. *The Instruction of Djedefhor*: Only the beginning of this instruction has been published. It was composed during the 4th or 5th Dynasty (ca. 2600-2350 B.C.) but the available copies date to the New Kingdom and to the Late Period.

Text: E. Brunner - Traut, "Die Weisheitslehre des Djedefhor," *ZÄS* 76(1940), 3-9, pl.1.

Text and translation: W. Helck, *Die Lehre des Djedefhor und die Lehre eines Vaters an seinen Sohn* (Wiesbaden 1984).

2. *The Instruction Addressed to Kagemni*: The work presumably belongs to the 6th Dynasty (ca. 2350-2180 B.C.) and has been partially preserved in the Pap. Prisse from the 11th or 12th Dynasty (ca. 2100-1990 B.C.).

Text and translation: A.H. Gardiner, "The Instruction Addressed to Kagemni and His Brethren," *JEA* 32(1946), 71-74; A. Scharff, "Die Lehre für Kagemni," *ZÄS* 77(1942), 13-21.

3. *The Instruction of Ptaḥḥotep:* This instruction, like that of Kagemni, was probably composed during the 6th Dynasty; among the manuscripts the most complete one is Pap. Prisse, originating in the 11th or 12th Dynasty, as stated above.

Text, commentary and translation: Z. Zába, *Les Maximes des Ptaḥḥotep* (Prague 1956).

4. *The Instruction Addressed to Merikare*: This was probably composed by one of the several kings bearing the name Akhtoi in the 9th-10th Dynasty (ca. 2200 B.C.) for his son Merikare. Three papyri have survived, the best preserved of which is Pap. Petersburg 1116A, dating from the 18th Dynasty (1580-1320).

Text: M. Golenischeff, *Les Papyrus hiératiques Nos.1115, 1116A et 1116B de l'Ermitage Impérial a St. Pétersbourg* (Leipzig 1913).

Text, commentary and translation: A. Volten, *Zwei*

altägyptische politische Schriften. Die Lehre für König Merikare (Pap. Carlsberg VI) und die Lehre des Königs Amenemhet (Copenhagen 1946), 3-82, pls.1-4; W. Helck, *Die Lehre für König Merikare* (Wiesbaden 1977).

Study (without translation): E. Blumenthal, "Die Lehre für König Merikare," *ZÄS* 107 (1980), 5-41.

5. *The Instruction of Amenemhet I*: Probably composed by Amenemhet's heir, his son Sesostris I, to legitimize his rule after the murder of his father (1970-1930 B.C.). Of the many copies on ostraca, writing tablets and papyri preserved from the time of the New Kingdom, Pap. Millingen is the most important. Its last page is damaged and has been complemented by Pap. Sallier II.

Text and translation: F. Ll. Griffith, "The Millingen Papyrus," *ZÄS* 34(1896), 35-51; A.Volten, *Zwei altägyptische politische Schriften*, 104-128.

Text, translation and study: W. Helck, *Der Text der "Lehre Amenemhets I für seinen Sohn"* (Wiesbaden 1969).

Study and translation: E. Blumenthal, "Die Lehre des Königs Amenemhet," *ZÄS* 111(1984), 85-107; ibid., 112 (1985), 104-115.

Publication of five new ostraca in Berlin Museum, synopsis of the available sources and repeated study of the text by H. Goedicke, *Studies in "The Instruction of King Amenemhet I for His Son,"* 2 vols. (San Antonio 1988).

6. *The Instruction of Anii*: The instruction, composed during the first half of the 18th Dynasty (1580-1400), is preserved in several copies with occasional variants. The main copy is Pap. Boulaq 4, from the 21st-22nd Dynasties (930-730 B.C.), which is extremely corrupt.

Text, commentary and translation: E. Suys, *La Sagesse d'Ani* (Roma 1935). A. Volten, *Studien zum Weisheitsbuch des Anii* (Copenhagen 1937-38).

Publication of a fragment: J. Černý, *Papyrus hiératiques de Deir el-Médineh*, T.I, Documents de Fouilles VIII (1978).

7. *The Instruction of Amenemope*: The connection between this instruction and the book of Proverbs changed the direction of

research of Biblical wisdom literature. The instruction has been preserved in many copies, the most complete of which is Papyrus 10474 in the British Museum. Scholarly opinion is divided over the date of composition of the instruction and over the period of the papyrus. One may assume that the author lived in the Ramesside Period while the Papyrus should be dated to the 20th or the 21st Dynasty (ca. 10th century B.C.).

Text, translation and interpretation: H.O. Lange, *Das Weisheitsbuch des Amenemope, aus dem Pap. 10474 des British Museum* (Copenhagen 1925).

Translation, commentary and study: I. Grumach, *Untersuchungen zur Lebenslehre des Amenope, Münchner ägptologische Studien* 23 (Berlin 1972).

8. *The Instruction of Ankhsheshonqy*: This Demotic instruction has been preserved on several papyri, the most important being Pap. 10508, in the British Museum. The partially corrupt papyrus dates from the late Ptolemaic Period (ca. 100 B.C.), but the date of composition goes back to an earlier period (4th century?).

Text, translation, and interpretation: S.R.K. Glanville, *Catalogue of Demotic Papyri in the British Museum*, vol. II, *The Instructions of 'Onchsheshonqy* (*B.M. Pap. 10508*) (London 1955).

Study and translation: H.J. Thissen, *Die Lehre des Anchsheschonqi*, (P. BM 10508) (Bonn 1984); Lichtheim, *LEWL* 13-92.

9. *The Instruction of Papyrus Insinger*: This Demotic text was mainly preserved on Pap. Insinger. The manuscript belongs to the 1st century A.D., while the composition itself goes back to the Ptolemaic Period (ca. 300 B.C.). Further fragments are preserved on six papyri.

Text, translation, and commentary: F. Lexa, *Pap. Insinger: Les enseignements moraux d'un scribe égyptien du premier siècle, après J.C.*, 2 vols. (Paris 1926). A. Volten, *Kopenhagener Texte zum demotischen Weisheitsbuch* (Copenhagen 1940-1941).

Study and translation: Lichtheim, *LEWL* 107-234.

10. *Demotic Wisdom Texts*: Fragments of collections of Demotic

wisdom sayings, three of which date to ca. 160 B.C. and are written on papyrus, are to be found in the Louvre (2377, 2380, 2414).

Publication: R.J. Williams, "Some Fragmentary Demotic Wisdom Texts," in *Studies in Honor of G.R. Hughes* (Chicago 1977), 263-271; A. Volten, "Die moralischen Lehren des demotischen Papyrus Louvre 2414," in *Studi in memoria di I. Rosellini* (Pisa 1955), vol.2, 271-280, pls. xxxiv-xxxv.

Study and translation: G.R. Hughes, "The Blunders of an Inept Scribe," in *Studies in Philology in Honor of R.J. Williams* (Toronto 1982), 51-67; Lichtheim, *LEWL* 93-106.[28]

The "Loyalist" Instructions

11. *The Stela of Seḥetep-ib-Ra:* This text (also known as *The Loyalist Instruction*) written upon the tombstone of the deceased urges loyalty to King Amenemhet III (12th Dynasty, 19th century B.C.). The inscription of this stela, completed by ostraca and wooden tablets dating to the New Kingdom, was published by: G. Posener, *L'Enseignement Loyaliste, sagesse égyptienne du Moyen Empire* (Geneva 1976).

12. *Instruction by a Man for His Son:* Like *The Instruction of Seḥetep-ib-Ra*, this work also urges support for the monarchy and was apparently written in the period of the 12th Dynasty. No whole copy has survived, although many fragments are preserved on papyri and ostraca.

Text, translation and commentary: K. Kitchen, "Studies in Egyptian Literature, I, The Instruction by a Man for His Son," *Oriens Antiquus* 8 (1969), 189-208; ibid., 9 (1970), 203-210. W. Helck, *Die Lehre des Djedefhor und Die Lehre eines Vaters an seinen Sohn* (Wiesbaden 1984).

Six new ostraca were published by J.L. Foster, *JNES* 45 (1986), 197-211, who attempts to construct the variety of surviving fragments into one complete composition. The most up-to-date translation of the instruction is presented by Brunner in *AW* 185-192.

Speculative-Pessimistic Wisdom[29]

13. *Admonitions of an Egyptian Sage* (*The Admonitions of Ipwer*): *Admonitions* was composed during the First Intermediate Period (ca. 2000 B.C.) or the late Middle Kingdom. The text is preserved on Papyrus Leiden 344, dating to the 18th or 19th Dynasty (1580-1200 B.C.).

    Text, commentary and translation: A.H. Gardiner, *Admonitions of an Egyptian Sage* (Leipzig 1909), 1-95.

14. *The Complaints of Khakheperre-sonb*: This work, which can be dated to the Middle Kingdom, has been preserved on a writing tablet from the 18th Dynasty. This tablet, No.5645 in the British Museum, is the single surviving copy.

    Text, translation and study: A. H. Gardiner, ibid., 95-112.

15. *The Prophecies of Neferti*: The single complete version deriving from the 18th Dynasty is preserved on Pap. 1116B recto in the Hermitage Museum, Leningrad. This is augmented by fragments preserved on writing tablets and ostraca.

    An integrated edition, translation and commentary is in W. Helck, *Die Prophezeiung des Nfr.tj* (Wiesbaden 1970).

    Translation and commentary: H. Goedicke, *The Protocol of Neferyt* (Baltimore 1977).

    Study (without translation): E. Blumenthal, "Die Prophezeihung des Nerfeti," *ZÄS* 109 (1982), 1-27.

16. *The Man Who Was Tired of Life*: This work was probably written either during the First Intermediate Period or at the beginning of the Middle Kingdom, although today some scholars believe that it should be ascribed to the days of the Hyksos (Second Intermediate Period). The surviving papyrus — Berlin 3024 — dates to the Middle Kingdom.

    Text and translation: R.O. Faulkner, "The Man Who Was Tired of Life," JEA 42 (1956), 21-40. W. Barta, *Das Gespräch eines Mannes mit seinem Ba* (Berlin 1969). H. Goedicke, *The Report about the Dispute of a Man with His Ba* (London 1970).

17. *The Eloquent Peasant*: This work is preserved on four papyri from

the Middle Kingdom. Three of these are now in Berlin (known as B1, B2 and R) and the fourth, Pap. Butler, is in London. Opinion is divided over the date of composition: some scholars date it to the Middle Kingdom (12th, 13th Dynasty), others to the Heracleopolitan Period (9th, 10th Dynasty).[30]

Text, commentary and translation: F. Vogelsang, *Kommentar zu den Klagen des Bauern* (Leipzig 1913); E. Perry, *A Critical Study of the Eloquent Peasant*, Ph.D. thesis, Johns Hopkins University (Baltimore 1986).

B. School Texts

18. *The Kemit*: This is a textbook composed at the beginning of the Middle Kingdom but based on earlier material. All surviving copies belong to the Middle Kingdom. *The Kemit* contains three sections — a formal greeting generally used to open a letter, a story and sayings similar in style and content to the Egyptian instructions and biographies.

Text: G. Posener, *Catalogue des ostraca hiératiques littéraires de Deir el Médineh* (Cairo 1951ff.), vol. II, pls. 1-21.

Text, translation: W. Barta, *ZÄS* 105(1978), 6-14.

19. *The Instructions of Amennakht*: Only the beginning has been preserved. The instruction, written by a scribe of the House of Life named Amennakht, centers on praising the scribal profession. It is probably of the same date as *The Instruction of Anii*, i.e., the 18th Dynasty.

Text, translation and study: G. Posener, "L'excorde de l'instruction educative d'Amennakhte," *Rd'E* 10(1955), 61-72.

20. *The Instruction of Kheti* (*son of Duauf*): The subject of this work is identical with the foregoing and its use as a school textbook is confirmed by hundreds of surviving copies. Its composition dates to the Middle Kingdom (12th Dynasty) but most of the copies are from the 19th Dynasty. The important papyri are: Pap. Sallier II, Pap. Anastasi III, and Pap. Chester Beatty XIX.

Text, commentary and translation: H. Brunner, *Die Lehre des Cheti Sohnes des Duauf* (Glückstadt 1944); W. Helck, *Die Lehre des Dw3-ḫtjj*, 2 vols. (Wiesbaden 1970).

21. *School Literature*: A collection of manuscripts dating to the Ramesside Period was published by Gardiner. In the present study only selected papyri are treated, namely: *Pap. Bologna* 1094, *Pap. Anastasi* III, IV, V; *Pap. Sallier* I, and IV verso; *Pap. Lansing*; *Pap. Koller*; *Pap. Turin* A and D.

Text, commentary and translation: A. H. Gardiner, R. Caminos, *LEM.*

22. *Pap. Chester Beatty* IV: The composition, whose main topic is the eternity of the scribes, was written during the New Kingdom. The surviving copy, *Pap. Chester Beatty* IV (= Pap. 10684 in the British Museum), can be assigned to the 19th or 20th Dynasty (ca., 1300-1000 B.C.).

A.H. Gardiner, *Hieratic Papyri in the British Museum, Third Series, Chester Beatty* IV, vol. I, 37-44, vol.II, plates 18ff.

23. *Letter to a Wayword Son*: An exhortation written in a form of a letter by the scribe Menna to his son and pupil. Only one copy has survived — ostracon 12074 in Chicago deriving from the workmen's village in Deir el Médineh. The topic, "a son gone bad," points to the possibility that it was used as a model letter in the village school during the Ramesside Period.

Text, translation and study: W. Guglielmi, "Eine 'Lehre' für einen reiselustigen Sohn," *WdO* 14(1983), 147-166;

J.L. Foster, "Oriental Institute Ostracon 12074: 'Menna's Lement' or 'Letter to a Wayward Son'," *JSSEA* 14(1984), 88-98.

24. *A School Exercise in Demotic*: The exercise was written on a papyrus known today as Pap. Berlin 13639, dating from the Ptolemaic Period.

Publication: W. Erichsen, "Eine Aegyptische Schulübung in Demotischer Schrift (Berlin 13639)," *Historik-Filologiske Meddelelser* 31(1945), 3-25.

25. *The Onomasticon of Amenemope*: Amenemope was a scribe in the House of Life at the end of the 20th Dynasty (11th century B.C.).

The onomasticon written by him includes about 2,000 items and is preserved in several manuscripts deriving from the 20th-23rd Dynasties; that of Golenischeff is the most complete.
Publication and study: A.H. Gardiner, *Ancient Egyptian Onomastica*, 2 vols. (Oxford 1947).

C. Royal Inscriptions and Autobiographies

Corpora of Texts[31]

26. *Inscriptions of the 18th Dynasty*: K. Sethe, *Urk.* IV.
27. *Texts of the Amarna Period* (14th century B.C.), pertaining to both royal and religious literature: M. Sandman, *Texts from the Time of Akhenaten* (Brussels 1938).

Studies and Monographs

(1) Old Kingdom

28. Phraseological study of the autobiographical inscriptions and addresses to visitors at tombs : E. Edel, "Untersuchungen zur Phraseologie der ägyptischen Inschriften des Alten Reiches," *Mitteillungen des Deutschen Instituts für ägyptische Altertumskunde in Kairo*, 13/1 (1955), 1-56.

(2) Middle Kingdom

29. A study covering the rhetorical as well as the lexical features peculiar to the inscriptions of the 11th Dynasty by: H.J. Polotsky, *Zu den Inschriften der 11 Dynastie* (Leipzig 1929; repr. Hildesheim 1964).
30. Research of the "royal" phraseology based on royal inscriptions, biographies and literary texts, wisdom works being treated in the last category: E. Blumenthal, *Untersuchungen zum ägyptischen Königtum des Mittleren Reiches*, vol. I (Berlin 1970).

(3) Old and Middle Kingdoms

31. A study of the evolution of the genre of "autobiographical inscription" beginning with the Old Kingdom up to the Middle Kingdom including translation and commentary of a variety of samples: M. Lichtheim, *Ancient Egyptian Autobiographies Chiefly of the Middle Kingdom: A Study and Anthology* (Freiburg-Göttingen 1988).

32. *The Stele of Mentuhotep Son of Hapu* dating from the 12th Dynasty, republished and studied by W. Schenkel, *JEA* 50(1964), 6-12.

33. An investigation of terms, phrases and idioms characteristic of the autobiographical texts: J. Janssen, *De traditioneele egyptische Autobiographie voor het Nieuwe Rijk*, vol.I: *Teksten*, vol.II: *Vertaling en Commentaar* (Leiden 1946).

(4) Autobiographies of the New Kingdom and the Late Period

34. *The Autobiography of Nufer*: A short text written on a statue of a man dating from the 18th Dynasty, published by G. Gaballa, *MDAIK* 26(1970), 49-54.

35. *Autobiographies from the Late Period* (from the 9th century to the 1st century B.C.)

Monograph and translation: E. Otto, *Die biographischen Inschriften der ägyptischen Spätzeit* (Leiden 1954): Inscriptions 1,3,5-10, 19, 22, 28, 39, 46, 48, 53, 57, 61, 75.

Publication of the above inscriptions in: *Kairo Catalogue Général* (Cairo 1914), Inscriptions Nos. 42231, 42213, 42225, 42208, 42210, 42230, 42227, 42226, 42236, 42237, 689; *Iret-Hor-aa*: K. Piehl, *ZÄS* 41 (1887), 120ff; *Petehor-neb-chen*: A. Scharff, *ZÄS* 62 (1925), 86ff; *Hor-Ra*: B. Turajeff, *ZÄS* 46 (1909), 75ff; *Hor*: W. Wreszinski, *Aegyptische Inschriften* (Vienna 1906), 85ff; *Taimhotep*: K.H. Brugsch, *Thesaurus*, 1968, 918ff; *Psamtich-sa-Neith*: H. Ranke, *MDAIK* 12 (1954), 112 ff.;

Petosiris: Excerpts from G. Lefebvre, *Le Tombeau de Petosiris*, 3 vols. (Cairo 1923-1924).

New edition of biographies of the 22nd and 23rd Dynasties, with translation, commentary and phraseology catalogue by K. Jansen-Winkeln, *Ägyptische Biographien der 22. und 23. Dynastie*, 2 vols. (Wiesbaden 1985).

D. Religious Literature

36. Selection of hymns and prayers from various periods. Translation and study: J. Assmann, *ÄHG*. Text: see ibid., for the sources for the following hymns — 20, 144, 148, 149, 150, 164, 173, 182, 195, 226, 227, 235.[32]

CHAPTER ONE

INSTRUCTION AND TEACHING TERMS

In Egyptian wisdom literature there are four terms denoting instruction and teaching — *sb3y.t*, *mtr(t)*, *tp rd* and *sḫr*. These terms are equivalent to *mûsār*, *tôkaḥat*, *tôrâ/miṣwâ* and *ʿēṣâ* respectively in Biblical wisdom literature. Examination of these words will shed light on the educative setting in both ancient Egypt and Israel, namely, on the identity of the teachers, the nature of the studied material and the methods of acquisition of knowledge in the Egyptian schools and within the Israelite didactic framework. Let us consider each term and its equivalent separately.

I. *sb3y.t* — *mûsār*

sb3y.t[1] which parallels *mûsār* in Biblical Hebrew, has a double meaning: (a) Instruction — mainly intended as training for a certain profession (such as carpentry, marksmanship, scribal arts, rules of administration — Blumenthal G2,21; *Urk.* IV 503, 13; 976, 13, 17; *Anastasi* IV 1a, 1; cf. also *Ankhsheshonqy* 19, 25) but also containing general educational aims (ethical-moral rules such as social conduct, table manners, behavior towards others, self-control, etc.; cf. *sb3 m/n ʿnḫ* below, and *sb3 sšm*, "to teach conduct" — *Les.* 74, 2); (b) Corporal punishment — in this sense the verb *sb3* is accompanied by the determinative of a man holding a stick, suggesting the method of teaching. Thus, *sb3y.t* refers to the reality of transferring information from teacher to pupil. Beating with a stick was common practice in ancient schools: "You have smote upon my back, your teaching has entered my ear," a pupil says to his teacher (*Lansing* 11, 1-2; *Anastasi* IV 8, 7); "Pleasant (*nḏm*) is the beating at school" another pupil says in adulation of his teacher (Fischer-Elfert, "Ich bin das Schiff," 11). That this is the significance of *sbꜣy.t* is verified by the use of the verb *sbꜣ* in reference to the domestication of animals. In the Egyptian school texts we read for example: "One teaches (*iri sbꜣy.t*) the lion" and "a monkey is taught (*sbꜣ*) to dance" (*Bologna* 1094 3,10; *Anastasi* V 8, 7-8; cf. *Anii* 10,1).[2]

The titles of Egyptian wisdom instructions, whose literary framework is that of father speaking to son, usually contain the term *sbꜣy.t* (*Ptaḥḥotep*, *Merikare*, *Anii*, *Amenemhet*, *Kheti*, etc.). But other kinds of compositions, associated with the wisdom tradition, are also named *sbꜣy.t*: the king's instructions to officials (*El Amarna*);[3] god's teaching to his believers;[4] encyclopaedic lists (*The Onomasticon of Amenemope*); last testaments (*Petosiris*); and even rules for letter-writing.[5]

It follows that the term *sbꜣy.t* indicates a literary genre[6] covering a variety of compositions, which differ from each other in form and content but all share a common aim — to transmit knowledge. All of these works served as textbooks in Egyptian schools.[7] This last fact illuminates the precise semantic field of the concept *sbꜣy.t*; as most of the works bearing the label belong to the didactic corpus, it becomes apparent that *sbꜣy.t* denotes primarily written, not oral, instructions (in contrast to *mtr*, see following section).[8]

Occasionally the usual label *sbꜣy.t* is replaced by the collocation *sbꜣy.t n/m ʿnḫ* — "teaching for life" (*Amenemope*, *El Amarna* — Sandman 60, 6; 80, 8-9; 92, 8). Elsewhere there are other, similar descriptions of teaching: "right conduct (*sšr*) of life" (*Seḥetep-ib-Ra* 1,7) or "sayings (*ṯsw*) of a way of life" (*Amennakht* 1). The attribute "life," which in the above examples accompanied "teaching," "conduct" or "sayings," stresses the ultimate goal of teaching, which is to guide man through life. It endows the man who follows its precepts with "life values," without which the enjoyment of life cannot be complete. Those values are longevity, good health, and honor. In the words of the Egyptian sage: "To direct him in the ways of life, to make him whole on earth, to let his heart enter its shrine and steer clear of evil. To save him from the mouth of the crowd, to let him be praised in the mouth of people" (*Amenemope*, Prologue, 1, 7 ff.).

The instructions were given in writing but the method of impressing them upon the mind was through oral repetition. The son of Anii protests that the pupil must learn the "scroll" by heart and claims that even then he will not be learned (9,17). It follows that the learning process connected with *sbȝ* did not consist in independent creative discovery but, rather, was a passive acquisition of knowledge.[9]

The educational framework was authoritarian, whether in the *informal* familial setting — where the father acted as teacher (for example, *Ptaḥḥotep*, *Ankhsheshonqy*, *Amenemope*), or the *official* one — within the king's court (where at times the king was the educator, as in the *El-Amarna* inscriptions and the autobiographical texts),[10] or in the school (as in the school writings). In the religious literature and the later autobiography, the god himself appears as a teacher bestowing knowledge (see above, n. 4).

mûsār,[11] like *sbȝy.t* in Egyptian, has a double meaning — reproof and teaching on the one hand and beating on the other.[12] Thus, *mûsār* in the first sense appears in the father's warning to his son: "My son, hear the instruction (*mûsār*) of your father and forsake not the law (*tôrâ*) of your mother" (Prov. 1,8). In another proverb it says: "A fool despises his father's instruction (*mûsār*), but he who heeds reproof (*tôkaḥat*) acquires prudence" (Prov. 15,5).[13] The didactic method which relies on the rod as a tool is clearly defined in a number of verses in which *mûsār* is parallel to *šēbeṭ* ("rod") or appears in association with it. For example, "He that spares his rod hates his son, but he that loves him chastises him" (*šiḥărô mûsār*) (Prov. 13,24). (See also ibid. 23,13; 22,15 — "the rod of reproof" [*šēbeṭ mûsār*]; and 19,18; 26,3; 29,19; cf. 1 Kgs. 12, 11, 14). The "punitive" authority in Israel, as in Egypt, comprises three factors: father and mother (real or fictional — Prov. 1,8; 13,1; 4, 1, 3; 31,1ff.), king (Prov. 31,1 [queen]; 1 Kgs. 12, 11, 14, 2 Chr. 10, 11, 14) and God (Prov. 3,11; Job 5,17; Ps. 94, 12). In this light, the roots of the Hebrew *mûsār*, as of the Egyptian *sbȝy.t*, seem to lie within the context of child upbringing. Only later was it applied to other areas of life, particularly to the religious-national and private sphere, where *mûsār* came to denote the relationship between God and believer, as well as the punishment inflicted by the God upon his people; but at times the "authentic" context of the word reappears in these passages (cf., e.g., Deut. 8,5).

To express the idea of gaining or acquiring instruction, Biblical wisdom makes use of verbs and expressions equal to those found in Egyptian wisdom: "take a lesson from" (*lqḥ mûsār*, Prov. 1,3; 8,10; 24,32); "hearken to" (*šᵉmaʿ*, ibid. 1,8; 4,1,10; 5,7 etc.); "apply your heart/pay attention to instructions" (*hābî'â lammûsār libbekā*, ibid. 23,12; *śym lēb*, and synonyms, ibid. 22,17; 24,32);[14] "'uncover' an ear to instruction" (*glh 'ozen lammûsār*, Job 36,10; cf. 33,16). Like Egyptian instruction, which guides man towards "a way of life" (*sbȝy.t n/m ʿnḫ*), so "reproofs of instruction" (*tôkᵉḥôt mûsār*) in the language of Proverbs are "a way of life" (*derek ḥayyîm*, Prov. 6,23); while "he who heeds instruction" (*šômēr mûsār*) attains "a way of life" (*'ōraḥ lᵉḥayyîm*, 10,17; cf. 8,33-35; etc.).

The question arises whether the word *mûsār* in the Bible denotes a specific literary genre, an instruction (*Lebenslehre*), as *sbȝy.t* does in the Egyptian wisdom. Some scholars find the genre of instruction in three collections of Proverbs entitled *mûsār* and which seem to have features characteristic of *sbȝy.t*, i.e., "The Proverbs of Solomon," 1-9; "The Sayings of the Wise," 22,17-24,22 (specially verses 23,12-26), and "Lemuel" 31, 1-9.[15] But even if the Hebrew *mûsār*, like its Egyptian counterpart, denotes the literary genre of instruction, the two are not identical. *mûsār* does not include a body of literary works differing from each other in content, as does *sbȝy.t*; nowhere in the Bible does *mûsār* imply a written instruction. It is essentially an oral exhortation. *mûsār* is not a guide for professional training accompanied by general ethical precepts in the manner of *sbȝy.t*.

II. *mtr(t)* — *tôkaḥat*

The polisemic word *mtr/mty* usually appears next to the term *sbȝy.t* in texts belonging to the wisdom literature.[16] The use of the noun is

common mainly in the instructions while the adjective is often used in the biographies and in the royal inscriptions.[17] The exact meaning of *mtr* and its relation to *sb3y.t* is difficult to determine for several reasons:
(a) The promiximity of the two terms, which stand in close association. Most Egyptologists have made no attempt to define them separately and translate them as follows: *sb3y.t* — instruction, *Lehre*; *mtr* — *Unter̄icht, enseignement.*[18]
(b) The term *mtr* is polysemic (*Wb.* II 171-174). Two main meanings are given in the dictionaries: (1) "to testify," "a testimony," "a witness" (Copt. ⲙⲛⲧⲣⲉ); (2) "be straightforward," "straightforwardness," "right." The spelling for both meanings is identical, as are the determinatives accompanying the term: two fingers, sometimes with the addition of a man sitting with his hand in his mouth (as adjective — "a straightforward man"; or as a verb — "to be precise," "to testify") or a rolled papyrus (representing a noun—"testimony," or a quality — "straightforwardness").

The meaning "straightforward" for *mtr* was more common in the wisdom literature of the Old Kingdom (*Kagemni, Ptaḥḥotep*) while the second usage, "testimony," "to testify," was more frequent in the Middle and the New Kingdoms. This fact may indicate a semantic development of *mtr*, which at first served to indicate a human trait and later referred to legal proceedings, since straightforwardness is essential in a witness. The semantic shift (metonomy) of the term from a general concept involving straightforwardness to one relating to a limited, specific situation is confirmed by the determinative common to both terms which, as described above, is a drawing of a bent finger, still having the meaning "precisely" (*maḍbūṭ*) in contemporary Arabic.[19]

Syntactic analysis, i.e., the examination of the corpus of texts on which this research is based, shows that *mtr*/*mty* embraces various spheres of life: on the social level it denotes one of the virtues of the ideal human type, e.g., "honesty";[20] appearing in a legal context it means "testimony,"[21] finally, in the learning-educational setting it stands in synonymous parallelism with *sb3y.t* and applies to education and reproof. Of the above three spheres only the last is relevant to our discussion. An examination of the texts belonging to this context reveals the following components as characteristic of *mtr* : *mtr* refers to an instruction in which relations between teacher and pupil are on a personal level, whether the reference is to study within the family, with the father acting as teacher (*Ankhsheshonqy* 4, 16-17; *Insinger* 8, 22; *Pap. Louvre* 2414 I 1; *Anii* 9,19), or to the acquisition of knowledge in a school (in school writings such as *Lansing* 8,3; 8,8; etc.).[22] In this context the paternal tone of the teachers and the pupils' undisciplined behavior, which may undermine the teacher's authority (cf. *Anii* 9,14-19), are remarkable.

Unlike *sbȝy.t*, *mtr.t* denotes oral instruction,[23] seeking to impart to the pupil general moral education and not necessarily professional skills. In *Anii* the father begins his instruction by saying that he intends to declare "*mtr.wt* of good character" (2,3), continuing on in more detail: not to be lazy, to avoid evil, etc. Further evidence is found in the school writings, where ethical reproofs (*mtr*) are directed at the idle scribe (*Sallier* I 7, 10).

It follows that *mtr* means reproof as a medium of teaching moral values, which may be acquired by study. However, study is not always the way to acquire values: in *Anii* the son complains that even a diligent pupil, well-versed in the writings, is incapable of fulfilling the father's *sbȝy.t mtr.wt* (9,17); but another text claims that a man may be endowed by nature with a good character without any training: "There is he who has not been taught (*mtr*), yet he knows how to instruct (*sbȝ*) another" (*Insinger* 9, 16).

When *mtr.t* appears in *parallelismus membrorum* with *sbȝy.t*, the latter term may well be understood to designate a manual for professional training, i.e., the two terms complement each other to form a single concept — a dual instruction embracing both professional training and rules of ethical conduct. Thus it becomes clear that the following two lines in *Pap. Bologna* 1094 are complementary: "One spends the whole night teaching you (*iw.tw ḥr mtr.t.k* — ethically, morally) and passes the whole day training you for a profession (*iw.tw ḥr sbȝ.k*)" (3, 7-8). This combination of professional training and educative teaching is expressed in the collocation *sbȝy.t mtr.w.*[24] This sometimes appears as the title of instructions — *Anii*, *Amennakht* — which combine both professional training (that of a scribe) and general ethical education.[25]

While regarding *mûsār* as the Hebrew equivalent of *sb3y.t*, scholars have tried to find in the Hebrew *'ēdût* an analogy with the Egyptian *mtr.*[26] *'ēdût*, like *mtr* has a double meaning: "to testify," "testimony," and "law" as inscribed on the tables of the testimony (source P). B. Couroyer believes that the original meaning of *mtr* is "testimony," "to testify," and that in Egyptian wisdom literature the term assumed a technical meaning of learning or education.[27] He bases his premise on the awareness that the Egyptian wisdom texts are biographies founded on testimony and personal experience; hence, *mtr* means advice based on successful personal experience, while *sb3y.t* refers to traditional data and technical knowledge. The noun *mtr* is therefore parallel to the Hebrew nouns *t*^{e}*'ûdâ* (Isa. 8,16,20) or *'ēdût* (Ps. 119) which in the Bible stand in parallelism with *tôrâ*. Thus the parallel Egyptian pairs *sb3y.t* — *mtr.t* and *sb3* — *mtr* are equivalent in Hebrew to *tôrâ* — *t*^{e}*'ûdâ* (*'ēdût*); *lmd* (pi'el) — *'wd* (hiph'il). The roots of this analogy, according to Couroyer, are already to be found in the books of Proverbs and Psalms, but they emerge clearly for the first time in Ben Sira 4, 11 where we read: "Wisdom instructs (*limm*^{e}*dâ*) her sons/And teaches (*wattā'īd*) all who give heed to her."[28]

While Couroyer is certainly correct in saying that in the Bible *'wd* (hiph'il) sometimes means "to teach,"[29] his claim that *mtr* parallels *'wd* is difficult to support for the following reasons:

(a) *'ēdût*, *t*^{e}*'ûdâ* and *lmd* (hiph'il), which are presented by Couroyer as equivalents to Egyptian wisdom terms, do not belong to Biblical wisdom phraseology.[30]

(b) In determining that the root *lmd* is the Hebrew equivalent of *sb3* in Egyptian, Couroyer relies, *inter alia*, on the Coptic translation of the Old Testament; according to him the verb in the pi'el — *limmēd* — is rendered in the translation *tsabo*, *tisbo*. But the Coptic translation of the Bible, at least most parts of it, are based on the Septuagint and not on the Hebrew Version.[31] Furthermore, the dictionary (Crum) shows that ⲥⲃⲱ, ϯ ⲥⲃⲱ is also used in Coptic for the translation of the noun *mûsār* and the verb *ysr* (in pi'el).[32]

(c) Couroyer's assumption that *mtr* is based on personal experience may be correct,[33] but it is difficult to accept that *mtr* is equivalent to *t^e'ûdâ*, *'ēdût*, in Hebrew, for nowhere in any Egyptian source is it explicitly stated that the reference is to a written document such as *t^e'ûdâ* or *'ēdût*. On the contrary, a survey of the sources shows, as we have seen in the above section, that *mtr* probably refers to "oral reproof."

While Couroyer's suggestion thus appears open to criticism, we propose an alternative possibility, namely that the Hebrew concept *tôkaḥat* (not *tôkēḥâ*, which does not belong to the wisdom vocabulary) is the equivalent of the Egyptian *mtr*. The word *tôkaḥat* belongs to the vocabulary of Biblical wisdom,[34] meaning "reproof, reproach, rebuke." This opinion is reinforced by the following linguistic usages and forms:
(a) The term *tôkaḥat* is close to the adverb *l^enōkaḥ* — "facing, in front of,"[35] while similarly *mtr* means, *inter alia*, "be present, in front of" (in Copt. — ⲙⲧⲟ; see *Wb*. II 171).
(b) Hebrew derivatives from the same root are the noun *n^ekōḥâ* and the adjective *nōkaḥ*, i.e., "straightforward," and "right," which also belong to the wisdom glossary.[36] Thus words of wisdom are "right to him that understands" (*n^ekōḥîm lammēbîn*), "there is nothing crooked (*niptāl*) and twisted (*'iqqēš*) in them" (Prov. 8,8-9). And elsewhere: "He will be kissed on his lips, that gives a right answer (*mēšîb d^ebārîm n^ekōḥîm*)," (ibid. 24,26; cf. BS 11,21). This Hebrew usage is analogous to the Egyptian usage of *mtr*, which when appearing as an adjective, means "straight," "precise."[37]
(c) The term *tôkaḥat* like the Egyptian *mtr*, has a legalistic connotation, but unlike *mtr* it does not include the meaning of "testify" or "testimony."[38] This does not negate the analogy between *tôkaḥat* and *mtr* for it is reasonable to assume that the meaning of "reproof" for *mtr* in the language of the Egyptian wisdom and school has its origins in the adjective "straight" and not in the verb "testify;" for "to straighten someone" means metaphorically, both in Egyptian and in Hebrew, to set someone on the right way, that is, "to educate."[39]

The semantic development of the term *mtr* may be reconstructed in the following way:

			(Couroyer:
1.	*adverb —	"be present"	————————
2.	*adjective —	"be straightforward	"to testify" [legalistic]
	/	\	|
3.	"to testify" "testimony"	"to teach/educative" "instruction"	"to teach" [testify — educational])

To summarize: *tôkaḥat* in the sense of "reproach" or "reproof" stands in parallelism with *mûsār* and appears to be a suitable analogy (rather than *ʿēdût*) to *mtr* which parallels *sbꜣy.t* in Egyptian. Thus, *mtr* is an oral reproof and *tôkaḥat* is a reproof expressed by mouth and lips (Job 13,6; 23,4); *mtr* is reinforced by beating with a stick and, similarly, *tôkaḥat* involves a beating (2 Sam. 7,14; Prov. 29,15; cf. wisdom Ps. 73,14). *mtr* is not directed at an incorrigible fool (*lḫ*); nor is *tôkaḥat* which is intended for a wise man (*ḥākām*) not a *lēṣ* (Prov. 9,8; 15,12; 19,25).[40]

III. *tp rd* — *miṣwâ, tôrâ*

In contrast to *sbꜣy.t* and *mtr(t)*, which belong to the didactic vocabulary, the term *tp rd* which stands in parallelism with them[41] originated in the phraseology of the court hierarchy and was borrowed by wisdom for its own use. *tp rd* denotes order or command of a teacher (father), king or deity.

The content of *tp rd* depends on the speaker. In the instruction, the teaching of the sage is termed *tp rd*: "*tp rd* of good speach" (*Ptaḥḥotep* 48), or "*tp rd* of relations with elders" (*Amenemope* 1,3). The instruction calling for loyalty to the royal house is also called *tp rd* (*Seḥetep-ib-Ra* 7,7); while in the inscriptions of the king's court, where the commander is the king or his high official, the orders are varied by nature, being directed towards both secular[42] and holy activities.[43]

Unlike *sbꜣy.t*, and even less like *mtr*, each of which contains a counseling element in the paternal tone of a man of experience rather than the character of an arbitrary order, in *tp rd* there is an uncompromising demand in the form of an ultimatum, usually issued by someone of high rank to a subordinate.[44]

In the search for an analogous term for the Egyptian *mtr* and *sb3y.t*, the word *tôrâ* has been suggested.[45] We, however, believe that *tôrâ*, in addition to another term, *miṣwâ*, is the equivalent of *tp rd*, i.e., *tp rd* = *tôrâ*, *miṣwâ*. Both the parallel linguistic usages of the Hebrew and Egyptian terms as well as their semantic determination confirm this assumption. In the Egyptian wisdom literature and outside it, *tp rd* stands in parallelism with *sb3y.t*, while in the Biblical wisdom literature both *tôrâ* and *miṣwâ* are parallel to *mûsār* (Prov. 1, 8 *mûsār* || *tôrâ*; Prov. 6, 23 *miṣwâ*, *tôrâ* || *tôk*^{e}*ḥôt mûsār*).

As we have already seen, the term *tp rd* has several meanings; in the Bible the terms *miṣwâ*/*tôrâ* cover an identical semantic field, while applying to: (a) a command of God (Gen. 26, 5; Deut. 8, 1-2; Wisdom Pss. 19, 9; 78, 7; Ezra 10, 3);[46] (b) a command by a king or a man (1 Kgs. 2,43; Jer. 39,11; Deut. 17,11, etc.); (c) wisdom instruction (Prov. 1,8; 3,1; 6,20, 23; 31,26; Qoh. 8,5; etc.).

Excursus

tôrâ, *miṣwâ* in Biblical wisdom literature — of God or wise man?

Bible scholars have long been preoccupied with the problem of identifying the authority lying behind the terms *tôrâ* and *miṣwâ* in Proverbs. Is it the Torah of God or that of a wise man? We believe that some of the distinctions presented in the preceding pages illuminate and contribute to the solution of this problem.

The derivation of the noun *tôrâ* is subject to debate. Lately, scholars have settled for the assumption that *tôrâ* is a nominalized form of the verb *yrh*, i.e., "to teach," "to direct," the basic meaning of which is "die Hand, die Finger ausstrecken um den Weg zu zeigen."[47] It seems that the primary meaning of *tôrâ* was therefore "guiding," "teaching," while the connotation of "law," "command," was a latter development. In general, scholars agree that the meaning of Torah, God's law, was absent from the early stages of the Hebrew wisdom literature, appearing only in the later Hebrew wisdom, in the postexilic Psalms (1; 94; 111; 112; 119, etc.) and in Ben Sira. In the latter, the natural, practical wisdom taught by a father or a teacher is replaced by a nomistic piety, and wisdom is identified with the Torah.[48]

Scholarly opinion is divided on whether the terms *tôrâ* and *miṣwâ*, in at least a part of Proverbs, may be identified with God's commands — the Torah. The prevailing opinion is that two layers or stages should be distinguished in Proverbs:[49] (a) Instructions based on wisdom as the fruit of experience and aimed at educating the individual towards a successful life. (b) Instructions and precepts pertaining to Yahwistic piety which explicate the instructions of type (a) above in a manner conforming to the spirit of the monotheistic faith.

In the first stage *tôrâ* and *miṣwâ* refer to the authority of a father or a wise man, and the instruction is set within a familial framework (real or fictional). In the second stage, which includes sentences identifying God's Law with wisdom (Prov. 1,7; 9,10; Job 28,28), the terms *tôrâ* and *miṣwâ* refer to God's Law.

While accepting the distinction of different stages in the development of Proverbs, Fichtner and other scholars[50] hold that *dābār*, *miṣwâ* and *tôrâ* always refer here to the sayings of wise men, never to God's Torah. As to Prov. 30,5: "Every word of God is pure. He is a shield to those who trust in him. Add not to his words lest he reprove thee and thou be found a liar" (|| Ps. 18, 31; 2 Sam. 22,31), generally considered to be a reflection of theological tradition, Fichtner argues that here we are not dealing with "words" of the Torah. Yet, the pupil is warned not to add to the "words" of the wise man, that is, to the collection of sayings. Fichtner concedes, however, that in this passage the wisdom words are, for the first time in the history of Hebrew wisdom, called "words of God," indicating the beginning of a process in which wisdom will be ascribed directly to God (Job 4,12 ff. and Prov. 8).

Comparison with the Egyptian material illuminates and confirms this gradual evolvement of Hebrew wisdom. As shown above, god does not appear in the guise of a teacher or mentor in the Egyptian wisdom texts — this belongs to religious literature and the autobiography inscriptions and appears at a relatively late stage.[51] Assmann, who investigated the connection between the Egyptian wisdom and Egyptian piety, showed that "personal piety" (*persönliche Frömmigkeit*), the beginnings of which were in the 18th Dynasty, gradually grew out of wisdom literature.[52] He points out stages belonging to this process: (1) In the wisdom literature of the Old Kingdom, "personal piety" is not a central subject and is present there only in the background. (2) Beginning with *The Instruction of Amenemope*, faith assumes major importance. In the literature of "personal piety" preceding and contemporary with *Amenemope*, we find the parallel concept that piety is not faith but knowledge, wisdom deriving from god (in the texts from *El-Amarna* and later, e.g., the *Hymn of Kiki*). (3) In the Ramesside Period the "knowledge of god" is the "fear of god" (e.g., *Bakenchons*).[53]

Hence, we may conclude that the theory of "chronological layers" in the Biblical wisdom literature is confirmed by a parallel development reflected in the Egyptian sources. In its initial stage the educational system both in Israel and in Egypt was natural and simple, i.e., the "instruction" and "command" were dependent on paternal authority, and education was conducted within the family; subsequently, or perhaps at the same time, instruction was given also at an official institution of education, most probably, the school.[54] This initial stage is reflected in the book of Proverbs which in spirit and character is closer than any other wisdom book in the Bible to the ancient Egyptian instructions. Here *tôrâ* is always that of the father and *mûsār* that of the teacher.[55] At a later stage faith in God became an inseparable part of wisdom; the *miṣwâ* and *tôrâ* of man became the Law and Torah of God. Signs of this development may already be found in Proverbs 30, 5.

IV. *sḫr* — *ʿēṣâ*

Several terms in our corpus serve to express the meaning of "to counsel," "counsel" in Egyptian,[56] but *sḫr* is the most important for comparative analysis with the Hebrew and the following discussion is restricted to this. The distribution of *sḫr*[57] is broad, covering all types of literature associated with the wisdom circle. Cazelles was the first to suggest regarding the Hebrew *'ēṣâ* to be the semantic equivalent of *sḫr.*[58] *'ēṣâ*, which derives from the West Semitic root *y'ṣ*, is not a wisdom term but occurs frequently in wisdom literature.[59] Like the Egyptian *sḫr*, *'ēṣâ* is a polysemic term, whose meaning is determined by its context. The semantic field of *'ēṣâ* and *sḫr* encompasses abstract meanings such as "thought," "way," "will," "intention," as well as concrete meanings emphasizing action, such as "plan," "command," "way of conduct."[60]

The usage of *'ēṣâ* and *sḫr* falls into three categories associated with various areas of life: education — instruction by the teacher and the words of the wise man denoted as "counsel;" the king's court — the king appears as counselor and his officials as bearers of counsel to the king; religious sphere — the counsel of god (*sḫr nṯr*) is on the one hand the divine plan reflected in the world order and in creation, and on the other it is "fear of god" and loyalty to him, which occupies a major place in the life of the believer.[61]

It is the first category i.e., the use of "counsel" within the didactic sphere, which is our concern. The other two categories do not belong to the subject of this chapter and we shall only note that the use of the term "counsel" within the setting of the king's court has played a central role in scholarly efforts to elucidate the figure of the wise man and to identify the creative circle responsible for wisdom in the Bible; thus some scholars have identified the "wise man" with the king's counselor.[62] As for the use of "counsel" in the religious context, this appears mainly in the prophetic writings and in Psalms, but it is not absent from the wisdom books.[63]

Returning to the didactic context, here *sḫr* — *'ēṣâ* assumes a meaning synonymous with *sb3y.t* — *mûsār* and *mtr(t)* — *tôkaḥat*, i.e., a sage's instruction.[64] This significance of *sḫr* is best expressed in the following examples: Ptaḥḥotep requests the king's permission to give his son "counsels (*sḫr.w*) of the fathers" (31) — a phrase directly related to the instructions that follow it; Seḥetep-ib-Ra gives "eternal counsels (*sḫr.w nj.w nḥḥ*), a correct method of life" (1, 6-7). Similarly in Proverbs, a father says to his son: "Hearken to counsel (*'ēṣâ*) and receive instruction (*mûsār*) that you may be wise in your latter end" (19,20). A teaching method predominant in both ancient Israel and Egypt is the giving and taking of counsel. Thus the high official praises himself as being one "who consults so as to be consulted" (*Intef son of Sent, AEA* 111, 19; ibid. 112, 12-13 and *Les.* 81,8).[65]

In the wisdom instructions the pupil is required to listen to the counsel of the teacher, the father. The obedient pupil "enters" (*'ḳ*) his teacher's counsel (*Anastasi* V, 23,5-6); while the foolish son acts counter to his father's counsel (*thi sḫr*) and disobeys his instruction (*sb3y.t*) (*Ptaḥḥotep* 207-208). "A wise man hearkens to counsel" says the sage in Proverbs (12,15). When Job was at the height of prosperity everyone hearkened to his counsel (Job 29,21).

Both in ancient Israel and Egypt the wise man serves as counselor adept at giving advice: The teacher is "versed in counsel" (*'m m sḫr.w, Lansing* 13b,9). Hence, in the autobiographic writings reflecting the values of wisdom, the high official appears as the possessor of "excellent counsel" (*AEA* 93,7; 98,8; cf. also ibid. 52,6 and *Urk.* IV 472, 13), as one of whom the king "is pleased with his counsels (*hrr.w ḥr sḫr.w.f*)" (ibid. 938,10; 1183,12; etc.).

In the Bible, *'ēṣâ* appears as the official form of expression for the wise man and stands in parallelism with "the law of the priest" and "the word of the prophet" (Jer. 18,18); the words of the wise men are *mō'ēṣôt wādā'at* ("wise counsel and knowledge," Prov. 22,20). The personified Wisdom in Proverbs, whose form in chapters 1 and 8 is close to the figure of the wise teacher, calls her words *'ēṣâ* (8, 14; cf. 1, 25,30). As noted above, Job appears in the days of his glory as the ideal wise man who bestows counsel on others, and Daniel, who is one of the wise men of Babylon (Dan. 2,12,13), replies to Arioch, captain of the king's guard, with words of *'ēṭā' wûṭᵉ'ēm* ("counsel and prudence," ibid., 2,14).

sḫr — *'ēṣâ* expresses a more liberal approach to education than that found in *sb3y.t* — *mûsār* and *mtr(t)* — *tôkaḥat.* The advice *sḫr* — *'ēṣâ*, which imparts to the pupil the possibility of making his own decisions, is the foundation underlying autodidactic learning.[66]

In conclusion, the Egyptian terms belonging to the semantic field of "instruction," "teaching" may be defined as follows:

sb3y.t	— an unshakeable tradition transmitted from generation to generation.
mtr(t)	— an oral instruction based on the teacher's experience.
tp rd	— a command given for a specific situation.
sḫr	— advice which can be appealed against.

Comparative analysis between these terms and the relevant terms in the Bible shows that the Egyptian term for instruction *sb3y.t* is a semantic equivalent of the Hebrew *mûsār*. *tp rd*, its partner in parallelism, is semantically identical with the words *miṣwâ* and *tôrâ* and like these has a threefold meaning, i.e., the command of a teacher, a king, or a god. The third term *mtr*, which is associated with the two former Egyptian terms, is equivalent to the term *tôkaḥat* in Hebrew and bears an identical meaning, namely, reproach and reproof. As to the Egyptian *sḫr*, it parallels the Hebrew *'ēṣâ* and both terms have a tone of liberality in education which is absent in the other terms.

CHAPTER TWO

TEACHING AND LEARNING ACTIVITIES

Chapter One considered terms signifying instruction and reproof and clarified various aspects of education. These terms, as we saw, related principally to the content of the material learned, but also touched upon the identity of the teachers and the nature of the educational framework. The present chapter deals with verbs and idioms concerning the activities of instruction and learning and completes the picture of the world of education in ancient Israel and Egypt.

I. VERBS CONNECTED WITH THE PROVIDING OF INSTRUCTION AND THE METHOD OF TEACHING

The semantic field of instruction in Egypt is covered with the three lexemes discussed at length in the preceding pages, *sb3*, *mtr*, *tp rd*, but here they occur either in verbal usage, that is, as verbs themselves or in the form of a combination of the verbs *rdi* ("to give") and *iri* ("to do") with the term "instruction" — *sb3y.t*, and its synonyms *mtr*, *tp rd*. In the language of Biblical wisdom the semantic field of the Egyptian *sb3*, *mtr* and *tp rd* is contained in seven verbs: *ysr* (niph'al, pi'el), *ykḥ* (hiph'il), *yrh* (hiph'il), *lmd* (pi'el), *byn* (hiph'il), *śkl* (hiph'il), and *'lp* (pi'el). Of these, only the last is characteristic of the language of the Hebrew sage. As the three Egyptian lexemes and their Hebrew semantic equivalents *ysr*, *ykḥ*, *yrh* were treated extensively in Chapter One,[1] we shall here first briefly turn our attention to the remaining four Hebrew lexemes and thereafter deal with further aspects that are relevant to teaching.

***lmd* (pi'el)**

lmd means "to teach," "instruct," and the participle *m^elammēd* designates a "teacher" (Prov. 5,13; BS 51, 17; cf. wisdom Ps. 119, 109). *m^elammēd* is exclusive to the wisdom literature and pertains to the wisdom vocabulary.[2] The root *lmd* in general is not part of this vocabulary, although it is connected with education. Thus, in some passages where the root *lmd* appears a vivid picture of the school's everyday life serves as a backdrop for the text. As in Isaiah 50,4 ff: "The Lord God has given me the tongue of those who are taught (*limmûdîm*) so that I know how to answer the weary with a word. Morning by morning he wakens; he wakens my ear, to hear as those who are taught (*kallimmûdîm*, i.e. pupils)." This description of rising in the morning to study is repeated in a cliché typical of Jeremiah: "I have taught (*w^elammēd*) them persistently but they have not listened to receive instruction (*lāqaḥat mûsār*)" (32,33). A feature common in these passages is the image of God as a teacher (cf. also Ps. 94,12).

Of all the terms found in connection with the subject of teaching and instructing in Egyptian, the closest to *lmd* is *sb3*, both from the viewpoint of its content as well as its form.[3] *lmd* also refers to animal training: in Jeremiah, Ephraim compares his suffering to those of a calf, saying: "Thou has chastened me and I was chastened like an untrained calf (*'ēgel lō' lûmmād*)" (31,17). Jeremiah probably borrowed this image from his predecessor, Hosea, who states: "Ephraim was a trained heifer (*'eglâ m^elûmmādâ*) that loved to thresh" (10,11).[4] The Hebrew nouns *m^elammēd*, *talmîd* and *limmûdîm* are derived from *lmd*, (like *sb3.w*, "a teacher," and *sb3y.t*, "pupil" which derive from *sb3*).[5]

The remaining terms — ***'lp*** (pi'el), ***byn*** (hiph'il), ***śkl*** (hiph'il) — have no semantic equivalent in Egyptian:

'lp The occurrence of *'lp* is limited to the wisdom books. In pi'el it means "to teach," and appears three times in Job (see below, Section b).[6]

byn In hiph'il it means "to endow somebody with understanding," "to teach."[7] The verbal form and the adjective *mēbîn*, i.e., "a teacher," belong to a later stage of Biblical Hebrew and do not appear in pre-exilic literature.

śkl The primary meaning of the root is "to look at," "to consider" (cf. Gen. 3,6), that is, observation aimed at understanding; the meaning "to teach," "to cause to discern," appears in the later Biblical books.[8]

So far we have dealt with the semantic analysis of terms relating to "the providing of instruction" in Biblical language. An examination of the context of these Hebrew words and of the terms which constitute an identical semantic field in Egyptian brings various details to light that prove useful in reconstructing the picture of education as it existed in Israel and Egypt.[9]

(a) The teaching authority: (1) Within a familial framework — a father (*Instruction by a Man for His Son* I 1; *Ankhsheshonqy* 4,16,17; etc.; Prov. 4,3,11 [*yrh*], cf. 5,13; Prov. 19,18; 29,17 [*ysr*]); a mother (Prov. 31,1 [*ysr*]; cf. ibid. 1,8; 4,3; 6,20 and Cant. 8,2). (2) The experienced elders (Job 8,8-10 [*yrh*]). (3) The teacher and the sage (*Lansing* 8,3; *Sallier* I 7,10 [*mtr*]; see also *Chester Beatty* IV, pl 18 verso 2, 8-9; Prov. 25,12; Job 6,25-26 [*ykḥ*]; 6,24 [*yrh*]; Qoh. 12,9 [*lmd*]; Job 33,33 [*'lp*]) or *mēbîn*, that is, the learned teacher who at times is one of the Levites (1 Chr. 15,22; 25,8; Dan. 11,33). (4) The high official — vizier (*Rekhmire*, *Urk.* IV, 1081,11) the district's governor (*Mentuhotep son of Hapu* 11). (5) The king (*El-Amarna*; and Blumenthal G 2,19-20, 22; 6,31). (6) The god, in the Egyptian hymn assumes the form of teacher (*Kiki* 1,2; *ÄHG* 150 B20; 149, 10,ff.); this image is also common in the Bible within and outside the educational framework: God "teaches" (*ysr*) his Law (Ps. 94,12 [a Psalm with wisdom features]; Deut. 8,5); God instructs, guides and teaches (*yrh*, *lmd*, *'lp*) (Job 36,22; wisdom Ps. 19, 102-103; Isa. 50, 4ff.; Ps. 25,4,9; 71,17; 94, 10 [a Psalm with wisdom features]; Job 35, 11);[10] He assumes the figure of a father "reproving" (*ykḥ*) his son (Prov. 3,11,12; Job 5,17; 13,10) and a teacher who *mēbîn* his commandments (wisdom Ps. 119, 27, 34, 73, 130, 144).

(b) The object of instruction: In the Bible the pupils are indicated in general terms — "sons of man" as distinct from animals; humans beings "are taught" (*'lf* — Job 15,5; 33,33; 35,11). While *yrh* in the sense of "to teach" is used for humans beings alone (wisdom Ps. 32,8-10), *ysr* and *lmd* like *sb3* and *mtr* in Egyptian (see the above discussion of *lmd*) are used both for training animals and instructing human beings.

The ideal recipients of the "reproof" are not only the "sage," who has a listening ear and is able to correct his ways (Prov. 9,8; 19,25), but also his opposites, the *na'ar*, *petî* (Heb.) and *ḫm* (Eg.), that is, "inexperienced youth" and "simple person." Thus *The Onomasticon of Amenemope* is defined in its title as "An instruction (*sb3y.t*) for understanding, a reproof (*mtr*) for the simple person (*ḫm*)" (cf. *Urk.* IV 1081,11; *ÄHG* 149, 7 ff.;[11] Prov. 1,4; 19,25; 21,11; etc.). The wise man moreover writes "instructions" for his young son (*Ankhsheshonqy* 5,16; cf. *Seḥetep-ib-Ra* reproaching his children, I 1-2). On the other hand, the opposite of the wise, the ignorant man, is likened to a deaf-mute (Blumenthal G 6,31; *Instruction by a Man for His Son* V 4-5).

(c) The method of providing instruction: The proven method for accelerating the learning process in the schools of the ancients consisted of threats or actual beatings. The verbs for instruction in Egyptian and Hebrew carry therefore a double meaning: *sb3* and *mtr* mean "to rebuke" with words as well as with blows: their equivalents in Biblical language are *ysr* and *ykḥ* (hiph'il).[12] Alongside these verbs with dual-meaning are Egyptian and Biblical Hebrew verbs which signify physical beating alone, *ḥwi* and *ḳnḳn* in Egyptian and their parallel *nkh* in Hebrew. At times they are accompanied by nouns: *šbd* in Egyptian and the parallel *šēbeṭ* (rod) in Hebrew, as well as the noun *sḫ.t* (blow) in Egyptian.[13] The threat of a beating recurs again and again in the Egyptian school writings. Thus in *Pap. Anastasi* III the pupil is warned: "Spend no day of idleness or you shall be beaten (*iw.tw ḥwi.k*), a boy's ear is upon his back, he hearkens to his beater (*ḥwi.f*)" (3,13 || ibid. V 8,5). Elsewhere the lazy scribe is compared to a beaten (*šsp ḳnḳn*) donkey (*Koller* 2,4); in *The Instruction of Anii*, a son's upbringing is compared to animal training (9,17-10,7), while the sage is referred to as "strong of arm" (10,15), suggestive of a threat to the obdurate son. The author of *Pap. Insinger* declares that "Thoth has placed the stick on earth in order to teach the fool by it... A son does not die from being punished by his father..." (9,6 ff).[14] Beating is effective, because the teachers had to endure it themselves at one time. The stick "fosters hope" towards a better future. "The rod (*šēbeṭ*) and reproof (*tôkaḥat*) give knowledge" (Prov. 29,15). "Folly is bound to the mind of a boy, but the rod of correction (*šēbeṭ mûsār*) will remove it" (Prov. 22,15). The Biblical sage, like his Egyptian counterpart, held that since the youngster or the fool were impervious to reason they had to be disciplined by corporal punishment, like an ass or a horse: "A whip for the horse, a bridle for the ass and a rod (*šēbeṭ*) for the back of the fools (*kᵉsîlîm*)" (Prov. 26,3). Evil, says the Biblical sage, is cleansed by flogging (Prov. 20,30).[15] This didactic stimulus is also hinted at by Qoheleth when he says: "For in much wisdom is much *vexation*, and he who increases knowledge increases *pain*" (1,18). However, while in the book of Proverbs and in the didactic Egyptian literature education and instruction are considered an efficient means of correcting the simple, this is not so in Qoheleth, who regards these means as useless: "What is crooked cannot be made straight, and what is lacking cannot be made up" (1,15). Wisdom is useless not only in the case of the "negative," incorrigible fool, the *lēṣ* and the *'ĕwîl* (cf. Prov. 19,25; 21,11; 27,22) but will not avail the "wise" either (Qoh. 2,11-22).

An attitude similar to that shown in the Egyptian didactic literature and the book of Proverbs is found in the later Hebrew literature and the wisdom of other peoples. Ben Sira says that he who spoils his child will lose him: "He who spoils his son will bind his wounds and with every scream will be upset in his belly. An untrained horse will be obdurate and an unrestrained child will be rebellious... crush his hips while he is still a youngster, bow his head in his youth and split his hips while little... chastise your son and increase his burden..." (30,7-13). The Assyrian sage Aḥiqar expresses a similar idea thus: "If I beat you, my son, you will not die; if I let you go your way — you will not live" (82).[16]

Summarizing, one may say that the components characteristic of the educational setting and the didactic method in Egypt and Israel — the identity of the teachers and pupils, the kind of material taught and the teaching method — are strikingly similar.

II. VERBS ASSOCIATED WITH ACQUISITION OF INSTRUCTION AND THE METHOD OF LEARNING

The verbs and phrases relating to the method of learning within the educational framework of antiquity — whether in the school institution or in another setting — point to the dual perception of study. It either takes the form of blind obedience, i.e., mere acceptance and assimlation of the teacher's instruction, or it is a more active learning method of understanding the material and "entering" the instructions so as to master and apply them.

The first aspect of this dual perception is covered by the following collocations: *iri sbȝy.t*, *smn sbȝy.t*, *šsp md.t*, *nḏr tp rd* in Egyptian and *qnh*, *nṣr*, *ṣpn*, *šmr*, *ḥzq* (hiph'il) + objects relating to *ḥokmâ* in Hebrew. For the second aspect, *wḥ'*, *'rḳ*, *'m*, *'ḳ sbȝy.t/sḫr* are used in Egyptian and *byn*, *śkl*, and *lmd* in Hebrew.

These two sides of learning are complementary, with no clear boundary dividing them, as is shown by the fact that some of the expressions have a double meaning relating to both aspects of learning. Examples are: Eg. *sḏm* — Heb. *šm'*, whose meanings are "to obey" and "to understand," Eg. *rdi ib* — Heb. *šyt lēb* and synonyms, meaning "to pay attention," "to hear" as well as "to think" and "to consider," and Dem. *ṯy sb'.t* — Heb. *lqḥ mûsār*, meaning "to obtain" and "to grasp, understand, instruction." Finally, *ḥqr* and *bqš* in Hebrew denote a higher level of inquiring after knowledge, i.e., pondering over and searching out things, for which the Egyptian verb *ḏ'r* forms only a partial analogy.

A. Verbs with a Double Meaning

Eg. *sḏm* (Dem. *stm*; Copt. [SF] ⲥⲱⲧⲙ) — Heb. *šm'*

The verb *sḏm*, which often collocates with the objects *sbȝy.t*, *mtr(t)* and *sḫr*, and its Hebrew equivalent *šm'* [17] are polysemic. Thus in texts belonging to the wisdom circle they both denote not only the act of "listening," i.e., a natural, automatic action, but also that in which it results — "obedience." Sometimes when the act of listening involves a certain mental effort, *sḏm/šm'* acquires the meaning of "to understand."[18]

One popular topic in Egyptian wisdom texts is the demand for attentiveness and obedience to the instruction of the father and the teacher and to people's words in general (*Kagemni* II 5; *Ptaḥḥotep* 49, 534ff.; *Amenemhet* ID; *Amenemope* 3,9ff.).[19] In the colorful language of the school writings the pupil is compared to domesticated animals: "The horse 'enters under' its harness, obedient (*p3 sḏm*) it goes out," says *Anii* and goes on: "The dog obeys (*sḏmw*) the word, and follows its master" (10,3-4 cf. *Bologna* 1094 3,8-10). Such complete obedience and unquestioning submission are also demanded of the pupil. In the epilogue of *The Instruction of Ptaḥḥotep*, where there is a play on words with the root *sḏm*, this intention is stated explicitly: "He who loves to hear is one who does what is said" (i.e., obeys, 554). This concept is also clearly reflected in the reproof of the pupil's bad behavior: "Listen (*sḏm*) to my words, do not neglect (*m wni*) my words" (*Instruction by a Man for His Son* I 2).

šm' in the sense of "obey" usually comes in conjunction with the indirect object, *b^eqôl*, or with the preposition *l^e* followed with another object (Prov. 1,33; 5,13; 23,22; etc.) and stands, like *sḏm* in Egyptian, in synonymous parallelism with the expression *haṭ 'ōzen* ("give your ear") (Prov. 5,13; 22,17; cf. *Amenemope* 3,8). *š^ema'* (imperative) recurs in this sense in the warnings throughout the first collection of Proverbs (1,8; 4,1,10; 5,7; 7,24; 8,6,32,33) as well as in the third collection (22,17; 23,19,22).[20] Since the third collection contains a direct parallel to *The Instruction of Amenemope*, and the first, like the Egyptian instruction, is constructed on the pattern of a father speaking to his son, it may be assumed that the Hebrew writer was influenced by the Egyptian model; but this idea requires further discussion and we will return to it at the end of this section. In any case, the Hebrew and the Egyptian forms confirm the opinion that *šm'*, in the imperative, is typical of the instruction genre.[21]

Bearing the sense of "hearing," *šm'* and *sḏm* relate at times to a legal setting. Job wishes: "Oh, that I had one to hear (*šōmēa'*) me! Behold, my desire is that the Almighty would answer me, and that mine adversary had written a book" (31,35). "A man who hears (*šōmēa'*)," in Prov. 21,28 is the opposite of "a false witness (*'ēd kᵉzābîm*)."[22] Hearing was the basic duty of the judge in ancient Egypt. He was obliged to listen to the plaintiff seeking a verdict. Rekhmire sings his own praise as "A leader, a prince who listens to his subjects" (*Urk.* IV 1158,10). The Eloquent Peasant protests against the high official "who should see" but "is blind," "who should hear" but "is deaf" (B1 113).[23] Sometimes in this context *sḏm* applies to a stage in the legal process and assumes the sense of "to investigate."[24]

The other significance of *sḏm*, "to understand," is expressed in the phrases "open of hearing" (*wb3y.f m sḏm.t*) (*Instruction by a Man for His Son* II 3) and "a hearing heart" (see following section). It also appears when *sḏm* stands in synomymous parallelism with the phrase "give your heart," common in the school texts. In this context "heart" functions as an instrument of understanding and acquisition of knowledge. Thus, in *Pap. Anastasi* III: "Give your heart, listen to my words" (4,3; cf. *Anastasi* V 23,6). *sḏm* assumes the latter sense also when it appears with the object "language," as in *The Story of Sinuhe*: "You hear (understand) the language of Egypt" (B 30 ff.; cf. *Wenamon* 2,77). Similarly, the Hebrew *šm'* means "to understand," applying to the objects *śāpâ* ("speech") or *lāšôn* ("language"). God, seeing the Tower of Bable, says: "Come, let us go down and then confuse their language, that they may not understand (*lō' yišmᵉ'û*) one another's speech (*'îš śᵉpat rē'ēhû*)" (Gen. 11,7; see also Deut. 28, 49). In the story of Joseph it says: "They did not know that Joseph understood (*šōmēa'*) them for there was an interpreter between them" (Gen. 42,23). But sometimes the verb used in this sense takes on other objects, for example, when Joseph is called one who "hears a dream (i.e., understands a dream), and can interpret it" (Gen. 41,15); and when in his disputation with his friends Job says: "Lo, my eye has seen all this, my ear has heard (*šāmᵉ'â*) and understood it" (13,1).

In ancient Israel, as in Egypt, "hearing" was a basic function of one who desired to learn. From the fairly frequent occurrence of the verb *sḏm* in the Egyptian wisdom literature it may be concluded that hearing was perceived as an important means of acquiring knowledge. Hearing was invested with a similar role in the world of Hebrew education: "Hear (*šimʿû*) instruction (*mûsār*) and be wise," Wisdom says in Proverbs (8,33); "Hear (*šᵉmaʿ*) my son and be wise," a father advises his son (23,19); and the maxim holds that "He who hears (*šōmēaʿ*) admonition gains wisdom" (15,32). In Israel, as in Egypt, hearing is a quality of the wise man (Prov. 1,5; 15,31; Job 34,2,34; *Ptaḥḥotep* 30-31; 41-42).

The ability to listen is a virtue equal to "straightness of the heart," i.e., honesty (*Ptaḥḥotep* 40), and is accompanied by moral integrity, "without blemish" in the words of *Seḥetep-ib-Ra* (8,7). This concept of hearing as a sublime virtue was preserved during all periods of ancient Egypt, with formulas and precepts lauḍing it recurring constantly: "Behold, to hearken is good for people," in the First Intermediate Period (*ZÄS* 44,87); "It's good to hearken," in the Middle Kingdom (*Wb.* IV 385,3-5) and as a term of respect for the officials of the 18th Dynasty, the roots of which go back go the 12th Dynasty: "A noble worthy of being hearkened" (*Seḥetep-ib-Ra* 8,3; cf. *Urk.* IV 415,13; 1033,7; 1194,10). In Israel the importance ascribed to hearing is shown by the proverb which compares it to sacrifice: "For it is better to hear (*lišmōaʿ*, i.e., "to understand") than to offer sacrifices like the fools" (Qoh. 4,17); "Behold to hear (*šᵉmōaʿ*, i.e., "to obey") is better than sacrifice," says Samuel (1 Sam. 15, 22).

The requirement "to hear" is accompanied by promise of reward for the obedient and punishment for the recalcitrant. In the Egyptian texts, the listener gains honor (*Ptaḥḥotep* 613-614), much good is bestowed upon him by the gods (*Insinger* 35,10) and the king awards him with advancement (Sandman 60,4); in Biblical wisdom he is endowed with the treasures of life, i.e., longevity, health and riches (Prov. 4,10,22; 8,21: cf. 8,8 ff.; etc.). He, who rejects wisdom, the disobedient, may expect a beating (*Insinger* 27,4) and destruction (Prov. 1,26ff.; 2,12ff.; etc.).

Among the parts of the body mentioned in this context are not only the ears, the natural tool of hearing, but also the heart (cf. Chapter 7 below); envisaged as the seat of mind and thought, the heart fulfils an important function here, as will be seen in the following section.

Finally, having enumerated the features common to the Egyptian *sḏm* and the Hebrew *šm'*, we may return to the question raised above: Can the use of the imperative forms *š^ema'*, *šim'û*, which are ubiquitous in Hebrew wisdom, be ascribed to Egyptian influence?[25] Since this form of address is also found in the Akkadian sapiential compositions, such as *Instructions to a Prince* and in *The Story of Aḥiqar* (57), one may conclude that these imperative forms were not borrowed from Egyptian wisdom but rather were characteristic of didactic settings in general.[26]

"A Hearing Heart"[27]

As noted above, the heart is connected with the function of hearing. Both the Hebrew and the Egyptian sages envisage it as the seat of thought and knowledge and as the instrument of understanding.[28] In texts where the heart appears in proximity with the root *šm'*—*sḏm*, two of the aspects connected with *šm'*—*sḏm* discussed above are discernible, i.e., will as manifested in obedience and ability as expressed in understanding. The first, obedience, accompanies "heart" when appearing in a formula common to the parlance of the Egyptian school: "Pay attention (lit. "give your heart"), listen to what I have said" (*Anastasi* III 4,1; 4,3; V 8,6). The epilogue of *The Instruction of Ptaḥḥotep* likewise praises obedience, relating it to the son's good will: "Useful is hearing to one who hears; hearing is better than all else when hearing is done with good will... It is the heart which makes of its owner a hearer or non-hearer. Man's heart is his life, prosperity and health! The hearer is one who obeys (lit. "listens to") what is said. He who loves to hear is one who does what is said. How good for a son to listen to (or obey) his father!" (540-542; 550-556). These verses present a paradox: hearing is described as a voluntary act on the part of the person addressed, yet, as the text goes on to say, it depends on a charismatic endowment beyond his control: "He who hears is beloved of god. He who does not hear is one whom god hates. It's the heart which makes of its owner a hearer or a non-hearer" (545-546; 550-551). In other words, the god is the one who bestows upon his beloved the ability to hear with his heart.[29] The heart's function as an instrument of understanding is also clearly reflected in the words of Amenemope to his son: "Give your ears, hear what is said, give your heart to understand it" (3,9-10; cf. Prov. 22,17). The same semantic coloring appears in *The Biography of Amenḥetep*, the architect of Amenophis III (18th Dynasty):

8. He has a hearing heart (*sḏm ib pw*),seeking counsel (*ḏ'r.f sḥ*)
regarding strange things, like one whose heart understands them (*nty ib ḫft.s*)
9. He finds a solution (*ṯs*) when in a corrupted situation
10. A master of wisdom, faithful to the ruler
11. He does that which benefits his Horus.

(*Urk.* IV 1817, 8-11)

In the above quotation the royal architect praises himself as possessing "a hearing heart," that is, through his heart he is able to understand and solve not only the routine, daily problems contained in the learning corpus but also "strange things" (8) or corrupt sayings "in a corrupted situation" (9).

The idiom "a hearing heart" which is mentioned only here, and the above passage from *Ptaḥḥotep* brings to mind King Solomon's request to God in Gibeon to give him *lēb šōmēa'*: "Give your servant therefore a hearing heart (*lēb šōmēa'*) to judge your people and to discern (*lᵉhābîn*) between good and evil" (1 Kgs. 3,9). God's reply to Solomon clearly defines what a "hearing heart" is: "And God said to him: Because you have asked for this... have requested understanding to discern in giving judgment (*hābîn lišmōa' mišpāṭ*) ... behold I give you a wise and discerning heart (*lēb ḥākām wᵉnābôn*)" (ibid. 11-12 cf. 2 Chr. 1,10); clearly, Solomon's wish is to have the ability to understand.

H. Brunner[30] was the first to point out the similarity between this passage and the Egyptian usage. In his opinion, 1 Kings 3 reflects a specific Egyptian concept of the heart as a means through which man receives god's precepts and instructions. As it appears in 1 Kings 3, the concept is indeed identical with that common in Egypt. But it is not otherwise foreign to the Bible, where the heart is generally regarded to be the seat of wisdom and thought.[31] Despite the remarkable affinity between the Egyptian source and 1 Kings 3, the difference between them is fundamental: Solomon did not request "a hearing heart" to receive God's instructions (Brunner); Solomon requested "a hearing heart" to enable him to fulfil his national obligation as king, that is to judge his people.[32]

Since the phrase "a hearing heart" appears only one time each in the Egyptian and Biblical literature it is difficult to see in 1 Kings 3 an adaptation of an Egyptian idiom.[33] Yet, the reverse, i.e., the borrowing of a Hebrew expression by the Egyptian scribe, also has to be ruled out. As we have seen, in Egyptian, "a hearing heart" appears in an inscription of the 18th Dynasty (ca. 1400 B.C.), far preceding the Solomonic period which initiates the consolidation of Hebrew culture and literature.

rdi ib / rdi m ib / rdi ḥ3.ty r — šyt / śym / hābē' / nṭh + lēb/ ntn 'et hallēb l^{e}/ ntn 'el lēb / śym bilbāb

These Egyptian phrases, like their equivalents in Biblical Hebrew, have several meanings, namely, "to hear," "to understand" and "to remember." In the sense of "hearing" the terms often stand in parallelism with *sḏm* in Egyptian and *šmʿ* in Hebrew and other terms belonging to the semantic field of "hearing" (*Anastasi* III 4,1; 4,3; Prov. 2,2; 23,12). The instruction "to pay attention" and "to hear" is common in the school writings, where the teacher customarily admonishes his pupil (e.g., *Anastasi* III 3,10; V 17,4). In the tomb inscription the deceased asks passers-by "to pay attention" to its content (*Petehor-neb-chen* D,10: Otto No. 75).

The Egyptian expressions *rdi m ib* (i.e., "to put in the heart") and *rdi ḥ3.ty r* ("give the heart to") reflect the concept prevalent in the wisdom literature that the heart is the organ of learning and understanding. "Give your ears, hear what is said / Give your heart (*imi ḥ3.ty.k r*) to understand them," says Amenemope to his son (3,9-10). In the school texts the pupil is ordered to take up the teachers words or the writings into his heart: "Be a scribe, put this in your heart and your fame (lit. name) will be similar (to that of the great scribers)"

(*Chester Beatty* IV pl. 18 verso 2,13; cf. *Petosiris*, in Lefebvre 61,14).

In Biblical wisdom the division between the two semantic aspects "to hear" and "to understand" is blurred: *šyt/śym lēb* (lit. "put the heart"), *hābē' lēb* (lit. "bring the heart") and *nṭh lēb* (lit. "incline the heart") mean not only "to pay attention," "to listen," but also "to consider" and "to reflect." So in Job 1,8, when God says to Satan: "*hăśamtā libbᵉkā* on my servant Job?" He is not only asking whether Satan had seen him, but whether he had also come to know him, had considered his personality (cf. ibid 2,3). The composer of the song about raising animals in Proverbs advises the owner of the flock to examine its condition: "Be then diligent to know the state of your sheep, *šît libbᵉkā* to the flocks" (27,23; cf. Job 7,17). The collocation *šyt lēb lᵉ* includes the awareness that the heart is the seat of thought and speech. At the beginning of "The Sayings of the Wise," which parallels the passage from *Amenemope* quoted above, it is said: "Incline your ear and hear the words of the wise, *wᵉlibbᵉkā tāšît* to my knowledge" (Prov. 22,17; cf. *Amenemope* 3,9-10 and the parallel introductory exhortation in Prov. 23, 12: "*hābî'â lammûsār libbekā* [i.e., apply your mind to instruction] and your ear to words of knolwedge").

The function of the heart as an instrument for investigation and gaining insight into the root of things appears in late wisdom literature: "*wā'ettᵉnā ('et) libbî lādda'at*" — this idiom is repeated in Qoheleth, where it signifies intellectual activity by means of the heart (1,17; 8,16; cf.: 7,25; 1,13). With it we find the expression *ntn 'el lēb*, denoting "to learn a lesson," "to gain personal experience" or "to gather impressions," for example: "and the living *yittēn 'el libbô*" (Qoh. 7,2); "For all this *nātattî 'el libbî*" (9,1; cf. 8,9).[34] Similar is the combination *šyt lēb*, which stands in parallelism with "to learn a lesson" (*lqḥ mûsār*) in Proverbs 24,32: "I beheld, *'āšît libbî*, I saw and I learned a lesson."

Finally, in a didactic context the Egyptian phrases *rdi m ib* and *rdi ḥ3.ty r* sometimes assume the meaning "to memorize things," "to learn by heart" — one of the foremost methods of study in the Egyptian school (*Amenemope* 3,11; *Lansing* 9,3; *Anii* 7,4).[35] At times the Hebrew phrase *śym lēb* also has the sense of "to memorize": Eliphas advises Job, "Receive direction from his mouth and lay up his words in your heart (*śîm 'ămārāyw bil^{e}bābekā*)" (Job 22,22); cf. "...and David laid up these words in his heart" (1 Sam. 21,13).[36]

ṯy sb'.t (Dem.) — *lqḥ mûsār*

The Egyptian collocation *ṯy sb'.t* (Copt. ϫι cƀω) means "to obtain" (lit. "to grasp," "to take" instructions). Its occurrence is limited in our corpus to *Pap. Insinger* (8,23; 9,18; 17,23), where *ṯy sb'.t* seems to replace the preceding collocations composed from the verb *šsp*, i.e., "to take," and terms denoting speech — *rȝ*, *ḏd*, *md.t*.[37] However, while *šsp* denotes a passive acquisition or reception of that which is said (cf. below, p. 60), *ṯy sb'.t* seems to indicate a more advanced stage — not only that of absorbing the teacher's words but of understanding them and being able to apply them in everyday life. In *Pap. Insinger* we find mention of different periods of man's life, among them a decade during which he is busy acquiring the necessary knowledge to plot his life's course (17,23). This activity depends on the free will of the pupil and is therefore more meaningful than hearkening and obeying instruction, which may be imposed by beating; as the Egyptian sage puts it: "It is a son's good and blessed portion to receive instruction (*ṯy sb'.t*) and to ask questions. No instruction can succeed if there is dislike" (ibid. 8,23-24). Acquiring facts (*šsp*) is not sufficient. There should also be understanding through the asking of questions (see below, *wḥ'*, p. 65).

The Hebrew idiom *lqḥ mûsār* (lit. "to take instruction") is analogous to *ṯy sb'.t* in Egyptian.[38] It appears as a verb, and as a noun, *leqaḥ*, which is a typical wisdom term.[39] "*lāqaḥat mûsar haśkēl* " is one of the declared purposes of the book of Proverbs (1,3); "*q^{e}ḥû mûsārî*" is what wisdom demands of passers-by (8,10); the wise man is he who "*lqḥ mûsār*" (24,32). Like its analogous expression in Egyptian, the primary meaning of *lqḥ* is"to obtain," "to acquire." *lqḥ*, in other words, first of all denotes the process of understanding the teacher's words, absorbing them and assimilating them to the already existing stock of personal knowledge. The noun *leqaḥ* applies to a person who has passed the initial learning stages, as may be seen from the following: "Let the wise man hear and add to his lesson (*leqaḥ*)" (Prov. 1,5); "Give (instruction) to a wise man and he will be wiser, teach a righteous man and he will add to his lesson (*yôsep leqaḥ*)" (ibid. 9,9; cf.16,21,23). *leqaḥ* in Biblical Hebrew also indicates a highly advanced level of learning: no longer obedience and passive acceptance of instruction, but acquisition of knowledge and learning lessons through personal experience. The wise man learns his lesson by observing the fate of the sluggard (Prov. 24,32); the father's lesson is based on his own experience as a pupil (Prov. 4,2).

There are uses of *leqaḥ* that have no equivalent in Egyptian. In some passages of Biblical wisdom the stress is not on he who learns, the pupil, but on the teacher. Since the pupil's ability to learn the material largely depends on the clarity of the teacher's presentation, *leqaḥ* at times refers to his powers of persuasion and expression. In Proverbs 16,21 we find: "and sweetness of the lips increases learning (*yôsîp leqaḥ*)" (cf. ibid. 23).[40] "I have given you a good lesson (*leqaḥ ṭôb*)" says the father to his sons (4,2); while the prostitute, assuming the role of a teacher in her attempt to seduce the youth speaks "...with her much fair speech (*b^erōb liqḥâ*)" (ibid. 7,21).[41]

B. Verbs of Obedience, Observance and Assimilation of Instruction

iri sb3y.t*, *smn sb3y.t*, *nḏr tp rd*, *šsp* + *md.t* and synonyms — *qnh*, *nṣr*, *ṣpn*, *šmr*, *ḥzk* (hiph'il) + *ḥokmâ

Having considered verbs with a double meaning — obedience and understanding — we now turn to the other verbs which are connected to only one or the other of these two aspects of learning. The Egyptian verbs denoting obedience and passive reception of instruction are: *iri sb3y.t*, meaning not only "to teach" (see above, Section I) but also "to carry out an instruction";[42] *smn sb3y.t* (lit. "to establish an instruction"), referring to obedience as a result of remembering a lesson;[43] *nḏr tp rd*, the primary sense of *nḏr* being "to hold," "grasp firmly," but in collocation with *tp rd* meaning "to obey," "to fulfil an order";[44] and *šsp r3/ḏd/md.t*, bearing the sense of "to grasp," "to obtain instruction."[45]

These verbs, except for the collocation *šsp* + object dealt with above (p. 59), are not characteristic of Egyptian wisdom language, at least not in the wisdom texts included in our corpus, and will therefore not be treated here at any length.

Let us now turn to the Hebrew phrases which approximate in content the four Egyptian collocations mentioned above, i.e., *qnh*, *nṣr*, *ṣpn*, *šmr*, *ḥzq* (hiph'il) + wisdom and its synonyms.

qnh originally belongs to the language of commerce and means "to acquire by paying." This primary meaning is still found in Proverbs 17, 16: "Why should a fool have a price in his hand to buy (*liqnôt*) wisdom when he has no mind (*lēb*)?" This would indicate that the *Sitz im Leben of qnh ḥokmâ* was the ancient school where the teacher was paid for his services.[46] In association with the acquisition of an abstract object, i.e., wisdom, or one of its synonyms, *qnh* occurs only in Proverbs, where it assumes the meaning of "to achieve," "to acquire." (cf. *qnh* + *ḥokmâ*, Prov. 4, 5, 7; 16, 16; 17, 16; 23, 23; *'ĕmet*, ibid. 23, 23; *mûsār*, ibid; *bînâ*, ibid., and 4, 5, 7; 16, 16; *da'at*, 18, 15; *taḥbulôt*, 1,5; *lēb*, 15, 32; 19, 8). This again expresses the concept of the ancients that "wisdom" is first of all tradition which is passed down through the generations and which can be acquired through effort.

The collocations *nṣr*, *ṣpn* + objects which emphasize the duty of the son to observe, keep and follow the father's instructions, are characteristic of wisdom literature.

nṣr, meaning "to observe," "to guard," and followed by the objects *tôrâ*, *miṣwâ* and synonyms, referrs usually to the commands of parent. It occurs seven times in Proverbs (3,1; 4,13; 6,20; 28,7; cf. 2,8; 3,21; 5,2). Its occurrence is especially frequent in the wisdom Psalm 119 (10 times), where its objects are associated with religious obligations, e.g., observing the divine law, the covenant, etc. (cf. *nṣr* + *miṣwôt*, Ps. 119, 15; *tôrâ*, ibid. 34; *ḥūqîm*, ibid. 33, 145; *'ēdôt*, ibid. 2, 22, 129; *piqqūdîm*, ibid., 56, 69, 100).[47]

The use of *ṣpn*, meaning "to keep," "to treasure," followed by objects relating to the wisdom instructions is exclusive to the parlance of wisdom[48] (*ṣpn* + *miṣwâ*, Prov. 2, 1; 7, 1; *da'at*, ibid. 10, 14; *'imrâ* [referring to God's law], Job 23, 12; wisdom Ps. 119, 11; *ḥokmâ*, BS 4, 23; 41, 15).

Both *nṣr* and *ṣpn* stand in synonymous parallelism with the verb *šmr* meaning "to observe," "to watch," which is also collocated with objects referring to wisdom dictates or divine commands (e.g., *mûsār*, *tôkaḥat*, *miṣwâ*, *tôrâ*, *'imrâ*, cf. Prov. 4, 4; 7, 2; 10, 17; 13, 18; 29, 18 etc.; Job 23, 11; Qoh. 8, 5; 12, 13). But *šmr* is not exclusive to wisdom and appears frequently in non-wisdom texts where it replaces the wisdom terms *nṣr* and *ṣpn*.[49]

The verb *ḥzq* (hiph'il), i.e., "to lay hold of," when collocated with the objects *mûsār*, *ḥokmâ* (Prov. 3, 18; 4, 13) also approximates *ṣpn* and *nṣr* in meaning. But the isolated occurrences of this phrase are inadequate to clarify its relationship to the wisdom vocabulary.

C. Verbs of Understanding and Knowledge

In Egyptian

'ḳ sb3y.t, 'ḳ sḫr

'ḳ sb3y.t, 'ḳ sḫr means "to enter," "to penetrate" the instruction or the method. This idiom appears three times within a didactic context. In *Pap. Anastasi* V 23,5-6 the pupil is commanded: "Enter (*'ḳ*) the plans (*sḫr.w*) of your teachers!" In *Pap. Chester Beatty* IV, pl.19 verso 4,6, it is said: "(only after) you are acquainted with the writings, do you enter (*'ḳ*) the instructions (*sb3y.wt*)." In a similar vein Anii tells his son: "Be proficient in the writings, go into the writings (*'ḳ m sš.w*), give them in your heart."[50] These examples clearly refer to an active form of study. Not obedience is demanded of the pupil but understanding: It is not enough to learn by heart, by rote; one must penetrate the meanings of the instructions, this being a higher level of learning than that of simply committing the writings to memory.

'rḳ[51]

The intransitive verb *'rḳ* means "to be clever," "to be skilled in" (sometimes followed by the proposition *m*). Only the verbal form of *'rḳ* relates to the semantic field discussed in this chapter, but its nominal (*'rḳw*) and adjectival (*'rḳ*, *'rḳ ib*) forms, also found in wisdom literature, help to clarify the semantic field of the verbal usage. *'rḳ* is connected probably with the homonym *'rḳ* (*Wb.* I 212, 3-7) meaning "to finish," "to complete" and from which the noun *'rḳy* is derived (ibid., 212,8), i.e., the last day of the month. Thus, *'rḳ* means "to comprehend to the end," "to gain full knowledge of." The adjective "clever" (*'rḳ*, *'rḳ ib*) may relate to ordinary mortals — a scribe (*The Instruction of Anii*, *Pap. Lansing*), a vizier (*Kagemni*, *Rekhmire*) or a high official (*Intef* — *Urk.* IV 970,5), or to the gods of wisdom — Sia (*ÄHG* 235,9) and Thoth (hinted indirectly in *Urk.* IV 1074,4-5). The reference therefore is not necessarily to wisdom which is attained by the hard method of learning and repetition of instruction but to another kind of knowledge, a perfect one, which naturally was identified with a trait originally attributed to the gods. This wisdom, known as charismatic wisdom, is bestowed upon mortal, by god. This concept underlies the words of Anii's son's: "Say to the god who gave you knowledge (*'rḳw*)" (10,11). He who is blessed with such understanding may be likened in his wisdom to the gods of wisdom: "My master, clever (*'rḳ*) in the image of Sia, a teacher who penetrates hearts" (*ÄHG* 235, 9). The nature of such wisdom is varied, ranging from an awareness of human character (*Kagemni* II 3) and knowledge of wise sayings (*Lansing* 14,10) to general proficiency in some area (*Rekhmire*, *Urk.* IV 1074,5; cf. *Kheti* XXVII E). There is no equivalent for *'rḳ* in the language of the Bible, but the root *byn* encompasses some of its aspects (see below).

wḥ'

The Egyptian term *wḥ'* is accompanied by a determinative depicting a cord. Its primary meaning is thus to "untie a knot." With an abstract object it means "to explain," "to solve" and was in use from the period of the Old Kingdom (*Ptaḥḥotep*) up to the New Kingdom Period (the school writings, *Amenemope*). Various terms denoting Egyptian wisdom words serve as its object, particularly *ṯs*, literally "knot," i.e., a well-constructed, well-worded saying. The clarification of a saying is therefore metaphorically compared to the act of untying cords.[52] This is well illustrated in Amenemope's words to his son:

> Give your ears, hear the sayings
> Give your heart to understand (*r wḥʿ*) them (3,9-10).

And in the epilogue:

> Fill yourself with them, put them in your heart
> And become a man who explains them
> (lit. "a man who unties their knots" — *rmṯ n wḥʿw.w*)
> One who explains (*iw.f wḥʿ*) as a teacher (27,13-15)
> (cf. *Instruction by a Man for His Son* II 6).

wḥʿ also applies to the interpretation of the writings: Intef is the explicator of the writings (*wḥʿ ḏrf*) (*Urk.* IV 969,14), while Amon's priest helped his master to clarify some obscure texts (*wḥʿ ḳsn.wt*, lit. "to loosen difficulties," Jansen-Winkeln I A1, B10; II 1, 9, 14).

wḥʿ pertains to the sphere of teaching. The teacher is the explicator (see above, *Amenemope*) while the gifted pupil and the proficient official are *wḥʿ ib*, i.e., intelligent, understanding[53] (*Lansing* 2,9; Prince Si-renpowet: Gardiner, "Incriptions," 123 ff. pl.8E; see also below). The collocation of *ib* ("heart") with *wḥʿ* is natural, since the heart, as the instrument of learning and understanding, participates in the mental activity associated with *wḥʿ*, i.e., explaining. Khakheperre-sonb requests his heart to explain (*wḥʿ*) what is taking place in the land (verso 1); Amenemope asks his son to "give your heart to understand them (i.e., my words)" (3,9-10).[54] Thus the meaning of a passage in *The Instruction of Ptaḥḥotep*, up till now considered incomprehensible, becomes clear. In this passage, in which the son who listens is praised and the one who does not is chastised, the following is said:

> 608. Don't take a word and then bring it (back)
> (i.e., don't say first one thing and then another)...
> 611. Beware of loosening cords (*wni ini*) in yourself...
> 615. Speak (only) after you have achieved the facility of an expert (*ḥmww*).

(Cf. the last line to ibid. 365-367:

> Be quiet because it's more profitable than *tftf*
> Speak (only) when you know you can explain
> It's the expert [*ḥmww*] who speaks in a council...)

Do not try to show off, says the Egyptian sage, do not attempt to expound words of wisdom ("to loosen the knots") before becoming a master of rhetoric. The above quotation reflects this ideal of restraint and self-control which characterizes the world view of the Egyptian sage.

wḥʿ therefore represents an advanced stage of learning. Listening (*sḏm*) and acquiring facts (*šsp*) are insufficient; there should also be understanding by way of "untying the knots" and solving problems. Understanding is achieved by asking questions. The author of *Pap. Insinger* 8,23 states: "It is the son's good and blessed lot to take instruction and *to ask* (*šn*)."[55]

wḥʿ presumably was borrowed from the educational sphere by the king's court. Common titles given a high official in the New Kingdom are "intelligent" (*wḥʿ ib*), and "one who explains (*wḥʿ ṯss.t*)." The steward of the palace (*imy r pr*) in the time of Amenophis I is so described, as are Prince Si-renpowet and King Tuthmosis III (*Urk.* IV 47,12, cf. ibid. 969,14; ibid. 554,16; Gardiner, above; see also Janssen I, 56-57, exx. 1ff.). Again, Biblical Hebrew does not have an equivalent verb containing the image of loosening knots, although the noun *taḥbulôt*, which semantically parallels the Egyptian *ṯs*, retains the figure of cord (see below, pp. 313–317).

ʿm (Copt. [S] ⲉⲓⲙⲉ)

The verb *ʿm* with or without the object *sḫr* means "to know." It first appeared in texts belonging to the New Kingdom Period and was preceded by the common verb *rḫ* which relates to the same semantic field.[56] *ʿm* is probably connected with the homonymous lexeme *ʿm* (*Wb.* I 183) meaning "to swallow" and used as a metaphor for "to know."[57] Knowledge, i.e., perfect mastery of the learned material, is compared to eating.

ʿm is found four times in the present corpus, all in a didactic context — *Anastasi* IV 4,11; *Sallier* I 4,5-6; *Lansing* 13b,9; *Amennakht* 8. In the latter two references the combination *ʿm m sḫr.w* is used. When spoken by the teacher in *The Instruction of Amennakht*, *ʿm sḫr.w* probably denotes mastery of various professions and teaching methods.[58]

For *ʿm*, too, there is no precise semantic equivalent in the language of the Bible. The closest we come to a parallel in the context of study and acquisition of knowledge is *byn* (see below). On the other hand, the connection between *'m*, "to know" and "to swallow," is reminiscent of similar imagery in the Bible. This usage is, however, not limited to the wisdom literature. In prophecy, the prophet's devotion to his mission is described as "eating God's words" — Ezekiel eats a scroll in his call: "So I opened my mouth and he fed me... and he said to me, son of man, your stomach will eat it and you will fill your innards" (Ezek. 3,1-3). Jeremiah in his lament addresses God thus: "Your words have been found and I have eaten them" (15,16). This metaphor recurs in the context of the relationship between the people and their God: Amos speaks of "hunger" and "thirst" for "God's words" (8,11; cf. Isa. 55,1-3). The object "Gods' words," which appears in prophecy, is replaced in the wisdom literature by "wisdom" and its synonyms. In Proverbs 24,13,14 knowledge is compared to honey: "My son, eat honey for it is good and honeycomb is sweet to your taste; so know wisdom to be to your soul..." Ben Sira (51,24) speaks of a thirst for knowledge. This figure, based on the concept that "Lernen ist..ein ebenso *rezeptiver* Vorgang wie Essen" (Lang),[59] achieves its fullest expression in Proverbs 9 where Wisdom is presented as a woman inviting the passers-by to come to her housewarming feast. This is a metaphor for a pupil being invited to go to school for the sake of intellectual pleasure and to eat a spiritual meal prepared for him by the teacher, here represented by Wisdom.[60] This image is also found in Ben Sira 15,3, where the reward given to him who adheres to wisdom is described: "...and she (Wisdom) will feed him the bread of the mind and slake his thirst with the water of understanding."

In the Bible

The Egyptian verbs *'rḳ*, *wḥ'* and *'m*, as already noted, have no exact semantic equivalents in Biblical Hebrew but in content they are close to the verbs *byn* (qal, hiph'il), *śkl* (hiph'il) and *lmd* (qal).[61]

byn (qal, hiph'il)

The verbal forms of qal and hiph'il (in the transitive) and the adjectival forms of *byn*, i.e., *mēbîn*, *nābôn*, are of special interest for the subject under discussion, viz., learning methods.

The root *byn* in the above forms is typical of the wisdom books (particularly of Proverbs and Job) but is not exclusive to them.[62] *byn* signifies an act of intellect, i.e., the achievement of comprehension by means of a mental effort. The hiph'il participle — *mēbîn* — when occurring in Proverbs is close in meaning to *nābôn*, but suggests a more active meaning.[63] In later biblical literature, not necessarily in wisdom texts, the term refers to proficiency in a certain area. The *mēbîn* here is a specialist in his profession, a master of his art or craft (poet, musician), and one capable of teaching it to his fellow men (1 Chr. 15,22; 25,7-8; 2 Chr. 34,12). In Egyptian *'rḳ*, which also denotes perfect knowledge, is comparable. With respect to the writings, the *mēbîn* is not only he who understands them but he who can explain them to others. *mēbîn* is the title given to a teacher (1 Chr. 25,8): the Levites *mēbînîm* "make (the people) understand" the Torah in the days of Ezra; in Psalms, the Lord *mēbîn* "makes understand" (wisdom Ps. 119, 130). This usage is close to the Egyptian concept of *wḥ'*, i.e., explanation, interpretation, as typical of the teacher (cf. *The Instruction of Amenemope* 27,14-15 cited above p. 64).

We have already observed that both the Egyptian and the Hebrew sage sometimes equate "listening" with "understanding," but in the Bible the former is usually perceived as a stage that precedes understanding. Not everyone who listens understands: "I heard but did not understand *'ābîn*," says Daniel (12,8). "Hear, indeed, but understand (*tābînû*) not," the prophet chastises his people (Isa. 6,9). The difference between these two stages is obvious in the words of Elihu to Job: "If now you have understanding (*bînâ*), hear this" (34,16), i.e., not everyone who hears understands, but only he who has achieved the higher level of understanding, hears.

As in Egyptian, he who has understanding, who comprehends, may be God (wisdom Ps. 119, 130) or a human being belonging to the group of sages, i.e., the intellectuals: the prudent (Prov. 14,8,15), the leaders (Job 32,9), the Levites (Neh. 8,7,8; 1 Chr. 15,22), the king's counsellor and the scribe (e.g., Jonathan, uncle of David, 1 Chr. 27,32; cf. *Urk.* IV 969,14). The object of "understanding" is also similar to that found in the Egyptian sources. The Egyptian pupil is enjoined to "penetrate" and comprehend the teacher's words and writings while the goal of the author of Proverbs is to make his readers understand "words of insight" (*'imrê bînâ*) (1,2), "proverb (*māšāl*) and parable (*m^elîṣâ*), the words of the sages and their riddles" (1,6).[64] In Proverbs 8,5, Wisdom orders fools *hābînû lēb*, i.e., have *lēb nābôn* ("a clever heart"). The latter expression, common in the language of Biblical wisdom (cf. Prov. 15,14; 18,15; and *lēb ḥākām w^enābôn*, 1 Kgs. 3,12), is reminiscent of the idiom *wḥ' ib* in Egyptian, both the Egyptian and the Hebrew expressions being based on the perception of the heart as the organ of understanding.[65]

Unlike its parallel in Egyptian, *byn* in Biblical language sometimes relates to faith in God. In Proverbs 2,5 we find: "...then you shall understand the fear of the Lord and find the knowledge of God"; and in Daniel, which is interspersed with many wisdom features, "understanding" of a vision is mentioned (8,16,27; 9,23; 10,1, etc.).

***śkl* (hiph'il)**

The root *śkl*, common in the Hebrew wisdom language, assumes in hiph'il the meaning of "to understand," "to grasp" (see discussion below p. 249).

***lmd* (qal)**

Surprisingly, *lmd* (in qal) meaning "to learn," "to study," an activity naturally located in the sphere of education and learning, is rare in the wisdom literature. The verb *lmd* (qal) appears just once in Proverbs (30,3) in connection with the stupid person (*ba'ar*) who does not learn.[66] On the other hand, expressions like *hābēn*, *lqḥ*, *nṣr*, *ṣpn*, *šmr* and *qnh*, dealt with above, are common. Two reasons could possibly account for this. One is that the root *lmd*, which occurs only in the later books of the Bible, belongs to a later phase of the Hebrew language. The second is that the meaning of the lexeme *lmd* contains an aspect of active learning. While the ancient sages of Egypt and Israel (apart from Qoheleth)[67] regarded human knowledge as a static mass, transferred from one generation to the next with virtually no possibility of expansion or addition, the verb *lmd* (qal) transcends the limitations set by passive acquisition of knowledge.[68]

D. Verbs of Quest and Pondering

In Biblical Hebrew the verbs *ḥqr* and *bqš* relate to a higher stage of learning, which has no parallel in the educational world of Egypt, although the meaning of the verb *ḏʿr* comes close to that of the Hebrew verbs.

In the Bible

ḥqr

The Hebrew root *ḥqr* has no semantic parallel in Egyptian wisdom literature. The verb and the noun (*ḥēqer*) are typical of wisdom vocabulary (particularly in the book of Job) but they also appear in other books.[69] Unlike most of the expressions mentioned so far, *ḥēqer* does not denote the acquisition of transferred knowledge or mastery of given material, but means independent study not subject to any specific authority. It denotes thorough examination and exhaustive thought on a given matter. God, when he examines something, reaches remote places unknown to man (Job 28,3-4; cf. BS 42,18). Elsewhere Job says that God is studying (*ḥôqēr*) wisdom (28,27), something which lies beyond the grasp of men.

Nevertheless, the son is asked to search for and to find wisdom (*dᵉrōš waḥăqōr baqqēš wûmᵉṣâʾ*, BS 6,27); and of the sage Qoheleth it is said that he "searched (*ḥiqqēr*) many proverbs" (Qoh. 12,9; cf. BS 44,5).

The negative form, *ʾên ḥēqer* ("it is unsearchable") refers to man's limited mental capacity. God is capable of great things *ʿad ʾên ḥēqer* (Job 9,10; cf. 5,9); but the people are not able to "grasp" his essence (ibid. 11,7; cf. BS 43,28); *'ên ḥēqer* to God's wisdom (Isa. 40,28) and the same is said of the thoughts of the king — "The king's heart is unsearchable (*'ên ḥēqer*)" (Prov. 25,3).[70]

***bqš* (pi'el)**

bqš (pi'el) is close in meaning to *ḥqr.*[71] This verb, collocated with the object "wisdom" or its synonyms and meaning "to seek knowledge," is unique to Biblical wisdom literature. The semantic development of the term reveals various stages in the approach to study in Hebrew education. At first it denoted the acquisition of knowledge but came to mean "observation" and "investigation," thereby diverging from the ancient system of passive acceptance and obedience to tradition. The older usage still appears in Proverbs[72] where *bqš* parallels *qnh da'at*, for example: "An intelligent heart acquires knowledge (*yiqneh da'at*) and the ear of the wise seeks knowledge (*t^ebaqqēš da'at*)" (Prov. 18,15; cf. 14,6; 15,14). But signs of the new attitude may already be present in Prov. 2,4: "If you seek it (*t^ebaqšennâ* wisdom) like silver and search for it (*taḥp^eśennâ*) as for hidden treasures..."

In Qoheleth the new approach attains full expression. Qoheleth, dominated as he is by his scepticism, cannot meekly accept conventional wisdom like his predecessors. Thus he comes closer to practicing critical observation on the basis of personal experimentation. This element, characteristic of Qoheleth, is especially evident in 7,23-29 and 8,16-17, where the key words are *biqqēš* ("search for") and *māṣā'* ("find") in both a positive and negative form. In these passages the subject of Qoheleth's study is wisdom or the order ruling the universe, "...every work that is done under the sun" (8,9,17); but "I did not find it" because "That which is, is... very, very deep, who can find it?" (7,24). "Man is not able to find the work that is done under the sun" (8,17).[73] True, the results of the search are negative, i.e., an inability to reach a solution and a feeling of helplessness, but the experiment has been done: "All this I have tested by wisdom" (7,23). In order to reach completeness and a final result the sage, though in vain, has tried to add up the details: "See this I have found... (adding) one to one to find the sum" (ibid. 27). This selfsame method characterizes modern research in our generation.

In Egyptian

ḏʿr (Copt. ϫⲱⲣ)[74]

According to the Egyptian concept, learning was the assimilation of wisdom and knowledge transmitted from generation to generation. The Egyptian recognized the possibility of acquiring this knowledge autonomously, independent of any educational framework,[75] but he did not recognize learning aimed at innovation or at addition to the conventional body of knowledge, the heritage of past generations.[76] Personal experience leading to fresh conclusions and results as occurs in Qoheleth was foreign to the Egyptian spirit. Nevertheless, the Egyptian verb *ḏʿr* approximates the sense of Hebrew *bqš*, "to go in quest of knowledge," and *ḥqr*, "to ponder over something." The primary meaning of *ḏʿr* is "to search out," "to seek" (*Wb.* V 539A), and this meaning is preserved in Coptic.[77] In medical texts it is used in the same sense as "to probe," "to examine a wound."[78]

In reference to abstract things it is used metaphorically, acquiring the sense "to ponder," "to wonder about things," "to investigate." Thus it is possible to "ponder over" the nature of man (*ḏʿr ḳd* — *Ptaḥḥotep* 463; cf. *The Biography of Sennufer*, in *Urk.* IV 1425,14) and his thoughts (*ẖ.t*, *ḥꜣ.ty* — see below), or "to seek advice" (*sḥ* — see below) and "the root of the problem" (*ḫnw* — see below).[79]

The concerns of the Egyptian priest Khakheperre-sonb of the Middle Kingdom and of the architect Amenḥetep of the 18th Dynasty are very similar to those of their Hebrew counterpart Qoheleth, who "examined (*ḥiqqēr*) many proverbs" (12,9). Khakheperre-sonb wishes "to investigate sayings (*ḏʿr ḫnw*)" by means of "searching of the heart (*m ḥḥy n ib*)" (recto 1); Amenḥetep sings his own praises as one who "has a hearing heart seeking counsel (*ḏʿr.f sḥ*) regarding strange things, like one whose heart understands them" (*Urk.* IV 1817,8-9). "The king's heart is unsearchable (*'ēn ḥēqer*)" declares the Hebrew sage (Prov. 25,3), while the Egyptian king is compared to the god of wisdom Sia who searches out (*ḏʿr*) every belly (*ẖ.t*) and heart (*ḥꜣ.ty*) and the innermost thoughts and secrets of man are laid bare before him (*Seḥetep-ib-Ra* 2, 5-6; cf. *The Tomb of Tutu*, Sandman 81,6: *ÄGH* 235,9).

III. A SUMMARY OF THE METHODS OF LEARNING AND ACQUISITION OF INSTRUCTION

The verbs and idioms related to ways of learning within the ancient educational system, whether within the school framework (as in Egypt) or under some other authority, indicate an ambivalent concept of learning. On the one hand, there is a demand for blind obedience, the acceptance and assimilation of the teacher's instruction. On the other hand, there is a more active way of learning, i.e., the need to understand things, "to enter into" the instructions, to master and use them.

Two parts of the body are useful in acquiring knowledge: the "ear," which relates to the first method of study, and the "heart," which relates mainly to the second (see Chapter 7).

These two aspects of study — the first involving the willingness of the pupil to learn and the second depending largely on his ability or talents — belong both to wisdom that is learned and acquired through experience. Beside this wisdom, the ancient Egyptian and Hebrew are familiar with natural or charismatic wisdom bestowed by God. Thus, God gives king Solomon a "hearing heart" (*lēb šōmēaʿ*); in the Egyptian texts god endows a human being with cleverness (*ʿrḳ*) and the high official claims that he "was born as one who knows (*rḫ*), one who is wise (*wḥʿ ib*)" (*Si-renpowet*, see above, p. 65).

The actual method of acquiring knowledge finds expression in the various terms dealt with above. The pupil can avail himself of the following means of learning: (1) Repetition and memorization of the lesson given by the teacher or the parent. This method is expressed by the terms *sḏm* — *šmʿ*, *iri sb3y.t*, *sšp md.t* — *qnh ḥokmâ* etc., *rdi m ib* — *śym lēb* and the like; (2) Learning the instructions through interpretation, asking questions, accepting advice and pondering. Here the following terms apply: *wḥʿ*, *ʿrḳ*, *ʿḳ* (with objects relating to instruction); *ṯy sbʿ.t*, *śym lēb* (second meaning) and synonyms, *lqḥ mûsār*, *byn*, *śkl* and *lmd*.

The fact that the verb "hear" and its synonyms occur with exceptional frequency in the wisdom literature, on the one hand, and that other verbs involving acquisition of knowledge seldom appear, on the other, leads to the conclusion that "hearing" was perceived as an important means of obtaining knowledge. Surprisingly, there is little reference in wisdom literature to practicing writing, which is mentioned only four times in the school writings and not at all in the Egyptian instructions. In the Biblical wisdom literature there are only six occurrences of the root *ktb* ("to write").[80]

Two aspects of the learning concept, obedience and understanding, have been described, which are dominant in the Egyptian and Hebrew didactic writings. Both Hebrew and Egyptian teachers apparently came to recognize that teaching by coercion and by application of authority was not always effective. Thus, they began to appeal to the pupil's good will and to stimulate his desire to acquire knowledge by having him ask questions, seek and receive advice or even through encouraging autodidactic study independent of all educating authority. But it seems that the Hebrew teachers went one step further: Unlike their Egyptian colleagues, they were no longer satisfied with conventional material passed down for generations and they tried to broaden the traditional boundaries by encouraging personal experimentation and individual quests. This is expressed in such terms as *lqḥ*, *ḥqr*, *bqš*, *ntn lēb* (Qoh.) and perhaps *lmd* as well, none of which has an equivalent in Egyptian, although *ḏʿr* assumes a similar sense in certain contexts.

These three learning methods — obedience and assimilation, interpretation and understanding, pondering and quest — complement each other, and, taken as a whole, point to different stages of knowledge acquisition (see Table 1).

Tables 2 and 3 present the following picture: Both Egyptian and Hebrew have a rich vocabulary relating to the *semantic field of study* (Table 3). Both languages tend to use a structure in which a verb is followed by various nouns designating the instruction to be learned, thus showing the importance of the material acquired. However, in the second area, that of *imparting knowledge* (Table 2), Hebrew evinces a more varied linguistic usage, which finds expression in the number of terms (10) pertaining to this semantic field. Egyptian stays with the structure of an auxiliary verb to which nouns denoting the instruction are added and is, therefore, in this case linguistically poorer than Hebrew (7 roots).

Table 1: Reconstruction of Learning Stages

Stage	Egyptian	Bible
Passive Learning ↓	*sḏm** *rdi ib* (‖ *sḏm*)	*šmʿ** *šyt lēb* and synonyms*
Obedience and Observance	*iri sbꜣ.t, nḏr tp rd* *rdi ḥꜣ.ty r*	*šmr, nṣr, ṣpn* + objects relating to *ḥokmâ*
	transition ↓	transition ↓
Assimilation	*šsp* + objects relating to words *smn sbꜣy.t, rdi m ib*	*qnh* + objects relating to *ḥokmâ* *bqš* + objects relating to *ḥokmâ**
Interpretation and Understanding	*ʿḳ sbꜣy.t, rdi ib* ("think," "consider")	*šmʿ*** *šyt lēb* and synonyms**
	ṯy sbʿ.t transition ↓ *wḥʿ* ↓	*lqḥ mûsār** transition ↓
Mastery	*ʿm, ʿrḳ, wḥʿ*	*byn* transition ↓
Searching/Pondering ↓ Active Learning	*ḏʿr*	*leqaḥ* (noun), *bqš***, *lmd, ntn* *ʾel lēb, ḥqr*

* 1st meaning.
** 2nd meaning.

IV. COMPARATIVE TABLES OF THE TERMS IN EGYPTIAN AND IN THE BIBLE FOR IMPARTING AND ACQUIRING OF INSTRUCTION

Table 2: Imparting Instruction — "To Teach"

Egyptian	Hebrew
1. *sb3* - - - - - - - - - - - - - - - - - - *rdi sb3y.t* (Copt. ϯ ⲥⲃⲱ) *iri sb3y.t* *iri sb3y.t mtr*	*ysr* (niph'al, pi'el); *lmd* (pi'el) *'lp* (pi'el) (?)
2. *mtr* - - - - - - - - - - - - - - - - - - *rdi mtr*	*ykḥ* (hiph'il)
3. *rdi tp rd*	*yrh* (hiph'il)
4.	*śkl** (hiph'il)
5.	*byn** (hiph'il)
6.	(*drk** [hiph'il])
7. *ḥwi* *ḳnḳn*	*ysr* (niph'al, pi'el); *ykḥ* (hiph'il); *nkh* (hiph'il)
8. *šbd*	*šēbeṭ*
9. (*ḫsf*)**	*'nš*
Characterized by: The use of auxiliary verbs (*rdi*, *iri*) + various terms denoting "instruction" as object.	Absence of auxiliary verbs.

* In the corpus under study no exact semantic equivalent has been found for these terms in the Egyptian language.

** The verb appears only once in a didactic context in the present corpus ((*Ptaḥḥotep* 495); *'nš*, its Hebrew equivalent, appears 5 times in Prov., which constitute half of its occurrences in the Bible.

Table 3: Acquisition of Instruction — "To Learn"

	Egyptian	Hebrew
	I. Verbs taking an object related to instruction and its synonyms	
1.	*šsp+rȝ/ḏd/md.t, ṯy sbʿ.t*	*lqḥ mûsār* (1st meaning)
2.	*iri sbȝy.t*	*lmd* (?)
3.	*smn sbȝy.t* (once only)	*šmr/ḥzq* (hiphʿil)+*mûsār* (?)
4.	*ʿḳ+sbȝy.t/sḫr* *sbȝy.t+ ʿḳ msḏr*	— *glh ʾōzen lammûsār* (Job 36,10)
5.	*nḏr tp rd*	*šmr + miṣwâ, tôrâ*, etc. *hẓq* (hiphʿil)+*mûsār, ḥokmâ* *nṣr, ṣpn+miṣwâ, ḥokmâ, daʿat*, etc.
6.		*qnh+ḥokmâ* and its synonyms
7.	*ḏʿr+ḫnw, sḥ, ḥȝ.ty, ẖ.t*	*bqš + ḥokmâ* and its synonyms (1st meaning)
	II. Verbs with or without an object relating to instruction	
8.	*sḏm, sḏm* + { *sbȝy.t* / *mtr.t* / *sḫr* } *sḏm ib*	*šmʿ, šmʿ* + { *mûsār* / *tōkaḥat* / *ʿēṣâ* } *lēb šōmēaʿ* (Solomon)
9.	*rdi ib, rdi m ib,* *rdi ib (ḥȝ.ty) r...*	*šyt, śym, nṭh, hābēʾ+lēb l^e* *ntn ʾel lēb* *ntn ʾet hallēb l^e* *śym bilbāb*
10.	*ʿm, ʿm m sḫr.w*; metaphorically — " to swallow"	*byn*; metaphor — *ʾkl* + God's words + wisdom words
	III. Verbs without an object relating to instruction	
11.	*ʿrḳ*	*byn, haśkēl*, (*ydʿ*)
12.	*wḥʿ, wḥʿ ib*	*byn*
13.	*sbȝ* (to teach oneself)	*lmd*
14.		*bqš*
15.		*ḥqr*

In this light, it may be assumed that the Hebrew sage valued the method of transmitting knowledge and teaching authority just as much as he was concerned about the pupil and the material taught. His Egyptian counterpart devoted more of his efforts to the pupil, for whom, after all, the didactic activity was intended, rather than to the teacher.

CHAPTER THREE

THE NEGATIVE HUMAN TYPE — TRAITS AND BEHAVIOR

Wisdom distinguishes between two categories of human beings, the negative and the positive type. Each has its own characteristic elements, expressed in contrasting traits and opposed actions, which are reflected in the wisdom vocabulary.

We shall begin with the negative human type. His character is recognizable by his attitude towards learning and teaching, a central theme in the wisdom literature (cf. Chapter 2), as well as by his general manners and way of life.

I. ATTITUDE TOWARDS TEACHING AND LEARNING

In Egyptian

A. Inattention and Disobedience

1. *sḏm* in the negative

As already stated, listening, i.e., obedience, appears as a most desirable quality in the wisdom writings from the early to the late period. By contrast, inattention, unwillingness to obey, are among the human characteristics that are scorned and derided. The incorrigible fool — *lh̯* (*Ankhsheshonqy* 7, 5-6), the stupid person — *wh̯3* (*Ptaḥḥotep* 575), and the wicked person — *bne* (*Insinger* 26,4) do not listen. Listening leads to moral perfection: "A son who listens will be without defect," says Seḥetep-ib-Ra (PL 8,7). On the other hand "The fault in every kind of character comes out from not listening" (*Insinger* 9,5). Reproof for inattention is of course common in the language of the schoolteacher: "I spend the whole day instructing you (but) you don't listen" (*Lansing* 8,3; cf. ibid. 2,4; 2,8; *Bologna* 1094 3,8). Those who refuse to listen are figuratively said to be deaf (*idw*, *s̱hy*). The following statement addressed to the pupil is frequent in the school writings but is found elsewhere too: "You are a deaf person who cannot hear, to whom they make (signs) with the hand" (*Koller* 2,5; cf. *Anastasi* IV 2,7). The high official who does not fulfil his duty is also represented as being deaf: "His face is blind to what he sees, deaf to what he hears..." (*The Eloquent Peasant* B1 188; cf. ibid. 113; and *The Prophecies of Neferti* 38).

B. Neglect and Abandonment of Learning and Wisdom

While sometimes the obstinate sons or pupils do not apply their ear and do not listen to the words of the father or the teacher, it also happens that they do apply their ear to the words spoken, but do not "enter (*'ḳ*) into them" (cf. above, p. 62) and neglect them. In *Lansing* 3,5-6 the teacher says to the pupil: "You have joined with me[1] as regards hearkening (but) you have neglected (*mḳḥ3*) my teachings (*mtr.wt*)."

To describe this manner of behavior in a pupil who instead of applying instructions in his daily life spurns and discards them, the Egyptian sage uses a series of verbs all similar in sense.

(a) Verbs relating directly to the words of the teacher and to wisdom:

2. *wni* — neglect (Dem. *wjn*;[2] Copt.[SA] ⲟⲩⲉⲓⲛⲉ)

wni and *ḫ3'* (see below) are the most common in this context (11 times). *wni* appears especially in writings from the Middle and New Kingdom. Its basic meaning, like that of the other verbs belonging to this semantic field (*thi*, *sni*), is an act of motion, i.e., "pass by," "go past." This sense is evident in the determinative of the word which depicts marching feet, but when *wni* has an abstract noun for an object it means "not to pay attention," or "neglect." It appears frequently at the beginning of the wisdom compositions in a warning addressed to the listeners. In the *Instruction by a Man for His Son* it is said: "Listen to my voice, do not neglect my words (*m wni mdw.i*)" (I 2); or "Turn your face to hear my words, do not neglect (*m ir wni*) what I say (to you) (*ḏd.tw.i*)" (*Amennakht* 4). Since spoken words (*ḏd.t*, *mdw*) almost always constitute the object — the words of a teacher, a scribe, or other official (cf. *Amenemope* 3,12; *Seḥetep-ib-Ra* [TC] 8,5 || 7,6; *Bologna* 1094 10,1; *Anastasi* I 6,8)[3] — it is possible that *wni* relates to abandoning oral, not written instruction.[4]

3. *ḫȝʿ* — abandon

The basic meaning is "set down," "place" (Copt. κω),[5] and when accompanied by an abstract object its meaning is "neglect," "abandon," "discard." While *wni* relates principally to neglect of oral teaching, *ḫȝʿ*, which has a similar frequency in our sample, apparently refers mainly to abandoning written instruction, that is, textbooks. A repeated formula in moral preaching to the scribe and to lazy pupils is, "I am told that you have abandoned writing (*ḫȝʿ.k sš.w*)" (*Anastasi* IV 2,4; ibid. 11,8; *Koller* 2,2; etc.); parallel to it appears the statement "You have turned your back (*ḫȝʿ.k ḥȝ.k*) upon god's words (*r mdw nṯr*)," that is, upon the hieroglyphs considered to be the words of the god (see *Anastasi* V 6,1-2 || 15, 6-7 || *Sallier* I 6,1-2).

4. *mkḥȝ* — turn the head

This verb at times replaces *wni* in writings of the New Kingdom and occasionally appears instead of *ḫȝʿ* in the school texts. Compared with the other two terms its frequency is limited (3 times only). Its literal meaning, as shown by the determinative of a man's head, is "turn the head,"[6] but its general meaning approximates *wni* and *ḫȝʿ*; in practice it is perhaps closer to *wni* as here too the words of the teacher are usually the object. Amennakht (9) says to his pupil: "Do not abandon (*m iri mkḥȝ*) my excellent sayings" (cf. *Lansing* 3,5; *Anastasi* V 17,3).

5. *sni* — not go beyond, not exceed, imitate (Dem. *snj*;[7] Copt. cine)

This verb originally involved the action of walking, and its general meaning is "to pass by," "go past" people and places.[8] In the school texts and the instructions it is commonly used as a prohibition directed to the second person: "Do not go beyond," "do not exaggerate." This subsequently developed a positive connotation, and became "imitate," "do as I do."[9] The father of Kagemni says to his children (II 5): "Heed it as I said it. Do not go beyond (*m sni*) what has been set down";[10] in *Ptaḥḥotep* (151) the messenger is warned to "keep the truth — do not go beyond it (*m sni.s*)," that is, he is to deliver the message exactly as it was given to him, without adding to it anything of his own.[11] In the *Instruction by a Man for his Son* it is stated: "Be perfect (*iri mi ḳd*) without being excessive in this (*nn sni im*)" (I 3). The passages from the *Instruction of Kagemni* and *Ptaḥḥotep* are preserved in *Pap. Prisse*, which belongs to the Middle Kingdom Period, while the *Instruction of a Man for his Son*, although preserved on copies from the New Kingdom, was also composed at the beginning of the Middle Kingdom. In these three sources, therefore, *sni* still bears its negative sense. But in *The Instruction Addressed to Merikare*, whose main copy (P 1116 A) is not earlier than the 18th Dynasty, the term appears in its new sense. Here the sage advises his son: "Copy (lit. imitate — *sni r*) your fathers, your ancestors... See, their words endure in books; open, that you may read them, copy (lit. imitate — *sni.k r*) the knowledge" (35-36). This semantic change of *sni* from a negative to a positive connotation is well attested in the variations between the different manuscripts of the *Instruction of Seḥetep-ib-Ra*, all of which belong to the New Kingdom: In line 7,6 the Egyptian sage requests his hearers to be like him and to follow in his ways: "Do not go beyond my example (*m sni ḳd.i*), do not neglect my words (*wni mdwt.i*)." This formulation, given by OAshm and other manuscripts, is different in PL manuscript where the expression *sni ḳd.i* in the sense of "do like, copy my example" replaces the negative *m sni* found in the other manuscripts. In line 8,5 the same sentence is repeated with a negation in PL and in positive form in the manuscript TC.[12] From the beginning of the New Kingdom Period, therefore, the meaning of *sni* is apparently "to do something exactly," "not to add and not to omit."

(b) A verb not relating directly to the instruction and words of the teacher but belonging to the semantic field of abandonment, neglect:

6. ***thi*** **(Dem. *th*) — (a) transgress, neglect, disobey**
(b) injure, attack
(c) err, go astray, mislead

Among the expressions listed in this section, the verb *thi* is the most frequent (about 35 times). It appears many times in the literary genre of instruction but can also be found in the phraseology of the king's court and in the pessimistic compositions. However, its total absence from the school texts in our collection shows that it does not belong to the sphere of education.

The term *thi* is polysemic and has the three meanings given above. The first belongs directly to the subject under discussion, namely, a person's attitude towards learning; the second defines a person's behavior in general, not necessarily with respect to teaching; the third is not connected to the subject of this chapter nor is it even characteristic of the Egyptian wisdom vocabulary and therefore will not be treated here.[13]

(a) The determinative of *thi* — marching feet — supports the conjecture that its primary meaning involved motion (like the verbs *sni* and *wni*) and can be translated "trespass," "go past a place." In time it acquired the abstract meaning "disobey," "transgress." This latter meaning is common in our sample (12 times out of 35 occurrences),[14] and in this context *thi* relates to negative behavior in the moral sense more than the foregoing terms do. Such behavior is deemed criminal and its perpetrators are called transgressors.[15]

He who follows this path is liable to severe punishment — "Knives are sharp against the transgressor" (*thi mṯn*, i.e., the disobedient — *Kagemni* I 2-3); similarly, Ptaḥḥotep says, "Woe to him who would transgress against (*thi*) it" (50). While in the sphere of wisdom people may "transgress" against the teaching of the sage, in matters of religion and ritual they "transgress against," neglect, the feast (*Anii* 3,4). In the phraseology of the king's court the expression indicates disobeying the king's orders (especially in the Middle Kingdom Period — *Seḥetep-ib-Ra* 5,13; Blumenthal G 8, 86-87).

At times *thi* appears with the object "way" — *thi wꜣ.t/mṯn* (see *Kagemni* above). Here the word "way" is used as a metaphor for "way of life," "proper behavior." Therefore, *thi wꜣ.t/mṯn* is an epithet for a man who does not walk in the right path, is disobedient, rebellious. Its antonym is *mḏd mṯn*, meaning the obedient man, he who submits.[16] In this sense *thi* is synonymous with *wni*, which sometimes replaces it in the later texts. The wisdom cliché cited above from *Ptaḥḥotep* (50) reappears in the *Instruction of Amenemope* (3, 12), with *wni* replacing *thi* of the former source: "Woe to him who neglects them (*pꜣ wn.w st*)."[17]

(b) The second use of *thi* — "harm," "attack" — is no less common than the first (about 14 times) and is present especially in the later wisdom literature — *Amenemope*, *Insinger* — where the object is usually a person.[18] For example, the scribe in *The Instruction of Amenemope* is warned: "Do not dip your pen to injure (*thi*) a man" (17,6; cf. ibid. 19,5); elsewhere in the same source the exhortation is "Do not shout against one you have attacked (*pꜣ thi.k*)" (4,10);[19] and in *Insinger* it is said that "He who does harm (*th*) for harm, his old age will be harmed (*th*)" (33, 20; etc.).

In contrast to the determinative accompanying the first meaning of *thi* (feet), the usual determinative here — from the Middle Kingdom on — is a knife placed on a knee and a man holding a staff in his hand, or — in a later period — a man with an axe (in *Insinger*).[20] These determinatives as well as the context in which the term appears in this sense indicate that *thi* here bears the sense of violent action, to injure physically, and refers to behavior in general. It is not surprising therefore that the sage often warns against this kind of behavior — Amenemope, for example, demands of his son not to injure (*thi*) people in various circumstances connected with his profession (5,11; 22, 2-4). Similarly, the author of *Pap. Insinger* speaks of the bitter end of the injurer (33, 20; 34,22) and states that the impatient man wishes to injure (ibid. 30,5), while the "man of god," the righteous man, acts in the opposite manner (ibid. 30, 10).[21]

Summary of the distribution of the verbs belonging to the semantic field of neglect and abandonment of learning in Egyptian (Table 4)

The verb *thi* which occurs in all literary genres except one (the school texts) is the most common.

sni appears in the instructions of the Old Kingdom and is used subsequently in the Middle Kingdom Period. In the New Kingdom it is then replaced by *wni*. The Middle Kingdom is a transitional period, when both terms appear together.

wni began to be used in the Middle Kingdom Period (*Loyalist Instruction* and pessimistic compositions). It reached its peak in the New Kingdom and disappeared immediately thereafter.

mḳḥ3 and *ḫ3ʿ* appeared in the New Kingdom only and exclusively in the school texts.

Table 4: Distribution of Verbs Belonging to the Semantic Field of Neglect and Abandonment of Learning in Egyptian

	Old Kingdom	Middle Kingdom	New Kingdom	Late Period
Instructions	*sni* *thi*		*wni* *thi* *mḳḥ3*	*thi*
Pessimistic Wisdom		*thi* *wni*		
"Loyalist" Instruction		*wni* *thi* *sni*		
School Texts			*wni* *ḫ3ʿ* *mḳḥ3*	
Autobiography				*thi*
King's Court Literature		*thi*	*thi* *wni*	

All verbs fell into disuse and disappeared from the wisdom corpus of the Late Period (*Ankhsheshonqy*, *Insinger*), with the exception of *thi*, which continues to be used in this period too.

In the Bible

A. Inattention and Disobedience

1. *šm'* used in negation

The son (*bēn*) and the simple man (*petî*) are without experience and do not listen to words of instruction. Likening himself to a youth, a pupil before his teachers, the father in Proverbs confesses: "I did not listen (*šāma'tî*) to the voice of my teachers nor incline my ear to my instructors" (Prov. 5,13). In the sarcastic language of the sage in Proverbs 19,27, the son is commanded "to cease to hear (*lišmōa'*) instruction," while the intention of the statement is to encourage the son to incline his ear only more to the words of knowledge. The youth (*na'ar*) and the simple person (*petî*) do not listen because they know no better, but the scorner (*lēṣ*) and the fool (*'ěwîl*) do not incline their ear intentionally: "A scorner (*lēṣ*) does not listen (*šāma'*) to rebuke" (Prov. 13,1; cf. 1,22,24); "The way of a fool (*'ěwîl*) is right in his own eyes, but a wise man listens (*šōmēa'*) to advice" (Prov. 12,15).

As in Egyptian, he who does not listen is metaphorically called a "deaf" person, but in the Bible this motif appears only in non-wisdom literature.[22]

B. Neglect and Abandonment of Learning and Wisdom

Even if not all verbs found in this context in the Biblical language are equivalent to the Egyptian verbs considered above, they are close to them in subject matter. The Egyptian terms *sni*, *wni* are especially close to *'zb*, *swr*, *nṭh* in Biblical Hebrew. The latter also originate as verbs of motion and are used figuratively when combined with an abstract object.[23] These expressions are common in Biblical wisdom literature but are not exclusive to it.

2. *'zb* ("forsake") is the opposite of "hearing" the words of wisdom, "acquiring" and "keeping" them (Prov. 4,2, 6; 10, 17; 28,4).

3. *swr* ("depart from") regularly appears in the wisdom vocabulary in a positive connotation through combination with an object of negative meaning: "departed/depart from evil (*rā'*)" (Prov. 13,19; 16,6,17, etc.). This collocation stands in synonymous parallelism with the expressions "to fear God" (Job 1, 1,8) and "to do good" (wisdom Pss. 34,15; 37, 27). A better analogy, however, to the Egyptian samples is contained in the following precept of a father to his sons: "Do not depart from the words of my mouth" (|| "listen to me") (Prov. 5,7).[24]

4. *nṭh* ("turn away") may replace *swr* in this context; for example, in Prov. 4,5 it is said, "Do not turn away (*tēṭ*) from the words of my mouth" (cf. ibid. 4,27); and Job states "I have kept his (God's) way and have not turned away (*'āṭ*)" (23, 11).

The following verbs, although not of motion, are similar to the Egyptian parallels:

5. *nṭš* ("forsake") appears with the object "mother's teaching" in the negative imperative (*'al tiṭṭōš*), following the positive imperative to "hearken to" (*š^ema'*) the father's instructions (Prov. 1,8; and cf. 6,20).

6. *pr'* ("neglect" instruction, advice): The primary sense of the verb is "unbind, loose,"[25] but in Proverbs in combination with an abstract noun it acquires the meaning "to neglect." Like the preceding verbs *pr'* comes in antithetic parallelism with "hear" (*šm'*), and "keep" (*šmr*) (Prov. 8,33; 13,18; 15,32). Here too the warning is directed to sons (*bānîm*) (ibid. 8,33; 4,15), the simple man (*petî*), the scorner (*lēṣ*) and the stupid person (*k^esîl*). Unlike most of the other verbs, the penalty for the neglecter is stressed: Proverbs 13,18 asserts that "poverty and disgrace come to him who neglects (*pôrēa'*) instruction" (cf. 15,32; 1,32ff).

7. *škḥ* ("forget"): While this term does not belong to the semantic field of abandoning and inattention to teaching, it is similar in meaning

to the preceding terms. The son is warned not to forget his father's instruction (Prov. 3,1) and "the words of his mouth" (ibid. 4,5).

In summary, the proximity between the terms in Hebrew and Egyptian concerning abandonment of teaching can be expressed as follows:

(a) These terms frequently appear in the negative imperative mood: "Do not," usually addressed to one lacking in experience — the son, the pupil, who has not yet acquired knowledge (*sni, wni*).

(b) A considerable part of the verbs in Hebrew (*pr‘, nṭš, swr, ‘zb*) appear like the Egyptian verbs (*sni, wni*) in antithetic parallelism with "hear" (Heb. *šm‘* — Eg. *sḏm*).

(c) The verbs *‘zb, swr, nṭh* are originally verbs indicating motion, but when combined with an abstract object — like their Egyptian equivalents *sni, wni* — they stand figuratively for leaving, abandoning something.

8. ***‘zb ’ōraḥ* and synonyms — *thi, thi wꜣ.t/mṯn***

An equivalent expression covering all three aspects of the Egyptian verb *thi* (see p. 82 above) does not exist in the Hebrew wisdom vocabulary, but the idiom *thi wꜣ.t/mṯn* "way" does have Hebrew parallels remarkably similar to the Egyptian.

The first sense of *thi*, namely, "trespass," "neglect," etc., is in essence approximated by the verbs listed in 1-7 above. The combination *thi* + way, which appears in this context, may be compared to the following expressions: *‘zb ’ōraḥ* — "forsake the way" (Prov. 15,10; cf. 2,13); *nṭh ’aššur minnî dārek* — "turn aside from the way" (Job 31,7), *derek* and its synonyms here being metaphors for "right way of life," "moral behavior."[26]

The Hebrew idiom *‘iqqēš* (*m*e*‘aqqēš, ne‘qaš*) *d*e*rākayim* approximates the Egyptian word *thw* — "transgressor." This adjective, which occurs several times in Proverbs (but does not appear in Job and Qoheleth)[27] indicates a person of bad behavior whose ways are crooked and whose morality is flawed (Prov. 10,9; 28,6,18; cf. also 2,15; 22,5). The antonym of *‘iqqēš d*e*rākayim* is *hôlēk tāmîm, hôlēk b*e*tummô*, that is, whose way is upright (Prov. 28,6,18; cf. the sapiential phrase *tāmîm,* *tām derek* — ibid. 11,20; 13,6; wisdom Ps. 119,1; cf. Job 4,6).[28] On the other hand, *hôlēk tāmîm* parallels the Egyptian *mḏd wꜣ.t/mṯn*, and if we accept Gardiner's suggestion[29] that the basic meaning of the verb *mḏd* in Egyptian is "to make straight," then we may consider the Hebrew wisdom phrases *yaššēr derek/ 'ōraḥ*, "to straighten the way," (Prov. 3,6; 9,15; 11,5), and *yᵉšar dārek*, "he whose way is straight" (ibid. 29,26; wisdom Ps. 37,14)[30] to be the semantic equivalents of the Egyptian term *mḏd wꜣ.t/mṯn*.

C. Verbs Indicating a Negative Attitude towards Teaching Without an Egyptian Equivalent

9-13. In addition to the Hebrew terms mentioned in sections (A) and (B) which have a parallel in the Egyptian wisdom lexicon, the language of the Biblical sage contains several verbs that also express a negative attitude towards teaching but which have no parallel in the Egyptian didactic literature.[31] These are distinguished by their sharp derogatory tone. Unlike the verbs considered above, they do not refer to the absence of obedience or to neglect but describe a graver degree of belittling study by the pupil, namely, scorn and hatred of learning.

The *'ĕwîl* ("fool") and *kᵉsîl* ("stupid person") *bāzîm*, i.e., "despise" wisdom and morals (Prov. 1,7; 23,9); ***bwz*** interchanges with its synonym the verb ***n'ṣ***.[32] The *petî* ("simple man"), the *lēṣ* ("scorner"), and the *kᵉsîl* "despise" (*n'ṣ*) the reproof of Wisdom (Prov. 1,30; cf. vss. 22 and 32). The *'ĕwîl* ("foolish") son despises (*n'ṣ*) the father's instruction (Prov. 15,5) and the obstinate pupil despises (*n'ṣ*) the "reproof" of his teachers (ibid. 5, 12).

The attitude of disparagement expressed by these two terms is replaced by still stronger feelings in the following ones. ***śn'***, "hatred" of knowledge, morality and reproof is a common emotion of the *kᵉsîl* (Prov. 1,22), the *ba'ar* (12,1) and the obstinate pupil (5,12). Such an attitude is conceived as a serious transgression, deserving capital punishment (ibid. 8,36; 15,10). Similar feelings are expressed by the terms ***m's*** and ***qwṣ***, each of which appears only once (3,11).[33]

Unlike his Egyptian counterpart, the Hebrew sage describing the negative attitude of the pupil towards study and teaching did not stop with a definition of the outward form of improper behavior (namely, inattention, disobedience, neglect and the like) but delved into the interior of the soul, i.e., into the feelings and emotions of the pupil (namely, scorn, hatred, disdain). Both aspects, internal and external, merge into one whole picture of the behavior of the negative human type towards teaching.

II. TRAITS RELATING TO THE EDUCATIONAL AND OTHER LEVELS

A. Idleness

In Egyptian

1. ***wsf***[34] **(v. n.; Copt.** ⲟⲩⲱⲥϥ; **qualitative —** ⲟⲩⲁⲥϥ **)**

This verb is first used in the Middle Kingdom Period[35] and in our sample occurs only in the pessimistic compositions and in the school texts. The determinative of marching feet accompanying the term in the Middle Kingdom is replaced in the New Kingdom Period by a drawing of a sparrow, a symbol of evil. This process most probably reflects a semantic change: in the first stage *wsf* has a positive connotation denoting slackness, inactivity, while later it is accompanied by a negative connotation of idleness.

Warnings repeated time and again in the school texts are: "Do not be idle" (*Anastasi* III 3,10; V 23, 1-2), "Spend no day of idleness" (ibid. III 3, 12-13; V 23, 5). These admonitions are reinforced with the threat of punishment. The idler is assured that he will fail (ibid. III 3,10) or will receive a beating (ibid. 3, 12-13).

Idleness of the pupil expressed itself in being seduced by pleasures, evading of the task of writing, and refusing to accept advice, which was one of the ways of learning in antiquity. Not only the lax pupil but also the bad leader who does not fulfil his duty is called *wsf* (*The Eloquent*

Peasant B1 257; B2 109). The plundered "peasant" threatens such leaders by citing the folk saying, "The sluggard has no yesterday," i.e., of him there will be no memory and his name will disappear among men (ibid. B2 109).[36]

2. ***ẖsy, ḫsy*** : The basic meaning of this is "be weak" (Copt. ϩⲓⲥⲉ), but it sometimes appears in *The Instruction of Ankhsheshonqy* in the sense of "to be lazy." The father repeatedly warns his son to avoid excessive eating, which will lead to laxity in his work. In Glanville's view the intention is laziness in connection with working the land (see ibid. 6, 18-19; 23, 17-18).[37]

In the Bible

1. ***'ṣl*** ("lazy"): The root *'ṣl* (adj. *'āṣēl*; n. *'aṣlâ*, *'aṣlût*, dual *'ăṣaltayim*) appears only in the wisdom books (16 times),[38] except for a single appearance in Judges (18,9). In Proverbs the use of *'ṣl* is concentrated in the second collection, but it is also mentioned in the poem "Woman of Valor" (31,27). Here the description of the idler (*'āṣēl*) is broader and more vivid than in the Egyptian sources. The Biblical author adopts a satirical tone and colorful images in his condemnation of idleness: "The *'āṣēl* dips his hand into the dish" (Prov. 19,24; 26,15); "Like vinegar to the teeth and smoke to the eyes so is *'āṣēl* to those whose messenger he is" (10,26); "*'āṣēl* says, 'There is a lion outside'" (22,13; cf. 26,13); "A door turns on its hinge and *'āṣēl* on his bed" (26,14).

Unlike the Egyptian sources, the problem of idleness in Proverbs is embedded neither in an educational-didactic framework nor in a social framework (as in *The Eloquent Peasant*). The sage in Proverbs is chiefly concerned with the fate of the idler as an individual.[39] The *'āṣēl* is not necessarily a pupil or a leader but any person characterized by the following traits: (a) inaction — he does not work with his hands (during a meal — Prov. 19,24 || 26,15; cf. 21, 25); he does not go out into the street (22,13; 26,13); he does not engage in farming (20,4; 24,30ff; cf.

Instruction of Ankhsheshonqy); he passes his time in complete inactivity — dozing, sleeping (Prov. 24,33; 19,15; 26,14; Qoh. 4,5); the ant does the opposite (Prov. 6,6ff; cf. the conduct of the "Woman of Valor," ibid. 31,34); (b) the idler justifies his indolence with spurious pretexts (Prov. 22,13; 26,13); (c) the idler is greedy, with an appetite that cannot be satisfied (Prov. 13,4; 21,25); (d) he is unreliable with respect to his fellows, and cannot serve as a messenger (Prov. 10,26).

Idleness is the trait of a fool, the *ḥăsar lēb* (Prov. 24,30). The way of the *'āṣēl* is crooked and "hedged with thorns" (ibid. 15,19). Types opposite to the *'āṣēl* are the *yāšār* ("straightforward person"), whose way is paved (ibid.), the *ḥārûṣ* ("diligent") (13,4) and the *ṣaddîq* ("righteous") (21,26). All these terms pair at times with *'āṣēl* in antithetic parallelism.

Like the Egyptian sources, the Hebrew texts threaten the idler with penalties, but here they are more severe: not just flogging or downfall, but poverty and loss of property (Prov. 6, 11 || 24, 34; cf. ibid. 28,19; Qoh. 10,18), hunger (Prov. 13, 4) and even death (Prov. 21, 25).

A synonymous expression to *'aṣlût* is *šiplût yādayim* (Qoh. 10, 18), close in meaning to *kap r^{e}miyyâ* and *yad r^{e}miyyâ.*

2. ***r^{e}miyyâ***: This noun, which derives from the root *rmh*, appears three times in Proverbs out of four appearances in the entire Bible.[40] *r^{e}miyyâ* means "laxity," "slackness," "idleness," and it is present in the collocation *kap r^{e}miyyâ* ("slack hand") (opp. *yad ḥārûṣîm*) and its synonym *yad r^{e}miyyâ*, which appear in Proverbs (10,4; 12,24; cf. *nepeš r^{e}miyyâ* [one who is slack] || *'aṣlâ* — ibid. 19,15). These are reminiscent of the Egyptian expression "idle fingers" (*Sallier* II 11, 10).[41]

B. Deafness, as a Metaphor

In Egyptian

In passing, mention has already been made to the metaphor of "deafness" for both the reluctance of the pupil to study and the wickedness of the bad leader. The motif of deafness is present in three expressions:

(1) The most common is ***sḫy*** (*sḫy*),[42] which appears six times in the school texts, the pessimistic compositions and the writings of the king's court beginning from the Middle Kingdom Period.[43]

(2) ***idi***,[44] is apparently linked to the Egyptian noun *idn* — *'ōzen* ("ear") in Hebrew — and appears only once, in *The Prophecies of Neferti*, and that in an ambiguous context.[45]

(3) ***msḏr.t dnrg*** appears twice in the school texts. Its exact meaning is unclear, but by virtue of its context it may be understood as having to do with deafness. Caminos interprets: "the ear is deaf(?)."[46]

The school texts and the pessimistic compositions refer to the "deaf" person in association with the "idler." In the school texts the behavior of the lazy apprentice of the scribe who does not listen to his teachers' words is likened to that of a "deaf" person. The expression "to have an ear that is deaf" is common in the school texts.[47] The image of deafness also appears in texts describing the duties of the ruler or the high official.[48] The vizier Rekhmire can praise himself with the declaration that he is not deaf to "one who has a weak arm" (cf. Prov. 21,13: "He who stops up his ear [*'ōṭēm 'oznô*] to the cry of a poor man"); and the wicked leader in *The Eloquent Peasant* is compared to a "deaf" man (B1 113; ibid. 188). His crime is great because his behavior constitutes an infraction of the cosmic-social order, i.e., the *mȝ'.t* . In the language of the Egyptian sage such a leader is said to be "deaf to justice" (ibid. B2 110). The reality of the anarchy which reigns in the land and which is the opposite of an orderly central government (symbolized by the *mȝ'.t*), is described by the sage thus: "When the listener is deaf," meaning he whose task it is to listen (the ruler) does not listen (*The Prophecies of Neferti* 38).

In the Bible

In Hebrew *ḥrš* has a double meaning: (a) "to be silent," "not to speak," and figuratively "to avoid action"; (b) "not to hear," "to be deaf."[49]

Only the second meaning, in which the word deaf often appears metaphorically, is relevant for our comparison with the Egyptian findings; this usage, however, does not appear in Biblical wisdom.[50]

III. NEGATIVE CHARACTERISTICS AND ACTIONS RELATING TO WAY OF LIFE AND GENERAL BEHAVIOR

Apart from "idleness" and "deafness," which signify the reaction of the obstinate pupil to teaching but which may also describe a negative way of behavior unconnected with the didactic framework, there are other characteristics typical of the behavior of the negative human type in daily life. While "idleness" and "deafness" are founded in inaction, these other traits involve activity. Therefore, wisdom often warns against them with the imperative "Do not do," and stresses the punishment meted out for this behavior. These traits are condemned not only in the wisdom literature but also in other literary genres (such as psalms, prophecy, royal texts). Therefore, most of the terms belonging to this subject are not exclusive to wisdom language, whether in Israel or Egypt.

A. Falsehood

In Egyptian

Two words, *(s)ʿḏꜣ* and *grg*, belong to the semantic field of falsehood and appear frequently in Egyptian wisdom literature. The first of these indicates flawed behavior while the second relates principally to false words. Consequently, *(s)ʿḏꜣ* appears to have a wider semantic field than *grg*, which is a hyponym of *ʿḏꜣ*.

1. ***(s)ʿḏꜣ*** **(Dem. *ʿḏ*)**[51]

The nominal form *ʿḏꜣ* begins to appear in the Middle Kingdom, its usage becoming more frequent in the New Kingdom (*Wb.* I 240-241). The verbs *ḏd* ("say"), *iri* ("do") are added to make the verbal form, and beginning with the New Kingdom the verb *s'd3* appears in this usage (*Wb.* IV 57). The adverb is *n 'd3*, "falsely."[52] The determinative, which is a hand grasping a staff or a sparrow, stands for violent and wicked action. In Demotic the determinative of a sparrow is augmented with a determinative designating an enemy (a bound man holding an axe). The occurrence of *'d3* in this corpus is restricted to the literary genre of instruction.

(s)'d3 indicates deceptive behavior and stress is usually laid on the damage it causes others. This behavior may be passive — concealment of the truth, pretence and hypocrisy. The false man (*rmt 'd*) in *Papyrus Insinger* is described as one who "does not tell to another what is in his heart" (25,22). But *(s)'d3* mostly relates to deliberate acts, which include the following: (1) theft of property (*Amenemope* 7,18; 14,9; 23,15); (2) forgery and falsification: of measures and accounts (ibid. 16,4); of written documents such as court records or the divine oracle copied by the scribe (ibid. 21,9,13); (3) lying, whether by blessing another in pretence and cajolery (ibid. 13,13-15; 14,2,3), or in giving a false answer (*Insinger* 22,21), by committing perjury in court (*Amenemope* 16,1; 20,9) or by giving a false oath (ibid. 7,18; 14,9; *Ankhsheshonqy* 16,13).

Every man can err through inappropriate behavior, but in particular danger of doing so is the high official with his wide powers, who may be drawn into wrongdoing by way of fulfilling his task. Therefore, most of the offenses listed above are given in the form "Do not do," addressed to the scribe or to some other figure of authority. Rarely does this trait involve a particular human type. For example, the "hot-tempered" man in *Amenemope* is spoken of as "laden with false words" (*mdy n 'd3*) (12,8; and cf. *Insinger* 22, 21). The behavior indicated by *(s)'d3* is deemed more sinful than the other transgressions against social morality enumerated in *The Instruction of Amenemope*, for only this one is termed an "abomination of god."[53] *mt.t 'd* is the opposite of justice, truth — *m3'.t*, and appears in antithetic parallelism with the latter (*Insinger* 24,17; 32,15; etc.).

The Egyptian sage is not sparing in his warnings and threats of punishment directed at those guilty of such behavior: he "will be caught by the might (*ba*) of the Moon" (*Amenemope* 7,19); he will suffer "poverty" (*Insinger* 32,15), or other trouble (ibid. 24, 17; *Ankhsheshonqy* 16,13).[54]

2. *grg* (Copt. [S] n. ϭⲟⲗ; v. ⲣ ϭⲟⲗ — "be false")

This term usually serves as a noun — "falsehood, lie."[55] In verbal usage it frequently collocates with the verb *d̲d*, "to say." The hieroglyph denoting this word, a pick excavating a pool (Gr U17), has no apparent connection with the meaning of the word. The determinative — a man sitting with his hand to his mouth — interchanges with the picture of a sparrow, indicating the negative connotation of the term.

grg is used more frequently than *ʿd̲Ꜣ* regardless of whether we analyze its usage diachronically or synchronically. *grg* first appears at the end of the Old Kingdom, and disappears in the Late Period. It is found in all genres of literature, from prose texts to hymns. *grg* and *ʿd̲Ꜣ* complement each other in terms of distribution: while *ʿd̲Ꜣ* is often present in the instructions of the New Kingdom Period, *grg* is found in the instructions from the Old Kingdom and the First Intermediate Period; it is also common in the pessimistic wisdom literature and in the *persönliche Frömmigkeit* writings. The primary meaning of *grg*, expressed in the determinative of a man sitting with his hand to his mouth, is "to speak falsely." As an abstract noun *grg* sometimes carries the sense of "wrongdoing," "injustice":

(a) In the sense of "falsehood," "lie," *grg* usually appears in antithetic parallelism with words denoting truth (*mꜢʿ.t*) (*Urk.* IV 438, 16-17; 971, 4-5; etc.).[56] The dwelling place of lying words before they are pronounced is like that of truthful words, the "heart." The high official Intef at the time of Tuthmoses III compliments himself for being "straight of heart" (*ʿḳꜢ ib*) since "it has no lie in it" (ibid. 970,10,11). "There is no falsehood in my heart," the pious one states (*ÄHG* 71,75). False speech is considered a crime, an "abomination" (*bw.t*) (ibid. 164, 12; 214, 106; *The Tomb of May*, Sandman 60, 2, *The Tomb of Ay*, ibid. 91,18). The ideal man keeps his distance from the liars and punishes them (*Urk.* IV 1078,16). The biographers repeat the following declarations: "(I am) a man of truth, without falsehood (*šw grg*)"; "I have not uttered a lie"; "there is no falsehood in ...." (*Urk.* IV 48,14; 119,14; 438,17; 970,11; cf. *Ptaḥḥotep* 532, and Jansen-Winkeln II 3,6,6).

The Eloquent Peasant accuses the high steward Rensi of not upholding this moral principle: "Speak not falsely (when) you are great" (B1 160; cf. *Instruction by a Man for His Son* IX 1). He compares him to a gardener who waters his garden with wrongdoing so as to make it grow with falsehood (*The Eloquent Peasant* B1 263; cf. also ibid. 67 and 298).[57]

(b) *grg* as an abstract noun, meaning "injustice," "wrong," stands in antithetic parallelism with the terms *mꜣʿ.t* — "truth," "justice" (ibid. 67; 240-241; 182-183, etc.), *bw nfr* — "good" (ibid. 198), and in synoymous parallelism with the terms *iy.t* — "mishap" (ibid. 298) and *isf.t* — "wrongdoing" (*Wb.* V 189,12). The meaning of *grg* in this usage is bound up with the religious-mythical concept underlying its antonym, *mꜣʿ.t*. Originally *mꜣʿ.t* was an abstract term standing for the cosmic order existing in the world since the creation.[58] This abstract value underwent a process of hypostasization, and *mꜣʿ.t* became a goddess, the daughter of Reʿ, the creator god who standing upon the primeval mound that emerged from the watery chaos first established the cosmic order — the *mꜣʿ.t*. The hieroglyph *mꜣʿ* depicts the primeval mound and shows the base of the throne of the Pharaoh who, as the god's regent on earth, is responsible for justice and order.[59] The wisdom instructions transmitted from father to son are firmly connected with the idea of *mꜣʿ.t* because their purpose is to assist a man in finding his place in the cosmic order. This is well illustrated in the following passage cited from *The Instruction Addressed to Merikare*: "No (crime) occurs when justice (*mꜣʿ.t*) comes to him distilled, after the manner of counsels said (i.e., given) by the ancestors" (34; cf. *Ptaḥḥotep* 641-644).

In an era of anarchy and a weakening of the central pillars of society, a state of disorder prevails, namely, "falsehood" replaces *mꜣʿ.t*. The pessimistic wisdom composition describes this condition thus: "Goodness is destroyed, none adhere to it. Flinging falsehood's (*grg*) back to the ground is also perished" (*The Eloquent Peasant* B1

197-198). "Falsehood," essentially an abstract concept, may like *mꜣʿ.t* become personified when linked to the latter: Falsehood sails in a boat (ibid. B2 98), is overwhelmed by truth (*Sallier* I 8, 9-10), is cast down upon the ground (*The Eloquent Peasant* B1 182-183).

In the Bible

The terms belonging to the semantic field of deceit, falsehood, in the Bible frequently appear in the wisdom phraseology, but their usage is common also in the non-wisdom literature. It is of interest that not one of them appears in Qoheleth.

1. *šqr*

šqr occurs more frequently than the other terms associated with falsehood both in the wisdom literature (Prov. 20 times; Job twice; BS 6 times), as well as in the other books of the Bible. In wisdom literature it is found only in the nominal form, *šeqer*. The word accentuates the practical side of deceit because it involves an action that harms the safety of people, and therefore is to be interpreted as "disloyalty," "treachery."[60] In wisdom literature *šeqer* is connected primarily with speech, rarely with another act and occasionally it bears the abstract sense of "worthlessness."

As an activity involving speech, *šqr* ("falsehood") is found in *legal contexts* such as (a) in giving testimony, (b) in disputation, and (c) in perjury:

(a) Injurious testimony: in Proverbs the word *ʿēd* ("witness") appears 6 times in combination with *šāqer*/*šᵉqārîm* (6,19; 12,17; 14,5; 19,5, 9; 25,18). The frequent warning against falsely testifying shows that this crime was common in Israel as well as in Egypt (see *ʿḏꜣ* above). In the Bible *šeqer*, when relating to testimony, does not refer only to the contents of the words spoken but is of more serious import: the *šeqer* denotes the anti-social behavior of the witness. The danger to a fellow-man arising from "false witness" is so great as to be compared to a "sword" and "sharp arrow" (Prov. 25,18). *'ēd šāqer* appears in Proverbs in synonymous parallelism with *yāpîaḥ k^ezābîm* (6,19; 14,5; 19,5,9) and interchanges with the terms *'ēd ḥinnām* (24,28) and *'ēd b^eliyya'al* (19,28).[61] The contrasting, is characterised by honesty and reliability and expressed in Proverbs in the collocations *yāpîaḥ 'ĕmûnâ* (12,17), *'ēd 'ĕmûnîm* (14,5) and *'ēd 'ĕmet* (14,25) which stand in antithetic parallelism with *'ēd šāqer/ š^eqārîm* and *yāpîaḥ k^ezābîm*.

(b) In legal disputation: in Job's debate with his friends, which is set in a legal framework, he accuses them of being "falsehood (*šāqer*) plasterers" (13,4; cf. 36,4). A similar charge is uttered by the righteous man against his enemies in Psalms (119, 69 [wisdom Ps.]; cf. 69,5; 35,19; etc.).

(c) Perjury in legal matters: a false oath, although not mentioned in the Biblical wisdom books, is pertinent to our discussion because of its parallel usage in Egyptian (see p. 94). The perjurious oath in the Bible is linked to the religious sphere and is perceived as an attack against God himself. The legal setting is still evident in the following passages: "Execute the judgment of truth and peace in your gates...and love no false oath, for all these I hate, says Yahweh" (Zech. 8, 16-17); "If there be any who does justice, who seeks truth that I may pardon her. Though they say, 'As Yahweh lives' yet they swear falsely" (Jer. 5,1-2, etc. — 5 times, and Zech. 5,4; Ps. 144,8, 11; etc.).

šeqer is also found in a *non-legal setting* and then means "unreliable speech." In this usage *šeqer* usually collocates with the words *dābār*, *lāšôn*, *ś^epātayim*, and stands in antithetic parallelism with the phrases *ś^epat 'ĕmet* ("truthful lips") (Prov. 12, 19), *'ōśê 'ĕmûnâ* ("act faithfully") (ibid. 12,22), these expressions signifying true, accurate and reliable speech.[62]

An inseparable feature of life in the king's court in Israel, as in Egypt, is talebearing and sycophancy: "If a ruler listens to falsehood (*d^ebar šāqer*), all his officials will be wicked," runs the saying in Proverbs (29,12), which is reminiscent of the warnings directed to the prince and the vizier in the Egyptian instructions and to the wicked leader in *The Eloquent Peasant.* Other verses associate speaking falsely with negative human types. Lying characterizes the "wicked man," who through his lies brings disgrace upon himself and others (Prov. 13,5). There is remarkable similarity between these words and the complaints of the Egyptian *Man Who Was Tired of Life*, who compares his stinking (disgraceful) name to that of a woman about whom lies were told to her husband (98). The *mēra'*, i.e., the evildoer appears in parallel with *šeqer*, i.e., false man (Prov. 17, 4); their antonym is the prince (*nādîb*), to whom "false speech is not becoming" (ibid. 7).

At times the sages stress the harm caused to others through falsehood. This motif is connected with acquiring wealth by guile: "The getting of treasures by a lying tongue" (Prov. 21, 6); "Bread gained by deceit is sweet to a man" (ibid. 20, 17). It is not surprising therefore that warnings against this sin recur frequently in Proverbs. *šeqer* belongs to a group of sins defined as "an abomination to Yahweh": "Lying lips are an abomination to Yahweh" (ibid. 12, 22; cf. Egyptian *s'ḏ3*, which is also perceived as an "abomination of the god," and *grg*, called an "abomination" — pp. 94–95 above). *šeqer* is mentioned in the list of seven crimes that endanger the very foundations of social morality: "There are six things which Yahweh hates, seven which are an abomination to him — haughty eyes, a lying tongue..." (Prov. 6,16).

Finally, *šeqer* sometimes does not relate to specific actions, nor does it have an active meaning, but appears in an *abstract sense*, with the meaning "worthlessness." The wicked man receives "deceptive (*šāqer*) wages" as his reward, but the wage of "one who sows righteousness" is "a sure reward" (lit. "fruits of truth") (Prov. 11, 18). When a man boasts of a present but does not give it: this is a "gift of *šāqer*" (25, 14). The beauty of a woman is *šeqer*, for it is an outer covering which says nothing about her inner qualities (31,30).[63]

2. *kzb*

kzb appears in the wisdom literature as a noun and as a verb (Prov. 10 times; Job 4 times; BS 6 times). The term is not exclusive to the wisdom language and is found frequently in the prophetic books and in the Psalms. As stated, *šqr* often relates to a negative way of behavior in general, but *kzb* has an even more negative connotation because it involves evil intent. In the course of time *kzb* underwent semantic development and assumed the sense of "to cause disappointment," "be unrealized."[64]

In qal and niph'al *kzb* means "to lie," "be a liar," or "be proven a liar"; in hiph'il it means "to disappoint," "fail." *kzb* appears in Biblical wisdom in usages similar to those observed for *šqr*, i.e., first of all as an activity connected with speech in a legal context:

(a) Matters between man and man: (1) Giving evidence — a term synonymous to *'ēd šāqer/šeqarîm* ("false witness") is *yāpîaḥ kezābîm*. The provenance of *yāpîaḥ* is Ugaritic, and in meaning and grammatical form (a participle) it equals the Hebrew *'ēd* (Prov. 6, 19; 14, 5; 19, 5, 9). *yāpîaḥ kezābîm* comes in antithetic parallelism with *'ēd 'ĕmûnîm* (14,5), *'ēd 'ĕmet* (14,25), that is, a witness who may be trusted.[65] He himself is worthless as a witness — "*yāpîaḥ kezābîm* (is) deception" (ibid.). (2) Legal disputation — Job argues before his friends that he is deemed a liar even though he is innocent: "I am counted a liar (*'ăkazzēb*) (34,5; see also 6,28; 24,25).

(b) Matters between man and God: The statements of Agur in Prov. 30, 5, 6 also elicit a legal setting: "Do not add to his (God's) word lest he *yôkîaḥ* you and you be found a liar (*wenikzābetā*)." The root *ykḥ*, which belongs to the court terminology, bears here the sense of "to accuse", i.e., God will accuse you and you will be found to be a liar.

Secondly, *kzb* refers to falsehood connected with other activities: Wealth acquired dishonestly is considered to be "deceit", and in Proverbs 30,8, Agur prays for a moderate life: "Remove falsehood and lying (*debar kāzāb*) far from me; do not give me poverty nor riches. Let me eat the bread that is my due (*leḥem ḥukkî*)." This verse becomes clear in the light of 20,17, which presents the opposite: "Bread of falsehood (*leḥem šāqer*) tastes sweet to a man." Agur on the one hand asks for *leḥem ḥukkî*, that is, the minimum necessary for survival; on the other, he begs to be put at a distance from *debar kāzāb*, that is, property accumulated not honestly, parallel in meaning to *leḥem šāqer* in 20,17. *kzb* is found in a similar context in a passage in Proverbs dealing with table manners and which has a direct parallel in *The Instruction of Anememope.* The Biblical sage counsels his son to behave with restraint should he be invited to dine at the ruler's table: "Do not desire his delicacies for it is deceptive food (*leḥem k*^{e}*zābîm*)" (Prov. 23, 1-3).

The Hebrew idiom *leḥem k*^{e}*zābîm* has a parallel in *Amenemope* (23, 15) in "chewing of deceit" (*wgꜣy n ʿḏꜣ*). *leḥem k*^{e}*zābîm*, like *leḥem šāqer* in Proverbs 20,17 and "chewing of deceit" in Egyptian means a meal acquired dishonestly. Elsewhere the sage adds, "A poor man is better than a false one (*'îš kāzāb*)" (Prov. 19,22), meaning that a poor man is better than a man who employs deceit in order to become rich.

3. *rmh*

This term, like *šqr* and *kzb*, is not characteristic of the wisdom lexicon, and refers to various acts of fraud, from mendacious talk to actual injury. *rmh* signifies cunning behavior, whose aim is to cheat others and to benefit the perpetrator. Therefore, such action is worse than *šqr* and *kzb*. In wisdom literature the nominal forms *r*^{e}*mîyyâ* (Prov. once;[66] Job twice) and *mirmâ* (Prov. 8 times; Job twice; BS once) appear. The verbal form appears once (Prov. 26,19). *r*^{e}*mîyyâ* generally stands for mendacious talk (Job 13,7; cf. ibid. 27,4); in one instance it signifies cunning behavior (Prov. 12,27). *mirmâ* has a wider meaning, namely, behavior intended to cheat and covers a variety of activities:

(a) Like *kzb* and *šqr*, *mirmâ* basically refers to speech, both inside and outside the legal framework. The sage says, "A truthful witness saves lives" and "One who testifies with lies (is) deceitful (*mirmâ*)" (Prov. 14,25). The form of antithetic parallelism in the verse emphasizes the disastrous nature of *mirmâ*. Proverbs 12,5 relates to a similar setting: "The thoughts of the righteous are just (*mišpaṭ*), the counsels of the wicked are deceit (*mirmâ*)." *mišpaṭ*, stands here in antithesis to *mirmâ* and signifies the norm of justice (cf. ibid. vs. 17: *mirmâ* [deceit] # *ṣedeq* [justice]). In a wisdom Psalm the son is advised to keep his lips from "speaking deceit (*mirmâ*)" (Ps. 34,14; cf. also "swore deceitfully [*l*^{e}*mirmâ*]," Ps. 24,4).[67]

(b) Falsification of weights and measures is also termed *mirmâ*. Like the Egyptian parallel, the phrase "an abomination to God" is connected with this practice: "Diverse weights are an abomination to Yahweh and false (*mirmâ*) scales are not good" (Prov. 20,23; cf. 11,1).[68]

(c) Hypocritical behavior and malicious intent furthermore are defined as *mirmâ*. As in Egypt[69] so in Israel the residence of deceit before it is uttered is the heart: "Deceit (*mirmâ*) is in the heart of those who devise evil" (Prov. 12, 20); "He who hates, dissembles with his lips, and sets deceit (*mirmâ*) in his heart" (26,24; cf. ibid. 23). Job in his "negative confession" states: "If I have walked with falsehood and my foot has hasted to deceit (*mirmâ*)" (31, 5). The sage in Proverbs says, "The wisdom of a prudent man is to discern his way, but the folly of fools is deceiving (*mirmâ*)" (14,8), that is, the folly of fools is expressed in their deceitful behavior.

4. *kḥš*

The verb *kḥš* when used in pi'el, means "to hide facts deliberately," "to deny a fact," or "not to acknowledge someone." *kḥš* does not belong to the wisdom lexicon nor does it have a parallel in the Egyptian material. For that reason we will not discuss it further, despite the fact that *kḥš* belongs to the semantic field of falsehood, in the Bible.[70]

Comparison between the findings in Hebrew and Egyptian

For the two lexemes (*[s]'ḏ3*, *grg*) which cover the semantic field of falsehood in the Egyptian wisdom literature, Biblical wisdom has four (*šqr*, *kzb*, *rmh*, *kḥš*). Both in Egypt and in Israel these terms are not characteristic of the wisdom terminology.

In view of our findings, it is difficult to determine exact equivalents in the two languages; but it seems that the term *šqr* in Biblical Hebrew is close to the Egyptian *grg*, while *kzb* and *rmh*, which complement the remaining semantic field, approximate in sense and usage the Egyptian concept *(s)'ḏ3*. This is attested by the following facts:

First, *šeqer* in Hebrew and *grg* in Egyptian are more common than the other terms belonging to the semantic field of falsehood. Both essentially involve (in the wisdom literature) speech but also appear in the abstract sense of "wrongdoing" or "injustice" in Egyptian and "worthlessness" in Hebrew. The terms even resemble one another with regard to linguistic usages:

	grg	*šeqer*
(1)	*grg* + *ḏd* (but also *’ḏꜣ* + *ḏd/mdy/mt.t*)	*d^ebar/’imrê/millāy* + *šeqer* (e.g. Prov. 13,5; Job 36,4; Isa. 32,7)
(2)	Synonymous parallelism: *grg*‖*isf.t* (wrongdoing, falsehood) *grg*‖*iy.t* (mishap)	*šeqer*‖*kāzāb*
(3)	Antithetic parallelism: *grg* # *mꜣ‘.t* (truth)	*šeqer* # *’ĕmet*, *ṣedeq* (+ *’ĕmûnâ*)
(4)	The expression "abomination": *bw.t* often occurs in relation to *grg* in the biographical and *persönliche Frömmigkeit* literature.	*šeqer* is "abomination to God." This idea is also expressed by the stems *śn’* (hate) and *t‘b* (abhor) followed by the object *šeqer*, the subject being the righteous (Prov. 13,5) or the pious man (Ps. 119,163).

Second, (1) The terms *kzb*, *rmh*, like *(s)‘ḏꜣ* refer to activity associated with the mouth as well as to other deeds intended to harm one's fellow man. These acts of deception are identical in the Bible and in the Egyptian sources and include: lying speech, whether hypocrisy and sycophancy (*rmh*) or false testimony (*rmh*, *kzb*) and perjury; becoming rich through dishonesty or robbery (*kzb*; but also *šqr*); and falsification of weights and measures (*rmh*).

(2) Evidence that the term *kzb* may be considered the equivalent of *‘ḏꜣ* in Egyptian is found in Proverbs 23, 1-3 which, as stated above, is parallel to *The Instruction of Amenemope*. The Hebrew has the phrase *leḥem k^ezābîm* for the Egyptian "chewing of *‘ḏꜣ*." Whether the Hebrew author was influenced by his Egyptian counterpart or vice versa, the writer of this text, Hebrew or Egyptian, regards the Hebrew term *k^ezābîm* as the equivalent of the Egyptian *‘ḏꜣ*. The Hebrew formulation in Proverbs 20,17, which does not parallel the Egyptian instruction, contains the phrase *leḥem šāqer*.

(3) Similarities in the linguistic usages of *kzb*, *rmh* in Hebrew and *‘ḏꜣ* in Egyptian:

	In Egyptian	In the Bible
(1)	A lying word: *‘ḏ3 + mdy/mt.t*	*d*^{e}*bar kāzāb* (Prov. 30,8)
(2)	False oath: *‘nḫy n ‘ḏ3* *‘rḳ ‘ḏ*	*nišba‘ l*^{e}*mirmâ* (Ps. 24,4)
(3)	Antithetic parallelism: *‘ḏ3 # m3‘.t*	*mirmâ # ṣedeq, mišpaṭ* *kāzāb # ’ĕmûnîm, ’ĕmet*
(4)	Falsehood (*[s]‘ḏ3*) is an "abomination to God" (*t3 bw.t n p3 nṯr*)	Acts involving *rmh* and *kzb* (Prov. 11, 1;20,23; 6,19) are "abomination (*tô‘ăbat*) to God."

Additional points of contact between Hebrew and Egyptian that are not restricted to any term in particular but relate generally to the semantic field of "falsehood" are the following:

(a) The practice mentioned most frequently is lying speech.

(b) Falsity is not associated with a particular human type; all are susceptible to this weakness. On the other hand, Egyptian and Biblical wisdom literature show similarity with regard to the identity of the people mentioned in this connection: the ruler or leader (cf. the accusations of *The Eloquent Peasant*, the declarations of the 18th Dynasty's high officials, the formulas of the autobiographical literature, etc., with Prov. 29,12); the scribe (cf. the exhorations directed at the scribe in *Amenemope* with the accusations voiced by the prophet Jeremiah, 8,8ff.); the foe, the enemy (in *Amenemope* the foe is at times "the heated man" who lies; the *persönliche Frömmigkeit* hymns contain complaints against people who speak falsehood [*ÄHG* 190, 38-39].[71] The proximity of these to the complaints of the believer in Psalms and of Job about the plottings of their foes, the false men, is indeed remarkable).

(c) Similar concepts are found in the Egyptian and the Hebrew wisdom:

(1) In the wisdom literature falsehood and lying are considered

despicable and thus called an "abomination to God." In Hebrew and Egyptian wisdom this phrase relates to matters of social morality, in this case wrongdoings towards fellow human beings. Outside the wisdom framework, in other literary genres, it is attached to religious-cultic morality and concerns transgressions between a man and the divinity (cf. Deut. 7,25; 12,31; 17,1; 18,12; 22,5; 23,19; 27,15; 24,4).[72] Sins deemed an "abomination to God" are identical in Proverbs and in *The Instruction of Amenemope*: Falsifications of measures and weights (*Amenemope* 18,23 - 19,1; Prov. 11,1; 20,22); false testimony (*Amenemope* 15, 20-21; Prov. 6,19); lying and hypocrisy, deceitful speech (*Amenemope* 13,15-16; 14, 2-3; Prov. 6,16; 12,22)

(2) In antithetic parallelism with "falsehood," stand the terms *'ĕmet*, *ṣedeq*, in Biblical Hebrew and their equivalent *mꜣʿ.t* in Egyptian. As stated, in Egypt this parallelism involves the perception of the *mꜣʿ.t* as a cosmic-mythic principle. Hints of a similar concept may perhaps be found in the first collection of the book of Proverbs in the sections containing the personification of Wisdom. This is said of Wisdom in 8,7-8: "For my mouth will utter *'ĕmet*; wickedness is an abomination to my lips. All the words of my mouth are *b^eṣedeq...*" In 3,19-20 it is said that "By Wisdom God founded the earth," that is, God created the universe with the help of Wisdom whose standards are justice and truth. In other words, God founded the universe on the tenets of order. In Israel, as in Egypt, the one responsible for the preservation of that order, called *ṣedeq* and *'ĕmet*, is the king. This concept is expressed in certain passages in Proverbs and Psalms. Underlying these texts is the Egyptian description of the king's throne, which is conceived as resting upon a base in the shape of the hieroglyph *mꜣʿ.t*, e.g., Proverbs 16,12: "It is abomination to kings to do evil, for the throne is established by *ṣ^edāqâ*" (cf. ibid. 20, 28; Ps. 89, 15; 97, 2).[73]

B. Covetousness and Desire

The terms belonging to the semantic field of covetousness and desire, are not characteristic of wisdom terminology, but the Hebrew and Egyptian sages warn frequently against this reprehensible trait.

In Egyptian

Four terms, which deal with desire and covetousness, appear in the Egyptian wisdom literature. They approximate each other in meaning and appear in similar contexts, but are distinguishable by the degree of negative connotation attached to them. We shall begin with the term representing the worst characteristic and continue on with the less serious offenses.

1. *ʿwn* (*ib*) — being rapacious, greedy

The most common term in this semantic field is *ʿwn* (19 times) meaning "to covet" in thought or — "to plunder" when pertaining to a deed. This last sense is well illustrated by the determinative of a man with an outstretched arm holding a stick, indicating violent action (Gr A24). *ʿwn* begins to appear in the Middle Kingdom (*Wb.* I 172) and in our sample it is present in texts from the Middle and New Kingdoms. This includes the instructions (*Ptaḥḥotep*, *Amenemope*), the pessimistic wisdom (*The Man Who Was Tired*, *The Eloquent Peasant*), and the royal court inscriptions (*Rekhmire*). The nominal and adjective forms are formed by the collocation of the verb *ʿwn* with the noun "heart" (*ib*): *ʿwn ib*. This collocation and other examples in which "heart" serves as the subject of the verb *ʿwn* (*The Man Who Was Tired* 105; 120-121; *The Eloquent Peasant* B1 117) seem to demonstrate that the basic meaning of *ʿwn* was covetousness in thought, lust for something. But in time the term acquired the sense of plunder and theft, as attested by its appearance in synonymous parallelism with "steal" (*ʿwꜣ* — ibid. B1 292-293) and "take" (*iṯi* — ibid. B1 165; *The Man Who Was Tired* 105).[74]

Covetousness thus involves an action that harms others and is intended to enrich the injurer. The objects coveted are always material things: an inheritance (*Ptaḥḥotep* 303-308; 316), another's property (*Amenemope* 8, 2; *The Man Who Was Tired* 105; *Peasant* B1 231). The coveter is a man not to be trusted, neither within the family (he seeks to deprive his relatives of their inheritance — *Ptaḥḥotep* 298ff.) nor within his profession (vis-à-vis his business partner — *Peasant* B1 169-170; cf. also *The Man Who Was Tired* 120-121). In *The Eloquent Peasant*, covetousness is numbered among a series of contemptible qualities which the wicked leader is accused of possessing, appearing there together with laziness (B2 110-111; B1 281), deafness (B2 110), gluttony (B1 281-282), pettiness (B1 66), and robbery (B1 164-165).

"Covetousness" is perceived as being antithetical to *mȝ'.t*, the social order. Thus, in the "negative confession" (Chap. 125, *The Book of the Dead*), whose purpose is to confirm that the deceased indeed upheld the tenets of *mȝ'.t*, "covetousness" is listed together with other negative acts that injure *mȝ'.t*. The deceased declares: "I have not stolen (*'wȝ*)... I have not coveted (*iri 'wn ib*)... I have not taken (*ṯȝw*)."[75] Similarly, in *Ptaḥḥotep* lines 84-99, 298-323, where the most detailed description of "covetousness" is given, the coveter is described as "a transgressor of the laws (of *mȝ'.t*)" (ibid. 91) and one who behaves in a manner opposite to one who is "precise in truth" (ibid. 312 ff.).[76] In *Amenemope* the coveter is contrasted with "the true silent man" (*grw mȝ'*), who is the ideal type of man (10, 10-11).

As "covetousness" symbolizes the weakening of the foundations of the social order (*mȝ'.t*), it frequently appears together with "falsehood" in the pessimistic wisdom literature. "Covetousness" and "falsehood" here have become the tokens of anarchy and instability. The "man who was tired of life" says, "To whom shall I speak today? Hearts are greedy (*'wn ib.w*)" (*The Man Who Was Tired* 105; 120-121; cf. *Peasant* B1 169-170; and ibid. 117).

In the instructions, which seek to preserve the *mȝ'.t*, there are warnings and condemnations directed against this negative attribute: covetousness is called a "painful sickness without cure" (*Ptaḥḥotep* 301); "It is a gathering of all evils (*bin.t*), a bundle of all hateful things" (ibid. 309-310 [P]). The gravity of the deed may be inferred from the punishment administered to its perpetrator. *The Instruction of Ptaḥḥotep* speaks of double punishment — in this world and in the next: The lot of the coveter is not good on earth (300ff.) for covetousness leads to quarrels among members of the family and results in the divorce of a woman from her husband (ibid. 303-308; cf. *Peasant* B1 291-292; B2

110). But beyond this, the coveter will not reach "safe shores," that is, will not reach the next world safely (*Ptaḥḥotep* 91ff.). Another formulation of this idea is the phrase "the greedy has no tomb" (ibid. 315).[77]

It is not surprising, therefore, that the vizier wishing to extol himself says: "I suppressed the coveter (*ꜥwn ib*)" (*Rekhmire*, *Urk.* IV 1078, 4); the leader "who desires perfect conduct" keeps his distance from covetousness (*Ptaḥḥotep* 298ff.).

The other lexemes belonging to the subject under discussion, ***ꜣfꜥ***, ***skn***, ***ḥnty***, are distinct from *ꜥwn* because they place the emphasis not on the action that arises from desire but on feelings of covetousness and rapacity and the inability to control it. In addition they are, unlike *ꜥwn*, accompanied by the determinative of a crocodile. The connection with this animal is clearly evident in the term *skn*, which differs from *snk* — crocodile — (*Wb.* IV 177) only in the order of the letters (metathesis).

2. *ꜣfꜥ*, *ꜣꜥfy*, *ꜥfꜥ* (Middle Eg. *ꜣfꜥ* ; Late Eg. *ꜣꜥfy*; Dem. *ꜥfꜥ* ; Copt. [B] ⲁϥϫⲓⲣ)

In Middle Egyptian *ꜣfꜥ* is characterized by the determinative of a crocodile,[78] while in Demotic there is a picture of an enemy. Both determinatives indicate the negative connotation of the term.

In our sample *ꜣfꜥ* (v., n., adj.) is found mainly in the literary genre of instruction and appears from *Kagemni* up to the late instruction of *Pap. Insinger* (12 times). It appears only once outside this genre. *ꜣfꜥ* signifies gluttony, the feeling of greed and the inability to control this desire. It refers either to voracity — "Do not be greedy (*m iry ꜥꜣfy*) to fill your belly," *Anii* 8,6-7, (cf. *Kagemni* I 4;8) — or to the desire for property and wealth. *Amenemope* warns his son: "Do not desire (*ꜣꜥfy*) a noble's wealth" (15, 9; cf. ibid. 6,15; *Insinger* 4,8; 16,22; 15, 7-18). The rapacious man is a fool (*Insinger* 5,18, without *ꜥfꜥ*) or impious (ibid. 4,8,9; 15,19). The opposite of greed is the ability to behave with restraint (during a meal — *Kagemni* I 4; in accumulating property — *Insinger* 15,16ff.).

The sages repeatedly warn of the uselessness of cupidity and of accumulating wealth: The goods of the greedy are ashes driven by the wind (*Insinger* 16, 22); his possessions are left behind after death and are given to another (4, 8-9). In the later wisdom the absurdity of cupidity is displayed against the background of the determinist concept that the god decides in advance who will be rich and who poor (ibid. 15, 7-20).[79]

Cupidity brings in its wake unpleasantness and punishment. It causes quarrels in the home (*Insinger* 15,12ff.); the rapacious man is subject to shame, his name "stinks" (ibid. 15,7); he is reproached (ibid. 25,15); sometimes he is even condemned to death (ibid. 15, 9).[80]

3. *skn*[81]

The root *skn* appears seven times in the present sample (v., n., adj.) and its occurrence is restricted to the instructions (beginning from *Kagemni* and ending with *Amenemope*). *skn* differs from the other terms belonging to the semantic field of covetousness because it originally pertained to the nature of the crocodile. In the wisdom literature, however, it is used figuratively for human beings (see *Wb.* IV 318, 9, 10).

The meaning of *skn* is "gluttony," "avidity," when the object lusted for, as with the foregoing terms, is for the most part inanimate: examples are food (*Kagemni* I 9); luxury items such as copper or cotton (*Amenemope* 18, 8); property (belonging to members of the lower class, the widow, the poor man — *Amenemope* 7, 14ff.). At times the appetite is for living objects — women (*Ptaḥḥotep* 277-297). Here too the lustful man is threatened with punishment. Property taken by robbery will lead to the downfall of the robber. He will be torn away from his children and his granaries will be ruined (*Amenemope* 7,12 - 8,8). The plundered goods will be a "block in the throat" (ibid. 14,7-8). Lust for strange women will cause death: "Death comes for having known them... No plans of his will succeed" (*Ptaḥḥotep*, above).

4. *ḥnty*

The meaning of this term (v., n., adj.) is similar to *skn*, and like the latter its occurrence is limited to the didactic instructions (from *Kagemni* to *Amenemope* — 6 times). Outside this literary sample *ḥnty* is found only once.

Like *skn*, *ḥnty* concerns desire for things belonging to others: food (*Kagemni* I 7); property (*Ptaḥḥotep* 317; *To Merikare* 40). Its antitheses are generosity and giving to others (ibid. 38-42; *Ptaḥḥotep* 481-488). The *ḥnty*, the greedy man, is called a "fool" (*ḫm ḫ.t* — *To Merikare* 40); he is identical with the "enemy" (*Amenemope* 8,2),[82] and appears in synonymous parallelism with *'wn ib* (*Peasant* B1 291; *Ptaḥḥotep* 317) and in proximity to *Sf'* (*Kagemni* I 7).

Summary (Table 5)

The terms relating to the semantic field of covetousneous in Egyptian have several common features:

(1) All terms, except *'wn*, are linked to the image of the crocodile.

(2) They appear most often in the genre of instruction (29 times out of a total of 44).

(3) The object of the covetousness is identical for all of them and is usually associated with the material world — food, property. Only *skn* refers to lust for women.

(4) All terms are accompanied by a warning regarding the uselessness of covetousness and the punishment that will befall the coveter.

(5) The nouns and adjectives belonging to the subject of covetousness always appear in proximity to other bad qualities and acts, e.g., wickedness, depravity, theft, extortion (in contrast with truth, kindness, restraint) and fool, wrongdoer, enemy, impious (in contrast with quiet man, honest man).

These common elements make it difficult to demarcate the semantic boundary between synonymous terms. Nevertheless, a certain gradation is evident in the seriousness of the wrong committed with covetousness. Most severe, is *'wn ib*, which involves real harm done to others, and least grave is *ḥnty*, which is in essence only the wish, the desire for the property of others but not the act of grasping for it.

Table 5: Terms Relating to the Semantic Field of Covetousness in Egyptian

Term (v. n. adj.)	Determinative	Meaning	Object	Degree of Transgression	Distribution: Instructions	Distribution: Pessimistic Wisdom	Distribution: School Texts	Distribution: Royal Court Inscriptions	Total
ꜥwn ib	man with a rod	robbery–the act itself not only the thought	property	grave ↓	*Ptaḥḥotep* *Amenenope*	*The Dispute* *The Peasant* (many)		*Rehkmire*	
					The widest distribution in the different literary genres				19
ꜣfꜥ/ꜣꜥfy/ꜥfꜥ	a crocodile	voracity, whose oppo–site is restraint	food property	l e s s	*Kagemni* *Anii* *Amenemope* *Insinger* (many)		*Sallier* I		12
skn	a crocodile	voracity of a crocodile	food property women	g r a v e	*Kagemni* *Ptaḥḥotep* *To Merikare* *Amenemope*				7
ḥnꜣy	a crocodile	cupidity for things owned by others	food property	↓ light	*Kagemni* *Ptaḥḥotep* *To Merikare* *Amenemope*	*The Peasant*			6

In the Bible

In the Bible, the semantic field of "covetousness" is covered by two lexemes, *'wh* and *ḥmd*, which do not belong to the wisdom lexicon. Therefore, the discussion of these terms will be restricted to a comparative analysis with the Egyptian material.

1. *'wh*

The root *'wh* is very common in the Bible in the sense of "to wish," "to desire." *'wh* (pi'el, hithpa'el), which signifies the feelings of desire arising from a man's own will appears in all the wisdom books.[83] *ta'ăwâ* ("desire") has a neutral meaning in the Bible and its negative or positive nature is determined by the context. Unlike the Egyptian, desire may at times have a positive connotation (see below). Far from being despised, this desire is spoken of in praise: "A desire fulfilled is a tree of life" (Prov. 13,12; cf. ibid. 19).

The noun "soul" (*nepeš*) is usually attached to the verb *'wh*. For example, Proverbs 13,4 speaks of the soul of the lazy man, which "desires" (cf. Prov. 21,10; Job 23,13; Qoh. 6,2, etc.). Sometimes "soul" is replaced by "heart" (*lēb*): the heart's desire of the king (Ps. 21,3). These collocations are close to the phrase *'wn ib* in Egyptian.

As in the Egyptian sources, the desired object belongs to the material world, e.g., food. Thus in Prov. 23,1ff, which directly parallels *The Instruction of Amenemope* 14,5 ff., the father counsels his son: "Do not desire the delicacies" of the ruler and of the "miser" (ibid. 6, 3; cf. BS 31, 12ff. [Gr.] and the parallel passages in *Kagemni* I).[84] The soul of man can also desire "wealth, possessions and honor," as in Qoheleth (6,2). But, in contrast to the Egyptian parallels, the object may also be an abstract thing: negatively — the wish to join bad company (Prov. 24, 1); the wish of the wicked man to harm his fellow man (Prov. 21,10); but also positively — the desire for *ṭôb* ("good") which is the lot of the righteous (ibid. 11,23), or the desire for *ḥesed* ("kindness") (ibid. 19, 22).

Since desire in the Bible may also bear a positive connotation, the desirer, as seen above, sometimes belongs to the category of positive human beings. Thus, Proverbs speak of the desire of the *ṣaddîqîm* ("righteous men") (Prov. 10,24; cf. 11,23 above). Usually, however, it is associated with the negative type. The *rāšā‘* ("wicked man") is possessed by desire (Prov. 21,10). "The desire of the wicked shall perish," states the wisdom Psalm (112,10; cf. 140,9, "the desires of the wicked"). Desire is one of the characteristics of the *‘āṣēl* ("lazy") (Prov. 13,4; 21,26), whose power is great in craving but little in action (cf. *Peasant* B1 282; B2 109-110).

Like his Egyptian counterpart, the Hebrew sage talks of the transience of wealth (Prov. 23,3,5, which parallels *Amenemope* 9,10ff.) and of the harm involved in desire (Prov. 21,25; 23,6-8). Also, the idea that God oversees the fulfilling of desire and that he is responsible for distributing material possessions among men recurs in the Biblical wisdom literature and is surprisingly close to the concept as expressed in the Egyptian *Instruction of Pap. Insinger.* Qoheleth argues that it happens that a man "lacks nothing for himself of all he desires; yet God does not give him power to eat of it" (6,2); and in Proverbs the sage says that God will satisfy the desire of righteous men (10,24; cf. Ps. 10,17).[85] However, in the present sample only in the Bible does God himself appear as one who desires (Job 23,13; Ps. 132,13; etc.).

Finally, although desire is essentially a human trait, it is transferable to animals ("the wild ass" in Jer. 2, 24). The opposite — unlike in Egyptian, where obviously gluttony was associated with the crocodile (see below) — is however not possible.

2. *ḥmd*

The verb *ḥmd*, "to covet," is synonymous with *'wh* in Biblical Hebrew (Gen. 3,6; also BS 5,1-2). They interchangeable (in the Decalogue: "You shall not covet [*taḥmōd*] your neighbor's house," Exod. 20,14 || "You shall not desire [*tit'awweh*] your neighbor's house," Deut. 5,18) and appear in a similar context (cf. "*ḥmd* the beauty" of a woman, Prov. 6,25, and "*yit'aw* beauty," Ps. 45,12).

ḥmd, like *'wh*, does not belong to the wisdom terminology and appears only five times in the wisdom books.[86] The basic meaning of *ḥmd* is remote from the Egyptian parallels, as the essence of *ḥmd* lies in sight which stimulates the desire and wish to possess the object seen and thus leads to action.[87] *ḥmd* therefore complements *'wh*: both concern "wanting" something — *ḥmd* through actually seeing and *'wh* through imagination. *ḥmd*, like *'wh* and unlike the Egyptian terms belonging to this field, may carry a positive connotation. The niph'al participle *neḥmād* serves as an adjective signifying the desired object. The laws of God are "more to be desired (*neḥĕmādîm*) than gold, even much fine gold" in the wisdom Psalm (19,11; cf BS 42,22 [M]); and in Proverbs the reward of the sage is "precious (*neḥmād*) treasure" (21,20; cf. BS 41,12[B]). But *ḥmd* for the most part, like the Egyptian terms, has a negative connotation when its object is material things: food (figuratively, in Job 20,20ff.; or [not in the wisdom context] clothing — Gen. 27, 15 [cf. Egyptian *skn*]; property — "your neighbor's house," Exod. 20,14; "silver and gold," Deut. 7,25; "fields" — Mic. 2,2 and "spoils" — Josh. 7,21). The object may even be human: "do not desire (*taḥmōd*) her (a woman's) beauty in your heart," says the sage (Prov. 6,25; cf. in the Decalogue, Exod. 20,14 || Deut. 5,18).[88] At times the object, as with *'wh*, is abstract, such as "scorn" (Prov. 1,22 — "and the scorners delight in their scorn") or "evil" (BS 14,14).

The desirer is usually a negative human type — the "wicked man" (*rāšā'*) (Prov. 12,12; Job 20,20, referring to verse 5 in the chapter) or the scorner (*lēṣ*) (Prov. 1,22; cf. Mic. 2, 1ff.).

The crocodile and covetousness in Egypt and in the Bible

Analysis of the Egyptian terms has shown that the trait of covetousness and gluttony is associated with the crocodile in Egypt. A picture of this animal accompanies the words *3f'*, *skn*, *ḫnty* as a determinative, or it is used figuratively to illustrate the rapaciousness of men. Thus the high official is rebuked, "You should have seemed less like a greedy crocodile" (*The Eloquent Peasant* B1 179; cf. ibid. 117-118; 223). In *The Instruction of Ptaḥḥotep*, one who accepts bribes is likened to a crocodile: "The thief is like a crocodile (*msḥ*) in court" (168).

This concept of the crocodile as a symbol of covetousness and gluttony goes back to a myth, vestiges of which are evident in ancient Near Eastern literature, including that of Egypt. The theme of this myth is the war of the god against the primal waters which strive to encroach on the dry land and engulf the man's habitat. It first appears in *The Instruction to Merikare*, composed, most probably, during the First Intermediate Period. In the passage describing the creation of the world it is said: "He (the god Re') subdued the water crocodile (*snk n mw*) for them (human beings)" (131).[89] Traces of this myth are also present in later Egyptian sources belonging to the New Kingdom Period[90] and in the Mesopotamian, Ugaritic and Hittite literature as well as in the Bible.[91]

In the Bible there is no etymological-linguistic, or even a conceptual connection between the terms *'wh, ḥmd* and the crocodile. But certain passages in Biblical poetry do refer to the voracious appetite of this reptile: prophecy, Psalms, and Job retain remnants of the ancient myth — parallel to that mentioned in the Egyptian *Instruction to Merikare* — which tells of God's war against the sea. In this myth the sea is often called a crocodile (*tannîn*) (Isa. 27,1,2; 51,9; Ps. 74,13ff.; Job 7,12; etc.) and its outstanding feature is its insatiable desire to rule the universe. This intention of the primeval monster was frustrated by God when he determined the limits of the waters. In the Israelite tradition this description of the crocodile, the enemy of God the Creator, became a metaphor for the enemies of Israel throughout the generations.[92] In Ezekiel, Egypt, which seeks to rule over the peoples, is likened to a rapacious crocodile (29,3ff.). Pharaoh is compared to a crocodile lying in the Nile, which has sinned in its pride. Here, too, God is to place a barrier and to limit the cupidity of the gluttonous reptile: "It shall be the most lowly of the kingdoms, and never again exalt itself above the nations; and I will make them so small that they will never again rule over the nations" (ibid. 15).

Of special interest for our discussion is the description in Jeremiah 51,34 which refers not to Egypt but to Babylon. Foretelling the destruction of that empire, Jeremiah likens Nebuchadnezzar to a crocodile: "... the king of Babylon has devoured me, he has crushed me; he has made me an empty vessel, he has swallowed me like a crocodile (*tannîn*), he has filled his belly with my delicacies, he has rinsed me out."[93]

Comparative summary of the subject of covetousness in Egypt and in the Bible

While the semantic field of "covetousness" is covered in the Egyptian wisdom literature by four lexemes, the Biblical wisdom vocabulary has only two terms for this field. It is difficult to find exact Hebrew equivalents for the Egyptian terms,[94] but it may be said that *'wh*, which relates not only to wish and thought, but also to action (robbery) is close to *'wn ib*. *ḥmd*, which primarily arises out of visual impression, has something in common with the other Egyptian terms whose meaning is wish, desire, but not necessarily action. The Egyptian terms have a negative connotation. In Hebrew the terms are neutral, and their positive or negative bias depends on the context. However, when these terms appear in a negative context the details forming the picture of covetousness in the Bible and in the Egyptian sources are greatly similar. The possessor of the attribute is a negative human type, and the object desired is usually a material thing. Covetousness is condemned, and in both places the penalty to be exacted for it is emphasized.

Finally, two details in which the Hebrew and the Egyptian sources differ should be noted: (1) In contrast to the Biblical wisdom in Egyptian wisdom this trait is bound up with the image of the crocodile. (2) In the Biblical wisdom an abstract value can also serve as object of desire (especially in the sphere between man and God), which is not the case in the Egyptian wisdom.

C. Anger, Strife

In Egyptian

The 14 terms belonging to this semantic field in Egyptian may be classified into three groups: (a) terms whose primary meaning is heat;

(b) words referring to the act of quarrelling; (c) lexemes expressing the emotion of anger.

1. Etymological and semantic analysis

(a) Terms borrowed from the semantic field of heat signifying a hot temper:

1. *šmm* (*ẖmm*)[95] (Dem. *ḫm*; Copt. [SA] n. ϩⲙⲙⲉ ; [S] v. ϩⲙⲟⲙ[96]

The determinative of this term, which is a brazier with a flame rising from it (Gr Q7), indicates its meaning, namely, "heat," "to be hot."[97] *šmm* in this sense appears from the Old Kingdom onwards, but it is used figuratively for human beings only beginning with the New Kingdom. In its latter application *šmm* bears the sense of "heated man" and the determinative of a brazier with flame is augmented by that of an enemy (a man with bound hands — Gr A13) or a man holding a stick (Gr A21).

šmm has cognates in the Semitic languages, indicating that its provenance is possibly Semitic.[98] Of interest for our purposes is only the attribute "heated man", which occupies a central role in *The Instruction of Amenemope* and in the *Deir el Médineh Ostracon* 1265[99] and also appears in other sources from the New Kingdom (*Chester Beatty* V recto 6, 7-12 || *Anastasi* V 6,5; *Sallier* I 8, 5-6; *Hier. Ostr.* I pl. 7,5). *šmm* is the only term in this semantic field that appears frequently in the wisdom writings together with a definite article or with possessive pronoun. This shows that the adjective *šmm* serves mainly to define a certain human type characterized by a hot temper. The *šmm* is a hot-tempered and quarrelsome man who is not able to control his mouth; hence he is at times called *šmw rȝ* — "hot- mouthed."[100]

šmm is synonymous with the following expressions: *tȝ rȝ*, identical in meaning to *šmw rȝ* (*Amenemope* 5,10; 12,16), *rḳw/s rḳw*, "the foe" (ibid. 5, 12; 15, 13-14), and *thw*, "the violent man," "attacker" (ibid. 5, 12). The antonym of *šmm* is "the silent man," "calm-tempered man," *grw mȝ‘* (*Amenemope*, chap. 4), *grw* (*Sallier* I 8,5-6).

2. *tꜣ* (adj. *tꜣw*, *tꜣ rꜣ* / *ib* / *ẖ.t*)

Like *šmm*, the primary meaning of *tꜣ* is "to be hot" (*Wb.* V 229). This is demonstrated by the writing of the word by means of the hieroglyph *tꜣ*, a potter's kiln (cf. ibid. 228), and by the determinative, a brazier with a flame (Gr Q7).[101] Figuratively *tꜣ* serves as an adjective, indicating a hot-tempered man. *tꜣ* appears from the Middle Kingdom Period onwards and it complements the occurrences of *šmm* in the pessimistic wisdom writings and in the instructions composed during the Old Kingdom and First Intermediate Periods. In the present sample the plain form, *tꜣw*, appears as an adjective only once (*Admonitions* 5,3); usually it is collocated with parts of the body — *ib* ("heart"), *rꜣ* ("mouth"), *ẖ.t* ("belly").[102] As adjective it stands in synonymous parallelism with *šmm* ("hot-tempered man"), *rḳw* ("enemy"), *thw* ("violent man") (*Amenemope* 5,10-15) and it occurs in proximity to *štm* ("quarrelsome man" — *Ptaḥḥotep* 373); in antithetic parallelism it is paired with *ʿn* ("gentle man" — ibid. 378-379).[103]

(b) Terms concerning quarrelling in word ("offend, insult") and in deed ("physical strife"):[104]

3. *štm*

štm[105] is accompanied by the determinative of a seated man, his hand at his mouth, which indicates some action involving the mouth. The meaning of *štm* is "to quarrel by means of the mouth," that is, "to provoke," "bear tales," "decry." *štm* usually appears in our sample as a verb and once as an attributive meaning "provoker": "The provoker gets into trouble," says the sage (*Ptaḥḥotep* 373). The occurrence of *štm* is restricted to the instruction genre beginning in the Old Kingdom and ending with the New Kingdom Period.[106]

4. *ṯṯṯ*, *s tyty*

The form *ṯṯṯ* serves as a verb and a noun. When used as an appellation the combination *s tyty* appears (*Anii* 5,6).[107] The meaning of *ṯṯṯ*, which occurs only in Late Egyptian, is "to quarrel" and "altercate" (*Wb.* V 413), and the determinative, identical to that accompanying *štm*, suggests that the term concerns a verbal dispute.

A synonym for *s tyty*, "a quarrelsome man," is "hostile man" (*rmṯ rḳy.t* — *Anii* 5, 7), and its antonyms are "straight" and "true" (*mtr.tw*, *mꜣʿ.w* — ibid. 5,7,8).[108]

5. *rḳ(w), rḳy(w)*

This term,[109] which appears in our examples principally as an adjective (*rḳw*, *s rḳw*, *rmṯ rḳy.t*) but also as a noun (*rḳw*), has the meaning "strife," the emphasis being on the *activity* of strife. The determinatives accompanying it — the picture of an enemy (a man with bound hands) and a sparrow — show its negative connotation. As an adjective *rḳw* is often collocated with the word "man" (*s* or *rmṯ*) meaning "hostile man," "adversary." The identity of the opponent varies and he may be the personal enemy of a god, a king or an ordinary man (*Urk.* IV, e.g., 556,16; 938,14; *Anii*, *Amenemope* — see below). Amenemope advises his son: "Do not befriend a heated man (*šmm*) and do not fraternize with a hostile man (*s rḳw*)" (15, 13-14; cf. *Anii* 2, 13-14; 8, 19). *rḳw* stands in synonymous parallelism with *šmm* (*Amenemope*, above), *thw* (*Amenemope* 5, 12) and *s tyty* (*Anii* 5,7) and in antithetic parallelism with *mtr.tw*, *mꜣʿ.w* ("straight," "true" — *Anii* 5,7,8).

6. *šnṯ* (v. *šnṯ*; adj. *šnṯy*; Copt. [SB] ϣⲱⲛⲧ)

The meaning of *šnṯ* is "to quarrel," "to insult," "to decry."[110] The adjective *šnṯy*, means "a foe,"[111] and its determinatives are a man holding a stick, a sparrow, a bound enemy holding an axe, and a crocodile (in the Greek Period, *Wb.* IV 520, 6).

šnṯ appears often in the writings of the 18th Dynasty both as an adjective and as a verb.[112] A common statement in these inscriptions is "I did not insult (*šnṯ*) him greater than I" (e.g., *Urk.* IV 1195,2; see *Wb.* IV 519,5). The antonym of *šnṯy*, "quarrelsome man," is *ḳb ẖ.t*, "cool-tempered man" (*Ptaḥḥotep* 323).

7. *sḫwn*

The meaning of the verb *sḫwn* is "to quarrel," and it involves the noun *ḫwn*, a bad quality (*Wb.* III 247). *sḫwn* begins to appear in the 18th Dynasty onwards, and disappears during the Late Period (*Wb.* IV 238,8-10). In our sample its occurrence is limited (*Instruction of Kheti* XXIII B [Dem 1013]; *Instruction by a Man for His Son* IX 2,4; XVIII 3; and *Urk.* IV 122,13; 505,5; etc.).

8. *thw*

The term *thw*, already mentioned above (see pp. 82–83, *thi*, meaning [b]), also belongs to the semantic field of "strife." *thw* means a "violent man," "eager to quarrel," as is shown by its special determinatives, namely, a knife lying on the knee and a man holding a stick. It appears in synonymous parallelism with *rḳw* and *t3 r3* and in proximity to *šmm* (*Amenemope* 5, 10ff.).

The following two lexemes are borderline cases between the semantic field of "strife" and the semantic field of "rebel," "perpetrate an act illegally."

9. *ẖnn* (v. *ẖnn*; n. *ẖnnw*; adj. *ẖnn*)

The term *ẖnn* occurs infrequently in the present corpus (6 times). The determinatives of a man holding a stick and the animal of Seth display the negative connotation of the term. The basic sense of *ẖnn* is "to do something bad," "to disturb" (*Wb.* III 383). As a noun its meaning is "strife," "tumult" (*Admonitions* 6,1; 12,13;[113] *Anii* 9,3; *Amenemope* 19,19). As an adjective its meaning is "contentious man" (*To Merikare* 24; *Amenemhet* IX B) and it frequently involves the figure of the god Seth (*Wb.* III 383, 11). *ẖnn* appears often in the context of rebel (*To Merikare* ibid.; *Amenemhet* ibid.) and it seems, therefore, that the term principally belongs to the phraseology of the king's court and not to wisdom. The meaning of the stem *ẖnn* changes gradually and it appears later in the Demotic instruction in the sense of "fool" (see pp. 191–192 below).

10. *sh3*

The noun *sh3* means "uproar," "confusion." The word appears once in reference to hostile talk: "Do not answer with hostility," the vizier advises his son (*Ptaḥḥotep* 476). The determinatives of *sh3* are identical to those appearing with the root *ẖnn*, which is often found in proximity with *sh3* (*To Merikare* 24; *Admonitions* 12, 12-13; cf. *Wb.* IV 206, 3). *sh3* appears in writings from the time of the Middle and New Kingdoms (*Ptaḥḥotep*, *To Merikare*, *Admonitions*, above, and *Neferti* 39-40).

(c) Expressions of emotions of anger and rage:

11. *3d* (v. *3d*; adj. *3dw*)

The meaning of the term, which comes into use beginning with the Pyramid Texts (*Wb.* I 24), is "to fume," "to rage." It seems that the word was used mainly to describe a trait of the crocodile and from this context it was converted into a description of human behaviour. The primary meaning is still reflected in the determinative which depicts a crocodile. It is also evident in the words of the Peasant: "I suppressed the wrathful (*ḫsf 3dw*), (but) the crocodile (*msḥ*) returns!" (B1 181). In the present sample, *3d* usually appears as a verb in the didactic literature (*Kagemni* I 9; *3d ib* — *Ptaḥḥotep* 76), or as an attribute (the "aggressor") in the pessimistic wisdom literature (*Peasant*, above, and ibid. 297) and in the writings of the 18th Dynasty (*Urk.* IV 969,7; 972,5; etc.).

12. *nšni*

nšni, as both verb and noun, occurs first in the Pyramid Texts, and appears in all the literary genres (*Wb.* II 340ff.). The determinative of the animal of Seth, which usually accompanies *nšni*, as well as its context show that the primary meaning of the term refers to the rage of animals (crocodile, snake, lion, e.g., *Anastasi* I 15, 2; *Anii* 10, 2). Figuratively, *nšni* relates to the anger of men (the king — *Anastasi*, ibid.; *Instruction by a Man for His Son* XVIII 2; Jansen-Winkeln I

A5,d,6; A6,e,13, II 1,8,3-4) and gods (principally Seth, see below, p. 127). *nšni* is attached to the verbs *ḫsf*, *sgrḥ*, *sḥtp*, to signify the driving out and suppression of fury (*Urk.* IV 1078, 2; Jansen-Winkeln above; Otto, below). Opposite terms are *ḥtp* — "to satisfy" (*KCG* 42210, p. 28 E6 || Otto No. 7) and *ḳbb fnḏ.w* — "to cool heat" (lit. noses) (*Seḥetep-ib-Ra* 3,5).

13. *ḫʿr*

The term *ḫʿr* does not appear until the 18th Dynasty (*Wb.* III 244). Most of the examples are from the *Instruction of Pap. Insinger* (10, 20; 21, 17; 22, 12, etc.). In *Insinger*, *ḫʿr* fills the same role as do the roots *šmm* and *tꜣ* in other instructions, with the similar meaning of "rage," "anger."

14. *fnḏ*

Like the Hebrew equivalent *'ap*,[114] *fnḏ* has a double meaning — a bodily part, "nose," and "rage, fury." In the latter sense, which belongs to the semantic field under review, *fnḏ* appears only once in a passage describing the king as a "cooler of rages (*ḳbb fnḏ.w*), he is far from rage (*nšn*) ..." (*Seḥetep-ib-Ra* 3,5).

2. The connection between the world of nature and the qualities of strife and fury

In Egyptian, all the terms presented denote a hostile quality or an act with negative implications. This is clearly indicated by the determinative accompanying these terms, which provides additional information as to their nature. Several recurrent determinatives can be recognized:

(1) The sparrow, or the "black bird," as the Egyptologists call it, which always has a negative connotation (*šnṯ*, *rḳw*).

(2) A man holding a stick, which indicates violent activity (*šmm*, *šnṯ*, *ẖnn*, *shꜣ*, *thw*).

(3) A bound man holding an axe in his hand, indicating an enemy (Gr A14*) (*thw*, *šmm*, *rḳw*).

(4) Various animals — crocodile (*ȝd*, *šnṯ*); animal of Seth (Gr E20) (*ḫnn*, *nšni*, *shȝ*); lion (*nšni*); snake (*tȝ rȝ*).
(5) Symbols of heat and flame — a brazier with a flame (*šmm*, *tȝ*); a potter's kiln (*tȝ*).

The fact that most of these determinatives involve animal characteristics or natural phenomena (fire, heat) reinforces the assumption that at first these concepts related to those objects, and only at a later stage were they adapted for usage relating to human actions and traits. A brief review of the significance of these animals within ancient Egyptian thought follows below which may help clarify their links with the concept of strife and fury.

The snake:

For the Egyptian the snake was a symbol of hostility and warfare. Sometimes this symbol is found in a positive context: the *i'rt* (or Uraeus), that is, the snake on the foreheads of the sun god and the king, protects them by shooting fire at their enemies.[115] At times the snake carries a negative connotation: the snake *'ȝpp* (or *Apopsis* in Greek) is the enemy of the universal order; it lies in wait for the sunship during its nightly journey through the underworld, and the god Seth, as protector of the sunship, battles with it. Moreover, the chaotic forces against which the creator god fights also appear in the image of a snake.[116] This dual significance of the snake, representing both good and evil, is expressed in *The Instruction of Amenemope* in a passage praising generosity:

> Set your goodness before the people
> Then you will be greeted by all
> As one welcomes the Uraeus
> And spits on Apopis (10, 17-20).

The snake is depicted in Egyptian literature as a reptile that spreads its terror all about. It is wrathful, furious and hostile. The snake became a metaphor for anger and wrath[117] and men in the hour of their fury were likened to it. Amenemhet was like "a snake of the desert" during his preparations for fighting the murderous traitors (VI F). The behavior of the man "whose heart begat strife" in *Insinger* is compared to that of a venomous snake (27, 14-15).

The crocodile:

The appearance of the crocodile both literally and as metaphor in the wisdom literature is more common than that of other animals. The list appended below which includes references to the reptile found in the corpus of our research, illuminates the characteristics of the crocodile.

The crocodile is known primarily for its rage, a characteristic expressed both in the orthography of the words that carry this sense and in the metaphoric use of the crocodile to designate various human types. Hence, the hieroglyphic representation (a crocodile) of the verb *3d* means "to rage like a crocodile." The crocodile appears as the subject of the verb *nšni*, which has a similar sense (*Wb.* II 340, 22).

It is figuratively said of the wicked leader that he is enraged (*3d*) like a crocodile (*msḥ*) (ex. 11 below); the scorner (*lḫ*) is compared to a "crocodile in fury" (ex. 9 below); one description of "the hot- mouthed," a negative human type, is that he "flips his tail like a young crocodile" (ex. 6 below).[118]

Sometimes this typical behavior of the crocodile takes on a positive sense. The king or the leader may be defined as an "enraged crocodile" to emphasize their greatness.[119] But the negative features of this reptile overshadow the positive ones: its smell becomes a byword and a taunt (ex. 15); its voracity knows no limits, therefore men who live to plunder and rob are equated with it (exx. 1, 3).

Often the "enemy" is described as a crocodile (exx. 3, 4, 8); this image may be understood against the background of the daily jeopardy in which the Egyptian found himself on account of crocodiles lying on the banks of the Nile. This fact is plainly evident in the writings of the Egyptian sage (exx. 5, 11, 14, 18, 19).

In the Egyptian myth, too, the crocodile is a symbol of enmity and evil. The creature belongs to the chaotic world of Seth, being the "messenger" and the "son" and the "creeping thing that Seth blew out of the entrails of Geb." The crocodile can also be called the "enemy of the god."[120]

Selected references to the crocodile

Instructions

1) *Ptaḥḥotep* 168. A bribe-taker is likened to a crocodile: "He is like a crocodile in court."

2) *Ptaḥḥotep* 257-262. Advice given to the leader who wishes to mend his ways — Perform noble acts, then you will be commended and not accused:

No strife will occur in the midst of honors
But where the crocodile enters hatred arises.

3) *To Merikare* 97-98. A description of the Asiatic:

The Asiatic is a crocodile on its shore
It snatches from a lonely road,
It cannot seize from a populous town.

4) *Amenemhet* XXI A. The might of the king is described thus:

I subdued lions, I captured crocodiles.
(The animals stand for the nations mentioned in the following line).

5) *Amenemope* 4, 16. The *šmm*, hot-tempered man, is like one sailing in a boat who cannot reach his destination:

The storm is tall, the crocodiles are vicious.

6) *Amenemope* 13, 4-7. The hot-mouthed man (*tȝ rȝ*):

flips his tail like a young crocodile... (cf. *AEA* 26)
His lips are sweet, his tongue is bitter
A fire burns in his belly.

7) *Amenemope* 22, 9. Quotation of a saying:

The crocodile that has no voice
Dread of it is small
("small" should be read instead of "old," "ancient" — Griffith).

8) *Ankhsheshonqy* 22, 15:

A crocodile does not take hold of a townsman.

9) *Insinger* 13,14-15:

The crimes of the scorner (*lḫ*) harm his brothers.
A crocodile in fury harms his divine brothers.

Pessimistic literature

10) *Peasant* B1 117-119. Words addressed to Rensi, son of Meru:

Your heart is greedy...
How miserable is the poor man whom you have destroyed!
You are like a messenger of the Crocodile.

11) *Peasant* B1 130 (cf. ex. 2):

Be a shelter, make safe your shore
See how your quay is infested with crocodiles!

12) *Peasant* B1 179-181. Words of the Peasant to Rensi, son of Meru:

You should have seemed less like a greedy crocodile (*msḥ skn*)...
I suppressed the wrathful (*ḫsf 3dw*), the crocodile (*msḥ*) returns!

13) *Peasant* B1 223-224. An appeal to the leader:

Shade, let not dry out
Shelter, let not the crocodile snatch.

14) *The Man Who Was Tired of Life* 70-80. The tale of a farmer whose life was endangered because of crocodiles.

15) *The Man Who Was Tired of Life* 96-98:

Lo, my name reeks.
Lo, more than crocodiles smell,
More than a shore full of crocodiles.

16) *Admonitions of an Egyptian Sage* 2, 12:

Lo, crocodiles are glutted (*3fy*) with what they have captured.

School texts

17) *Kheti* IV C. The nails of the coppersmith are like the claws of the crocodile and he smells like fish.

18) *Kheti* XIX A-B. The hazard of the profession of launderer is the proximity to the crocodile.
19) *Kheti* XXI C-F. The profession of the fisherman is dangerous owing to crocodiles.

The animal of Seth (*st*, *swti*, *swtḫ*, *stḫ*):

Unlike the other animals presented in this context, neither Seth nor the animal that symbolizes him are used as metaphors or images in the Egyptian wisdom literature. The animal of Seth, the identity of which is controversial,[121] appears only as a determinative of some of the expressions signifying "rage," "fury."

The semantic field of "anger," like other expressions having to do with confusion and disorder, is associated in Egyptian with the stormy world of the god Seth. The most outstanding feature of Seth, apart from his immense strength, is his anger. The anger of Seth, "lord of the tempest," is manifested in thunderstorms and the Egyptian king is compared to Seth in his rage.[122] Seth is also the god of the desert and of the dark forces that emanate from the wilderness, which in time came to be identified with the enemies of Egypt (including the Hyksos). Thus Seth himself became the "enemy" of the gods. He is the rival and slayer of Osiris and the foe of the sun god. Animals abhorred by the Egyptians, such as the crocodile, became his animals and all the negative qualities of man became associated with him. This outlook is expressed in a book of dreams from the Middle Kingdom. In this book mankind is divided into two groups: the people of Horus and the people of Seth. A warning is given to avoid the company of the members of the latter, and even that they should be offered as sacrifices. According to the conception of the Egyptian myth, the angry, infuriated man who cannot control his temper belongs to the category of "the people of Seth." "Seth-like" rage is a quality of the evil-tempered man, and in the words of the vizier Rekhmire, "I expelled the anger (*nšn*, with the determinative of the animal of Seth) of the evil-tempered man (*ḏw ḳd*)."

The lion:

The determinative of the lion appears in fact only for a single term (*nšni*) and then only once (*KCG* 42210, p. 28 E6 || Otto No. 7). The image of the lion, however, appears often in this corpus. The outstanding characteristics of the lion are its anger and wrath, which are unleashed against its enemies, and its courage and fearlessness in battle. The author of *Anii* presents it as a model for uncontrolled rage and wildness: "The savage lion abandons his wrath (*nšni*)" (10,2). Pharaoh is compared to an enraged lion (*mȝi nšni*) (*Anastasi* I 15,2). From here stems the concept which either identifies the king with Sekhmet, the goddess of war in the form of a lion, or regards him as her son. In *The Instruction of Seḥetep-ib-Ra* it is said of the king that "he is Sekhmet to those who disobey him" (5, 13).[123]

Determinatives signifying fire and heat:

Like the determinatives signifying animals given above, those denoting heat are linked to the world of nature as well as to the world of religion. The likening of anger and strife to heat of fire (Eg. *ḫ.t*, *srf*,[124] *nsr* [=*nswt*]), which is common in the Egyptian wisdom, apparently arises from the observation of human habits and conduct and their subsequent comparison with natural phenomena. In the world of the gods there is also a connection between fire, war and strife. Fire is perceived here as the weapon of the goddesses of war such as Sekhmet and Tefnut.[125]

The terms *tȝ* and *šmm*, discussed earlier, originally belong to the semantic field of heat, were adapted for use in the semantic field of "strife" and "anger." The comparison of quarrel and dispute to a raging fire can be seen in the following examples:[126] Idle chatter is compared to "fire" (*ḫ.t*) (*Instructions of a Man for His Son* XIV 1), all the more so angry words — the "hot-mouthed man" (*tȝ rȝ*) has "flames" (*Ptaḥḥotep* 378) and "fire burns in his belly" (*Amenemope* 13,7); the flurry of words of "the heated man" (*šmm*) is "like fire in straw" (ibid. 5,14-15).[127]

In time, fire becomes the common symbol for the angry, hot-tempered man. In *Amenemope* the word "fire" (*ḫ.t*) is accompanied by the determinative of a bound man (5,15; 13,7), usually depicting the *šmm*, the hot-tempered person.

Opposite images serve to describe men belonging to the positive category. The leader who performs his duties properly is the "extinguisher" of fire (*ʿḫm ḫ.t*, Otto No. 7, see above; cf. Jansen-Winkeln I A5,d,6-7; II 1,8,5), the "suppressor of the flame" (*dr srf*, *Urk.* IV 1180, 6; Janssen I p. 35, Ba 2). A subject loyal to his king is a "cooler of heat" (*ḳbb srf*), that is, possessor of a calm temperament (Blumenthal G 3, 36; Janssen, above, 6, etc.).[128] This human type, which is the opposite of "the heated man" (*tꜣ rꜣ*, *šmm*), is called "the silent man" (*grw*) in the wisdom literature (cf. Chap. 4, below).

3. Subject matter analysis: The "heated man" and the motif of anger and strife in the Egyptian sources

The use of heat as a metaphor for a human type has a long tradition in Egypt, beginning with the early instructions. *The Instruction of Kagemni* speaks of "expanding the place of the silent man" (*grw*), and in contrast to him appears the man "who strays from the path" (*thw*) (I 1ff.) who plays a role parallel to *šmm* in *The Instruction of Anememope* (5, 12-15). *The Instruction of Ptaḥḥotep* presents the "hot-bellied" man (*tꜣ ẖ.t* 352), whose opposite is the "cold-bellied" man (*ḳb ẖ.t* 323), and who spreads gossip and tells tales. Elsewhere "hot-hearted" (*tꜣ ib*) appears, specifically referring to a man given to anger and who ultimately is destroyed in the flames of his own speech (378).

Later, in the *Admonitions*, the adjective *tꜣw* appears as an attribute of those who deny the existence of god, saying "If I knew where god is I would serve him" (5,3).

The "hot-tempered man" is a central theme in *The Instruction of Amenemope*. The term recurs throughout the work and is contrasted with its antonym the "silent man" in chapter 4 (see below). The "heated man" (*šmm*) is depicted here, as in *The Instruction of Ptaḥḥotep*, as one whose foremost feature is his irascibility, expressed in his manner of speech. Its synonym is the *tꜣ rꜣ*, "hot of mouth" (*Amenemope* chap. 3, cf. ibid. chap. 9, and the collocation *šmw rꜣ* in *Hier. Ostr.* I pl. 7, 5), a man quick to anger and ready for a quarrel. Due to this tendency towards quarrelling he is called "enemy" (*rḳ*) (*Amenemope* chaps. 3 and 12). It becomes clear from chapters 9 and 10 in *Amenemope* that the "hot-tempered" man is "laden with falsehood" and "entraps with his speech," that is, "cunning." It is also assumed that he is higher in rank than the scribe. He is incorrigible to the point where the sage sees fit to appeal to the creator god Khnum to refashion him on the potter's wheel (ibid. 12, 15ff.).

In the *Ostracon Deir el Médineh* 1265, which like *The Instruction of Amenemope* dates to the Ramesside Period, the "hot- tempered" man plays an equally central role. As in chapter 4 in *Amenemope* the setting is religious and he is presented as one who has failed to fulfil his various ritual duties. However, the emphasis here is on the social framework. The *šmm* is perceived as an outsider to society and as one being pursued so that he may be beaten (I 4).[129] His negative traits include "impatience" (*wȝḥ ib*) and "obstinacy" (*dns ib*) (II 6-7).[130] He is undoubtedly a very dangerous man against whom society must be safeguarded not only in this world but also in the next. This may be concluded from *Ostracon Leipzig* 8 (*Hier. Ostr.* I pl. 7,5) which contains a curse aimed at driving him away from "the west," the dwelling place of the dead.

Images from the plant and animal kingdom are used to vividly describe the fate of the hot-tempered man. At times he is equated to a tree that soon withers (*Amenemope* chap. 4 and *Deir el Médineh* 1265, II 4-5); occasionally he is compared to animals — a mouse, a bird — which are doomed to die (*Anastasi* V || *Chester Beatty* V).[131]

The expression *šmm* (like its parallel *tȝ rȝ*) usually appears in the New Egyptian language accompanied either by a definitive or by a possessive pronoun ("your hot-tempered man" — *Deir el Médineh* 1265, *Hier. Ostr.* I pl. 7,5, *Chester Beatty* V, *Anastasi* V). This to some extent confirms the view, obtained from an analysis of the literary sources, that the issue here is not a single characteristsic, *but a human type who became a symbol for the bad-natured man par excellence* in the Egyptian wisdom literature.[132] The "hot-tempered" man was encumbered with a range of traits and flaws condemned by the Egyptian sage, namely, anger, fury, lying, lack of restraint, and uncontrollable temper.

The warning to avoid contention and show restraint recurs in the majority of the wisdom texts. In this context, apart from the expressions given above which involve the *šmm* figure, other terms appear which likewise concern anger, strife and hostility: *štm*, *ṯṯṯ*, *sḫwn*, *nšni*, *ḫnn*, *sh3*, *3d*, *šnṯ*, *ḫ'r* (see above).

Often "strife" and "anger" are closely accompanied by other negative qualities and actions, such as lying (*Anii* 5,5-9), insulting (*Ptaḥḥotep* 375ff.), covetousness (ibid. 316-323) and even inciting rebellion (*To Merikare* 24). Anger belongs to "the possessor of bad nature," says the sage (*Urk.* IV 1078, 2). Therefore, he counsels to avoid strife by keeping clear of the quarrelsome man (*Kheti* XXIII B, *Amenemope* 5,10-11; 11,13ff.; *Anii* 5, 7, cf. *Ptaḥḥotep* 476) or through submission and obsequiousness (*Amenemope* 5,12). In this context the warning "do not rage" (with the terms *ḫnn*, *3d*, *ḫ'r*) appears frequently. It is addressed principally to one in a higher position who must take care not to insult (*šnṯ*) either his superior or those under him: the saying "I did not insult anyone greater than I" (*n šnṯ.i '3 r.i*) is common in the writings of the 18th Dynasty; the vizier lauds himself as one who eschewed anger (*Urk.* IV, above; cf. *Ptaḥḥotep* 76); and the king is described as the "cooler of rage, himself far from rage (*nšni*)" (*Seḥetep-ib-Ra* 3, 5-6). This caution is reinforced with the threat of punishment, which at times takes the extreme form of the death penalty (see above, *Amenemope* 12, 15ff; also *Anii* 5,6).

In contrast with the "silent man" (*grw*), the "heated man" (*šmm*) appears only in chapter 4 in *Instruction of Amenemope* and in *Pap. Sallier* I (8,5-6). In both places the background is religious;[133] in *The Instruction of Amenemope* the setting of the events is the temple, while in *Pap. Sallier* I there is a hymn to the god Thoth. Whether the sense of *šmm* is identical here with that appearing in the passages (given above) whose background is social morality, or whether it takes on a different meaning in the context of religious morality, will be considered in the next chapter.

Summary

Anger and strife are presented in the Egyptian wisdom literature as signs of a flaw in the human character. The terms belonging to this semantic field are illustrated through metaphors taken from the realm of nature, some of which belong to the world of everyday reality and others to the world of myth and Egyptian religion. The appellations appearing in this context — "hostile" man, "quarrelsome" man, and the like — do not signify a negative type of man but one of the traits that compose his character. This is not the case with *šmm* (and its synonym *tȝ*), which stands for a negative human type in Egyptian wisdom. Of the 13 (without *thw*) lexemes belonging to the semantic field of "anger," "strife," only four (*šmm*, *tȝ* [in collocation], *štm*, *t̠t̠t*) belong to the Egyptian wisdom vocabulary and their distribution is evident in compositions of the instruction genre. The remaining terms also are frequent in other literary genres (the king's court, autobiography), although they too are well represented in the instructions. These findings are set forth in Table 6.

In the Bible

1. Semantic determination of terms involving anger and strife compared with the Egyptian

In the Bible, as in Egyptian texts, three groups may be distinguished among the words belonging to this semantic field: (a) Words with a double meaning which belong to the semantic field of "heat", on the one hand, and carry the sense of "to be angry," "to quarrel" on the other; (b) words relating to the act of quarrelling, usually a verbal dispute; (c) words expressing the feeling of anger.

(a) Terms belonging to the semantic field of heat — *ḥmm*, *ḥrh*, *zwd* (|| Eg. *šmm*, *tȝ*):

1. ***ḥmm***

The root *ḥmm* is semantically and even etymologically equivalent to *šmm*. *ḥmm* like *šmm* signifies natural, meteorological heat, and figuratively describes emotions. Our concern is with the nominal form *ḥēmâ*, meaning "heat," "anger," which is not characteristic of the wisdom language[134] except when it constitutes a component in the

Table 6: The Distribution of Terms Belonging to the Semantic Field of Anger and Strife*

		šmm	*šmm r3*	*t3*	*t3 ib*	*t3 r3***	*t3 ẖ.t*	*štm*	*ṯtṯt (s tyty)*	*rk(w)*	*šnṯ*	*ẖnn*	*sh3*	*3d*	*sḫwn*	*nšni*	*ḫ'r*	*fnḏ*
Instruction	*Kagemni*													+				
	Ptahhotep				+		+	+			+		+	+				
	To Merikare			+	+			+				+	+					
	Amenemhet											+	+					
	Anii	+							+	+		+						
	Amenemope	+				+		+	+	+		+						
	Insinger																+	
"Loyalist" Instructions	*Sehetep-ib-Ra*														+	+		+
	Man for His Son							+							+	+		
Pessimistic Wisdom	*The Peasant*										+			+				
	Admonitions			+								+	+					
	Neferti												+					
	Khakheperre-sonb									+								
School Texts	*Kheti*														+			
	Chester Beatty V	+																
	Anastasi V	+																
Royal Court Inscriptions (18th Dyn.)	*Urk.* IV									+ many	+ many			+ many	+	+	+	
Late Auto-biography	*Otto*															+		
Religious Literature	*Sallier* I	+																
	Deir el Medineh 1265	+ 11x																
	Hieratic Ostraca I	+	+ 2x															

* *thw* is omitted being basically related to the semantic field of "neglect of learning", see Table 4, above.
** The form *r3 t3* occurs once in *The Autobiography of Anhurmose* (19th Dyn.), pl. 25, l. 35 (Ockinga, *El Mashayikh*).

idioms *'îš ḥēmâ/ḥēmôt* and *ba'al/gᵉdal ḥēmâ*, which signify an irascible man and which appear only in Proverbs. These are discussed in detail below (see pp. 144–149 below). *ḥēmâ* refers to the anger of both man and God: regarding the anger of man, there are many examples both within and outside wisdom literature, for example, "A soft answer turns away wrath (*ḥēmâ*), but grievous words stir up anger" (Prov. 15,1; cf. ibid. 6,34; 16,14 and wisdom Ps. 37,8). Regarding the anger of God, the term *ḥēmâ* appears in Job (21,20) in this usage,[135] as well as in the wisdom Psalms (78,38; 106,23; cf. also BS 16,6; 33,8 [B]); but it is more common outside wisdom literature (in prophecy, Psalms, and Chronicles), where it parallels *'ap* ("anger") of God (e.g., Mic. 5,14), his *qeṣep* ("anger") (e.g., Ps. 38, 2), his *ḥărôn 'ap* ("heat of anger") (Nah. 1,6) and appears in conjunction with *bᵉ'ap wûbᵉḥēmâ wûbᵉqeṣep* (Deut. 29,27, etc.). It is also used often in this context as the object of verbs signifying burning, igniting *ḥēmâ*, namely: *b'r* ("burn") (e.g., Jer. 4,4); *yṣt* ("kindle") (e.g., 2 Kgs. 22,13); *'lh* ("stir up") (Ezek. 38, 18); *špk* ("pour out") (e.g., Ezek. 7,8); *ntk* ("pour out") (e.g., Jer. 7,20); and *yṣ'* ("go forth like fire") (e.g., Jer. 4,4). When the term *ḥēmâ* is used in the wisdom literature to define the anger of man or God, it often collocates with verbs bearing the opposite meaning, namely, "cover over" and "nullify" the *ḥēmâ*: *hēšîb* ("turn away") (Prov. 15,1; wisdom Ps. 106,23), *'ăzōb* (wisdom Ps. 37,8), *lō' yā'îr* (wisdom Ps. 78,38).[136]

2. *ḥrh*

The basic meaning of *ḥrh*, which does not belong to the wisdom terminology (7 times in the wisdom texts out of 93 times in the Bible), is "to burn." Later it came to mean "to become angry, inflamed."

In Proverbs the root *ḥrh* appears once only. In a verse, which recurs with slight changes in the wisdom Psalm, the sage counsels not to become angry (*titḥar*) through brooding over the behavior of evildoers (Prov. 24,19; cf. wisdom Ps 37, 1,7-8).[137]

In Job the verb *ḥrh* serves several times to indicate the reaction of Job and his friends, and it also refers to the anger of God (e.g., 32,2,3,5; 19,11, etc.).

The noun *ḥărôn* means "burning anger," and its subject is always

God. In the wisdom literature it appears once in Job: "God will send forth his fierce anger (*ḥărôn 'appô*) into him" (20,23), as well as in the wisdom Psalm (78,49) and in Ben Sira (45,19; 46,7).

3. ***zwd, zyd***

The basic meaning of *zwd* is "bubble, boil"; this sense is preserved in the form of the noun *nāzîd*, "boiled food" (Gen. 25,29).[138] Metaphorically *zwd* describes human behavior as shown by the derivatives: *zēd* means an irate man who behaves insolently, and the noun *zādôn* refers to arrogant and wicked conduct.[139]

The root *zwd* is not characteristic of wisdom literature. *zēd* appears once in Proverbs (21,24), while the plural, *zēdîm*, belongs to the terminology of Psalms and signifies people who spurn God and his commandments.[140] The word is present in this sense in Ben Sira too: "The arrogant and the scorner will not take a commandment" (32,18; cf. ibid. in proximity to "wicked men" — 12,4).

The noun *zādôn*, which occurs in Proverbs three out of the 13 times in the Bible refers to social morals: *zādôn* is the opposite of "modest" (Prov. 11,2; cf. BS 10,18). It produces strife (Prov. 13,10) and is one of the traits of the *lēṣ* ("scorner") (ibid. 21,24). The term appears often in Ben Sira both in a social setting, as in Proverbs, and in a religious setting, as in Psalms (see, e.g., 15,7; 16,2-3).[141]

(b) Terms concerning strife — *mādôn, ryb, maṣṣâ, z'm* (|| Eg. *štm, ṯṯt, rḳ[w], šnṯ, ẖnn, sḫwn*):

The sages repeatedly warn against strife and discord. Over 20 statements on this subject are made in Proverbs, demonstrating its importance for the sapiential thought.

4. ***mādôn***

The singular *mādôn* and the plural *midyānîm* are characteristic of the language of Proverbs[142] but are absent from the vocabulary of Job and Qoheleth. To create the verbal form, *mādôn* combines with the verbs *grh* ("stir up") (Prov. 15,18; 29,22), *'wr* ("awaken") (ibid. 10,12) and *šlḥ* ("spread") (ibid. 16,28; 6,14,19).[143] *mādôn* is synonymous in meaning with *rîb* and stands in parallelism with it (ibid. 15,18; 17,14, etc.). The difference between the two is that *mādôn* stresses the emotional state preceding the quarrel or fight, namely, the feeling of anger and aggressiveness. The subject of the action is always a person belonging to the negative category — *'îš ḥēmâ* (Prov. 15,18); *'îš 'ap* (29,22); *r^e^ḥab nepeš*, ("greedy man," — 28,25); *'îš tahpukôt* (16,28); *lēṣ* (22,10); and in combinations: *'îš*, *'ēšet m^e^dônîm* (*Q^e^rê*: *midyānîm*) (ibid. 25,24; 26,21; 27,15; cf. 19,13).

5. *ryb*

The root *ryb*, used as a verb and as a noun, may describe in the Bible a physical[144] or a verbal clash. *ryb* is not confined to the wisdom language but when employed in a wisdom context it usually has the sense of a dispute either in or outside a legal framework.[145]

In Proverbs the dispute is usually between human beings (3,30; 17,14; 25,8-10 [legal background]; 26,17; etc.), and there is a recurrence of the warning "Do not contend" (3,30; 25,8); but God too appears here as a participant in a dispute: He pleads the cause of the orphans and the needy (22, 23; 23,11).

Job is involved in a dispute (legal) with both God (9,3; 10,2; etc.) and mortals (13,19; 31,35; etc.). In this context the following collocations are found in Job: *'îš rîb*, i.e., an opponent in litigation (ibid.; cf. Isa. 41,11; etc.) and *rîbôt śpātay* ("pleadings of my lips" || *tôkāḥ^e^tî*) (Job 13,6). In addition to its verbal usage, *rîb* as a noun appears as the object of the following verbs in wisdom literature: *ḥarḥar rîb* (Prov. 26,21), *hitgallā' b^e^rîb* (20,3; 17,14), *yṣ' l^e^rîb* (25,8). For the opposite idea the following expressions are used: *hašqēt rîb* (15,18), *n^e^ṭôš rîb* (17,14).[146]

6. *maṣṣâ*

The root *nṣh*, concerning physical struggle, appears only as a noun, *maṣṣâ*, in the Biblical wisdom books. *maṣṣâ* comes twice in Proverbs (out of 4 times in the Bible) and is not found in Job and Qoheleth.

The term bears a negative connotation and involves the wickedness and delinquency of human beings (Prov. 13,10; 17,19). *maṣṣâ* stands in synonymous parallelism with *peša'* (ibid.) and *rîb* (Isa. 58,4). In Ben Sira *nṣh* appears as a verb, in a verse that —like the Egyptian parallels — compares contention to fire: "Do not struggle (*tînnāṣ*) with a quarrelsome man and do not place wood on the fire" (8,3).

7. *z'm*

In contrast to the previous term, *z'm* relates not to physically but to orally expressed anger. It means "to speak angrily," "rebuke," "curse."[147] Thus, it is close to the terms *štm*, *šnṯ*, *ṯṯṯ* in Egyptian. The root *z'm* is not exclusive to the wisdom books in which it appears only nine out of 35 times in the Bible.[148] In Proverbs it is found in verbal use (qal): *yiz'āmûhû* || *yiqqbuhû* (24, 24) and as an adjective in the passive form: *z^e'ûm* of God, that is, "cursed by God" (22, 14) and *pānîm niz'āmîm* (niph'al), that is "angry face" (25,23). In Psalms and Ben Sira the noun *za'am* has an abstract sense in reference to the fierce anger of God (cf. *za'am* together with *ḥărōn 'appô* (of God), *'ebrâ* and *ṣārâ* in Ps. 78, 49 [wisdom Psalm]; BS 5,7; 39,23).

(c) Terms referring to anger and fury — *'np* (*'ap*), *ka'as*, *'br*, *qeṣep*, *z'p* (|| Eg. *fnḏ*, *3d*, *nšni*, *ḫ'r*):

8. *'np* / *'ap*

The root *'np* is most commonly used in the Bible to signify anger, but does not belong to the wisdom vocabulary. The wisdom literature contains only the noun *'ap* (in Proverbs and Job) which is the semantic equivalent of *fnḏ* in Egyptian and like it has a double meaning — a bodily organ and anger. Flash[149] believes that the semantic development was from the original meaning *'ap* — "nose" to the sense of *'ap* — "anger," the nose playing a part in the feeling of anger.

In the Bible the noun *'ap* is usually associated with the anger of God (ca. 170 times) and less frequently with the anger of men (ca. 40 times). But in Proverbs the situation is reversed: *'ap* refers to the anger of God once (Prov. 24, 18), and the remaining times its subject is the fury of man. In this usage the following idioms are found in Proverbs: *ba'al 'ap* (22,24; cf. BS 8,16), *'îš 'ap* (Prov. 29,22),[150] and *mîṣ 'ap* "squeezing of anger," (ibid. 30,33). However, *'ap* also appears here in plain form (ibid. 24,18; especially in parallelism with *ḥēmâ*, ibid. 15,1; 21,14; 27,4; cf. wisdom Ps. 37,8).

In Job, as in the other books of the Bible, *'ap* often relates to God (9,13; *ḥărôn 'appô* — 20,23,28; etc.). In Ben Sira *'ap* signifies both anger of men (BS 8,16; 10,18; 30,24; 45,18) and anger of God (ibid. 5,6; 33,8[B]; 45,19; etc.).

9. *ka'as*

In the Biblical wisdom only the nominal form *ka'as* (*ka'aś* in Job) is employed.[151] In the wisdom language *ka'as* relates to one of the human emotions — anger.[152] This feeling frequently arises from the sense of deprivation and its meaning approximates "vexation," "grief."[153] A stupid son elicits *ka'as* ("grief") in his father (Prov. 17,25). In Qoheleth *ka'as* is parallel to *mak'ôbîm* (2, 23) and *ḥolî wāqāṣep* (5,16; cf. also ibid. 1,18; 11,10). The term *ka'as* is also found in a similar sense in passages in which Job describes his suffering (6,2-3; 17,7).

Outside wisdom literature, especially in the Deuteronomist phraseology in Kings and in Jeremiah, the root *k's* regularly appears (in hiph'il) to signify God's anger towards the people provoked by their apostasy.[154]

10. *'br*

The root *'br*, which means "outburst of anger," "overflow of fury" and which appears in our texts as a verb — *hit'abbār* (hithpa'el) and as a noun — *'ebrâ*, does not belong to the wisdom lexicon.[155] Scholars are divided as to whether *'br* in this sense derives from the root *'br*, "to pass over, through,"[156] or if there are two different roots.

In the Biblical literature the term is frequently used to describe the anger of God,[157] but it is less common with respect to men. The opposite picture appears in Proverbs, where *'br* always comes in reference to human beings. These are usually consigned to the negative human category — the *rāšā'*, *zēd*, *lēṣ*, and *kᵉsîl* . In this context *'br* sometimes carries the notion of arrogance, haughtiness, as, for example, in Proverbs 14,16: "The wise man fears and avoids misfortune, but the stupid man is arrogant (*mit'abbēr*) and is confident" (cf. also ibid. 21,24, and BS 16,8). A passer-by who shows anger (*mit'abbēr*) in a quarrel that is originally not his concern is compared to a man seizing a dog's ear (Prov. 26,17);while he who infuriates the king (*mit'abb*^{e}*rô*) will bring misfortune upon himself (ibid. 20,2).

The meaning of the phrase *yôm 'ebrâ* in Proverbs 11,4, repeated in Job 21,30 (*yôm 'ăbārôt*) in parallelism with *yôm 'ēd*, is "a day of evil, trouble, calamity" (cf. also BS 5,8; 34,6 [B]).[158] In Job and in the wisdom Psalms the root *'br* is applied to God. In God's second reply to Job he is called on "to shed abroad the outburst of his anger (*'ebrôt 'appô*)," that is, to pour out his rage if he has strength like God (40, 11). In wisdom Psalm 78 the verse "When God heard, he was full of anger (*yit'abbār*)," signifying rage sparked by the sinning of his people against him, is twice repeated (vss. 21,59); and the noun *'ebrâ* appears there together with *ḥărôn 'appô*, *za'am* and *ṣārâ* in the description of the plagues against Egypt (vs. 49).

11. *qṣp*

The root *qṣp*, which appears in both verbal and nominal form belongs to a later stage of Biblical language. The noun *qeṣep*, "anger," stands in synonymous parallelism with *'ap*, *za'am*, *ḥēmâ*, and *ka'as*. *qṣp* appears only twice in the wisdom literature, viz., in Qoheleth. Here it serves both as a verb (qal) in reference to the anger of God (5,5) and as a noun, in reference to the toiling person: his lot is *ka'as*, *ḥolî* and *qāṣep* (ibid. 16). The verb occurs once in the wisdom Psalms applying to past infuriation of God by the children of Israel (106,32).

12. *z'p*

z'p signifies the emotion of rage. The term appears twice in Proverbs, as a noun and as a verb: 19,12 states "The wrath (*za'ap*) of a king is like the roaring of a lion" (cf. 20,2, where the "wrath of a king" is replaced by the "fear of a king");[159] and Proverbs 19, 3 says, "And then he (the fool) is angry (*yiz'ap*) with God."

Addenda:

13. *rgn*

The root *rgn*, which means to "slander," "whisper," does not belong to the semantic field of strife and anger. But *rgn* does in the Bible concern matters of strife and anger (Prov. 26, 20-22; 17,28) and is therefore essentially close to the Egyptian *šnṯ*. *rgn* is frequent in Proverbs than in any other book (three times out of six in the Bible).

The participial form *nirgān* (niph'al), "backbiter," appears here accompanied by images and pictorial descriptions, reminiscent of the Egyptian parallels: the activity of the *nirgān* is likened to "fire" (26,20-22); the *nirgān* separates close friends (16,28).[160] (Cf. the description of the *tȝ rȝ* in *Amenemope* 13, 1ff., "who causes brothers to quarrel.") In Proverbs 18, 8 it is said that "the words of the *nirgān* are like delicious morsels;[161] they go down into the inner chambers of the belly." In this passage the belly is presented as the dwelling place of words and thoughts, an image common in the Egyptian thought, but unusual in the Hebrew sphere.[162]

14. *rûaḥ*

rûaḥ ("spirit") in the sense of "anger" appears 6 times in the Bible, including, according to the Gesenius-Buhl dictionary, two references in Proverbs.[163] In Proverbs 16,32 "one who rules his spirit (*mōšēl bᵉrûḥô*)" parallels one who is "slow to anger (*'erek 'appayim*)," and in 29,11 the stupid man is said to "give full vent to his spirit (*rûḥô*)." These two verses, cited by Gesenius-Buhl, may be augmented by at least two more: "A man whose spirit (*rûaḥ*) lacks restraint" is compared to a city broken through, without a wall (ibid. 25, 28), and the phrase *qᵉṣar rûaḥ* (lit. "short-tempered," ibid. 14, 29), meaning a man looking for a quarrel. These descriptions in Proverbs are close in essence to passages in the Egyptian wisdom literature that speak about quenching and suppressing the flame of discord (see above, pp. 128–129 and below, pp. 153, 156).

To sum up, the above analysis shows that only three out of 14 terms concerning anger and strife (*rgn*, *mādôn*, *ḥēmâ* [+ *'îš/ba'al*]) are characteristic of the language of the Biblical sage. The remainder do not belong to the wisdom vocabulary. However, the abundance of terms relating to this semantic field in Biblical wisdom reveals that shunning the feeling of anger and the act of quarrelling played a central role in the ideology of the wise men in Israel.

2. Subject matter analysis of terms referring to anger and strife in relation to the Egyptian

(a) The motif of anger and strife in the Biblical wisdom literature:

The attitude of the Hebrew sage and his Egyptian counterpart to traits and activities pertaining to the sphere of anger and strife is similar. In Proverbs, as in the Egyptian wisdom literature, people who provoke quarrel — *'îš ḥēmâ*, *'îš 'ap*, *'îš bᵉlîyya'al*, *'îš midyānîm*, the *nirgān* and *'îš tahpukôt* (Prov. 6,14; 15,18; 16,28; 26,20-22; 29,22; etc.) — are condemned. The sage in Proverbs accuses the greedy man, literally the "wide of soul," of creating dispute (Prov. 28,25), as did before him, albeit in more moderate tones, the Egyptian author of *The Instruction of Ptaḥḥotep* (316-323). The quarrelsome man is called *zēd* or *'îš rîb* in the Bible, parallel to *rḳw* ("enemy") and *thw* ("violent man") in Egyptian. Both texts contain interspersed warnings not to get involved in a quarrel and to avoid the company of people with this negative tendency (Prov. 3,30; 17,14; 25,8; Qoh. 7,9; etc.). The wisdom ideal in Egypt and in Israel is the cool-tempered man — *qar rûaḥ*, he who calms anger (Prov. 17,27; 29,8,11); the adversary should be met with silence and words of appeasement (Prov. 15,1; cf. wisdom Ps. 37,7-8 and *Amenemope* 5,10-17; 22, 1ff.; also *Anii* 3,17-4,1; 8,16-20; etc.). In Egyptian literature there is frequent mention of the danger inherent in the deeds of the hot-tempered man. In the Bible this danger is thrown into relief through vivid metaphoric language: the *mit'abbēr* is compared to one who seizes a dog by his ears and thus will be bitten (Prov. 26,17); or a man who starts a quarrel is likened to one who breaches a dam (17,14; cf. also 22,8; Job 5, 2). The link between strife and anger is well expressed in the saying in Proverbs 30,33 which puns on the root *'ap*, using it in its different senses as an organ of the body or pertaining to anger: "For pressing milk brings out curd and pressing the nose (*'ap*) brings out blood, and pressing anger (*'ap*) brings out strife (*rîb*)."

Although there is great similarity between the Hebrew and the Egyptian material, in certain details the Hebrew wisdom differs from the Egyptian. In the Bible, the activity of quarrelling and the feeling of anger are associated with the *k^esîl* ("stupid man") (Prov. 14, 16; 18, 6; Qoh. 7,9) and his synonyms: the *'ĕwîl* (Prov. 12,16; 19,3; 20,3; 27,3; Job 5, 2) and the *lēṣ* (Prov. 22,10). In the Egyptian sources the "stupid man" does not appear in this context.[164] Furthermore, the terms concerned with anger and strife in Biblical wisdom literature are rarely involved with the world of nature, as we shall see in the following section.

(b) Images from the realm of nature:

(1) Animals associated with anger:

The association between strife and anger and the natural world, so abundantly expressed in Egyptian myth and religion and clearly evident in the literature of the inhabitants of the land of the Nile, rarely appears in Biblical wisdom literature. Here only one example is found, the lion. The king and the ruler in their fury are likened to a lion, e.g., "The wrath of the king is like the roaring of a lion" (Prov. 19,12 || 20,2; cf. 28,15).[165]

In this connection it is worth mentioning the *tannîn* (crocodile), depicted in Job 41 as an animal that spreads terror. However, since the description of the crocodile directly follows that of the Leviathan in the previous chapter (Job 40, 25ff.), it is difficult to distinguish between them. This also makes it impossible to decide whether the verses 11-13 in chapter 41, which might have been of interest for our discussion, speak of the crocodile or the Leviathan, or even of some other mythological creature.[166] Whatever its identity, this animal is described in its rage thus:

> Out of his mouth go burning torches,
> (And) sparks of fire leap forth.
> Out of his nostrils a smoke comes forth,

As of a boiling pot and rushes
His breath sets coals ablaze
And a flame goes forth from his mouth.

(2) Heat and fire as a metaphor for anger in the Bible:

The image of heat and fire for anger was common in the languages of the ancient Near Eastern peoples. The vivid use of the incandescence of fire to signify human emotion in Biblical literature is expressed on two levels: the terminological level and the conceptual level.

We already observed above that the basic meaning of the three terms *ḥmm*, *ḥrh*, *zwd* involves heating, boiling and burning, and that they are used figuratively to describe the anger of man and God. The wisdom books, prophecy and the Psalms are interspersed with images and descriptions based on this usage. In the wisdom literature these images refer to the human sphere, to the interaction between human beings. Strife and contention are likened to fire and irate words to wood used to set a fire. He who ignites off the quarrel is like charcoal and wood that keep the fire blazing: "Where there is no wood the fire goes out, and when there is no backbiter (*nirgān*) strife will cease. Charcoal for embers and wood for fire, and a quarrelsome man (*'îš midyānîm*) to make strife hot" (Prov. 26,20-21); cf.: "Do not contend with a loud man and do not put wood on the fire" (BS 8,3). The words of *'îš b^{e}liyya'al* are like a "scorching fire" (Prov. 16,27).

Outside wisdom literature these images always involve a description of God; thus God is depicted in the moment of his rage: "Smoke went out from his nostrils, and devouring fire from his mouth; glowing coals flamed forth from him" (Ps. 18,8-9). In Psalms and in prophecy the following phrases and clichés describing God's fury recur often: "a fire is kindled in my anger" (Jer. 15,14; 17,4); "the fire of my wrath" (Ezek. 21, 36; 22, 21, etc.); cf. "the fire of my jealousy" (Zeph. 3, 8); "his anger is poured out like fire" (Nah. 1,6; Lam. 2,4); "his fury comes forth like fire" (Jer. 4,4; 21,12; etc.); "his fury burned like fire" (Ps. 89,47; cf. 79,5). Of the king's enemies in Psalm 21 it is said that God "will make them as a blazing oven, ...he will swallow them up in his wrath (*'appô*) and fire will consume them" (vs. 11).

As the above discussion of the relevant Biblical material shows, there is great similarity, on the linguistic as well as the stylistic level, in the use of "fire" in the language of the Hebrew and the Egyptian wise man. The words *ḥmm*, *ḥrh*, *zwd*, like their parallels in Egyptian, initially involved fire and only later served to signify human emotions and feelings. In Biblical wisdom, as in the Egyptian, the image of fire is presented within the setting of social morals and its concern is the relations between man and his fellow man. There are, however, some important differences. The image of fire in the context of social morality is limited in the Bible to the wisdom literature, and here, too, occurs only sparsely (twice altogether). Outside the wisdom literature there is widespread use of the image to illustrate the rage of God in a religious context. Furthermore, not only is the use of this metapahor in the wisdom rhetoric limited, it is also incomplete: Comparison with the Egyptian wisdom, where the complete picture is evident, shows that in the Bible only half of the image has been preserved. "Fire," which is the symbol of evil and of the negative traits of anger and rage, is in the Egyptian sources contrasted with "coolness" and "water," symbolizing the ideal way of life and the noble character of a man. There is no parallel to this in the Biblical literature.[167]

In light of these differences, it may be assumed that if there was any literary contact, the Hebrew sage was influenced by his Egyptian counterpart, and not vice versa. However, the figurative use of "fire" or "flame" in connection with dispute is found in the literature of other ancient peoples;[168] therefore when not attached to a human type the image does not necessarily derive from the Egyptian concept but from a common universal motif.

(c) *'îš ḥēmâ* in the Biblical wisdom and accompanying expressions:

(1) *'îš ḥēmâ*, the Hebrew equivalent of *šmm*

Several expressions have been suggested in research for the Hebrew parallel of the Egyptian terms *šmm* or *tȝw*:

Drioton, who found clear evidence of the influence of the Semitic language in the Egyptian *Instruction of Amenemope*,[169] sought to demonstrate this for the term *šmm* as well which, according to him, appears only in *Amenemope*. He claimed that *šmm* is the semantic equivalent of the Hebrew term *zēd*. *zēd*, like *šmm* is derived from the verb "to boil," "seethe" (i.e., *zwd*). Therefore, *zēd* is a violent man boiling with rage, who in Proverbs 21,24 is defined as follows: "Scorner (*lēṣ*) is the name of the proud, arrogant man (*zēd*), he who acts with insolent pride (*'ebrat zādôn*)."[170]

Drioton's suggestion is not acceptable, for three reasons. First, *šmm* is obviously an Egyptian term. It appears not only in *The Instruction of Amenemope* but in at least five more Egyptian sources (see above). Second, the root *zwd* does not belong to the Biblical wisdom lexicon. The adjective *zēd* appears in Proverbs only once (see above; twice in BS) and is absent from Job and Qoheleth. *zēdîm* in the plural belongs to the terminology of religious morality and is present in prophecy and particularly in Psalms.[171] Third, the characteristic quality of the Egyptian *šmm*, that is, strife and anger, is not mentioned in connection with *zēd* in Proverbs; although in one instance it accompanies the noun *zādôn* there: "Pride (*zādôn*) causes only strife (*maṣṣâ*) but with those who take counsel is wisdom" (Prov. 13,10).[172]

As early as 1924 Humbert suggested, that the expressions *'îš ḥēmôt* (Prov. 22,24), *'îš ḥēmâ* (15,18), *ba'al ḥēmâ* (29,22), *g^edāl ḥēmâ* (19,19), *ba'al 'ap* (22,24) and *'îš 'ap* (29,22) be regarded as the Hebrew parallels of the Egyptian *šmm*.[173] This suggestion has been accepted by most scholars,[174] and indeed it seems most likely that these expressions are the precise equivalents of the Egyptian concept and that they were coined under the influence of the Egyptian wisdom. The grounds for this are as follows:

(a) The root *ḥmm* in Hebrew is phonetically, etymologically and semantically parallel to *šmm* in Egyptian. Appearing in the collocations *'îš/ba'al/g^edāl ḥēmâ* it has a figurative sense, "heat," serving as a metaphor for "anger" and "hot temper," like the Egyptian *šmm*.

(b) This usage is, as already stated, indeed not only known from the literature of Israel and Egypt, but also from that of other ancient peoples

— Sumer and Babylon. However, with respect to a human type it is frequent only in the Egyptian literature and in the passages cited from Proverbs.

(c) It seems that the Hebrew author drew upon an Egyptian source, and not vice versa. *'îš ḥēmâ* and its synonyms appear only in Proverbs with respect to man, while in the other Biblical books they usually involve a description of God (see above). The expression *'îš ḥemôt* in fact appears in the third collection of Proverbs, where direct parallelism with *The Instruction of Amenemope* has long been recognized and attributed to the dependence of the Hebrew author on the Egyptian (Prov. 22, 24, 25 || *Amenemope* 11, 13-14).

Bryce, who also maintains the view that Proverbs was influenced of Egyptian wisdom, concluded that the Egyptian material was borrowed by the Hebrew writer and gradually modified to fit the new setting.[175] This process of adaptation contained three stages: the adaptive, assimilative and integrative.

Bryce's theory, as applied to *'îš ḥēmâ* and its synonyms, may be summarized as follows:[176]

(a) The *adaptive stage*: At this stage there is verbal correspondence between the Hebrew and Egyptian material:

1. Proverbs 22,24-25
   Make no friendship (*'al titra'*) with a man
   given to anger (*ba'al 'ap*),
   Nor go (*tābô'*) with a wrathful man (*'îš ḥēmôt*)
   Lest you learn his ways
   And bring destruction on yourself.

This parallels *Amenemope* 11,13-17:

13. Do not associate (*snsn*) with a hot man (*šmm*)
14. And do not approach (*ḫnḫn*) him to converse...
17. Let him not cast his speech to catch you.

Bryce suggests that the proximity is expressed here (a) in content: the human type characterized by the association between heat and quarrel; (b) in form: (1) "The unusual use of *r'h* in hithpa'el to signify 'make friends with' may be accounted for by its close equivalence to the Egyptian word *snsn* which also means 'befriend.'"[177] (2) The verb *tābô'* approximates in form (imperative) and even in meaning ("to approach") *ḫnḫn* in Egyptian.

2. Proverbs 29,22:

> A man of wrath (*'îš 'ap*) stirs up strife (*mādôn*)
> And a man given to anger (*ba'al ḥēmâ*)
> causes much transgression (*rab pāša'*).

Amenemope 13, 1:

> He causes brothers to quarrel (*ṯṯṯ*).

Amenemope 5, 10:

> Do not start a quarrel (*ṯṯṯ*) with the hot-mouthed man (*pꜣ tꜣ rꜣ*).

Bryce states that here too there is adaptation of an essentially Egyptian type. *ba'al ḥēmâ* is "an exact equivalent of the Egyptian image," as attested by the features that characterize him, especially his being *rab pāša'* (cf. above, *Amenemope* 11, 17). He also finds in the phrase *qar rûaḥ* ("cool of spirit") (Prov. 17,27) a literal parallel to the Egyptian *ḳb ḫ.t* (lit. "cool of body"), that is, "cool tempered," which is the antonym of *tꜣ ḫ.t*, meaning "hot tempered" in Egyptian. The "hot-tempered man" in Egyptian contrasts with the "silent man." The latter expression is purely Egyptian and has no representation in Biblical Hebrew. But the verb *šqṭ* (hiph'il) appears once in the Bible in connection with strife, in Proverbs 15,18:

> A hot tempered man (*'îš ḥēmâ*) stirs up strife (*mādôn*)
> But he who is slow to anger (*'erek 'appayim*)
> Quiets (*yašqîṭ*) contention (*rîb*).

Here too, according to Bryce the Egyptian image is adapted.

(b) The *assimilative stage*: Instead of a term constituting verbal correspondence with the Egyptian parallel, an equivalent Hebrew idea is introduced. In Proverbs 15,18 and 16,32 the phrases *'erek 'appayim* ("slow to anger") and *mōšēl bᵉrûḥô* ("one who rules his temper") appear to signify the positive human type, while in Proverbs 14,29 *qᵉṣar rûaḥ* ("short-tempered") symbolizes the negative type.

(c) The *integrative stage*. Integration of the Egyptian motif into the Hebrew tradition occurs, but it is still possible to trace the foreign sources. The inspiration of Ps. 1 and Jer. 17, 5-8 was undoubtedly the poem in chapter 4 of *Amenemope* concerning the "hot" and the "silent" man.[178]

Bryce's theory, while indeed innovative, does not withstand criticism. It is impossible to suppose that, after an interval of thousands of years from the time of the composition of the works under discussion, a precise diagnosis of the kind presented above can arrived at — the result can never be more than conjecture and inevitably remains subject to the arbitrary judgment of the researcher.[179]

(2) Nouns synonymous or conceptually associated with *'îs ḥēmâ*

(a) *'îš/ba'al ḥēmâ* appears in synonymous parallelism with *ba'al/'îš 'ap* (Prov. 22,24; 29,22; see also BS 8,16) and interchanges with it (cf. Prov. 15,18 with 29,22). The collocation *ba'al/'îš 'ap* like *'îš/ba'al ḥēmâ*, is constructed from a noun expressing anger, *'ap*, together with the words *'îš*, *ba'al*. Like *'îš ḥēmâ*, *ba'al/'îš 'ap* serves as an epithet for a human type only in the wisdom literature (Prov., BS). Outside this genre it usually refers to the anger of God.[180]

The collocation *'îš/ba'al 'ap*, unlike *'îš ḥēmâ*, is an independent Hebrew linguistic usage and should not be seen as the result of external influence. The use of the term *'ap* in reference to anger is rare or absent in other languages. In Egyptian, as we have seen, the term *fnḏ* does indeed appear in the double sense of a bodily organ and anger, but the use of *fnḏ* to signify anger is rare in the Egyptian wisdom literature (only one occurrence).[181]

ba'al/'îš 'ap, like *'îš ḥēmâ*, is a man ready for a quarrel (Prov. 29,22; 22, 24,25). His antonym is *'erek 'appayim*, literally a man "long of face," that is, a man who is slow to anger and in control of his temper. *'erek 'appayim* appears in antithetic parallelism with *'îš ḥēmâ* (15,18) and *qᵉṣar rûaḥ* (14,29).[182]

(b) The phrases *'erek rûaḥ*, *qar rûaḥ*, *qᵉṣar rûaḥ/'appayim* also belong to the subject under survey, although they do not stand in parallelism with *'îš/ba'al ḥēmâ* or *'îš/ba'al 'ap*. *'erek rûaḥ* and *qar rûaḥ* have a similar meaning to *'erek 'appayim*,[183] while *qᵉṣar rûaḥ* is similar in sense to *qᵉṣar 'appayim* (Prov. 14,17) and appears as an attributive of a man only in Proverbs 14,29.[184] (Cf. also *'ên ma'ṣār lᵉrûḥô*, "he who has no rule over his own spirit," Prov. 25,28).

(c) Finally, the motif of the negative human type characterized by qualities of anger and the tendency towards contentiousness also includes the terms *'îš midyānîm* and *zēd*, mentioned in the above.

(3) Conclusion

The human type *'îš/ba'al ḥēmâ* may be seen as the Hebrew counterpart of the Egyptian *šmm*. *'îš ḥēmâ* is the phonetic, etymological and semantic equivalent of the Egyptian term. Moreover, what we have before us is probably a case of borrowing or imitation of the Egyptian linguistic usage and concept. Regarding the expressions synonymous with it, *ba'al/'îš 'ap* and *qeṣar/rûaḥ, 'appayim*, these are close to the Egyptian parallel in terms of content but do not indicate a direct contact. We cannot regard them as confirmation for any stage (Bryce) of adaptation of the original Egyptian material to the Hebrew sphere. As we have shown, such a determination involves conjecture and lacks solid support.

CHAPTER FOUR

THE POSITIVE HUMAN TYPE — TRAITS AND PRACTICES QUIETNESS, CALMNESS, COOLNESS

The number of terms belonging to the semantic field of quietness, calmness, and coolness is considerably lower than of those relating to the opposite semantic field of strife and anger discussed in the previous chapter. It follows that the sage's doctrine is less a paean to the fine qualities of the wise man than a collection of moral admonitions directed at the person whose character is flawed and wanting. Nevertheless, the ideals of quietness and self-control hold pride of place in the *Weltanschauung* of the Egyptian sage and of his Hebrew counterpart. Words in praise of restraint — evinced principally in silence and in the avoidance of dispute and quarrel — are a consistent theme in Egyptian and Biblical wisdom, as we shall see in the following.

In Egyptian:

I. SEMANTIC ANALYSIS OF THE TERMS

1. *gr* (Dem. *g'*; Copt. [SAF] ϭω)[1]

gr[2] is the most common term in Egyptian for expressing "quietness," beginning with the Pyramid Texts and continuing up to the Late Period (*Wb.* V 179). In our corpus *gr* serves as verb or noun mainly in the instructions (33 times), the pessimistic wisdom (11 times) and the writings of the king's court (11 times). The principal meaning of *gr* is "to be quiet," "not to talk," as indicated by the determinative of a man sitting with his hand to his mouth. Used in this way, *gr* is in antithetic parallelism with "to talk": "If there is a quarrel do not talk, keep quiet (*gr.tw*) and it will be well for you," says Anii (4,1; cf. 3,11; *Kagemni* I 1; *Ptaḥḥotep* 365; *Insinger* 3,7); sometimes it stands with "mouth," "to be quiet with your mouth" (*Kagemni* II 1) and sometimes with the preposition *n* in the sense of "be silent in the presence of..." (*Ptaḥḥotep* 425; *Bologna* 1094 11,7).

"Quietness" usually carries a positive connotation, and it signifies avoidance of negative action, e.g., quarreling — Anii advises his son, "Stay away from hostile people, keep your heart quiet among fighters" (8,19-20; cf. *Amenemope* 22,7-8). "Quietness" also includes refraining from garrulity — in this context *gr* stands in parallelism with phrases consisted of a verb and the term *ib*, "heart":[3] "If you are a man of worth, who sits in his master's council, set your heart (*sȝḳ ib*) on excellence, be quiet, because it is profitable..." (*Ptaḥḥotep* 362 ff.; cf. the synonymous expression *ḫrp ib*, Janssen I p. 115, Gd 1; and its antonym *fḫ ib*, "release the heart," *Instruction by a Man for His Son* VII 4).

But at times there is condemnation of silence, when silence implies non-performance of positive acts; for example, being silent toward the violent man (*To Merikare* 110) or silence in response to the anarchy prevailing in the land (principally in the pessimistic literature — *Khakheperre-sonb* verso 2,4,5; *Neferti* 20; 38).

gr concerns not only social morality between man and man but also belongs to religious terminology and serves to describe the relationship between the believer and his god. The quality of "quietness" is one of the traits of the pious man, "the silent in the temple" (*Amenemope* 7,7). Gods too are qualified by this term, for example, Thoth (he is *pȝ ġrw* — *Sallier* I 8,5) and Osiris.[4] The god often appears in the hymnal literature as one who loves and protects the quiet man.[5] The epithet *grw*, *grw mȝʿ* plays a special role in Egyptian wisdom literature, which we shall discuss below.

1a. *sgr*

The causative form of *gr*, *sgr* appears as a verb and noun especially in the king's court writings and in the pessimistic literature.

As a verb its meaning is "to silence," its object having a negative connotation: the talkative mouth (*Neferti* 48), noise in the palace (*Urk.* IV 967,12), or a man whose behavior is crude — "loud of voice" (*kȝ ḫrw* — Janssen I p. 108, Fe 1). It has the meaning of "to becalm" when its object carries a positive connotation — a defenseless person or one of lowly rank, such as "weeping person," "child" (Janssen, ibid. 3; *To Merikare* 47; Blumenthal G 6,32).

As a noun, *sgr* usually appears in collocations in a religious context: *nb.t sgr* means "the realm of the dead" (*Wb.* IV 323,18); and *s.t sgȝ*, "a place of silence," appears once in our corpus (in *Anastasi* III 1,2).[6]

The epithet *nb sgr*, "lord of silence," designating Osiris, the god of the dead, is common: "The voice is not raised in the house of the 'lord of silence,'" says the vizier of Thutmosis III (*Urk.* IV 1031,9; cf. *The Peasant* B1 27-29).[7] The expression *s.t sgr* signifies the palace: Intef is "the silencer of noise" and "controller of foot (*ḫrp rḏ*) in the place of silence (*m s.t sgr*)" (*Urk.* IV 967, 12,14).

2. *sgrḥ* (Copt. [S] ⲥϭⲣⲁϩⲧ)

sgrḥ is the causative form of the verb *grḥ*, "to cease, complete"; the meaning of *sgrḥ* is "to make peaceful, pacify" in matters of war and conflict. As a noun it means "silence."[8] The determinative, like that of the foregoing terms, is a man with his hand to his mouth; but this may be replaced by a picture of forearm with the palm held downwards, indicating actions involving a hand movement (Gr D41), and in Demotic a drawing of a sail (Gr P5) designating a calming, pacifying action.

sgrḥ therefore is situated on the boundary between the semantic field of silence, rest, and the semantic field of pacification and peace. In the Coptic Version of the Bible ⲥϭⲣⲁϩⲧ is used for the phrases "the land is at rest" and "the land had rest" of the Masoretic text, describing a condition opposite to war.[9]

sgrḥ, which appears from the Middle Kingdom Period on, does not belong to the wisdom terminology, but it occurs extensively in the late *Instruction of Pap. Insinger.*[10] Here it has a similar function to that of *gr* and indicates quiet speech (22,7), calm conduct, which is the manner of the sage (10,3; 23,7,12; the opposite behavior characterizes the fool [*lḫ*] who is restless — 23,17) and the way of the pious man at divine service (23, 10, etc.).

3. *ḳb, ḳbb, (ḳbḥ)*[11] (Dem. *ḳb, ḳbꜥꜣ*; Copt. [S] ⲕⲃⲟ)[12]

The primary meaning of *ḳb*, also evident in the determinative — a water-pot from which water is pouring, sometimes accompanied by a sign for water (Gr W15) — is "coolness" in weather and cold water. The term became a metaphor applied to human beings, and in this usage it acquired the sense of "be calm, quiet, cool tempered." *ḳb* is found with this meaning in wisdom literature, where it has wide distribution in various literary genres, including the didactic and "loyalist" instructions, the school writings, the autobiographies and the king's court inscriptions. But it does not appear in the instructions of the New Kingdom Period (*Anii*, *Amenemope*) and the Late Period (*Ankhsheshonqy*, *Insinger*) and it is rare in the pessimistic wisdom (twice).

The original meaning of *ḳb* (*ḳbḥ*) is still recognizable in the metaphor describing the savior king in *The Admonitions of an Egyptian Sage*: "He will bring coolness (*ḳbḥw*) upon the heat (*tꜣw*)" (11, 13). The image is quite clear in light of similar passages: in *Seḥetep-ib-Ra* "he (the king) cools anger (lit. "noses" — *ḳbb fnḏ.w*),[13] he being far from rage (*nšni*)" (St 3,5); and in *Instruction by a Man for His Son* the mouth of the quiet man (*rꜣ n grw*) "makes coolness (*ḳbḥw*) among gabblers (*ꜥšꜣ.w ḫrw*)" (XIV 2).[14]

In figurative usage the verb *ḳb* indicates calm behavior, inactivity: while the enemy cannot keep quiet (*To Merikare* 68), the son, on the contrary, is asked to behave like a deaf person with restraint and coolness (*Instruction by a Man for His Son* XVIII 5). The biographers, furthermore, congratulate themselves for adhering to this way of behavior: "I am cool-tempered, I am calm" (*iw ḳbb.kwi hri.kwi* — Janssen I p. 35, Ba 3).[15] As an adverb, *ḳb* ("calmly") qualifies the verbs "sit" (*Bologna* 1094 4,7) and "speak" (*Anastasi* I 5,4).[16] The noun *ḳb*, "calmness," always has a positive connotation: the teacher is "a magistrate in calmness (*m ḳb*)" (*Lansing* 14, 3). In the collocation *gr ḳbb* it means "calmness of spirit" which is one of the qualities of the believer (cf. *R3jj's Stele*: Assmann, "Die 'loyalistische Lehre,'" 2; and *Urk.* IV 1195,11). Of importance and special interest is the attribute *ḳb*, "calm-tempered," which is found in the combinations *ḳb m3ʿ*, *ḳb ẖ.t*, *ḳbb srf*, *ḳb nmt.t*, and which couples with *grw*, the "silent man," in synonymous parallelism (see pp. 163–164).

4. *hrw* (Copt. [S]ϩⲣⲣⲉ)

The basic meaning of *hrw* is "be pleased, satisfied," and it is in synonymous parallelism with the term *ḥtp*, "be pleased";[17] but *hrw* also is found in the sense of "to calm, to be quiet." In Coptic ϩⲣⲣⲉ means "to cease, to quiet, to be still," and in the Coptic Version it stands for the stems *rgʿ*, *šqt* (hiphʿil) in the Masoretic text of the Bible.[18] *hrw* is not characteristic of the wisdom lexicon, its occurrence in the instructions and the school writings is relatively sparse and it is found frequently in the autobiographical and the king's court writings (Janssen; *Urk.* IV). But *hrw* is juxtaposed to and connected with the terms listed above belonging to the semantic field of "quietness, calmness." Therefore, the following discussion is restricted to examples in which *hrw* appears in this context.

One such example is the pairing of *hrw* with the "silent man" (*grw*) in synonymous parallelism: "The tent is open to the silent, the seat of the quiet (*hrw*) is spacious" (*Kagemni* I 1-2); it also appears in synonymous parallelism with *ḳb* (see the discussion of *ḳb* above).

In the sphere of quietness and calmness *hrw* is principally used as an adjective, in plain form (*hrw*) or in collocation (*hrw ib*, "of calm temperament";[19] *hrw nmt.t* "steady of pace," "of measured step" — see p. 164 below) and stands in contrast with *r3 t3* "the possessor of a hot mouth" (*The Autobiography of Anhurmose*, pl. 25, l. 35).

hrw is frequently involved with the art of speech. Our area of interest includes passages in which *hrw* refers to calming talk that settles the mood of those hearing it, its opposite being hasty, ill-considered speech, or irritative words. A priest of Amon of the 22nd Dynasty says: "I am he who extinguishes fire of speaking (*ʿḫm ḫ.t md.wt*) with calmness (*m hrw*)" (Otto No. 7 || *KCG* 42210 p.28, E6-7); while Rekhmire, who excels in self-adulation, says, "I am balanced (*srf ib*) in giving counsel, calmness to the listener" (*hrw r sḏm*) (*Urk.* IV 1082,9).[20]

4a. *shri*

Beginning with the Middle Kingdom the causative verb *shri* appears, meaning "to satisfy, to gladden" and also "to becalm" (*Wb.* IV 207-208). *shri* is not characteristic of the wisdom literature but belongs to the phraseology of the king's court. Here the idiom "calming mouth" (*rꜣ shrr*) is common, serving regularly to qualify the judge in the New Kingdom Period (many times in the inscriptions of the 18th Dynasty: *Urk.* IV 482,2; 486,16, etc; cf. also *KCG* 42236 p.85,B3 || Otto No. 19). The king appears as "the becalmer of the two lands" or the servant loyal to him is he who "quietens the land" on his behalf (Blumenthal 183, 384-385).

Summary

The resultant picture, therefore, is the following:

(1) The semantic field of quietness, calmness and coolness has six[21] terms in Egyptian, of which two are the causative form of the basic stem — less than half the number in the opposite semantic field of quarrel and anger.

(2) Most of the determinatives accompanying the terms carry the sense of quietness, calm and coolness: "quietness" is depicted by a man sitting with his hand to his mouth (*gr*, *sgr*, *sgrḥ*); "calm" and "coolness" are illustrated by a sign of water, a pot from which water is being poured out (*ḳb*), and a sail, signifying a gust of wind (Dem. *sgrḥ*).

(3) The significant proximity among the lexemes belonging to this semantic field is expressed not only by the external sign of common determinatives but also in linguistic usages and style:

(a) The terms are combined with identical words:

with *nmt.t*, "stride"— *ḳb nmt.t*; *hrw nmt.t*
with *mꜣꜥ*, "justice" — *gr mꜣꜥ*; *ḳb mꜣꜥ*.

(b) The terms are coupled in synonymous parallelism or appear in collocation:

hrw || *gr* ; *ḳb* || *gr* ; *gr ḳbb*

(c) The terms stand in conjunction, in parallelism, or in contrast with idioms and phrases that are identical or similar:

(i) *ḳ3 ḫrw*, "loud of voice," appears in antithesis to *grw*, *sgr* and *ḳb* (see above and also p. 163 below), while *ʿš3 ḫrw*, "large of voice," i.e., "prattler," appears in antithesis to *hrw*.

(ii) *fḫ ib*, "to release the heart" appears in antithetic parallelism to *gr*, while *pri.t ib*, bearing a synonymous meaning, "to take out the heart," appears antithetically to *hrw*.

(iii) The term *srf*, "fire," "flame," is connected with three of the terms: *gr* is the opposite of *srf* — the *grw* ("silent man") appears as one who suppresses a flame — *d3r srf*; *ḳb* is collocated with it — *ḳb srf*, "of easy temperament," and *hrw* stands in synonymous parallelism with *d3r srf*, "he who suppresses a flame."

(iv) *ḳmi sp.ty*, "sealed of lips" is an expression synonymous to *grw* and *hrw* (*ib*).

(4) Table 7: Semantic Definition of the Egyptian Terms Relating to the Field of Quietness, Calmness, Coolness

		gr	*sgr*	*sgrḥ*	*ḳb(ḳbḥ)*	*hrw*	*shri*
Causitive verb			+	+			+
Refers to speech		+	+	+	+	+	+
Expresses restraint and self control		+			+	+	
The opposite: strife, anger		+		+*	+	+	+
Refers to:	man	+	+	+	+	+	+
	god	+	+	+			
Religious Connotation		+	+	+	+**	+	+
Signifies a human type		+			+	+	

* In the sense of "war."

** *ḳb nmt.t* .

(5) Frequency of the terms: *gr* is the most common for the idea of quietness and restraint (65 times), followed by *hrw* (50 times).

Over half the appearances of *gr* (i.e., 28) are concentrated in the instructions beginning with the earliest (*Kagemni*) and ending with the latest (*Ankhsheshonqy*, *Insinger*). Therefore, there is no doubt that *gr* belongs to the vocabulary of the Egyptian sage. This term also has a wider distribution than the other terms and is found in all genres relating to wisdom.

hrw, which is not characteristic of the wisdom language, is second to *gr* in frequency. It appears in all literary genres of our sample except for the "loyalist" instructions and the religious literature.

ḳb, which is the third most frequent term (28 times), is already found in the didactic literature linked to the Old Kingdom Period (*Ptaḥḥotep*) and the First Intermediate Period (*To Merikare*), but its use intensifies in the New Kingdom in compositions not relating to the instruction genre. *ḳb* is found principally in the rhetoric of the king's court during the 18th Dynasty (11 times) and in the school writings (5 times).

sgrḥ, which occurs seldom in the present corpus, appears in the late *Instruction of Pap. Insinger* and in the king's court inscriptions.

shri does not pertain to the wisdom vocabulary and appears only in the biographical writings of the king's court.

The following terms are used to signify the "silent," "cold-tempered" human type (see discussion Section IIB below):

grw, *grw mȝʿ* (23 times) — mainly in the instructions (8 times) and the biography of the the king's court (8 times);

hrw, *hrw ib/nmt.t* (20 times) — mainly in the royal biography (19 times) and in the instructions (once);

ḳb, *ḳb/ẖ.t/srf/mȝʿ* (14 times) — mainly in the royal biography (8 times), late autobiography (3 times), instructions (twice) and school writings (once).

II. SUBJECT MATTER ANALYSIS OF THE TERMS

A. The Motif of Quietness and Accompanying Circumstances

Quietness is a central concept in the Egyptian sage's world of values. Since it has been treated as such in a comprehensive article by E. Brunner-Traut which contains quotations from a variety of Egyptian sources,[22] the following discussion will be restricted to representative examples from the wisdom writings.

The circumstances under which quietness receives its important value show a wide variance.

1. Quietness for social reasons

(a) A wish not to injure others:

(i) Gossip is considered a crime in the wisdom outlook. In the school writings the pupil is admonished with the following: "Do not slander and refrain from speaking..." (*Bologna* 1094 11, 7); in *The Instruction of Ptaḥḥotep* the son is told: "Do not repeat slander nor should you listen to it, it is the spouting of the hot-bellied..." (350-353; cf. *Anii* 3,11).[23]

(ii) Recourse to silence is recommended in matters of strife and dispute; in the colorful language of the author of *Amenemope*: "Sit yourself in the arms of god and your silence will destroy them (your opponents). The crocodile that makes no sound, dread of it is ancient" (22, 7-10). This means that silence during an argument rewards the silent one with general attention and brings honor, the crocodile, with which the silent man is compared being the best proof of this;[24] likewise *Anii*: "If there is a quarrel, do not talk, be silent and it will be well for you" (3,17-4,1; and cf. 8,16-20; 9,7-10). Coolness of temperament is a quality that appears repeatedly in the autobiographical and the king's court writings. The ideal king is he who "cools noses" (i.e., anger) (*Seḥetep-ib-Ra* St 3,5; cf. *Admonitons* 11, 13ff.).

(iii) The talkative man stirs up rebellion: "A talker is a mischief-maker; suppress him, kill [his children], erase his name... The hothead is an inciter of citizens, he creates factions among the young... suppress (him), he is a rebel; a talker is a mischief-maker for the city; bend the multitude and drive out hot temper (*tꜣw*) from it" (*To Merikare* 23ff.; 27ff.).

(b) Silence out of politeness:

Silence is one of the principles of table etiquette. Thus the Egyptian sage states: "If you are one of the guests at the table of one greater than you... do not speak to him until he summons..." (*Ptaḥḥotep* 119-126). "You sit with your hand on your mouth, do not ask anything of him (the master)..." (*Kheti* XXIV C-D).

2. Silence as self-discipline

The wisdom lexicon is rich in phrases and formulas referring to restraint and self-control. "Conceal your thoughts, control your mouth," says Ptaḥḥotep to his son (618). The ideal official is "he who conceals his thoughts, hides the counsel of his belly" (*Urk.* IV 1198, 12, 13). The explanation for this requirement is given in *The Instruction of Amenemope*: "Better is a man whose speech is in his belly than he who tells it to cause harm" (22, 15-16). To express this idea the wisdom language employs phrases which combine a verb and parts of the body, such as: "Control one's mouth" (*ḥn rꜣ*), "closed of mouth" (*ḥꜣp rꜣ*), "sealed of lips" (*ḳmi sp.ty*), "control of one's thoughts" (lit. "heart") (*sꜣḳ ib*), "suppress one's desires" (lit. "sink the heart") (*ḫrp ib*), "suppress once's thoughts" (lit. "heart") (*dꜣr ib*), "hide one's belly" (*ḥꜣp ẖ.t*).[25]

3. Silence on account of religion

The Egyptian believer displays his faith and his devotion in quiet and calm behavior during divine service. The instructions repeatedly call for silence while offering sacrifices in the temple (*Anii* 4,1-4; *Insinger* 23,10[26]) or while engaged in activity at the necropolis, whose epithet is "the place of quiet." The gods — Amon, Osiris and Sobek-Reʿ — are "lords of silence."[27] The priest whose behavior follows this pattern may take pride in being the "possessor of balanced steps" (*ḳb nmt.t*) in the holy of holies and in not "raising his voice" (Otto No. 70,8; 75,9).[28]

The examples given above indicate that "quietness" means avoidance of an act or speech that are injurious, but it does not mean silence out of helplessness or submission. Therefore, together with statements in praise of silence there are others that condemn silence when it is not appropriate and untimely. In the pessimistic wisdom literature (*The Peasant*, *Neferti*) the leaders are condemned for their silence and unwillingness to act against rife injustice. And in the didactic instruction the sages laud apt speech spoken at the right time. The author of *Pap. Insinger* advises "Do not let yourself be called an 'idiot' (*bne*) because of silence when it is time to speak" (3,7).[29]

B. The "Silent Man"

What is the meaning of *grw* in Egyptian? Does it refer to a trait, one of the qualities of the ideal human type in the Egyptian wisdom? Or is "silent" a general definition of this type, covering all his characteristics? Does the way of life embodied in this figure belong to the social sphere or the religious sphere, or to both? Is *grw* identical with the collocation *grw mȝʿ*, which begins to appear in the New Kingdom Period? These questions may be answered by way of an analysis of the context wherein the term "silent man" appears. The most useful references for this purpose are those in which the "silent man" appears in contrast or as a complement to terms signifying human types or human characteristics (Sections 1 and 2, below) and passages whose *Sitz im Leben* and creative circle are certain, whether the king's court, the school or the temple (Section 3).

1. The *grw* and the *šmm*

In two passages the "silent man" (*grw* or *grw mȝʿ*) appears together with the *šmm*,[30] in *The Instruction of Amenemope* and in *Pap. Sallier* I.

The important section is chapter 4 of *The Instruction of Amenemope*,[31] where the setting of the events is clear and indicated in the opening line of the chapter, namely, the "temple." This is the only passage in the Egyptian instruction compositions where the "silent man" appears in direct contrast with the "hot-tempered man."

The *šmm* and the *grw mꜣ‘* are compared to trees: the *šmm* is a tree growing in a forest (or within the temple), while the *grw mꜣ‘* is like a tree growing in a garden (or a place bathed in sunlight). The contrast is thus between a tree growing wild and one that has been cultivated (or between a sickly tree growing in the shade without sun and a tree growing in sunshine in a garden).[32] The fate of the *šmm* is bitter. Its burgeoning is brief and its end is sudden. Its loss is two-fold — it is inundated by water and burnt in fire, and in the end is buried far from the place of its growth.[33] The destiny of the "silent man" is the opposite. He prospers (lit. "greens") and sends forth a double quantity of sweet fruit. He is placed before "his lord" (the god) and his end is natural — in the place of his growth, the garden.

The text does not elucidate the misconduct of the *šmm*. This is indirectly suggested, however, by the contrastive structure of the passage. The "silent man" is described as one who "sets himself apart" (line 7), that is, he is a modest man who keeps to himself. We may infer that the *šmm* possesses opposite traits and different manners.[34] The *šmm*'s way of life and attitude to divine service (which is the setting of chapter 4) are set forth in the wisdom literature in verses all concerned with the ritual procedures and the conduct of the believer in the temple:
Anii 4, 1-4:

> Do not raise your voice in the house of god
> He abhors shouting.
> Pray with loving heart, whose every word is hidden.
> He will grant your needs
> He will hear your words
> He will accept your offering.

Insinger 23, 10:

If there is no calm in a temple its gods abandon it.

Pap. Chester Beatty IV pl. 20 verso 5, 1-2:

> Do not ask the god. The god does not approve of him
> who approaches too closely.

(Cf. also *Amenemope* 25, 5; Otto No. 75, 9).

The concept underlying these statements is that the believer must ensure that his intention is pure during divine service; external ceremony is no proof of devotion to the god. The *šmm*, who parades his faith by shouting and through constant presence in the temple, is rejected and sent away empty-handed. But the "silent man" (*grw m3ʿ*) of humble mien, who prays silently with a loving heart, wins grace owing to his moral virtues.[35]

Chapter 4 of *Amenemope*, then, shows the "silent man" as a pious man, devout in his heart to the god, while the "hot-tempered man" is one who only makes a pretence of believing, whose piety is external. A similar description of the "hot-tempered man" is found in *Ostracon Deir el Médineh* 1265, where he is depicted as one incapable of fulfilling the cultic instructions and who fails in his ritual enterprises.[36]

The idea that the god is revealed to the "silent" believer but remains concealed from the "hot-tempered" man is expressed in the hymn to the god Thoth in *Pap. Sallier* I:

> Come that you may rescue me, the silent one (*p3 grw*)
> Thoth (you are) a pleasant well (*ẖnm.t nḏm.t*)
> to the thirsty man [in] a desert;
> It is sealed to him that finds its mouth
> (but) it is open to the silent one(*p3 grw*).
> The silent one came and found the well
> and the heated man (*p3 šmm*)... (8, 5-6).

At the beginning of the passage (8,4ff.) the god of wisdom is compared to a palm tree whose fruit has kernels containing water. This image refers to wisdom which is hard to attain. Wisdom pictured as hidden water[37] is repeated later: the god Thoth, the god of wisdom, is compared to a well of sweet water that quenches a man's thirst in the wilderness;[38] the "hot-tempered" man cannot find the well, but the "silent man" finds it. The moral here is identical with that of *Amenemope* chapter 4: the "silent man" can look forward to a happy fate while the end of the "hot-tempered man" is bitter.

2. Expressions other than *šmm* attached to *grw* (syntagmatic analysis)

By examining of the expressions associated with *grw* that serve as its antonym, synonym or complement, it is possible to determine its semantic field.

(a) Lexemes with which *grw* stands in contrast:

thi mtn — the "disobedient man"; when juxtaposed to the "silent man" his habit of excessive talking is emphasized (*Kagemni* I 2-3).

ʿwnty — the "greedy man" who accumulates property by theft (*Amenemope* 10, 6ff.).

ḳ3 ḫrw — the "loud of voice," namely, he who is noisy during divine service in the temple (*ÄHG* 195, 56) and makes himself heard in the cemetery, the "house of silence" (Otto p. 68; No. 41; No. 65, 10-11).[39]

(b) Expressions with which *grw* stands in synonymous or complementary parallelism:

snḏw — the "modest, humble man" (*Kagemni* I 1).

mty/mty ḥ3.ty — the "precise, straight-thinking man" (ibid. and *Urk.* IV 993,7) and *ʿḳ3 s.t ns* — "straight of speech" (ibid. 6).

hrw — "calm" (*Kagemni* I 2).

ḳb/ḳb srf — "cool-tempered" (*Urk.* IV 1181, 14; Janssen p. 35 Ba 7).

nb ḳd — "man of character" (*Ptaḥḥotep* 167); *nfr bi.t* — "good character" (*To Merikare*, in the colophon; *The Autobiography of Anhurmose*, pl. 25, l. 34 [Ockinga, *El Mashayikh*]).

w3ḥ ib — "kind" (Anhurmose, ibid.).

šw grg — "without falsehood" (Janssen I p. 115, Gd 5).

ḳb and *hrw* are exceptions in this list. Unlike the other terms, they do not relate to a particular human trait but define a human type. *ḳb* and *hrw* are found in this sense together with *grw* principally in the autobiographical writings beginning with the Middle Kingdom and in the inscriptions of the 18th Dynasty (*Urk.* IV). Here both *ḳb* and *hrw* refer to the high official in the service of the king.

The cool-tempered man, the *ḳb*[40] — which is also found in the combinations *ḳb(b) srf* ("cool-tempered," lit. "extinguisher of heat"),[41] *ḳb ẖ.t*[42] ("cold-bellied"), *ḳb mꜣʿ* ("the truly cool-tempered")[43] and *ḳb nmt.t* ("cool, calm of stride")[44] — is the antonym of *šmm* and *tꜣ*.[45]

ḳb in plain form and in collocations stands in antithetic parallelism with "man of strife" (*šnty*), "high of temperature" (*ḳꜣ srf*) and "loud of voice" (*ḳꜣ/šd ḫrw*).[46] *ḳb* is synonymous not only with *grw* but also with *hrw*.[47] The following attributes indicate his qualities: he "suppresses heat" (*dꜣr srf*), that is, he is restrained;[48] he is one "without haste" (*šw m ḥꜣḫ*) who "goes according to his steps" (*šm r nmt.t.f*).[49]

ḳb, then, is a man restrained in his conduct, with calm prevailing in all his actions, one who considers his actions and avoids loud speech and altercations.

The calm man — the *hrw* — is present also in the collocations *hrw ib* ("of calm temper")[50] and *hrw nmt.t* ("of calm step").[51] *hrw* is in synonymous parallelism with the adjectives "modest," "exact," "silent" (*Kagemni* I 1-2). The adjective *hrw ib* is especially common in the phraseology of the king's court of the 18th Dynasty, but it is already amply represented in the biographical writings of the 12th Dynasty.

A man described as *hrw* has the following virtues: "efficacious in speech" (lit. "excellent of sayings" — *mnḫ ṯsw*), "controlled" (lit. "extinguisher of heat" — *dꜣr srf*), "possessor of patience" (lit. "free of taking out the heart" — *šm m pri.t ib*),[52] and "sealed of lips" (*ḳmi sp.ty*).[53] The expression *hrw nmt.t*, which is abundant in the biographical writings of the 12th Dynasty, is synonymous with the idioms "obedient" (*mḏd wꜣ.t/mṯn*),[54] "steady of sandal" (*mn ṯb.t*) and "excellent of speech" (*iḳr s.t ns*).[55]

The figure that emerges here is remarkably similar to the human type depicted by the previous term *ḳb*. *hrw* is a man who keeps a secret, obeys his superiors, is versed in the art of speech and is able through his counsel and statements to instil calm in his listeners. *hrw* is a person accomplished in his manners and actions, and one who causes pleasure and satisfaction in others.

3. The ideal human being

The characteristics described above together constitute the image of the ideal man: The *grw*, the *hrw* and the *ḳb* signify a man who is perfect in his behavior in all areas of life — the "silent man." This human type is the embodiment of all the qualities and traits that are sought by the sage on the social level as well as in the sphere of religion and faith.[56]

The "silent man" is he who is thoughtful in manner and modest in conduct; he eschews strife and garrulousness; he is kind and gives of his possessions to others; he is honest and obedient towards his superiors. The "silent man" is the devoted pious man, and his lips and heart are one. The contrasting type is not merely the prattler but one possessing a whole set of negative traits and flaws manifested in excessive activity and covetousness. The "silent man" is not an ideal restricted to a particular class, status or profession: The epithet and its synonyms apply equally to the high officials in the king's service (the vizier — *Ptaḥḥotep*, *Kagemni*; courtiers of the 18th Dynasty [*Urk.* IV] and of the later dynasties [*The Autobiography of Anhurmose*, pl. 25, l. 34; Jansen-Winkeln I B 28,1; B 29,1]); the scribe (*To Merikare*,[57] *Amenemope*, *Hatnub*, *Anastasi* II [11,2]); and the common folk: the Eloquent Peasant describes himself and his peers as "silent men" (B1 285, 298). From this early definition of the downtrodden class as "silent," the term "silent man" apparently developed later to signify the pious man, he who faithfully performed the divine service. The believer wishing to appear before his god in humility and meekness of spirit would call himself "silent" and "poor."[58]

To sum up, the "silent man" is not an ideal only of the officialdom or the court, as several scholars have claimed.[59] It refers to every class of people in various walks of life whether in the country, the school,[60] the king's court, or the cultic institutions. This image constitutes a central motif in Egyptian wisdom, one with an ancient tradition starting in the Old Kingdom (*Kagemni*) and whose imprint is still evident in the writings of the Coptic church.[61]

4. The development of the motif of the "silent man" — the *grw* and the *grw mȝ'*

Our survey shows that the Egyptians in order to describe the human ideal had at their disposal a set of phrases and figures of speech. This vocabulary changes and undergoes transformations according to the concepts and considerations prevalent in different periods. In the early period social behavior stood very much in the forefront, as is evident in the didactic instruction and the pessimistic wisdom of the First Intermediate Period and the Middle Kingdom. During this period all the positive attributes of social morality were attached to the figure of the ideal man, the "silent" one. Later, when the emphasis shifted to the relationship between man and his god and with the growth of personal piety — the first signs being evident in *The Instruction of Amenemope* — the "silent man" began to appear in religious context. The "silent man" now bore the sense of "pious man."[62] Not that the "silent man" had altered in significance, but stress was now laid on his personal contact with the god. The god Thoth is described as imparting his wisdom to him and the god Amon is defined as his savior. This development found its expression in the terms *grw* and *grw mȝʿ*.

The "silent" and the "truly silent" — the *grw* and the *grw mȝʿ*:

The term *grw mȝʿ*, less common than *gr* (6 times in the present sample), stands, as stated, in contrast to *šmm* in *Amenemope* chapter 4. It is also present there as an epithet for the scribe *Amenemope* (2,7) and it is an attribute of the scribe who copied *The Instruction to Merikare* (colophon 145, 149).[63] Menkheperre-sonb, Amon's priest at the time of Thutmosis III, styles himself as *grw mȝʿ* (*Urk.* IV 993,3) and similarly the Libyan prince of the seventh century B.C. who is "*grw mȝʿ* ... expert in praising the gods" (Jansen-Winkeln I A23,a2, II 3,6,2;3,6,20). *grw mȝʿ* appears yet again in chapter 7 of *The Instruction of Amenemope*, this time in contrast with the "greedy" (*ʿwn ib*): "The boat of the greedy is left (in) the mud, while the bark of the truly silent sails in the wind" (10,10-11). As in chapter 4, here too the theme, expressed metaphorically, is the good fortune of the silent man and the evil fortune of the opposite type, but this time the image is not taken from the world of nature but from that of sailing. Again the background is religious, as shown by the subsequent lines which state that god is the bestower of life's necessities and therefore there is no need for covetousness (ibid. 12-15).

From the sources presented above it is clear that *grw mꜣʿ* is not found prior to the 18th Dynasty and it does not replace *grw*, which continues to appear together with it. Since in four out of the six times the term occurs in a religious context we assume that *gr.w mꜣʿ* belongs to religious terminology;[64] *grw* applies to both the social and the religious sphere since (a) *grw* is found in a religious setting in synchronistic use with *grw mꜣʿ* (cf. *Amenemope* chapter 5 — "All the silent in the temple"; and *Sallier* I, p. 162 above); and (b) we find a parallel linguistic development in the use of the terms *ḳb* and *ḳb mꜣʿ*. *ḳb* is already found in the El Amarna texts in a religious context (*The Rꜣjj's Stele* [pp. 153–154 above], *KCG* 917), but in the late autobiography it appears in the collocation *ḳb mꜣʿ* (Otto).[65]

In sum, the term *grw* refers to social morality and is also associated with religious belief. The *grw mꜣʿ*, which appears together with it from the New Kingdom onwards, belongs to the ethical- religious terminology and reflects the development of the Egyptian outlook from a focus on social to religious ethics. The *gr* then becomes not only the ideal man in the social context but also the ideal pious man, i.e., a *grw mꜣʿ*, a man who behaves according to the laws of order, which apply to the entire world, the *mꜣʿ.t*.[66]

In the Bible

I. SEMANTIC ANALYSIS OF THE BIBLICAL TERMS AS COMPARED WITH THE EGYPTIAN

The ideal of silence and calm is also expressed in the vocabulary of Hebrew wisdom, but, unlike the Egyptian, the topic here is not central, and the relevant terminology is not characteristic of the wisdom literature. The following discussion, therefore, will be limited to a comparison with the Egyptian material (Section A). However, the ideal of restraint and self-control embodied in the Egyptian "silent man" does occupy an important place in the thinking of the Biblical sage. The terms belonging to this sphere are typical of the wisdom lexicon and the subsequent analysis (Section B) is devoted to them.

A. Terms Belonging to the Semantic Field of Silence in the Bible but not Characteristic of the Sage's Vocabulary

1. *ḥrš*

ḥrš, as noted above (Chapter 3, pp. 92–93), has a double meaning "to be silent," "not to speak," and "to be deaf" (cf. Aram., Arab.). We believe that the semantic development of *ḥrš* was from the concrete sense of being deaf to the abstract sense of being silent. Thus *ḥrš* only partially parallels the corresponding Egyptian words.

However, *ḥrš* — the subject of which is usually man, rarely God — is the most common term in the Bible expressing the concept of quietness.

ḥrš is far more frequent in Job than in any other wisdom book (9 times), where it appears as an intransitive verb in contrast to "to speak" (*dbr*) (13,13; 33,31). Once it is present as a transitive verb meaning "to silence" (11,2). For our purposes the following verses are important: "Teach me and I will be silent (*'aḥărîš*)" (6,24); "Be silent (*haḥărēš*) and I will teach you wisdom" (33,33). In these verses the didactic tone is evident, being reminiscent of the command directed at the pupil in the Egyptian school: "You will make calculations quietly (*gr*); let no sound from your mouth be heard" (*Anastasi* V 23,4).

In Proverbs *ḥrš* appears twice as a quality of the sage, similar to *sgrḥ* in *The Instruction of Pap. Insinger* (cf. above): "A man of understanding remains silent (*yaḥărîš*)" (11,12; cf. 17,28; Job 13,5).

The roots closest to the Egyptian *gr*, *sgr*, and *sgrḥ* are *štq* and *šqṭ* in Hebrew, but these are rare in the wisdom language as is shown below.

2. *štq*

štq belongs to Late Biblical Hebrew (*BDB* 1060). It appears only four times in the Bible — once in Proverbs 26,20, which resembles the passages cited in Egyptian: "Where there is no slanderer, strife is quieted (*yištōq*)"; cf. *Anii* 4,1: "If there is a quarrel do not speak, be silent (*gr.tw*) and it will serve you well" (and also ibid. 8,19; *Instruction by a Man for His Son* XV 6; *Seḥetep-ib-Ra* 3,5; etc.).

3. *šqṭ*

The use of *šqṭ* is rare in wisdom literature (5 times in Proverbs and Job out of 38 times in the Bible). In Job it is present as an intransitive verb (qal), meaning "to be silent": Job, cursing the day of his birth, says, "I have no ease and no quiet (*šāqaṭtî*) and no rest and torment comes" (3,26; cf. ibid. 13); and as a transitive verb (hiph'il), meaning "to quiet someone": God is described as one who quiets the cry of the poor and the needy (ibid. 34,29), like the Egyptian god who appears as the "redeemer of the poor" and the "lord of the silent."[67] In Proverbs *šqṭ* is found only once, as a transitive verb: "He who is slow to anger quiets (*yašqîṭ*) strife" (15,18). In this usage *šqṭ* is close to *sgrḥ* in Egyptian, both serving to describe the land in times of peace (see, e.g., Zech. 1, 11, and cf. *sgrḥ* above).

4. *ḥšh*

ḥšh appears in poetic language, predominantly, in the later texts (16 times). Its primary meaning is "to remain silent" in contrast to "to speak." Thus in the famous catalogue of the seasons in Qoheleth 3,7 it is said: "A time to keep silence (*laḥăšôt*) and a time to speak." (Cf. the Egyptian awareness of the "timing" of silence: "Do not let yourself be called 'idiot' [*bne*] because of silence when it is time to speak" — *Insinger* 3,7).

5. *dmy/dmm/dwm*[68]

The root *dmm* is frequent in the Bible (62 times), but in the wisdom literature it is found only in Job (4 times) and in the wisdom Psalm (Ps. 37). Its primary meaning is probably silence through fear and dread: Job says, "Because I dreaded the great multitude, and the contempt of clans terrified me, I kept silent (*wa'eddōm*), not going out of the door" (31,34). *dmm* has several meanings, all having inactivity of speech and movement in common:[69] in the description of Job's days of splendor, the silence of the people in expectation of his words is mentioned: "Men listened to me, and waited, and kept silence (*weyiddemû*) for my counsel" (29,21; cf. Ps. 37,7); while in Job 30,27 *dmm* has the meaning of "stillness," "silence" — as opposed to excitement, described there as "boiling of bowels."

The noun *d^e^māmâ* appears once in Job 4,16 and concerns the theophany, which is accompanied by "a still (*d^e^māmâ*) small voice" (cf. 1 Kgs. 19,12).

There is no similarity between the Biblical use of *dmm* and the Egyptian terms apart from the nominal form *dûmâ*. This appears as an epithet for She'ol in Psalms (94,17; 115,17) and parallels the Egyptian *nb.t sgr*, signifying the abode of the dead as "the realm of silence."

6. *šlw*

Among the Hebrew terms belonging to the semantic field of "silence," "quietness," *šlw* is the closest to the Egyptian *hrw*. *šlw* (adj. *šalēw*; n. *šalwâ*) commonly appears in later Biblical literature and is present eight times in the wisdom texts.[70]

šalwâ is found here, as in the Egyptian, in contrast to *rîb* ("strife"): "Better is a dry morsel with quiet (*šalwâ*) than a house full of sacrifices with strife (*rîb*)" (Prov. 17,1). *šalwâ* is a quality of the successful man (BS 41,1); on the other hand, in the pessimistic literature the wise man bemoans the *šalwâ* of wicked men (Job 21,23; wisdom Ps. 73,12; the opposite in Job 20,20). *šalwâ* is found once in a negative connotation, meaning inactivity through irresponsibility: "And fools are destroyed by their complacency (*šalwâ*)" (Prov. 1,32).[71]

B. Terms Characteristic of Hebrew Wisdom that Have a Link with the Egyptian

1. Hebrew parallels of the Egyptian human types — *grw*, *hrw*, *ḳb(b)*

While the antonym of the "silent man," namely, the "heated man" (*'îš ḥēmâ*), is mentioned in Proverbs, a figure identical to the Egyptian "silent man" is absent from the wisdom books of the Bible. Nevertheless, the Hebrew sage uses several terms which are coupled in antithetic parallelism with *'îš ḥēmâ*. These terms expressing the motif of self-control and restraint are in fact the parallels of the Egyptian ideal human type, the "silent man," as is shown in the following lines.

(a) *'erek 'appayim* ("slow to anger"): This adjective applies to a man of self-discipline, he who is tolerant and restrained. In this usage it appears only in Proverbs (14,29; 15,18; 16,32).[72] In other books it usually refers to God. In Proverbs it appears in various circumstances concerned with restraint in a social setting:

(i) Suppression of strife and anger: Anger and contentiousness are among the traits of the *'îš ḥēmâ*, *qeṣar rûaḥ* and *gebah rûaḥ*, the antonyms of *'erek 'appayim*, in the following words of the sage: "a hot-tempered man (*'îš ḥēmâ*) stirs up strife but *'erek 'appayim* quiets contention" (Prov. 15,18); "*'erek 'appayim* has great discernment but the short tempered man (*qeṣar rûaḥ*)[73] exalts folly (*'iwwelet*)" (14,29) (cf. also BS 1,23 [Gr.]).

The phrase *'erek rûaḥ*, found in Qoheleth, is synonymous in meaning to *'erek 'appayim* and contrasts with *gebah rûaḥ* ("proud man"). "Better is the slow in spirit (*'erek rûaḥ*) than the proud in spirit (*gebah rûaḥ*)," says Qoheleth (7,8). Here too the sage tends to preach control of anger which (cf. Prov. 14,29, above) is the business of fools: "Do not be quick to anger for anger lodges in the bosom of stupid men" (Qoh. 7,9).

(ii) Forgiveness for offense: The stature of a man is reflected in his ability to forgive an injury. "Good sense makes a man slow to anger (*he'ĕrîk 'appô*), and it is his glory to overlook an offense" (Prov. 19,11; cf. BS 30,22).

(iii) Proficiency in rhetoric: He who is expert in the art of speech is not quick to use his tongue, a quality which is important in the king's court, as the sage asserts: "With patience (*'ōrek 'appayim*) a ruler may be persuaded and a soft tongue will break a bone" (Prov. 25,15; cf. BS 5,11).

(b) *qar rûaḥ*: Coldness and water symbolize ideal behavior in Egyptian wisdom. The expression *qar rûaḥ*, which is the semantic equivalent of the Egyptian *ḳb(b)*,[74] appears once in the Bible in Proverbs 17,27. *qar rûaḥ*, called here "man of understanding," stands in parallelism with the "one who *ḥôśēk 'ămārāyw*," i.e., he who restrains his words. *qar rûaḥ*, like *'îš ḥēmâ*, is undoubtedly a term borrowed from the Egyptian wisdom and adapted for Hebrew by the combination of the noun *rûaḥ* and the adjective *qar*. The opposite of *qar rûaḥ* is *qᵉṣar rûaḥ* ("short-tempered") (Prov. 14,29) and a man who has no *ma'ṣār lᵉrûḥô* ("curb to his spirit," i.e., is without self-control), who is like a breached city without a wall, defenseless (Prov. 25,28).[75]

(c) *šᵉpal rûaḥ* ("low of spirit"), *ṣanûa'* ("modest"), *'ānāw* ("humble"): Modesty and humility also are listed among the virtues of the ideal human type in the Egyptian sapiential outlook.[76] The same motif is found in Biblical wisdom in the following expressions: The collocation *šᵉpal rûaḥ*, which is exclusive to Proverbs (16,19; 29,23);[77] the adjective *ṣānûa'*, which appears once in the Bible, in Proverbs 11,2; the adjective *'ānāw* (*Qᵉrî*), which interchanges with *'ānî* (*Kᵉtîb*) in Proverbs[78] (3,34; 14,21; 16,19; also Job 24,4), and the noun *'ănāwâ*, which is found three times in Proverbs (out of six times in the Bible).

In Proverbs modesty and humility are an essential condition for the attainment of honor which is one of life's values according to the wisdom concept: "A man's haughtiness brings him low, but one who is lowly in spirit (*šᵉpal rûaḥ*) will obtain honor" (ibid. 29,23), and "Humility (*'ănāwâ*) goes before honor" (15,33; cf. 18,12; 22,4); not only is honor the reward of the lowly, but also wisdom: "But wisdom is with those who are modest (*ṣᵉnû'îm*)" (ibid. 11,2).

2. Other expressions involving restraint and self-control

One of the reasons for "silence" in Egyptian, as we have seen above, is the application of self-discipline. This principle assumes an important place in the normative world of Biblical wisdom, and in expressing this concept the sages make use of a set of phrases and terms that recall the Egyptian usage:

(a) In Egyptian, expressions occur in this context composed of the collocation of a verb and bodily organs (noun) — in the Biblical language the verbs *nṣr* and *šmr* are combined in the same way and have a similar meaning:

nṣr, meaning "keep," "watch," "guard with fidelity," is found together with *peh* ("mouth") ("He who guards his mouth [*nōṣēr pîw*] keeps his life, but he who opens wide his lips comes to ruin" — Prov.

13,3); and with the noun *lēb* ("heart") ("Keep your heart [*n^e ṣōr libbekā*] with all vigilance for from it flow the springs of life," ibid. 4,23).[79]

šmr, similar in meaning to *nṣr*, is also juxtaposed to *peh* ("He who keeps [*šōmēr*] his mouth and his tongue keeps himself out of trouble," Prov. 21,23) and with *lēb* (in recommendation of securing things in the heart: "My son, listen to my words... keep them [*šām^e rēm*] within your heart," ibid. 4,20,21). Cf. also "He who restrains his lips (*ḥōśēk ś^e pātāyw*) is prudent" (ibid. 10,19); "He who closes his lips (*'ōṭēm ś^e pātāyw*) is thought to be perceptive" (ibid. 17,28).

(b) Other expressions in the wisdom literature concerned with self-discipline:

The phrase *ksh dābār*, meaning "to keep a thing hidden," is the opposite of "He who goes about as talebearer," he who "reveals secrets" (Prov. 11,13). The contrary trait characterizes the stupid man, and is expressed in the collocations *glh lēb* and *yṣ' rûaḥ*: "A stupid man has no pleasure in discernment, but only in expressing his own mind (*hitgallût libbô*)" (Prov. 18,2); "A stupid man gives full vent (*kōl rûḥô*) to his anger" (ibid. 29,11).

II. SUBJECT MATTER ANALYSIS OF THE TERMS

A. The Motif of Silence in Biblical Wisdom

Words in praise and in favor of "silence" and "restraint" are voiced in the Hebrew as well as in the Egyptian wisdom literature. The grounds for silence in the Hebrew texts largely correspond to those in the Egyptian sources.[80]

1. Silence out of adherence to social norms

(a) Unwillingness to harm others: In the Bible "silence" does not always mean the opposite to prolixity in speech. Sometimes it is the antithesis of slandering and idle gossip. The prattler goes about telling the secrets of others, while thc trustworthy man conceals what has been said (Prov. 11,13; 20,19); "Do not be in a hurry to bring into court... Argue your case with your neighbor and do not reveal another's secret," says the sage (Prov. 25,7-10), that is, do not give away the secret of another person when you quarrel with your fellow man.[81] An intelligent man is silent about the flaws of others: "He who lacks sense belittles his neighbor, but a man of understanding remains silent" (Prov. 11, 12).

(b) Care not to give offense or injure through speech: "When words are many, transgression is not lacking, but he who restrains his lips is prudent," the sage asserts (Prov. 10,19). Elsewhere he warns: "If you act the fool by exalting yourself or if you have been devising evil, put your hand on your mouth.[82] For pressing milk produces curds, and the pressing of the nose produces blood, and the pressing of anger produces strife" (30, 32-33).[83] Ben Sira prays to God to enable him to control his desires and his tongue (22,27-23,2 [Gr.]).

2. Silence through reserve and holding one's tongue

(a) Taciturnity is one of the qualities of the sage: "He who is sparing with his words understands what knowledge is" (Prov. 17,27; cf. ibid. 28 and 10, 19, and BS 1,23, 24 [Gr.]).

(b) Hasty and impulsive speech is one of the shortcomings of a man with bad manners: "You have seen a man who is hasty in his words? There is more hope for a stupid man than for him" (Prov. 29,20; cf. ibid. 15,18).

(c) Concealment of things: Wise men conceal their knowledge while the fool puts no curb on his tongue (Prov. 10,14); the man who controls his mouth and his tongue keeps himself out of troubles (ibid. 21,23; cf. 13,3).

3. Silence in a cultic setting

To this belongs a passage in Qoheleth that describes the behavior of the wise man and the stupid man when offering a sacrifice: "To draw near to listen is better than to offer the sacrifice of fools; for they do not know that they are doing evil. Be not rash with your mouth, nor let your heart be hasty to utter a word before God, for God is in heaven and you upon earth; therefore let your words be few. For a dream comes with much business and a fool's voice with many words" (4,17-5,2). Part of this passage is obscure, and several suggestions for its interpretation have been put forward.[84] For our purposes the following details are important: (a) The conduct of the fool during sacrifice is censured, and it is said that obedience (*šmʿ*) is preferable to the sacrifice of fools (4,17); (b) The nature of this reprehensible behavior is expressed in the statement "a fool's voice with many words," that is, the fool prattles on noisily at the time of divine service; (c) The wise man is warned not to behave like the fool, viz., not to speak hastily ("be not rash with your mouth") nor to pour out his soul before God, on the grounds that God is too distant and elevated for human understanding: "For God is in heaven and you are upon earth."

Qoheleth's words are remarkably similar to the warnings of the Egyptian sages to keep silent in the temple on the one hand, and to their declarations on the gods' love of silence and dislike of him who approaches them too closely on the other (see pp. 152, 159, 161 above).

4. The "timeliness" of silence

Like his Egyptian counterpart, the Hebrew sage recognizes the importance of the timing of silence and commends speech at the proper time: "To make an (apt) answer is joy to a man, and a word in season how good it is!" (Prov. 15,23). BS 20,7 asserts that "a wise man keeps silent until the right time and a fool takes no note of the time" (cf. ibid. 1,23 [Gr.], 4,23-24; and also Qoh. 3,7).

B. Parallels to *Amenemope* Chapter 4

Parallel in subject matter to chapter 4 of the Egyptian *Instruction of Amenemope* are Psalms 1 and Jeremiah 17, 5-8. As in *Amenemope*, two human types are contrasted in the Bible, positive and negative: the "righteous man" and the "wicked man" in Psalms; the "man who trusts in God" and the "man who trusts in man" in Jeremiah. As in the Egyptian composition, both are compared to plants: a tree planted by streams of water and chaff in Psalms 1; a tree planted by water and a shrub in the desert in Jeremiah 17. Their fate is identical to that of their Egyptian equivalents: the positive type will win long life while the negative type will be destroyed.

Gressmann was the first to point out the resemblance between these Biblical passages and *The Instruction of Amenemope* (1924).[85] He claimed that two points of contact exist between the Hebrew and the Egyptian material: the imagery of trees and the "Judgement of the Dead,"[86] which he believes is intimated in Ps. 1,5 but found nowhere else in Psalms. To these Blackman[87] adds a third point of contact — verse 2 in Ps. 1, in which it is said of the righteous man: "And in his Law he studies day and night." In his view this verse is close to the admonitions addressed to the pupil in the Egyptian school texts of the 19th and 20th Dynasties, such as "Spend the whole day writing with your fingers whilst you read by night."[88]

Both Gressmann and Blackman argue for an Egyptian influence on these Biblical passages. But while the closeness of *Amenemope* chapter 4 and Psalms 1 and Jeremiah 17 is undeniable, there are also equally significant differences between the passages:

(1) The negative human type is compared in Psalms and in Jeremiah to chaff and to a shrub, while in *Amenemope* he is compared to a tree.[89]

(2) The positive type in the two Hebrew sources is compared to a tree "planted by streams of water" and "by water." In the Egyptian text the term *tẖn.t*  , which refers to the place of growth of the *grw m3ʿ*, is indeed subject to debate, but from the determinative it is clear that it is cultivated land and not water.

(3) The background of all three passages is religious,[90] but the nature of the activity differs in each. In *Amenemope* it is worship of the god in the temple; in Jeremiah the stress is laid on social behavior and the conflict is between a man who trusts in God, who will be his savior, and a man who trusts in his fellow men and will be disappointed; and in Psalms we find the ideally pious man devoted to the study of God's Law, as distinct from the wicked man who sits idly in the seat of the scornful.

The first two differences may be explained by the contrasting physical features of Israel and Egypt. In Israel, where water is not abundant, the image of the flourishing, successful, righteous man is that of a tree planted by waters (see Job 29,19; cf. Ez. 47,12 and also the simile without water in Ps. 92, 13-14; Ps. 52,10; etc.). By contrast, in Egypt the Nile is the main source of water and its flooding signifies catastrophe; therefore the destruction of the "heated man" in *Amenemope* is brought about through a deluge of water. In the Bible destruction of the wicked man is often likened to "chaff" blown by the wind (cf. Hos. 13,3; Isa. 29,5; Ps. 35,5).

The connection between the three passages is clear, even if it is difficult to determine whether the Hebrew source influenced the Egyptian or vice versa (the latter, as stated, being the claim of Gressmann, Blackman, and others),[91] or whether they shared a common source.

Should the latter be correct, it may explain an additional variance noted in the three passages, i.e., the different circumstances, which would then stem from the treatment of common material by these separate authors, each shaping it to suit his own particular purpose: the prophet (Jeremiah) as a social critic emphasizing the social aspects; the Psalmist, as standard-bearer for the fear of God, stressing the religious element; and the author of *Amenemope*, whose instruction combines early wisdom tradition with the later concept of *persönliche Frömmigkeit*, impressing both of these aspects upon the material at his disposal: social morality as embodied in the types *grw* and *šmm*, and piety as expressed in the religious setting of ritual service in the temple.

C. The Ideal Man

In the early Egyptian wisdom the concept "silent man" and its synonyms do not involve the figure of the sage. The first time that quietness and calmness appear as qualities characterizing the wise man is in *The Instruction of Pap. Insinger* (10,3; 23,7,12).

The picture is different in Biblical wisdom literature. Even though *štq* ("be silent") is not characteristic of the wisdom vocabulary, motifs connected with this ideal consistently accompany the wise man. Self-control, reserve, patience, cool temper, sparingness of speech,

Table 8: The "Silent Man" and the "Heated Man" in Egyptian and Biblical Wisdom

		Egyptian	Hebrew
I) Social setting	Positive human type	*grw* (*ḳb*)–the "silent man," cool-tempered, is the "ideal human type." In later stage (*Insinger*) the virtue of "silence" becomes attached to the "sage"–*rmt n rḫ*.	1) *ḥākām* and its synonyms–"ideal human type." 2) *qar rûaḥ*–borrowed from Egyptian; *'erek 'appayim/rûaḥ* express the same idea in Hebrew
	Negative human type	*šmm* (*tȝw* + bodily parts) – the "hot-tempered man."	1) *k^esîl* and its synonyms. 2) *'îš ḥēmôt/ḥēmâ, ba'al ḥēmâ* – borrowed from Egyptian; *'îš/ba'al 'ap, q^eṣar 'appayim/rûaḥ* express the same idea in Hebrew.
II) Religious setting	Positive human type	*grw, grw mȝ'*– pious man (beginning from *Amenemope*). In later sources–*rmt nṯr* *	*ṣaddîq* *
	Negative human type	*šmm*–whose piety is pretense. (*Admonitions*; *Amenemope*, chap. 4; *Deir el Médineh* 1265; *Sallier* I). In later sources–*sȝbe**	*rāšā'* *

*See pp. 258 ff. below.

holding one's tongue, avoidance of quarrel — these are the features that mark out the "man of understanding" and the "prudent man" (Prov. 10,19; 11,12 ; 12,23; 14,29; 17,27; etc.; cf. pp. 174–175 above), as well as the Egyptian *grw*.

Opposite habits and traits, similar to those of the Egyptian *šmm*, are the mark of the "fool": he is a man of anger and strife (Prov. 18,6,7; 20,3; 29,9; etc.; Qoh. 7,9); he is a gabbler who reveals his inner secrets (Prov. 18,2; 29,11; etc.); the silence of a fool is likewise unnatural, to the extent that "a fool who keeps silent is considered wise" (ibid. 17,28; cf. Job 13,5).

The role of *grw* and the *šmm*, symbolizing the positive and negative human types in the Egyptian wisdom, is filled in the Biblical wisdom by the *ḥākām* and the *k^esîl*. Together with the *k^esîl* and the *ḥākām*, the terms *'îš ḥēmâ* and *qar rûaḥ* are used. These lexemes reflect obviously Egyptian concepts, which were adopted by the Hebrew writer.

In the wisdom Psalm (Ps. 1,6) the *ṣaddîq* and the *rāšā'* replace the *ḥākām* and the *k^esîl*. As stated, the connection between this Psalm and chapter 4 of *The Instruction of Amenemope* has led some scholars to assume that the Hebrew writer borrowed from the Egyptian source. Thus, the psalmist, who adopted the Egyptian material and reworked it into its new Hebrew dress, identified the "heated man" and the "silent man" in Egyptian with the central figures in his own normative world, namely, the *ṣaddîq* and the *rāšā'*.

Whether or not the author of Psalm 1 was influenced by the Egyptian motif, it is obvious that the *ṣaddîq* and the *rāšā'* here take the place of the *ḥākām* and the *k^esîl* of the "classical" wisdom books. Two stages in the development of the motif of the "ideal man" and his opposite may therefore be discerned in the Bible: (a) in the wisdom literature *ḥākām* — *k^esîl*; (b) in the Psalter *ṣaddîq* — *rāšā'*. These stages parallel the history of the terms "heated man" and "silent man" in the Egyptian literature.[92] The *ḥākām* and the *k^esîl* in the Bible, like the *grw* and the *šmm* in the Egyptian sources, changed from the two contrary human types in the social context in the early wisdom literature to the major figures in the ideology of personal piety, which emphasizes

Table 9: The Motifs "Anger-Strife," "Silence-Restraint" in the Egyptian Wisdom and the Bible

Aspect		Hot Temper, Strife: Egypt	Hot Temper, Strife: Bible
Linguistic	Characteristic Vocabulary	*šmm*; *tꜣ(w)* (+ part of body); *štm*, *ṯṯṯ* — are characteristic of the instruction genre. The remaining terms are common in all genres.	*'îš ḥēmâ/ḥēmôt*; *ba'al ḥēmâ*; *'îš/ba'al 'ap*, in reference to humans, are unique to the wisdom books. The remaining terms are common in all genres.
	Etymological-semantic Analogy	*šmm* ⟷	*ḥēmâ* (*ḥmm*)
		fnḏ ⟷	*'ap* (*'np*)
	Distribution and Frequency of Terms	Terms denoting "coolness," "suppression of strife and anger," e.g., *ḫsf*, *dꜣr ḳb(b)* + object — occur with high frequence. A few phrases signify the opposite.	Terms referring to "igniting strife," e.g., *hst*, *b'r*, *grh*, *gl'* have wide distribution (in wisdom books and elsewhere). Fewer expressions signify the opposite sense, e.g., *šqṭ* (hiph'il), *nṭš*, *škk*.
Stylistic	Metaphors	Animals Fire	Animals — hardly any (lion once). Fire — especially in respect of God's anger (outside wisdom literature); anger of man (twice in wisdom literature).
Subject Matter	Human Traits	The contemptible traits — contentiousness and anger — related to a recognized human type: *šmm*, *šm rꜣ* (+ a definite article) and *tꜣ(w)* (+bodily organ).	Contentiousness and anger are contemptible traits attached to the *kᵉsîl* and its synonyms (*'ĕwîl*, *lēṣ*); with it come in this context *'îš tahpukôt*, *'îš/'ēšet midyānîm*, *nirgān*, *rāšā'*.
	Human Type	*šmm* is the embodiment of all negative human traits: contentiousness, hot temper, lying, slandering, covetousness.	*kᵉsîl* is the negative human type paralleling the Eg. *šmm*; *'îš ḥēmâ*, *ba'al 'ap* being secondary types. *'îš ḥēmâ* derives from from the adaptation of the Eg. *šmm* (mentioned only 4x in connection with "strife" while *kᵉsîl* and its synonyms appear 9x).
	Subject of Behavior and Emotion	A human being is usually the subject of anger and strife in the wisdom texts. In other genres also gods may be the subject.	The same as in Egyptian literature. Outside wisdom literature but also often in Job God usually appears as the subject. (He becomes angry at his people, the nations, the wicked men).

Aspect		Silence, Restraint Egypt	Bible
	Characteristic Vocabulary	*gr* (mainly in the instructions); *ḳb(b)* (in the instructions and royal court texts); *sgrḥ* (frequently in *Insinger*); *hrw* (*ib*), *sgr* (occasionally in the instructions mainly in other genres).	*ḥrš*; *štq* ; *šqṭ*; *šlw*, *ḥšh*; *dmm* — are close in sense to the Eg. parallels, but do not belong to the wisdom vocabulary.
Linguistic	Etymological-semantic Analogy	*ḳb(b)* — cool-tempered *nb.t sgr* — the realm of the dead	*qar rûah* (1x in Prov.) derives from adaptation of the Eg. concept. *'erek 'appayim/rûah* used to express this sense in Hebrew. *dûmâ* — She'ol (Ps.)
	Distribution and Frequency of Terms	Many expressions to signify "restraint" "holding the tongue" — verb + bodily organs: mouth, lips, heart, and belly.	In a similar sense — *nṣr*, *šmr*, *ḥśk* etc. + mouth, lips, heart, and tongue.
Stylistic	Metaphors	Trees designating human types — *Amenemope* 4, *Deir el Médineh* 1265. Water—the word *ḳb(b)* itself and Thoth as a palm tree in whose fruit is water and as a well of water — *Sallier* I.	Plants referring to human types in Ps. 1 and Jer. 17, 5-8 paralleling *Amenemope* 4. Wisdom is compared to a spring of water.
	Human Traits	Most valued characteristics are silence and self-control (*gr* and synonyms).	Restraint and self-control are appreciated as well by the Hebrew sage; but the use of the Heb. equivalents to the Eg. *gr*, i.e., *šqṭ and štq* is rare in this context.
Subject matter	Human Type	*grw*, *grw mȝ'*, the silent man, is the ideal human type in both social and religious settings.	The *ḥākām* is the human ideal in the social sphere. Together with him appear *'erek 'appayim/rûaḥ*, *šᵉpal rûaḥ*, *ṣānûa'*, *'ānāw*, but these are only secondary figures to *ḥākām*. The *ṣaddîq* is the ideal human type in the religious sphere (Ps. 1).
	Subject of Behaviour and Emotion	God and humans appearing as the subjects of silence.	As subject of restraint and self-control man appears usually in the wisdom literature, but elsewhere God is *'erek 'appayim*.

not the relationship between man and man but that between man and his god.

To conclude, one of the most important virtues in Biblical wisdom, as in the Egyptian wisdom, is moderation and restraint. The ideal man is tolerant, cool-tempered, balanced in his conduct, sparing of speech, keeps secrets and eschews quarrels. However, the lexemes *šqṭ* and *štq*, which are the semantic equivalents of the Egyptian terms belonging to the central Egyptian sapiential topic of the "silent man," do not belong to the lexicon of the Hebrew sage. "Silence," as part of the proper behavior of the believer who submits to the god, expressed in the later Egyptian literature beginning with the New Kingdom Period (especially in the hymns of personal piety), is present in the Bible only in non-wisdom books.[93]

CHAPTER FIVE

THE CONSEQUENCES OF FAILING TO ACQUIRE LEARNING: FOOL AND FOOLISHNESS

In Egyptian

I. LINGUISTIC-SEMANTIC AND CONTENT ANALYSIS OF THE TERMS

The relatively large vocabulary at the disposal of the Egyptian sage for the expression of foolishness attests to the subject's importance. The words included are characteristic of the sage's language and are complementary in distribution: in the early wisdom compositions the terms *ḫm*, *wḫꜣ* appear; later, the lexemes *iw.ty ḥꜣ.ty*, *šꜣšꜣ*, *ḫn* and *gwš*; and finally, in the Demotic instructions, the three synonymous words *lḫ*, *swg* and *ẖn*.

1. *ḫm*

ḫm,[1] whose basic meaning is "know not," serves as the antonym of the stem *rḫ*, "to know." The determinative of two outstretched arms that accompanies *ḫm* signifies negation in Egyptian (Gr D35). At times there is an additional determinative, a sparrow, which stands for something evil.

ḫm serves as a verb, a noun, and an adjective in the Egyptian wisdom, but only the last form is characteristic of the sapiential vocabulary. The adjective derives from the verb, which usually states a neutral fact of "not to know," "be ignorant of";[2] but cases occur of the verb carrying a negative connotation, meaning "to deny something," whether in a political or a religious context.[3]

ḫm (*s ḫm*) is the most common term signifying a foolish man in the early instructions (cf. Table 10). Appearing in all the literary genres of wisdom (except the autobiography), its use gradually declines in New Egyptian until it disappears in Demotic (which continues to use only the verb).[4] *ḫm* is coupled in antithetic parallelism with *rḫ*, "wise," (e.g., *Ptaḥḥotep* 54; *Admonitions of an Egyptian Sage* 4, 7), i.e., mankind is divided into two categories, *ḫm.w* and *rḫ.w* — fools and wise men (*Mentuhotep* 5; cf. *Chester Beatty* IV pl. 20, verso 6,6). *ḫm* usually has a positive connotation: his flawed behavior arises from ignorance while his improvement lies in the acquisition of knowledge. Hence, the *ḫm* is the target primarily of the Egyptian instruction: *Ptaḥḥotep* defines his essay as "instruction for the *ḫmw* so that he may know" (47); and the epilogue of *The Instruction of Amenemope* states: "Look to these thirty chapters... they cause the *ḫm* to know. If they are read to the *ḫm* he will be purified through them" (27, 10-12); the *Onomasticon* of the Ramesside Period is also intended as "instruction of the *ḫm*" (*Onomasticon of Amenemope* 1,1).

The task of educating the *ḫm* falls to the leaders of society — the king and the high official. In praise of the king it is said that "he brings up the *ḫm* to become wise (*rḫ*)" (*Instruction by a Man for His Son* IV 5; cf. *The Eloquent Peasant* B1 287).

At times the adjective *ḫm* carries a negative tone, when it serves as an epithet of condemnation against the leader who does not fulfil his duties properly — the judge who usurps justice in *The Eloquent Peasant* (B1 218, 219) or the quarrelsome superior official (*Ptaḥḥotep* 66). This negative nuance intensifies in the later sources. Intef, the herald of Thutmosis III, lauds himself as one who "holds in esteem the artisan (*ḥmww*) who turns his back on the *ḫm*" (*Urk.* IV 970, 2,3). The negative connotation is already plain in *Khakheperre-sonb*, who asserts that it is useless to answer the *ḫm* (verso 4,5). Here lie perhaps the seeds of the later concept rejected in *Papyrus Chester Beatty* IV: "Beware of saying: 'every man according to his nature; simpletons (*ḫm.w*) and sages (*rḫ.yw*) are the same; Destiny and Fortune are the character inscribed in god's own writing'" (Pl. 20 verso 6,6); that is, the effort invested in studying is pointless as a man's character and lot, be he fool or sage, have long since been fixed by the god.

In the religious literature the Egyptian believer presents himself as a *ḫm*, "an ignorant," before his god, and thereby expresses his obedience and devotion: "I was like a *ḫm*, without understanding (*iw.ty ḥ3.ty*) I knew not between good and evil" (*ÄHG* 149, 7,8).

2. *wḫ3*

The root *wḫ3*, depicted by the determinative of a sparrow, appears in our sample as a noun, an adjective and a causative verb (*swḫ3*). The most frequent usage, characteristic of the language of the Egyptian sage, is again in the adjectival form, meaning "fool." *wḫ3* is coupled with *ḫm* in synonymous parallelism and like it stands in antithetic parallelism with *rḫ* ("wise man").[5]

The adjective *wḫ3* appears in the didactic and pessimistic wisdom literature, of the Old and Middle Kingdoms and in the biographical writings of the 18th Dynasty and the Late Period. Analysis of the sources shows that *wḫ3* has a more negative connotation than *ḫm*. While *ḫm* derives from the verb "know not," the adjective *wḫ3* does not derive from a verb signifying a neutral fact but refers principally to the unwillingness to know.

The most detailed description of the *wḫ3* is found in *The Instruction of Ptaḥḥotep* (575ff.), in a section contrasting two figures: the son who listens, the wise one, and the son who does not listen, the *wḫ3*. The bad son, the *wḫ3*, does not obey (lit. listen), does not distinguish between good and evil. He occupies himself with everything that is hateful and is of perverted speech. His reward will be in keeping with his acts: he will not acquire property; instead of honor he will receive beatings and rebukes; and instead of longevity and health he will be subject to injury and punishment. A son of this sort is spoken of elsewhere in the same source: "Turn him out, he is not your son, you did not beget him" (ibid. L2 207ff.).

The ignorance of the *wḫ3*, unlike that of the *ḫm*, does not stem from not learning or the absence of means of acquiring knowledge but from his unwillingness to learn and his rejection of social norms. A characteristic feature of the *wḫꜣ* is his inability to distinguish between what is useful and what is harmful, between good and evil. This feature, mentioned in the above quotation from *Ptaḥḥotep*, is repeated in *The Admonitions of an Egyptian Sage* (6, 13) and in a quotation of this source in *The Instruction of Amenemhet* (XIV B, C).[6] The *wḫꜣ* is depicted here as one who through the twisted mirror of his thought sees the anarchy reigning in the land in a positive light, while the proper social order and accepted beliefs appear intolerable to him.[7] Beating and punishment, which are not mentioned with respect to the *ḫm*, are a proven means of correcting the *wḫꜣ*. The "*wḫꜣ* is hard pressed," says Ptaḥḥotep above (574; cf. also 587). As the *wḫꜣ* is not the ideal object for instruction, the ruler will not pride himself on having taught him (as he did regarding the *ḫm*) but will compliment himself on the fact that he himself is not a *wḫꜣ* (*To Merikare* 115). The high official who does not fulfil his task properly will be shamed with the insulting appellation *wḫꜣ* (*The Eloquent Peasant* B1 218-219; cf. ibid. 286-287).

Even though the atmosphere around the *wḫꜣ* is always critical and negative, he does not emerge as one who endangers the social order or abuses other people. Through his distorted way of thinking, the *wḫꜣ* brings injury primarily upon himself, or at worst injures his family's honor.

3. *iw.ty ḥꜣ.ty* (Copt. ⲁⲧϩⲏⲧ)

This expression, which is composed of the noun "heart" (*ḥꜣ.ty*) and the negative relative adjective (*iw.ty*) and sometimes augmented by the word "man" (*s*), belongs to the Egyptian wisdom terminology.

iw.ty ḥꜣ.ty is the semantic equivalent of the Hebrew adjective *ḥăsar lēb* ("senseless"). In the Coptic Version ⲁⲧϩⲏⲧ [8] stands for the terms *k^{e}sîl* and its synonyms in the Masoretic text.[9] The occurrence of the term is restricted (6 times in our sample), and it appears beginning from the time of the New Kingdom in *The Instruction of Anii*, the school writings, the religious literature and the late biography. *iw.ty ḥꜣ.ty* is thus associated with two frameworks — didactic and religious. In the didactic framework the lazy scribe, pupil or son, who refuses to learn and to work, is labelled with this attribute, and the following warning occurs frequently: "Do not be a senseless man" (*m iri iw.ty ḥ3.ty.f*) (*Bologna* 1094 3, 6-7). In *The Instruction of Anii* (6,6-10) the son is advised to build a house and to accumulate wealth and not to sit idle like a *iw.ty ḥ3.ty* (cf. *Sallier* I 5,9). In the language of prayers and hymns *iw.ty ḥ3.ty* — like *ḫm*, with which it is paired in synonymous parallelism — serves to describe the humility and devotion of the believer before his gods (*ÄHG* 149, 7-8). In the prayer to Reʿ-Harakhti the pious man actualizes his devotion to the god by likening himself to an ox going after grass and presenting himself as a man *iw.ty ḥ3.ty* ("without understanding"), who sins through ignorance (*Anastasi* II 10,7-11,1).

The meaning of *iw.ty ḥ3.ty* is thus close to that of *ḫm*, in the sense of passive foolishness, a less grave form than that expressed in the attribute *wḫ3*. The lack of knowledge of the *iw.ty ḥ3.ty* may indeed draw him into sin, but by error, not by design.[10]

The following two terms are also attached to the didactic sphere but owing to their infrequent occurrence are difficult to define semantically.

4. *ḫn* (*ḫini*)

The adjective *ḫn* is found in our sample only in the New Kingdom literature (9 times — in the school writings and in *The Instruction of Anii*). Like the other terms belonging to this semantic field, it is accompanied by the determinative of a sparrow (*Wb.* III 290, 1). In the school writings *ḫn* is a term of censure applied to the pupil who refuses to study (*Pap. Turin* D2, 6 || *Lansing* 8,3). Of the *ḫn* son, who does not heed his father's words, it is said that his destiny is to labor hard hauling ships (Posener, "Ostraca inédits," 175ff.). The meaning of *ḫn* may be "a man without education"[11] since in *Anastasi* I 13,2 a scribe scorns his colleague as being "*ḫn*, without a teacher," and in *The Instruction of Anii* the masses, who are compared to beasts devoid of knowledge, are called *ḫn* (10, 9ff).[12]

5. *šȝšȝ*

The usage of the adjective *šȝšȝ* is also limited to the New Kingdom Period. *šȝšȝ*, like the other lexemes belonging to "foolishness," is accompanied by the determinative of a sparrow, at times augmented by a drawing of a man with arms outstretched, signifying exhaustion (Gr A7).

The present corpus includes only a single mention of *šȝšȝ* in a passage berating the lazy scribe (*Pap. Anastasi* V 7,4), from which little can be deduced. The meaning of the word, according to Erman-Grapow, is "*unfähig, leistungsunfähig, unzuverlässig*" (*Wb.* IV 414, 1). In his article on *Pap. Salt* Černý presents other examples of the use of the term.[13] Two of these, which are taken from *Pap.* 10052 (3, 16; 10, 8) in the British Museum, shed light on its meaning. Here *šȝšȝ* is accompanied by the determinative of a dancing man (Gr A32), from which it may perhaps be inferred that *šȝšȝ* means a madman. Since in the latter references the trait is attached to an old man, *šȝšȝ* may have to do with silliness, folly, brought on by old age.[14]

6. *lḫ* (Dem. *lḫ*;[15] Copt. [S] ⲗⲁϣⲓⲉ[16])

lḫ appears only in Demotic, and its occurrence is restricted to the Demotic instructions (in *Pap. Insinger* 40 times out of 52; the remainder in *Ankhsheshonqy* and *Pap. Louvre* 2377, 2380).[17] Its determinative is a bound man holding an ax (i.e., the enemy), indicating the negative connotation of the term. *lḫ* emerges as a fool worse than all those mentioned so far. The *lḫ* is not talentless or weak-minded, incapable of absorbing knowledge, but someone who casts off all restraints, including educational authority. The *lḫ*, who refuses to study and does not listen to instructions (*Ankhsheshonqy* 27, 10), is compared to a statue of stone (*Insinger* 8, 22; cf. *Anakhsheshonqy* 21,20). Of him the writer of the Demotic instruction repeats what was already said by his predecessor, the sage Ptaḥḥotep, about the *wḫȝ*: "Better the son of another" (*Insinger* 9, 15). Any attempt to teach him is pointless as it will only lead to hatred of the teacher: "Do not instruct a *lḫ*, lest he hate you" (*Ankhsheshonqy* 7, 4). As with the *wḫȝ*, the rod is the most effective means of disciplining him (*Insinger* 14,6).

The *lḫ* possesses a "bad character" (*Insinger* 29,6), evinced in his conduct and traits, which stem from his incapacity for self-restraint: gluttony (ibid. 3,4; 6,1, 19; etc.), pursuing women (6,1; 8,12), impatience, vengefulness (3, 23; 21, 18; 27, 15), miserliness (10, 4) and restlessness (23, 17; 29,17; etc.). The evil nature of the *lḫ*, moreover, leads him to crime (*bt3* — *Insinger* 29,6). Since his crimes bring injury to others (ibid. 13, 10-14), the wise man counsels keeping away from him (*Ankhsheshonqy* 13, 6) and trusting him neither with missions (*Insinger* 14, 7) nor with material possessions (ibid. 12, 10-13).

On the religious level the *lḫ* is shown as an impious man, one who mocks the service of the god (*Insinger* 30, 21) and in times of trouble does not trust in the god (ibid. 19,13).

The *lḫ* is remediable only through punishment, which is mentioned repeatedly in connection with him; harm comes to him (ibid. 5, 14; 7,6; 21, 18; etc.), he is despised (ibid. 26, 1; 27, 15; see also *Ankhsheshonqy* 18, 11; 25, 23); his traits may even cause his own death (*Insinger* 28, 2). Not surprisingly, therefore, the *lḫ* parallels and is juxtaposed with other negative attributes, "fool" (*swg*/*rmt swg* — 6 times; *ẖn* — 4 times); "wicked," "impious" (*s3be* — 4 times); "bad man" (*rmt bn* — twice); "inferior man" (*rmt ḫm* — once).[18] The *lḫ* then is not the "semantic successor" of the Middle Egyptian *ḫm* or *wḫ3* but signifies a more acute level of foolishness, bordering on wickedness.

As distinct from the terms presented so far in this chapter, the description of the *lḫ* is vivid and varied in its use of metaphors taken from the natural world: the *lḫ* son is compared to a "statue of stone" (see above); in his violent behavior the *lḫ* is like the crocodile (*Insinger* 13,15) or the snake, which spews out poison (ibid. 27, 14, 15; cf. 13,10) and in his lust for women he resembles "a fly on blood" (ibid. 7,23; see also *Ankhsheshonqy* 22, 12-13).

7. *swg* (Dem. *swg*;[19] Copt. [SB] adj. ⲥⲟϭ ; n. ⲙⲛⲧⲥⲟϭ)

swg, which in our sample appears chiefly as an adjective but also as a noun and verb, is not unique to the sapiential lexicon. It is synonymous with *lḫ* in the Demotic wisdom,[20] but unlike *lḫ*, the usage of *swg* is already evident in the New Kingdom Period (*Wb.* IV 76, 8). It is found in *The Instruction of Ankhsheshonqy* (7 times), in *Insinger* (20), and a few times in *Pap. Anastasi* I and in *Pap. Louvre* 2380. The determinatives of *swg* in our sample are a fish in Egyptian and an enemy in Demotic. According to *Wb.* (ibid.) an additional determinative appears in New Egyptian, i.e., a child with a finger in his mouth, which for the word's meaning is most important as it suggests "the silliness of a child."[21] In the Coptic Version of the Bible ⲥⲟϭ stands for the terms *nābāl* and *ba'ar*, which belong to the semantic field of "foolishness" in Biblical Hebrew.[22]

As an abstract noun, *swg* appears several times in *The Instruction of Pap. Insinger* as a characteristic of the *lḫ* (14, 13), the "inferior man" (*rmt ḫm* — 15, 4) and the "avaricious man" (*'f'* — 15, 17).

As an adjective, *swg* (in plain form or collocated, *rmt* [*rm*] *swg*)[23] is synonymous with *lḫ*, and like it stands in synonymous parallelism with the "bad man" (*bn* — ibid. 3,7,8) and "stupid man" (*ẖn* — ibid. 14,23), and in antithetic parallelism with "wise man" (*rmt rḫ* — *Ankhsheshonqy* 13, 6). But *swg* differs in meaning from *lḫ* in that it describes a man who is to a lesser degree foolish than the latter: *swg*, like *lḫ*, is a person of mental ability, an ability which he fails, however, to realize because of his wicked nature. In the words of the sage, "When the *swg* acts according to his *heart* (i.e., mind), he acts like a wise man" (*Ankhsheshonqy* 19, 8). The *swg*, then, does possess intelligence, even though he does not make use of it, and it is hard to see in him "the born fool, 'idiot'" as Glanville suggests.[24]

swg does not appear in an educational context except on one occasion, in an argument between two scribes in *Pap. Anastasi* I: "You are more foolish (*tw.k swg.tw*) than Kasa, the reckoner of the cattle" (9, 6-7).[25]

swg refers principally to a man with disreputable traits where social morality is concerned. These traits are in part like those associated with the *lḫ*, that is, gluttony (*Insinger* 7, 9; 15, 17), contentiousness (ibid. 13, 16, 17); but the *swg* goes particularly astray in matters of speech — he talks much and loudly (ibid. 3, 8; 22, 23; cf. 4, 5). As he does with regard to *lḫ*, the sage advises to stay away from him (*Ankhsheshonqy* 13, 7; *Insinger* 13, 12ff.; *Pap. Louvre* 2414 II 3, III 11). But while there is remedy for the *lḫ* and his foolishness may be extirpated by punishment and beating, the *swg* on account of his bad nature cannot be changed — in the words of *Insinger*, "to slay (?)[26] the fool (*rmt swg*) is to draw him away from his evil character" (14,5).

8. *ẖn* (*ẖnnw*)

In the Demotic instruction an additional term for "foolish man" appears, *ẖn*, which is synonymous with the two preceding terms, the *lḫ* and the *swg*. This term, whose occurrence is limited to *The Instruction of Ankhsheshonqy* (twice) and *Insinger* (18 times), derives from the verb *ẖnn*, "do something bad, disturb" (Erichsen 385), and in the earlier instruction its meaning is "quarrelsome man" (see p. 120 above).[27] The basic meaning of *ẖn* was thus "troublemaker," "a man eager for a quarrel," and in time the meaning changed to "foolish man." This semantic shift in *ẖn* attests to a transition in the portrayal of the negative human being in the Egyptian wisdom: from a negative human type embodied in the "heated man" (*šmm*) and its synonyms (including *ẖn*) in the early instruction (see ibid.) to a negative human type expressed in "foolish" and its synonyms (*ẖn*, *swg*, *lḫ*) in the later Demotic instruction. *ẖn* thus belongs to the semantic field of "quarrel," "anger" on the one hand and "foolishness" on the other.[28] The "foolish" type represented in the *ẖn* may be seen as a form of integration of *lḫ* and *swg*.

The Egyptian sage refers to the behavior and characteristics of the *ẖn* chiefly in the context of social morality and says little about his mental qualities:

— It is not possible to trust the *ẖn* with affairs of property, work, or errands (*Insinger* 12, 12-13; 14,23; 21,22 cf. *lḫ*).

— He is without patience, does not pay heed, does not take counsel (ibid. 21, 19-22; 21, 12; 26,4).

— He has a bad nature: He hates (ibid. 26,13 cf. *swg*, *lḫ*); is synonymous with "wicked" (*sȝbe*, ibid. 14, 23 cf. *lḫ*, *swg*) and "bad man" (*rmt bn* — ibid. 23, 15-16).

— He is not versed in the art of speaking, is silent when one should talk (ibid. 3,7 cf. *swg*).

— As for mental capacity, the *h̲n* is without intelligence and is ignorant: antonyms are the "wise man" (*rmt rḫ* — *Insinger* 9, 6-7; 22, 3-4; cf. *Ankhsheshonqy* 27,3) and the "man of heart," the sensible man (*wʿ ḥ3t.t*, ibid. 13, 2-3); on the other hand *h̲n* is synonymous with terms signifying "foolish" in Demotic: *swg* (ibid. 14, 23; *h̲n* interchanges with *swg* in the mss. of *Pap. Insinger*: see Volten II, 59; 96-97) and *lḫ* (ibid. 12, 11-12; 21, 19; 22, 4;23, 16-17). At the same time he is remediable: "Thoth has placed the stick on earth in order to teach the fool (*ḫn*) by it," says the author of *Pap. Insinger* (9, 6).

Excursus

9. ***gwš*** in Egyptian and the ***ʿiqqēš*** in Biblical wisdom literature — "the crooked."

The primary meaning of *gwš*, which appears in Egyptian from the New Kingdom Period onwards, is "to be crooked." But when present in didactic context it is used metaphorically to describe human nature which according to Brunner is "a child unfortunate from birth in terms of character or intellect."[29] *gwš* thus belongs to the semantic field of "foolishness" in Egyptian. The accompanying determinatives, like those found with the other terms belonging to this field, signify something negative.[30] ϭⲱⲟⲩϭ , ϭⲱⲟⲩϫ in Coptic (SAB) stand for terms denoting something crooked in the Masoretic text — *ʿiqqēš*, *ʿăqalqallôt*, *tahpukôt*, *nālôz*.[31]

In compositions belonging to wisdom literature the term *gwš* is found as an adjective qualifying a human being in two passages:

(a) *Instruction of Anii* (10, 13-14) — Anii compares his son to a "crooked" stick, saying, "The crooked stick (*p3 ḫt gwš*) is left on the ground, the sun and shade attacking it." The son who refuses to study is compared to a branch that grows crooked and is thrown away because there is no use for it; but since a good craftsman can find use even for a crooked stick, there is still hope for the son: "If the carpenter takes it, he straightens it (*sʿḳw.f*), making it a noble's staff."

(b) A more pessimistic approach appears in the ostracon from the Egyptian school of the New Kingdom where it is said: "Do not (try to) straighten what is crooked (*s'ḳ3 gwš*), do as you like (but) each man is drawn (i.e., raised) according to his nature as are his limbs."[32] This text assumes that everyone is endowed from the start with a particular nature that cannot be altered, revealing a clearly determinist world view and implying the denial of the fruitfulness of any attempt at education. In contrast, the author of *Pap. Chester Beatty* IV warns to "Beware of saying: 'every man according to his nature; simpletons and sages are the same'" (pl. 20 verso 6,6).

Brunner has stated that these two texts — in which the youth is likened to a crooked tree, and must be set straight by his educators — hark back to the traditional picture of education. True, the term *gwš* first appears in the New Kingdom Period, but in Brunner's view the image it reveals is early and already underlies maxim 12 in *The Instruction of Ptaḥḥotep*: "If you are a man of worth, beget a son who will make god well disposed; if he is straight (*mty*), he takes after you" (197ff.).

It is noteworthy that in *The Instruction of Ptaḥḥotep* the author uses the word *mty* to describe the "positive" son and not *s'ḳ3*, which appears in the two passages cited above. The primary meaning of *mty* is indeed "be straight," but in the didactic context it has the sense of "to reprove," "to educate."[33] It is reasonable to suppose that in the section from *Ptaḥḥotep* the term *mty* also has a didactic connotation; the upright son is the educated one, who accepts his father's precepts and follows in his path, as distinct from the "crooked" son who does not. The confrontation between *mty* and *gwš* also may be traced in *Anii* 9, 18-19, where the father answers his son thus: "According to my opinion (*m ib.i*) your complaints are twisted (*gšw*). I shall set you right (i.e., instruct you) (*iw.i mtr.k tw.k*) about them."[34]

The term *'iqqēš*, which is characteristic of the Hebrew wisdom lexicon,[35] is the closest Hebrew parallel to *gwš* in Egyptian. *'iqqēš* means "twisted," "crooked," "perverted" (*BDB* 786). The primary meaning of *'qš* is an uneven area of ground. This is a topographical term as evident from the noun *ma'ăqāš* (i.e., twisted place) and from the verbal use of the root *'qš*, of which the word *derek* ("way") is frequently the object. Like *gwš* in Egyptian, *'qš* stands as a metaphor for human nature, but, unlike *gwš*, *'qš* has no connection with the plant world — the image of the pupil as a crooked branch that the teacher straightens and corrects is not found in the Bible.

'iqqēš in the Bible and *gwš* in Egyptian serve to define a negative human type; but *'iqqēš*, unlike *gwš*, relates not to the mental and scholastic abilities of a man but to his moral flaws.[36] The most detailed and vivid description of this type occurs in Proverbs 2,12ff.: the *'iqqēš* is "evil," "a man of perverted speech," who "forsakes the paths of uprightness." His sinning is so great that elsewhere he is considered an "abomination to God" (ibid. 11, 20). The vocabulary used to describe this figure includes the combinations *'iqqēš* and *lēb* ("heart") / *derek*, *'ōraḥ* ("way") / *peh* ("mouth") and synonyms, which exemplify the disgraceful traits of the *'iqqēš*. The *'iqqēš* is a man corrupt in his ways and behavior (*'ōr^{e}ḥōtāyw 'iqqšîm*).[37]

To conclude, both *gwš* and *'qš* have the primary meaning "crooked," both serve as antonyms to "straight"[38] and both are used metaphorically for human beings; but the similarity between them ends there.

II. THE SCALE OF FOOLISHNESS

The above analysis has shown that most of the terms belonging to the semantic field of "foolishness" have a similar sense, making it difficult, therefore, to distinguish between them semantically. On the other hand, applying the criteria of chronology and literary genre, three groups can be discerned among these terms (cf. Table 10):

(1) Terms whose occurrence is usually limited to didactic works composed in the New Kingdom Period (mainly the school texts and *The Instruction of Anii*) — *iw.ty ḥ3.ty*; *ḫn*; *š3š3* and *gwš*.

(2) The terms *ḫm* and *wḫ3* which exceed the others in duration (from the Old Kingdom to the Late Period) and in the variety of literary genres in which they appear.

(3) Terms prevalent in the Demotic wisdom but rare or absent in earlier literature — *swg*, *lḫ*, *ẖn*.

In light of this division an attempt may be made to define the range

Table 10: Distribution of Terms Relating to the Semantic Field of Foolishness in Egyptian

		ḫm**	wḫꜣ	iw.ty ḥꜣ.ty	lḫ	swg	ḫn	šꜣšꜣ	ẖn(nw)	gwš
Instruction	*Kagemni*									
	Ptaḥhotep	+	+							
	To Merikare	+	+							
	Amenemhet	+***	+							
	Anii	+		+			+			+
	Amenemope	+								
	Ankhsheshonqy				19x	7x			2x	
	Insinger				36x	20x			19x	
	Pap. Louvre 2414*				+	+				
"Loyalist" Instruction	*Seḥetep-ib-Ra*									
	Man to His Son	+	+							
Pessimistic Wisdom	*Admonitions*	+	+							
	Khakheperre-sonb	+								
	Neferti									
	Man Who Was Tired	+	+							
	Eloquent Peasant	+	+							
School Texts	*LEM*	+		+			+	+		
	Anastasi I	+				+	+			
	Onomasticon	+								
	Petrie Ostracon									+
	Chester Beatty IV	+								
	Posener (*Rd'E* 8)						+			
Royal Inscriptions	*Urk.* IV Blumenthal	+	+							
Late Autobiography	Otto		+	+						
Religious Literature	*IHG*	+		+						
	Total	29	13	6	60	29	4	1	21	3

* See item 10 in the Corpus above.
** Adjective and noun; verb included only if it clearly stands in wisdom context.
*** Verb

of each term within the semantic field of "foolishness." This can be done in two stages: (a) by examining a term's relationship to terms with which it is grouped (above); and (b) by determining its positions within the general array of the semantic field of "foolishness".

(a) — Group 1: The restricted occurrence of these terms makes it difficult to determine their precise meaning, although the impression is that *iw.ty ḥꜣ.ty*, which appears more often than the other terms, and *ḫn* have a more optimistic tone than *šꜣšꜣ* and *gwš*, which refer to a man who — owing to a defect from birth (*gwš*) or some other factor — lacks the faculties necessary for learning.

— Group 2: *ḫm* is the most widespread term for "fool" in the period prior to the Demotic writings. *ḫm* is the "good fool," the simple man, lacking in experience, who may be improved by acquiring knowledge. The *wḫꜣ*, who fills the "semantic gap" left by the *ḫm*, stands for the "bad fool," who is capable of learning but has no desire for it. The *ḫm* signifies the objective fact of ignorance while the *wḫꜣ* stands for unwillingness to obtain knowledge.

The distribution of *ḫm* covers almost all the literary genres included in our corpus, while that of *wḫꜣ* is limited. It is not found in the instructions from the New Kingdom Period and the Later Period, in the school writings or in the religious texts. Its absence from the latter is understandable: we would not expect the believer, who wishes to express his devotion to his god and to win his grace, to present himself before the divinity with the negative epithet *wḫꜣ*. The *wḫꜣ* is similar in his behavior and manners to the "heated man," the *šmm* (and synonymous terms), who "play the role" of the *wḫꜣ* in *The Instruction of Amenemope.*

— Group 3: The terms *swg*, *lḫ* and *ẖn* highlight areas of life that other terms only marginally touch upon. Social morality is central here, while the educational level, previously given emphasis, is pushed aside. Social morality in the Demotic wisdom is identified with religious morality and the god appears as a factor of decisive importance. The first signs of this new approach already make their appearance in the literary devices of works predating the Demotic instruction, in which the terms *iw.ty ḥꜣ.ty* and *ḫm* are used metaphorically in religious contexts. This process reaches its peak with the identification of the *lḫ* with the "wicked" (*s3be*) and his representation as an impious man.

The *swg* and the *ẖn*, which are paired with *lḫ* in synonymous parallelism, lay stress on other aspects of "folly": *swg* is the incompetent youth, unable to acquire knowledge owing to a defect in his character, while the *ẖn* combines the traits of both *swg* and the *lḫ*.

(b) All the terms belonging to the semantic field of "foolishness" in Egyptian refer to a man's intellectual capacity. A gradation is detectable here, moving from terms signifying ignorance owing to some irremediable flaw to labels linking lack of knowledge with unwillingness to learn, the most grave of these being the *lḫ*. The *lḫ*, who rejects the educational authority and deliberately refuses to learn, stands at the summit of the pyramid shown below, which illustrates the semantic field of the terms according to the criterion of intellect.

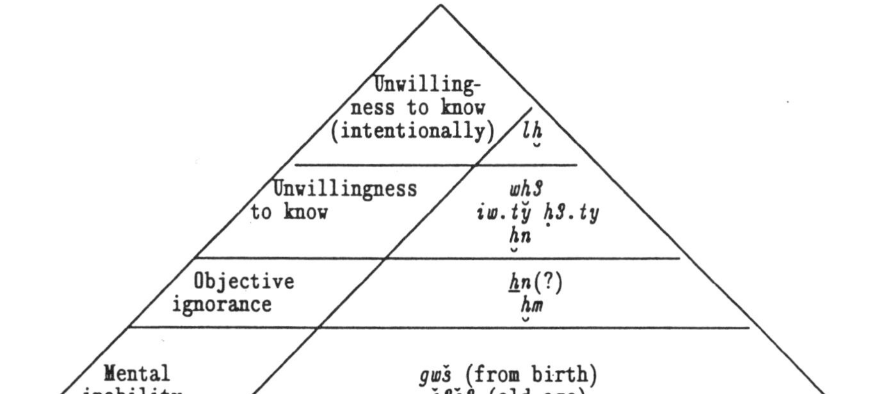

The Semantic Field of Foolishness in Egyptian
according to the Aspect of Intellect

Wisdom docs not distinguish between the intellectual and the moral aspects. In the sage's view, the individual is part of the community, and his acts are evaluated in terms of the good or ill they cause others.

"Foolishness" is therefore not merely a mental but also a moral deficiency.

Seven of the terms in the sources before us involve a social setting and define man according to his social conduct. According to the criterion of social morality these terms may be delimited thus:

moral criterion

good fool ——————————→ **bad fool**

ḫm *iw.ty ḥ3.ty* *swg* *wḫ3* *ẖn* *lḫ* *s3be*

Here, too, *lḫ* proves to be the most negative quality ending up on almost the same level as the *s3be* — the impious man — with regard to social morality.[39]

III. FOOLISHNESS AND LEARNING ABILITY

Examination of sources dealing with the motif of foolishness in the Egyptian literature shows that the Egyptians devoted much thought to the notion of a person's ability to study and his intellectual capacity. Experience in education taught them that not everyone is able or willing to learn, and they were aware of the "limitations of education."

An analysis of the words belonging to the semantic field of foolishness indicates, as we have seen, that a clear distinction exists between people who possess the qualities necessary for acquiring knowledge and those with a mental or physical defect who cannot be put right by learning. Instructions and admonitions are directed in particular to the members of the first group, and the wisdom language is rich in phrases signifying them (*ḫm*, *wḫ3*, *iw.ty ḥ3.ty*, *ḫn* and *lḫ*). But even with respect to this group, the Egyptian teacher gives up and admits failure if the object of the exercise spurns the instruction: "Do not instruct a *lḫ* lest he hate you" (*Ankhsheshonqy* 7, 4). The obstinate and recalcitrant pupil is compared in his ignorance with a mindless animal (the terms fish, beasts, goose are applied to the *lḫ*, the *ḫn*, the *iw.ty ḥ3.ty* and the *swg*).

The decision as to which of the above categories the pupil belongs obviously lies with the teacher and not the pupil, who may excuse his indolence and refusal to learn on the grounds that he was born an idiot. This, indeed, is the claim of the son of Anii: "If I were like (you), as learned as you, then I would carry out your instructions.... But each man is led by his nature" (9, 14-15). The author of *Pap. Chester Beatty* IV, as we have already seen, takes a sharply-worded stand against this approach: "Beware of saying: 'every man according to his nature; simpletons and sages are the same'" (pl. 20 verso 6,6).

However, as early as *Pap. Chester Beatty* IV we find signs of the concept expressed in later Egyptian sources that man does not control his destiny but all is in the hand of the god; in the words of the Egyptian sage, "Shayt and Renenutet (Destiny and Fortune) are the character inscribed in god's own writing..." (ibid.); cf. *Insinger*: "The heart and the character and their owner are in the hand of the god" (15, 5).

Not everything, then, is in the hand of man, not even the acquisition of knowledge. Together with wisdom obtained through study and experience the Egyptian recognizes "charismatic wisdom," endowed by the god:[40] "There is one who has not been taught, yet he knows how to instruct another; there is he who knows the instruction, yet he does not know how to live by it" (*Insinger* 9,16-17).

In the Bible

ANALYSIS OF BIBLICAL TERMS AS COMPARED WITH THE EGYPTIAN

In the Bible, as in Egyptian, a gradation of terms signifying "fool" may be discerned. Here the terms are divided into two groups:

(1) Terms indicating the "positive" fool — *ḥăsar lēb*, *petî*.

(2) Terms indicating the "negative" fool — *k^esîl*, *'ĕwîl*, *lēṣ*, *nābāl*, *sākāl*.

1. *ḥăsar lēb*

The adjective *ḥăsar lēb* (lit. "one who lacks sense") is the semantic equivalent of the Egyptian *iw.ty ḥ3.ty*. In both languages this idiom reflects the concept of the heart as the seat of thought and mind. *ḥăsar lēb* appears only in Proverbs (10 times, once as a noun) and in Ben Sira (once), and is unique to the sage's vocabulary.

ḥăsar lēb is an innocent youth without experience and education, who is exposed to dangers: he is tempted by a "strange woman" (Prov. 6, 32; 7,7) or by Wisdom and Stupidity personified in her image (9,4,16); he gives a pledge (17,18); is credulous (BS 19,4 [Gr.]). His behavior causes harm not only to himself but also to others: he is impolite and scorns his fellow man for his failings (Prov. 11,12).

The *ḥăsar lēb* resembles his Egyptian counterpart *iw.ty ḥ3.ty*: he "follows useless pursuits" (Prov. 12,11) and his bent is for comfortable indolence rather than working his vineyard or his land (24,30). The *ḥăsar lēb* is intent on his "folly" (*'iwwelet*) (Prov. 15,21), but is still remediable through the tested means of stimulating the learning processes, i.e., beating: "On the lips of him who has understanding (*nābôn*) wisdom is found, but a rod is for the back of *ḥăsar lēb*" (Prov. 10,13).[41]

2. *petî*

The *petî*, the "simple man," is the semantic equivalent of the *ḫm* in Egyptian, but is not close to him etymologically. The adjective *petî* derives from the root *pth*, which means "be spacious, wide, open" (*BDB* 834).[42] *petî* belongs to the wisdom vocabulary and is found in Proverbs (14 times), the wisdom Psalm (twice) and Ben Sira (as the participle *pôteh* — 4 times); outside the wisdom literature *petî* appears only twice. The wisdom lexicon also contains the nouns *petî* (Prov. 1,22) and *p^etayyût* (ibid. 9,13), which appears as the personification of foolishness in parallel with *'ēšet k^esîlût* and in contrast to *ḥokmôt*.

The *petî*, who stands in synonymous parallelism with *ḥăsar lēb* and *na'ar*,[43] is a foolish man whose folly stems from lack of knowledge and experience. He is an innocent youth, subject to danger and temptation: he is easily seduced by the "strange woman" (Prov. 7,7; 9,4,16); he "believes everything" (14,15); he fails to see danger ahead (22,3 || 27,12).

The antonym of *petî* is not *ḥākām* ("wise man") but *'ārûm* ("prudent man"), who not only has the knowledge of the *ḥākām* but is capable also of applying this knowledge to order his life securely (see Prov. 14,18; 22,3 || 27,12). The Egyptian instruction is intended to impart knowledge to the *ḫm*, and the sage in Proverbs likewise directs his words primarily to the *petî*: "That prudence may be given to the simple (*p^etā'îm*), knowledge and discretion to the youth" (1,4). The *petî*, willing to acquire knowledge is the ideal pupil for he learns from the punishment of others: "Strike a scorner (*lēṣ*) and the simple (*petî*) will learn prudence" (19,25; cf. 21,11). Not only the sage, but also the personified Wisdom and God (in wisdom Pss.) appear as teachers of the *petî* (Prov. 8,5; wisdom Pss. 19,8; 119,130).[44]

3. *k^esîl*

The *k^esîl* — who appears in synonymous parallelism with *petî*, *ba'ar*, *nābāl* and *lēṣ* and in antithetic parallelism with *ḥākām* and its synonyms (*nābôn*, *mēbîn*, *'ārûm*) and *ṣaddîq* — is the most common term in the Biblical wisdom denoting the "stupid man." The use of *k^esîl* is exclusive to the wisdom language and is present in Proverbs (49 times, especially chapters 18 and 26), Qoheleth (18 times), Ben Sira (5 times) and the wisdom Psalm (Ps 49,11).[45] The etymology of *k^esîl* is subject to debate. Some link it to the Arabic "to be clumsy," others hold that its original meaning is "to be/become fat," hence "to have confidence."[46] The verb *ksl* does not belong to the wisdom vocabulary, while the noun *k^esîlût* is found once in Proverbs (9,13).

It is hard to pinpoint a precise semantic equivalent for *k^esîl* in Egyptian; as will be seen below, it has some similarity to *wḫ3* on the one hand and to *lḫ* and *swg* on the other.

The *k^esîl* is not the worst type of foolish man and may yet be set right:[47]

(a) The *k^esîl* stands in synonymous parallelism with the *petî*, the "positive" fool (Prov. 1,32): see, e.g., the appeal full of hope by Wisdom in Proverbs 8,5: "O simple ones (*p^e tā'îm*) learn prudence; O foolish men (*k^e sîlîm*) understand wisdom!"

(b) The *k^e sîl* is capable of recognizing authority and submitting to discipline, even if it is done the hard way, by being beaten like a household animal (Prov. 26,3;[48] cf. 17,10; 19,29).

(c) The family framework is mentioned often in connection with the *k^e sîl*; it seems that the subject here is a young boy whose manners can still be corrected (ibid. 10,1; 15,20; 17,21; 19,13).

(d) There are human types whose negative behavior exceeds that of the *k^e sîl* : He has more hope than he who is "wise in his own eyes" (Prov. 26,12) and "a man hasty in his words" (ibid. 29,20).

More than any other term belonging to the theme of "foolishness," the description of the *k^e sîl* is embellished with graphic language, imagery and metaphor taken from everyday life and nature. The *k^e sîl* is compared to household animals and to deformed persons, etc. (chiefly Prov. 26, 1-12; Qoh. 7,6). Through these linguistic and stylistic devices the character of the *k^e sîl* is illustrated in various life situations.

In the didactic-educational setting, the *k^e sîl* has no wish to learn (Prov. 17,16; 18,2), hates knowledge and is devoid of understanding (ibid. 1,22; 23,9; Qoh. 2,14; 10,2); he lacks concentration — "his eyes are on the ends of the earth" (Prov. 17,24). The "proverb," the device whereby the sage expresses himself, is meaningless in the mouth of the *k^e sîl* (Prov. 26,7,9). The form of expression characterizing the *k^e sîl* is *'iwwelet* ("folly"): "The mouth of the stupid (*k^e sîlîm*) pours out folly (*'iwwelet*)" (Prov. 15,2; cf. 12,23; 26, 4,5; etc.). The *k^e sîl* does not learn from experience and repeats his folly (26,11).

Some of the *k^e sîl*'s negative traits involved in other levels, furthermore, are: sinning through speech (cf. *swg* in Egyptian), i.e., he utters slander (Prov. 10,18), talks much (ibid. 18,2,6,7; 29,11; Qoh. 5,2; 10,12; BS 20,7) and loudly (Qoh. 9,17); he is *'iqqēš ś^e pātāyw*, that is, a liar (Prov. 19,1); he is attached to pleasure and a life of merrymaking and idleness (Qoh. 7,4-6;[49] BS 27,13 [Gr.]; Qoh. 4,5; cf. also Prov. 19,10); he is arrogant, self-confident (Prov. 14,16;[50] 28,26; cf. 1,32ff), quarrelsome (Prov. 18,7; Qoh. 7,9), and he is a wrongdoer (Prov. 10,23;

13,19). Finally, he is rich, having enough money to "buy wisdom" (Prov. 17,16) — when wealth is juxtaposed with *kᵉsîl* it has a negative connotation. In this context the terms *'ānî* (parallel to *ḥākām* — Qoh. 6,8) and *rāš* (Prov. 19,1), both meaning "poor," appear in contrast to *kᵉsîl*.

In the social setting, the *kᵉsîl* is an obstacle to others — he is unreliable; therefore he should not be allowed to perform any service (Prov. 26,10), particularly not as a messenger (ibid. 6) nor as a guardian of property (ibid. 21,20; cf. *lḫ* and *ẖn* in Egyptian, especially in *The Instruction of Pap. Insinger* 5,12-17; 12, 12-13; 21,22). The sorrow the *kᵉsîl* brings upon his parents is great (see p. 202, c).

The recommended attitude towards him is keeping distance and not becoming friendly (Prov. 13,20; 14,7; 17,12; BS 27,12 [Gr.]; cf. the attitude towards the *swg* and the *lḫ*). He is not to be spoken to (Prov. 23,9; 26,4), although in certain cicumstances he should be answered (ibid. 5)[51] and even, as we saw above (see p. 202, b), beaten.

In Qoheleth, two new elements accompany the figure of the *kᵉsîl*. One of them is peculiar to the skeptical character of this book — Qoheleth is dubious about the advantage of wisdom over folly: "And I applied my heart to know wisdom and to know madness and folly. I perceived that this also is but a striving after wind. For in much wisdom is much vexation, and he who increases knowledge increases sorrow" (1,17-18). Elsewhere he says that "one fate comes to all of them" — the wise and the *kᵉsîl* (2,14); the wise will die with the *kᵉsîl* (ibid. 16; cf. Ps 49,11 [wisdom Ps.] and Qoh. 6,8).

The second element, which as the previous has no parallel in Proverbs, is the reference to foolishness against a cultic background (Qoh. 4,17-5,6). The sins of the stupid man regarding the cult included in this passage are: sacrifice accompanied by wicked deeds (Qoh. 4,17); delay in paying a vow (5,3); making noise in the temple (5,2).[52] It is possible that already Qoheleth reflects the later stage of wisdom, in which wisdom and the divine Law are identical. In this context the *kᵉsîl*, who refuses to accept the authority of wisdom, has become an enemy of the Law, and the word's meaning approaches that of *rāšā'* ("wicked man"): "Wickedness is folly (*kesel*) and foolishness (*siklût*) is madness," says Qoheleth (7,26).[53]

In Ben Sira, which belongs to a later phase in the development of wisdom, the term *k^esîl* is not found in a religious context but its use is linked with the educational and social spheres. Only once in the Greek Version of Ben Sira does *k^esîl* parallel *ṣaddîq*, viz., "godly man" (27,11 [Gr.]).

In the wisdom Psalms the *k^esîl* comes in parallelism with *ba'ar* (49,11; 92,7; 94,8) and the specific feature that aligns him with the "wicked man" is the non-recognition of God.

4. *'ěwîl, 'iwwelet*

'ěwîl, "foolish," and *'iwwelet*, "folly," belong to the wisdom vocabulary and derive from the root *'wl*, whose primary meaning is to "become fat," "grow thick."[54] *'ěwîl* is found in Proverbs (19 times), Job (twice), Ben Sira (4 times) and five times outside the wisdom literature.[55]

Concerning the *'ěwîl* it is said: "Though you crush a fool (*'ěwîl*) in a mortar with a pestle along with crushed grain, yet his folly (*'iwwaltô*) will not depart from him" (Prov. 27,22). Thus, the *'ěwîl* is an incorrigible ignoramus and therefore worse than the *k^esîl*. Like the latter, the *'ěwîl* stands in antithetic parallelism with *ḥākām*, *'ārûm*, and *ṣaddîq* (in Proverbs) and in synonymous parallelism with *ḥăsar lēb* and *pôteh* (in Ben Sira).

It is difficult to determine the semantic equivalent of *'ěwîl* in Egyptian, but his traits are reminiscent of the *swg*. The *'ěwîl* despises the instruction (*mûsār*) of the wise (Prov. 1,8; 15,5; cf. BS 6,20); his *mûsār* is folly (*'iwwelet*) (Prov. 16,22); he is prideful and self-assured about his ways (12,15; 14,3); he is contentious (12,16; 20,3; 27,3; Job 5,2); he is often accused of sinning through speech, i.e., babbling; he is not expected to keep silent, and therefore, if he does keep silent, he "is considered wise" (Prov. 17,28; cf. *The Instruction of Pap. Insinger* 3,7-8). In this connection we find the collocations *pî* ("mouth of") *'ěwîl* (Prov. 14,3), *'ěwîl ś^epātayîm* ("of lips" — 10,8,10),[56] and his mouth is said to be *m^eḥittâ* (i.e., "a disaster" — 18,7).

The *'ĕwîl* is indeed without wisdom (Prov. 10,21; 16,22; 24,7), but at the same time he is not without intellectual ability, even if this is channeled in negative ways: "A fool's (*'ĕwîl*)[57] intrigue is sin," states the sage in Proverbs (24,9).

'iwwelet, which appears in Proverbs (22 times) and Ben Sira (5 times),[58] denotes an attribute characteristic of human types usually relating to the negative category according to the sapiential perception. *'iwwelet* is a trait common to the *k^esîl* (Prov. 12,23; 15,2, 14; etc.), the *'ĕwîl* (16,22; 27,22), the *q^eṣar 'appayim* (14,17), the *q^eṣar rûaḥ* (14,29), the *rāšā'* (5,23), the *ḥăsar lēb* (15,21), the *petî* (14,18), as well as the *bēn* and the *na'ar* (Prov. 22,15; BS 30,13).

'iwwelet is bound up with sins of speech (see Prov. 15,2 where the opposite is "the tongue of the wise"; and also 12,23; 13,16; 26,4,5), and causes swindling and misleading (Prov. 14,9; 19,3; 24,9).

The folly of the *na'ar* (youth), whose ways are still amenable to correction, is driven out by beating (Prov. 22,15; cf. BS 30,13). Once *'iwwelet* is personified as a woman who demolishes her house in contrast to "Wisdom" who builds and maintains it (Prov. 14,1).[59]

The noun *'iwwelet* stands in antithetic parallelism with terms belonging to the semantic field of wisdom — *ḥokmâ/ôt*, *t^ebûnâ*, *bînâ* and *da'at* — and is in synonymous parallelism with *k^elimmâ* ("shame") (Prov. 18,13). The use of *'iwwelet* recalls the use of the noun *swg* in the Egyptian sources. *swg* is one of the traits of the *lḫ*, just as *'iwwelet* is a trait of the *'ĕwîl*, the *k^esîl*, the *petî*, etc., in the Biblical wisdom.

5. *lēṣ*

lēṣ (qal, participle; pl., *'anšê lāṣôn*)[60] belongs to the Biblical wisdom vocabulary and is found in Proverbs (14 times), Ben Sira (8 times), and the wisdom Psalm (once). The etymology of the term is not certain. Some believe that it derives from *lyṣ*, "to mock," and *lēṣ* (qal) is "a mocker, man of scorning"; others define him as one who talks incessantly, the babbler, adducing the Arabic root *laṣ* ("to turn aside") and the hiph'il participle *mēlîṣ*, meaning "spokesman," "interpreter".[61] Be that as it may, the chief failing of the *lēṣ* is connected with speech (see BS 35,18 [B,H]).

The *lēṣ* is a serious type of fool, worse than the *petî* and worse, even, than the *k*^e^*sîl*. While the Hebrew educator has not lost hope of improving the *k*^e^*sîl*, this is no longer the case with the *lēṣ*; for him who spurns reproof and rebuke (Prov. 13,1; 15,12; cf. BS 15,8) beating too is ineffectual (Prov. 19,25; 21,11): whoever attempts to teach him only brings "abuse" upon himself (9,7). Therefore, the sage advises, "Do not reprove a scorner (*lēṣ*) lest he hate you" (ibid. 8). These words are remarkably similar to what is stated about the Egyptian *lḫ*, who parallels the *lēṣ* in behavior and manners: "Do not instruct the *lḫ* lest he hate you" (*Ankhsheshonqy* 7,4).

It is the wicked nature of the *lēṣ*, "the bad shoot" in the language of Ben Sira (3,28), which prevents his access to knowledge. Even when he wishes to do so "a scorner (*lēṣ*) seeks wisdom in vain" (Prov. 14,6).[62]

Proverbs 21,24 contains a "definition" of the term: "*lēṣ* is the name of the proud, hot-tempered man (*zēd*), he who acts with insolent pride."[63] Besides insolence, a second trait is characteristic of the *lēṣ* in the social framework: he creates strife — "Drive out a scorner (*lēṣ*) and strife will go out, and quarrelling and abuse will cease" (Prov. 22,10; cf. 29,8); therefore, the *lēṣ* is a candidate for condemnation (Prov. 19,29).[64] The wise man counsels avoidance of his company, his isolation and even expulsion from the community (Prov. 22,10; Ps 1,1 [Wisdom Ps.]; cf. also BS 13,1). His negative conduct is reviled to such extent that it is said: "The *lēṣ* is an abomination to man" (Prov. 24,9).

Unlike the other varieties of fool listed so far, the *lēṣ* is involved prominently in the religious setting. The *lēṣ* is found in synonymous parallelism not only with the *petî* ("simple"), the *k*^e^*sîl* ("stupid"), but also with the *rāšāʿ* ("wicked") (Prov. 9,7; Ps. 1,1) and the *ḥăttāʾîm* ("sinners") (Ps. 1,1); and in antithetical parallelism it pairs with *ḥākām* (wise), *nābôn* ("man of understanding"), as well as *ʿănāwîm* ("humble persons") (*Q*^e^*rê*, Prov. 3,33). The *lēṣ* rejects and scorns all authority, secular or sacred. In the wisdom Psalm he is presented as an impious man who despises the Law, in contrast to the Godfearer, the student of the Law (Ps. 1); Ben Sira states explicitly that "the *lēṣ* does not uphold the Law" (35,18 [B] || "the *lēṣ* does not follow a commandment," 35,18 [H]).

To conclude, the *lēṣ* is the incorrigible fool, not necessarily on account of any intellectual inability but owing to his inherent bad nature. He is insolent and despises both the educational authority and the principles of religion, and the only way therefore to obviate his harmful influence is to expel him from the community.

6. *ba'ar*

The adjective *ba'ar*, which belongs to the language of Biblical poetry, appears only five times in the Bible and its occurrence is restricted to the wisdom books (Proverbs — twice; wisdom Psalm — 49,11; 73,22; Psalm with wisdom features — 92,7).

ba'ar derives from the noun *b*e*'îr*, "beast," "animal," and its primary meaning is a brutish man, stupid as a beast, a man whose stupidity stems from ignorance.[65] This image is presented in Psalm 73,22, where the pious man says, "I was brutish (*ba'ar*) without knowledge, a beast I was with you." It is also evident in the refrain in Psalm 49,13,21: "He is like the beasts that perish," referring to the *ba'ar* in verse 11.

ba'ar is synonymous with *k*e*sîl* (Ps. 92,7; 49,11) and stands in contrast with *ḥākām* (Ps. 49,11). It belongs to the supplicatory language of the Hebrew believer, who, like his Egyptian counterpart, desires to highlight his submission and insignificance before God. While the Egyptian pious man describes himself as "senseless" (*iw.ty ḥȝ.ty*) and compares his way of life to that of an ox (see p. 187 above), his Hebrew counterpart, to express a similar notion, simply applies the term *ba'ar* (Prov. 30,2; Ps. 49,11; 73,22; 92,7). In the relations between human beings *ba'ar* appears only once as one who "hates reproof (*tôkaḥat*)," in contrast to one "who loves reproof (*tôkaḥat*)" (Prov. 12,1).

7. *nābāl*

In wisdom language the adjective *nābāl*, although not a characteristic wisdom term, is used to denote another type of fool, which parallels *k*e*sîl* (Prov. 17,21).

Besides being an adjective the root *nbl* functions as a verb and a noun: in Proverbs (adjective 3 times, verb once), Job (adjective twice, noun, *n^ebālâ*, once) and in Ben Sira (adjective 4 times). To this should be added three passages outside the wisdom books that have wisdom features — Deuteronomy 32,6, Isaiah 32,5 and Jeremiah 17,11.[66]

Scholars are divided as to the etymology and semantic field of the *nābāl*. Some link the word to the Arabic *nabal*, i.e., "wretched things," or the Arabic *nabīl*, i.e., "noble" while others connect it with the Akkadian *napālu(m)*, meaning "to destroy"; Some derive it from the verb *nbl* ("to sink," "to drop down," "to languish"). Still others point to its proximity to the noun *n^ebēlâ* ("corpse") or connect it with the noun *n^ebālâ* ("disgrace"). This is not the place to enter into this debate,[67] and the discussion that follows focuses upon the definition of the adjective *nābāl* in relation to the other terms belonging to the semantic field of "foolishness" in the Biblical wisdom literature. Appearances of the *nābāl* outside wisdom texts are mentioned only if they shed light on the sapiential concept of *nābāl*.

In the familial setting, the *nābāl*, like the *k^esîl*, brings his father sorrow by rejecting his authority and teaching (Prov. 17,21; cf., ibid. 25; 10,1; 13,1; 15,5). Such a situation is depicted in Deuteronomy 32 where God assumes the image of the father, while the people appear as his disobedient sons, being described as a "stupid (*nābāl*) and senseless people" (Deut. 32,6).

In the social framework the *nābāl* appears as a person of inferior origins, called by Job "son of the nameless" (Job 30,8). Belonging to the lower social class *nābāl* comes in proximity to the "slave" and the "maid" (Prov. 30,22,23) and is an antonym of *nādîb*, a member of the upper class, a noble (Prov. 17,7).[68]

In the sapiential context *nābāl* primarily signifies a man of flawed character in terms of social morality; his weak traits are miserliness, arrogance and lying:

Miserliness, greed: the *nābāl*'s being "filled with food" is listed among a series of intolerable occurrences: "Under three things the earth trembles, under four it cannot bear up ... and a stupid man (*nābāl*) when he is filled with food" (Prov. 30,21-22). This statement may be interpreted in light of what is said of the *nābāl* in Biblical prophecy and historiography, where the foremost feature of the *nābāl* is his miserliness and greed. For example, "The stupid man (*nābāl*) will no more be called noble (*nādîb*) nor the knave (*kîlay*) said to be honorable (*šôa'*)... to leave the craving of the hungry unsatisfied and to deprive the thirsty of drink" (Isa. 32,5-6). Nabal of Carmel, true to his name, refuses to give of his food to David and his young men (1 Sam. 25,10ff); and the *nābāl* in Jeremiah 17,11, is described as "he who gets riches but not by right" (cf. BS 18,18 [Gr.]). Likewise Agur, in the passage quoted above (Prov. 30), states the traditional dogma that it is not seemly for the *nābāl* to be rich;[69] where this happens it is a sign of the collapse of universal order and the reign of anarchy.

Pride, arrogance: Proverbs 30,32 says, "if you act the fool (*nābaltā*) by exalting yourself or if you have been devising evil, put your hand on your mouth" (i.e., be silent, desist from these actions) for "pressing anger produces strife" (i.e., lest this stir up anger and result in strife) (ibid. 33);[70] Job attributes similar behavior to the young men, the "sons of *nābāl*," who mock his misfortune (Job 30,1-14).

Lying speech: "Honest speech"[71] does not correspond to *nābāl*, just as "false speech" does not fit with the *nādîb* (Prov. 17,7). The language characterizing the *nābāl* is that of *n^ebālâ* ("folly"); his words are of *ḥōnēp* and *tô'â*, i.e., hypocrisy and misleading falsehood (Isa. 32,6). This section in Isaiah concerns dealings between man and man but is set in a religious context; the *nābāl* is charged with uttering lies to God. Job, chapter 2, also makes use of the root *nbl* in a religious setting: Job accuses his wife of talking "as one of the foolish women" (*n^ebālôt*) (2,10), that is, of lying to God (cf. Ps. 14,1: "The *nābāl* says in his heart, 'There is no God'" || 53,2).

The *nābāl* therefore belongs only marginally to the semantic field of "foolishness" in the Biblical wisdom. Rather than pointing to the intellectual powers of a man it refers to his moral values with respect to of social and religious spheres. On the religious plane the meaning of *nābāl* approximates that of *rāšā'*, the "impious man" (in the same way as the term *nādîb*, which stands in antithetic parallelism with it, parallels *ṣaddîq* in Prov. 17,27). In this the *nābāl* brings to mind the Egyptian *lḫ*, who in his apostasy against the god stands close to the

Egyptian "wicked man" — the *s3be* (in *The Instruction of Pap. Insinger*).

8. *sākāl*, *siklût*, *sekel*

The root *skl*, which belongs to the late phase of Biblical Hebrew, is characteristic of the vocabulary of Qoheleth. The adjective *sākāl* appears in Qoheleth (5 times), but it appears in Jeremiah (4,22; 5,21),[72] and in Ben Sira (51,23) as well. The nouns *siklût* and *sekel*,[73] however, are unique to Qoheleth (7 times and once respectively).

As the *sākāl*, together with the *k^esîl*, covers the semantic field of "fool" in Qoheleth, it is possible to clarify the image of the *sākāl* by comparing it with the *k^esîl*.

From the verses in Qoheleth in which the *sākāl* is mentioned, it is evident that some of the traits inherent in him are identical with those which mark out the *k^esîl*, that is, lack of wisdom ("his heart is absent" — Qoh. 10,3; cf. BS 51,23ff.) and garrulity (Qoh. 10,14). Two features, on the other hand, distinguish the *sākāl* from the *k^esîl*. First, of all the terms for "fool" in the wisdom books only the *k^esîl* is singled out for his attitude towards cultic duties and his behavior in the temple. This is not the case with the *sākāl*; in Qoheleth 7,17 the *ṣaddîq* is indeed presented as the *ḥākām* and the *rāšā'* is termed *sākāl*, but this is not in context of cultic activity. Second, as Mandry has already suggested,[74] the *sākāl* is depicted in Qoheleth as one who has gained authority and power by illegal means. This is seen in the section describing the anarchy reigning in the land: "A fool (*sākāl*) is appointed to great heights while rich men sit in lowly places" (Qoh. 10,6);[75] and in 2,18-19 Qoheleth complains of the pointlessness of property gained through toil for upon his death "I must leave it to a man coming after me, and who knows whether he will be wise or foolish (*sākāl*)? And he will control all my wealth for which I had toiled in wisdom under the sun."

In overall features, then, the *sākāl* resembles the *k^esîl* in Qoheleth, with the former referring mainly to the plane of social morality while the latter also relates to the religious-moral sphere.[76]

The abstract noun *siklût*, found in the Bible only in Qoheleth, serves as an antonym for *ḥokmâ* and invariably accompanies it, together with the noun *hôlēlût/lôt* (1,17; 2,12; 7,25). Qoheleth wishes "to observe *ḥokmâ wᵉhôlēlôt wᵉsiklût*," namely, to experience them (2,12; cf. 1,17), and his conclusion is that *siklût* is identical with *hôlēlôt* (7,25).

9. ***hôlēlût*, *hôlēlôt***

The stem *hll* is polysemic and scholars are divided over its etymology. Most of them assert that its primary meaning is "shout," and point to Arabic, Aramaic and other Semitic languages. This meaning is preserved in the verbal forms in pi'el (*hillēl*) and hithpa'el (*hithallēl*), which carry the sense of "praise," "rejoice."[77]

The hithpo'el form *hithōlēl* means "to act like a madman" (see 1 Sam. 21,14-16 and cf. BS 3,27 — *mitḥôlēl* which, perhaps, should be *mithôlēl*); in po'al its meaning is "to be a fool," "to cause someone to act like a fool or madman," as expressed in Qoheleth 7,7, where *yᵉhôlēl* appears in synonymous parallelism with *wî'abbēd 'et lēb*, that is, "to destroy the mind" (see also Job 12,17). *hll* in the sense of "to be a fool" is found only in Qoheleth (once) and Job (once), in the verses cited above. The noun *hôlēlôt*[78] is found in the Bible only in Qoheleth (5 times).

hôlēlôt appears here always together with *siklût* and it is difficult to distinguish between the meaning of "folly" and "madness" which are both attached to the term.[79] *hôlēlôt* is thus situated on the boundary between the semantic fields of "folly" and "madness" (cf. *šȝšȝ* in Egyptian).

In Qoheleth 7,25 *hôlēlôt* and *siklût* are shown to be identical in the expression "the folly (is) madness"; in 10,13 *siklût* is juxtaposed with "evil *hôlēlût*" and elsewhere it is stated that it signifies "evil" (Qoh. 9,3; see also 1,17; 2,12).

Summary

The terms belonging to the topic of "foolishness" refer to different types of fools, who may be distinguished according to their intellectual capacity and their social and religious behavior. On the other hand, their descriptions in the wisdom books evince a uniformity and repetition of traits which appear common to them all. The descriptions relate to two levels: the social, which is more in prevalent, and the religious, which is less emphasized.

On the social level the individual is always presented as a part of a whole and his attitude to others as belonging to two frameworks — the narrower one of the family, where the attitude toward father and mother is scrutinized, and the broader one of the community. In this context the sage is concerned chiefly with two flaws in character that are found in the various kinds of fool — a refusal to accept educational authority (*k^esîl, 'ĕwîl, lēṣ*), and sins of speech (*'ĕwîl, k^esîl, petî, lēṣ, sākāl, nābāl*).

On the religious level, the terms at times indicate the erroneous way of the believer, who knows no better (*petî, ba'ar*), but more often they point to deliberate denial (*nābāl, lēṣ*).

As to the distribution of the terms (see Table 11), the smallest number of terms appear in Job, while the largest number with the most variety are found in Proverbs, especially in the fifth collection. However, *k^esîl* and *'ĕwîl* are also frequent in the second collection, and *petî, lēṣ* and *ḥăsar lēb* are common in the first collection. In the view of most scholars these collections belong to the early phase of wisdom in Proverbs.[80]

Terms whose usage disappeared after Proverbs (*ḥăsar lēb, petî*) or became rare (*lēṣ*) surface once more in Ben Sira. This book also contains the stem *skl* (in plural), which, as we have seen, is exclusive to Qoheleth among the Biblical wisdom books.

Comparison of the Egyptian and Hebrew terminology

(1) Semantic parallels

It is difficult to determine precise semantic equivalents in Egyptian for all the Hebrew terms, and vice versa. *ḥăsar lēb*, as we have seen, is the linguistic and semantic equivalent of *iw.ty ḥ3.ty* in Egyptian. In terms of subject matter the *petî* may be said to approximate the *ḥm* while the image of the *lēṣ* recalls the *lḫ*. In both Egyptian and Biblical Hebrew two groups of "fool" are distinguishable, the "positive" and the "negative": the former is open to correction, and the latter is not. In

Table 11: Distribution of Terms Relating to the Semantic Field of Foolishness in the Bible

	Term	Prov. (main collections)	Qoh.	Job	BS (Hebrew MSS)	Wisdom Ps.	Total
1)	*k^e sîl*	49 x (coll. 2,5)	18 x		5 x	3 x (49,92*,94*)	75
	kesel		1 x			1 x (49)	
	k^e sîlût	1 x					
2)	*'ĕwîl*	19 x (coll. 2,5)		2 x	4 x		25
	'iwwelet	22 x			5 x		27
3)	*lēṣ*	14 x (coll. 1,5)			8 x	1 x (1)	23
	lāṣôn	(*'anšê*) 1 x					
4)	*petî*(adj.)	14 x (coll. 1,5)			*pôteh*-4 x	2 x (19,119)	20
	petî(*n.*)	1 x					
	p^e tayyût	1 x					
5)	*ḥăsar lēb*	10 x (coll. 1,5) (1 x n.)			1 x		11
6)	*nābāl*	3 x		2 x	4 x		9
	n^e bālâ			1 x			
7)	*sākāl*		5 x		1 x		6
	sekel		1 x				
	siklût		6 x				6
8)	*ba'ar*	2 x				3 x (49,73,92*)	5
9)	*hôlēlût/ôt*		5 x				5

* Psalm with wisdom features (Whybray, see Corpus n. 17, above).

both languages the distinction between different types of "fools" can be understood in the form of a graded scale based on the intellectual-moral condition of the person.

Based on the foregoing, a tentative comparison of the Hebrew and Egyptian terminology shows the following gradation:

Positive fool (corrigible)

In the Bible:	**In Egyptian:**
1) *ḥăsar lēb, petî*	1) *ḫm, iw.ty ḥȝ.ty*
2) *k^{e}sîl* (*sākāl*?)	2) *wḫȝ*
3) *'ĕwîl*	3) *swg* (?)
4) *lēṣ*	4) *lḫ*
5) *nābāl*	

↓

Negative fool (incorrigible)

Some of the terms belonging to the semantic field of "folly" are, in both Egyptian and the Bible, cases on the borderline between this field and the semantic fields of "wickedness" and "madness." *nābāl* and *lēṣ* in the Biblical wisdom and *lḫ* in the Egyptian sources are close to "wickedness," while *hôlēlôt/ût* in Hebrew and apparently *šȝšȝ* in Egyptian have the basic meaning of "madness."

(2) Parallels in subject matter

The Egyptian and the Biblical wisdom do not deal with defining the various types belonging to this field — their nature and quality are evidenced by *different* ways of behavior in *similar* life situations. The Biblical sage refers more to the social and less to the intellectual aspect involved in these terms; the Egyptian wisdom places greater emphasis on the educational-didactic aspect. But according to both the Hebrew and the Egyptian concept the mental state is an inseparable part of a man's character and moral traits. A man devoid of intellect and without knowledge is also defective in his moral nature on both the social and religious levels. The more limited a man's faculties in terms of acquiring knowledge the greater the danger he poses to the social and religious life of the community.

In the didactic wisdom literature in the Bible, as in the Egyptian wisdom, great attention is paid to education. From the above investigation of "folly" emerge several common points:

(a) The Hebrew and the Egyptian sage recognize the limitations of education; the *'ĕwîl*, possessing as he does a wicked nature (cf. *swg*), cannot be taught; anyone attempting to teach a *lēṣ* (cf. *lḫ*) brings disgrace upon himself.

(b) Although in Israel, unlike in Egypt, texts belonging explicitly to the school institution have not been discovered, at least part of the Biblical wisdom texts may be related to this framework indirectly (see pp. 349ff below). Thus, e.g., if one accepts the view of scholars that the first collection in Proverbs is an educational text intended for pupils,[81] the terms contained in it — *petî*, *ḥăsar lēb*, and *lēṣ* — may be regarded as the terminology of the early Hebrew school, like *šꜣšꜣ*, *iw.ty ḥꜣ.ty*, *gwš*, *ḫn*, which appear in the texts of the Egyptian school.

(c) One of the central themes of Proverbs (especially 10,2-11,6) is the confrontation between the "fool" and the "wise man." The topic is also dominant in the Demotic instructions, and its origins can even be traced back to the early Egyptian wisdom.

In light of this, Licht's assertion that since "in the wisdom literature of the peoples the conflict between the wise man and the fool is not mentioned at all ... the image of the fool is characteristic, and unique to the Israelite wisdom literature"[82] seems to be incorrect and needs to be re-examined.[83]

(3) The exclusive nature of the Hebrew material

Two features stand out in Hebrew wisdom with respect to "foolishness":

(a) Only in Israel is there personification of the abstract nouns "wisdom" and "folly," in both cases in the form of a woman.[84] In Proverbs 9,1-6, 13-18 *ḥokmâ* and *kᵉsîlût* appear as houseowners who invite passers-by to participate in their meals. In Proverbs 14,1 "wisdom" (*ḥakmôt nāšîm*)[85] is set against "folly" (*'iwwelet*) and again both appear in the guise of women, one who destroys her house, the other who builds it.

In Egypt we do find personification of abstract qualities — especially relevant for our purposes is the personification of the Ma'at, whom some identify with the female figure of wisdom in Proverbs[86] — but there is no personification of "foolishness" in the Egyptian wisdom sources.

(b) The Hebrew wisdom makes greater use of abstract nouns than the Egyptian: *'iwwelet* (22 times), *k^{e}sîlût* (once), *siklût* (7 times), *p^{e}tayyût* (once), *hôlēlût/ôt* (5 times).[87]

Synopsis

Similarity and dissimilarity in Egyptian and Biblical wisdom in the semantic field of foolishness:

	Similar		Dissimilar
1.	Gradation in seriousness of mental-moral condition of the fool.	1.	Lack of reference to the of formal pedagogical framework (school) in the Bible.
2.	Distinction between two main groups — positive and negative fool.	2.	Lack of personification of "foolishness" in the Egyptian wisdom.
3.	Confrontation between the fool and the wise man.	3.	Limited use of abstract nouns in the Egyptian wisdom literature.
4.	No definition of the type but concern with behavior and various activities.		
5.	The pious man represents himself as a fool, ignorant like a beast.		
6.	The borders of the semantic field of "foolishness" are "wickedness" on the one hand and "madness" on the other.		

CHAPTER SIX

THE CONSEQUENCES OF ACQUIRING WISDOM: WISE AND WISDOM

I. SEMANTIC ANALYSIS OF THE TERMS

The number of terms relating to the semantic field of "wise," "wisdom" is relatively large. This is not surprising since the topic stands at the pinnacle of the sapiential ideology. Who is the wise man? What is the distinction between him and the fool? What are the sources of wisdom? Is wisdom purchased, endowed, or is it a natural skill? Are there boundaries to man's intellectual abilities? — These are only some of the issues that absorb the wise man's mind.

In Egyptian

1. *rḫ* (Dem. *rḫ* ; Copt. ϣ-)

The most common root in the semantic field of "wisdom" is *rḫ*, meaning "to know," "to recognize" (*Wb.* II 442). Its antonym is *ḫm*, "know not", "to be ignorant of" . The word is preserved in Demotic and in Coptic ϣ- means "to know," "to be capable of."[1] *rḫ* appears in this corpus as verb, noun and adjective.

Verb:

As a verb *rḫ* has the general sense of "to know" and is not limited to the wisdom vocabulary. Therefore, the discussion below is restricted to thosc applications of *rḫ* that are characteristic of the Egyptian wisdom sources and that may serve for comparison with the Biblical material.

Usually *rḫ* is transitive and is associated with various kinds of objects, e.g., eloquence (*Wb.* II 443,23; Jansen-Winkeln I A10, e,3; II 3,6,12), skill at reading and writing (in the school writings — *Kheti* XXII A; *Lansing* 2,2); and, in particular, knowledge of the future: the formula "Behold, man cannot know what will happen" (*Kagemni* II 2) recurs in different versions in the wisdom sources and serves to emphasize man's impotence as compared to the divine omnipotence (cf. *Ptaḥḥotep* 343; *The Eloquent Peasant* B1 183; *Amenemope* 23,8-9 || 22, 5-6).

Another common topic is knowledge of human nature, knowing "the name" of a man, "the excellence of his heart," "the excellence of his advice." This awareness is especially important in the sphere of those who are in the service of the king: in praise of himself the high official declares that "his master" or "the king" knows his "name" (Janssen I p. 77, Bl 80; *Urk.* IV 514,9; Blumenthal G4,46); the opposite view is stated in *The Instruction of Amenemope*: "A man at the side of an official, his name should not be known" (24, 6-7). The phrase "to know the god" signifies faithful behavior towards him, the conduct of the pious man (*Wb.* II 442, 12-14);[2] and likewise "to know his plans (*sḫr*)" (*Amenemope* 23, 8 || 22,5; Janssen I p. 75, Bl 44; etc.).

At times *rḫ* in Egyptian, like *yd'* in the Bible, has a sexual sense: "to know a person carnally" (*Ptaḥḥotep* 288; *Ankhsheshonqy* 20,23).[3] *rḫ*, with or without the preposition *r*, occasionally takes on the sense of "to discern," "to distinguish between" (*Urk.* IV 970,1, "fool" and "wise man"; *ÄHG* 149,8, "good and evil"; cf. *Wb.* II 444,1). The collocation *rdi rḫ*, meaning "to cause someone to know," "to teach," is set as the goal of instruction and the function of the high official. In the epilogue to *The Instruction of Amenemope* it is written, "They (the thirty chapters) teach (*rdi rḫ*) the fool (*ḫm*)" (27,10) (cf. *Seḥetep-ib-Ra* 1,5; *The Eloquent Peasant* B1 287; *Kheti* XXII G; etc.). The official of the 18th Dynasty causes "every man to know his duty" (*Urk.* IV 967,9; 1006,5; etc.).

The active participle, *rḫ*, serves as an attributive, indicating the mastery of the artisan (*Wb.* II 445,4); the skilled, learned scribes are *sš.w rḫyt* (*Sallier* I 1,6 according to *Wb.* ibid.).[4] The passive participle *rḫḫy* means "well-known," "renowned" (*Urk.* IV 119,3).

As to the question of possession of knowledge or the lack of it, man usually is portrayed as one who is ignorant (of the future, see above, of the day of his death, etc. — *Anii* 5,2; 10,9; *Admonitions* 2,3). The "fool" (*ḫm*, *wḫ3*) is particularly notable for his lack of knowledge (*Peasant* B1 287; etc.). By contrast, the god appears as "knowing": Amon knows the future (*Urk.* IV 244,15); the god knows the nature and thoughts of man (*To Merikare* 123; *Urk.* IV 1083, 6ff); he knows "the silent man" (ibid., 1083, 11) and him who serves him faithfully (*To Merikare* 67); he is acquainted with "the heated man," "the foe" (ibid. 49; *Amenemope* 5, 17); and, finally, the god knows and determines man's fate (*Anii* 6,9).

Among men, the king takes first place as one who knows (mainly in the phraseology of the king's court — *Urk.* IV 429,1,5; 514,9, etc.; Janssen I p. 76; Blumenthal 325-327). The high official, too, lauds himself as "one who knows": the future (Hatnub is "the knower of tomorrow before its advent" — Janssen I p. 75, Bl 41; cf. *Rekhmire* — *Urk.* IV 1129,12); his social position in the king's court (to which belong the phrases "recognizes the place of his foot" [*s.t rd.f*], or "his steps" [*nmt.t.f*], Janssen I p. 74, Bl 15ff.); and palace rules, matters of law and justice, the advice of the god, etc. (see Janssen I pp. 74ff.; Blumenthal 408; etc.).

Noun:

The noun *rḫ* is less common than the verb in our sample. *rḫ*, which is antithetical to *ḫm*, and in synonymous parallelism with *šs3* and *ḥmww ib*, refers to "knowledge" originating in the tradition of the ancestors and transmitted by way of instruction acquired through learning. Therefore, the instruction itself is termed "knowledge" — in *To Merikare* it is said: "Copy your forefathers... See, their words endure in books; open, read them and copy the knowledge (*rḫw*)" (35-36); at the close of *Papyrus Insinger*, too, the work is called "the end of giving knowledge in order that one might know" (*n ty rḫ ʿme*) (35,13; cf. *Kheti* XXIII A). But *rḫ* may also relate to innate wisdom possessed by man from the moment of his birth (see below). *rḫ* is usually the practical knowledge that equips one to carry out his duties properly. Antef is an excellent scribe who interprets the writings skillfully and is "equipped with knowledge" (*Urk.* IV 969,14,16). The officials of the king's court in the 11th and 12th Dynasties succeeded in averting wrongdoing by virtue of "the greatness of their knowledge" (Janssen I p. 74, Bl 7-10). The topic of "knowledge" is thus usually bound up with daily affairs and practical information; rarely does *rḫ* in our examples concern religious matters or some form of abstract knowledge: the inscription of the father of Petosiris speaks of "knowledge of the powers" (*rḫ b3.w.f*) of the god (Lefebvre 116,4 || Otto No. 46), while elsewhere knowledge of the "mysteries" is mentioned (*Urk.* IV 1209, 1).

The natural aim of "knowledge" is indeed the "fool" (*ḫm*) (*Ptaḥḥotep* 47; cf. ibid. 577); but also one who already possesses "knowledge," namely, the "wise man" (*rḫ* or *šs3*) must continue to learn, for there is no limit to wisdom (ibid. 52-54, 573; *Ankhsehshonqy* 8,3).

Adjective:

The active participle *rḫ* is used adjectivally for "wise" beginning in the Middle Kingdom (*Wb.* II 445). Sometimes *rḫ* is collocated with *ḫ.t*, "thing," to form *rḫ (i)ḫ.t*, literally "he who knows something," i.e., "wise," whose antithesis is the *ḫm (i)ḫ.t* (*Peasant* B1 219). The passive participle (imperfect) *rḫḫ* expresses the sense of "learned man,"[5] and in Demotic *rmt rḫ*, literally "wise man" (fem. *sḥm.t rmt rḫ.t*), appears.

The adjective *rḫ*, "wise," is in synonymous parallelism with other adjectives having the same meaning — *s33*, *si3*, *wḥ' ib* — and in antithetic parallelism with terms signifying the "fool" — *ḫn*, *lḫ*, *swg*, *wḫ3* — and other negative human types — *rmt bn* (Dem. "bad man"), *s3be* (Dem. "wicked man").

The *rḫ* occurs in all genres belonging to the wisdom literature. Its limited appearance, therefore, in the school writings and its complete absence from the "loyalist" instructions are remarkable.

The *rḫ*, the "wise man," is principally one who has acquired knowledge and does not cease storing up wisdom (*Ptaḥḥotep* 52-54, 573; cf. *To Merikare* 36). Himself the possessor of knowledge, he is capable of teaching others (Janssen I p. 73, Bl 2,3,4,6) and he is a master of rhetoric: Neferti, the "wise," utters "fine words, choice phrases" to the king (*Neferti* 13). *rḫ* may denote not only a man who satisfies the norms presented in the didactic instructions but also someone expert in a particular pursuit, e.g., a craftsman, a scribe, a magician[6] and a soothsayer (*Wb.* II 445,4; 443, 28ff.).[7]

As the concept of wisdom makes no distinction between intellectual faculties and moral virtue, the *rḫ* also fulfils all the requirements of sapiential morality: he controls his emotions, displays restraint (*Insinger* 6,8; 9,23; Otto No. 39 || *ZÄS* 46, 75ff. l.1; etc.). In the social setting he brings benefit to others by giving good counsel (*Ptaḥḥotep* 54); the *rḫ* is a reliable and honest man, both as messenger and in other matters (*Ankhsheshonqy* 6,13; *Insinger* 10,2; 26, 19, 22, 24). Therefore, the sages advise to seek association with him (*Ankhsheshonqy* 13,6) and counsel marriage to him (ibid. 25,15).

In the later wisdom the *rḫ* is the pious man, who follows the way of the god (*Insinger* 29,3-5) and wins his reward (ibid. 5,15; 35,11; 29,5; see also *Ankhsheshonqy* 18,11; 21, 7-8). In the Demotic instructions statements are made in praise of the wise woman (*Ankhsheshonqy* 8,22; *Insinger* 8,5; cf. "a woman of valor," Prov. 31,10ff.).

The king and the high official represent themselves as "the ideal wise man." Merikare's father describes the king thus: "The Lord of the Two Banks is one who knows (*rḫ iḫ.t*). A king ... is not ignorant (*wḫ3*). As one wise (*s33*) did he come from the womb" (115-116; cf. Blumenthal G1 40); the officials of the 11th and 12th Dynasties pride themselves on being wise men (Janssen I pp. 73-74), even "wise from the womb" — like the king (ibid. p. 73, Bl 3).[8]

The epithet *rḫw*, i.e., "the sage" par excellence, is applied to Thoth, the god of the scribes and of wisdom.

To illuminate and more sharply delineate the figure of the *rḫ*, the Egyptian sage juxtaposes him with his opposite, the "fool" (*wḫ3*, *lḫ*, *swg*, *ẖn*).[9] The employment of this contrast begins to appear in early wisdom, *The Instruction of Ptaḥḥotep*, continues in *The Admonitions* and attains its fullest expression in the Demotic *Instruction of Pap. Insinger*.

The fool is the opposite of the wise man in conduct and manners: The wise man learns, the fool (*wḫ3*) is hard pressed (*Ptaḥḥotep* 573-574); the wise man says "yes," the fool (*wḫ3*) says "no" (*Amenemhet* XIV B;

Admonitions 6, 13); the wise man displays self-control, the fool (*lḫ*) is greedy (*Insinger* 5, 16-18); the wise man is impeccable, the fool (*lḫ*) reveals his stupidity through his tongue (ibid. 12,23-24); one should keep the company of the wise man and not of the fool (*swg*, *lḫ*) (*Ankhsheshonqy* 13,6,7); the wise messenger is preferable to the foolish (*lḫ*) one (ibid. 6,13 and cf. *Insinger* 21,22); the fool (*lḫ*) is without recompense while the wise man receives his reward (*Ankhsheshonqy* 18,11; 21, 7-8; cf. *Insinger* 29, 5-6).

In the later wisdom sources a note of uncertainty begins to appear in this traditional outlook dividing mankind into two clear-cut categories of "wise" and "fool," good and bad.[10] In *The Instruction of Pap. Insinger* the boundaries between "wise" and "fool" are blurred. The author of the later instruction presents facts firmly based on reality that serve to dislodge the conventional axioms: There is a "wise man" who does not know (*Insinger* 4,19); he who lives like a wise man is not always wise, and he whose life is hard is not a fool (*lḫ*) (ibid. 5,5,6; see also 22, 3-4; 25,11; 27,18).

In sum, the *rḫ* is one who has learned, has acquired knowledge, and is able to make his knowledge benefit him in his daily life; this takes place both in the relationship between man and his fellow men and in that between the pious person and his god.

2. *s33*

s33 appears in the present sample as a verb, an abstract noun (*s3.t*; *s33*), and the participle form is used as an adjective.[11] The determinatives accompanying *s33* are identical with those of *rḫ*, i.e., a man with one hand to his mouth and a rolled papyrus, signifying thought and spiritual activity (Gr Y1). *s33* apparently has a connection with the root *s33* whose meaning is "to be satisfied, sated with" (*Wb.* IV 14-15); that is, *s33* has the literal meaning of "to be full of wisdom" and it involves the comparison of the process of acquiring wisdom with eating, which appears often in the wisdom sources.[12]

s33 is characteristic of the king's court writings and common in the early instructions (*Ptaḥḥotep*, *To Merikare*, *Instruction by a Man for His Son*), it is not found in the school writings and the instructions of the

New Kingdom (*Anii*, *Amenemope*).[13] *s33* is synonymous with the lexemes *rḫ* and *s3r*[14] and at times interchanges with them.

The wisdom to which the concept *s33* relates is multifaceted. On the one hand, *s3.t*, like *rḫ*, is acquired wisdom, studied in an educational framework. The sage *s33*, therefore, may be defined as "school[15] for the nobles" (*To Merikare* 33); Ptaḥḥotep tells his son, "Teach (*sb3*) the great (man) what is useful to him ... Thus you let his knowledge (*s33*) impress his ... lord" (399-401).

On the other hand, *s33* signifies wisdom which is not acquired but is innate wisdom, wisdom which is the property of the gods. The father of Merikare says, "As one wise (*s33*) did he come from the womb" (117). This formula is also common in the language of officialdom. It is said of the chief treasurer Icher-Nofret that "he came out of the womb as a wise man (*s33*)" (Janssen I p. 32, Ar 6 cf. p. 31, Ar 4 and Blumenthal G1,40). The author of *The Instruction of Ptaḥḥotep* contradicts this concept, asserting that "no one is born wise (*s33*)" (41). Among the gods this wisdom is primarily the property of Thoth, the god of wisdom. Therefore, kings, who liken themselves to this god, are termed *s33* — "wise"; Thutmosis III boasts with the words "I became wise in the wisdom of the gods (*ss33.kwi m s3r.t*)" (*Urk.* IV 160,6).

This wisdom, which is acquired by study or originates in a natural talent, relates to the practical skills of a man, demonstrated in a particular post which he fills or in his professional expertise: *s3.t* is wisdom manifested in the capacity for administration and rulership in both the high official and in his master the king; the official is wise (*s33*), conducting negotiations with the great and being versed in court protocol (*Ptaḥḥotep* 399-401; cf. the biography of Amon's priest — Janssen-Winkeln I A9,d2; II 3,5,5); in this connection appear the expressions "knows procedure," "obeys," "wise in understanding" (*s33 sbḳ*) (Janssen I pp. 31-32, Ar 1,3,5,8). The king is termed *nb s3.t*, "lord of wisdom" (see Blumenthal G1,41; *Sinuhe* B 48 — Sesostris I; cf. *Wb.* IV 16,1). Less frequently *s33* is concerned with technical or professional proficiency. The professions included here are the scribe — the scribe Intef, entitled *s33*, is described as an interpreter of written texts and equipped with knowledge (*Urk.* IV 969,14,16)[16] — and the soothsayer — Neferti, the wise lector-priest, utters "fine words" before the king, depicting the future (*Neferti* 7).

From the above analysis it appears that *sꜣ.t* is wisdom possessed by both gods and human beings, and that, where men are concerned, this virtue is limited to the upper class. The common folk are not among the fortunate who merit the epithet *sꜣꜣ*, unlike *rḫ*, which can be applied to all people. Another distinguishing feature is that in the present corpus only *rḫ* relates to the aspect of social morality.

3. *sꜣr*

sꜣr, which is in use only from the Middle Kingdom onwards, appears in our corpus mainly as a noun, *sꜣr.t* (12 times) and twice as a verb. The determinatives are identical to those appearing with the foregoing terms except one which is "a string of a bow."[17] The expression *sꜣr*, which stands in synonymous parallelism with *rḫ*, is not characteristic of the wisdom vocabulary but belongs to the language of the biographical writings of the king's court.

sꜣr.t is wisdom that stems primarily from life experience. It is the understanding of the adult, inexistent in the child. *The Admonitions* speaks of "a child without knowledge" (*nḫn n sꜣr.t.f* — 16,1). This is repeated in the description of Haremhab's coronation ceremony: "Food was given him in abundance while he was yet a child without understanding" (*iw.f m ḥwn nn sꜣr.t.f*) (line 3 — Gardiner, *JEA* 39, 13ff.). But *sꜣr.t* may also be gained through learning: the author of *Kemit* studied the books of his ancestors and "after that I became wise (*m-ḫt sꜣr.i*)" (pl. 19).

sꜣr.t is a characteristic quality of the gods; like *rḫ* and *sꜣꜣ* it refers principally to the god of wisdom, Thoth (*Wb.* IV 18,12). *sꜣr.t* is also the possession of men of the higher social class. The king is called "lord of understanding," *nb sꜣr.t*, an understanding imparted to him by the gods (Haremhab, above, line 11). In addition, this epithet is applied to the vizier and treasury keeper of the 18th Dynasty (*Urk.* IV 67,10; 513,6); others are "excellent" or "of good understanding" (*iḳr*/*nfr sꜣr.t*) (ibid. 481,13; 527,7; 993,4; 1183,3), while Seḥetep-ib-Ra, who holds the post of high official in the temple, is he whose "lord recognized his wisdom (*sȝr.t.f*)" (PL 8,4; cf. *The Biography of Neb-neteru*, the 22nd Dyn. — Janssen-Winkeln I A10, d,2).

4. ***siȝ***

The term *siȝ*, meaning "perception," "knowledge," and appearing from the Pyramid Texts onward (*Wb.* IV 30), is not characteristic of wisdom language and is usually found in the terminology of the biographical writings.[18] It appears in the present corpus as a verb and as an abstract and proper noun, and is accompanied by three determinatives. One, identical to that of the previous term, is a man with one hand to his mouth, while the other two portray the particular meaning of the term, namely, an eye, signifying discernment, penetration, and a god, signifying personification of the abstract value *siȝ*.[19]

siȝ means "knowledge of," "insight into" an object. In our sample this object is usally a person. The authors of the biography flaunt the fact that the king "knew them" for their superior qualities (*Urk.* IV 429,2; 898,14; Blumenthal G4 53,54; etc.). The special significance of the word comes to the fore when *siȝ*, is collocated with the term "heart," meaning discernment of the feelings and thoughts harbored within it: "You do not know (*n siȝ.n.k*) my heart," says the Eloquent Peasant to the official (*The Eloquent Peasant* B1 298); Intef, enumerating his own talents, calls himself "one who knows the heart" (*siȝ ib*, i.e., is perceptive) (*Urk.* IV 971,1; cf. Janssen I p. 95, Cz 1; etc.).

siȝ is also a proper noun, referring to the knowledge of the god Reʿ who created the world assisted by Sia, "wisdom" and Ḥu, the "creative word." In its hypostatic form *siȝ* is then perceived as a virtue possessed by the king, who is the representative of the creator god on earth. The formula "*ḥw* is in (your) mouth, *siȝ* is in (your) heart" is common in the Egyptian literature when mention is made of the god or the king (Blumenthal G 1,43,44).[20] At times Ḥu and Sia are joined by Maʿat (truth), and these denote three divine attributes in possession of the king; in his words of reproof addressed to the King the Egyptian sage says, "Ḥu, Sia and Maʿat were with you" (*Admonitions* 12,12; etc.).

siȝ is thus charismatic wisdom, pertaining to gods (Amon-Reʿ —

see Blumenthal G 1,43; Thoth — *Urk.* IV 498, 2-4) and kings (of Sesostris I it is said in *Sinuhe*, "Lord of knowledge (*siꜣ*) who knows people..." [B 214-215]; cf. the descriptions of the following kings: Amenemhet III — *Seḥetep-ib-Ra* 2,5; Akhenaten — *ÄHG* 235, 9; and see also Blumenthal G 1,44).[21]

To sum up, *siꜣ* means "to know someone thoroughly." As a noun it has a double sense: that of an abstract quality — perception, sagacity — and that of endowed, charismatic wisdom, possessed by gods and kings but never by ordinary mortals.

5. ***šsꜣ***

šsꜣ, meaning "to be expert," "skilled," appears in our corpus as a verb, noun and adjective. The determinative is a rolled papyrus, indicating spiritual activity, sometimes accompanied by the drawing of the head of a bubalis (Gr F5). *šsꜣ* pertains most probably to the terminology of the school for scribes in Egypt, as 14 of its 35 occurrences refer to the scribal profession. It is not frequent in the instructions (only twice in *To Merikare* and *Anii*) but appears often in the school writings and in the king's court phraseology. The stem *šsꜣ* stands in synonymous parallelism with some of the terms belonging to the subject of wisdom, such as *rḫ*, *sbꜣ* and phrases such as "a useful noble," "an excellent man," indicating a positive human type. On the other hand it appears in antithetic parallelism with the fool, *ḫm*. *šsꜣ* signifies expertise through experience and practice. The verb is generally accompanied by the preposition *m* or *ḥr*, followed by the object of expertise. The area of expertise is varied, ranging from the ability to read and write to mastery of a specific profession or subject. In *Papyrus Chester Beatty* IV the pupil is told: "After you are well versed in the writings (*iw swt šsꜣw.k m sš*) you enter into the instructions" (pl. 19, verso 4,6 || 4,9) (cf. *Anii* 7,4); of the *šsꜣ* scribe it is said, "The instruction of books is graven in his heart" (*Anastasi* I 11,2; cf. *Urk.* IV 1083,16). The high official is proficient in building (*Rekhmire*, *Urk.* IV 1152,12), in matters of law (Janssen I p. 34, Ay 4), in work (ibid. Ay 5), in the writings (*Urk.* IV 121,2 || 151,15 || 509,22 || 1223,13; *Wb.* II 181,4;), and the like.

Sometimes the *šsꜣ* is joined to a noun and serves as an attributive with the meaning of "expert," "skillful": in *Papyrus Anastasi* I, *sš šsꜣw* is a master scribe (14,5; 18,1); in *Papyrus Lansing* mention is made of *šsꜣ ḏbʿw*, "skillful fingers," that is, a scribe whose fingers are experienced in the craft of writing (3,1); in *Urk.* IV the collocation *šsꜣ ḥr*, meaning "gifted," is frequent (118,4; 509,2; 555,4; 1017,1; etc.). In the religious context *šsꜣ* expresses the relationship between the god and the pious man. The god is well acquainted (*šsꜣ*) with him who offers sacrifices (*To Merikare* 130); while the godfearer is intimate with the "plan of god" (*sḫr n nṯr* — inscription of the father of Petosiris, Lefebvre 116,4).

6. *ḥmw* (Dem. *ḥm*; Copt. ϩⲁⲙ)[22]

The hieroglyph signifying the term *ḥmw* is a stone-worker's drill (Gr U24), which indicates that the primary meaning of *ḥmw* was connected with handicraft, and from there was transferred into the sphere of abstract knowledge.

The root *ḥmw*, which begins to appear in the Old Kingdom, has two principal meanings: (a) "to create," "build," e.g., the construction of a chariot, goldsmithing, etc.; (b) "skill," "to be expert, skilled" (*Wb.* III 82-86).

In our corpus *ḥmw* is present as a verb, meaning "to create," "to build"; as a noun, *ḥm.t*, has the double sense of "craftsmanship" and "skill" while the adjective *ḥmww* signifies a craftsman or one who is skilled.[23] In New Egyptian and Demotic (*ḥm*) it means "carpenter" (*Instruction of Anii*, *Ankhsheshonqy*); and in Coptic ϩⲁⲙ has the sense of "craftsman" (Crum 673-674).

Only in the sense of "skill" does *ḥmw* belong to the semantic field under review, and this therefore lies at the center of the following discussion. *ḥmw* in this sense appears in synonymous parallelism with *sbꜣ*, *rḫ*, *šsꜣ ḥr* (|| *ḥmww ib*), and in antithetic parallelism with *ḫm*.[24]

The distribution of *ḥmw* is wide — it is found in texts ranging from the Old Kingdom to the Late Period (30th Dynasty), and while it is common in the biographical writings (21 times), it also appears frequently in the instructions (from *Ptaḥḥotep* to the Demotic instructions — 11 times).

ḥmw relates to two levels: (a) On the professional level *ḥmw* denotes the qualifications required of the high official. In this context the common formula in the texts is "the best craftsman in his trade" (*ḥmww n wnw.t.f*, lit. "the skilled one, competent, in his trade" — Janssen I pp. 29-30, Al 1,4,6,9). Of the excellent scribe it is said that he is "skilled with his fingers" (ibid. Al 7). (b) On the level of general education *ḥmw* — primarily in the instructions but also in the biographical texts — refers to the principles of education and general knowledge:

Mastery of the art of speaking. This is evident not only in the way one speaks but also in the ability to listen to others. A detailed definition of a man so gifted is given in an inscription from the Late Period written by the priest of Amon in Thebes: "His saying was select, there was no hatred in his words.... an expert in speech, who balances the hearts, his utterance was like milk" (Janssen-Winkeln I A7, e,3-4 || Otto No. 3 || *KCG* 42212, p. 35 E 3-4). Ptaḥḥotep, wishing to stimulate these talents in his son, commands him to "speak (only) after you have mastered the craft" (lit. "have entered the act of a craftsman" — *sp n ḥmww*) (615); "He who hears becomes a master-hearer (*ḥmww*)" (518). Here too belongs the phrase *ḥmww mdw* (or *ḥmww m md.t*), "skilled in speaking" (*To Merikare* 32; cf. *Ptaḥḥotep* 367).

Mastery of knowledge. Out of one who is taught (*sbb3yw*) develops the expert (*ḥmww*), says the Egyptian sage (*To Merikare* 36). This expertise can refer to any form of knowledge, whether derived from books (ibid.) or obtained otherwise (*Ptaḥḥotep* 56; *The Eloquent Peasant* B1 260). The idiom *ḥmww ib*, "gifted," is common in this context (*Urk.* IV 555,3; *KCG* above; *Wb.* III 83,4).

ḥmww is first and foremost the epithet of the high official, who appears as the master leader of the artisans (*ḥmww*) or of "every craft (*ḥm.t nb.t*)," or as the one "standing at the head of the artisans" (*Urk.* IV 411,17; 434,12; 1173,2; etc.). On a few occasions *ḥmww* is applied to the god (the creator god Ptah, ibid. 555,3; see *Wb.* III 82,14), or to the king (*Urk.* IV 555, 3 and *Wb.* III 83, 16).

7. *‘rḳ*

‘rḳ, meaning "to be clever, skilled," "to gain full knowledge of," is present as a verb, adjective and noun in our corpus. The noun *‘rḳw*, "skill," and the adjective *‘rḳ*, "skilled, clever," pertain to the subject under review, while the verb *‘rḳ*, "to be skilled," belongs to the semantic field of learning, acquiring knowledge. The root *‘rḳ* in all its forms is discussed in Chapter 2 (see pp. 62–63 above).

Summary

The terms belonging to the subject "wise," "wisdom" complement each other in range of distribution (diachronic and synchronic [i.e., literary genres]) and in semantic field.

At the head of the table of distribution (Table 12) stands the root *rḫ*, which appears most frequently (97 times) and covers almost all the genres belonging to wisdom literature, beginning with the Old Kingdom texts and ending with the Demotic instruction. The other terms occur less in the instructions and more in the biographical literature of the king's court (*sꜣr*, *siꜣ*, *šsꜣ*, *ḥmw*) and in the school texts (*šsꜣ*). These lexemes appear mainly in texts of the Middle and New Kingdoms, and are not found in Demotic.

The terms are alike in meaning and have similar linguistic usages. They are all in synonymous parallelism with *rḫ* and some are interchangeable in collocations. For example, the expression "lord of wisdom" has three variants: *nb* + *sꜣ.t*/*sꜣr.t*/*siꜣ*; the phrase "wise from birth" may be rendered by the stems *rḫ* or *sꜣꜣ*, while the expert scribe is he who has skillful (*šsꜣ*) fingers (*ḏb‘.w*), or who is *ḥmww m ḏb‘.w.f* or *rḫ ḏb‘.w.f*.[25]

At the same time, various nuances of meaning may be discerned:

rḫ — its primary sense is knowledge obtained by learning and intended for a practical purpose. Sometimes *rḫ* may also refer to innate wisdom.

siꜣ — means "to gain full knowledge of," "to penetrate" into something. *siꜣ* is charismatic wisdom, belonging to the god and the king, and as

Table 12: Distribution of Terms Relating to the Semantic Field of Wise, Wisdom in Egyptian

Literary Genre	Name of Composition or Source	*rḫ* (v.,n.,adj.)	*s3ꜣ* (v.,n.,adj.)	*s3r* (v.,n.)	*si3* (v.,n.)	*šs3* (v.,adj.)	*ḥmw* (v.,n.,adj.)	*ʿrḳ* (v.,n.*,adj.*)
Instruction	*Kagemni*							
	Ptahhotep	6	4		1		5	
	To Merikare	1	3			3	3	
	Amenemhet	1					1	
	Anii	1				1		1
	Amenemope				3			
	Ankhsheshonqy	24					1	
	Insinger	34** (67)					1** (11)	
"Loyalist" Instruction	*Man for His Son* *Sehetep-ib-Ra*		1	1	1	1		
Pessimistic Wisdom	*Admonitions* *Man Who Was Tired* *Khakheperre-sonb* *Neferti*	5	1	1	3	3	4	1
School Texts	*LEM* *Anastasi* I *Chester Beatty* IV *Demotic Pap.* (Williams)	4		1	1	10	2	1
Royal Court Literature & Biography	*Urk.* IV Blumenthal Janssen	17	11	9	15	18	21	1 (*ʿrḳ ib*)
Late Biography	Otto Jansen-Winkeln	4	1		2	2	1	
Religious Literature	*ÄHG*		1	1	1			1
	Total	97	22	13	27	37	38	5

* The only grammatical forms belonging to the semantic field under discussion.

a proper noun it is the hypostasis of the knowledge of the creator god.

ʿrḳ — perfect, thorough knowledge of a certain object, and as such first of all an attribute of the gods, and then bestowed by them on human beings.

s33 — charismatic wisdom possessed by gods and kings, but also acquired wisdom concerned with practical talents, such as administrative skills.

s3r.t — understanding chiefly stemming from experience, but also acquired through learning (*Kemit*), and bestowable by the gods (Haremhab).

šs3 — capability, expertise, acquired through practice and experience.

ḥmw — professional talent and ability.

Finally, to round off our synopsis, we may note that the subject of the knowledge is found to vary: *rḫ* and *ḥmw* are attributed to the common folk and the upper class, which is not the case with the other terms — their subjects are exclusively the social elite (the king and his officials) and the gods.

In the Bible

The vocabulary relating to the subject of "wise", "wisdom" plays an important part in the Biblical wisdom lexicon, and includes 11 terms. As their occurrence is also common in non-wisdom sources, references are given only when they are of interest for clarifying the term or for the purpose of bilingual comparison. The focus, however, is on a comparative analysis with the Egyptian material.

1. *ydʿ*

ydʿ, which is found throughout the range of the Semitic languages, is the semantic equivalent of the root *rḫ* in Egyptian.[26] *ydʿ*, like *rḫ*, is not specific to the wisdom books, but is present in all the phases of the Hebrew language and in all its literary genres. In the wisdom sources the root *yd‘* is found as a verb, a noun — *da‘at/dā‘at* — and as an adjective (active participle) — *yōdēa‘*.

Verb:

As a verb *yd‘* has several meanings similar to the Egyptian usage: (1) "to recognize," "to know"; (2) "to distinguish"; (3) "to know a person carnally." Since the last sense does not appear in the wisdom literature the following discussion concentrates on the other two.

In wisdom literature the object of knowledge is at times people (to Job come "all who had known him [*yōd^{e}‘āyw*]" — Job 42,11; in the wisdom Psalm God appears as one who cares about his faithful and distinguishes between righteous and wicked — wisdom Pss. 1,6; 37,18).[27] At other times the knowledge is of the future (Prov. 27,1; Qoh. 8,7; 10,14). But the verb *yd‘* for the most part has as its object the word *da‘at* and its synonyms, such as *bînâ*, *ḥokmâ*; occasionally these relate to the instruction of the sage (Prov. 1,2; cf. 4,1; 22,17); or they signify wisdom in the general sense (ibid. 17,27; 24,14) or the order prevailing on earth (Qoh. 7,25; 8,16) and the work of creation (Job 38,4).

Outside the wisdom literature *yd‘* concerns professional competence (see adj. *yōdēa‘*, below). In the prophecy the root *yd‘* is applied in the national religious framework and denotes recognition by the people of their God (e.g., Isa. 1,3; *yd‘* + *bînâ* signifying the worship of God — Isa. 29,24, etc.; cf. *da‘at q^{e}dōšîm* — Prov. 30,3).

The second meaning of the root *yd‘*, "to distinguish," "to perceive" by means of experience, appears in the frequent formula in Qoheleth: "And I applied my mind (lit. heart) to know wisdom..." (1,17; 8,16); "I turned my mind (lit. heart) to know and to search out and to seek wisdom..." (7,25). The formula is followed by the outcome of this quest, opening with "I knew" (or "I saw") (3,12-14; 8,17; etc.). *yd‘* also means "to distinguish" in the phrase "to know (*yd‘*) good or evil" (Deut. 1,39; 2 Sam. 19,36); as such it forms the main theme in the story of Genesis 2 and 3, which scholars associate with the wisdom tradition,[28] and in which the fruit of "the tree of the knowledge of good and evil" confers the ability "to know," that is, to distinguish between good and evil.[29]

As in the Egyptian parallels, the verb *yd‘* commonly appears in the

Hebrew wisdom sources with a negation, in order to emphasize the insignificance of man as compared to the omnipotence of God. This negative connotation of *yd'* is typical of the pessimistic tone of Qoheleth where it relates both to knowing the future as well as to understanding the cosmic order as it exists in the present, both of which are beyond human comprehension (9,1,12; 10,14; 11, 2,5,6). The same idea is expressed in the negative formulation that recurs in Proverbs: "Do not boast about tomorrow for you do not know what a day may bring" (27,1; cf. also Job 37, 15,16). In Qoheleth the rhetorical question, "Who knows?" resounds again and again (2,19; 3,21; 6,12; 8,1).

Noun:

da'at, "knowledge," is characteristic of the wisdom vocabulary (Prov. 40 times, Job 11 times, Qoh. 8 times) but also occurs frequently outside the sapiential circle (31 times). *da'at* stands in synonymous parallelism with other terms belonging to the sphere of wisdom and instruction (such as *t^{e}bûnâ*, *ḥokmâ*, *m^{e}zimmâ*, *mûsār*, *'ormâ*) and in antithetic parallelism with *'iwwelet*. *da'at*, like the Egyptian *rḫ*, is primarily knowledge *transmitted by teaching*:

- *da'at* is imparted by the teacher: Qoheleth "taught the people *da'at*" (12,9); in Proverbs Wisdom plays the part of the teacher in her effort to educate the fools who hate *da'at* (1,22,23).
- As in Egyptian, instruction is termed "knowledge" (*da'at*) (Prov. 22,20) and in this context it is synonymous with the term *mûsār* (ibid. 12,1; 23,12). *'imrê da'at* are words of knowledge voiced by the teacher before his pupils (Prov. 19,27; 23,12).
- *da'at*, as its equivalent in the Egyptian instructions, is directed to those devoid of knowledge: the *na'ar* ("youth") (1,4) and the *k^{e}sîl* ("stupid man") (1,22). The *rāšā'* ("wicked man") is without knowledge (Prov. 29,7). Those possessing knowledge are the *'ārûm* (who is crowned with *da'at* [Prov. 14,18]), the *ḥākām* (who receives it [21,11], lays it up [10,14], masters it [15,2] and teaches it [Qoh. 12,9]) and the *nābôn* (who seeks it [Prov. 15,14], spreads it [ibid. 7] and acquires it [18,15]).

- He who has *da'at* is a master of rhetoric: "He who is sparing of words is wise (*yôdēa' dā'at*)" (Prov. 17,27; cf. 14,7; 15,2,7; Job 34,35); the phrase "lips of knowledge" signifies lips that speak words of wisdom (Prov. 14,7; 20,15) (cf. the Egyptian expression *rḫ r3.f* — "knows his mouth").

Like *rḫ* in Egyptian, the root *yd'*, as we have seen above, may also be present in a religious setting, denoting the relationship between the believer and God. God "knows" his faithful, while the believer is termed "one who knows his God."[30] Thus, *da'at* on the one hand is knowledge acquired by learning and experience and on the other *a divinely endowed gift* (Prov. 2,6-7). Wisdom is the property of God, who created the universe by it (3,19ff.). Knowledge is identified with "the fear of Yahweh," a motif that has no parallel in the Egyptian wisdom. This conception is evident in several verses of the first collection in Proverbs: "The fear of Yahweh is the beginning of knowledge" (Prov. 1,7; cf. ibid. 29); "Then you will understand the fear of Yahweh and find the knowledge (*da'at*) of God" (ibid. 2,5); "The beginning of wisdom is the fear of Yahweh, and the knowledge (*da'at*) of the holy is understanding" (9,10; cf. 30,3).

In non-wisdom sources *da'at*, like the Egyptian equivalent, may signify knowledge of prediction, wisdom of magicians and astrology. Bil'am represents his words as prophetic utterances: "The oracle of him who hears the words of God and knows the knowledge (*yōdēa' da'at*) of the Most High" (Num. 24,16).[31] In the reproach directed at Babylon in Deutero-Isaiah, the prophet indicts her for trust in "her wisdom" and "her knowledge" (*da'at*) (Isa. 47,10), which are the "sorceries" and "enchantment" mentioned in the previous verse; that is, using augury and astrology for the purpose of making political decisions (cf. ibid. 44,25). It is said of Daniel and the children with him that they were "endowed with knowledge (*yōdᵉ'ê da'at*), understanding learning." This knowledge is defined later as "the letters and the language of the Chaldeans" (Dan. 1,4); "language of the Chaldeans" standing for the art of astrology.[32]

Qoheleth expresses his habitual skepticism regarding the usefulness of *da'at* and *ḥokmâ* (1,16-18), which are granted by God's free will (2,26). In She'ol there is neither *ḥokmâ* nor *da'at*, he affirms.[33]

From the above investigation it appears that *da'at*, like *rḫ* in Egyptian, is primarily wisdom gained by learning and intended for practical purposes: "by knowledge are the righteous delivered," asserts the author of Proverbs (11,9; cf. 19,2).

Adjective:

It is difficult to distinguish between the adjective *yōdēa'*, and *ḥākām* — the latter is the more common; both are equivalent to the Egyptian adjective *rḫ*, and in grammatical form (participle) *yōdēa'* parallels the Egyptian term.

In the Biblical wisdom literature *yōdēa'*, when not in collocation, always appears in the plural, *yōdᵉ'îm*, mostly in synonymous parallelism with *ḥăkāmîm* ("wise men") or *nᵉbōnîm* ("intelligent men") (Qoh. 9,11; Job 34,2). In this context *yōdᵉ'îm* refers to a general quality, parallel to the "strong" or the "fleet-footed" (see Qoh. ibid.).

By contrast, outside the wisdom books the adjective *yōdēa'* denotes "skill," "technical knowledge," for example, in hunting, letters, funeral lament, sailing, lyre-playing (Gen. 25,27; Isa. 29,11; Amos 5,16, cf. Jer. 9,16; 1 Kgs. 9,27; 1 Sam. 16,16,18; etc.). Once the collocation *'îš da'at* appears in Proverbs (24,5), being synonymous with *ḥākām* and *yōdēa'*, while its form parallels to the Demotic *rmt rḫ*.

2. *ḥkm*

The stem *ḥkm* (Aram., Akka., Arab.) is characteristic of the wisdom language, though its occurrence is not restricted to the wisdom books.[34] In the latter it is found as a verb — in qal, meaning "to act wisely," "to become wise" (e.g., *ḥākamtā* — Prov. 9, 12); in pi'el, meaning "to make wise," "teach wisdom" (e.g., *yᵉḥakkᵉmēnû* — Job 35,11); in pu'al, meaning "made wise" (e.g., *ḥăkāmîm mᵉḥukkāmîm* — Prov. 30,24); as an adjective — *ḥākām*; as a noun — *ḥokmâ* (fem.); *ḥokmôt* (pl. abst.)[35] (Prov. 1,20; 9,1; 24,7; Ps. 49,4 [wisdom Ps]; BS 4,11; here too belongs *ḥakmôt*, in Prov. 14,1, which should be pointed *ḥokmôt*).[36]

From the above analysis of the relevant Egyptian material it appears that when referring to knowledge the Egyptian mainly focused upon the fact of knowledge, i.e., being a wise man — only rarely is the reference to an action performed by means of knowledge, that is, acting wisely or making someone act in such a way.[37] This latter sense, which in the Bible is expressed through use of the verb *ḥkm*, is therefore not dealt with in the following survey, which is restricted to the adjectival and nominal forms, *ḥākām* ("wise") and *ḥokmâ* ("wisdom").

Adjective:

The adjective *ḥākām*, "wise," found in all the wisdom literature (beginning with Prov. 46 times, Qoh. 21 times, Job 8 times, wisdom Ps. once, and ending with BS 19 times), commonly stands in parallelism either synonymously with other adjectives belonging to the semantic field of wisdom — *nābôn*, *mēbîn*, *yōdᵉʿîm*, (*ṣaddîq*) — or, more frequently, antithetically with *kᵉsîl* (12 times), *'ĕwîl* (6 times), *lēṣ*, *'ănšê lāṣôn*, and *sākāl*. Together with the form *ḥākām* — which at times also functions as a noun — are found combinations meaning "wise man," i.e., *geber ḥākām* (Prov. 24,5; Job 34,34), *'îš ḥākām* (Prov. 16,14; 28,9), which are parallel to *rmt rḫ* in Demotic.[38]

ḥākām, which is the semantic equivalent of the Egyptian *rḫ*, belongs to the terminology of the educational framework in Israel, whether it be the school or some other creative circle.

(1) Who is the *ḥākām*?[39]

The *ḥākām* is one who has acquired knowledge, who uses his knowledge in everyday life and is able to impart it to others. As the transmitter of knowledge, the sage is the teacher:

It is said of Qoheleth that "he taught the people knowledge" (12,9; cf. Job 15, 17,18).

The sage teaches by means of "rebuke" (*gᵉʿārâ*) (Qoh. 7,5; Prov. 13,1) and "reproof" (*tôkaḥat*) (Prov. 15,12; 25,12).

As it is a source of knowledge and information aimed at guiding the pupil in the proper course of life, the teaching of the sage is compared to a "fountain of life" (Prov. 13,14; cf. also 3,1-2; 7,2; etc.).

The sage furthermore is the writer, the author of instructions:

He is engaged in the literary pursuit of collecting sayings and writing books (Qoh. 12,9b). The instruction of the sage, put into writing, is called "the words of the wise":[40] "The words of the wise are like goads, and like well-fastened nails are the collected sayings" (Qoh. 12,11; cf. Prov. 1,6; 22,17, and also 24,23).

The sage, then, is a man who has acquired knowledge, but continues his pursuit of wisdom — this makes him the ideal pupil:

In Proverbs such a pupil is termed "a wise son" (10,1 || 15,20; 13,1; 23,24), the opposite being the son who is *lēṣ*, *k^esîl*, etc. (13,1; 17,25; 19,13; etc.). The Hebrew *ḥākām*, like the Egyptian *rḫ*, studies throughout his life: "Let the wise man hear and add to his learning" (Prov. 1,5); "The ear of the wise seeks after knowledge" (Prov. 18,15; cf. 21,11; 9,8-9).

Since according to the wisdom concept, the ideal man is he who learns and acquires knowledge throughout his life, it is not surprising to find that the old man, advanced in years, is looked upon as a sage:

In Job it is stated that "wisdom is with the aged and understanding in length of days" (12,12). Elihu later opposes this conventional position: "I said, 'Let days speak and many years teach wisdom'... It is not the old that are wise, nor the aged that understand what is right" (ibid. 32, 7-9). Qoheleth, in his habitual paradoxical style, presents a confrontation between the old and foolish king and a wise child (4,13) — which would have been impossible in the early wisdom. Advanced age is one of the characteristics of the sage in the Egyptian sources also. Ineni, a high official in the time of Thutmosis I, says, "My deeds were with knowledge (*rḫ*), an order (*tp rd*) was not given to me by an old man..." (*Urk.* IV 57,17 - 58,1). The Egyptian instructions were on the whole composed by older men — e.g., the vizier Ptaḥḥotep writes an instruction for his son at the ripe old age of 110 years; and Kheti, in the epilogue of his work, speaks of his lifelong experience.[41]

(2) The characteristics of the *ḥākām* ("wise man") and *k^esîl* ("fool") contrasted:

The sage is characterized by both his intellectual faculties and his moral nature, which in sapiential thought are inseparable. Most of the virtues attached to the *ḥākām* are expressed in verses in which *ḥākām* and *k^esîl* (and its synonyms — *'ĕwîl*, *lēṣ*, *sākāl*) are presented in contrast.[42] Found chiefly in Proverbs, but also in Qoheleth, this literary device is applied to various aspects of life and well illustrates the images of the *ḥākām* and the *k^esîl* (and his synonyms).

(a) Intellectual faculties:

The *ḥākām* is the ideal object of instruction, while the *k^esîl* refuses to gain knowledge (Prov. 10,1; cf. 15,20) and hates *tôkaḥat* (*lēṣ*, ibid. 9,8; 13,1; 21,11).

The *ḥākām*, who is prudent in his behavior, does not remain satisfied with the knowledge he has thus far acquired, but continues to seek more; the *k^esîl* is prideful (14,16), confident in himself (*'ĕwîl* — 12,15; cf. 14,3).

The *ḥākām* possesses *da'at* ("knowledge") while the *k^esîl* adheres to *'iwwelet* ("foolishness") (Prov. 14,8,24).

The *ḥākām* is skilled in rhetoric[43] while the *k^esîl* is much given to error in his speech ("the mouth of the fool brings perdition" — ibid. 10,14; "pours out *'iwwelet*" — ibid. 15,2; cf. Qoh. 10,12).

The *ḥākām* is able to accumulate property, while the *k^esîl* lacks the necessary acumen (Prov. 21,20; 14,24; cf. *sākāl* — Qoh. 2,19).

(b) Moral virtues:

The *ḥākām* brings blessing upon the community in which he lives — his wisdom saves a city in time of war (Prov. 21,22; cf. Qoh. 9,15,18); the *k^esîl* causes injury to others — he grieves his parents (Prov. 15,20) and brings no comfort to mourners (Qoh. 7,4).

The *ḥākām* displays restraint and self-control, while the *k^esîl* is hot-tempered, unrestrained (Prov. 29,11); he rages (*'ĕwîl*, ibid. 29,9); he does wrong (*k^esîl*, ibid. 10,23). Therefore, one is counseled to seek the companionship of the *ḥākām* but to keep a distance from the *k^esîl* ("He who walks with wise men [*ḥăkāmîm*] becomes wise, but the companion of fools [*k^e sîlîm*] will suffer harm," Prov. 13,20; cf. *Ankhsheshonqy* 13,6-7; and also Qoh. 7,5). The *ḥākām* wins a reward but the *k^e sîl* receives punishment: the *ḥākām* gets "honor," the *k^e sîl* "disgrace" (Prov. 3,35); the *'ĕwîl* is the servant of the *ḥākām* (ibid. 11,29).

In late Hebrew wisdom we find a development similar to that observed in the late stage of Egyptian wisdom. Qoheleth casts doubt on the traditional conception that distinguishes between the wise man and the fool: "For what advantage has the wise man over the fool?" he asks (6,8); after death the fate of both is identical, "for of the wise man as of the fool there is no enduring remembrance" (2,16; cf. wisdom Ps. 49,11). Qoheleth, as does the author of *Pap. Insinger*, asserts that, like any other man, the sage is subject to error and temptation: Oppression turns a wise man into a fool, just as bribery results in loss of mental ability (Qoh. 7,7; cf. *Insinger* 7,11; 23,7; 34, 12).

Noun:
ḥokmâ is multifaceted and encompasses various walks of life. It can designate technical skill or manual work, which relate to the common folk, as well as legal acumen and leadership qualities in the king and his aides, or knowledge, i.e., fear, of God. In many of these references it is difficult to distinguish between the use of the term *ḥokmâ* in the wisdom sources and its use in non-wisdom sources. This being the case, both are dealt with here together, while the present discussion naturally centers on different aspects of *ḥokmâ* in wisdom and does not attempt to cover the term's applications and connotations in the whole of the Bible.

ḥokmâ stands in parallelism with synonymous terms such as *bînâ* (4 times), *t^e bûnâ/ôt* (3 times), *da'at* (twice), but also with *yir'at* ("the fear of") Yahweh (twice) and *'ēṣâ* (advice);[44] it is also juxtaposed to terms such as *maddā'* ("learning") (in the later literature — Dan. 1,4; 2,21; 2 Chr. 1,11-12), *kišrôn* ("skill") (Qoh. 2,21), *ḥešbôn* (ibid. 7,25) and *mûsār* ("instruction") (Prov. 23,23). *ḥokmâ* serves as a supernym for a considerable number of terms belonging to this semantic field, namely, *da'at*, *bînâ*, *t^e bûnâ*, *'ormâ* (the last in a positive connotation) and as a polysemic word it refers to the following types of wisdom:

(1) Practical wisdom

(a) Technical skill: The art of building is perceived as wisdom: "By wisdom a house is built and by understanding it is established," says the sage (Prov. 24,3; cf. 14,1); the craftsmen responsible for the Tabernacle, the Temple and their various furnishings are also termed "wise men" (Exod. 28,3; 31,3,6; 35,25; 35,31-36,2; 1 Kgs.7,14; 1 Chr. 28,21; etc.). This corresponds to the Egyptian, where, as we have seen, a special lexeme is used to signify the craftsman's skill — *ḥmww*. On one occasion the sailor is called *šsꜣ* in Egyptian (*Anastasi* IV 2,7), and in the Bible, too, we find that the mastery of the ship's pilot is considered *ḥokmâ* (Ps. 107,27; Ezek. 27,8-9).

(b) The capacity for administration, the ability to rule and dispense justice: This wisdom is in the possession of the king, the prince and the advisor. David is wise, like the angel of God, "to hear good and evil" (2 Sam. 14,17,20), as is Solomon (1 Kgs. 3,9,12).[45] This is the wisdom granted to the messianic king at the end of days (Isa. 11,2-4). It is also found among strangers — the men of Edom (Jer. 49,7); the king of Assyria, bragging about his ability to rule and create an empire, is "wise in his own eyes" (Isa. 10,13ff.); Azitawadda, king of Danuna, vaunts himself similarly in an inscription from Karatepe. Aḥiqar, who is "a wise and skillful scribe" (line 1) and "counselor of all Assyria" (lines 2, 12), teaches Nadin the art of counseling and the skill of administering affairs of state (line 19). Wisdom lauds and praises herself in Proverbs 8, declaring that "By me kings reign, and rulers decree what is just, by me princes rule..."

(c) Understanding of trade and accumulation of property: Qoheleth talks of the paradox of accumulating property which the sage has to leave behind on his death without knowing who will inherit it (2,19ff; cf. 6,7). In Ezekiel the prince of Tyre is described as one who did well in commerce and enlarged his treasure through his wisdom (Ezek. 28,4,5).

(2) Cleverness, wit

Small animals possessing natural wit (*ḥăkāmîm mᵉḥukkāmîm*)are referred to in the numerical saying in Proverbs 30,24-28 and also in 6,6ff. Such wit is possessed by the wise women who appear in the Biblical historiography — the woman from Abel Beth-Ma'achah, who saved her city, and the woman of Tekoa', who was sent by Joab to David (2 Sam. 20,16,22; 14,2). In the wisdom books intelligence in the sense of "cleverness" always has a positive connotation, but not outside them, where "wisdom" may be invested with a negative tone, taking on the meaning of cunning: "Come, let us deal shrewdly with them" (*niṯhakkᵉmâ lô*), say the Egyptians, planning to destroy the Children of Israel through hard labor (Exod. 1,10). David speaks of this kind of slyness when advising Solomon to kill Shime'i (1 Kgs. 2,8-9); the counsel of Jonadab, "a very crafty man (*'îš ḥākām mᵉ'ōd*)," to Amnon (2 Sam. 13,3) likewise bears a negative connotation (cf. Jer. 4,22).

(3) Divine wisdom

Wisdom is in the possession of God: "With God are wisdom and might, he has counsel and understanding" (Job 12,13; cf. also *da'at*, p. 234 above); Job speaks of the wisdom of God's "council" (15,8). In the book of Job the belief that God alone knows wisdom (28,23) and that no human being is able to find it stands out in all its sharpness (ibid. 12-20). Qoheleth, too, relentlessly seeking divine wisdom, is unable to attain it (8,17). Divine wisdom is manifested in the perfection of the universe (ibid.) and in the work of creation. God created the world by means of his wisdom (Prov. 3,19; 8,22ff.; cf. Job 9,4ff.; 38,36-37; and also cf. with Re', the creator god in Egypt).[46]

Wisdom as a divine attribute is hypostasized in the first collection of Proverbs (see Appendix B below, cf. Eg. *siȝ*). Since wisdom originates with God, the "fear of God" may be identified in the wisdom literature with wisdom and knowledge. "The fear of Yahweh is the beginning of wisdom and the knowledge of the holy is understanding," says the sage in Proverbs (9,10), adding that "the fear of Yahweh is instruction of wisdom" (15,33; cf. 1,7); as the book of Job puts it, "Behold, the fear of Yahweh that is wisdom" (28,28; see also wisdom Ps. 111,10, and cf. *da'at* p. 234 above).

Since wisdom is multifaceted its *sources* are varied. There is wisdom gained through *learning* — wisdom passed from teacher to pupil, father to son, through teaching and instruction (Prov. 1,2; 19,20), proverbs, and the words of the wise (ibid. 1,6; 22,17). The pupil also has at his disposal encyclopaedic lists (onomastica), which systematically set forth groups of terms intended as mnemonic devices. The sayings in Prov. 30,15-31, Job 38,4-39,30, and also 1 Kgs. 5,13, probably are based on such lists.

Apart from wisdom acquired through study there is wisdom gained through *experience*: wisdom arising from personal experience or the experience of past generations — Qoheleth frequently refers to his personal experience (e.g., 1,13a, 16-17a; 2,1, 3a, 4-8, 12a, 24; etc.); Job and Elipaz also speak of their personal discoveries (Job 5,3,27; 15,17; 21,6).

The elders, the possessors of experience, as already stated, are considered to be wise men. In Egypt the tradition of the ancestors is the principal source of wisdom (see *To Merikare* 34-35). This Egyptian concept is well reflected in a passage in Isaiah 19, which speaks of the wisdom of Egypt: Pharaoh's advisers claim that "I am a son of the wise, a son of ancient kings" (11), that is, they lean on the tradition of antiquity. In Israel the tradition of ancestors is only one of the sources of wisdom. The speeches of Job's friends are based on this tradition: Elipaz talks of the purity of the wisdom in an age when there were no strangers in the land (Job 15,18ff.); Bildad invokes the wisdom of generations that lived in the past (8,8-10).

Occasionally the path to acquisition is less arduous. Wisdom is not won through study or experience but is endowed, *charismatic*. As wisdom is the possession of God, he may impart it to men. "For Yahweh gives wisdom," it is said in Proverbs (2,6), and Qoheleth states: "For to the man who pleases him God gives wisdom and knowledge" (2,26). It is first of all kings who are gifted with this charismatic wisdom: David is wise as an "angel of God" (2 Sam. 14,20); "And God gave Solomon wisdom" (1 Kgs. 5,9; cf. 10,24); the ideal king in Isaiah possesses "the spirit of Yahweh, the spirit of wisdom" (11,2). Then, it is also a property of leaders: Joseph (Gen. 41,38-39), Joshua Deut. 34,9); and of artisans: the Tabernacle craftsmen (Exod. 31,3,6; 35,31,35;36,1ff.).

3. *byn*

The basic meaning of *byn* is "to become separated," which applies to the ability to discern between alternatives[47] and to understand perfectly through insight (cf. Eg. *siꜢ*). *byn*, which emphasizes the mental effort involved in understanding, is situated on the border between the semantic fields of "wisdom" and "learning." The word belongs to the wisdom terminology, but is found in non-wisdom literature as well.[48] The use of *byn* in the wisdom sources is varied: it is present as a verb (qal, niph'al, hiph'il), an adjective — *nābôn* (niph'al), *mēbîn* (hiph'il), and a noun — *tᵉbûnâ*, *bînâ*.

The forms of the verb and noun in hiph'il belong partly to the semantic field of teaching and learning and were discussed in Chapter 2. Here items relating to the subject of wisdom are presented.

Verb:

In qal, *bîn*, *yābîn*, means: (1) "to understand" by means of the senses — the "eyes" (Prov. 7,7;[49] and also Job 9,11; cf. Eg. *siꜢ*, accompanied by the determinative of an eye) and the "ears" (*byn*||*šm'* — Job 13,1; 34,16; etc.; cf. p. 67 above); (2) "to understand," "to discern," by means of the intellect — "understand (*tābînû*) and then we will speak" (Job 18,2); in this context *byn* stands in synonymous parallelism with *yd'* and *ḥkm* (Ps. 92,7 [Ps. with wisdom features]).

In niph'al, the meaning is "to have understanding." The participle form, *nābôn*, is especially common, serving as an adjective (see below).

In hiph'il, the verb has a threefold meaning: (1) "to discern between" — "to discern (*lᵉhābîn*) between good and evil" (1 Kgs. 3,9, which parallels ibid. verse 11 — *hābîn lišmōa' mišpāṭ*, i.e., "to discern what is right," relating to the role of the king as judge of the people [see p. 56 above]); (2) in the later Biblical wisdom books its meaning is "to be expert" in the interpretation of dreams and visions (Dan. 1,17; 2 Chr. 26,5) and in playing a musical instrument (2 Chr. 34,12) (cf. Eg. *ḥmww*); (3) "to instruct": see Chapter 2 above, p. 67.

In a religious context man is often presented as "one who has no understanding" (wisdom Ps. 32,9; cf. Psalms with wisdom features: 92,7; 94,8); Job does not understand (23,8), likewise the wicked man (*rāšā'*,

Prov. 29,7) and evil men (*'anšê rā'*, Prov. 28,5). God, by contrast, appears as understanding the deeds and ways of man (Prov. 24,12; cf. Ps. 139,2; 5,2).

Adjective:

nābôn

The definition of *nābôn* is given in Proverbs 16,21: "The wise of heart is called *nābôn*," that is, the wise man with "heart" (i.e., mind), who weighs and examines things, is the *nābôn*. This term, which refers to the intellectual ability of a human being and never appears as an attribute of God, is characteristic of the wisdom language (Prov. 9 times, Qoh. once, BS 7 times).

nābôn is close in meaning to *ḥākām*, and in 18 of the 21 occurrences in the Bible it is associated with this word (either in parallelism or in conjunction).[50]

The *nābôn*, like the *ḥākām*, is the ideal pupil: one who seeks knowledge — "*nābôn* acquires sayings (*taḥbulôt*)" (Prov. 1,5 || *ḥākām*; and 15,14; 18,15), he has a facility for learning (14,6) and accepts reproof (19,25). The heart serves as the instrument whereby he acquires knowledge — "The heart of *nābôn* seeks knowledge" (Prov. 15,14; cf. 18,15; 14,33).[51] Like the *ḥākām*, the *nābôn* is master of rhetoric: "On the lips of *nābôn* wisdom is found," states the sage in Proverbs 10,13 (cf. *n^{e}bôn dābār*, i.e., "prudent in speech," in 1 Sam. 16,18). The *nābôn* "closes his lips," keeps silent, when necessary (Prov. 17,28).[52]

mēbîn

The *nābôn* is an intelligent man, possessing discernment more than just in the passive sense — while "*le* mēbîn *est un émule du* nabûn *mais de manière plus active*"[53] Unlike *nābôn*, *mēbîn* serves as an adjective for man and also for God and is not a term characteristic of the wisdom literature. *mēbîn* is present in Proverbs (6 times), the wisdom Psalm (once — 119) and Ben Sira (5 times) but is not found in Job and Qoheleth.

When contrasted with *k^{e}sîl*, the "stupid man," *mēbîn* is set in a didactic background. The *mēbîn* is an easy pupil: "He who keeps the instruction is a *mēbîn* son" (Prov. 28,7), a reprimand is sufficient to correct his ways (17,10 — the opposite is the *k^esîl*, who is beaten); he is a man whose concern and business is wisdom; he is not content with learning but examines and delves into the meaning of things (Prov. 17,24; cf. 8,9; 28,11).

As guardian of justice, the *mēbîn* appears against the background of social morality. Wisdom takes pride that her words are straight and "right to the *mēbîn*" (Prov. 8,9); the *mēbîn* is described here as one who recognizes the value of justice and rejects "twisted" and "crooked" speech. His description as "prolonger of the life of the state" in Proverbs 28,2 may be understood in this light.[54]

Outside the wisdom literature, *mēbîn* in late Biblical prose usually appears as a teacher who is a specialist in certain arts (poet, musician: see p. 67, above).

Noun:

The nouns *t^ebûnâ*, *bînâ*, stress the capacity for mental discernment and the reliance of the sage on his intellectual qualities.[55]

t^ebûnâ

The term is characteristic of the wisdom vocabulary (Prov. 19 times; Job 4 times; wisdom Ps. once [49,4] and 18 times in other books). *t^ebûnâ*, meaning "understanding," signifies the mental ability of a man and is difficult to distinguish semantically from *ḥokmâ*. *t^ebûnâ* stands in synonymous parallelism with *ḥokmâ*, as well as *'ēṣâ*, *bînâ*, *m^ezimmâ*, *lēb*, and in antithetic parallelism with *'iwwelet*. *t^ebûnâ* also appears once as personification coupled in parallelism with *ḥokmâ* (Prov. 8,1). In the wisdom literature the term *t^ebûnâ* relates to the following:

— *t^ebûnâ* is primarily instruction which has to be acquired (especially that of the father in the first collection in Prov., e.g., 2,3; 3,13; 5,1).
— *t^ebûnâ* is also wisdom arising from experience and may be found in the old man: "Wisdom is with the aged and understanding in length of days" (Job 12,12).
— *t^ebûnâ* refers to technical skill, that is, the work of building or other craftsmanship. This application appears many times outside the

wisdom literature and once in Proverbs 24,3 (cf. building the Tabernacle and the Temple: Exod. 35,31; 36,1; 1 Kgs. 7,14).

— *t*^{e}*bûnâ* is a quality of God. Common outside the wisdom literature, it is a motif which is mentioned in the wisdom books also. Job states: "With him are wisdom (*ḥokmâ*) and might, he has counsel (*ʿēṣâ*) and understanding (*t*^{e}*bûnâ*)" (12,13; cf. Prov. 21,30; and also Isa. 40,28; Ps. 147,5). Therefore, God can bestow them on man, "For Yahweh gives wisdom (*ḥokmâ*), from his mouth come knowledge (*daʿat*) and understanding (*t*^{e}*bûnâ*)" (Prov. 2,6; cf. Exod. 35, 31-32; 36,1: where God grants it to the artisans of the Tabernacle; and 1 Kgs. 5,9, where Solomon is the recipient). God works by means of *t*^{e}*bûnâ*: thus he accomplished the creation (Prov. 3,19; cf. Ps. 136,5; Jer. 10,12 || 51,15) and overcame *rahab*, the mythic sea monster which in Biblical poetry symbolizes Egypt (Job 26,12; see also Ps. 87,4; Isa. 30,7).

— *t*^{e}*bûnâ* as a human quality: a man full of understanding is termed *ʾîš t*^{e}*bûnâ/ôt* (|| *yôdēaʿ dāʿat*, Prov. 17,27) and his opposite is *ḥăsar lēb*, the senseless (Prov. 11,12; 15,21). Beside his intellectual ability (Prov. 10,23), the moral virtues of "the man of *t*^{e}*bûnâ*" are stressed: he is honest (Prov. 15,21) and restrained (*qar rûaḥ* — 17,27), accepting the advice of others (20,5) and keeping silent about their shortcomings (11,12); his opposite in this context is the *k*^{e}*sîl*, "the fool" (10,23; cf. 18,2); an opposite way of behaviour also signifies the *ḥăsar t*^{e}*bûnôt* ruler who is "a great oppressor" (28,16).

bînâ

The term belongs to the wisdom language (Prov. 14 times; Job 8 times; BS 3 times; and 15 times in other books).[56] *bînâ* comes in conjunction and in synonymous parallelism with *ḥokmâ* and other terms belonging to the semantic field of wisdom and learning, namely, *mûsār*, *t*^{e}*bûnâ*, *leqaḥ*.

bînâ refers primarily to mental ability, understanding, in man. Agur, who represents himself as stupid (*baʿar*), states: "I have not the *bînâ* of a man" (Prov. 30,2); the teacher says to his pupil, "Trust in Yahweh with all your heart and do not rely on your own *bînâ*" (Prov. 3,5). The goal of the book of Proverbs is to impart words of *bînâ*

(|| *ḥokmâ*, *mûsār* 1,2). The father's instruction, besides *ḥokmâ* and *t*^{e}*bûnâ*, is also designated *bînâ* (Prov. 4,1); admonitions recur again and again to acquire *bînâ*, to cry out for it, to adhere to it (Prov. 2,3; 7,4; 16,16; 23,23).

When human understanding is in conflict with divine omnipotence, the latter prevails. Proverbs 3,5, cited above, and also Proverbs 23,4 — "Do not toil to acquire wealth, desist from your *bînâ*" — reflect the doubt and skepticism regarding the effectivity of human *bînâ*.[57] Traces of a doubting tone are also evident in Job, where it is said that man does not know the place of *bînâ* (Job 28,12,20); and God declares that *bînâ*, which is the knowledge of the wonders of creation and the universe, is beyond human capacity (ibid. 38,4ff; cf. 39,26).

These two motifs — the limits of human understanding and the omnipotence of God — led to an awareness that "the fear of Yahweh is the beginning of wisdom, and the knowledge of the holy is *bînâ*" (Prov. 9,10; cf. 30,2,3); "Behold, the fear of Yahweh that is wisdom and to depart from evil is *bînâ*" (Job 28,28). In the description in Isaiah 11, the messianic king is filled with "a spirit of wisdom and understanding (*bînâ*)" granted to him by God (2).

Like *ḥokmâ* and *t*^{e}*bûnâ*, *bînâ* appears in personification. Wisdom calls herself *bînâ* (Prov. 8,14), and Proverbs 7,4 states that she is to be called *mōdā'*, that is, "a relative" (cf. 2,3).

4. *śkl*

śkl[58] (v. [hiph'il]; n.) though frequent in the sages' parlance, does not belong to the wisdom terminology (Prov. 19 times; Job four; wisdom Ps. 6 times; Ps. with wisdom features once [94]; BS 19 times); it appears mainly in the late Biblical literature (61 times outside the wisdom books).[59]

The term *śkl* is polysemic and scholarly opinion is often divided as to which meaning fits a given context. Five principal meanings may be distinguished: (a) "to give attention," "to consider"' (b) "to be prudent," "act prudently"; (c) "to prosper," "have success," the result of behavior mentioned in (b); (d) "to teach," "give insight" to someone; and (e) "to understand," "have comprehension."

A feature common to all these applications is that the subject of *śkl* is always man and not God: God is never said to be intelligent (*maśkîl*) or the possessor of prudence (*śēkel*). Since of the meanings listed above only the second, "to be prudent," and the fifth, "to understand," belong to the subject of wisdom, the discussion that follows is restricted to these two. (The first and fourth meanings are associated with matters of teaching and were presented in Chapter 2 above.)

śkl in the sense of "to be prudent" is found as a verb and a noun. The hiph'il participle form, *maśkîl*,[60] (appearing principally in the second collection of Proverbs) applies to the prudent man, endowed with intelligence, of which he makes use to improve his social standing and to safeguard his way of life. The poor man, a member of the lower class, succeeds through being *maśkîl* in inheriting an estate (Prov. 17,2; cf. BS 10,23,30). His opposite is the *mēbîš* (one "who brings disgrace"): a *maśkîl* slave has mastery over a *mēbîš* son (ibid.; cf. Prov. 10,5; 14,35; BS 7,21; etc.); such a slave is the heart's desire of the king (Prov. 14,35).

The *maśkîl* knows how to choose the proper course in life and to escape death (Prov. 15,24, the opposite condition is described in 21,16). Family members who are *maśkîlîm* (wife, son) are considered a blessing (Prov. 19,14; 10,5; cf. BS 7,19).

As abstract noun *śēkel/śekel* (Prov. 6 times; Job once; other books 8 times), bears the meaning of practical acumen that brings a reward. "Prudence (*śēkel*) is a fountain of life to its possessor," says the sage in Proverbs 16,22. The possessor of *śēkel* wins praise (Prov. 12,8); therefore, *śēkel* has at times the sense of success; the son who obeys his father's teaching will find "favor and good success (*śēkel ṭôb*) with God and man" (Prov. 3,4). The collocation, *śēkel ṭôb*, used in this context appears twice more in the wisdom literature (cf. Prov. 13,15; wisdom Ps. 111,10) and relates to the sapiential vocabulary.[61] The antithesis of *śēkel* is *'iwwelet* ("folly") (Prov. 16,22) and *na'ăwēh lēb* ("distortion of the heart," i.e., mind, intellect) (12,8). A clear example of prudence of this kind is Abigail, wife of Nabal, described as a "woman of good understanding (*ṭôbat śekel*)" (1 Sam. 25,3), who through her sensible way of behavior is able to avert the threat of annihilation by David and his men that looms over her house.

śkl used verbally (hiph'il) in the sense of "to understand," "to have comprehension," is connected with the semantic fields of both wisdom and learning. The object of the comprehension is usually God's Law in the wisdom Psalm: "Thy commandment makes me wiser than my enemies... I have more understanding (*hiśkaltî*) than my teachers... I understand more than the aged" (119,98-100). In another Psalm, with wisdom features, the following question is raised: "Fools, when will you be wise (*taśkîlû*)?" i.e., possess knowledge of God's will and way (94,8). The combination *śôm śekel* in Nehemiah 8,8 has identical meaning: in the time of Ezra and Nehemiah the people read "the Law of God clearly, and they gave the sense (*śôm śekel*), so that the people understood."

The infinitive absolute *haśkēl* means "grasp," "insight." Elihu accuses Job of "speaking without knowledge; his words are without insight (*lō' b^e^haśkēl*)" (Job 34,35). In Daniel God appears as the bestower of this insight: "As for these four youths, God gave them learning and insight (*haśkēl*) in all letters and wisdom" (1,17). The purpose of the book of Proverbs is "to receive instruction of *haśkēl*" (Prov. 1,3).

A capacity for careful thought and intelligent consideration are thus deemed lofty virtues in man and are expressed in the terms *bînâ*, *t^e^bûnâ*, *śēkel*. The first two of these may be acquired by study while the third is a natural quality, also called *'ormâ* or *m^e^zimmâ*. Like the other words, *'ormâ* and *m^e^zimmâ* denote cleverness involving practical understanding, but at times they have a negative connotation. *'ormâ* and *m^e^zimmâ* are on the boundary between the semantic fields of "wisdom"-"cleverness" and "cunning"-"lying." The negative tone that sometimes accompanies these terms distinguishes them from *bînâ*, *t^e^bûnâ*, *śēkel*, which in the wisdom books generally appear in a positive light.

5. *'rm*

The root *'rm*,[62] which is used in the wisdom literature as a verb, adjective (*'ārûm*) and noun (*'ormâ*), always appears in Proverbs with a positive connotation, while in the other books it has a negative note.

Like *maśkîl* and *nābôn*, it is a quality which applies only to human beings (and one animal: the snake in the story of the Garden of Eden) and is never found in reference to God.

As a verb (twice in Prov., once in BS, and 3 times in other books) its meaning in the wisdom sources is "to become wise," "to acquire wisdom," through study and education. "He who heeds reproof acts wisely (*ya'rîm*)," states Proverbs 15,5 (cf. ibid. 19,25 and BS 6,32).

The adjective *'ārûm* is unique to the wisdom vocabulary (Prov. 8 times; Job twice, cf. Gen. 3,1).[63] The *'ārûm* "is the product of education, the graduate of the wisdom school."[64] In Proverbs *'ārûm* has a positive significance and its antonym is the *petî* (4 times), but it also stands in antithetic parallelism with *kesîl* (3 times) and *'ĕwîl* (once).

The figure of the *'ārûm* is similar to the *ḥākām*: he possesses practical sense which guides him in his daily life (Prov. 13,16). His conduct is the epitomy of restraint, caution and moderation (he escapes danger — 22,3 || 27,12; he "conceals knowledge"[65] — 12,23; he "conceals an insult" — ibid.,16; cf. also 14,15); the nature of the *'ārûm* is summed up in the verse, "The wisdom of *'ārûm* consists in understanding his way" (Prov. 14,8).

In Job the setting is different: *'ārûm* is found in a religious- moral context and in a negative connotation. The *'ārûm* is one who on account of his cunning and trickery is seen as the enemy of God and man. Eliphaz accuses Job of choosing the "tongue of *'ărûmîm*," i.e., lying (15,5); while in chapter 5 God appears as he "who frustrates the devices of *'ărûmîm*" (v. 12).

The noun *'ormâ* (Prov. 3 times; Job once; other books twice) is practical wisdom accruing from experience of life, but which can be transmitted through teaching and education. Like its parallels *da'at* and *mezimmâ*, it is intended primarily for the *petî*, the innocent and inexperienced youth. One of the main goals of the book of Proverbs is to impart *'ormâ* to the *petî* (1,4; cf. 8,5). In Proverbs 8 personified Wisdom asserts that she possesses the intellectual qualities required by a ruler since she "dwells in *'ormâ*" (ibid. 12). In Job *'ormâ* appears with a negative connotation: of God it is said, "He takes the wise in their *'ormâ* and the counsel of the tortuous is carried headlong" (5,13); the critical tone is clearly evident from the parallelism between "wise" and "tortuous."

6. *m^ezimmâ*

The noun *m^{e}zimmâ* derives from the root *zmm*,[66] meaning "think upon," "purpose." The expression is characteristic of the wisdom language (Prov. 8 times; Job twice; BS twice; 9 times in other books) and has both a positive and negative connotation.

In its positive connotation *m^{e}zimmâ* carries the sense of neutral planning, and is synonymous with the terms *da'at*, *t^{e}bûnâ*, *tûšîyyâ* (and *meḥqār* — BS 44,4). As such it is common in the first collection of Proverbs. The instruction of the father and the words of the teacher addressed to a son are termed *m^{e}zimmâ* (Prov. 1,4; 3,21; cf. 5,2; 2,11); personified Wisdom boasts that she possesses *m^{e}zimmâ* (8,12).

In its negative connotation *m^{e}zimmâ* means "device," "evil thought," occurring in the second and third collections of Proverbs and in Job. *'îš m^{e}zimmôt*, *ba'al m^{e}zimmôt* is a negative human type whose special nature is that, with him, evil is planned and thought out. This makes him an enemy of society, and he is thus defined in the language of Proverbs: "He who plans to do evil will be called *ba'al m^{e}zimmôt*" (Prov. 24,8; cf. ibid. 12,2; 14,17; Job 21,27).[67]

In one instance in the wisdom sources *m^{e}zimmâ* does relate to God, viz., God's plan to punish the wicked man (Job 42,2; cf. Jer. 23,20).

7. *tûšiyyâ*

The root *yšh*, which is also found in Arabic, meaning "assist," "support," is a technical term of wisdom literature.[68] The noun *tûšiyyâ* occurs 10 times in Biblical wisdom (Prov. 4 times; Job 6 times; BS once) out of a total of 12 occurrences.

tûšiyyâ is "practical wisdom," "ingenuity," which leads to success or deliverance. The emphasis is on its effectiveness. The sense of *tûšiyyâ* alters according to its context:[69] at times it is found in synonymous parallelism with *'ēṣâ*, *ḥokmâ*, or with *'ezrâ*, *māgēn* ("shield"), and *maḥš^{e}bôt 'ărûmîm*, and at times it is in conjunction with *m^{e}zimmâ* and *'ōz*.

In father-to-son admonitions *tûšiyyâ* means "wisdom" (Prov. 3,21). The isolated man, "one who separates himself, rages against all *tûšiyyâ*" (18,1); elsewhere *tûšiyyâ* is the ruler's understanding, which Wisdom prides herself on possessing (8,14).

tûšiyyâ in this sense of a human virtue also appears in Job, but here doubt is cast on the benefits that may be gained from it. Thus, Job rebukes Bildad for his entirely unhelpful statements: "How have you helped him who has no power...? How have you counseled him who has no wisdom, and plentifully declared *tûšiyyâ*?" (26,2-3). The *tûšiyyâ* of men is restrained by God, who appears as he who "frustrates the devices of the crafty (*maḥšᵉbôt ʿărûmîm*), and their hands achieve no success (*tûšiyyâ*)" (Job 5,12). *tûšiyyâ* is the exclusive quality of God: "But oh! that God would speak... And that he would tell you the secrets of wisdom. For he is manifold in understanding (*tûšiyyâ*)" (ibid. 11,6).

The sage in Proverbs likewise recognizes that *tûšiyyâ* originates with God, who bestows it on human beings. In the following passage the meaning of *tûšiyyâ* is close to that of *ʿezrâ*, "help," *māgēn*, "shield," and *ʿōz*, "strength": "For Yahweh gives wisdom, from his mouth come knowledge and understanding, he stores up *tûšiyyâ* for the upright and he is a shield (*māgēn*) to those who walk in integrity" (Prov. 2,6-7). This meaning is also reflected in Job: Job accuses God of preventing his deliverance, and he calls for "help" — *tûšiyyâ* (|| *ʿezrâ* 6,13; 30,22 [*Qᵉrê*]).[70] Like the sage in Proverbs, Job admits in his reply to Zophar that "with him (God) are strength (*ʿōz*) and *tûšiyyâ*" (12,16).[71]

In the sapiential sources, then, *tûšiyyâ* is practical wisdom, wisdom for administration and rule, or the ingenuity to escape from troubles.[72]

8. *kišrôn*

The Hebrew noun derives from Aramaic and its meaning is "ability," "skill," "success." *kišrôn* appears only in Late Biblical Hebrew, and its occurrence is limited to the book of Qoheleth (2,1; 4,4; 5,5).[73]

In his characteristically paradoxical style Qoheleth declares on the one hand that "with wisdom, and knowledge and skill (*ḥokmâ, daʿat, kišrôn*) a man accumulates property" (Qoh. 2,21), and he posits that all successful work is accomplished with skill — *kišrôn* (4,4);[74] but on the other hand he asks, what is the profit in *kišrôn* ("success") for those who possess it? (5,10)

Summary

A. The Semantic Aspect

(1) Of the plethora of lexemes belonging to the semantic field of wisdom in the Bible, only five are apparently exclusive to the wisdom books — *bînâ*, *nābôn*, *'ārûm*, *tûšiyyâ*, *kišrôn*.

The roots *ḥkm* and *yd'* are the most common in the sapiential sources (each ca. 200 times).

(2) Some of the terms go beyond the framework of the semantic field of wisdom and are situated on its border with another semantic field: (a) *'rm*, *zmm*, in negative connotation approaches the semantic field of cunning, lying; (b) the stems *śkl*, *kišrôn* and *tûšiyyâ* are located between the semantic fields of wisdom and success; (c) some of the forms of *śkl* and *byn* belong to the subject of teaching and study.

(3) The link between a man's capacity for understanding and his senses is expressed in two terms, *byn* and *śkl*; both involve the act of seeing (*hitbônān*, *haśkîl*) and show that, according to the wisdom conception, observation and visual scrutiny are a part of the process of understanding.[75]

(4) Some of the terms have a double connotation, negative and positive, which may reflect a diachronic development from the positive conception to the negative, or two different synchronic approaches. Thus *'ormâ* is a quality that is praised in Proverbs but condemned in Job and the other books of the Bible; *m^{e}zimmâ* is found in a positive and negative context in Proverbs but in a negative context in Job and in the non-wisdom books. This duality applies equally to the term *bînâ*.[76]

B. A Tentative Subdivision within the Semantic Field of Wisdom

It is difficult to classify semantically the terms belonging to the subject of wisdom: Most of them are synonyms (e.g., *da'at*, *t^ebûnâ*, *bînâ*, *tûšiyyâ*, and *kišrôn* stand in synonymous parallelism with *ḥokmâ*, while *m^ezimmâ*, *ḥokmâ*, *t^ebûnâ*, and *śekel* are synonymous with *da'at*); they are antithetical to identical lexemes relating to the semantic field of "folly" (viz., *pth*, *ksl*, *'wl*), and are associated with the same major topics (see Section C below). Tables 13 and 14 contain suggested criteria for the semantic demarcation of the above terms.

Table 13 shows that all the terms (except one, *tûšiyyâ*) refer to the instruction of a father or teacher, i.e., denote taught wisdom. From this it emerges that in the Biblical wisdom literature wisdom is conceived primarily as didactic and as something which is taught, while wisdom granted by God and wisdom acquired through life experience take second and third place. Thus, for the acquisition of wisdom, the means which stands out above all others is mental effort.

Sapiental activity requires a mental effort or a definite investment. An examination of the various terms shows that some of them entail an amount of active engagement and reflect great mental effort, while others involve the more passive state of mere absorption and acquisition, the effort thereby being minor (see Table 14).

A third criterion is that of social morality. As we have seen, the Hebrew and Egyptian sages do not distinguish a man's intellectual qualities from his moral behavior. It is therefore worth noting to what extent there exists a gradation of the different terms within the context of social morality. It appears that such a gradation is clear only regarding three expressions:

good ——————————————————————> bad

ḥākām(|| *ṣaddîq*) *'ārûm*, *ba'al/ 'îš m^ezîmmôt*

Although *mēbîn*, *nābôn*, *yōdēa'*, *maśkîl* have a positive connotation, the gradation of these and other terms under review remains vague.

Table 13: The Source of the Wisdom as Criterion for Terminological Demarcation of the Semantic Field of Wisdom in the Bible

Source	*ḥokmâ*	*da'at*	*bînâ*	*t^{e}bûnâ*	*'ormâ*	*m^{e}zimmâ*	*tûšiyyâ*	*śekel*
Didactic, taught wisdom (*mûsar 'ab*)	+	+	+	+	+	+		+
"Natural" (from birth) wisdom or gained through life experience	+				+			+
Endowed, "charismatic" wisdom	+		+	+			+	

Table 14: "Mental Effort" as Criterion for Terminological Determination of the Semantic Field of Wisdom in the Bible

Mental effort: minor ——————————————————> great			
Acquisition of wisdom (through instruction or experience)	Insight, perceiving delving into matters	Thought, consider-ation, planning	Great mental effort and sapiential activity: teaching, writing, exegesis
ḥokmâ *da'at* *t^{e}bûnâ* *'ormâ*	*bînâ* *tûšiyyâ* *śekel*	*m^{e}zimmâ* *'ormâ/'ārûm* *tûšiyyâ* *nābôn*	*ḥākām* *mēbîn* (*śôm*) *śekel*

C. The Thematic-Conceptual Aspect

ḥokmâ and its synonyms — *t^ebûnâ, bînâ, tûšiyyâ, da'at* — are virtues possessed by man and God. But other attributes belonging to this subject — *nābôn, 'ārûm* and *maśkîl* — signify human understanding alone and are not among the qualities of God.

The areas of life covered by the terms belong to the semantic field of wisdom are many and varied:

The intellectual field: (a) literary creativity — the collection and composition of proverbs, onomastica (Qoheleth — Qoh. 12, Solomon — 1 Kgs., etc.) (*ḥokmâ, t^ebûnâ*); (b) exegesis (*byn* [hiph'il], *maśkîl, śôm śekel*); (c) teaching, study (*ḥākām, mēbîn, maśkîlîm*); (d) being steeped in information, knowledge, writing (*yōdēa'* — Daniel); (e) eloquence (*ḥākām, da'at, nābôn*).

Administration and government: (a) judgment — Solomon, David, the messianic king (*ḥākām, bînâ, lēb nābôn*); (b) administration — Solomon, David, Joseph (*ḥākām, nābôn, tûšiyyâ*); (c) counseling — Aḥiqar, Jonadab, Amnon's friend (*ḥākām*), Jonathan, uncle of David (*mēbîn, nābôn, ḥākām*).

Professional qualifications: (a) building and other trades outside the wisdom literature: navigation, soothsaying, interpreting dreams, playing musical instrument, lamentation (*ḥākām, yōdēa', byn* [hiph'il], *nābôn, t^ebûnâ*); (b) the scribal profession (Aḥiqar, Qoheleth, Ben Sira).

Religious affairs: (a) fear of God (*ḥokmâ, da'at, bînâ*); (b) understanding the vision of God (*byn* [hiph'il] — Daniel);[77] (c) God's Law and scriptures (*byn* [hiph'il], *haśkēl*).

II. COMPARISON BETWEEN THE HEBREW AND THE EGYPTIAN FINDINGS

A. Semantic Parallels

It is difficult to determine semantic equivalents between terms belonging to the semantic field of wisdom in Hebrew and in Egyptian, but some affinity can be pointed out. The semantic field covered by the verb *rḫ* in

Egyptian is covered in the Bible by the root *yd'*, which matches it in meaning and linguistic usages, while the adjective *rḫ* ("wise") parallels the adjectives *ḥākām* and *yōdēa'* in Biblical Hebrew.

Other expressions in the Bible are conceptually close to the Egyptian terms. *byn*, which among other things means "discernment," "recognition through vision," is on the one hand close to *siꜣ* and on the other to *'rḳ*, which like it signifies proficiency through delving deeply into matters and comprehending them wholly.

'ormâ is a quality not possessed by the *petî*, who lacks experience; similarly, *sꜣr.t* in Egyptian is a quality absent in the inexperienced youth.

The term *ḥm.t* in Egyptian is partly parallel to *kišrôn* in Hebrew, but unlike the latter it does not refer to success.

B. Thematic-Conceptual Parallels

In Egypt and Israel the "wise" man is he who has acquired wisdom through study and who continues to do so throughout his life — the "wise man" is the "eternal student."

In the conception of the ancient sage, intellectual and moral aspects are complementary. Therefore, the term "wise man" denotes not only mental powers but moral norms as well: he unites in his image intellectual and moral perfection. The "fool," who stands in contrast to him, is not only the recalcitrant pupil who rejects educational authority, but also the man who strikes out against the social conventions, the accepted moral norms of the community (see Appendix A, below). In Egypt the "wise man" is part of the social elite and belongs to the professional class of scribes; in pre-exilic Israel too, the sages were scribes who engaged among other things in writing wisdom literature (see Appendix D).

"Wisdom" is, first of all, practical wisdom, utilized by man in his daily affairs, and it has many facets. Apart from studied and acquired wisdom the Hebrew and Egyptian sages recognize wisdom of another kind: technical, professional wisdom, e.g, skills used in building a house or steering a ship; wisdom accumulated through lifelong experience, i.e., the wisdom of the aged; and charismatic wisdom originating with God, who bestows it on his favored. In the late wisdom sources the latter concept of wisdom predominates and wisdom is identified with the fear of God (see Appendix C). Wisdom as an attribute of the divinity is hypostasized in the literature of Egypt and in the Biblical wisdom books. Thus, in the first collection in Proverbs wisdom appears in the form of a woman, who speaks out to all who pass by (see Appendix B).

APPENDIX A

THE FOOL AND THE WISE MAN, THE WICKED AND THE RIGHTEOUS MAN

Dividing mankind into opposite categories and placing these side by side in order to illuminate and delineate them, is characteristic of the Hebrew sage as it is of his Egyptian counterpart. Since both contrast the fool with the wise man and the wicked man with the righteous, we may ask whether these two antithetical sets are identical: Are "righteous—wise" on the one hand and "fool—wicked" on the other synonymous epithets, indeed intended to denote the positive and the negative human type? Or are we dealing here with two independent contexts, each different in content and vocabulary?

In research on Proverbs several scholars have treated the problem extensively. The Egyptian material, however, has enjoyed less attention, and the question was first raised in the studies of M. Lichtheim and O. Keel.[78] A thorough comparison of the Hebrew and the Egyptian findings may aid us in finding a solution to this problem, each side shedding light on the other.[79] The semantic discussion of the terms in the preceding sections already described the features of the "sage—fool" dichotomy in the Egyptian and Hebrew material (pp. 221–222, 238–239). The following analysis of the typical features of the antithetical pair, the "righteous—wicked" man, in Biblical and Egyptian wisdom will complete the picture. Finally, a comparison will be made between the Biblical and Egyptian findings, after which the conclusions arising from it will be presented.

A. The Egyptian Findings

M. Lichtheim states:

> The concepts of "wise man" and "fool" already occur in the Instruction of Ptaḥḥotep, but only as a side glance in the epilogue. The terms are absent from the Instructions of Any and Amenemope. It is in Ankhsheshonqy that they make a conspicuous appearance and the words used are the same as those of Pap. Insinger... In Pap. Insinger the terms are at the very center of the teaching and their meanings have been deepened.[80]

We accept the first part of Lichtheim's comment — with one reservation: The contrast between "fool" and "wise man" makes its mark not only in *The Instruction of Ptaḥḥotep* but in other instructions belonging to the First Intermediate and the Middle and New Kingdom Periods as well. True, the contrast is not made by means of the adjectives "wise" and "fool," but is expressed in the verbal form of *rḫ* ("to be wise," "to know") accompanying the antonym *wḫꜣ* ("fool") (see *The Instruction of Amenemhet* XIV B and *The Instruction to Merikare* 115,116, treated above, pp. 221-222; and also the epilogue of *The Instruction of Amenemope*, in which the contrast between the "fool" and the "wise man" is an underlying concept: "They (the thirty chapters) cause the fool (*ḫm*) to know (*rdi rḫ*)" [27,10]). This pattern has also left its mark in works that are not among the didactic instruction but belong to the wisdom circle (such as *The Admonitions of an Egyptian Sage* 4,7-8; 6,13 [Cf. pp. 221–222 above]; *The Instruction of a Man for His Son* IV 5; *The Eloquent Peasant* B1 287; *Pap. Chester Beatty* IV pl. 20, verso 6,6; *The Stele of Mentuhotep* 5 [see p. 184 above]; *Urk*. IV 970,1; etc.).

The division of humanity into fools and wise men thus appears already in the wisdom literature belonging to the Old Kingdom and continues, in a less obvious way, during the Middle and New Kingdoms.

In the instruction from the New Kingdom (*Amenemope*) the contrast of wise man — fool, *rḫ* — *wḫꜣ*/*ḫm*, in the earlier instruction is replaced by the contrast between the "heated man" and the "silent man," *grw* — *šmm*, and their synonyms (see pp. 160ff., and cf. p. 196 above).

The dichotomy between wise man — fool returns in the Demotic instruction, first in *Ankhsheshonqy* and later in *Insinger*, where this topic finds its full expression. The terms used in the late wisdom are *rmt rḫ* for "wise man" and three words for "fool" — *ẖn*, *lḫ*, *swg*. Apart from these antithetical pairs, another one occurs in *Insinger*, the "man of god," *rmt nṯr*, and the "wicked man," *sȝbe*. Lichtheim believes that the "man of god" is essentially the same as the "wise man" and that the "fool" is coupled with impiety (*sbȝ*). In her view the author of *Papyrus Insinger* employs these terms to enlarge the dichotomy of "wise man" and "fool."[81]

Since a semantic analysis of the terms and comparison of the passages in the Egyptian literature with parallel material in the Biblical wisdom may decide the issue, we shall turn to this in the following lines.
The wicked man — *sȝbe*, in the form *sbi* — already appears in the Middle Kingdom Period (*Wb.* IV 87), and its meaning is "foe," "rebel," against the king or the god. *sbi* therefore belongs originally to the political context,[82] and not to the vocabulary of wisdom. There is no connection between *sbi* and the terms denoting "fool," "wise man" and "man of god" in the early wisdom literature.

The picture changes in *The Instruction of Pap. Insinger*, where *sȝbe* appears in antithesis to "the man of god" — *rmt nṯr*. The *sȝbe* is an impious man who is oblivious of god (19,10; 31,18). In the social setting he is depicted as one who violates moral norms: he is intolerant, a miser, violent, vindictive and resentful (15,19; 23,24; 29,18; 31,3; 34,11).
The man of god — *rmt nṯr* — who does not appear in the wisdom context prior to *The Instruction of Pap. Insinger*, is the god-fearing, pious man (2,11; 18,3; 19,12). In social categories he is described as patient and gentle (18,16; 19,9-12; 30,10; 33,12). The term "man of god" *rmt nṯr* is also found in Coptic — ⲣⲙⲛ ⲛⲟⲩⲧⲉ, where it stands for *ṣaddîqîm* ("righteous men") in the Bible (e.g., Prov. 13,22; Isa. 26,7).[83] The phrase *rmt n nṯr* may therefore be seen as the semantic equivalent of *ṣaddîq* in Hebrew.

The above analysis shows that the setting for the contrast between the pious and the impious man is a dual one: social and religious morality. *sȝbe* stands in parallelism and in conjunction with terms belonging to the semantic field of evil, "evil man" — *rmt bn* (*Insinger* 13,5; 20,3; 30,24) and "inferior man" — *rmt ḫm* (ibid. 15,1,2). True, *sȝbe* stands in parallelism with and appears in proximity to the terms *lḫ* ("fool") and *rḫ* ("wise man"), but the background of these references is moral (social or religious), not educational (*lḫ* — ibid. 14, 13-14; 28,9-10; 30,22-23; *rḫ* — ibid. 23, 23-24; 34,11). The expression *rḫ* is never coupled in parallelism with "man of god." It seems, therefore, that the two groups, "wise man — fool" and "man of god — wicked man," in the Egyptian perception belong originally to two different spheres, the one concerned with the intellectual and didactic field, the other with the religious. As the Egyptian wisdom shares this motif with the Biblical wisdom, we shall now turn to the Hebrew material which may have a bearing on the above assumption.

B. The Biblical Findings

In the Biblical wisdom literature (Prov. 10-15 and Qoh. 7,8,9, see below), as in *The Instruction of Pap. Insinger*, there are two pairs of contrasting human types, "wise man — fool," *ḥākām* — *k^esîl*, and "righteous man — wicked man," *ṣaddîq* — *rāšā'*. At times these two pairs intermingle: the "wise" — *ḥākām* equals the "righteous" — *ṣaddîq* and the "fool" — *k^esîl* is analogous with the "wicked man" — *rāšā'*.

(1) The history of research:

Among the scholars who have dealt with this problem three main approaches are discernable: (a) one which identifies righteous man with wise man and wicked man with fool; (b) another which rejects this identity and claims that the terms are distinct; (c) an intermediate position, which states that a connection exists between the two groups, but that they relate to different semantic fields.

(a) U. Skaldny (1962)[84] conducted comprehensive research on this question with regard to the book of Proverbs. In Skaldny's view, the contrast between *ṣaddîq* and *rāšā'* and the identity between *ṣaddîq* and *ḥākām* depend on the chronology of the collections in Proverbs: the earlier the collection, the more evident the contrast and degree of identity. Thus, in chapters 10-15, which in his view are the earliest, the contrast between the righteous and the wicked man forms the central theme and the identity between *ṣaddîq* — *ḥākām* and *rāšā'* — *k^esîl* is total; but in 25-27, which belong to the later collection, this identity does not exist.

Many scholars, however, do not accept Skaldny's method of relative chronology. The chief flaw in Skaldny's analysis is his assumption that all the virtues enumerated in Proverbs belong to the *ṣaddîq* and all the vices to the *rāšā'*, even when these traits are attached to other subjects than the *ṣaddîq* or *rāšā'*.

H.J. Hermisson (1968)[85] on the whole follows Skaldny, and his sole innovation is in relating *ḥākām* and the *k^esîl* to the wisdom vocabulary. However, he sees *ṣaddîq* and *rāšā'* as characteristic of an early Israelite definition for which hardly a parallel can be found in the wisdom of the ancient Near East, a claim that requires revision in light of the findings in *The Instruction of Pap. Insinger.*

In contrast to Skaldny and Hermisson, most scholars who posit an identity between the two groups *k^esîl* — *rāšā'* and *ḥākām* — *ṣaddîq* relate the contrast between *ṣaddîq* and *rāšā'* to a later stage in the history of the development of wisdom (e.g., McKane, Loader).[86]

(b) J. Conrad (1967)[87] is a proponent of the theory which proposes an absence of identity between *k^esîl* — *rāšā'* and *ḥākām* — *ṣaddîq.* True, the distinction between the two pairs is difficult to make in terms of content, as *ḥākām* — *k^esîl* involves not only the intellectual aspect but also moral behavior. Nevertheless, there is a thematic distinction between them, which is confirmed by two arguments — one technical: it is possible to separate the two groups without affecting their unique nature; and the other conceptual: the attitude to God is secondary in the *ḥākām* — *k^esîl* pair but dominant in the *ṣaddîq* — *rāšā'* pair.

Scott (1972) likewise holds that two separate pairs are present here, each associated with its own vocabulary and set of ideas;[88] *ḥākām* — *k^esîl* are taken from the context of education and the school, while *ṣaddîq* — *rāšā'* belong to the level of "ritual orthodoxy" and their concern is the acceptance, or rejection, of God's command.

(c) B.W. Kovacs (1974)[89] adopts the intermediate position, asserting that Proverbs reflects the ethic of the professional class, the sages-scribes, the intellectual elite. Behind the contrasting proverbs of righteousness — wickedness and wisdom — foolishness is an awareness of the existence of method and order that govern the world, to which man is obliged to adapt. Like Scott and Conrad, Kovacs holds that the two groups cover different semantic fields, but that they are conditional upon each other. According to the ethical concept of the sages-scribes righteousness is a precondition for wisdom, as foolishness is for wickedness.

(2) Analysis of the Biblical material and comparison with the Egyptian findings:

The dichotomy between wise man — fool and righteous man — wicked man is found in Proverbs and Qoheleth but not in Job. Having examined the first pair (see above, pp. 238–239) we are now in a position to have a closer look at the second.

In Proverbs: The contrasting pairs *ḥākām* — *kᵉsîl* and *ṣaddîq* — *rāšāʿ* are found principally in chapters 10-15. In chapters 14-15 the contrast between the partners of the first pair is often presented, while the contrast between the *rāšāʿ* and the *ṣaddîq* is common in chapters 10-11.[90]

The subjects raised in Proverbs in order to demonstrate the contrast between *ṣaddîq* — *rāšāʿ* are multifaceted and concern various aspects of life. In the following list certain themes are seen to be more common, hence more important for reconstructing the motif of the *rāšāʿ* — *ṣaddîq* contrast in Proverbs. Presented in order of their frequency these subjects are:[91]

(a) Reward and punishment: these are the consequences of the conduct of the *ṣaddîq* and the *rāšāʿ* respectively (e.g., 3,33; 10, 16,24,25,27,28,30; 11,8,10; mainly in the second collection).

(b) Conduct on the social level: that of the *rāšāʿ* consists of harming others, cruelty, destruction of the city, murder, lying and hypocrisy (e.g.,

Prov. 12, 5,6,10,12,21; 24,15; 10, 11,31,32). That of the *ṣaddîq* is honesty, righteousness, mercy, offering help; he is a blessing to others (11,11; 12, 5,10; 13,5; 29,7).

(c) Matters of justice and law: the *rāšā'* is presented as guilty, the *ṣaddîq* as innocent (17,15; 18,5; 24,24).

(d) Religious background: ritual and religious morality involving the terms *ṣaddîq* — *rāšā'* as in the Psalms and in prophecy are rare in Proverbs. In one instance God appears against a ritual background as one who hears the prayer of the righteous and who keeps far from the wicked (15,29). The identical idea is expressed (ibid. 8) by the antithetical pair *r^{e}šā'îm* — *y^{e}šārîm*: "The sacrifice of the wicked (*r^{e}šā'îm*) is an abomination to Yahweh, but the prayer of the upright (*y^{e}šārîm*) is his delight." Furthermore, God is the executor of retribution: the *ṣaddîq* receives his reward, the *rāšā'* his punishment (3,33; cf. 10,27).

(e) The didactic background: only rarely does the pair *ṣaddîq* and *rāšā'* refer to intellectual powers or involve an educational background: the *ṣaddîq* speaks out only after thought and consideration; not so the *rāšā'*, whose mouth "pours out" evil things (15,28; cf. not in antithetic parallelism 10,31: "The mouth of the righteous (*ṣaddîq*) brings forth wisdom," 11,9 and wisdom Psalm 37,30). In this context the *ṣaddîq* stands in synonymous parallelism with *ḥākām* and in contrast to *rāšā'*, *lēṣ*, *'ĕwîl*. The *ṣaddîq* , like the *ḥākām*, is the ideal pupil, unlike the *rāšā'*, whose behavior in this respect is like that of the *lēṣ* (Prov. 9,7-9: *rāšā'* || *lēṣ*; *lēṣ* # *ḥākām*; *ḥākām* || *ṣaddîq*). Cf. also: "The lips of the righteous feed many, but the fools (*'ĕwîlîm*) die for lack of wisdom" (ibid. 10, 21).[92]

The topic of the contrast between the *ṣaddîq* and the *rāšā'* in Proverbs therefore relates chiefly to social behavior, and to a lesser degree involves the religious sphere. The *rāšā'* is a negative type as he violates the social order and denies God. But the *ṣaddîq* possesses lofty qualities on both the social and religious levels. The terms that are synonymous and interchangeable with them as components in parallelism also refer to these two levels: *rāšā'* is synonymous with *ḥaṭṭā'îm*, *bōgēd*, *mᵉrē'îm*, *'îš rā'*, *pō'ălê 'āwen*, and *ḥānēp*, while the synonyms of *ṣaddîq* are *yāšār*/*yᵉšārîm*, *ṭôbîm*, *tāmîm*/*tᵉmîmîm*, *nᵉdîbîm*.

The picture thus obtained is the following: *ṣaddîq* — *rāšā'* in Proverbs are rarely mentioned in the religious context and they are also foreign to the world of study and education; where present in Proverbs these terms relate to social behavior. By contrast, the *kᵉsîl* and the *ḥākām* belong to the wisdom vocabulary and the educational and didactic spheres. As Hermisson states, the *kᵉsîl* and the *ḥākām* are "vivid" characters here, while the *rāšā'* and the *ṣaddîq* are merely "pale" personalities, borrowed from a different area of life, religion and ritual. The two settings relate therefore to two separate worlds but in Proverbs the borders between them are blurred.

In Qoheleth: The picture is similar in Qoheleth where the contrast between the *ṣaddîq* and the *rāšā'* invariably entails the problem of retribution — reward for the *ṣaddîq* and punishment for the *rāšā'*. The traditional dogma expressed in Proverbs causes skepticism in Qoheleth. The doubts, which were raised in *The Instruction of Pap. Insinger* in a humble and diffident voice and only by intimation (see p. 222 above), are here stated explicitly: "One fate comes to all, to the righteous and the wicked," asserts Qoheleth: "death" (9,2; cf. 8,14). "There is a righteous man who perishes in his righteousness, and there is a wicked man who prolongs his life in his evildoing," he declares (7,15ff.).

Only once is the pair *ṣaddîq* — *rš'* (as verb) juxtaposed to the pair *ḥkm* (as verb) — *sākāl*. This is however not against a didactic background, and here, too, the contrast involves issues characteristic of Qoheleth — retribution and death:

> Be not overly righteous (*ṣaddîq*) and do not make yourself
> overwise (*tithakkam*). Why should you destroy yourself?
> Be not overly wicked (*tirša'*), neither be a fool (*sakal*);
> why should you die before your time?
> It is good that you should take hold of this, and from that do
> not withhold your hand; for he who fears God shall come
> forth from them all (7, 16-18).

It is good to take hold of this and of that, says Qoheleth, because "he who fears God" escapes the two extremities. Here, for the first time in the history of Hebrew wisdom, the righteous man is parallel to the wise man and the wicked man to the fool; in Qoheleth it is explicitly stated for the first time that the wicked man and the fool are identical and that the righteous man is identical with the wise man, at least regarding their fate (9,1: "the righteous and the wise and their works are in the hand of God"). Qoheleth reaches this conclusion after much seeking and exploring as he reveals in 7,25: "I turned my mind (lit. heart) to know and to search out and to seek ... and to know that wickedness (*reša'*) is foolishness (*kesel*)..."[93]

In Ben Sira: While in Qoheleth the roots *rš'* — *śkl* and *ḥkm* — *ṣdq* are in synonymous parallelism, in Ben Sira *rš'* — *ḥkm* stand in antithetic parallelism, 15, 9-10: "Praise is not fitting in the mouth of the wicked... In the mouth of the wise praise is uttered."[94]

To conclude, the pairs "wise man — fool," "righteous man — wicked man" (or "pious — impious man") are found not to be identical, i.e., each belongs to a different semantic field, the one to the sphere of education and study, the other to that of religion and ritual. But since no division exists in the thinking of the sage between a man's mental qualities and his socio-religious behavior they meet on the level of social morality, which makes it difficult to separate them. The type that harms the soundness of society may be designated "fool" and also "wicked man," and he who contributes to the foundations of the community is termed either "wise man" or "righteous man."

In Egyptian wisdom the pair "righteous man — wicked man" appears at a relatively late period and was obviously preceded by the pair "wise — fool."

In Hebrew wisdom the chronology of these two pairs is less clear since the two pairs appear side by side from the very beginning. While scholarly opinion is divided as to whether their occurrence is synchronic or diachronic, we are inclined, in the light of the Egyptian material, to accept the latter view, i.e., that they relate to two different stages in the development of the Hebrew wisdom: the "wise — fool" belonging to the earlier stage and "righteous — wicked man" to the later stage.

APPENDIX B

THE PERSONIFICATION OF WISDOM

The personification of Wisdom in the Bible appears in the first collection of Proverbs only (1,20-33;8;9,1-6); later the motif develops and is expressed in a more extensive form in the Apocryphal wisdom literature, in Ben Sira (chaps. 1, 4, 14-15, 24, 51) and also in the Wisdom of Solomon (e.g., chaps. 7 and 8).

In chapters 1, 8 and 9 of Proverbs, Wisdom is presented as a woman standing at the gate of the city and inviting the passers-by to partake of the teaching she has to offer. In chapter 1, adopting the prophetic form of address, she admonishes the audience. In chapter 8 she makes greater claims for herself: it is she who gives nobles and rulers the authority and capacity to rule (14); her powers stem from the fact that she was the first to be created by God (22); she was *'āmôn*, i.e., an artisan,[95] who helped God at the time of creation. In 9,1-6 *ḥokmôt* stands in contrast with Lady Stupidity (*'ēšet k^esîlût, p^etayyût*, ibid. 13ff.), and both invite the passers-by to dine in their house. The description of Wisdom's rival is reminiscent of the image of the "strange woman" in chapters 1-9, especially the passage in 7,14ff — "A vow-offering was due from me / Today I have paid my vows" — in which she tempts the youth to participate in the feast she has prepared to mark the fulfilling of a vow.

Since this figure of Wisdom personified as a woman delivering speeches appears neither in the other Biblical books nor in the extra-Biblical literature, the following questions arises: What is the nature of this mysterious image of Wisdom? What is the relation between her and the *ḥokmâ — mûsār* ("wisdom — instruction") that the teacher wishes to impart to his pupils in chapters 1-9 of Proverbs?

Does chapter 9 hint at a possible solution? Here Wisdom appears in contrast to Stupidity, which may be interpreted on the basis of the similar figure which appears in chapter 7, i.e., the "strange woman."

The most acceptable perhaps among the answers suggested is the one which sees here the personification of an abstract idea, a well-known device both in and outside the Bible. In the Bible, for example, the book of Psalms offers the image of Righteousness and Truth kissing each other (Ps. 85,11-13), and in Proverbs the description of Prudence and Understanding watching over the obedient son recurs (e.g., Prov. 2,11-12; 3,22-25; 4,8-9; cf. also 2, 11-12). Outside the Bible, "Ägypten in der östlichen Mittelmeerwelt [kann] das klassische Land der Hypostasen gennant werden," states Donner.[96] Especially close to our subject is the personification of the Egyptian virtues Ma'at and Sia. Ma'at, which originally designates an abstract value, namely, "order," "righteousnes," changes in the course of time into a separate goddess, the daughter of the the creator god Re', who imposed this order on earth. Sia, meaning "knowledge," "insight" (see pp. 225–226 above), was at first an abstract value, also attributed to the god Re'. But later it became a personified value belonging to all the creator gods, Amon and Atom as well as Re', and even to Thoth, the god of wisdom.[97] Albright finds a similar phenomenon in the Canaanite epic, where, according to his view, "wise," the attribute of El, the head of the pantheon, became a goddess of wisdom.[98]

It is therefore reasonable to suppose that in Proverbs, too, the issue is personification of a divine quality, for whose construction characteristics of foreign gods were employed. Various gods have been mentioned in this connection,[99] but the closest in traits and features to Dame Wisdom are the Babylonian goddess of love, Ishtar, and the Egyptian goddess of justice Ma'at (*mȝ'.t*).

In view of the framework of our study and its focus on the relevant sapiential Egyptian material, we shall deal here only briefly with the theory regarding Ishtar offered by Boström[100] and discuss at greater length the possible influence of the Egyptian Ma'at, which was studied extensively by Kayatz.[101]

The Ishtar theory is based mainly on the assumption that the "strange woman" in Proverbs is to be identified with Ishtar, the goddess of love, who represents sacral prostitution. Wisdom, who is the rival of and stands in contrast to the "strange woman" was also invested with the characteristics of the goddess of love.

Traces of the description of Ishtar are found in chapters 1-9. In chapter 7 the "strange woman" is described (in the Septuagint) as looking through the window (a common description of Ishtar) and inviting the youth to a sexual rite, just as Ishtar invites her faithful to a similar ceremony. The seven pillars of Wisdom's house in chapter 9 are the seven stars of Ishtar, the goddess of heaven. The "strange woman," whose ways lead to She'ol, is Ishtar, whose descent to She'ol is related in the myth. Wisdom, who appears frequently as bestower of life and is linked with to the tree of life 4,23; 8,35) is Ishtar, who is associated with this tree.

Regarding the Egyptian sources, Kayats enumerates the following features and motifs characteristic of the Egyptian Ma‘at that might have influenced the Biblical Wisdom:

(1) Wisdom delivers her speech in the first person. This speech, whose main thrust is self-praise, is structured on the pattern of the Egyptian's gods' songs of self-praise (but not of Ma‘at).

(2) The existence of Wisdom prior to the creation of the universe and her description as the favorite child of the god, who plays before him (Prov. 8, 30-31), is similar to the description of Ma‘at.

(3) Wisdom in Proverbs is described as the beloved, as is Ma‘at, who is the beloved of various gods and kings and who in return loves kings and men.

(4) Wisdom is presented as endower of life and protection. Proverbs 3,16 states, "Long life is in her right hand; in her left hand are riches and honor." This description is remarkably similar to that of Ma‘at and other Egyptian gods who are presented holding the symbol of life, the *‘nḫ*, in one of their hands and in the other the scepter of rule and honor, the *w3s*.

(5) Wisdom is compared to a "garland," a "wreath," and a "necklace" (Prov. 1,9; 3,3; 4,9; 6,21). According to Kayats, this reflects a custom of the superior judges in Egypt who wore a chain from which hung a likeness of Ma‘at; and also furthermore the Egyptian belief that the deceased having undergone the trial of the dead is crowned with a garland called *m3ḥ n m3‘ ḫrw* and is declared a *m3‘ ḫrw*, that is, "one who is vindicated."

(6) A connection between Wisdom and the king is revealed in the statement by Wisdom in Proverbs 8,15: "By me kings reign" (and ibid. 23). In Egypt Ma‘at is conceived as the foundation of the throne, and the king, as the representative of the god Re‘ on earth, is entrusted with her protection.[102]

We are inclined not to accept the position of scholars who claim the exclusive influence of either the Babylonian or the Egyptian goddess. It seems that in elaborating the image of the female Wisdom in the Bible, the Hebrew author was influenced by both or more accurately shares here an ancient Near Eastern heritage — personification of Wisdom is also found in the Hellenistic world in the figure of Isis-Sophia and in the Assyrian setting, as attested by *The Story of Aḥiqar* (lines 94-95).[103]

The assumption that Wisdom incarnate in Proverbs originates in an abstract value which then became personified offers a solution to the problems presented at the beginning of this section. Wisdom, an abstract value with multiple meanings, was presented in human form for didactic purposes. This anthropomorphological presentation, which was intended to attract and hold the attention of the pupil, was accomplished by using elements and motifs from extra-Biblical mythology. This novel personified image of Wisdom was principally influenced by the characteristics of the Egyptian goddess of justice and the Babylonian goddess of love. The borrowings from the Babylonian myth left its imprint not only on the image of Wisdom but also on her antonym, Stupidity, identified with the "strange woman." These foreign elements were then modified to fit the Hebrew framework and the monotheistic conception; no longer an independent goddess to whom all the universe is subject (the Ma'at), but "Dame Wisdom," who herself is subject to God and serves him.[104]

APPENDIX C

STAGES IN THE DEVELOPMENT OF THE CONCEPT "WISE MAN," "WISDOM" IN EGYPT AND IN THE BIBLE

From the very start the Egyptian perception recognizes various sources of wisdom. Wisdom is knowledge acquired by study and experience, but sometimes it happens to be a natural gift, endowed from birth. Wisdom also occurs as understanding bestowed by god. Thus, the father of Merikare advises his son: "Copy your forefathers... See, their words endure in books; open, read them and copy their knowledge" (35ff.). Ptaḥḥotep, too, urges his son to acquire wisdom through the difficult way of studying; not necessarily from books, however, but from men:

> Consult the ignorant (*ḫm*) and the wise (*rḫ*)
> The limits of skill are not reached...
> Good speech is more hidden than greenstone
> Yet may be found among maids at the grindstones (54ff.).

Natural wisdom is found among common people as well as the members of the upper class. The king and his high officials may claim that they are "wise from birth," that is, possess natural cleverness (see pp. 221, 223, etc., above).

At times this wisdom is presented as a divine gift. The budding of this perception is found as early as *Ptaḥḥotep*, where it is stated: "He who hears is beloved of god; he whom god hates does not hear" (545-546; cf. pp. 55–56 above). It also underlines the words of the author of *Pap. Chester Beatty* IV (pl. 20 verso 6,6: p. 193 above), and it finds its fullest expression in the late *Instruction of Pap. Insinger*. It is the god who determines a man's nature, whether he is to be wise or foolish. Therefore, external circumstances do not attest to a certain kind of character (*Insinger* 5,3-8; 25,11-13; 27,18-21): Wisdom and ignorance, poverty and riches — all are subject to and determined by god, says the sage; therefore, there is a wise man who fails for lack of knowledge (*Insinger* 4,19) and there is a wise man who lives sparingly but becomes a pauper (7,15-17).

Thus, from acquired wisdom, attained through study and experience, and from natural wisdom, transmitted through inheritance, wisdom in the course of time becomes a charismatic gift possessed exclusively by the god. The "wise man" is merely a mortal, limited in his powers and liable to err (to be caught in love of women — *Insinger* 7,11; to be drawn into an act of vengeance — ibid. 34,12-13). The only way leading to prosperity and success in the opinion of the Demotic sage, is fear of god: "The wise man who goes and comes will place the greatness of the god in his heart" (ibid. 29,3ff.).

This development found in the Egyptian literature has an astonishing parallel in the history of the Hebrew wisdom.[105] The early wisdom in Israel, too, was multifaceted: natural wisdom, possessed by certain human beings (the wise women from Abel Beth-Ma'achah and from Tekoa') and also among animals (Prov. 6,6-7; 30,24ff.); technical and professional wisdom, the talent of the craftsman (artificer, graver, builder, etc.); and wisdom learned through proverbs, encyclopaedic lists, and songs (Prov. 1-9; Solomon, 1 Kgs. 5,12-14). But already in the early stage this wisdom is determined by God: "There is no wisdom (*ḥokmâ*) nor understanding (*t^ebûnâ*) nor counsel (*'ēṣâ*) against Yahweh. The horse is made ready for the day of battle, but to Yahweh belongs the victory" (Prov. 21,30ff.); "A man's mind plans his way but Yahweh directs his steps" (16,9); "The plans of the mind belong to man, but the answer of the tongue is from Yahweh" (16,1).

Man, then, may have his own inner thoughts, but his external conduct is ultimately decided by God (cf. ibid. 16,2; 19,21; 20,24). These verses are very close in content and spirit to what is stated in *The Instruction of Pap. Insinger.* Henceforward, wisdom is the possession of God; she was created (*qānānî*) by him (Prov. 8,22ff.) and he grants her to those cherished by him (Solomon, Joseph, etc.). Natural wisdom turns into charismatic wisdom. Job admits his inability to find this wisdom, while Qoheleth standing before divine wisdom, which has mastery over the world, cannot comprehend it.

By the end of this process wisdom is identified with religious belief. "The fear of Yahweh is the beginning of wisdom" (Prov. 9,10; 1,7; 15,33; Job 28,28; wisdom Ps. 111,10; BS 1,14 [Gr.]). Wisdom is the gift of God to mankind, it has descended from heaven to dwell among them (BS 24).

Thus, a parallel development can be discerned in wisdom in Israel and Egypt. However, the process in Egypt differs from that in Israel in two details: (a) The god does not appear in the Egyptian sources under review as the direct bestower of wisdom to man, it is only stated that god determines who will be wise; (b) the later stage in the development of the Hebrew wisdom has no parallel in the Egyptian. We have not found in the Egyptian wisdom literature anything like the concept that fear of god is wisdom, though such a development is found by Assmann in the "*persönliche Frömmigkeit*" literature, where it grew out of the Egyptian wisdom literature beginning from the Amarna Period.[106]

APPENDIX D

WISDOM — ATTRIBUTE OR PROFESSION?
WISE — ADJECTIVE OR OCCUPATIONAL LABEL?

The prevalent view in scholarship is that the "wise men" form a defined group of people holding a particular occupation.[107] Regarding the nature of this occupation opinion is divided: Some state that the wise men had technical skills such as building, engraving, sailing, etc.; others hold that they were the men and officials of the king's court: the counselor, the judge, the messenger;[108] still others regard them as possessing superhuman powers: fortune-tellers and sorcerers; some identify them with the class of scribes,[109] or believe the *ḥăkāmîm* were professional teachers.[110]

Since *ḥākām* in the Bible has various meanings, the problem cannot be solved by focusing on the Biblical context — extra-Biblical material should also be considered. We shall begin with the Biblical finding and then move on to the relevant Egyptian material which may shed light on the subject under review.

The expression *ḥākām* is multifaceted in the Biblical literature:

(1) The epithet *ḥākām* is not attributed usually to a particular class or group, but to anyone qualified in some field (Exod. 31,3,6; 36, 8; Isa. 40,20; Jer. 9,16; 10,9; etc.) or one possessing general knowledge (Isa. 5,21). One may assume, therefore, that *ḥākām*, is an adjective, indicating a virtue and not a particular profession or social class. Qoheleth says, "Again I saw that under the sun the race is not to the swift, nor the battle to the strong, nor bread to the wise, nor riches to the intelligent, nor favor to the learned" (9,11). Here "wise" parallels a list of virtues: "swift," "brave," "intelligent," etc., none of which can be said to denote groups of people with a particular profession.

In Jeremiah 18,18 it is said: "For Law (*tôrâ*) shall not perish from the priest, nor counsel (*'ēṣâ*) from the wise man (*ḥākām*), nor word (*dābār*) from the prophet." Here there is also no evidence that the wise men spoken of are a distinct professional class, that is, political advisers; in the parallel verse in Ezekiel 7,26 the "wise men" are replaced by "elders": "They shall seek a vision from a prophet and Law (*tôrâ*) from the priest and counsel (*'ēṣâ*) from the elders (*z^eqēnîm*)."[111] In this verse the concept of "wise men" is rendered so as to remove the sense of an occupation, and *ḥākām* is an attribute, not a profession.

(2) The "human ideal" formulated in Proverbs is not directed to a limited circle but to everyone: the youth (1,4; etc.), the farmer (24,30ff.;

cf. 31,16), the shepherd (27,23ff.), the witness (14,5; 19,5,9; etc.), the messenger (13,17; 25,13; etc.), and the drunkard (23,29ff.).

On the other hand, instruction in Proverbs is intended for a certain social class, the aristocracy surrounding the king: the wise men, the experts, are functionaries at the royal court — judges, counselors, messengers, and the like. Wisdom is associated with a certain circle, that of the educated, and it is they who are responsible for wisdom literature.

(3) Should the "educated" be identified with the professional class of scribes (Kovacs) or not (Whybray)?[112] Study of the Biblical texts shows that the office of the king's scribe is a permanent and well-known one during the period of the Monarchy.[113] However, in the period of the First Temple the title "scribe" — *sôpēr* — does not bestow the epithet *ḥākām* on a man. The scribes Ezra (7) and Baruch (Jer. 36,26,32) are not named "wise men." In Jeremiah 8,8 also there is no absolute proof of identification of the scribe with the *ḥākām*. Jeremiah asks: "How can you say, 'We are wise and the Law (*tôrâ*) of Yahweh is with us?' But, behold the pen of the scribes has been made to no purpose (*laššeqer*), the scribes have written in vain (*šeqer sōpᵉrîm*)." The prophet applying the language of Deuteronomy, which defines the *tôrâ* as "wisdom" and the people as "understanding" (see Deut. 4,6), does not condemn the *sôpᵉrîm ḥăkāmîm*, the writers of the book of Deuteronomy;[114] it is the people whom he castigates for not observing the teaching committed to writing by the scribes: "From the least to the greatest... every one deals falsely" (ibid. v. 10).

Evidence of the existence of the profession of a scribe who engages in teaching (the Torah) dates only from the time of the Second Temple.[115] Such scribes were Ezra (Ezra 7,12,21; Neh. 8,1-3,7,8), Ben Sira (BS 51,23) and the wise men mentioned in Qoheleth 12,11 as "masters of collections," Qoheleth himself being one of them. Nevertheless, we assume that the "wise men" were scribes and that the scribes constituted the circle that created and imparted the Hebrew wisdom literature as early as the First Temple period. This assumption is confirmed by the extra-Biblical testimony.

In Egypt the writing and transmission of wisdom literature involves the class of scribes attached to the king's court or the Egyptian school. The didactic wisdom compositions, *The Instruction of Anii*, *The Instruction of Amenemope* and *The Onomasticon of Amenemope*, were written by men who called themselves "scribes." In *Papyrus Chester Beatty* IV the eight famous scribes of Egypt are mentioned; these are described as "wise scribes" (*sš.w rḫ iḫ.t*) and are presented as the authors of a considerable part of the wisdom writings. In *The Prophecies of Neferti*, Neferti has the titles lector-priest, and scribe "excellent with his fingers"; and in *Papyrus Westcar* the miracle-worker Djedi, renowned as a wise man, is certainly a scribe and teacher too, for he requests a barge to carry his books and his pupils (*Les.* 30,10). Thoth, the god of scribes, was furthermore the god of wisdom. In Egypt, therefore, it seems impossible to separate the institution of the scribes from the creative circle of wisdom.

A similar situation is revealed in the Akkadian sources. Palace and temple scribes, responsible for administrative records, royal chronicles and collections of laws, were also creators of wisdom literature.[116]

These considerations lead us to believe that in pre- exilic Israel there also was a class of educated scribes who constituted the creative circle of Hebrew wisdom. To this class of wise men engaged in composing, compiling, editing and writing down the sapiential material belong "the men of Hezekiah," who are said to have "copied" the Proverbs of Solomon (Prov. 25,1).[117]

In conclusion, it may be stated that *ḥākām* in the Bible is a multifaceted concept denoting a highly skilled master of a particular profession but who is also any mortal gifted with natural understanding. At times he acquires his knowledge through study and experience, and at times he belongs to the class of scribes and the intellectual elite responsible for writing, studying and teaching the wisdom literature (Qoh. 12,9ff.).

CHAPTER SEVEN

THE PARTS OF THE BODY INVOLVED IN INSTRUCTION AND WISDOM

The terms presented in this chapter, denoting organs of the body, do not of themselves belong to the wisdom lexicon but in certain contexts constitute an inseparable part of the world of education and wisdom. These terms — the ear, tongue, mouth, belly and heart — are associated with various stages in the mental process of learning and can be divided into three groups:

(a) The organ associated with the acquisition of knowledge: The ear is the instrument both of hearing and understanding; its function is to receive information from the outside and to convey it to a person's interior.

(b) The organs used in expressing knowledge and thought: The tongue and the mouth are organs of speech and, contrary to the ear, their function is to pour out from within a man's thoughts and feelings.

(c) The organs in which received knowledge is stored in between the two stages of transmission from the outside inwards and vice versa: the belly and the heart.

While a remarkable affinity is found in the usage of these terms in Hebrew and Egyptian in respect to both subject matter and literary devices, this does not always indicate a link between the two cultures or the impact of one upon the other. The closeness of the Hebrew and Egyptian terms in groups (a) and (b) usually stems from common concepts that prevailed throughout the ancient Near East and which were part of the educational framework and the ancient method of study. As to the terms in group (c), certain applications of these terms in the Biblical wisdom literature are indicative of a borrowing and imitation of

Egyptian concepts and phraseology, which were modified and adapted to the Yahwistic spirit.

I. THE EAR

'ōzen — *msḏr, ʿnḫ.wy* (Dem. *msḏʿ, msḏ [r]*; Copt. [S] ⲙⲁⲁϫⲉ)[1]

The organ of hearing, *'ōzen* in Hebrew, is designated in Egyptian by two terms: *msḏr*, which appears beginning with the Pyramid Texts and whose occurrence is restricted to the school writings; and the form in dual *ʿnḫwy*, which is used from the Middle Kingdom onwards, for the most part juxtaposed to other organs of the body. In our sample it occurs in the instructions and the autobiographical inscriptions.[2]

A. The Ear as an Organ of Hearing and Obedience

The function of the ear as an organ of hearing and obedience is illustrated in an image which recurs in the Egyptian school texts: "The pupil's ear is upon his back, he hears when he is flogged" (*Anastasi* III 3,13; cf. ibid. IV 8,7-8, and *Lansing* 11, 1-2).[3]

An important official function is to be the "ear of the king,"[4] an expression that occurs frequently in the writings of the 18th Dynasty (parallel to the "mouth" and the "eyes of the king," *Urk.* IV 486,7-8; 540,9,10,16,17; etc.). In the Bible, the expression *'ōzen šōmāʿat* ("an ear that hears") refers to the ideal situation between teacher and pupil, and it is among the sages that such a hearkening ear dwells (Prov. 15,31; cf. 18,15 and *'ōzen maqšebet* in BS 3,29). The sage's reproof to a pupil who is graced with such an attentive ear is compared to precious ornaments (Prov. 25,12).

In appeals for obedience addressed to youth the word "ear," which collocates with the verbs "to give" in Egyptian (*rdi*) and in Hebrew (*ntn*) and with "to inclinc" (*nṭh*) in Hebrew, stands in synonymous parallelism with the verb "to hear" (*Amenemope* 3,9 || Prov. 22,17;[5] Prov. 4,20; 5,1; similarly 2,2; cf. BS 6,33 and 51,16).

About the pupil who is not disposed to listening, we read: "I did not listen to the voice of my teachers, nor incline my ear to my instructors" (Prov. 5,13). This sort of pupil, "who turns his ear from hearing" (28,9), is regarded as a fool, and of him it is said, "Speak not in the ears of a fool (*k^esîl*)" (23,9). In Egypt, the lazy pupil is similarly censured, where he is spoken of as being "deaf" or as one having a "deaf ear" (*Anastasi* IV 2,5; 2,7; *Koller* 2,5; 2,3).

B. The Ear as an Agent of Understanding

The ear was not considered merely a passive organ for hearing that which is spoken and conveying it to the interior of a person. Sometimes it was also conceived as an instrument for understanding and evaluating words, and as such its function resembles that of the heart, which in the wisdom tradition was regarded as the organ of understanding and acquiring knowledge. This meaning for the ear is principally found in the Biblical wisdom literature but also occurs in Egyptian sources. Thus, the scribe Amenemope addresses his son in the following words: "Give your ears (*imi ʿnḫ.wy.k*), hear what is said, and apply your heart to understand it." In the parallel passage in the collection of the "Sayings of the Wise" in Proverbs we read: "Incline your ear and hear the words of the wise, and apply your heart to my knowledge" (Prov. 22,17; cf. 2,2; 23,12). And in Ben Sira (3,29) we are told: "The heart of the wise man understands the proverbs of the wise, and an attentive ear rejoices at wisdom" (cf. ibid. 6,32-33).

In asking, "Does not the ear try words as the palate tastes food?" (12,11) Job takes issue with the uncritical acceptance of conventional wisdom on the part of his companions. The sage does so by proposing that the ear's function is not confined to the mere reception of the words it hears, but that it also "tastes" them, in the same way food is tasted when eaten. In other words, its function is to examine what is said and to distinguish good from bad, the truth from a lie.[6] Moreover, Job himself is in possession of this very faculty, for he goes on to say, "Lo, my eye has seen all this, my ear has heard and understood it" (13,1).

C. The Deity as Teacher

In the early didactic literature there is a prevailing recognition that the will to hear is in man's control, since he can use his ears as he wishes. Together with this awareness, there appears already in the early wisdom writings in Egypt and later in Israel the concept that hearing is a gift endowed by the deity. In *The Instruction of Ptaḥḥotep* it is said:

> He who hears is beloved of god
> He whom god hates does not hear (550-551).

The words of Ptaḥḥotep parallel those of the sage in Proverbs:

> The hearing ear and the seeing eye
> Yahweh made them both (20,12).

In this light the image of God as a teacher who "opens the ear" (*glh 'ōzen*) of men becomes clear. Thus, in Job God "opens their ears to instruction (*mûsār*)" (36,10; cf. 33,16). And in the poems of the "Servant of God" and other prophecies of Deutero-Isaiah, both of which bear the imprint of wisdom tradition, we encounter the didactic setting, with the Deity assuming the guise of teacher, while the Servant (or the people) takes the role of pupil, and the ear is represented as the instrument of learning. Thus we read in Isaiah 50,4-5:

> Morning by morning he wakens
> He wakens by ear (*yā'îr lî 'ōzen*)
> to hear as the pupils.
> The Lord Yahweh has opened my ear (*pātaḥ lî 'ōzen*),
> and I was not rebellious,
> I turned not backward...

Elsewhere the prophet reproves the people, who are described as a rebellious pupil: "...from of old your ear has not been opened (*lō' pittᵉḥâ 'ōznekā*)" (48,8); "You see many things, but do not observe them; his ears are uncovered (*pāqôaḥ 'ōzᵉnayim*), but he does not hear" (42,20; cf. 35,5).

God's role, then, is to "waken" the ear of the pupil (the people) who refuses to "open" his ear. This combination, of the verbs "open" (*ptḥ*, *pqḥ*) and "waken" (*'wr*) with the noun "ear" (*'ōzen*), is not usual in Biblical Hebrew. Expressions such as these were common, on the other hand, in Mesopotamian literature, and it would appear that Deutero-Isaiah, who spent at least part of his life in Babylon, borrowed them from there. In Akkadian the word for ear (*ḫasīsu*) means both "hearing" and "understanding," for the "ear" was conceived as the seat of intelligence and wisdom. Thus the Akkadian expression *pīt ḫasīssi* signified "opening the ear" and "wisdom"[7] and is equivalent to the expressions *ptḥ*, *pqḥ*/ *'ōzen* appearing in Isaiah.[8]

II. THE TONGUE

***lāšôn* — *ns* (Dem. *ls*; Copt. λας)**
***šsȝw* (Dem. *šs*)**
šsr

The semantic field of *lāšon*, "tongue," in the Bible is covered by several terms in Egyptian, one of which is *ns*, the etymological and semantic equivalent of the Hebrew *lāšôn*[9] and the most common term bearing this sense in our sample. It appears in the instructions from *Ptaḥḥotep* to *Ankhsheshonqy*, in the pessimistic wisdom literature, the school texts and the biography (about 25 times). Two other expressions are *šsȝw*, whose use in the present corpus is limited to Demotic (*šs*) and which is found only in *The Instruction of Pap. Insinger*, and *šsr*,[10] which does not appear until the 22nd Dynasty and which in our sample occurs only in the autobiographical texts.

The tongue has two aspects — the physiological and anthropological. It is the second element which is prevalent in the wisdom literature: the tongue signifies primarily an organ of speech, a means of expressing a man's thought. The phrases, metaphors and motifs associated with it in the Hebrew and Egyptian wisdom are strikingly similar.

A. The Tongue as an Organ of Speech and Knowledge

Since the tongue is an organ of speech,[11] and eloquence is conceived as an art, some of the sayings concerning the tongue are devoted to praise of the latter faculty.

In *The Instruction to Merikare* it is said: "Be skilled in speech so that you may be strong; the strength of the king is the tongue; speaking is stronger than any fight" (32; cf. *Anii* 2,8; 7,8-9). With eloquence and the ability to give advice counted among the virtues required in the king's service, the official so gifted is termed *spd ns*, "keen of tongue"[12] (Janssen I p. 32, At 10,11; *Rekhmire*, *Urk.* IV 1084,2; *Wb.* II 320,13). In the rich imagery of Proverbs such an accomplished tongue is compared to a precious treasure, "choice silver" (Prov. 10,20) and "a tree of life" (15,4; cf. 12,18) and it is called "the tongue of the wise" (ibid. and 15,2), or "the tongue of the righteous" (10,20). In the late Egyptian inscriptions it is compared to "oil of myrrh" (Otto No. 9 || Jansen-Winkeln I A12, c,9; II 6,2) and in the Bible to "honey" and "milk" (Prov. 16,24; cf. wisdom Ps. 119,103 and Cant. 4,11).[13]

In the didactic context the tongue appears as instrument of learning. In *Anii* the son asserts: "A boy does not follow the moral instructions though the writings are on his tongue" (*Anii* 9,17). Here Anii's son challenges the traditional teaching method, which is based on memorizing the material taught. He argues that while the writings are "on the tongue" of the pupil, i.e., while he knows them by heart, he may still fail to understand them and be unable to apply them. In the Bible the tongue has a similar role: in one of the poems of the "Servant of God," in which wisdom imprints are evident, the Servant, likened to a pupil, says: "The Lord Yahweh has given me the tongue of pupils (*l^ešôn limmûdîm*) that I may know to answer him that is weary" (Isa. 50,4). Here *l^ešôn limmûdîm* denotes eloquence, which makes it possible to give suitable advice to one in need of it.

B. The Tongue as Source of Power and Harm

A second motif is the power of the tongue and the harm it can unleash.[14] This theme, common in the instructions and the autobiographical writings of Egyptian literature, occurs often in the sayings of the second collection in Proverbs.

In *The Instruction of Pap. Insinger* (4,5) the tongue is compared to a knife that cuts through the life of its owner when misused. The father of Merikare says, as noted, that the power of the king is in his tongue and that speaking is stronger than any fight (32). These truisms closely resemble the saying in Proverbs 25,15, "a soft tongue will break a bone" and its variation in *The Story of Aḥiqar*, "the [king]'s tongue is soft, but it breaks a dragon's ribs" (lines 105-106; cf. ibid. 100: "A king's word is soft, [but] keener and more cutting than a double-edged dagger"; cf. also BS 28,17 [Gr.]).

In Hebrew literature, the tongue of the wicked man is likened to a weapon that wounds others: "the arrows of a false tongue" (BS 51,6[B]; cf. Ps. 57,5; 64,4; Jer. 9,2,7; Prov. 12,18; 25,18). Anii likewise mentions the harm caused to the individual when he uses his tongue improperly: "A man is ruined by his tongue" (7,8-9). Like his colleague Anii, the scribe Amenemope warns against the "heated man," who "ruins and builds up with his tongue" (12,3). The verbs "build" and "ruin," appearing here are taken from the sphere of the building trade and are used in *Amenemope* to describe the work of creation. In chapter 25 the god Khnum appears as a potter who fashions human beings on his wheel: "Man is clay and straw and god is his builder; he ruins and builds daily" (24,15). In light of this, "to build" and "to ruin" in *Amenemope* 12,3 mean to grant life and to cause death. In other words, according to the sapiential concept, words can be used in such a way as to create life and to cause death. The words of the Egyptian sage match closely those of his Hebrew counterpart, who says, "Death and life are in the power of the tongue and those who love it will eat its fruits" (Prov. 18,21); "Good and evil and life and death — and the tongue rules over them completely" (BS 37,18 [B,D]).

C. The Tongue as a Tool of Rhetoric

Rhetoric, expressed by means of the tongue, is based on two principles: reticence and sincerity.

The Egyptian sage believes that a man must behave with restraint and not pour out his heart before a stranger (*Anii* 7,7-9; cf. 2,8). The "prattler," whose "tongue is everywhere," is censured (*Insinger* 3,6). The scribe commands his son:

> Give your ears, hear what is said...
> Let them rest in the casket of your belly
> May they be a lock in your heart
> When there rises a storm of words
> They will be a mooring post for your tongue
> (*Amenemope* 3,9-16).

Ankhsheshonqy even prefers dumbness to a hasty tongue (15,16). The speech of the negative human type, the hot-tempered man, is swift (*Amenemope* 12,1;[15] cf. *Insinger* 21,14-16; 22,10). Also in the Bible does restraint belong to the wisdom ideal. "He who keeps (*šōmēr*) his mouth and his tongue keeps himself out of trouble," says the sage in Proverbs (21,23) and the psalmist demands: "Keep (*n^eṣōr*) your tongue from evil and your lips from speaking deceit" (wisdom Ps. 34,14).[16] It is not enough for a man to speak at the right time and place — he must also be sincere. In the words of the Egyptian sage, "His heart matches (?) his tongue" (*Ptaḥḥotep* 528); "Do not separate your heart from your tongue," Amenemope instructs his son (*Amenemope* 13,17); and after about a millennium the author of *Pap. Insinger* advises the youth in similar words, "Do not let your tongue differ from your heart" (25,21). What is in the heart of the wise man is found, unchanged, on his tongue (ibid. 26,22), that is, he has "a straight tongue" (*mty* — Otto No. 5 || Jansen-Winkeln I A10,d,12; II 3,6,10; *ʿḳ3 s.t ns* — *Urk.* IV 993,6; cf. *The Eloquent Peasant* B1 131 and *Instruction by a Man for His Son* IX 7).

In the Egyptian literature the warning that arises in this contcxt is usually associated with the fate of the individual. By contrast, Biblical wisdom emphasizes the harm caused to society as a whole by those who misuse their tongues. This topic is expressed in a number of collocations consisting of adjectives and nouns with negative connotations attached to the word *lāšôn*; for example, *l*ᵉ*šôn šāqer* ("lying"), *mirmâ* ("deceit"), *tahpukôt* ("perversity"), *ʿărûmîm* ("craft"), *hawwōt* ("mischief"). Thus the wicked possess a tongue of *tahpukôt* (Prov. 10,31; cf. 17,20) — a perverse tongue, which causes a "break in the spirit," that is, loss of life[17] (Prov. 15,4) — or *l*ᵉ*šôn hawwōt*, which brings destruction in its wake (Prov. 17,4). The "strange woman" speaks to the inexperienced youth with a "smooth tongue," a cajoling tongue (ibid., 6,24; cf. 2,16; 5,3; 7,21). The enemies "make the tongue smooth," i.e., are flatterers (Prov. 26,28; 28,23; 29,5; cf. Ps. 5,10). In other cases *l*ᵉ*šôn šāqer* or *l*ᵉ*šôn ʿărûmîm* are applied to denote untrustworthy behavior (Prov. 12,19; cf. Job 15,5; Ps. 109,2), and in Proverbs 6,17 *l*ᵉ*šôn šāqer* is listed among the social abominations.

D. The Tongue and the Heart in Egyptian Wisdom

The tongue and the heart are closely associated in Egyptian wisdom: The tongue and the heart make up the total picture of a man's spiritual state, which not only finds expression in the instructions concerning honesty cited in the foregoing section but also is reflected in metaphors based on Egyptian religious belief and mythology. Since this notion has no parallel in the Biblical wisdom, a brief outline of the Egyptian material will follow.[18]

A picture that recurs in our sample is the comparison of the tongue and the heart to parts of a scale: The heart is likened to the weight, for it is the instrument used in the weighing up of things, considering and pondering matters while a man's tongue is portrayed as the plummet, for it expresses what is concealed in the heart, just as the plummet indicates the results of weighing. As the scale is the symbol of justice and honesty, this image appears often in the description of the leader or the high official responsible for these social norms: "Your tongue is the balance of the two lands, it is the weight of the Ennead (*Urk.* IV 533,14; cf. *Les.* 81, 6-7). *The Eloquent Peasant* uses this metaphor for the opposite purpose, i.e., when demonstrating the leader's failure to carry out his task:

> Speak not falsely — you are the balance...
> Your tongue is the plummet,
> Your heart the weight,
> Your two lips are its arms
> (B1 160-166; cf. ibid. 148-150; 322-325; B2 92ff.).

In another sapiential tradition a man's life is compared to a voyage on a boat, whereby his tongue is likened to the rudder that steers the boat according to the man's own wishes. Traces of this tradition are evident in *The Instruction of Amenemope* 20, 3-6:

> Keep firm your heart, steady your heart
> Do not steer with your tongue;
> If a man's tongue is the boat's rudder,
> The Lord of All is yet its pilot.

That is, be steady in your heart, firm in your decision, so that the tongue may express what your heart thinks (cf. *The Eloquent Peasant* B1 54-62; ibid. 91; 126-129; B2 98-103; *Admonitions* 12,5).[19]

The passage of *The Instruction of Amenemope* cited above contains an additional notion which is characteristic of the late wisdom: a man's tongue is here no longer independent, but the pilot of the ship of his life is the god. The awareness that a man's way of life is no longer subject to his own considerations, but his plans and their implementation are in the hands of the god, is clearly reflected in the words of the author of *Pap. Insinger*. He declares that the god "directs the heart and the tongue by his commands" (31,11; cf. 31,5).[20] The Hebrew sage articulates the same idea thus: "To man belong the plans of the heart (i.e., the mind), but from Yahweh comes the answer of the tongue" (Prov. 16,1; cf. 19,21; cf. also pp. 310 ff.).

III. THE MOUTH

peh — r3

In Egyptian and in Hebrew "mouth" is a polysemic term.[21] Among the meanings found in the wisdom literature are the following: The mouth is a bodily organ used for eating, drinking and speaking; "mouth" carries the sense of "speech," "saying" (cf. Chapter 8, pp. 312, 321, 328); and, finally, "mouth" means "opening," "gate."

In the framework of our study only the meaning of mouth as an instrument of speech comes under consideration. The mouth appears in this usage in parallelism with other parts of the body both in Egyptian — heart, tongue, eyes, ears — and in the Bible — heart, tongue, lips — and also in construct or in conjunction with words meaning "say," "speak," "saying" (*mdw*, *ḏd*, *ṯsw* in Egyptian, *dbr*, *'mr*, *māšāl* in Biblical Hebrew).[22]

A. Eloquence and Officialdom

rȝ is usually found in sayings and aphorisms concerned with rhetoric in general and giving advice in particular. As such it is common in the collocation *spd rȝ*, literally, "sharp of mouth," that is, skilled in speech. Pertaining to the king's court phraseology this phrase concerns the official's ability to give advice.[23] An official of the 12th Dynasty boasts that he is "skilled of speech (*spd rȝ*) in the place of meanness," i.e., that he is able to give sound counsel in cases of loss of wits (Janssen I p. 32, At 5); another says that he is "skilled in speech (*spd rȝ*) among the courtiers" (ibid. At 9; and see ibid. 6,7; cf. *rȝ spd mdw*, Jansen-Winkeln I A 10,d,2; II 3,6,11 || *KCG* 42225 p. 58 D2; etc.). This quality of excellence in the official is notably similar to that mentioned regarding God's Servant in Deutero-Isaiah 49,2: "He (God) made my mouth like a sharp sword."

Eloquence is conceived in Proverbs as wisdom. Of the *'ĕwîl*, the ignoramus, it is said, "In the gate he does not open his mouth" (Prov. 24,7). One man keeps silent out of ignorance and another owing to his mastery of eloquence: "If you have been devising evil, put your hand on your mouth," says the sage (Prov. 30,32).[24] Speech at the appropriate time causes joy: "Joy comes to a man through an (apt) answer of his mouth, and a word in season, how good it is!" (ibid. 15,23).

A regular title for courtiers of the 18th Dynasty and the Late Period is "a mouth that calms (*r3 shrw/shrr*) all the land to its extremities" (*Urk.* IV 482,2; 486,16; 527,5; etc.; Jansen-Winkeln I A14,z,2; A19,j,h,2; II 2,1,21-23);[25] or "the mouth of the king of Upper Egypt" (*Urk.* IV 540,9; 899,2; 900,8; etc.). This title, which persists until the Late Period (Otto No. 19 || *KCG* 42236 p. 85 B2; Jansen-Winkeln I A11,h,4; II 2,1,6; I A1,b,9; II 1,9,11), signifies the role of the high official as advisor to the king in various matters of government. From the 18th Dynasty onward the title *r3 ḥry*, "supreme mouth," appears (*Urk.* IV 58,6; 426,6; etc.), which refers to the high official, usually the keeper of the king's property or the supervisor of the treasury. At times, in case of emergency, this functionary was appointed to direct construction work and crafts connected with the palace.[26]

The title also appears in the Bible. When Joseph was elevated to eminence in Egypt, Pharaoh said, "By your mouth shall all my people be ruled" (Gen. 41,40). Among the titles accorded to Joseph at this ceremony was thus "mouth of the king." There is no doubt that in the story of Joseph, the Egyptian background of which is obvious, this title is one of the Egyptian features woven into the narrative. The title also appears in the book of Exodus but here it is hard to determine whether its source is Egyptian or not. Moses, who is hesitant about responding to God's call on the grounds that "I am heavy (*k^{e}bad*) of speech and heavy (*k^{e}bad*) of tongue" (source J — Exod. 4,10),[27] is assisted by his brother Aaron who serves as his "mouth" (ibid. 16), just as the officials of Egypt are the "mouth" of their king.

The term "mouth" becomes a central motif in Hebrew prophecy, where the prophet acts as the "mouth" of God. In the "scroll of rights" of the prophet in Deuteronomy 18,18 it is said, "And I (God) will put my words in his mouth and he shall speak unto them all that I command him." Since it is used to transmit God's words, the mouth comes to occupy a major place in the ceremony of the prophet's call (see Isa. 6,6-7; Jer. 1,9). To Jeremiah, the reluctant prophet, God says that if he repents of his wicked ways — "If you utter what is precious and not what is worthless" — he will be re-sanctified as a prophet, the renewal of the divine call being confirmed by the words "You shall be as my mouth" (Jer. 15,19).

In the story of the call of Moses, which serves as the prototype for later divine calls, the Hebrew conception is predominant; nevertheless the early Egyptian sense of the term still seems to underlie it. According to source J, Aaron acts as Moses' mouth and Moses for him is God (Exod. 4,16). The sense of "mouth" as a title of officialdom is still present, and the epithet "God" — often used to refer to the Egyptian king — is given to Moses, who in this context functions as a king. However, in the parallel verse in source P "mouth" is replaced by "prophet" and Moses is "God to Pharaoh": "See I make you as God to Pharoah and Aaron your brother shall be your prophet" (Exod. 7,1). Here an attempt appears to have been made to obliterate the foreign elements, but this intrudes again in the words "I make you as God to Pharaoh," which in effect contains a veiled polemic against the Egyptian king-god concept which is unacceptable to the monotheistic faith.

B. Loquacity vs. Verbal Restraint

One of the topics accompanying the use of "mouth" in the Hebrew wisdom and the Egyptian sources is condemnation of loquacity on the one hand and praise of verbal restraint on the other.

He who speaks much brings calamity upon himself: "He who guards his mouth preserves his life. He who opens wide lips, it is a ruin to him" (Prov. 13,3; cf. 21,23). Very similar to this are the words of Aḥiqar (98): "More than all watchfulness watch thy mouth and [over] what [thou] h[earest] harden thy heart. For a word is a bird: once released no man can re[capture it]."

In the Bible emphasis furthermore is placed on injury to others caused by verbal wickedness. "The mouth of the wicked (utters) perverse words", that is, the twisted words of the wicked mislead others[28] (Prov. 10,31), and likewise: "The impious (lit. "profane") with his mouth destroys his neighbor" (ibid. 11,9); "Wise men conceal knowledge but the mouth of the fool is near destruction" (ibid. 10,14; cf. 18,7; 15,28).

"Mouth" occurs also, though less frequently, in a positive context: a "mouth" that brings blessings to its possessor (Prov. 12,14; 13,2; 18,20; Qoh. 10,12) and to others (Prov. 10,31; see also 10,11; 18,4).[29] The Egyptian wisdom, too, lauds the ability to keep a secret and to be circumspect in speech. This virtue is perceived primarily as one of the qualities of those belonging to the higher circles of the king's court. The supervisor of the treasury of Queen Hatshepsut boasts that he "covers his mouth (*ḥ3p r3*) on any matter regarding the palace" (*Urk.* IV 429,3; cf. ibid. "seals his mouth," *ḫtm r3.f*, 47,10. The opposite is *ḫ3ḫ r3*, "hasty in speech" — *The Eloquent Peasant* B1 208; *Instruction by a Man for His Son* XIV 4). Ptaḥḥotep, preparing his heir for his role of vizier, advises him: "Conceal your heart, control your mouth (*ḥn r3.k*)" (618). This advice recurs in *Instruction by a Man for His Son*, where it is said, "He who controls his mouth (*ḥnn m r3.f*) is prosperous" (XVIII 6), and in the autobiographies of the 22nd-23rd Dynasties, where the high official is praised as one who controls (*ḥn*) his mouth (Jansen-Winkeln I A 1,b,4; 10,d,12-13; II 3,6,5-6).

C. The "Gate" of the Heart

In this connection, "mouth" appears together with "heart," for the mouth gives voice to that stored in the heart. The Eloquent Peasant describes his wretchedness in these words: "But my belly is full, my heart is burdened, therefore it comes out from my belly... so my mouth opened to speak" (B1 275ff.), the mouth articulating the feeling of suffering and the thoughts residing in the heart. A mouth "burdened with complaints" is a "full mouth" (*r3 mḥ* — *Neferti* 45); a man who complains is said to be "open of mouth" (*wn r3* — *The Eloquent Peasant*, ibid.; or *wpi r3* — *The Man Who Was Tired of Life* 3-4, 55).

Similar usages are found in the Bible. The mouth speaks what the heart ponders: "The heart of the wise informs his mouth," says the sage in Proverbs (16,23); the righteous man weighs his words and examines them in his heart before he opens his mouth (Prov. 15,28;[30] cf. Qoh. 5,1ff.)

Elihu, "burdened" with admonitions like the Egyptian Eloquent

Peasant, describes his condition in similar words: "For I am full (*mālēti*) of words, the spirit of my belly constrains me... I must speak, that I may find relief" (Job 32,18-20). The "mouth" (in Egyptian) "is full" with complaints; Job, complaining against God, says, "I fill (*'ămallē'*) my mouth with arguments" (23,4).

Man opens (*pṯḥ*) his mouth, in order to voice what is within him (his belly, his heart). His words may be words of wisdom: "I open my mouth in *parable*" (wisdom Ps. 78,2); the woman of valor "opens her mouth with *wisdom*" (Prov. 31,26; cf. BS 51,25); or words connected with litigation, as in *The Eloquent Peasant*, above, and in the admonition of Lemuel's mother: "Open your mouth for the dumb... Open your mouth, judge righteously" (Prov. 31, 8,9).[31]

The downtrodden, the rejected person, is deprived of the right to speak: "closed of mouth" in Egyptian (*The Eloquent Peasant* B1 286). Similarly, in the instruction to Lemuel the poor, the oppressed man, is "dumb," and his mouth has to be opened (Prov. 31,8; cf. Ps. 38,14).

D. Words Flowing like Water

The Hebrew and the Egyptian sage both depict speech by the image of running water. The Eloquent Peasant says:

> But my belly is full, my heart is burdened,
> therefore it comes out from my belly.
> As a dam is breached and water escapes,
> so my mouth opened to speak
> (B1 275ff.).

The mouth is compared to the breach in the river dam, and the Peasant's words of stifled anger and pain burst forth like water gushing through a crack in a dam.

In Proverbs speech is frequently compared to the water of a spring but not necessarily in describing distress and suffering, as in the Egyptian *Peasant*. At times the metaphor is inherent in a single verb deriving from the root *nb'*, "spring, flow": "The mouth of the wicked pours forth (*yabbîa'*) evil" (Prov. 15,28); or the metaphor is a fountain:

"The mouth of the righteous is a fountain of life" (ibid. 10,11). At other times the figure expands to include a series of images all connected with water: "The words of man's mouth are deep waters, a flowing brook, a wellspring of wisdom" (ibid. 18,4), that is, speech that emerges from the depths of a man is like "deep waters". Words described as a "flowing brook" are words fresh as stream water which is continually replenished. Such words are also compared to a "wellspring of wisdom," i.e., an inexhaustible source of wisdom.

IV. THE BELLY

beṭen — *ẖ.t* (Dem. *ẖ[t]*; Copt. [SBA] ϩн)

ẖ.t in Egyptian is the semantic equivalent of the Hebrew *beṭen.* These terms are not unique to the wisdom vocabulary in either Egyptian or Biblical Hebrew, but out of approximately 70 instances in the Bible about 25 occur in the wisdom literature. In both Egyptian and Biblical writings the term "belly" bears three main meanings: (a) a part of the body: the digestive organ, the stomach;[32] (b) the maternal belly: the womb;[33] (c) the inner parts of the body, the innards, as the residence of thought and feeling.[34]

The last of these meanings is of particular interest for comparative research as it provides an example of evident Egyptian influence on the Hebrew wisdom language — even though its foreign origins later became blurred. It therefore stands at the focus of the following discussion.

A. In the Bible

The belly, *beṭen,* is used mainly in two senses, as digestive organ and as the organ of birth. As a receptacle for man's thoughts and feelings, belly is rarely found, since in the Bible heart, *lēb*, usually serves as the residence of the mind, thoughts and feelings.[35] However, in some passages the belly explicitly fulfils the fuctions of the heart. These passages, rare as they are, appear mainly in the wisdom literature.[36] It may be assumed, therefore, that they echo the Egyptian conception in which this aspect of the belly occupies center stage.

The belly's function as *seat of the mind and thoughts* is well illustrated in Proverbs 22,18 (paralleling *Amenemope* 3,9-10), where the son is warned to guard the words of the wise in his belly: "For it will be pleasant if you keep them in your belly (*bᵉbiṭnekā*) if they be ready on your lips," i.e., words are stored in the belly, released at will by the speaker. Thus, Elihu (Job 32,18-20) compares the rebukes he has been suppressing in his belly to wine fermenting inside a tightly closed skin that inevitably must burst. His words are markedly similar to the lament of the Egyptian Peasant bewailing his suffering: "But my belly is full, my heart is burdened, therefore it comes out of my belly... after I have bailed out my waters and emptied what was in my belly" (*The Eloquent Peasant* B1 275-280). The same image recurs in Job 15,2 where Eliphaz, who considers Job's innermost thoughts as useless as the east wind that brings nothing but harm, asks: "Would a man of sense answer with windy knowledge and fill his belly (*biṭnô*) with dry wind?" And similarly, evil-doers are described as those whose "belly (*wûbiṭnam*) prepares deceit" (ibid. 35).

Evil thoughts bring perdition, while good ones, conversely, carry reward: "From the fruit of his mouth a man's belly (*biṭnô*) is filled, he is satisfied with the produce of his lips" (Prov. 18,20).

The image of the belly as a dwelling place for words, so common to wisdom literature, also appears in the prophets, although the word "belly," *beṭen*, is not present. Ezekiel in his call is commanded to eat a scroll "written all over on both sides with dirges and laments and words of woe"; he ate it and "it tasted as sweet as honey" (Ezek. 2,8-3,3).[37] Jeremiah speaks of eating the words of God which were joy and happiness to him (Jer. 15,16).

Another aspect of the belly as the *seat of the emotions* of lust and avarice is evinced in Job 20,20: "Because he (the wicked) knew no quietness in his belly (*biṭnô*) he will not escape with his valued possessions" (cf. *Ptaḥḥotep* 235ff.). The belly quakes and the lips quiver at the news of the destruction of the Temple (Hab. 3,16); and in a Psalm with sapiential features (31,10) the pious man's belly is wrathful because of persecution by his enemies.[38]

B. In Egyptian

The belly is regularly used to denote man's innermost soul, the seat of his intelligence, thoughts and emotions. In this sense *ẖ.t* serves as a synonym for "heart," with which it is coupled in parallelism.[39]

The function of *ẖ.t* as *a reservoir for human thoughts* is well illustrated in the prologue to *The Instruction of Amenemope*, where the father counsels his son, saying:

> It is profitable to put them (my words) in your heart...
> Let them rest in the casket of your belly (*hnw n ẖ.t.k*)[40]
> May they be a lock in your heart.
> When there arises a storm of words
> They will be a mooring post for your tongue
> (*Amenemope* 3,11-16).

This passage finds its parallel in Proverbs 22,18: "For it will be pleasant if you keep them in your belly, if they are ready on your lips."

A wonderful simile comparing a man's belly to a great granary in which are stored his replies, readily awaiting his choice, appears in *Anii* 7,9-10:

> As to a man's belly, it is wider than a granary
> filled with every kind of answer.
> Choose the good, say the good,
> while the evil is locked in your belly.[41]

ẖ.t, being the residence of thought, can sometimes represent thought itself. "The best of my belly" is how the father of Merikare describes his instructions, meaning his deepest thoughts (Epilogue, *To Merikare* 144-145).

As a near synonym of "thought," the belly is also the source of inspiration for the creative person. In describing his vain efforts in this respect, Khakheperre-sonb says, "I have wrung out my belly of what it holds in releasing all my words" (recto 3).

The belly — the center of man, his innermost essence — is seen as a precious treasure which should be well guarded and wisely used. In this context the expression "to hide the belly" (i.e., thought), *ḥ3p ẖ.t*, is common. The loyal official who conceals the secrets of the palace is said to be "a leader of citizens, a truly sublime vizier, whose belly hides the plans of the palace" (*Wb.* III 357,3; cf. *Urk.* IV 47,10; 971,2; 1198,13). Where the ideal functionary is characterized by his self-restraint and ability to keep silent, the "hot-tempered man" is apt to burst out in wrath and argument, and it is on account of this despicable habit that he is called "hot-bellied," *t3 ẖ.t* (see p. 118 above); of him it is said in *Amenemope*: "The fire burns in his belly" (13,7; cf. Job 15,1 above). The hypocrite, who does not say what is in his belly, is termed "sick of belly" (*šnn ẖ.t*):

God hates him who falsifies his words
And his great abomination is the sick of belly
(*Amenemope* 14,2-3; cf. 22,11-16; 23,4).

However, silence and the muzzling of the belly are not always the correct way of behavior. The belly is also the *seat of pain and sorrow*, and the sufferer should be permitted to have his say. In this connection there appears in Egyptian the phrase "to empty the belly," *fḫ*, *sk*, *šw* / *ẖ.t*. Ptaḥḥotep advises his son, in case he becomes a leader of whom a request is made:

Keep silent while listening to an appellant
Do not reprimand him till he has emptied his belly (*sk.t ẖ.t.f*)
of everything that he intended to say to you.
The victim of injustice desires to pour out his heart
more than the carrying out of actions for which he has come
(*Ptaḥḥotep* 265ff.).

And similarly, the Eloquent Peasant, one of these very victims of social injustice, says:

Having bailed out my waters,
Emptied what was in my belly (*snf.n.i ntt m ẖ.t.i*),
and washed my linen,
My complaints are done, my suffering is over
(*The Eloquent Peasant* B1 278-280).

Fear, joy, bitterness, love, greed and lust are seated in the belly. The faithful servant who restrains his impulses, "does not follow the dictates of his belly," while he who "obeys his belly" is considered an enemy (*Ptaḥḥotep* 235-248). Love of the leader is in his subjects' belly (ibid. 412-413); joy fills the belly (*Urk.* IV 894,14) as does bitterness (ibid. 1077,11). A man will bless his hated counterpart because of the fear in his belly (*Amenemope* 13,14).

C. *ḥadrê bāṭen* — *hnw n ẖ.t*

The Hebrew idiom *ḥadrê bāṭen*, lit. "the rooms of the belly," meaning "the innermost belly," is unusual in Biblical Hebrew, appearing only four times in the Bible, all in the second collection of Proverbs:

(1), (2) Prov. 18,8 || 26,22: "A gossip's whispers are gulped savory morsels[42] and they go down into the rooms of the belly."

(3) ibid. 20,27: "The soul of a man is the lamp of Yahweh, searching his rooms of the belly."[43]

(4) ibid. 20,30: "The sins of the evildoer are purged by bruises, and the rooms of his belly by blows."[44]

The Hebrew idiom *ḥadrê bāṭen* originates in the Egyptian phrase *hnw n ẖ.t*, "casket of the belly." The Egyptian expression appears in *Amenemope* 3,13, which parallels Proverbs 22,18, as mentioned above (see p. 293). In this passage the father urges his son to keep the sage's words in "the casket of your belly" (*hnw n ẖ.t.k*). The term denoting "casket," *hnw*, appears in the Egyptian sources in the sense of a box, a receptacle for books.[45] It seems, therefore, that in the Egyptian image the belly is a casket containing thoughts, plans and words, instead of books. Since the heart in the Egyptian perception is the seat of wisdom and intellect, it naturally dwells within the belly.[46] In the Late Period the term denoting casket (*hn*) in Egyptian came to describe the belly as the residence of the heart: "Your heart is within its casket."[47] The lazy pupil is like the ass "whose heart is not in his belly" (*Sallier* I 3,9 || *Anastasi* V 10,7-8); Amenemope warns against the desire for a poor man's property, for he has accumulated it while "his heart sinned within his belly" (14,10). The heart of "the heated man" is parched in his belly (*Ostracon Deir el Médineh* 1265II4). When a man expresses his thoughts and speaks aloud, it is as if his heart was going out of his very depths, his belly. A garrulous man is therefore described as one whose "heart is going out" (*pri ib*):

> Don't empty your belly to the crowd
> And you will not harm your dignity.
> Don't scatter your words to the crowd
> Or join the company of him *whose heart goes out.*
> Better is the man whose message is *in his belly*
> Than he who tells it to cause harm
> (*Amenemope* 22,11-16).

This may be compared with *Kheti* XXV B-C:

> Don't utter secret words, he who hides
> his *belly* (i.e., keeps silent)
> makes himself a shield
> Don't say words that go out of the heart
> when you are sitting with an opponent.

Since the heart is at times described as a divine power dwelling inside man (cf. p. 309 below), the belly may be presented not only as the heart's casket but also as its shrine, its temple. We read in the inscription of the priest Neb-neteru of the 22nd Dynasty: "The heart is a god whose shrine (*k3r.f*) is in the intestines (*m r3 ib*)."[48] The author of *Amenemope* means the same when he describes the aim of his work in these words: "... to cause his heart to descend to his shrine (*k3ri.f*)," namely, to his belly (*Amenemope* 1,9).

In light of the foregoing discussion, the expression *ḥadrê bāṭen* in Proverbs should be seen as a Hebrew "translation" of the Egyptian idiom "casket of the belly."[49] This idiom, which is rooted in the life of the Egyptian school but foreign to the Israelite sphere, was probably first adopted and then adapted to the Hebrew background. The casket of books (*hnw*), a common piece of equipment of the Egyptian scribe but not of his Hebrew counterpart, was replaced by the word "room" (*ḥeder*), common in the Israelite environment; the "casket of the belly" was changed to *ḥadrê bāṭen*, "rooms of the belly." Cf. Prov. 24,4: "Rooms are filled with knowledge."[50]

V. THE HEART

lēb, lēbāb — *ib* (Dem. *ib*); *ḥ3.ty* (Dem. *ḥ3.t*; Copt. ϩⲏⲧ)

A. Terminology and Basic Meaning (Physiological Aspect)

In both Egyptian and Biblical Hebrew two terms denote "heart": *ib* and *ḥ3.ty* in Egyptian and *lēb* and *lēbāb* in Hebrew. The semantic distinction between the two terms is difficult in both languages.

ib, which appears together with *ḥ3.ty* and in parallelism with it, is the semantic equivalent of the Semitic *lb*.[51] *ḥ3.ty* is apparently the *nisbe* form of *ḥ3.t*, "front," "forehead." Some scholars maintain that the primary meaning of *ḥ3.ty* is a physical organ, the chest, while *ib* originally stands for "mind," "intelligence," and synonymous qualities;[52] others hold that *ḥ3.ty* signifies a larger organ.[53] However, these distinctions cannot be verified with certainty, and the significance and application of the two terms overlap in the literary sources. Therefore, in the following discussion we treat them as a single term.

In time, the term *ḥ3.ty* long superseded *ib* and in Coptic only the form ϩⲏⲧ remains. This development is evident in our sample also. In works of the Old Kingdom Period *ḥ3.ty* occurs rarely. It becomes prevalent in the New Kingdom (*Anii*, *Amenemope*), and in the Demotic instructions it predominates and replaces *ib*.

The basic meaning of *lēb* in Hebrew is "chest"[54] (cf. *ḥ3.ty*). Together with *lēb* is found the secondary form *lēbāb*, which appears frequently in certain books (First-Isaiah, Deuteronomy, Chronicles). The two forms do not differ in usage and in the present framework we refer to them as a single term. The term *lēb* is more common in Biblical wisdom than in any other Biblical literary genre.[55]

In Egyptian and in Hebrew the "heart" signifies the innermost being, on which a man's life depends. The heart controls the other bodily parts which, as portrayed in the theology of Memphis, depend on it for their proper functioning.[56] Health and contentment prevail when the heart is in its place. The aim of *The Instruction of Amenemope* is, among other things, "to let his heart enter its shrine" (3,13). The opposite condition, lack of contentment, or sickness, is indicated in Egyptian by the phrase, "the heart has gone out." This is the situation of the Eloquent Peasant whose heart has come out (*prì*) of his belly (B1 275-276). Similarly the pupil, who yearns for the city of his birth, expresses his distress as follows: "No task can I accomplish since my heart has moved away (*tfy*) from its place" (*Anastasi* IV 5,2).

In Israel, as in Egypt, the secret and essence of a man's existence lie in the heart. After telling Delilah "all his heart" (Judg. 16,17) Samson loses his life.[57] The sick man, whose physical powers have left him, uses an expression equivalent to the Egyptian to describe his distress: "my heart *'ăzābānî*" (i.e., failed me) (Ps. 40,13; cf. "his heart died within him," (1 Sam. 25,37).

However, although it is the center of man, the heart is not identified with him, but conceived as an independent and separate entity. Therefore, in Egyptian, the heart may bear witness against its possessor in the Judgment of the Dead. The proverb states that "a brave heart in distress is the companion of its lord" (*Khakheperre-sonb* recto 13). In the late instruction it is said that the "wise man" is he who "takes his heart for a companion" (*Insinger* 21,5). The heroes of the wisdom composition at times speak to their heart (*Khakheperre-sonb* verso 1,5; cf. *Neferti* 20). The sense of "heart" is similar in this context to the "soul," the *bȝ* in Egyptian — a dialogue between a man and his soul forms the setting of *The Man Who Was Tired of Life*. The heart, together with the terms *bȝ* and *kȝ* marks the inner spiritual being of the man.[58]

A common figure of speech in the Bible, especially in Qoheleth, is "to speak with the heart," "to say (*'mr*) in the heart" (Qoh. 1,16; 2,1; 2,15; 3,17-18; cf. Ps. 10,6; 14,1; etc.), "to meditate (*śyḥ*) with the heart" (Ps. 77,7; cf. ibid. 27,8). As in Egyptian, several terms signify a man's soul — besides *lēb* are found *rûaḥ* and *nepeš*.[59]

The brief review presented above shows that there is an analogy between the basic meaning of the term "heart" in Egyptian and in Biblical Hebrew. In both languages "heart" is a polysemic, multifaceted term. The different meanings of the word and the expressions associated with it are remarkably similar in Hebrew and Egyptian wisdom, but this does not always attest to reciprocal influence or linkage.

Comprehensive and detailed studies have been published on the theme of "heart" in both Egyptology and Biblical scholarship.[60] The discussion that follows is limited to details important for the subject under examination, namely, to aspects referring to wisdom and learning (Section B 1). The remaining material concerning the term "heart" appearing in the wisdom literature, will be introduced only when referring to Egyptian characteristic terminology and concepts, whose appearance in the Bible may show an Egyptian connection or influence (Sections B 2,3,4).

B. Additional Meanings of Heart in the Egyptian and Hebrew Wisdom Literature

1. The heart as seat of reason and understanding

For the Egyptian and the Hebrew the heart is primarily the seat of understanding. Amenemope opens his instruction with these words:

> Give your ears, hear what is said
> Give your heart (*ḥ3.ty*) to understand them...
> May they be a lock in your heart (*ib*)...
> If you make your life with these in your heart (*ib*)...
> (*Amenemope* 3,9ff.)

Two tenets of wisdom are expressed here: words of wisdom are stored in the heart, and the heart is an instrument for understanding them. These ideas occur again and again in the Egyptian wisdom literature, attached to the following phrases: *rdi/di/imi+m ib*, "to put in the heart" (see p. 57 above); *wḥ'+ib/ḥ3.ty*,"to understand," "to be intelligent" (see pp. 64–65 above); *ip(t) m ib, ḥ3.ty ip*, "to understand in the heart," "understanding heart" (*Wb.* I, 66,16ff.; *Anii* 2,1; cf. ibid. 5,4).

As the seat of man's reasoning the heart is in charge of the intellect — understanding, memory, consideration, planning. The Egyptian describes his old age thus: "The heart has stopped and cannot remember (*tm sḫ3.n.f*) yesterday" (*Ptaḥḥotep* 16); "to take to heart" means to memorize, to learn by heart (see p. 58 above); the heart knows (*rḫ* — *Anii* 2,14-15) or does not know (*ḫm* — *Anastasi* V 6,2); the heart thinks (*k3i* — *Urk.* IV 434,8), plans and implements (*k3.t ib* — ibid. 1213,14).

Intellectual activity depends on the heart, which makes its owner one who hears or does not hear (*Ptaḥḥotep* 550-551). The heart of a fool does not hear (*Turin* D 2,6), and he is compared to an ass which has "no sense in his belly" (*Anastasi* V 10,7-8 || *Sallier* I 3,9; cf. *Anii* 10,9). "Destitute of heart" (*iw.ty ḥ3.ty*) is a common term for fool (see pp. 186–187 above), while "man of heart" is the title of the wise man (*Insinger* 13,2).

The loyal official may boast that he is "the heart of the king" or the "heart of the master of the palace" (*Urk.* IV 968,9; ibid. 1076,14; *Wb.* I 59,15; III 27,10; see also Otto No. 9 || *KGC* 42227 p. 66 C/4). Before such a servant one "opens" the heart (*sr n wb3 n.f ib*) (*Urk.* IV 538,14; 1129,5; 1169,13). But usually the opposite command appears, forbidding — in accordance with the ideal of "silence" and "self-restraint" which dominates the wisdom literature — the outpouring of the heart, the residence of thought and speech. Regular idioms in this usage are: *hrp ib*, "sink the heart," that is, "conceal thought" (*Ptaḥḥotep* 618); *s3ḳ ib*, "pull together the heart" (ibid. 364; Polotsky par. 64). And in negation: "Do not wash (i.e., pour out) your heart," *i' ib*[61] (*Ptaḥḥotep* 79; cf. ibid. 152). "Do not bare your heart," *pri ib* (*Kheti* XXV C; *Amenemope* 22,14). Metaphorically, Amennakht says, "Let your heart be like a dam" (5); the "hasty of heart," (*ḫ3ḫ ib*) who behaves in the contrary way, is condemned (*The Eloquent Peasant* B1 211).

In the Bible, as in Egyptian, the heart, *lēb*, is the seat of wisdom and instruction as well as the instrument for acquiring knowledge and understanding. Wisdom and counsel dwell in the heart (Prov. 2,10; 14,33; 20,5); the words "are uttered from the heart" (Job 8,10). As the heart is the place of wisdom it may also be synonymous with it — the sage says, "O you simple ones, understand prudence; and you fools, understand *lēb* (i.e., wisdom)" (Prov. 8,5); elsewhere he says, "He who acquires *lēb* (i.e., wisdom) loves himself" (ibid. 19,8; cf. 15,32). He who possesses "heart," is *ḥăkām*, wise (Job 12,3; 34,10,34 — Job and his friends), or *ḥăkam lēb*, "wise of heart" (Prov. 10,8; 11,29; etc.); the opposite is *ḥăsar lēb*, the simpleton (see p. 200 above) or the fool, who is said to "have no heart" (i.e., mind) (Prov. 17,16; cf. Hos. 7,11).

The role of the heart as an instrument for the acquisition of knowledge is emphasized in the following verse: "Why should a fool have a price in his hand to buy wisdom when he has no heart?" (Prov. 17,16), that is, the situation of a rich fool is a paradox: on the one hand he has the means to pay for studies, but on the other he lacks the organ that alone makes learning possible. The central role played by the heart in the process of study and perception is well illustrated in Qoheleth (1,16-17; 2,15; 7,25; etc.). Regular expressions in this context are: *ntn 'et hallēb l^e*, *šyt/śym/nṯh lēb*, in both, the sense of "to pay attention" and of "to consider," "to learn" (see pp. 58–59 above); the heart "acquires (*qnh*) knowledge" (Prov. 18,15; cf. ibid. 17,16) and "seeks (*bqš*) knowledge" (ibid. 15,14).

The heart is the center of intellectual activity, it, therefore, *yaśkîl* the wise man's mouth, adding *leqaḥ* to his lips, in other words, through it the sage increases his knowledge (Prov. 16,23; cf. Job 17,4). The heart "understands": "The heart of the wise man understands the sayings of the sages" (BS 3,29).[62] The heart "knows" (*yd'*) (Qoh. 7,22; 8,5); the heart is "wise" (*ḥkm*) (Prov. 16,23; cf. 23,15; etc). The contrary occurs when a man loses his heart, that is, he loses his intellect, his wits (Job 12,24). The heart "thinks" (*ḥšb*), "devises" (*ḥrš*), "reflects" (*hgh*) (Prov. 16,9; cf. 19,21; 6,18; 24,2; 15,28).

Here also belong the expressions *hegyôn lēb* ("reasoning of the heart") (wisdom Ps. 19,15), *hāgût lēb* ("meditations of the heart") (wisdom Ps. 49,4), *maśkîyyôt lĕbāb* ("imaginations of the heart") (wisdom Ps. 73,7),[63] *ma'arkê lēb* ("the plans of the heart") (Prov. 16,1; cf. also BS 37,17).

As in Egyptian, the heart in the Bible controls memory. This function is expressed in the phrases: *śym bilbab* (see pp. 58–59 above), *šmr, nṣr, ṣpn,* "in the heart" (Prov. 4,21; 3,1; Job 10,13; wisdom Ps. 119,11), and in images reminiscent of Egyptian customs: the instruction is compared to a chain attached to the heart of the pupil: "Bind them upon your heart always; tie them about your neck" (Prov. 6,21). The origin of this image may lie in the Egyptian custom of wearing talismans consisting of a rolled and tied papyrus placed in a holder, although, as attested by the silver plates containing the "Blessing of the Priests" recently discovered in the Hinnom Valley in Jerusalem, such talismans were not absent from Israel either.[64] Another metaphor, possibly taken from the world of the Egyptian scribe — but it, too, could be Hebrew — appears in the teacher's exhortation to the pupil to remember his words: "Bind them about your neck, *write them on the tablet of your heart*" (Prov. 3,3; 7,3).[65] These words approximate the mocking statements made by the rival of the scribe Amenemope: "You are wise at the head of your friends, the instruction of books is graven in your heart (*sb3y.t n sš.w ḫty.ti ḥr ib.k*)" (*Anastasi* I 11,2-3).

As the residence of wisdom, thought and counsel, the heart constitutes a precious treasure. Both the Hebrew sage and his Egyptian counterpart ordain that it be preserved and not readily revealed to others: "Keep your heart with all vigilance, for from it flow the springs of life" (Prov. 4,23); "Do not reveal your heart to all flesh" (BS 8,19[A]; cf. Qoh. 5,1 and *Amennakht* p. 300 above). Contrary behavior is characteristic of the *k^{e}sîl*, the "stupid man": "A stupid man has no delight in understanding but in expressing his own heart" (Prov. 18,2).

2. The heart as the residence of feelings

The heart is the center of feelings: pain, hatred, fear, anxiety, but also joy, pleasure and satisfaction dwell in the heart. The latter notion finds expression in Egyptian in a series of phrases, which include: *ib nfr* — "good, happy heart" (*Ankhsheshonqy* 12,8; *Admonitions of an Egyptian*

Sage 3,12); or *nfr ḥr ib*, "pleasing, good in the heart" (*Kagemni* II 6; *Amenemope* 5,7-8); *hrw ib/ḥ3.ty*, "please, satisfy the heart" (*Anii* 9,9 - 16; *Insinger* 16,3), and also *ḥtp/sḥtp ib* (*Kagemni* I 9; *Anii* 9,7-8; *Urk.* IV 1071,17).

An important idiom in this connection is *(s)nḏm ib*, "sweet, pleasant to the heart." This idiom, which is repeated in the instructions (*Amenemope* 9,7-8 || 16, 13-14), the royal inscriptions (Blumenthal 125, 329-330) and the autobiographies (Otto p. 70), reflects an ideology that regards a life of pleasure without sadness and anxiety as essential.[66]

The sages in the Bible also encourage the seeking of joy in life. This theme attains fullest expression in Qoheleth, but elements of it are already considerable in Proverbs, as evinced in such expressions as *lēb śāmēaḥ*, "joyous heart," and *ṭôb lēb*, "glad heart": "Joyous (*śāmēaḥ*) heart makes cheerful face" (Prov. 15,13; cf. ibid. 30), says the sage, declaring that to a man who is joyful, all his days are a continual feast (ibid. 15,15). Elsewhere it is said, "A cheerful (*śāmēaḥ*) heart is a good medicine but a broken spirit dries up the bones" (ibid. 17,22; cf. 27,9; Qoh. 2,10 and *Insinger* 24, 23-24).

The collocation *ṭôb lēb*, common in Qoheleth, appears in parallelism with the root *śmḥ*. Joy and pleasure are the command of God to man is Qoheleth's conclusion in light of his life experience: "Go eat your bread with joy, and drink your wine with a glad heart (*lēb ṭôb*), for God has already approved your actions" (9,7; cf. 3,12,13).

In the same context we find in Qoheleth the expression "to follow the ways of the heart" (*hlk b^edarkê hallēb*), which parallels the Egyptian idiom *šms ib*. *šms ib* — a key word in the Egyptian perception of life — means basically "fulfil the heart's wishes," and appears in the early instructions (*Ptaḥḥotep* 186ff; *To Merikare* 58, 80) as well as in the later autobiographies (e.g., *Petosiris*).[67] *šms ib* is an ambivalent expression:[68] bound up with the early Egyptian ideology of life, its meaning shifted throughout the generations to suit the various conceptions of life and belief in different periods.

There is no doubt that some of the occurrences of *šms ib* constitute a call to pleasure and to a life of joy in this world. This meaning is attached to *šms ib* principally in works composed in an atmosphere of skepticism and pessimism, such as the instruction written during the First Intermediate Period (*To Merikare*, above) or the "Make Merry" songs sung at funeral banquets. At times of crisis and misery, when conventional boundaries crumble and traditional beliefs are challenged, the need to live for the moment intensifies.

The atmosphere encompassing these works is like that evident in the book of Qoheleth, the passage in 11,9 being particularly close to the Egyptian sources: "Rejoice, young man, in your youth, and let your heart cheer you in your youthful days. Walk in the ways of your heart (*b^e^darkê libb^e^kā*) and in the sight of your eyes" (cf. ibid. 5,18-19; 3,22). The opposite instruction given by the sage in Proverbs — "guide your heart in the way" (23,19) — is roughly pushed aside here in language unmistakably reminiscent of the contemporary Egyptian tomb inscriptions (*Petosiris*). If one assumes that the author or editor of Qoheleth was familiar with the Egyptian literature,[69] one may possibly infer that the Hebrew idiom "to walk in the ways of the heart," bears the traces of the Egyptian terminology and motif.

3. The heart as the character, nature of man

Since the heart is the symbol of man's inner life, it frequently assumes the sense of "character," and in Egyptian it parallels or comes in proximity with this term (Eg. *ḳd*, Dem. *3my.t*) (e.g., *Ptaḥḥotep* 463-470; *Insinger* 12, 14-22; 25,16-17).[70]

In the Judgment of the Dead, too, the role of the heart is to symbolize the character and moral quality of the man: "The god places the heart on the scales over against the weight. He recognizes the wicked man and the righteous by his heart" (*Insinger* 5,7-8). The traits and features of a man, both negative and positive, are associated with the heart. In Egyptian, as in Biblical Hebrew, the term "heart" joins other words to form adjectives referring to different human types. For example, *wnf ib* is "light-minded," he whose heart is "joyous"; *'3 ib* is "insolent" while *srf ib* is "cautious," "patient" and *'ḳ3 ib* is "precise," "straight." In the Bible we find *'iqqēš lēb*, "twisted man," "not straight," and in contrast with him the *bar lēbāb*, "honest," "pure" man.

One of man's ideal virtues in the Egyptian conception is strength of character. This quality is also expressed by combinations in which one of the components is the heart, *ib*. Two idioms are present in this context: *dns ib* and *sḫm ib*. These are of particular importance as they have parallels in Biblical literature. Both expressions are ambivalent and may be found with a positive and a negative connotation.

dns ib[71] (lit. "heavy of heart"), "firm of heart," refers to a man who is restrained and in control of his senses. The high official is "*dns ib*, hiding his intentions" (*Urk.* IV 64,7). "Keep firm your heart (*dns ib.k*), steady your heart (*smn ḥ3.ty.k*)," the sage instructs his son (*Amenemope* 20,3).

Sometimes the expression is found in a negative context. Of the obstinate pupil who does not obey his teacher it is said, "How conceited you are! You do not hearken when I speak. Your heart is heavier (*dns ib.k*) than a great monument..." (*Lansing* 2,4). "Heavy of heart" is also one of the negative traits of the "heated man," together with "broadness of belly" and "lack of patience" (*Ostracon Deir el Médineh* 1265 II 6-7).

sḫm ib,[72] "stout-hearted," has a double meaning. It can refer to a positive trait, the opposite of weakness and cowardice: Senmut, one of Hatshepsut's nobles, prides himself on being "stout of heart and not weak" (*Urk.* IV 410,5; cf. the titles of Thutmosis ibid. III 556,1 and Intef ibid. 968,16). The expression *sḫm ib* also means precision and honesty in conjunction with the image of the scales. Thus, "the scales of the Lord of the Two Lands, the stout of heart of the Good God" is a description of a 18th Dynasty official (ibid. 454,2).

sḫm ib can appear in a negative connotation also, denoting violence and insolence, the opposite of modesty and respect. The noble praises himself for being "without insolence (*sḫm ib*)" (ibid. 66,12). The violent man, the *sḫm ib*, is the antonym of *snḏ*, the modest man (ibid. 1092,13-14; 1082,17; *Admonitions* 11,13). This last meaning, however, is not important for the purpose of comparative research.

The expressions denoting "firmness, hardness of heart" are connected with the Egyptian tradition of the next world and the judgment after death, as has been demonstrated by A. Hermann.[73] The heart plays an important role in the Egyptian Judgment of the Dead. It voices the "negative confession" in which the deceased declares his innocence, and it is weighed on the scales against the symbol of the goddess Ma'at (justice). Therefore, in order to safeguard the heart's reliable performance at the dead man's trial, the ancient Egyptians placed a heart-shaped scarab on the left side of the mummy's chest. Made of precious stone, this heart helped the Egyptians to overcome the problem of providing evidence of the innocence of the deceased; if anything happened to the natural flesh-and-blood heart, the scarab simply replaced it. From the religious sphere, the "heart-of-stone" motif was transferred to everyday life, denoting correct human behavior expressed by the idioms *dns ib*, *sḫm ib* (formerly *nḫt/rwḏ ib*), which appear in the instructions and the autobiographies.

Hardness of heart and stubbornness, usually praised in the Egyptian sources as traits of strong character and resolution, are condemned in the Bible. Here words meaning "hardness," "firmness," when connected with the term "heart," have a negative connotation. The king of Egypt appears as a model of the negative human type in the book of Exodus, the relevant phrases being found in the stories of the enslavement and the Exodus from Egypt, which have a clearly Egyptian setting. These phrases are as follows: *ḥzq lēb*, "to harden the heart" (parallel to *sḫm ib*) (Exod. 7,13,22; 8,15; etc., sources P and E); *kbd lēb*, "heavy, hard of heart" (parallel to *dns ib*) (Exod. 7,14; 8,11,28; etc., source J); *qšh lēb*, "harden the heart" (parallel to *rwḏ/nḫt ib*) (Exod. 7,3, source P).

Two of these idioms, *kbd lēb* (6 times in J) and *ḥzq lēb* (8 times in P and 4 times in E), are not common in the Bible, their appearance being limited to sections which have an Egyptian background. *kbd lēb* appears only once outside Exodus, in 1 Samuel 6,6, and then, too, in a reference to the story of the Exodus: "Why should you harden your hearts as the Egyptians and Pharaoh hardened their hearts?" the Philistines are asked. *ḥzq lēb*, too, appears once more,[74] in Ezekiel — in whose prophecy Egyptian elements are more evident than in any other prophet — where the people's perverse behavior is described as being "hard of heart," in parallelism to "stiff, hard of face" (Ezek. 2,4). Thus, we come to the conclusion that these two idioms reflect the adaptation of an Egyptian motif.

This, however, is not the case with the third idiom, *qšh lēb*, which is found only once in Exodus (J) but appears in other Biblical passages without an Egyptian background (Prov. 28,14; Ps. 95,8 and Ezek. 3,7). The combination of the root *qšh* ("hard") and a bodily organ or a synonym of "heart" is in the Bible the usual way of rendering "stubbornness" (cf. "hard of face," "stiffen the spirit," "stiffen the neck" in Deut. 2,30; Jer. 19,15; Ezek. 2,4; etc.). This expression should therefore be regarded as the authentic Hebrew equivalent to the various Egyptian terms.

kbd lēb and *ḥzq lēb* indicate not a direct borrowing of the Egyptian terminology, but rather a manipulation and adaptation of the foreign material to the Hebrew sphere, i.e., the Egyptian motif was adjusted to fit the Hebrew concept and therefore subjected to the following changes: (1) "hardness of heart," symbolizing restrained behavior and self-control in Egyptian, assumed in the Bible the aspect of a negative characteristic — stubbornness and disobedience; (2) *dns ib* and *sḫm ib* usually function as adjectives in the Egyptian examples available to us. The root *dns* when in combination with "heart" may sometimes act as a verb ("harden your heart" — *Amenemope* 20,3), but we have not found a case where the god appears to harden someone's heart. We do find this in Exodus. Here, as in the Egyptian sources, man (Pharaoh) appears often as the one who can harden his heart (8,11,28; 9,34), or his heart (Pharaoh's) may harden itself (7,13,14,22; 8,15; 9,7,35), but in the Biblical text there is a far higher number of cases where God is the one who hardens someone's, i.e., Pharaoh's, heart (9 times: 4,21; 7,3; 9,12; 10,1,20,27; 11,10; 14,4,8). As such, the formula is in direct contradiction to the Egyptian concept, which perceives the king as a god and the heart as the seat of the divinity in man (see Section 4 below).

Not only in the description of Pharaoh's behavior at the time of the Exodus do we find the traces of the Egyptian motif in the Bible. It is also discernable in Ezekiel in the idiom "hard of heart," referrred to above, as well as in another unusual expression, "a heart of stone" (*lēb 'eben*) (Ezek. 11,19).[75] This expression appears only once again, in Job 41,16: "his heart is as hard as a stone," used in describing the crocodile, a description probably also deeply rooted in the Egyptian environment.[76]

4. The heart as the source of moral strength in the individual and of divine inspiration

From the wisdom compositions of the Old Kingdom Period on, a two-fold concept of the "heart" appears in the Egyptian literature. The "heart" is on the one hand an independent entity, which determines the decisions of a man and affects his way of life, and on the other hand it is the residence of divine inspiration in man, the organ that transmits god's will.[77] The first concept apparently reflects the role of the heart as portrayed in the sphere of myth and religion. In the Memphitic theology,[78] the heart is presented as the ruler over the other bodily organs thus actually determining the wholeness of the body and its proper functioning. The Egyptian sage indeed recognizes the importance of the heart in charting the course of a man's destiny. This is well illustrated in the following statements: "Man's heart is his life, prosperity, health" (*Ptaḥḥotep* 552). "He who knows his heart (i.e., acts according to its decisions), the fate knows him (*Insinger* 4,23); "The good [fate] of the good man is given him by his own heart" (ibid. 2,19; cf. 5,1). From the 11th Dynasty on sayings begin to appear which depict the heart as guiding a man along the course of his life: "It is my heart that advanced my status" (*Les.* 72,15; cf. Otto p. 38 n.1); or "My heart led me to the path"; or "It is my heart, which causes me to do this by directing my affairs (*sšm.f ḫr.i*)" (*Urk.* IV 119,1; 504,7; 974,1; 1223,4).

The ambivalent concept of the heart is already found in *The Instruction of Ptaḥḥotep*. Together with the awareness that it is the heart which guides man in his life, expressed in the motto "follow your heart" (*šms ib*) (186; cf. pp. 303–304 above),[79] comes the following statement: "He who hears is beloved of god. He who does not hear is one whom god hates. It's the heart which makes of its owner a hearer or a non-hearer" (cf. pp. 55–56 above) — thus, hearing, which depends on the heart, is ultimately granted or not granted to man by god. This awareness, that the fate of man is in the hands of god, developed gradually. Beginning from the New Kingdom the heart is mentioned as the residence of the divinity in man, and the heart itself becomes compared to god. In the prologue to his instruction, Amenemope announces that the purpose of his words is to make "the heart enter its shrine," an idea expressed more clearly in the words of the priest Neb-neteru, of the 22nd Dynasty: "The heart is god. His residence is in the innards, he is pleased when the organs are rejoicing (Otto No. 5 || *KCG* 42225, p.60E10)."[80] In other references a man's heart is compared to an organ of God's body and therefore it is forbidden to harm it (*Amenemope* 24,3-4).[81]

In the following stage, in the autobiographical writings and the later instruction, the heart becomes the organ that transmits the will of god to man and the means by which the god directs man. Thus "god's way," implanted in man's heart, is mentioned frequently in the writings of the Petosiris family (Otto No. 46 || Lefebvre 61,14,28).

From this point on, the heart no longer controls the other bodily organs, but it is the god who "directs the heart and the tongue by his command" (*Insinger* 31,11). The god looks into the heart, and knows what is in the heart (*Anksheshonqy* 26,11; *Insinger* 31,17; cf. 31,4; 35,2). The heart is the abode of the "greatness of god" (*Insinger* 18,23; 29,3; 31,4; cf. 30,18), of "his fear" (*Ankhsheshonqy* 14,10; Otto No. 46 || Lefebvre 81,25) and of "his plans" (ibid. 81,22). These expressions continue the tradition of the hymns of *persönliche Frömmigkeit* of the time prior to and during the Amarna Period. In these hymns the formula "to put god into the heart (*rdi m ib*)" to signify fear of god, and the phrase "trust (*mḥ ib*) god" to signify recognition of him, are common.[82]

Finally, in the Demotic wisdom, where, as in the religious literature, the personal relationship between the god and man stands out, the supremacy of the god and the insignificance of man are expressed by sayings that highlight the absolute dependence of the heart on god. "The heart and the character and their owner are in the hand of the god" (*Insinger* 15,5), or "It is the god that gives the heart, gives the son, and gives the good character" (ibid. 9,19; cf. 23,23).

From the outset, monotheistic belief denies the heart the role of a kind of private god for each and every man. However, in the Bible, as in Egyptian, the heart may be seen as the agent for transmission of God's will. Indeed, God implants certain attributes and emotions in the heart of man: primarily he grants charismatic wisdom (to Solomon; to the craftsmen of the Shrine; etc.), God even put "fear" (Jer. 32,40), "joy" (Ps. 4,8) and "the (love) of the world" (Qoh. 3,11)[83] into the human heart.

Like the Egyptian god, the Hebrew God directs men to carry out an action by means of their heart (Ezra 7,27; Neh. 2,12; 7,5);[84] God may also grant a "heart" (to Solomon he imparts a "wise and discerning heart" [1 Kgs. 3,12]) and he may "fashion a heart" (Ps. 33,15). But in the Bible *it is not possible for the heart of a man to be defined as "God."* On the contrary, often a man's heart is in conflict with the will of God: "A man's heart plans his way, but Yahweh directs his steps," says the sage in Proverbs (16,9). The prince of Tyre is rebuked by the prophet Ezekiel because in his pride he sinned in thinking that his heart was the heart of a god: "You have set your heart as the heart of God" (28,2, cf. ibid. 6). The motto "follow your heart," which is found once or twice in Biblical wisdom literature (Prov. 23,19; Qoh. 11,9) and is probably the outcome of Egyptian influence, is utterly rejected and condemned in the religious sphere. The formulas "to follow one's stubborness of heart," "who stubbornly follows his own heart," denote apostasy and a lack of fear of God.[85] "Trust in Yahweh with all your heart and do not rely on your own insight," says the sage (Prov. 3,5). In those passages where man's heart confronts God, the latter's supremacy is invariably stressed. God sees into the heart (Prov. 15,11; BS 42,18; cf. also 1 Sam. 16,7; Ps 44,22; 2 Chr. 6,30). God tests (*bôḥēn*) and measures (*tōkēn*) hearts, that is, he is capable of assessing man (Prov. 21,2; 24,12; cf. 16,2; 17,3).[86]

The Hebrew sages go even further than their Egyptian counterparts in establishing the absolute superiority of God, and do not allow man "free choice".[87] "Many are the plans in the heart of man, but it is the counsel of Yahweh that will stand" (Prov. 19,21; see also 16,1,9). These verses may be a concealed polemic against the Egyptian concept. Such a polemic is certainly present in the following verse from Proverbs: "The king's heart is channels of water in the hand of Yahweh; he turns it wherever he will" (21,1); the Egyptian background, that of agriculture based on irrigation through canals, is obvious here (cf. Deut. 11,10-12). The Biblical text takes issue with the Egyptian conventions — neither the heart is God, nor is the king, says the Hebrew sage; the heart does not guide a man in his life's way, but God guides the heart. The heart of a king, then, (regarded as god in Egypt) is in God's hand, which moves it according to his will, just as the farmer diverts the water channels according to the needs of the land. In the Biblical wisdom the heart is no longer depicted as an organ that transmits the will of God and allows man "free choice" — the heart is an instrument in the hand of God to do with as he pleases, and all that man has left to do is to fulfil this will (cf. Qoh.3,11-15).

CHAPTER EIGHT

WISDOM WORDS

In Egyptian

At the beginning of his instruction the Egyptian priest Khakheperre-sonb, who lived during the 12th Dynasty, writes as follows:

> Had I unknown phrases (*ḫn.w*)
> maxims (*ṯs.w*) that are strange,
> novel untried words (*md.wt*)!

This utterance, bemoaning his inability to create words never spoken previously, stands in chiastic parallelism with the title of the work, which directly precedes it:

> The collection of words (*md.wt*)
> the gathering of maxims (*ṯs.t*)
> the quest of phrases (*ḫn.w*) with a searching heart.

The three terms that are repeated here — *md.wt*, *ṯs.w* and *ḫn.w* — belong to the semantic field of "wisdom words," which also includes the noun *r3*, a group of collocations in which *r3* is one of the components — *tpy r3*, *s.t r3*, *pri n/m r3* — and collocations with adjectives, e.g., *ḏd nfr/mnḫ/iḳr*, *ns*, *s.t ns/iḳr*.

The introduction to *The Complaints of Khakheperre-sonb* calls to mind the beginning of the book of Proverbs. In both works the opening passage includes the name of the composition ("The collection of words" and "Proverbs"), the name of the author (Khakheperre-sonb and Solomon), and the purpose of the composition. In the Egyptian work the latter is stated with a note of despair and disappointment (recto 2ff.)

arising from the author's personal experience, while the Hebrew Proverbs, by contrast, exudes optimism and even pretentiousness:

To know wisdom and instruction
to perceive the words of understanding (*'imrê bînâ*)...
to give prudence to the simple
to the young man knowledge and discretion.
A wise man will hear and increase learning and a
man of understanding will attain maxims (*taḥbulôt*)
to understand a proverb (*māšāl*) and parable (*m^{e}lîṣâ*)
the words of the sages (*dibrê ḥăkāmîm*) and their
riddles (*ḥîdōtām*).

Parallel to the Egyptian terms for wisdom words are six Hebrew expressions: *'imrê bînâ*, *taḥbulôt*, *māšāl*, *m^{e}lîṣâ*, *dibrê ḥăkāmîm*, and *ḥîdâ*.

In light of the above, the following questions arise:

1) Are there analogies between the Egyptian terms for wisdom words and those present in the prologue to Proverbs?

2) If the Hebrew terms signify different patterns of wisdom, do the Egyptian terms refer to different literary forms as well?

I. TERMS FOR WISDOM WORDS IN EGYPTIAN THAT HAVE AN ANALOGY IN BIBLICAL HEBREW

1. *ṯs* — *taḥbulôt*

The word *taḥbulôt* is one of the terms in Biblical language used in particular to denote wisdom sayings. *taḥbulôt*, which is always plural, is distinct from all the other terms in the semantic field of "wisdom words" in that its distribution is restricted to the wisdom books.[1]

In the introductory verses of Proverbs, the wisdom spoken of is intended not only for the "simpleton" (*petî*) and the "young man" (*na'ar*) but also for the wise man: "Let the wise man hear and increase knowledge, and the man of understanding acquire *taḥbulôt*" (Prov. 1,5). In Proverbs the term *taḥbulôt* occurs in three further instances in the context of warfare: "For by *taḥbulôt* can you wage war" (24,6; see also

11,14;20,18). In Job, which describes the greatness of God in nature, the word is applied to God: "The cloud scatters his lightning; it is turned about by his (God's) *taḥbulôt*: that they may do whatever he commands them on the face of the habitable world" (37,11-12). The cloud[2] and the flash of lightning[3] revolve in accordance with God's *taḥbulôt*, which activate them.[4]

In these verses the term has a positive tone: *taḥbulôt* are meant to save people or to express the authority of a ruler. Once the word appears with a negative connotation in connection with evil-doers: "The thoughts of the righteous are just; the *taḥbulôt* of the wicked are treacherous" (Prov. 12,5).

Interpreters of the Bible, both ancient and modern, have followed the Septuagint, which translates the word with *ḥôbᵉlût* (the art of piloting a boat, Gr. κυβερνησις), and linked *taḥbulôt* with the title of sea captain, *rab ḥōbēl*, a derivative from the Hebrew noun *ḥebel* ("rope," "cord").[5] Thus the term *taḥbulôt*, when used as a form of wisdom, is considered to be a metaphor: Just as a sea captain (*rab ḥōbēl*) grasps his ship's ropes (*ḥăbālîm*) which support the mast and sails and guides it through a sea of obstacles,[6] so does the man gifted with *taḥbulôt* know how to guide his ship through narrow straits to safe shores and find his direction through the breakers of life.[7]

In fact, the Bible does consider seamanship, the technical knowledge of navigation, to be a function of wisdom along with other professions (such as craftsmanship, mourning, and sorcery). They are wisdom acquired by study, as opposed to charismatic wisdom. Thus, in Ezekiel 27,8: "Thy wise men, O Tyre, were in you, they were your pilots (*ḥōbᵉlāyik*). The elders of Gebal and her wise men were in you, the repairers of thy seams" (see also ibid. 27-29). Similarly, in Psalms 107,23-27, sailing is described as wisdom: "They that go down to the sea in ships...they reeled and staggered like drunken men and were at their wits' (*ḥokmâ*) end".[8] In Jonah 1,6 the term *rab haḥōbēl* is mentioned once again, but without any special information attached to it.

However, the traditional interpretation of *taḥbulôt*, based on its association with the profession of *rab ḥōbēl* ("pilot"), seems to be far from the literal meaning of the word and, indeed, inadequate:

(a) As a special characteristic of the pilot or sea-captain, we would have expected *taḥbulôt* to appear in conjunction with *ḥōbēl*, as we find *g*^{e}*bûrâ* ("might") in conjunction with *gibbôr* ("a mighty man"), *'ōšer* ("riches") together with *'āšîr* ("a rich man"), *'ēṣâ* ("counsel") with *yô'ēṣ*, or *ḥākām* ("a wise man"); also the conjunction of *ḥāzôn* ("vision") or *dābār* ("word") with *nābî'* ("prophet") appears, as does *tôrâ* ("law") with *kōhēn* ("priest") (Ezek. 7,26; Jer. 9,22; 18,18; 2 Sam. 16,23, the counsel of 'Aḥitopel). However, in Ezekiel 27 and in Psalms 107, where *ḥōbēl* appears, the intellectual capacity required for competent navigation is expressed by the general term *ḥokmâ* ("wisdom") while the word *taḥbulôt* does not occur.

(b) The verses in Ezekiel which mention the *ḥōbēl* are thought to have been written later than the rest, after the exile of Jehoiachin (ca. 600 B.C.),[9] and similarly Jonah is thought to have been written after the destruction of Nineveh.[10] But the word *taḥbulôt*, which belongs to the vocabulary of wisdom, appears in earlier passages. Collections I-III of Proverbs, in which the word appears, are dated earlier than the sixth century B.C.[11] Admittedly it appears in Job — in the speech of Elihu — but even assuming the speech is a later addition to Job the ideas it contains nevertheless belong to the authentic material of that book.[12]

Thus, it would appear that the title *ḥōbēl* is posterior to the noun *taḥbulôt*, which makes it more likely that *ḥōbēl* derived from *taḥbulôt*, and not vice versa, as is generally assumed. However, as we shall see, it is almost certain that both words are derived from a third, shared noun.

Egyptian literature comes to our aid in solving this problem. In Egyptian, the transmission of counsel from teacher to student and from father to son or the imparting of a sage's experience to someone else, are all accomplished by means of well formulated maxims, words that are "tied and bound together." As H. Brunner first showed, those maxims are called "knots" — *ṯs(t)*  in Egyptian.[13] A wise saying is a "knot," represented by the ideogram for a tied belt with the determinative for rope. *ṯs* appears both in wisdom texts and in non-wisdom texts influenced by sapiential tradition. The term first appears in the Old Kingdom and continues through to the Late Period (ca. seventh century B.C.).[14]

For example, *The Instruction of Ptaḥḥotep* is called "*ṯsw* of good speech" (42). The priest Khakheperre-sonb expresses his literary ambitions[15] in the following words: "Had I unknown phrases, *ṯsw* that are strange, novel untried words" (recto 1,2). Neferti, another lector priest, a scribe and wise man, is summoned before the king, Snefru, because of his ability to speak "good words, choice *ṯsw*" (*The Prophecies of Neferti* 7).

The man who understands and interprets is called "he who unties knots," — *wḥ‘* 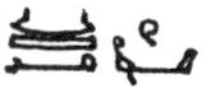 .[16] The verb is accompanied by the determinative of a rope, and its literal meaning is "to loosen ropes or knots." *wḥ‘* not only accompanies the term *ṯs*, whose literal meaning is "knot," but also other terms that denote wisdom. For example, in the prologue of *Amenemope* (3,10) we find:

Give me your ears
Hear what is said
Give your heart to understand them (*r wḥ‘.w*)
(lit. to loosen their knots).

And the epilogue ends with similar words (28, 14-15):

Look to these thirty chapters
They please, they instruct
Be filled with them, put them in your heart
And become a man who expounds them (*rmṯ n wḥ‘.w*)
(lit. who looses their knots)
One who expounds as a teacher.[17]

Now let us return to the word *taḥbulôt* in Biblical Hebrew. Like its Egyptian counterpart, *ṯs*, it is probably connected to the word for knot or a tied rope, *ḥebel* in Hebrew. Figuratively speaking then, *taḥbulôt* is a saying that is tightly phrased, well constructed, a pithy maxim made like a series of knots and loops. Such a saying is the work of a craftsman, and only a craftsman expert in the craft of speech can understand it.

Thus the vizier Ptaḥḥotep (second millennium B.C.) admonishes his son:

Do not take a word and then bring it back.
Do not put one thing in place of another.
Beware of loosening the cords in you (*wni ini im.k*)
(*Ptaḥḥotep* 608-611).

Here instead of the more common figurative expression *wḥʿ*, he speaks literally of untying ropes, and the image is concrete and vivid. The pupil must refrain from undoing ropes, that is, from trying to clarify things before he has full mastery of the craft of speech; he must restrain and control himself until he reaches the stage of the expert craftsman. In the words of Ptaḥḥotep: "Speak (only) after you have mastered the craft (*ʿḳ.n.k m sp n ḥmww*) (lit. after you have reached the action of a craftsman)" (615).

Similarly in the Bible, the craftsman, he who knows *taḥbulôt*, who is a master of wise words and whose tongue is sharp in speaking, cannot be overcome by his foes in war (Prov. 11,14; 20,18; 24,5).[18] He is a powerful and effective leader, as is God in Job. By contrast, "the wicked, their *taḥbulôt* are treacherous" (Prov. 12,5); they have not mastered the art of speech.

What, then, is the connection between *taḥbulôt* and *ḥōbēl* in Biblical Hebrew? Both derive from the same noun, *ḥebel* ("rope"), but their ways parted and, as we have tried to show, an independent semantic development took place. The traditional explanation can be diagrammed as follows:

ḥebel ("rope")
|
ḥōbēl ("sea-captain")
|
taḥbulôt

Our hypothesis, in the light of the Egyptian evidence is:

ḥebel
/ \
ḥōbēl *taḥbulôt*

2. *md.t*, *mdw* — *dābār*

In Egyptian: *md.t*, *mdw* (Dem. *mt.t*)[19]

md/w/t is the most common term in Egyptian for "speech," "word." Being polysemic, it also has other meanings: "matter," "affair," "spell," "legal plea."[20] *mdw* is not characteristic of the wisdom language and its occurrence is not limited to this literature,[21] but it concerns one of its major themes, viz., the art of rhetoric. The significance of *mdw* and its uses in this context will be in the center of the following discussion.

mdw, which appears in synonymous parallelism with other terms involving education and eloquence such as *sb3y.t*, *ḫn*, *ṯs*, *pri n/m r3*, *ns* and *ḳd* ("character," "nature"), occurs in the wisdom sources as (a) the spoken word, speech, and (b) as a saying written in a book (or originally oral sayings which were then committed to writing):

(a) One of the recurrent statements in the instructions is that speech is an art that has to be learned: "Speaking (*md.t*) is harder than all other work," Ptaḥḥotep tells his son (368; cf. ibid. 510-512). In *The Instruction Addressed to Merikare* speech is compared to a weapon that assures its owner victory in battle (32; see p. 281 above; cf. Prov. 24,6; 11,14; 20,18; Qoh. 9,14-16). The writers of biographies flatter themselves as being endowed with this quality: one of them was "the tongue of speech (*ns mdw*) of him in the palace" (*Urk.* IV 968,7) and another high official (Rekhmire) employed his tongue to whip people and thus was named the "scourge of speech" (*mdw n md.t*).[22] The latter expression recalls the Biblical image "You shall be hidden from the scourge of the tongue" (Job 5,21) and "He shall strike the earth with the rod of his mouth" (Isa. 11,4; cf. BS 51,2[B] and Jer. 18,18). Neb-neteru, the priest of Amon, has a "sharp speaking (*spd md.t*) mouth," while his colleagues are presented as "builder of monuments of speech" (Jansen-Winkeln I A20,d || II 3,6,18) and "bow-wrap of speech" (ibid. I A20,c || II 3,6,17; cf. also 3,6,16).

The speech of an eloquent man is "choice" (*stp*), "sweet" (*nḏm*), "excellent" (*iḳr*), "pleasurable" (*sḏ3y ḥr*) and "satisfying" (*hrw m ib/ḥr ib*).[23]

Knowing when to speak and when to keep silent also belongs to the art of rhetoric. "Do not let yourself be called an idiot because of silence when it is time to speak (*mt.t*)" (*Insinger* 3,7; cf. *Pap. Chester Beatty* IV pl. 18 verso 1,3; *Urk.* IV 1083, 11). To what extent the Egyptians valued eloquence and way with words may be judged from the following saying: "A speech (*md.t*) grows more than a *smnyt* plant" (*The Eloquent Peasant* B1 153).

However, speech does not always appear in a positive light. Occasionally the Egyptian sage counsels avoidance of speech when it is harmful, as in the case of quarrel and strife (*Ptaḥḥotep* 149; 376; 608) — the metaphors "a storm of words" (*Amenemope* 3,15) and "a blaze of speech" (Otto No. 7 || *KCG* 42210 p. 28,E6-7) relate to "words of strife" in the wisdom texts. Similarly, the sages do not approve of excessive speech or chatter: "Be moderate in the function of speech" and "sleep before speaking," the sages advise their sons (*Amenemope* 5,13; cf. ibid 5,8; 12,1; 22,13,14; *Anii* 2,6; *Ankhsheshonqy* 14,12; *Kheti* XXV C).[24]

(b) A wisdom instruction in its final written form is *mdw*. This may be traditional wisdom of ancient times handed down by ancestors: "Copy your forefathers... See, their words (*md.wt.sn*) endure in books (*sš.w*); open, read them and copy the knowledge" (*To Merikare* 35-36). In the same way the king says to the vizier: "Instruct him (your son), then, in the sayings of the past (*md.wt ḫr ḥ3.t*)" (*Ptaḥḥotep* 37).[25] It may also refer to recent wisdom, of only one generation, which is passed down from father to son, as it is said, e.g., of Ankhsheshonqy: "He wrote on the sherds of the jars the matters (*mt.w*) that he could teach his son" (5,19). Amennakht addresses his pupil saying: "Turn your face to hear my words (*md.wt.i*)... Do not turn your back on my speech of value" (3-4; cf. 9); a similar injunction is voiced by the teacher in the school writings: "Give your heart, (i.e., pay attention) listen to my words, you may find them advantageous" (*Anastasi* III 4,3; cf. V 17,4).[26]

The collocation *mdw nṯr*, meaning "god's scripts" and not exclusive to the wisdom books, also indicates the use of *mdw* as a written word.[27]

Thus, *md/w/t* signifies "word" in Egyptian. In wisdom literature it may refer to the spoken word, especially choice speech used in the art of rhetoric, but it may also be a written word, conventional wisdom tradition written in hieroglyphs (*mdw nṯr*).

In the Bible: *dābār*

Parallel to the Egyptian *mdw*, the Hebrew *dābār*[28] is the most common term in the Biblical language denoting "word," "speech." *dābār*, like *mdw*, is polysemic, identical in its various meanings and in some of its uses to the Egyptian equivalent; *dābār* also means "matter," "affair," "language," "royal edict," "sentence of judgment," "word of God," etc.[29] It stands in parallelism to *'ămārîm* ("words," "speeches"), *'ēṣâ* ("advice"), *millîm* ("words"), *miṣwâ* ("command"), and, like the Egyptian *mdw*, it serves as the object of verbs having to do with hearing, speaking and writing. *dābār* is mostly attached to other words, which determine its positive or negative connotation.

In a *positive* connotation *dābār* is found in construct with "wise men", i.e., *dibrē ḥăkāmîm*. This collocation, exclusive to the sapiential lexicon, signifies words of wisdom, words that are to be learned.[30] In the the father-to-son address which appears in the first collection of Proverbs *dābār* is synonymous with *miṣwâ*, *mûsār* and *tôrâ* (1,23; 4,4,20; etc.); the speeches of Job to his friends are defined as *d^ebārîm* (Job 29,22; 31,40; 32,11), as are the utterances of other sages: Lemuel, Agur, Qoheleth (Prov. 30,1; 31,1; Qoh. 1,1; etc.).[31] Two features of this usage stand out:

(a) The speech is authoritative; like *mdw* in Egyptian it may be oral (Prov. 22,17: "Hear *dibrê ḥăkāmîm*") or written (Qoh. 12,11: "*dibrê ḥăkāmîm* are like goads, and like well- fastened nails are the collected sayings").

(b) The speech is given in cultured language, indicating eloquence. These sayings are described as "a word fitly spoken," "a good word" (see pp. 325ff. below), "words of delight" (*ḥēpeṣ*)" (Qoh. 12,10) and "fine (*yāpîm*) words" (BS 35,5 [B]). These formulations define the well-constructed speech of the sage, which causes delight (*ḥēpeṣ*) to the ear and is delivered at the right time: "A word (*dābār*) in season how good it is!" (Prov. 15,23).

Thus, in reference to wisdom sayings *dābār* always has a positive sense. In the following cases *dābār* is found in a *negative* connotation:

(a) When attached to another word of negative shading which signifies anti-social activity: "the words of a slanderer (*nirgān*)" (Prov. 18,8 || 26,22); "the words of the treacherous (*bōgēd*)" (22,12); "a false (*šeqer*) word" (13,5; 29,12); "a false (*kāzāb*) word" (30,8); "words of wind (*rûaḥ*)" (Job 16,3; etc.).

(b) When used independently: in the Bible, as in Egyptian, excessive speech is condemned; for example, "but the talk (lit. word) of the lips tends only to want" (Prov. 14,23); "When words are many, transgression is not lacking" (10,19; cf. Qoh. 5,1,2; 10,14; BS 32,11 [Gr.]).

3. *pri n/m r3* — *mippri pî 'îš*

r3 is a polysemic term with one of its meanings, "speech," belonging to the semantic field under discussion (see pp. 285ff. above). In our sample this usage is limited to four or five instances. Therefore, it is difficult to determine the precise sense of the term and to what extent it may refer to a particular literary form of wisdom saying.[32] However, *r3* frequently functions as a component in collocations with the meaning of "speech": *pri m/n r3*, *s.t r3*, *tp(y) r3*. The following discussion centers on *pri m/n r3*. Contrary to *tp(y) r3* and *s.t r3*, which have no parallel in Hebrew and are not characteristic of the wisdom language either,[33] *pri m/n r3* has a remarkable analogy in the Hebrew wisdom — *mippᵉrî pî 'îš* .

The idiom *mippᵉrî pî 'îš*, lit. "from the fruit of a man's mouth," meaning "speech,"[34] appears only in the second collection of Proverbs. It is found in three versions of one proverb, to which (in the second part of the verse) three different proverbs have been attached:

12,14:	From the fruit of his mouth a man will be satisfied with good, and the recompense of a man's hands will be rendered to him.
13, 2:	From the fruit of his mouth a man eats good, but the desire of the treacherous is violence.
18,20:	From the fruit of his mouth a man's stomach is satisfied, and from the produce of his lips he is filled.

In Biblical language *p^{e}rî*, when used metaphorically, is generally accompanied by abstract nouns: *ma'ălālîm* ("actions") (Jer. 17,10; Mic. 7,13; etc.), *ma'ăśîm* ("deeds") (Ps. 104,13), *maḥăšābôt* ("thoughts") (Jer. 6,19), *derek* (in the sense of "conduct," Prov. 1,31); or by bodily parts: *kap* ("palm") (Prov. 31,16), *yād* ("hand") (31,31).[35] Therefore, the collocation *p^{e}rî pî 'îš*, while exclusive to Proverbs, is not exceptional in its grammar and linguistic form, but it is exceptional because of the narrow and specific meaning attached to it. While all combinations mentioned above carry the sense of recompense, consequences, result, *p^{e}rî pî 'îš*, means "speech".[36]

A collocation common in Egyptian beginning with the Pyramid Texts in the Old Kingdom Period (third millennium B.C.), continuing through the Middle Kingdom and ending in the New Kingdom (first millennium B.C.) is *pri n/m r3*,  , lit., "that which emerges from the mouth," i.e., speech.[37] The Egyptian expression is constructed from the common verb of motion *pri*, "to go out," "to leave." From this verb derive *pr.t*, lit. "that which goes out," namely, seed, fruit,[38] and *pr.t*, the season of growth of seeds, i.e., winter.

pri n r3 is often associated with the words of the dead. The saying "It emerges from the mouth of the deceased" means "He says such-and-such" (*Pyramid Texts* 162; *Thebes Tomb* 106).[39] Later, in the New Kingdom, and especially in the biographies of the 18th Dynasty, this formulation appears in connection with the description relating to a high official: "He, what comes out of his mouth is found satisfactory" (*hr.tw/ḥtp.tw ḥr pr.w n r3.f*) (*Urk.* IV 546,9; 1011,7; etc.; cf. also *Lansing* 15,3). At times it also refers to the king's utterance: "I performed what issued from his (the king's) mouth (*pr.t m r3.f*)," says Tutu, a high official in Amenhotep IV's court (Davies, *El Amarna* VI, pl. XIX,6). The phrase is also present in the school texts where it signifies the prediction of the sages: "The sages who foretold the future, what came from their mouth (*pri m r3.sn*) occurred" (*Chester Beatty* IV pl. 19 verso 3,7-8).

Hence, what is an unusual combination with a foreign meaning in Biblical language appears to be a common and frequent expression in the Egyptian literature of the dead and in the language of its officials. Thus it would seem[40] that the author of the sayings in Proverbs (12,14; 13,2;

18,20) knew Egyptian and was acquainted with the phraseology that prevailed in the court of the "Great House" during the New Kingdom. The Hebrew author borrowed the phrase from Egyptian, but during the borrowing process a corruption took place. Possibly due to his incomplete mastery of Egyptian writing, he derived the expression *p^e^rî pî 'îš* from the noun "fruit" (Heb. *p^e^rî*, Eg. *pr.t*) and not from the verb "leave" (Heb. *yṣ'*, Eg. *prì*), and instead of the literal translation *môṣā' peh*,[41] rendered *p^e^rî peh*. Or, he may have introduced this change deliberately — to impart to the foreign material an Israelite coloration and to adapt it to the Biblical vocabulary, in which the metaphorical use of *p^e^rî* ("fruit") in combination with other nouns was common.[42]

At a later stage in the development of Hebrew the term *nîb ś^e^pātayim* appears, meaning "fruit of the lips," parallel to *p^e^rî pî 'îš* in Proverbs; cf. "create the fruit of the lips" in Deutero-Isaiah (57,19).

In light of the use of "fruit of the mouth" both in Proverbs and Egyptian literature a solution presents itself for the cryptic verse in Hosea, "and we will render *pārîm ś^e^pātēnû*" (14,3). *pārîm* should not be understood here as sacrifices of bulls but as deriving from *p^e^rî*, "fruit of the lips," speech, prayer; the people are required to offer not sacrifices but words of praise and thanks and to utter a prayer to God. This is also the rendering in the Septuagint and the Syriac Version.[43]

The third stage in the development of the term, which began with *p^e^rî peh* ("speech") in Proverbs and continued with *p^e^rî ś^e^pātayim* ("prayer") in prophecy, is found in the Qumran Scrolls. In the Manual of Discipline (*Serek Hayyaḥad*) the phrase *t^e^rûmat ś^e^pātayim* is a common term for "prayer":[44] "And the *t^e^rûmat ś^e^pātayim* ("prayer") will be as a soothing odor of righteousness (man's sacrifice) in the (God's) judgment and a perfect way of life as a pleasing freewill offering" (1QS 9,4-5). There is a repetition here of the idea, holding pride of place in Biblical prophecy, of prayer and uprightness instead of offering and sacrifice: "For I desire righteousness and not sacrifice, and the knowledge of God more than burnt offerings" (ibid.). It is at this point also that the history of this expression comes to its conclusion: having begun, possibly, in the world of the dead and the Egyptian king's court, it culminates in the setting of the Israelite faith, where the spiritual is elevated over the material, i.e., prayer over cult. The phrase, therefore, which in the beginning belonged to the sphere of human relations (literature of Egypt, Proverbs), ended up referring to the relationship between man and his God.

II. EGYPTIAN EXPRESSIONS WHICH HAVE NO CLEAR ANALOGY IN THE HEBREW VOCABULARY

4. *ḫn*

The term *ḫn* appears in texts from the Middle Kingdom onwards, but it disappears in Demotic and is not to be found in the late autobiography.[45] *ḫn* is connected with the verb *ḫni*, "to land," "to glide," "to fall,"[46] as seen by the determinative of an alighting duck (Gr G41). The primary meaning of *ḫn* is therefore that of something coming down to earth, falling, and in the language of the Egyptian sages it serves to signify eloquent, superior speech, which on being heard gives the impression that it has come down from some abode high-above.[47]

The Egyptian expression recalls the Hebrew phrases *nṭp millâ* ("the word drops") (Job 29,22), *nṭp śᵉpātayim* ("the lips drip [honey]") (Prov. 5,3), where speech also is related to something that descends. In Egyptian, though, the metaphor is taken from the world of living creatures, the flight of birds, while in the Bible it is associated with the phenomenon of rainfall.

The term *ḫn*, which stands in synonymous parallelism with other terms indicating speech (e.g., *ḏd.t*, *md.t*, *mdy*), has a positive note and stands for a stylish phrase, the mark of a learned man, one skilled in rhetoric. Such a man, e.g., is the scribe in *Anastasi* I, "at whose utterances (*ḫn.w.f*) men rejoice when they are heard," and who is praised as one "skilled in hieroglyphs" (1,1; cf. III 4,8); *ḫn.w* are the words of the Eloquent Peasant, who is a master of rhetoric (B1 280).[48]

The term has a negative tone only when it is joined to an adjective or noun with a negative connotation, e.g., "mean sayings" (*ḫn.w ḫwr*: *Instruction by a Man for His Son*, II 6), "obscene sayings" (*ḫn.w dydy*: *Lansing* 14,8; cf. also *Amenemope* 12, 4).

ḫn is usually the spoken word, but at times it is a saying written in a scroll, a traditional wisdom saying found in the texts. The son of the scribe Anii claims that the youth who does not understand words of wisdom rehearses and quotes the text in the scroll without reaching an understanding of its depths. In the language of the instruction, "the son, he understands little, and says (i.e., recites) the sayings in the books" (*y ḏd.f ḫn.w m ʿrw*) (9, 15-16). Khakheperre-sonb defines his essay as "the quest of phrases (*ḫn.w*) with searching of heart" (recto 1,2).

In the sense of "proverb," "folk saying," *ḫn* comes in the collocation *ḫn n md.t* (which in the mss. interchanges with *ṯs n md.t* and *p3 pw ḏd.w*: cf. *The Eloquent Peasant* B1 37 to R 86 and also ibid. B1 19 to R 69).[49]

Expressions constructed with an adjective: *nfr* ("good," "beautiful"), *mnḫ* ("efficacious") and *iḳr* ("excellent")

5. ***nfr/t + md/w/t***

6. ***nfr + ḏd***

While the word *md/w/t*, as stated above, is not a specific wisdom term, the collocation *md/w/t nfr(t)* does belong to the wisdom terminology.[50] The great value that the Egyptians placed on the spoken and written word is expressed in the fact that wisdom instructions and eloquent speech are called "fine speech" *md/w/t nfr(t)* or *ḏd nfr*. *nfr*, "good," is to be understood here as signifying esthetic as well as ethical perfection.[51]

The Instruction of Ptaḥḥotep is called "maxims of good speech" (*ṯs.w n md.t nfr.t*, 42) or "standard (lit. command) of good speech" (*tp rd n md.t nfr.t*, 48). The words of the "prophecy" of Neferti are "fine words, choice formulations" (*md.wt nfr.[w]t ṯs.w stp.w*, 7 || 13).

The man who has mastered "good speech" is a sage, fluent in eloquence. This fluency is acquired through study — "hearing well is speaking well" (*nfr sḏm nfr md.t*), says Ptaḥḥotep in the epilogue to his work (537) — but it may also be the fruit of a simple man's natural talent. Thus, it may be found in maids at the grindstone (*Ptaḥḥotep* 58-59) and in the Eloquent Peasant, whose words are described as "good speech, which comes out from the mouth of Re' himself" (B1 319; cf. ibid. 75).

Whether learned or the outcome of life experience and natural skill, eloquence belongs to the set of qualities that make up the figure of the ideal sage. Not surprisingly, therefore, the writers of the autobiographies, who see themselves as the embodiment of all wisdom values, appear in their inscriptions as "good of speech" (Janssen I p. 25, Af 29; Otto No. 8 || *KCG* 42230 p. 74 l.5).

Besides the phrase *nfr md/w/t*, which is usual in the wisdom literature but less widespread in the phraseology of the autobiography, the variant *nfr ḏd*, common in the latter genre, appears — in parallelism with "good reporter (*whm nfr*)"[52] or juxtaposed to "informer of what is desired (*whm/smi mrr.t*)"[53] — first in the Old Kingḍom (6th Dynasty) disappears in the Saitic Period.

The following collocations — *mnḫ* + *ḏd/ṯs(w)* and *iḳr* + *ḏd/ns/s.t ns/ṯs(w)* — are used similarly to those constructed with *nfr*. The first is prevalent in the didactic wisdom sources. The second is common in the king's court phraseology (during the Middle Kingdom) and the late autobiography, and we shall therefore deal with it only briefly.

7. *mnḫ* + *ḏd*, *ṯs(w)* [54]

mnḫ qualifies the noun *ḏd* ("efficacious speech"), and *mnḫ ḏd* qualifies a man ("efficacious of speech"). At times *mnḫ* serves as the object of a verb ("to state something useful"). It occurs frequently in a didactic context, chiefly in the teacher's addresses to the pupil in the school texts of the New Kingdom. Sometimes it is also found in the king's court writings, as an epithet for the high official.[55]

It seems that the adjective *mnḫ*, when in connection with speech, highlights the knowledge and understanding that form the basis for correct speech. Anii says to his son that if he is familiar with books, that is, has knowledge, then "everything you say will be excellent" (*y ḏd.tw.k nb.t mnḫy*, 7,5; cf. ibid. 2,6); the wisdom sayings of Anii are "excellent" (*n3y spy mnḫ.t*)" (5,4). The words of Amennakht to his pupil should be similarly understood: "You will know the plans[56] in order to state the excellent" (8), that is, the speech of the pupil who is versed in the writings will be efficient and excellent.

The efficient high official is praised as being "excellent of speech," beside having other qualities that are important for his function: "Excellent of speech (*mnḫ ḏd*), who 'conceals belly' regarding, the conduct of the palace" (*Urk.* IV 47,9-10; cf. Janssen I p. 22, Aa 45, ibid. 49, *mnḫ ṯs.w*; see also *Anastasi* II 4,7).

8. *iḳr + ḏd, ns, s.t ns, ṯs*

The collocations *iḳr* ("excellent") + "speech" (*ḏd*), "tongue" (*ns*), "tongue's place" (*s.t ns*), "formulated saying" (*ṯs*) interchange with *md/w/t nfr/t, ḏd mnḫ*, and appear together with them in the royal and biographical inscriptions.

The adjective "excellent of speech" (*iḳr ḏd*), parallel to "excellent of heart" (*mnḫ ib*), is attributed to the master builder of the 26th Dynasty.[57] Others are termed "excellent of tongue" (*iḳr ns, iḳr s.t ns*),[58] by which is meant a man whose word can be trusted. This expression is common in the 12th and 13th Dynasty in parallelism with "true of heart" (*mtr/mty ib/ḥ3.ty*).[59]

III. SUMMARY OF THE TERMINOLOGY IN EGYPTIAN

Nine terms, appearing either independently or in varying combinations, constitute the semantic field of "wisdom words" in Egyptian. The most common — albeit not exclusive to the wisdom phraseology — is *mdw* (*md.t*) (94 times in our sample, of which 48 occur in the instructions). The characteristic expressions in the wisdom lexicon are *ṯs* (25 times), *ḫn* (15 times), and the collocations *ḏd* + *mnḫ* (11 times) and *md.t nfr.t* (10 times). The remaining expressions, *pri n/m r3*, *ḏd* + *nfr*, *tp(y) r3*, *ḏd/ṯs/ns/s.t ns* + *iḳr* are not part of the wisdom vocabulary. They are common in wisdom literature especially the king's court inscriptions and the autobiographies, but are missing in the didactic compositions (except for *tp[y] r3*, which is found once). A clear semantic distinction between the various terms is difficult to make, and hence the question posed at the beginning of the discussion, whether the Egyptian terms relate to different literary patterns, remains unanswered. All that can be stated with certainty is that *ḫn* concerns high-level speech and eloquence. *ṯs* chiefly denotes well-constructed wisdom sayings, whether it be a proverb or a quotation from the writings. As for *md/w/t*, which appears in all the literary genres belonging to wisdom texts from the Old Kingdom to the later periods, it should be regarded as a supernym of the other terms. In collocation with the adjective "good" (*nfr*) it becomes an eponym and is employed only to denote "words of wisdom."

We found no term or literary form parallel to the Biblical Hebrew *ḥîdâ* in the Egyptian wisdom.[60] The Hebrew term *māšāl*, refers to a wide range of literary forms,[61] one of which is a succinct saying containing a truth based on life experience, which is common in both Hebrew and Egyptian wisdom literature (see [1] below); common too is the use of figurative language (see [2] below).[62]

(1) To express this meaning of the Hebrew term *māšāl*, "succinct saying," "popular folk saying," the following words are used in Egyptian:

— *ḫn n md.t.* This appears once, in *The Eloquent Peasant*: "This Nemtynakht said: It is not the saying (*ḫn n md.t*) people say (*ḏd*): 'A poor man's name is pronounced for his master's sake'" (B1 19-20).[63]

— *rꜣ.* *Mentuhotep*: "I heard a saying of men (*rꜣ n rmṯ*): 'The tombstone of a man is his good (character), he of the wicked character is forgotten'" (15-16).

— *ṯs.* *Ptaḥḥotep*: Beware of approaching women when you enter a strange house, because "a poor saying (*ṯs pw ḫsy*) is 'shoot the opponent.'[64] When one goes to do it, the heart rejects it" (292).

Although there is no regular term in Egyptian to denote a proverb[65] the sage often does make use of this literary device to express his thoughts. For example:

— In *Kagemni* and *Ptaḥḥotep* two versions of one maxim appear. *Kagemni* II 2 has: "One knows not what may happen, what god does when he punishes"; *Ptaḥḥotep* 343 has: "No one knows what may happen when he perceives tomorrow."

— In *The Instruction of Amenemope* the stanzas usually end with a quoted maxim, inserted without an introduction (e.g., 9,7-8 || 16,13-14;

11,10-11 [|| 22,15-16]; 22, 5-8 || 23,8-11), or maxims are woven into the body of the text (e.g., 10,8-11).[66]

— *The Instruction of Ankhsheshonqy* is a rich source of Demotic sayings that in part repeat Middle Egyptian proverbial sayings, as Lichtheim has recently shown in her wide-ranging study.[67]

(2) Similarly, there is no term in Egyptian for metaphor and simile, although these literary devices do embellish the sayings of the sages. Subjects are many and varied and are taken from the natural and human world. In *The Eloquent Peasant* there are images relating to trade and shipping (B1 91-92; 148-151; 189ff.; etc., see p. 285 above). Comparisons deriving from the animal and plant world are worked into *The Instruction of Amenemope* (chapter 4: image of trees; see p. 161 above; chapter 9: image of the wolf, etc.); the four poems ending *The Dispute between a Man and His Ba* are laced with similes, as is *The Instruction of Ankhsheshonqy* (see, e.g., 22,12; 23,24; 24,20, and cf. also *Anastasi* V 7,8-8,1).

Allegory is used in *The Man Who Was Tired of Life*, both in the words of the man and in the replies of his conversation partner, his *ba*. Two allegorical tales or parables appear in lines 68ff: one is about a peasant who is saved from the perils of a nocturnal storm, but loses his wife and children in a lake; the other about a peasant who is disappointed when he asks his wife for a meal. Both stories intend to teach a moral lesson.[68]

In the Bible

I. SIX TERMS DEFINING WISDOM WORDS IN THE PROLOGUE TO PROVERBS

Three of the six terms in the prologue to Proverbs denoting wisdom words — *māšāl*, *mᵉlîṣâ*, and *ḥîdâ* — are considered by Biblical scholarship to be typical wisdom patterns, but the frequency of these terms in the Biblical wisdom literature is less than in non-wisdom literature. Thus, the noun *māšāl*, used in the title of the book of Proverbs (*mišlê*) and present in its prologue (1,6) and in the headings of two of its collections (*mišlê š^elōmōh*: 10,1; 25, 1), is referred to as a literary pattern[69] only 10 times in Proverbs, Job and Qoheleth, and twice in the wisdom Psalms, while in the rest of the Bible it is found about 20 times.[70] The term *m^elîṣâ* occurs once in Proverbs (1,6)[71] and once in Habakuk (2,6). *ḥîdâ*, which also appears in Proverbs (1,6), is found twice more in the wisdom Psalms (49,5; 78,2) and 14 times outside the wisdom literature.[72] However, they persist and continue to appear in the Apocrypha (Ben Sira), alongide new terms such as *pitgām* (BS 5,11; 8,9).

In contrast, the remaining three — *'ămārîm*, *taḥbulôt*, *dibrê ḥăkāmîm*, occur more frequently in the wisdom books than outside them (see Table 15).[73]

Be this as it may, the most common term in the Biblical wisdom to signify "word of wisdom" is *māšāl*, which is present in all the wisdom books, followed by *'ămārîm*, which is absent only from Qoheleth (see Table 15).

The verb that precedes the terms (apart from *taḥbulôt* and *pitgām*) in the prologue to Proverbs is "to understand" (1,2,6); hence, the common feature of these terms is that they indicate words which are difficult to understand, cryptic, requiring illumination.

Many detailed studies analyzing the meaning and use of *māšāl*, *m^elîṣâ* and *ḥîdâ* in the Biblical literature have been written,[74] and even if scholars dispute the basic sense of a particular term, no one doubts that they are of Semitic origin. However, none of these terms — apart from *māšāl* in the sense of "succint saying," "maxim," considered above — have parallels in Egyptian and they therefore do not enter into our discussion.

Our analysis, on the other hand, concentrates on the words *dābār* (especially in the collocation *dibrê ḥăkāmîm*, discussed above pp. 320–321) and *'ămārîm* (see below), neither of which has received its deserved place in research, and also on the terms, collocations and images that are close to the ones found in the Egyptian literature (see *taḥbulôt*, *mipp^erî pî 'îš* above; and Section III below).

Table 15: Distribution of Words Denoting "Wisdom Sayings" in the Biblical Wisdom Books (and Ben Sira)

	Term	Prov.	Job	Qoh.	Wisdom Pss.	BS (Heb.MSS)	Other Books
1.	*māšāl* (noun)	6	3	1	2	4	20(ca.)
2.	*m^elîṣâ*	1	—	—	—	1	1
3.	*ḥîdâ*	1	—	—	2	2	14
4.	*taḥbulôt*	5	1	—	—	3	—
5.	*'ămārîm*	21	16	—	4	2	12
6.	*dibrê ḥăkāmîm*	2*	—	2	—	—	
(7.	*pitgām*	—	—	—	—	2	2**)

* Once (24,23) without *dibrê*.
**I.e., in Ezra and Daniel, as "decree."

II. *'ămārîm* — WORDS

This term, which refers to the words of man and only rarely to the words of God, is characteristic of Biblical poetic language. Deriving from the verb *'mr*, *'ămārîm*, unlike *dbr*, which stresses the action of speaking, emphasizes the content of the words spoken. This content is clarified by means of adjectives and nouns that commonly accompany the term.[75] In Proverbs, Job and the wisdom Psalms the words of the sage are called *'ămārîm*.

'ămārîm in Proverbs (1,2,21; 2,1; 4,5,10,20; 22,21; etc.) are words of the teacher-father and personified Wisdom, synonymous with *mûsār*, *miṣwâ*, *maḥăšābôt* and *d^ebārîm*. The ill-intended words of "the strange woman," uttered in stylish language which pleases the ear of those who hear them (Prov. 7,5), can also be called *'ămārîm*.

The wisdom psalmist calls his words *'ămārîm* (19,15; 78,1). Job's words of complaint and dispute with God (34,37) and the statements of his friends, which are mainly words of admonition and reproach (32,14; 33,3) are also described with this term.

On rare occasions is the term present in a negative connotation. In Job it is attached to *rûaḥ*, "wind," to signify the insignificance and vainness of Job's words (6,26; 8,2).

The words of God are called *'ămārîm* in Job and in "The words of Agur" in Proverbs, which are part of the wisdom of the "Sons of Qedem" (Job 6,10; 22,22 || *tôrâ*; 23,12 || "commandment [*miṣwat*] of his lips"; Prov. 30,5 || Ps 18,31, 2 Sam 22,31).

III. FIGURES OF SPEECH AND COLLOCATIONS OF LIKE MEANING TO EGYPTIAN EXPRESSIONS CONSTRUCTED WITH AN ADJECTIVE

As we have seen, the Egyptian sage uses a series of collocations to describe a saying which is perfect in form as well as content. These collocations are constructed with nouns referring to "speech" combined with the adjectives "good" (*nfr*), "excellent" (*iḳr*) and "efficacious" (*mnḫ*). In the Biblical wisdom, "speech" occurs in connection with similar expressions and imageries:

Elegance. Like his Egyptian counterpart, the Hebrew sage stresses the elegant form of the well-made expression; the wisdom saying is compared to a precious jewel fashioned by a craftsman: "A word fitly spoken (is like) apples of gold in settings of silver" (Prov. 25,11);[76] "fine words" spoken at a feast are likened to a necklace adorned with precious stones, turquoise and sapphire (BS 35,5).

The Hebrew *dābār ṭôb*, like the Egyptian equivalent *md/w/t nfr/t*, denotes the eloquent speech of the sage and the poet: "My heart is overflowing with a *dābār ṭôb*, I address my verses to the king; my tongue is like the pen of a ready scribe," says the psalmist (Ps. 45,2). The able tongue of sages expresses their knowledge in beautiful words: "The tongue of the wise uses knowledge rightly (*têṭîb da'at*), but the mouth of fools utters folly" (Prov. 15,2).[77]

To the adjectives *yāpeh* and *ṭôb*, which are equivalent to the Egyptian *nfr*, may be added the noun *ḥēn*, "grace," "favor," which is used in much the same way to express eloquence in speech. It is common in Biblical wisdom[78] and mostly refers to the external form of an object: "The words of the wise man's mouth bring him *ḥēn*" (Qoh. 10,12). The man gifted with this kind of eloquence has a king for a friend (Prov. 22,11), or he is himself a king, for *ḥēn* is counted among the king's virtues: in the words of the psalmist, "*ḥēn* is poured upon your lips" (Ps. 45,3). Ben Sira says that "lips of *ḥēn*" multiply "those that give greeting," that is, friends (6,5).

Moral perfection. As in Egyptian, "good word" not only refers to the artistic, graceful form of the saying, but also defines the moral perfection inherent in it: The felicitous saying is one that contains moral purity — "Evil thoughts are an abomination to Yahweh but pleasant words (*'imrê nō'am*) are pure" (Prov. 15,26). "Pleasant words," as distinct from evil thought, satisfy hunger and impart health, in the vivid language of Proverbs 16,24: "Pleasant words (*'imrê nō'am*) are like honeycomb, sweetness to the soul (i.e., the palate) and health to the bones." Egyptian has an etymological and semantic parallel in the expression "*nḏm* (sweet) speech" (*Amenemope* 25,12; *Anii* 7,11 [*Pap. Boulaq* IV] and in *Pap. Deir el Médineh* No. 1 recto 8,7; *Urk.* IV 510,14), *nḏm* being the equivalent of the Hebrew *n'm.*[79]

Delight. "Good speech" causes pleasure and joy. The priest Neferti speaks "choice phrases, over which the king rejoices (*ḏ3y*)" (13); the thirty chapters in *The Instruction of Amenemope* delight (*sḏ3y*) him who reads them (27,6-8). A good word is one of encouragement which gladdens its hearers, in contrast to the anxiety that generates depression: "Anxiety in a man's heart bows it down, but a good word (*dābār ṭôb*) makes it glad" (Prov. 12,25).

Precious object. Speech accompanied by the adjective *iḳr* in Egyptian means "excellent, efficacious speech." The root *iḳr* is common to Egyptian and the Semitic family of languages,[80] but in Hebrew the meaning of *yāqār* is wider and has both the sense of "splendid," "influential," as in Egyptian, and that of a "prized" and "precious" object.[81] This meaning applies when *yāqār* is placed together with "speech" in the Biblical wisdom literature. In Proverbs 20,15 it is said: "There is gold and a multitude of corals, but the lips of knowledge are a precious jewel (*k^eli yāqār*)." Lips of knowledge are compared to a precious object, and the "tongue of the righteous" is "choice silver" (Prov. 10,20). These metaphors are surprisingly close to the words of Ptaḥḥotep, who says, "A good speech is more hidden than greenstone" (58).

IV. THE IMPORTANCE OF THE MASTERY OF "GOOD SPEECH" AND THE ART OF COMMITTING IT TO WRITING IN ISRAEL AND EGYPT

The abundance of terms in the Biblical and ancient Egyptian languages for "speech" and "word" indicates the central place held by eloquence and the rules of rhetoric in Israel and Egypt.

The Egyptians highly valued the art of fine speech, especially in the king's court and the school circles.[82] *The Instruction of Amenemope* declares that its goal is to teach as follows:

All the rules of official procedure
The duties of the courtiers
To know how to answer one who speaks
And to reply to one who sends a message
(Prologue 1, 3-6).

(|| Prov. 22,21:
To inform you about truth and truthful words
so that you may return answer, truth,
to him who sends you).

In *The Prophecies of Neferti* the king desires a man who will speak "fine words, choice phrases," at the hearing of which the king "may be entertained."

The epithets "good of speech," "one, the utterances of whose mouth are satisfying," occur repeatedly in the biographical inscriptions. *Pap. Anastasi* I is in fact a paean to eloquence and the art of debate. The Egyptian wisdom instructions, used as learning material at school, are replete with words of exhortation and admonition concerning the rules of speaking and praise for him who masters them, for example, *Ptaḥḥotep* 624-627:

Be deliberate when you speak,
so as to say things that count;
then the officials who listen will say:
'How good is what comes out of his mouth'

(cf. ibid. 249-256; 362-369; 370-371; 507ff.; 537);

Instruction to Merikare 32ff.:

Be skilled in speech so that you may be strong;
the strength of the king is the tongue;
speaking is stronger than any fight.

A warning to speak neither much nor fast appears in *The Instruction of Pap. Insinger* (3,6; 22,21), as well as an exhortation to speak in an interesting way: "Do not let (yourself) be called 'stupid' because of the weariness which your words cause" (3,8; cf. 3,1; 12,24); "Speech is plentiful (but) the span of life is short," says Anii (*Pap. Deir el Médineh*, No. 1, recto 5,4).

In Proverbs, especially the second and fifth collections, there are many statements in praise of correct speech and good advice (e.g., 15,1,23; 16,24; 25,11,12,15; 26,4ff.). This motif is also expressed in statements which encourage restraint and moderation or reject fast talk and verbal transgressions such as divulging a secret, gossiping and tale-telling. Although the ideal human type termed "prudent of speech" (*n^{e}bôn dābār*, 1 Sam. 16,18) had its origin in the king's court, it was not lacking in popular circles either: The Egyptian *Eloquent Peasant* is "good of speech"; "good speech" is present in maids at the grindstone (*Ptaḥḥotep*);[83] in Israel the two women from Tekoa' and Abel Beth Ma'achah are expert in eloquence (2 Sam. 14; 20,16ff.).

The sage is not only he who is capable of expressing words of wisdom and masters the art of speaking; he also composes, collects and investigates wisdom sayings. Investigation is prevalent in Qoheleth, whose author relies on his personal experience, as expressed in the words "And I applied my heart to search and to explore" (1,13; cf. 7,25 and p. 70 above); "I saw... (and lo)..." (1,14; 3,22; 5,17; etc.); "And I said to myself" (2,15); "I then turned... (and lo...)" (2,11-12); "... and see all the activity taking place on the earth" (8,16); "All this I tested in wisdom" (7,23). The epilogue to the book relates to this search and exploration, and sums up the literary activity of Qoheleth thus: "And he weighed, and searched and fashioned many Proverbs. Qoheleth sought to find attractive words and to set down the truth honestly" (Qoh. 12,9-10). A similar literary pursuit occupies the sages in the days of Hezekiah, as stated in Proverbs 25,1: "Proverbs of Solomon, which the men of Hezekiah, king of Judah, copied."

The professional aim of the sages both in Israel and Egypt was the same, to find "new words" and commit them to writing. The Egyptian priest Khakheperre-sonb, like Qoheleth, wishes to find new, original, sayings, which had not been known to the forefathers. This quest for the ability to say "a good word" is also present in *The Eloquent Peasant*, where the official informs the king that he has found a peasant "good of speech."

In Egypt the teaching of fine speech and eloquent writing was provided at the school. Composed in the 11th-12th Dynasty and essentially a collection of formulations and expressions intended to serve the needs of the Egyptian scribe, the handbook known as *Kemit*[84] opens up a window to this world for us, as is shown in the following example, part of the *Kemit*'s opening formula:

> The servant speaks to his master whom he loves
> May he live, prosper, be healthy for ever and ever
> as wishes the servant who is there.
> May you be justified by the *Baw* of Heliopolis and by all the Gods
> May they give that you live
> May they make for you every good thing as wishes the servant who is there...

CHAPTER NINE

CONCLUSIONS

Contemporary philosophers, linguists, and anthropologists are in general agreement that the vocabulary of the speakers of a given language reflects their socio-cultural circumstances, i.e., that a people's language is the expression of the sum total of their geographical environment, activities and modes of thought.[1]

This principle as formulated by modern linguistics can also be seen at work in the Biblical and Egyptian wisdom vocabularies. As our study has shown, phrases and terms that are typical of Hebrew and Egyptian wisdom literatures and which express the respective perceptions and world-view of the latter, are repeated constantly throughout the genre.

In both Israel and Egypt wisdom phrases and terms — when appearing outside wisdom literature and found together with other elements peculiar to wisdom, i.e., literary form and subject-matter — may be used as criteria to indicate a "wisdom influence" in other literary genres.

Before discussing this subject further we shall first give a summary of the phraseology characteristic of the Hebrew and Egyptian sages and draw some appropriate conclusions.

I. WORDS CHARACTERISTIC OF HEBREW WISDOM LITERATURE

Words characteristic of Biblical wisdom may be divided into two groups: (a) words found only in wisdom literature; (b) words with a higher frequency in wisdom literature than in other genres.

(a) The following expressions and collocations appear exclusively in the Hebrew wisdom books:

1. *'lp* ("to teach": once in Prov., 3 times in Job)
2. *m^e^lammēd* ("teacher": once in Prov., in wisdom Ps., and in BS)
3. *qnh* ("to acquire") + objects relating to wisdom (12 times in Prov.)
4. *ṣpn* ("to treasure") + objects relating to wisdom (3 times in Prov., once in Job, twice in BS)
5. *ḥadrê bāṭen* ("chambers of the belly": 4 times in Prov.)
6. *ḥăsar lēb* ("one who has no sense [lit. heart]": 11 times in Prov., once in BS)
7. *ḥārûṣ* ("diligent": 4 times in Prov.)
8. *'ēšet k^e^sîlût* ("foolish woman": once in Prov.)
9. *'ṣl* (adj., n., "lazy, laziness": 14 times in Prov., once in Qoh.)
10. *p^e^rî pî 'îš* ("fruit of the mouth": 3 times in Prov.)
11. *taḥbulôt* ("a well-constructed saying," "a maxim": 5 times in Prov., once in Job, 3 times in BS)
12. *dibrê ḥăkāmîm* ("words of wise men": twice in Prov., twice in Qoh.)
13. *'erek 'appayim* ("slow to anger":[2] 3 times in Prov.)
14. *qar rûaḥ* ("cool-tempered": once in Prov.)
15. *q^e^ṣar 'appayim* ("short-tempered": once in Prov.)
16. *q^e^ṣar rûaḥ* ("short-tempered": once in Prov.)
17. *'îš ḥēmâ/ḥēmôt* ("heated man": twice in Prov.) and synonymous expressions:
    18. *ba'al ḥēmâ* (once in Prov.)
    19. *g^e^dal ḥēmâ* (once in Prov.)
    20. *ba'al 'ap* (once in Prov., once in BS)
    21. *'îš 'ap* (once in Prov.)
22. *nirgān* ("slanderer": 4 times in Prov.)
23. *kišrôn* ("skill," "success": 3 times in Qoh.)

To this list should be added the collocation:

24. *tōkēn libbôt* (an epithet for God as one who weighs the hearts: twice in Prov.), which we treated elsewhere.[3]

Eight of the terms listed above show an affinity with forms of speech and expressions found in the Egyptian literature. Some of these are literal translations of Eygptian terms (*'îš ḥēmâ*, *qar rûaḥ*, *tōkēn libbôt*, *taḥbulôt*); others are adaptations, modified to suit Hebrew style and usage (*ḥadrê bāṭen*, *'erek 'appayim*, *qᵉṣar 'appayim*, *qᵉṣar rûaḥ*). As such these Hebrew expressions can be fully understood only when considered in the light of comparable Egyptian usages. On the other hand, two of the terms (*ḥăsar lēb* and *pᵉrî pî 'îš*), despite the existence of analogies in Egyptian sources, need not necessarily be linked with Egypt, i.e., we may be dealing here with an independent parallel development in both languages.[4]

As to the distribution of the above eight terms, there are 33 occurrences in Proverbs, mostly concentrated in the second collection (21 in chaps. 10-22,16), but they are also found in the other didactic collections (chaps. 1-9; 22,17-29,27). In Job there are 5 instances, and one in Qoheleth.

The findings in the five didactic collections of Proverbs (1-29), support the assumption that these collections exhibit terminological-linguistic contact with Egypt.[5] As to the other wisdom books in the Bible, the findings are inadequate to determine whether here, too, contact indeed existed with the Egyptian sources.

The relatively extensive degree of lexical contact with Egyptian found in the second collection of Proverbs sheds light on the chronological aspect of the book's composition and perhaps also on its *Sitz im Leben*. The traces and imprints of Egyptian phraseology in the second collection reinforce the assumption that the sources of Proverbs date back to the pre-exilic period (i.e., probably to King Solomon's time), and they also support the thesis that Proverbs — or at least part of it — served as a textbook in the ancient Israelite didactic setting[6] (see section V below).

(b) The terms dealt with so far are, as stated, exclusive to the wisdom books. It is, therefore, not these but words and phrases belonging to the second category which can serve to reveal "wisdom influence" in other genres. The words of this category, which are given below, occur more frequently in Biblical wisdom literature than in other litrary genres:

'ĕwîl; *'iwwelet*; *ba'ar*; *kesîl*;[7] *petî*; *lēṣ*; *sākāl*; *'iqqēš*; *hôlēlôt/ût*; *ka'as* (n.); *mādôn*; *rgn* (v.);[8] *ḥkm* (v.); *ḥākām*; *ḥokmâ/ôt*; *tebûnâ*; *bînâ*; *nābôn*; *mēbîn*;[9] *śēkel ṭôb*; *'ārûm*; *'ormâ*; *mezimmâ*; *tûšiyyâ*; *tôkaḥat* (not *tôkēḥâ*); *leqaḥ*; *mûsār*; *dibrê ḥăkāmîm*; *melîṣâ*; *'ămārîm*; *ḥēqer*; *bqš* + *ḥokmâ* and synonyms; *nṣr* + *tôrâ*, *miṣwâ* and synonyms; *nṣr* + *lēb*, *lāšôn*, *peh* (as objects);[10] *yāšār*, *tām* + *derek*; *swr mērā'*.[11]

It is the accumulation of several words, or the appearance of a single term together with other characteristic wisdom features in a passage outside the wisdom books, which may indicate a relationship of the passage to the wisdom literature (see Section VI below).[12]

II. WORDS BELONGING TO THE EGYPTIAN WISDOM VOCABULARY

There is no autonomous corpus of Egyptian texts such as we have in the Bible. The corpus we have selected for our research is, of necessity, based on a limited number of sources (cf. Corpus). A *definitive* lexicon of Egyptian sapiential words cannot as yet be compiled — this will become possible only after *all* known Egyptian texts (published so far or awaiting publication) are analyzed. Nevertheless, even if no final ruling can be made as to which of the words listed below are unique to the Egyptian wisdom literature, they clearly appear to be characteristic of the genre.

1. *sb3* ("to teach," Heb. *ysr* *)[13]
2. *sb3y.t* ("instruction," Heb. *mûsār* *)
3. *mtr(t)* ("to reprove," "reproof," Heb. *ykḥ** [hiph'il], *tôkaḥat**)
4. *sḫr* ("counsel," Heb. *'ēṣâ**)
5. *'rḳ* ("be proficient," "wise," "wisdom," Heb. *byn** [qal, hiph'il], *tebûnâ**)
6. *wḥ'* ("explain," "resolve," Heb. *byn*, *śkl* [hiph'il])

7. *rdi ib, rdi m ib, rdi ḥꜣ.ty r* ("put in the heart," "give the heart to," Heb. *ntn 'el lēb*, ntn 'et hallēb* l^{e}* and synonyms)
8. *šsp* (+ *md.t* and synonyms as an object, "to take," "to accept," Heb. *lqḥ mûsār*)
9. *ṯy sbꜥ.t* (Dem. "to grasp instruction," Heb. *lqḥ mûsār*)
10. *wni* (+ "instruction" as an object, "to neglect," "abandon," Heb. *ʻzb*, nṭš**)
11. *(s)ʻḏꜣ* ("to lie," "a lie," Heb. *kzb*, rmh*)
12. *grg* ("falsehood," "lie," Heb. *šqr **)
13. *ʻwn ib* ("greedy," "avarice," Heb. *ḥmd, 'wh*)
14. *skn* ("be greedy," Heb. *ḥmd, 'wh*)
15. *ḥnt* ("be greedy," Heb. *ḥmd, 'wh*)
16. *ḥnty* ("greed," Heb. *ḥmd, 'wh*)
17. *štm* ("be angry," Heb. *zʻm, kʻs*)
18. *ṯṯṯ* ("to quarrel," Heb. *maṣṣâ, rîb*)
19. *tꜣw*
20. *šmm, šmw*

} ("heat" as a metaphor for "anger," "quick-tempered," Heb. *ḥmm*, 'îš ḥēmâ** and synonyms)

21. *gr* ("to be silent," Heb. *štq*)
22. *grw* ("silent man")[14]
23. *grw mꜣʻ* ("truly silent man")

} (Heb. *'erek 'appayim qar ruaḥ*)

24. *ḫm* ("simpleton," Heb. *petî**)
25. *wḫꜣ* ("fool," Heb. *k*^{e}*sîl **)
26. *iw.ty ḥꜣ.ty* ("stupid," "lacking understanding," Heb. *ḥăsar lēb**)
27. *ḫn* ("fool," Heb. *k*^{e}*sîl, sākāl* [?])
28. *lḫ* (Dem. "fool," Heb. *lēṣ**)
29. *swg* (Dem. "stupid," Heb. *'ĕwîl*)
30. *ẖn* (Dem. "fool," Heb. *k*^{e}*sîl*)
31. *gwš* ("crooked," Heb. *ʻiqqēš*)
32. *rḫ* ("to know," "knowledge," "wise man," [*rmt rḫ, rḫ ḫ.t*] Heb. *ydʻ *, yōdēaʻ **)
33. *rḫ iḫ.t* ("wise man," Heb. *ḥākām**)
34. *ḥmww* ("skilled," "craftsman," Heb. *kišrôn*)
35. *sꜣꜣ* ("be wise," "wisdom," Heb. *ḥkm, ḥokmâ*)

36. *si3* ("wisdom," Heb. *byn*, *bînâ*)
37. *ḥn* ("speech," "saying," Heb. *'ămārîm* [?])
38. *ṯs* ("well constructed saying," "maxim," Heb. *taḥbulôt* *)
39. *md.t nfr.t* ("good speech," Heb. *dābār ṭôb**/*yāpeh**)
40. *mnḫ ḏd/ṯsw* ("excellent saying," Heb. presents no parallel)

III. COMPARISON OF HEBREW AND EGYPTIAN FINDINGS

A. Differences, and an Attempt to Explain Them

Some of the features common to the words characteristic of the Hebrew and Egyptian wisdom vocabularies have been indicated above, and the remaining ones are presented in the second part of this section (see B below). Besides the similarities there are also differences resulting from the different nature of the two languages, from the different world-views and fields of interest, as well as from distinct areas of literary activity and types of target audience.

1. Terms commonly used by the Egyptian sage that have no parallel in the vocabulary of his Hebrew counterpart and vice versa

The verb *gr*, "to be silent," and its derivatives "silence," "silent man," express a central concept in Egyptian wisdom literature which has no real equivalent in Biblical wisdom literature. The Hebrew sage is not called "the silent," an epithet typical of the Egyptian sage, and *štq*, the Hebrew equivalent of *gr*, appears only once in Proverbs. The concept of "silence" is associated in Egyptian with the ideal of restraint and self control. This value does appear in Biblical Hebrew, but rather is expressed by words relating to the semantic field of "restraint" and "self-control,"[15] that is, in Hebrew wisdom the central topic is not the polarity of "silence" and "speech" but the confrontation between "restraint" or "self-control," and the "lack of self-control." The emphasis is not on the contrast between the "silent" and the "hot-tempered" man but between the "wise man" and the "fool." As

Lanczkowski has shown, the "silence" motif is connected with the internal historical and political development of Egypt,[16] so that its absence from the Israelite scene is not surprising.

Another important theme in Egyptian wisdom, expressed by a variety of terms, is the warning against greed and avarice. In Biblical wisdom this motif is marginal, although we do find similar warnings in the legal texts and in prophecy. Here, the difference seems to arise from the different nature of the respective audiences addressed by the Egyptian and the Hebrew sage: the creative circles of Eygptian instruction and its readers belonged predominantly to the upper classes (vizier, king, scribe), who in their professional capacity enjoyed extensive powers — as tax collectors, judges, executives, etc.; the Egyptian instructor, therefore, felt the need to warn them against the abuse of their powers.[17] The Hebrew maxims, on the other hand, are addressed to all social classes, from king, judge and counsellor to peasant and shepherd.[18]

Against this background another difference between the Egyptian and the Hebrew wisdom vocabulary comes to light: The adjective "diligent," *ḥārûṣ*, which designates the mode of behavior recommended in Proverbs, has no parallel whatever in the Egyptian instructions, or, still more surprisingly, in the Egyptian school writings.[19] Contrary to the Egyptian instructions, most of which are clearly aimed only at the well-off, Proverbs is a didactic book presumably intended for *all* strata of society, including the lower classes where lack of diligence and hard work could lead to hunger and poverty. This difference in target audience may, perhaps, explain the absence of an equivalent term to *ḥārûṣ* in the vocabulary of the Egyptian sage.

Finally, the Hebrew and Egyptian wisdom vocabularies differ also with regard to the creative activity of the sages: one of the functions of the Hebrew sage was to compose proverbs and *riddles*, but a term paralleling the Hebrew *ḥîdâ*, "riddle," is not found in Egyptian. Here, a possible explanation may lie in the fact that the custom of posing riddles obviously derives from an Semitic background.[20]

2. A theme expressed in one language by a larger number of words than in the other

It is generally accepted that the number of different words in a given language referring to a certain subject indicates the degree of importance the speakers of the language attach to that subject. Accordingly, there appear to be certain semantic fields of particular interest to the Hebrew sage that are of less concern to his Egyptian counterpart, and vice versa. The subject of teaching and educating is covered in Egyptian mainly by three stems, *sbꜣ*, *mtr* (independently or with auxiliary verbs) and *rdi tp rd*, while Biblical wisdom has seven: *ysr*, *yrh*, *lmd*, *ʾlp*, *byn*, *śkl*, *ykḥ* (see Chapter 2, Table 2). This may indicate that while teaching methods are of importance to the Hebrew sage, the Egyptian sage is more interested in the acquisition of knowledge and study per se. The Hebrew sage turns his attention to those in charge of dispensing instruction while the Egyptian searches for a way to reach the hearts of its recipients, the pupils.[21] This assumption is reinforced by another detail differentiating the Egyptian vocabulary from the Hebrew one. In our discussion we have had frequently observed the Egyptian sage's predilection for words with a negative connotation.[22] This suggests that the Egyptian sage was more interested in correcting the youth or the man whose behavior showed obvious flaws rather than in praising the one gifted with talents and virtues.

This evaluation is further supported by the fact that the Egyptian wisdom compositions belong to the corpus of school texts. Scholars have concluded from this (see Section V below) that the Hebrew wisdom literature, likewise, was intended as study material in Israelite schools. From the foregoing, however, it is apparent that the use of the Hebrew texts was not limited to school circles — they were also available to educational authorities outside that framework, namely, parents, master craftsmen and to those few literate men who had reached the stage of self-education. The autodidactic method is reflected in the terms *ḥqr*, *bqš*, which are unique to the Hebrew wisdom vocabulary and indicate an advanced stage of study beyond the school level: a constant accumulation of knowledge based on life experience and self-instruction rather than on the repetition of traditional material handed down by the authorities, a method characteristic of the Egyptian school. Naturally, self-instruction was the domain only of educated people engaged as teachers or scholars, either officially or privately (cf. Qoh. 12,9; 7,23-29; 8,16-17).[23]

It was mentioned above that a larger number of words for a single concept implies a greater importance attached to that concept. However this is not always so. For example, the Hebrew word *'ōzen* has in our corpus two corresponding Egyptian words, and the Hebrew *lāšon*, has two corresponding Egyptian terms. The reason, here, is not that "ear" and "tongue" have greater importance in Egyptian than in Hebrew but, as my corpus offers to show, that in certain fields Egyptian is richer in concrete words than Hebrew and vice versa. Thus abstract nouns such as the Hebrew *'iwwelet* ("folly"), *siklût* ("foolishness"), *hôlēlût* ("madness," "folly"), and the like (cf. p. 216 above) are infrequent in the language of the Egyptian sage. Moreover, where Hebrew expresses an abstract concept in a single word Egyptian requires a combination of two or more words, for example, *m^elîṣâ*, *māšāl*, *'ămārîm* in Hebrew are parallel to *ikr* + *ḏd*, *ns*, *s.t ns*, *ṯs(w)*; *mnḫ* + *ḏd*, *ṯs(w)*; *nfr* + *md/w/t* in Egyptian.

3. Terms analogous in the language of the Hebrew and Egyptian sages but generated by different conceptions

Occasionally Hebrew and Egyptian wisdom words display a close formal similarity but beneath this external resemblance reveal a different content. This may be explained by the differences between ancient Egypt and Israel with respect to religion, physical environment, and way of life, which led to divergent concepts and outlooks.

Both in Egypt and Israel, wisdom is personified. The Hebrew *ḥokmôt* is close to the Egyptian *SiꜢ* and perhaps also to *MꜢ'.t* (see pp. 268ff. above), but conceptually the image of Wisdom in Hebrew differs from the Egyptian images: *ḥokmôt* is God's assistant and emissary while *MꜢ'.t* is an independent being to whom the gods are subservient. *ḥokmôt* also differs from *SiꜢ*, which is the incarnation of the knowledge of the creator god and as such pertains to the king, god's representative on earth; nor is *ḥokmôt*, like *SiꜢ*, the partner of the "creative word" (*Ḥw*), though, being

God's "assistant" in the act of creation, it is, as *SiꜢ*, associated with the latter: "Then I was by him *'āmôn*" (Prov. 8,30).[24]

Further instances of different religious concepts involve Egyptian mythology, which has no parallel in Biblical literature. Thus the Egyptian terms: *nšni*, *shꜢ*, *ẖnn*,[25] relating to quarrel, all reflect the Egyptian belief that the god Seth symbolizes the forces of evil, and are accordingly accompanied by the determinative representing the "animal of Seth."

A similar phenomenon underlies the attribute *tꜢ rꜢ*, "one who has a hot mouth," referring to a negative way of conduct. *tꜢ rꜢ* is marked by the determinative *'Ꜣpp*, a snake, described in the myth as the enemy of the sun which it seeks to swallow.[26]

"Tongue" and "heart," moreover, are associated with the Egyptian cosmology and the belief in the Judgement of the Dead (which appear to be alluded to in the Biblical wisdom).[27]

"Falsehood," *grg*, and "avarice," *'wn ib*, which are key words in Egyptian wisdom, do not occupy an analogous place in Hebrew wisdom. As central concepts in Egyptian theology, *'wn ib* and *grg* are contrasted with universal order, the *mꜢ'.t*: falsehood and avarice replace the *mꜢ'.t* as order breaks down and the state is taken over by anarchy. Hence, both terms also signify "chaos," "disorder," thus extending far beyond the meaning of their Hebrew parallels.

As to the physical background, imagery in the Egyptian sage's language is often taken from a world of nature which is markedly different from that of Israel. Thus, terms in the semantic field of "avarice" and those concerning "dispute" and "anger" are accompanied by determinatives of animals with which the Egyptian was familiar — crocodile, snake, or lion. Terms for "silence" and "restraint," which represent highly positive values in Egyptian wisdom, are followed by the symbol of life, the image of water flowing or being poured, natural to a land where the Nile is the source of life. On the other hand, the ant, eagle, goat, locust, ibex, etc., typical of the Israelite landscape and occasionally appearing in the Hebrew wisdom, find no mention in the Egyptian wisdom.

Finally, the following may briefly serve as examples of differences in life style and ideals. In Egyptian (not only in the wisdom literature) the expressions *dns ib*, *sḫm ib*, literally meaning "firm of heart," "heavy of heart," i.e., brave, stubborn, stand for models of correct human behavior, whereas their (non-wisdom) Hebrew counterparts, *ḥzq lēb*, *kbd lēb*, *qšh lēb*, which occur almost exclusively in the story of the Exodus with reference to Pharaoh, have a negative connotation.

B. Features Common to the Hebrew and Egyptian Wisdom Terminology

Alongside this diversity in Hebrew and Egyptian wisdom terminology, some general lines of similarity are discernible. Thus, in some cases equivalent terms in the two corpora undergo the very same semantic development or change.

Most Bible scholars have long accepted the theory of a gradual development of Biblical wisdom: at first wisdom focused on the human individual and his daily affairs, and only later became theological and identifiable with "the fear of God."[28]

The picture emerging from the Egyptian sources, which indicates stages of development which run markedly parallel to the Hebrew, may confirm this view of a gradual transition of wisdom: its roots lie in wisdom deriving from practical experience and passed down from father to son. Later, faith becomes pivotal to instruction (in *Amenemope*) until, finally, in the "personal piety" writings, the god himself is represented as the sole source of knowledge and wisdom.[29]

This process of change in the nature and image of wisdom, the gradual transition from one form to another, is reflected in the semantic development of terms characteristic of both the Hebrew and Egyptian wisdom vocabulary. This semantic development corresponds to the various stages in the evolution of wisdom:

(1) The Egyptian terms *sbꜣy.t*, *sbꜣ*, *mtr*, parallel to the Hebrew *tôrâ*, *miṣwâ*, initially denote human wisdom, that of a father or teacher, but later they refer to divine law and command.

(2) The terms belonging to the semantic field of "wisdom" first stand for empirical wisdom or wisdom attained by study; in the final stage they denote charismatic wisdom bestowed by God (cf. Chapter 6, Appendix C, above).
(3) The contrast between positive and negative human types is expressed in the early stage of wisdom by the pair "wise"—"fool," which is later replaced in Hebrew and Egyptian wisdom by "righteous man"—"wicked man" (in Egyptian only in the Demotic instructions).[30]

IV. THE INFLUENCE OF THE EGYPTIAN LANGUAGE ON BIBLICAL LITERATURE

When two societies speaking different languages come into contact, conditions can under certain historical or cultural circumstances arise which facilitate linguistic influence. This may be either a one-way or a mutual process. Our study has led to the conclusion that where the contact between Biblical and Egyptian wisdom literature is concerned, it was Hebrew that was influenced by Egyptian and not vice versa. This, of course, does not preclude the possibility of a reversed situation in other areas, so that, for example, contact with the monotheistic sphere may have exerted an influence on the Egyptian world.[31]

Besides the examples given in Sections I and III of this chapter, there are others dispersed throughout our study, which show that also in Biblical books outside the wisdom literature there appear expressions and idioms which have a close affinity to the Egyptian. Such expressions are *lēb šōmēaʿ*, "a hearing heart," in the story of Solomon's dream at Gibeon; *lēb ʾeben*, "heart of stone," in the prophetic books; "to go after the heart" (*bᵉʿiqbôt hallēb*), is a positive notion in Qoheleth but negative in the religious literature; the title *peh*, "mouth," given to Aaron on account of his function as speaker for his brother Moses, and to the prophets in general because they are the "mouth" of God; and, finally, perhaps even the expression *ʾnp*, "to be angry," which parallels *fnḏ* in Egyptian.

V. THE *SITZ IM LEBEN* OF HEBREW WISDOM

Can the proven terminological contact between Biblical and Egyptian wisdom literature help solve the problem of the *Sitz im Leben* of Biblical wisdom? Biblical literature contains no information about the function and use of wisdom compositions. Most scholars believe that the Hebrew wisdom was connected with a school setting, although neither the Bible nor archeological findings offer any kind of unequivocal evidence of the existence of such an institution in ancient Israel.[32] The conclusion that schools did exist has been reached in the following ways:

— By analogous projection. It is an established fact that there were schools in Egypt and Mesopotamia. We may reasonably assume that the establishment of the monarchy in Israel under David and Solomon and the attendant emergence of a class of officials, created a need for schools of the kind we know to have existed in the neighboring regions of the ancient Near East.[33]

— By backward projection based on examples in the later wisdom genre. Thus, we are told that Qoheleth was a teacher who "taught the people knowledge" (Qoh. 12,9); and of Ben Sira (51,23) we learn that he was a teacher at his *bêt midrāš* (school).

— By pointing out allusions in the Bible to the existence of schools. Such references may be found, for example, in Isaiah 8,16; 28,9ff.; 50,4-9; Proverbs 5,13; 17,16, and elsewhere.

— School "exercises." Recently a new argument has been put forward which suggests that a number of short, fragmentary inscriptions found at various sites in Israel (e.g., Gezer, Lachish, Arad, Kadesh-Barnea, Kuntilat Ajrud), and dated from the twelfth century B.C. onward are in fact the school exercises of pupils and therefore evidence of the existence of schools at these sites in antiquity.[34]

Our research has indeed been able to confirm the premise that, like the Egyptian wisdom, the Hebrew didactic compositions were connected with a certain educational framework, for we have shown (a) the existence of terminological contact between Hebrew and Egyptian wisdom literature (the latter involved in school teaching), and, more important, (b) the existence in the Biblical sage's vocabulary of semantic equivalents to terms usually found in writings associated with the Egyptian schools, as follows:[35]

(1) The teacher's instruction is *sb3y.t* in Egyptian (31 times in the instructions, 22 times in the school writings)[36] and *mûsār* in Biblical wisdom.

(2) Terms indicative of the teaching method used, i.e., beating, are the Egyptian *ḥwi*, *ḳnḳn* and also *šbd*, meaning "rod," "stick." The Hebrew verb *nkh*, "to beat," occurs frequently in Proverbs either with or without the object *šēbeṭ*, "rod." The latter word appears 3 times in Job as well.

(3) The "idle pupil," *wsf* in the Egyptian school writings, is called *ʿāṣēl*, "lazy," in the Bible (in Prov., Qoh.).

(4) The "ignorant pupil," *iw.ty ḥ3.ty* (3 times in the Egyptian school writings, once in the instructions) is the equivalent of *ḥăsar lēb* in the language of the Biblical sage (Prov., BS).

(5) Besides *iw.ty ḥ3.ty* appears in Egyptian *ḫn*, which is close in meaning (4 times in the school writings; once in the *Instruction of Anii*).

(6) The man of positive character, the "calm-tempered," is called *ḳb* in the Egyptian school writings (4 times in the school writings; 3 times in the instructions) and parallels the adjective *qar rûaḥ* in Proverbs (once).

(7) The "ear" as an instrument of learning is characteristic of the educational sphere both in Egypt and Israel (although it is also present in the Mesopotamian school writings).

The outcome of the discussion thus far is that in the vocabulary of the Biblical wisdom books we find features that recall the ambience and didactic approach of the Egyptian schools. To this we may add that of the terms associated with the vocation of the scribe in Israel we find (a) that the name of David's scribe, *šîšāʾ*, *šawšāʾ* (1 Kgs. 4,3; 1 Chr. 18,16; cf. 2 Sam. 8,17; 20,26), is a transliteration of the Egyptian *sš š*ʿ*t*, i.e., "scribe of letters";[37] and (b) that the Hebrew terms for ink and inkwell, *d*^{e}*yô* and *qeset*, are clear adaptations of the Egyptian *ry.t* and *gsti*.[38]

It would therefore seem reasonable to assume that the first educational institutions in Israel were inspired by an Egyptian archetype, and that the book of Proverbs — especially its second collection — served as learning material in these institutions. This, of course, gives us only indirect and not absolute proof of the existence of an independent educational institution in Israel along the lines of the Egyptian school. Nor should it be taken to mean that the didactic methods and study materials at schools in Israel were identical with those in Egypt — after all, the Canaanite alphabet and Egyptian hieroglyphics represent two entirely different systems of writing. Neither does the assumption of the existence of schools in Israel preclude the possibility that alongside the educational activities in the official school setting education was also pursued privately, viz., with master craftsmen or within the family,[39] and that knowledge was also acquired by individuals autodidactically as we find, for example, in Qoheleth.

Wisdom composition in the ancient Near East involved not only school circles or private education but also the king's court. In Egypt, the king's court contained a school for princes and the sons of the high officials. There, too, the scribes, actually the king's officials, carried out their creative work. The firm link between wisdom and the king's court is expressed also in the attribution of some of the instructions to kings and their use in certain periods as propaganda for the king's house (e.g., the "loyalist" instructions). A similar phenomenon is found in the Hebrew tradition which ascribes the composition of wisdom to King Solomon and asserts that King Hezekiah's men were involved in it (Prov. 25,1). The frequent mention of sage-counsellors in the kings' courts both in Biblical literature and the Egyptian sources[40] also points to the king's court as a setting for the flourishing of wisdom.[41]

Presumably, therefore, in Israel and Egypt wisdom activity was associated with *several* circles, including the king's court as well as other educational frameworks, both official and private.

VI. SAPIENTIAL TRACES OUTSIDE THE WISDOM BOOKS

The assumption that Hebrew scribes, like their counterparts in Egypt, were educated in schools or in some other educational setting in which wisdom compositions served as learning texts, may furnish a solution to another problem in Biblical research, viz., the presence of traces of the wisdom tradition in texts which are not usually counted to wisdom literature.[42] A similar situation exists with respect to Egyptian literature, where we find formulas and expressions that echo ideals and concepts characteristic of wisdom literature reappearing in the rhetoric produced by the royal court (as in official inscriptions and biographies), and in autobiographies, some of which were composed as late as two millennia after the instruction texts were written.

Actually, there is nothing surprising about the existence of wisdom vocabulary in non-wisdom texts, and the phenomenon is common to both Hebrew and Egyptian literature. All of these works were the creations of a single type of author, namely, the scribe. That the wisdom tradition influenced literary works otherwise unrelated to the Biblical wisdom literature appears therefore as quite a legitimate assumption, and there seems to be no reason for rejecting it, as a number of scholars in the field have attempted to do. The opinion that the sapiential ideology reflects an approach to reality that was shared by *all* Israelites[43] as well as the argument of an absence of agreed criteria for measuring "wisdom influence"[44] cannot eliminate the fact that such influence existed.

This influence is expressed in subject matter, literary forms and a characteristic vocabulary. Separately, none of these is sufficient for determining wisdom influence, but when appearing together they form a tested and efficient criterion for the identification of such influence.[45] Thus, we concur with Whybray and many others that "the intellectual (i.e., wisdom) tradition" made its mark on passages outside the Biblical wisdom books.[46]

VII. THE HISTORICAL BACKGROUND OF THE CONTACT BETWEEN HEBREW AND EGYPTIAN WISDOM LITERATURE

The number of terms common to the Egyptian and Israelite wisdom is not very large, and its demarcation is not always certain, especially where the foreign coloring has become blurred through extensive modification by way of adapting it to the Hebrew sphere. This is at times so expertly done that the foreign provenance is indeed difficult to detect. However, the evidence accumulated in our study is sufficient to show that the Hebrew authors were closely acquainted with at least part of the Egyptian wisdom literature. Egyptian phrases and words, found in no other wisdom compositions in the ancient Near East, left their imprint on the Biblical wisdom literature.

What might have been the conditions and circumstances under which Hebrew scribes came into contact with the products of the Egyptian scriptorium?

The first contacts between Hebrew and Egyptian culture probably took place during the reign of Solomon, who is reported to have established close ties with Egypt. Solomon married Pharaoh's daughter, and adopted Pharaonic practices and customs by building chariots and storage cities and by organizing expeditions to obtain luxury goods from Africa. These relations with Egypt were maintained during the reign of Hezekiah, to whose circle the compilation of the Proverbs of Solomon is ascribed (Prov. 25,1). Since Hezekiah was the leader of the pro-Egyptian faction opposed by Isaiah (Isa. 30,1-17; 31), some of the evidence of literary contact with the Egyptian wisdom tradition found in Proverbs and Job may be attributed to his period. Be this as it may, the connection between the Hebrew and Egyptian wisdom tradition seems best illustrated in the setting of the Solomonic period.

Support for this view is found in the comprehensive article by Williams,[47] in which he examines the Egyptian elements underlying the institution of the monarchy in the era of David and Solomon — from the design of the throne, the coronation ceremony and the list of royal officials to tax-collecting methods and commercial procedures. All these show the impact of the highly developed Egyptian culture.

Furthermore, if one assumes that with the establishment of the monarchy in Israel a need arose for a class of officials and that such personnel would have been trained for their tasks in an educational setting similar to the Egyptian, it is reasonable to conclude that the first

Israelite school was founded as early as the time of King Solomon and consequently modeled on the Egyptian schools. It was through this, for Israel novel institution, that Egyptian influence infilitrated into the Hebrew wisdom, which — at least partially — served as learning material in the school and other educational settings.[48]

EPILOGUE

In the end we return to the beginning, where it was said that as yet little has been done in the field of comparative terminological research of Biblical and Egyptian literature. Once more, let us quote the words of the priest Khakheperre-sonb:

> Had I *unknown* phrases, maxims that are strange,
> *novel* untried words, not transmitted sayings...

The Egyptian priest, living in the second millennium B.C., complains of his inability to find new words and say something that has never been said before. Fifteen centuries later, Qoheleth, for purely prosaic reasons warns against writing too many books and excessive study saying:

> Furthermore, my son, be warned: of making many books there is no end; and much study is a *weariness of the flesh.*

Fortunately, neither the words of the Egyptian priest nor those of the Hebrew sage apply to the contemporary state of comparative research of Egypt and the Bible, where the unexplored territory is vast and continues to invite scholarly attention.

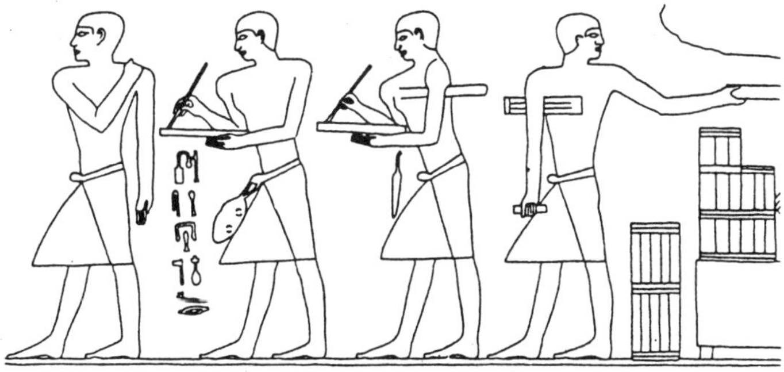

NOTES

INTRODUCTION

1. See below, pp. 146—148.

2. In this connection we should also note the study of W. Bühlmann (1976) on the concept of right speaking and silence in Proverbs 10-30 (omitting 22,17-24,22). Bühlmann analyzes the Hebrew relevant terminology and gives numerous comparative examples from Egyptian literature, particularly of the instruction genre, but he depends on secondary sources for the Egyptian, so that notwithstanding its importance his work contains nothing new on the comparative terminology of Hebrew and Egyptian. Kayatz (1966) is more valuable for our purposes; this study analyzes the form and content of the first collection of Proverbs (chaps. 1-9) with a bias towards Egyptian literature, and compares Biblical terms and formulas with Egyptian ones (see esp. 34 ff., 42, 51-52, 125 ff.). Also, a number of Egyptian concepts and their Hebrew analogies are referred to marginally in the lectures of J. Leclant and A. Cazelles in *SPOA* (5 ff., and 27 ff., respectively).

3. See, e.g., Brunner, "Review of G.E. Bryce"; also Murphy, "Hebrew wisdom," 27.

4. See Whybray, *The Intellectual Tradition*; Baumgartner, "The Wisdom Literature"; Schmid, *Wesen und Geschichte*.

5. For the use of quotations in Egyptian literature see Brunner, "Zitate"; also Fecht, *Der Habgierige*, und Volten, *Weisheitbuch des Anii*, 46 ff. For the corresponding device in Hebrew literature see, e.g., Gordis, *Koheleth*, 95 ff.; Baumgartner, "The Wisdom Literature," 224; Whybray, *The Intellectual Tradition*, 61, 67, 68.

6. Whybray was preceded by Scott, *The Way of Wisdom* (1971) 121-122, who counted 77 wisdom terms and claimed that these furnish a criterion for identifying wisdom influences in other parts of the Old Testament. Unlike Whybray, Scott does not concern himself with the semantic aspect of these terms. See also Kuntz, "The Canonical Wisdom Psalms," 200 ff. for this use of the terminological criterion in identifying wisdom Psalms; and similarly, recently, A. Hurvitz, whose working hypothesis is that "if there is in fact such a thing as 'Wisdom Psalms'... we may assume that these texts have absorbed words and expressions which were current specifically in Wisdom Literature," see "Wisdom Vocabulary," 41.

7. See Crenshaw, in *SAIW* 481-494, who is followed by Fontaine, *Traditional Sayings*, 168-170. Also Murphy, in *Isr. Wisd.* 35-42 and "Hebrew wisdom," 27-28; and Kuntz, "The Canonical Wisdom Psalms," 199ff.

8. See Hurvitz, *Wisdom Language,* 17 n. 69.

9. I have been guided in this by the common assumption of semanticists today that languages reflect the intellectual ambience of their users. See, e.g., Ullendorff, ("Thought Categories," 287), who cites the philosopher E. Cassirer's statement: "Language is not a simple reflection of the world of objects, but rather embodies the results of an intellectual remoulding of this world."

10. Other scholars have also attempted to compose a list of wisdom phraseology (see n. 6 above), but in view of his caution and meticulousness Whybray's list is to be preferred. To Whybray's lexicon, which is restricted to words, should be added the collocations and pairs of words collected by Hurvitz, *Wisdom Language*.

11. See my reservation in Chap. 9, p. 340.

12. See Lyons, *Semantics*, 240-243, 261-266, 268; Kedar, *Biblische Semantik*, 46; Sawyer, *Semantics in Biblical Research*, 28-29.

13. See Lyons, *Semantics*, 244. Also Barr, *The Semantics*, 109, 158-159; and idem *Comparative Philology*, 170 ff.

14. Etymologies of Egyptian are dealt with, although only to a limited extent, in A. Erman's and H. Grapow's *Wörterbuch der aegyptischen Sprache.* Their work in this field was extended by W. Westendorf in his dictionary (*Koptisches Handwörterbuch*) which deals with the etymology of Coptic. Both dictionaries have been used in this study.

15. Concerning the theoretical basis of the concept of the semantic field and its uses and development, see Ullmann, *The Principles of Semantics*, 152 ff. and idem *Semantics*, 243-253, also Lyons, *Semantics*, 250-261, Nir, *The Semantics*, 168-178; and Sawyer, *Semantics in Biblical Research*, 28-59.

16. Some of the terms referring to the methods of instruction in ancient Egypt can be found in Brunner, *Erziehung*. Others appear in the publications of Janssen, Otto, Blumenthal, and Jansen-Winkeln dealing with literary genres indirecty connected with wisdom literature. Most important for our investigation are, of course, sapiential terms dealt with in Lichtheim (1983) and Brunner (1984), but both cover a limited quantity of terms and literary sources and do not use semantic tools.

17. See Corpus, pp. 12ff.

18. Cf. Bloomfield, *Language*, 139-140.

19. We have used in particular the translations published by M. Lichtheim in *LEWL*, see Corpus, p. 23.

20. For a complete understanding of the technical aspect of our research note the following: (a) The system used for Hebrew transliteration is that recommended by *Biblica*. (b) The Masoretic Version of the Bible and other Hebrew texts have been translated directly from the original unless otherwise stated. (c) The distinction between noun and adjective is difficult in Biblical Hebrew as well as in Egyptian. There are many words which take both noun and adjective patterns. Hence, as applied in this research, these categories are not absolute, but are based on the semantic analysis of the terms.

CORPUS

1. The following brief review of current research and of the sources, on which this work is based, intends only to provide an introduction to our corpus necessary for a complete semantic determination. Bibliographical information complementing this survey are given in the notes.

2. For the semantic determination of the Hebrew words, one must look beyond the bounds of wisdom literature and rely on other Biblical books. This is due to the importance of using the general language system for semantic determination, and is particularly important when defining terms which are common in the wisdom literature but appear also as a *terminus technicus* in other literary genres (e.g., *miṣwâ*, *tôrâ*).

3. For the direct parallelism between the two sources see, Gressman, "Die neugefundene Lehre"; Oesterley, "The Teaching of Amen-em-ope"; Humbert, *Recherches*, 17-26; Williams, "The Alleged Semitic Original"; Bryce, *A Legacy*, passim; Römheld, *Wege*, 151-181; Shupak, "Comparative Aspects," 7-9.

4. Alt, "Die Weisheit Salomos," 139 ff., has shown that the numerical sayings in Prov. 30, 15ff., the description of Solomon's knowledge related to the world of flora and fauna in 1 Kgs. 5,13 and the depiction of the animals' behavior in Job 39, are based on ancient onomastic lists.

5. The above division of Proverbs, based on the book's latest editing, is accepted by most scholars. A comparative study of literary forms and formulations of the instructions of the ancient Near East carried out by Kitchen, led him to different results, according to which the book contains only four collections: (1) Solomon I: 1-24 (1, 1-6 title; 1, 7-9, 18 prologue; 10, 1 — subtitle; 10, 2-24, 34 — main text; supplements: "Words of the Wise" I: 22,17-24,22; "Words of the Wise" II: 24, 23-34); (2) Solomon II: 25-29 (25, 1 — title; 25, 2-29 — text); (3) Agur: 30 (30,1a — title; 30,1b-33 — text); (4) Lemuel: 31 (31, 1 — title; 31,2-31 — text: section I: 2-9; section II: 10-31); see idem "Proverbs" and "The Basic Literary Forms."

6. See Kaufmann, *Religion*, vol. 2, 631-646, who rejects the accepted ideas of 19th century scholars; see also Grinz, *Studies in the O.T.*, 81-82; idem. *The Book of Proverbs*, 76 ff.; and Lang, *Lehrrede*, 52-55. A detailed discussion of formal criteria accepted by 19th century scholars in dating wisdom literature and their refutation is presented by McKane, *Proverbs*, 1ff.

7. See Lang, Lehrrede, 58-60; and lately: Whybray, "Wisdom Literature in the Reigns of David and Solomon," Crenshaw, "The Sage in Proverbs," esp. 216.

8. Some scholars found Aramaic elements here, others, expressions in Arabic. Tur Sinai, following Ibn Ezra, went further and considered Job to be a Hebrew translation of an Aramaic work.

9. For the refutation of both arguments see Kaufmann, *Religion*, vol. 2, 623, 637-642. Hurvitz, "The Date," has shown that at least the language of the prose tale in Job is late post-exilic, sharing common features with the Aramaic.

10. For the affinity of Job with the Mesopotamian wisdom compositions see,

e.g., Gray, "The Book of Job"; on further parallels between Job and the Egyptian literature see Humbert, *Recherches*, 75 ff., von Rad, "Hiob 38," and Gray, ibid. Especially striking is the similarity between Job 31 and the "Confession of the Dead," Chap. 125 in *The Book of the Dead.*

11. For a more exact date of the composition of Job see: Scott, *Proverbs*, XX (6th century B.C.); Terrien, "Job," (early exilic period); Albertz, "The Sage," 248, 250 ff. (postexilic Jewish community).

12. See Gordis, *Koheleth*, 69 ff., 95 ff., Crenshaw, *Ecclesiastes*, 48-49; Whybray, *Ecclesiastes*, 18-19; Fox, *Qoheleth and his Contradictions*, 19-28, and most recently Murphy, "The Sage in Ecclesiastes," 263-264. This conflict of different points of view, characteristic of Qoheleth, is termed by Loader a "polar structure" in his book *Polar Structures.*

13. Thus the sceptical atmosphere and the argument of the meaninglessness of life is close to the Babylonian *Dialogue between Master and Servant* and the Egyptian work, *The Man Who Was Tired of Life*, while the subject of the topsy-turvy foundations of society and social criticism are characteristic of the Egyptian speculative wisdom literature (see p. 19 below). So, too, the call for pleasures and the search for life's delights remind us of the Babylonian *Epic of Gilgamesh* and *The Songs of the Harper* in Egypt (cf. pp. 303—304 below). There is evidence of the Hellenistic conception in only one section, 3,21, in which Qoheleth brings up the idea of the ascendancy of man's spirit after death and goes on to refute it. For further discussion of the connections of Qoheleth with Egyptian literature see Galling, "Kohelet," 276 ff., Humbert, *Recherches*, 107-124, Gemser, "The Instructions," 125-126, and Crenshaw, *Ecclesiastes*, 51-52.

14. Cf. Fox, "Qohelet," and Gordis, "The Original Language."

15. See Loader, *Polar Structures*, 124-131.

16. Hurvitz's innovation is the finding that every characteristic wisdom term is regularly replaced by another term bearing the same sense outside the wisdom literature. Hurvitz convincingly uses this tool to demonstrate that six psalms belong to the wisdom corpus. The weakness of his method, however, is his exclusive reliance on linguistic criteria, whose efficiency remains limited; the fact, e.g., that a term appearing in a psalm can also be found once in a wisdom text does not necessarily prove its relationship to the wisdom vocabulary. Hurvitz himself recognizes this weakness and does not deny that with different tools, such as subject-matter and literary form, additional wisdom Psalms may be identified; see Hurvitz, *Wisdom Language*, 122.

17. Thus Murphy ("A Consideration") lists seven wisdom Psalms — 1, 32, 34, 37, 49, 112, 128; Kuntz ("The Canonical") adds two — 127, 133; von Rad (*Wisdom in Israel*, 47 ff.) adds 111, 119, 139 (excluding 32) and Sarna (in "T^{e}hîlîm," *The Biblical Encyclopaedia*, vol. 8) adds 53, 91, 133 (and excludes 32, 34); Whybray (*The Intellectual*, 154) includes among them 90, 92, 94, 104, 107 — which are not commonly regarded as wisdom Psalms; Hurvitz mentions six — 19, 32, 34, 37, 112, 119. A comprehensive summary of this "chaotic" situation in research is given by Luyten "Psalm 73," 59-64. See also Fichtner, *Die altorientalische Weisheit*, 9; Scott, *Proverbs*, XXI; Eissfeldt, *Introduction* 124-127; Mowinckel, "Psalms and Wisdom," 205 ff. and Kaufmann, *Religion*, vol. 2, 518-522, and the synoptic table in Hurvitz, *Wisdom Language*, 128.

18. The Greek Version of BS is also pertinent to the present inquiry, when it consistently translates a specific Hebrew term with one and the same Greek word.

19. For more differences between BS and proverbial wisdom tradition see Sanders, *Ben Sira*, 12-26.

20. The roots of BS lie not only in Biblical traditions but also in extra-Biblical wisdom. The relation of BS to the Hellenic and Egyptian wisdom traditions and especially his connection with Theognis on the one hand and with *Pap. Insinger* on the other was recently discussed by Sanders, ibid. 27-106.

21. A variety of literary genres from this category belonging to as many periods as possible are included, since the broader the extra-wisdom comparative sphere, the more exact and complete will be the determination of the wisdom glossary.

22. The chronology appearing in this work is based on the table of dates included in the article "Egypt," *Encyclopaedia Hebraica* (Jerusalem-Tel Aviv 1982), vol. 24, 182-185.

23. Most scholars, e.g., Erman, Gardiner and lately also Kitchen, are of the first opinion, but Lichtheim supports the opposite view, in *Literature*, vol.1, 139, 145-146, and cf. Fôti, "Prophecies of Neferti," 3ff. Inclusion of the speculative texts in the category of Egyptian wisdom will not be generally accepted; however, in my "Egyptian 'Prophecy' and Biblical Prophecy" I have tried to show that the five works, listed below (pp. 25-26) under "Speculative- Pessimistic Wisdom" constitute an independent unit within the Egyptian wisdom literature, while in "Egyptian 'Prophetic' Writings" I discussed the proximity between these works and the Biblical wisdom literature as evinced in patterns, literary forms, vocabulary and content.

24. It is often difficult to differentiate between texts belonging to the school writings and instructions because the content of some of the latter (such as *The Instruction of Kheti* or that of *Amennakht*) is identical to those of the school writings (namely, praise of the scribal profession), although they bear the title *sb3y.t* (instruction).

25. See Brunner, "Zitate," 169-171; idem "Eine neue Entlehnung," 17-19; idem "Ein weiteres," 53 and lately in *AW* 253-254, 403; see also Lichtheim, *AEA*, esp. 98-99, 110-111; Gilula, "Review," 504-506 and E. Blumenthal, in *Festschrift für G. Fecht*, eds., J. Osing and G. Freyer, *ÄAT* 12 (Wiesbaden 1987), 93-96.

26. J. Assmann, "Weisheit."

27. Since the available Egyptian texts usually have been preserved not in the original manuscript but in later copies, the dates of the relevant copies were also given below. The English translation of most of the texts appears in the following books: *ANET* 405-421; 431-446; J.H. Breasted, *Ancient Records of Egypt*, 5 vols. (Chicago 1906-7); A. Erman, *The Ancient Egyptians*, ed. M. Blackman; W.K. Simpson (ed.), *The Literature of Ancient Egypt*; M. Lichtheim, *Ancient Egyptian Literature*, 3 vols. The latter is the most comprehensive publication in English, containing a review of research and a bibliography; but the most up-to-date study of Egyptian wisdom literature appeared recently in German: H. Brunner, *AW*, which includes an annotated translation of the works with an introduction to each of them, a discussion of the literary genre, and a bibliographical review.

28. A complete list of published Demotic wisdom texts is to be found in Smith's "Weisheit, demotische," *LÄ* VI, 1197-1204.

29. Further thorough discussion of the works relating to the Egyptian speculative literature may be found in my article "Egyptian 'Prophecy' and Biblical Prophecy," esp. 4-9.

30. Recently two studies of *The Eloquent Peasant* have convincingly demonstrated that its date of composition is late 12th or perhaps 13th Dynasty; Berlev, "The Date of the Eloquent Peasant," pointed out that the title *imy r3 pr wr* of Rensi is not regularly attested until late in the 12th Dynasty, and Vernus, "Le date du Paysan Eloquent," indicated that the verbal system reflects a similar date.

31. Due to the restricted scope of our study, the important corpus by K. Kitchen, *Ramesside Inscriptions* (Oxford 1968ff.), is not included.

32. Naturally all comparative study of Biblical and Egyptian wisdom texts must take into account similar texts from other regions of the ancient Near East; our references are normally to the editions of Lambert, Kramer, Gordon, Cowley, and Lindenberger (see Bibliography).

CHAPTER ONE

1. *sb3y.t* is derived from *sb3*, "gate." In ancient times, both in Egypt and in Israel, it was at the town gate where the judges sat and trials were held; see *Anastasi* IV 4,7; *Pap. Abott* 7,1.

2. Cf. the root *lmd* similarly used in the Bible see below, p. 47, n.4.

3. Assmann, "Die 'Loyalistische Lehre' Echnatons," 1ff.

4. Otto, 25-26; *ÄHG* 149, 5ff.; *Hymn of Kiki* 1, 2 (Vernus, "Kyky," 120); Jansen-Winkeln I A5, d8; II 4, 1, 18, 21.

5. E.g., *Anastasi* IV 1a, 1; *Sallier* I 3,4.

6. The search for an exact determination of this genre and its component parts is still in its infancy (see Blumenthal, "Neferti," 28-30), but our knowledge has lately been widened thanks to the research of Kitchen ("The Basic Literary Forms" and "Proverbs"). A close scrutiny of the above mentioned texts shows that they have common features, as expressed in their construction, literary forms, style and vocabulary. A large part of these texts has a uniform structure which includes: (1) title — *sb3y.t* + name of the writer and of the person for whom it is intended; (2) the purpose of the work; (3) prologue — the circumstances surrounding the delivery of the instruction or the composition of the work; (4) the text of the instruction; (5) epilogue — at times referring back to the prologue. As to their stylistic characteristics, the wisdom sayings are composed of two main patterns — general maxims in the 3rd person (*Aussagen*) and admonitions in the 2nd person (*Ermahnungen*); and typical formulas are used — comparisons "better than," and the truism "good for..." This genre also has a characteristic vocabulary (discussed below).

7. Many copies of the instructions of *Kheti*, *Amenemhet* and *Amenomope* made by school pupils are preserved; see H. Brunner, *Erziehung*, 85ff. and also his article "Die 'Weisen.'"

8. The assumption that *sb3y.t* denotes a written instruction is corroborated by both form and content: (a) These compositions are written in the form of a last

testament left behind by the deceased for his heirs — *Ptaḥḥotep* is described as man of advanced years; *Amenemope* addresses the youngest of his sons; sometimes the writer is no longer among the living — *Merikare*, *Amenemhet*, *Petosiris*, and at times the narrative informs us that the writer believes he will die far from his family — *Ankhsheshonqy*. These examples create the impression that the writer assumes his message will not reach its destination unless it be written down. (b) The term *sb3y.t* often stands in parallelism with something written. In *Pap. Chester Beatty* IV the following is said to a pupil: "Only after you become proficient in what is written do you enter (i.e., understand) the instructions" (pl. 19 verso 4,6; 4,9). Of the scribes it is said that "they made heirs for themselves (in the form of) books of instructions which they had composed" (pl. 18 verso 2, 8-9). The excellent scribe is wiser than his peers, for "the instruction of books (*sb3y.t sš.w*) is graven in his heart" (*Anastasi* I 11, 2-3). (c) Sometimes the determinative denoting *sb3y.t* is the sign of a papyrus book (Gr V12) (*Amenemope* 27, 8, 15; *Bologna* 1094 3,7; cf. *Chester Beatty* IV pl. 20, verso 6, 14). (d) Elsewhere a written instruction is explicitly spoken of, or it may be understood from the context that *sb3y.t* indicates written matter. Thus, in a passage from a Demotic wisdom text, a "copy of an instruction" (*ẖ.t wʿ.t sbʿ.t*) given by a scribe of the House of Life is mentioned (Thissen, *Anchscheschonqi*, 5). Also the sayings written by Ankhsheshonqy for his son are termed *mtr.t* (4,11-12; 4,17), before they are written, and *sb3y.t* (5, 14-17) after.

9. This is verified by the verbs that collocate with *sb3y.t*: "to take" (*ṯy*) (*Insinger* 8, 23; 17,23; cf. 9,18); "to hearken" (*sḏm*) (*Ptaḥḥotep* 507ff.; *El Amarna* — Sandman 60,6; 80, 89; etc.); "to pay attention" (*rdi[m]ib/ḥ3.ty*), comes often in this context but does not collocate with *sb3y.t* (*Amenemope* 3,10,11; *Anastasi* III 4,1,3; *Anastasi* V 17,4 etc.); and "to enter the ear" (*ʿḳ msḏr*) (ibid. IV 8,7)); for a discussion of these verbs, see Chap. 2.

10. Cf., e.g., Jansen-Winkeln I, 74-75 n. 38.

11. P. Humbert, in *Recherches*, 67-68, was the first to determine that *mûsār* is the Hebrew equivalent of the Egyptian *sb3y.t*, an idea which has generally been accepted by scholarship; the exception is Couroyer, for whom the equivalent of *sb3* is *lmd* (see following section).

12. This double meaning appears both in wisdom books and elsewhere. The noun *mûsār* — 30 times in Prov. ; 4 in Job; none in Qoh.; 8 in Jer.; 8 times in other books — Deut., Isa., Ezk., Hos., Zeph., and Ps. The verb *ysr* appears 9 times in the wisdom books (5 times in Prov.; twice in Job; twice in wisdom Psalms) out of 44 times in the Bible.

13. With the meaning "teaching" and "reproof," *mûsār* usually appears with the following terms: *tôḵahat* — in parallelism (Prov. 5,12; 10,17; 12,1; 13,18; 15,10,32) and in construct state (ibid. 6,23); in parallelism with *ʿēṣâ* (ibid. 19, 20), *ʾimrê dāʿat* (ibid. 19,27; 23,12), *daʿat* (ibid. 8,10); and in conjunction with *ḥokmâ* (ibid. 1,2,7; 23,23).

14. For the Egyptian parallels see n.9 and cf. also Chap. 2, (pp. 51ff., 57ff., 59ff.) which deals with both Egyptian and Hebrew equivalents enumerated here.

15. Cazelles, "Les débuts," 29, finds this genre in Prov. 1-9; similarly Whybray and others; see McKane's summation, in *Proverbs*, 6 ff.

16. *mtr* stands in parallelism with *sb3y.t*, in *Amenemope* 1,1-2; *Onomasticon* 1; *Bologna* 1094 3,7-8, etc; or comes in juxtaposition with it — *Anii* title and 9,17; *Amennakht* 1; *Kiki* 1,2; etc.

17. In the present corpus the noun *mtr(t)* appears about 40 times in the instructions and 14 times in the school writings; it is also a common adjective in the king's court literature, appearing 24 times.

18. In recent research the view has been put forward that the difference between *mtr.t* and *sb3y.t*, in Demotic wisdom at least, is that the former means "'testimony' which is based on practical experience" while the latter means "work of theoretical nature" (Thissen, *Anchscheschonqi*, 1-8, and following him Smith, *LÄ* VI, 1195). This theory was dismissed by Ritner (*Bibliotheca Orientalis* 44 [1987], 642-643), who argued that "it is difficult to see a difference between the two terms appearing in *Onchsheshonqy*." Ritner is correct with respect to Thissen's distinction, but the two terms are in fact distinct even in *Anksheshonqy*: see n. 8(d) above.

19. Even if the theory about the metonomy of the term is uncertain, it still seems to us that *mtr(t)*, *mty*, should be treated as one polysemic lexeme, not as two homonymous lexemes as do *Wb.* II 171 ff. and Faulkner, 120-121.

20. This "honest man" may be a vizier (*Kagemni* I 1; *Ptaḥḥotep* 199), a scribe (*Anii* 4,13; cf. 5,8) or an official in the royal court (*Urk.* IV 890,13; 993, 7 — *mty ib*; Janssen I p. 23, Ac 3,7; Blumenthal 300-301).

21. See *Anii* 8,18 and *Amenemope* 16,1 where the term involves the giving of evidence in court, and in *A Letter to a Wayward Son* 70-71, where it appears in a testimony formula at the end of the letter (cf. Guglielmi, *WdO* 14 [1983], 161).

22. In the hymns the god appears as a teacher, *Kiki* 1,2: "but now his god has taught him (*mty*) and made him wise according to his teaching (*sb3y.t.f*)" (*ÄHG* 374).

23. This is indicated by the accompanying determinative of a man sitting hand in mouth and perhaps also by the determinative of two fingers. This is due to the fact that speech in the Orient is usually reinforced by manual gestures. Cf. also the words of the prince of Byblos in *The Report of Wenamum* (2,60) — "Words of great reproof (*mtr.t '3.t n md.t*) which you addressed to me..." This last reference is given by Brunner, *Bibliotheca Orientalis* 12, 66, as proof that the collocation *sb3y.t š'w.t* (in Sallier I 3,4) refers to written instruction; *sb3y.t š'w.t* also appears in Černý-Gardiner, *Hier. Ostr.* I, 105/4 recto. These last citations reinforce the premise made in our discussion that *mtr* is essentially oral instruction while *sb3y.t* is written; however, we have failed to find the inverted combination: *sb3y.t nj md.t* * ("oral reproof") or *mtr.t š'w.t* *("written reproof").

24. This explanation differs from that of Spiegelberg, who translated "*Erziehungslehre*" in *ZÄS* 53 (1917), 115.

25. Thus, in *The Instruction of Amennakht*, beside the general moral admonitions, there appears praise for the scribal profession, while in *Anii* the instructions referring to this profession are combined with "instruction of good character" (i.e., moral values).

26. Drioton, in his essay on *The Instruction of Amenemope* (*MBR* 258), argued that *mtr.wt wḏ3* (*Amenemope* 1,2) is a translation of the Hebrew *'ēdût šālôm*; Williams does so as well, although he, in contrast to Drioton, believes that the

Egyptian work exerted an influence upon the book of Proverbs ("The Alleged Semitic," 102).

27. See his detailed study "Un égyptianisme," 206-217 and also idem "L'origin égyptienne," 214-215.

28. This opinion is accepted also by Sanders, *Ben Sira*, 91 n.132.

29. For this connotation of *'wd* (hiph'il), cf. Weinfeld, *Immanuel* 8 (1978), 10.

30. The noun *'ēdût* does not appear in Prov., Eccl., or Job at all, while the verb, in hiph'il, appears in Job just once (29,11). *lmd* is mentioned only four times in the wisdom books, out of ca. 80 times in the Bible.

31. Cf. A. Shisha Halevy, "Coptic Translations," 131.

32. See Crum 319b regarding Prov. 1,2; Job 5,17 and ibid. 320b for Job 4,3; Deut. 8,5 and Ps. 118,17.

33. Cf. Thissen's similar explanation, n.18 above.

34. *tôkaḥat* appears 16 times in Prov. ; 2 times in Job and 6 times in other books (Ps., Ezra, Hab.).

35. Stemming from the fact that combatants in argument face each other, see Mandelkern, *Corcondantiae*, 476d.

36. So also Terrien and Wolf, but Whybray, *The Intellectual*, 140-142, refutes this opinion.

37. The trait of honesty, expressed by *mtr* or its synonyn *'ḳ3*, is of central importance to the Egyptian wisdom literature. The opposite of "honest" is "crooked," *gwš*, which parallels *'iqqēš* in the Bible, see below, pp. 192—194.

38. For the forensic usage of *ykḥ* see, e.g., Isa. 29, 21; Amos 5,10; cf. Bühlmann, *Von rechten Reden*, 108 and the detailed discussion by G. Mayer, in *TDOT* VI, 65-68, 70. As stated above *tôkaḥat* does not bear the sense of "testimony" although in one instance *ykḥ* is associated with the activity of a witness, see Ps. 50, 7-8 and cf. Mayer, ibid. 66.

39. See below and cf. Spiegelberg, *ZÄS* 53 (1917), 115.

40. *tôkaḥat* is used similarly to *mtr* as the following examples show: (a) in parallelism with *mûsār* (|| *sb3y.t*) — Prov. 3,11; 5,12; 10,17; 12,1; 13,18; Job 5,17; 40,2 etc.; (b) in construct state with *mûsār* — *tôkᵉḥôt mûsār* (|| *sb3y.t mtr.w*) Prov. 6,23; (c) in the collocation *tôkaḥat ḥayyîm* — Prov. 15,31; cf. the beginning of *The Instruction of Amennakht* 1).

41. *tp rd* || *sb3y.t* — *Ptoḥḥotep* 47,48; *Urk.* IV 503, 12-13; *tp rd* || *sb3y.t* || *mtr* — *Amenemope* 1,1-3.

42. For orders directed to carpenters and craftsmen, see *Urk.* IV 503, 12, 13; 1149, 10, 11; to inspectors, ibid. 1152, 13; to him "who is in charge of the town" and the vizier, ibid. 1103, 14; 1086, 10; to judges, ibid. 482, 1; to the army, ibid. 1112, 16; and for marksmanship, ibid. 976, 13,17.

43. For duties connected with ritual ceremonies and temple administration see ibid. 1148, 14; 1187, 10; 1208, 9; *Petosiris* 81, 38.

44. The relatively "gentle" tone of *sb3y.t* and *mtr* as compared with *tp rd* is shown by the following facts: (a) While the former two terms approximate the word *sḫr* (counsel), *tp rd* usually appears in the court's inscription in parallelism with *hp* — "law, ordinance," which sometimes is fixed in writing (*Wb.* II 488,8; *Urk.* IV 936,5; 1045,4; 1087,10,11; Jansen-Winkeln I A11,h,5). (b) *mtr* and *sb3y.t* are the

objects of the verb *sdm* which expresses obedience to instruction. The verb *sdm*, originally meaning "hearken," designates a natural, sensual act with no compulsion involved. In the royal phraseology *sdm* is replaced by the verb *ndr*, which collocates with *tp rd* as an object when a demand for obedience is referred to. (c) The hard tone accompanying *tp rd* is hinted at by the word's orthography — a drawing of a head and a foot, symbolizing servility(?) as well as from its presumed etymology; it may derive from the expression appearing in the *Pyramid Texts* — *tp rdwy*, i.e, "before the feet" (*Wb.* II 462,8); or *rd* may be connected with the Hebrew root *rdh* — "to rule," "to trample," "to stamp on" — which usually carried a negative connotation (Lev. 25,53; 26,17; Neh. 9,28; etc.). Cf. Calice §245; Vycichl, "Grundlage," 397 No. 59.

45. Thus Couroyer, "Un égyptianisme."

46. It is true that the equivalence is not complete. In the Bible it is God himself who gives the command, unlike in the Egyptian (in this corpus), where he "gives" *mtr*, *sb3y.t*, but not *tp rd*. Nevertheless, the content of the commands is identical in Hebrew and Egyptian because both refer to commands dealing with sacrifices and ceremonial ritual.

47. See *KBL*³ 416-417, 1573; Liedke and Petersen, "*tōrā* — *Weisung*," *Theologisches Handwörterbuch zum A.T.* (Munich-Zurich 1976), 1032. Another suggestion, dismissed in research, was to derive *tôrâ* from *yrh* "to shoot," "to throw" (cf. ibid.; also see Duesberg and Fransen, *Les scribes inspirés*, 231; Smith, *AJSL* 46 [1929],1). Also, the possibility of considering *tôrâ* to be a loanword from the Akka. *têrtu(m)*, i.e., "teaching," "instruction" has been taken into consideration (*KBL*³, 1573; Liedke and Petersen, ibid., Duesberg and Fransen, ibid.).

48. On the close connection between postexilic psalmic wisdom and the Torah, see lately Ceresko, "The Sage in Psalms," 220-221, 224, 227; for the identification of Wisdom with the Torah in BS see Sanders, *Ben Sira*, 24-26.

49. The following works are based on this opinion: Whybray, *Wisdom*; idem *The Intellectual*; Scott, *Proverbs*; idem *The Way*; Zimmerli, "Zur Structur;" McKane, *Proverbs*, 17-18; Fichtner, *Die altorientalische Weisheit*, 81-97; Oesterley, *Proverbs*; Lindblom, "Wisdom," 196. Some of the scholars named speak of a diachronic evolvement and some of a synchronic one: (a) Diachronic — Stage I: Biblical wisdom literature as part of the literature of ancient Near East; stage II: the assimilation of the wisdom literature into other Biblical traditions, resulting in a Yahwistic piety which reached its peak in Ben Sira (McKane, Fichtner, Scott). (b) Synchronic — One cannot speak of different stages in the evolvement of wisdom, but there are various types of wisdom — empirical and theological — which existed side by side (Zimmerli, Oesterley, etc.). Some scholars even distinguish between two different synchronic circles active simultaneously and producing different kinds of wisdom (Baumgartner, Gemser, Rankin).

50. Fichtner, *Die altorientalische Weisheit*, 81-97; a similar opinion is held by Whybray in *Wisdom*; also cf.: Duesberg-Fransen, *Les scribes inspirés*, 231-232; Perdue, *Wisdom and Cult*, 269-271, 303 and Küchler, *Frühjüdische Weisheitstraditionen*, *OBO* 26(1979), 33ff.

51. See p. 33 above, and n.22.

52. Assmann, "Weisheit," 12ff.

53. Fox, "Aspects of the Religion," challenges the theory of a chronological

development of Egyptian wisdom. According to his view, even if the above opinion is correct, this development had no influence upon Israelite wisdom; see below Chap. 9, n. 29.

54. Cf. below, pp. 349ff.

55. Nevertheless, the opinion of McKane (*PWM* 48ff.) and others, claiming that ancient wisdom was secular and without a religious basis, is unacceptable. Wisdom in Israel and the ancient Near East has always been founded on religion: see Kitchen, "Proverbs," 103 n. 78; Hermisson, *Studien*, 106-107.

56. These terms are *nḏ/nḏnḏ*, *sḥ*, and *sṯny*(*sḏny*).

57. The *nisbe* adjective *sḫry*, counselor, does not appear in our corpus, but *sḫr*, often collocates with other words thus constructing an adjective: *s sḫr.w.f*, lit., "man of advice," i.e., an active man; *ʿm m sḫr.w* "adept in giving counsel"; *dns sḫr.w*, lit., "heavy in advice," i.e., balanced in his views; *iḳr sḫr*, "excellent in giving advice," etc.

58. Cazelles, *SPOA* 36; Humbert in *Recherches*, 72, suggests the noun *m*^{e}*zzimôt* (Prov. 8,12) as an equivalent of *sḫr.w*, but this term does not always fit within the semantic field of *sḫr* especially not within its religious context.

59. Cf. *BDB* 419, *TDOT* VI, 157. *ʿēṣâ* is used 22 times in the wisdom literature (Prov. — 20; Job — 9; wisdom Pss. — 3; BS — 7) out of 86 times in the Bible.

60. Cf. *BDB* 420, *Wb.* IV 258ff., and *TDOT* VI, 157 ff.

61. For other aspects of the terms *ʿēṣâ* and *sḫr* see the detailed discussion of de Boer, "The Counselor;" Whybray, *The Intellectual*, 15-31, 132-133; McKane, *PWM* 15-22; Barucq, "Une veine de spiritualité," 198-202; Brunner, *Erziehung*, 51-52; Blumenthal 389-390, 395 and recently L. Ruppert in *TDOT* VI, 157-185.

62. For a summary of views on this subject and their refutation see Whybray, ibid., and lately idem *SIANE* 134ff., *pace*, van Leewen, ibid. 295ff. esp. 303-304. The *ʿēṣâ* in the Bible and in the Egyptian sources often involved activity at the king's court. Selected references are, in Egyptian: On the figure of the king as counselor and possessor of counsel — *Sinuhe* B 48-49; *Sallier* I 3,7; *Anastasi* V 10,4; Blumenthal 389-390; Otto, *Gott und Mensch*, 34; on the counsel given to the king in the council of officials — *Ptaḥḥotep* 250; 619; see also *sḥ* — Polotsky par. 76, A-G; *Ptaḥḥotep* 363 ff.; cf. Isa. 19,11 — "Wise men counselors of Pharoah." In the Bible: see Job 3, 14; Isa. 9,5; on the use of *ʿēṣâ* in practice see the counsel of Ahitophel and Hushai the Archite — 2 Sam. 16,17; the story of Rehabeam taking counsel — 1 Kgs. 12; cf. Prov. 15,22; 12,20; for counsel in a context of war see Prov. 20,18; 21, 30-31, etc.; cf. 2 Kgs. 18,20 — Isa. 36, 5. Also belonging to the technical terms of this semantic field are *dābār*, *hašēb dābār*, or *dabbēr dābār*, meaning "to give counsel" (Prov. 18,13; 24,26; 25,11; 26, 16, etc. Cf. Judges 20,7; 1 Kgs. 12,6,9; Job 29,21-22, in which *ʿēṣâ* || *dābār*).

63. The same meanings for *sḫr* and *ʿēṣâ* and the motifs connected with them are to be found in the religious context. The principal ones among them are: (a) The counsel of god: *sḫr nṯr* is the plan which rules the world and determines the world order (*Khakheperre-sonb*, recto 11, *Amenemope* 21,14; Isa. 25,1; 46,10, etc.). (b) The counsel of God is the measure by which the wise man conducts his life in

Israel and Egypt (*Instruction by a Man for His Son* VI 2; wisdom Ps. 73, 24); therefore, God may be described as the counselor of his believers (Ps. 16,7, cf. 20,5 and wisdom Ps. 119). Similarly, the family of Petosiris states that "they followed the plans of the head of the gods" in their endeavor to indicate their loyalty to god (Lefebvre 81, 23-26; 116, 2-6; cf. Ps. 73 above). (c) In the instructions from the New Kingdom there is a conflict between "the plan of god" and human thought: in these sources man is presented as one not being privy to god's plan, similar to the hero of the book of Job, who is exposed by God as being equally ignorant (see the repeated saying in *Amenemope* 22, 5-8; 23, 8-11; cf. *Anii* 8, 9-10 and Job 38, 2; 42,2; and cf. Prov. 19,21 to 20, 24; 21,30). In the Demotic instruction the wise man goes a step further and declares that counsel is the exclusive domain of the god (*Insinger* 22,5), while the wise men of the Bible go even beyond their Egyptian counterparts and describe God as "violating" human counsel (Job 12,17; cf. 5,13). The conflict between human counsel and the counsel of God is also expressed in Biblical historiography and reaches a peak in the prophetic literature; on this subject see: Von Rad, *Wisdom in Israel*, 97-104; idem "Josephsgeschichte," 120-127; McKane, *PWM* 48ff. and *TDOT* VI, 171 ff.

64. See Brunner, *Erziehung*, 51-52. This is also the opinion of Zimmerli, *SAIW* 178-184, 320-321; but Gemser, ibid. 208-219 argues that *'ēṣâ* when appearing in the wisdom literature means a command against which there is no appeal; similarly, Kovacs "Is there class-ethic," 185.

65. But here the root *nḏ* is used and not *sḫr* see, n. 56 above.

66. In the autobiographies the high officials often claim to be "knower (*rḫ*) who taught (*sbꜣ*) himself knowledge (*rḫ*) by accepting counsel;" see, e.g., *AEA* 111, 19; 112, 12-13 and Brunner, *Erziehung*, 51-52.

CHAPTER TWO

1. For the nominal forms of *ysr, ykḥ, yrh* see there. Here we provide only some brief complementary notes on the verbal forms: *ysr* — unlike the noun *mûsār* the verb *ysr* is not typical of wisdom lexicon (cf. Chap. 1, n. 12). Like the analogous Egyptian verb *sbꜣ*, *ysr* has a double meaning (in niph'al and pi'el): "to teach" (ex. Prov. 19, 18; 29,17, Job 4,3; etc.) and "to punish by physical chastisement" (1 Kgs. 11, 14; 2 Chr. 10, 11, 14; Deut. 21, 18; 22, 18; Ps. 6, 2; 38, 2; etc; Jer. 31, 17). *ykh* — this verb (in hiph'il) is not exclusive to the Biblical wisdom vocabulary either. It appears 25 times in the wisdom literature out of 54 times in the Bible. The primary meaning of *ykḥ* is "to straighten," from which derives "to accuse," "to reprove," and also "to punish" in order to correct (e.g. Prov. 3, 12; 25, 12; Job 5, 17; 6, 25-26; 13, 10 and cf. p. 38 above). *yrh* — the root *yrh* (in hiph'il) means "to teach," "to direct towards the right way." Its occurrence is not limited to the wisdom books, where it appears only 13 times out of 49 times in the Bible (e.g., Prov. 9, 8; 25, 12; Job 6, 25-26; 13, 10; etc.).

2. Cf. Hurvitz, *Wisdom Language*, 116-117.

3. However, we reject Couroyer's suggestion to regard *lmd* as the Hebrew equivalent of *sbꜣ*; see above, pp. 37ff.

4. Cf. the expression *malmad habbāqār*, i.e., "the goad of the ox" (Judg. 3, 31)

and Weinfeld, *Deuteronomy* 303 n. 3. For a similar connotation of the verb *sb3* in Egyptian see above, p. 32.

5. Cf. Prov. 5, 13; Ps. 119, 99 with *Amenemope* 27, 15; *Anastasi* V 23, 6 and Isa. 50, 4; 54, 13; 1 Chr. 25, 8 with Blumenthal G2 23,24; for further discussion on the root *lmd* see below, p. 68—69.

6. *'lp*, which appears once in qal, means "to learn" (Prov. 22, 25). The common connotation in modern Hebrew, i.e., animal training, is not found in the Bible.

7. *byn* (hiph'il) stands in synonymous parallelism with *drk* (hiph'il) and *yrh* (hiph'il) in Ps. 119, 34-35; Job 6, 14 and with *lmd* (pi'el) in Isa. 40, 14; cf. *BDB* 107/3; for further discussion on *byn* see below, pp. 67ff., 243ff.

8. For further discussion of the verb *śkl* see below, p. 68.

9. The summary presented here is general and does not distinguish between the lexemes except where this is relevant to the subject.

10. Besides God, who appears as the instructor of the congregation (further exx.: Exod. 24, 12; Isa. 2, 3; Mic. 4, 2; Ps. 27, 11; cf. 25, 8, 12), the representatives of the religious-ritualistic establishment, namely, the priests, the prophets and the Levites, also function as teachers of God's laws: 1 Sam. 12, 23; Isa. 9, 14; 28, 9 ff; Lev. 10, 11; 14, 56; Deut. 24, 8; Ezek. 44, 23; Neh. 8, 7-9; 2 Chr. 35, 3.

11. Cf. also *Ankhesheshonqy* 4, 16-17; *Insinger* 8, 21; *Instruction by a Man for His Son* I 1.

12. See pp. 2, 4 and n. 1, above.

13. *šbd* in Egyptian (Copt.[B] ϣⲃⲱⲧ) is borrowed from the Semitic, see *Wb.* IV 442, 13.

14. See also *Lansing* 11, 1; *Anastasi* V 8, 5-6; *Sallier* I 7,11, etc.

15. Cf. also Prov. 17, 10: "A reproof enters more into a wise man than a hundred stripes into a fool" with *Sallier* I 7,11: "to get a hundred stripes as punishment."

16. Beatings were also common practice in the schools in the times of the Mishna and the Talmud. See M. Arzt, "The Teacher in Talmud," in *Kaplan Jubilee Volume*, 35 ff. To the verbs in the Bible belonging to the semantic field of "to teach," one can add the verb *drk* (hiph'il) meaning to "guide" (lit. "to show the way"). Although it appears just once in Prov. 4, 11, it stands in synonymous parallelism with other verbs mentioned above, namely, *yrh* (ibid.), *byn* (see n. 7), and *lmd* (Ps. 25, 5; Isa. 48, 17). Usually the sage functions as the guide while the object of the guidance is wisdom, but in the religious context God is the guide, teaching his precepts (Ps. 107, 7; 119, 35 [wisdom Ps.]; Isa. 42, 16; 48, 17; etc).

17. The objects of Heb. *šm'* are diverse: some of them parallel the objects of the Eg. *sḏm*: *'ēṣâ* (|| *sḫr*, Prov. 12, 15; 19, 20; Job 29,21); *mûsār* (|| *sb3y.t*, Prov. 1, 8; 4, 1; 8, 32; 19, 27; Job 20, 3); *tôkaḥat* (|| *mtr*, Prov. 15, 32; Job 13, 6); *dibrê ḥăkāmîm* (Prov. 22, 17; Qoh. 9, 17); *'ămārîm* (Prov. 4, 10); *gᵉ'ārâ* (Prov. 13, 1, 8: Qoh. 7, 5); *millâ* (5 times in Job); *ḥokmâ* (not explicitly in Prov. 1, 33; 8, 34).

18. At times it is difficult to decide between these three meanings. The meaning of *sḏm*/*šm'* can be determined only according to the context; cf. Brunner, *Erziehung*, 131-132.

19. Cf. also *Amennakht* 2,3; *Instruction by a Man for His Son* I 2, etc.

20. The call "to hear" is also repeated in Job 13, 6,7; 15,17; 21,2; 33,1; 34,2,10,16; etc. and in Ben Sira 30,27(H); 34,22(B); 41,14; etc. The same usage of *šmʿ* is found in Biblical texts which do not belong to the wisdom literature but have wisdom features. Thus Weinfeld (*Deuteronomy*, 175-176, 304-306, 355) has pointed out that in Deuteronomy *šmʿ* has the sense of listening, obeying a parent's instruction (Deut. 21, 18), and that the imperative form *šᵉmaʿ*, with which the teacher addresses his pupil (Prov. 5, 7; 7, 24, etc.), was adapted and used by the Deuteronomist to address the people "and now, O Israel, hear..." (Deut. 4, 1; cf. 5, 1; 6, 4; 9, 1 etc. and also *haskēt wûšᵉmaʿ*, ibid. 27, 9).

21. Cf. Lang, *Die weisheitliche Lehrrede*, 29 n. 11.

22. See Bühlmann, *Von rechten Reden*, 200 ff. For the legal sense of *šmʿ* cf. 1 Kgs. 3, 11; Deut. 1, 16-17 and also section "A Hearing Heart," below. *šemû* also appears in Akkadian in a legal context see Caselles, *SVT* 15, 109-110 and cf. the imperfective active plural participle in Eg. of *sḏmyw*, meaning "judges," (Gr 593).

23. Cf. also *The Eloquent Peasant* B2 114; *Urk.* IV 1114,3,7 (*Rekhmire*) and *Wb.* IV 386, 3-13.

24. This sense of *sḏm* is clear when it parallels *wḏʿ* ("to pass judgement"); thus in *The Eloquent Peasant* B1 234: "You were appointed in order to investigate (*sḏm*) and to judge between two (*wḏʿ snwj*)"; cf. *Mentuhotep* 12. More on this subject can be found in my article "A New Source."

25. Kayatz, *Studien*, 129-134, has pointed out the different and common features regarding the "hearing" motif in the first collection of Proverbs and in the Egyptian instructions and school writings.

26. A unique usage of the root *šmʿ* in the Bible, not found in the Egyptian sources under discussion, is its adaptation to the religious sphere: the warning to hear God's commands appears frequently in Deut. (9, 23, etc. cf. n. 20 above), in prophecy (e.g., Jer. 7, 28), in historiography (1 Sam. 15, 22; 1 Kgs. 20, 36) and in Ps. (e.g., 106, 25).

27. For more extensive treatment of this subject see my article "Some Idioms," 203-206.

28. On this function of the heart, see also the next section and pp. 299—302 below.

29. Cf. Prov. 20, 12 for a similar idea that God bestows "a listening ear" (without mentioning "heart").

30. H. Brunner, "Das hörende Herz," who did not refer to the above section from Amenḥetep, not yet available to him. I wish to thank Professor Brunner for calling my attention to this reference; cf. also idem "Zentralbegriffe," 411-412.

31. On this concept of "heart" in the Bible, see pp. 299—302 below.

32. Cf. the usage of *šmʿ* in a legal context in the Bible and see n. 22 above. In the light of Deut. 1, 16-17 where *šmʿ* means "to judge," Weinfeld (*Deuteronomy*, 246 ff.) regards the paragraph in 1 Kgs. 3 as belonging to the Deuteronomist; see also McKane (*PWM* 108-109), who translates *lēb šōmēaʿ* as "legal acumen" and understands (ibid. 59) the words of the woman of Tekoaʿ to David — "for as an angel of God so is my lord the King to discern (*lišᵉmōaʿ*) good and bad, therefore the Lord, thy God, will be with thee" (2 Sam. 14, 17) — as a reference to David's ability to pass judgement.

33. Of this opinion are Brunner, Liver and others; cf. my article "Some Idioms," 211 nn. 6, 7.

34. A different interpretation is given by Johnson, *The Vitality*, 78 n.3 who assumes that *ntn 'el lēb* in Qoh. 7,2; 9,1 means "to bear in mind."

35. *Amenemope* 3, 11: "It is profitable to put them in your heart (*di.t st m ib.k*), woe to him who neglects them"; *Anii* 7, 4: "Enter the writings, put them in your heart (*imi sn m ib.k*)"; cf. Brunner, "Das Herz," 83. Gardiner's interpretation (Gr §184, §303), followed by Faulkner (155), that *rdi m ib* means "to determine," does not conform with the examples mentioned above.

36. In the Egyptian religious sphere the "giving of god's way" or the presence of the god himself in the heart are mentioned. Hence, the writer of the biography advises living mortals that: "it is useful to walk in the way of the god. He who encloses it in his heart (*di.s m ib.f*) will achieve greatness; a monument in this world is the one who puts his (the god's) way in his heart" (*di wꜣ.t.f m ib.f*, *Petosiris* above); "I will put the god in my heart" says the believer (*di.i...m ib.i*) (*Naos des Nefer*, Assmann, *SAL* 18); see also ibid. 26 — *Turin Stele* 196; cf. *ÄHG* 75, 23 and below, pp. 308ff.

37. E.g., *Ptaḥḥotep* 543: "How good for a son to grasp (*šsp*) his father's words"; also ibid. 564; *Amennakht* 6; *Anii* 9, 16.

38. Outside wisdom literature the verbs *'ḥz* and *tpś*, semantic parallels of *ṯy* and *šsp* are used. These verbs in certain contexts assume the meaning of "being skilled" and have equivalents in Akkadian; cf. Cant. 3, 8: *'ăḥuzê ḥereb mᵉlummᵉdê milḥâmâ*; Jer. 2, 8: *tōpᵉśê hattôrâ*; see also Gen. 4, 21; Amos 2, 15 and the usage of *'ḥz* in Qoh. 2, 3 and 7, 18; cf. Weinfeld, *Deuteronomy*, 163 n. 3.

39. *leqaḥ* appears 6 times in Prov., once in Job, 5 times in BS, and twice in other books (Deut. Isa.); the Hebrew phrases *qabbēl mûsār* (Prov. 19, 20) and *haḥăzēq bammûsār* (ibid. 4, 13) also belong to this context and should be compared to *ṯy sbꜥ.t* in Dem. and *šsp* + object in Eg.

40. Thus McKane, *Proverbs*, 489; cf. also *zak liqḥî* — Job 11, 4.

41. It seems that *lqḥ mûsār* was taken from the wisdom vocabulary and adapted for use in prophetic vocabulary where it has a negative connotation — disobedience to God (Jer. 17, 23; 32, 33; 35, 13; Zeph. 3, 2, 7) and refusal to learn from God's punishment (Jer. 2, 30; 5, 3).

42. In our examples *iri sbꜣy.t* appears only in *El Amarna* inscriptions, where it denotes obedience to the king's instruction: "My master has advanced me for I have carried out his instruction by listening to him," says the high official (Sandman 60, 4-5, cf. ibid. 77, 5-6).

43. *smn sbꜣy.t* appears only once in the present corpus in *Anii* 10, 7, and refers to bull training: "remembering his lesson," the bull obeys his master. "Lesson" (*sbꜣy.t*) in this context relates to the practice of mastering an animal by means of beating; cf. Lichtheim, *Literature*, vol. II, 144.

44. *nḏr tp rd* belongs to the milieu of the king's court (see *Urk.* IV 384,10; 489, 4) and appears only once in an Egyptian wisdom text in our corpus (*Admonitions* 11, 4).

45. See p. 59 and n. 37, above.

46. Cf. Dürr, *Das Erziehungswesen*, 110; Lang, *Frau Weisheit*, 172-173.

47. *nṣr* is a semitic root (*BDB* 665; *KBL* 631; *TWAT* V, 578) whose cognate in Egyptian is the verb *nḏ*, "to protect" (see Hodge, "Egyptian and Survival," 407) and not *nḏr* (*ÄgHWb* 91). Outside the wisdom literature *nṣr* + objects appears only twice in a religious context referring to observing and keeping the covenant (Deut. 33, 9; Ps. 25, 10).

48. Cf. Hurvitz, *Wisdom Language*, 106-108.

49. Cf. ibid. 196. *nṣr* and *ṣpn* stand in antithetic parallelism with the following stems: *nṣr* # *lwz* (Prov. 3, 21), *ntš* (ibid. 6, 20), *škḥ* (ibid. 3, 1); *ṣpn* # *mwš* (Job. 23, 12) — all relating to the semantic field of "neglecting," "forgetting." For the construction *nṣr*, *šmr* + parts of the body as objects relating to the semantic field of "silence" see pp. 172—173 below.

50. Cf. the words of a pupil in a Ramesside text: "I have (now) entered into your instruction (*ʿḳ r sb3y.t*) and I did consider the counsel (*sḫr*) when I was with you" (Fischer-Elfert, "Ich bin das Schiff," 8).

51. According to Calice § 15, *ʿrḳ* is connected to the Semitic root *ʿḳl* meaning "to understand" in Arab.; see also Cohen, *Essai comparatif* §46.

52. Cf. *Wb.* I 348-349 and see the discussion on *ṯs* below, pp. 313—317

53. Cf. *Wb.* I 348, 15.

54. *The Onomasticon of Amenemope* is defined at its beginning as "An instruction for understanding of the heart (*sb3y.t wḥʿ ib*)," i.e., an instruction for understanding by means of the heart.

55. This reading accords with Volten II,25 and with Lichtheim, *Literature* III, 192. In *Pap. Anastasi* I the scribe also asks questions of his friend in the same manner in which God asks Job (38, 1 ff.). In Job the questions cannot be answered for they deal in subjects which lie beyond the scope of man — "Therefore I have declared without understanding things too wonderful for me without knowing" (Job 42, 3). Whether the material in Job is taken from an onomasticonic list, as suggested by von Rad ("Hiob 38," 293ff.), or not, the scheme of "questions and answers" takes us back to the teaching methods of the ancient school.

56. See, for example, a letter formula in which the verb *ʿm* replaces *rḫ* which is commonly used in this context — "See, this letter is for the information (*r rdi.t ʿm*) of my master" (*Sallier* I 4, 5-6).

57. *ʿm* means "to know," particularly when the reference is to secret information which must "be swallowed," i.e., hidden; cf. *Wb.* I 184, 10ff.; ibid. 14 *ʿm ib* — "to swallow, to hide in the heart."

58. See Posener, *RdÉ* 10 (1955), 61 ff.

59. Lang, *Frau Weisheit*, 127.

60. See Whybray, *Wisdom in Proverbs*, 13-14; Lang, *Frau Weisheit*, 122, 127-131, 140.

61. Cf. also the Hebrew verb *ydʿ* below, pp. 232ff.

62. See Whybray, *The Intellectual*, 126-127; for a discussion of other forms of *byn* and further details regarding its meaning see below, pp. 243ff.

63. *mēbîn* appears 6 times in Prov. out of 21 times in the Bible.

64. Further objects of understanding are "knowledge" (*dāʿat*, Prov. 19, 25; 29, 7 etc.), "riddle" (*ḥîdâ*, Dan. 8, 23), "books" (*sᵉpārîm*, ibid. 9, 2), "learning" (*maddāʿ*, ibid. 1,4) and "Torah" (Neh. 8, 8).

65. Cf. also Isa. 6, 10; Dan. 10, 12.

66. For *lmd* in pi‘el see discussion above, p. 47. The root *lmd* appears only 4 times in Prov., Job. and Qoh., but 11 times in BS, 26 times in Ps. (14 of them in wisdom Pss.) and 17 times in Deut. where the sons figure as those who learn (4, 10; 11, 19; 31, 13).

67. See discussion of *ḥqr* and *bqš* below.

68. Outside the wisdom literature *lmd* often appears in a religious context. It refers to the relationship between God and his believers, the objects of learning being the knowledge of God (Jer. 31, 34) and God's laws and commands (wisdom Ps. 119, 71, 73; cf. Deut. 5, 1 etc.); and another object common in this setting, but a negative one which "should not be learned," is "the ways of the nations" (Deut. 18, 9; wisdom Ps. 106, 35).

69. The verbal form appears 10 times in Biblical wisdom books (6 in Job, 3 in Prov., once in Qoh.), 9 times in BS, and 16 times in other books; the nominal form seems to be typical of wisdom parlance, appearing 8 times in Biblical wisdom literature (6 in Job, 2 in Prov.), twice in BS, and 4 times in other books. Only those examples relevant to the subject of the chapter will be treated.

70. See also the discussion of this verse in the section on *ḏ‘r* below.

71. In this context the verb *ḥpś* ("to look for") appears once as synonym of *bqš* see, Prov. 2, 4; and cf. Lam. 3, 40 where *ḥpś* parallels *ḥqr*.

72. See Westermann, *Die Begriffe*, 167-169.

73. Cf. Job 28, 12 ff, where a similar idea is expressed.

74. Cf. Meeks I, 445.

75. See Chap. 1, n. 66, and cf. also Mentuhotep (pl. 22 l. 3) who states that he was "one instructed by his (own) nature (*sb3.n bit.f*) like a child who grows up with a father," i.e. that he was a self-made man; see Petrie, *Tombs of the Countries and Oxyrhynkhos* (London 1925), 19, pl. xxii.

76. Cf. Brunner, *AW* 221; Crenshaw, *O.T. Wisdom*, 214. Khakheperre-sonb's desire to create new words is, as far as I can see, exceptional in ancient Egyptian literature, cf. Chap. 9, n. 23.

77. Cf. Num. 13, 2 and Gen. 42, 34 where Copt. ϫⲱⲣ replaced the roots *twr* and *rgl* in Hebrew: see Crum 781.

78. *Wb.* V 540; C. Ockinga, "*Kha‘kheperrēsonbu*," 90 n. 10.

79. Outside wisdom literature *ḏ‘r* also refers to "investigation" of "message" (*wpw.t*) and of the "truth" (*m3‘.t*); cf. *CT* V 269; *Urk.* IV 1344, 20 and also ibid. 57, 15, Faulkner 320 and Goedicke, *Neferyt*, 57 n. g.

80. See *Anastasi* III 3, 10-11; V 8, 3; 9, 1; 10, 3: Cf. Prov. 3, 3; 7, 3; 22, 20, etc. The verb "to read" in Eg. *šdi* should also be mentioned in this context. It appears only twice in the present corpus (*Anastasi* III 3, 10 || V 8, 3).

CHAPTER THREE

1. Our translation of the expression "*itḥ.k* <*tw*> *m-di.i*" differs from that of Caminos and Lichtheim, who translate: "You have dragged yourself from me as regards hearkening" (*LEM* 381-382); "you resist listening to me" (*Literature* II, 169); to the meaning "to tie up" for *itḥ*, see Lesko I 61.

2. Erichsen 80; the term does not appear in the Demotic sources included in this corpus.

3. Only twice is the object different: In *Rekhmire* (Sethe, *Die Einsetzung des Veziers* 11), the theme is the function of the vizier to receive petitions and in this context he is ordered not to disdain those who appeal to him; and in *Khakheperre-sonb* (recto 11) it is "the ordinances of the gods (*mẖr.w*)" which "are neglected (*wni*)."

4. This is confirmed by the fact that *sḏm* stands in antithetic parallelism with *wni* (see *Amennakht* 4; *Instruction by a Man for His Son* I 2; cf. also *Amenemope* 3, 12; *Seḥetep-ib-Ra* 8, 5).

5. *Wb.* III 227.

6. *Wb.* II 163.

7. Erichsen 437.

8. *Wb.* III 454.

9. This use is common principally in the Greek Period when the verb *sni* comes with the preposition *r*. On the semantic development of *sni* cf. Ockinga, "The Burden," 93-94; unlike Ockinga, we do not separate *sni* and *sni r* in our discussion since it seems that the Egyptian scribe considered them to be a single lexeme, which, e.g., is confirmed by the fact that in the identical verses in *Seḥetep-ib-Ra* (7,6 and 8,5) *sni* and *sni r* appear interchangeably, having the same sense — "imitate my example."

10. There is a remarkable similarity between these utterances and sayings that appear in the Biblical wisdom, albeit not necessarily in reference to learning or wisdom but rather in connection with the commandments of God and his deeds. Cf. the words of Agur: "Every word of God is pure... Do not add to his words" (Prov. 30,5,6); or Qoheleth: "Whatever God does endures forever; nothing can be added to it, nor anything taken from it" (3,14). Also BS 18,6 (Gr.): "Nothing is to be taken away and nothing added" (cf. Deut 4,2 ; 13,1).

11. Cf. Brunner's translation — "übertreibe sie nicht" (*AW* 115). This passage has been preserved as a remnant of ancient Egyptian wisdom in the writings of the Coptic monastery. Here too the teacher desires "not to overlook matters." See Brunner, "*Ptaḥḥotep* bei den koptischen Mönchen," 145ff. In Coptic the verb ⲟⲩⲱⲧⲃ̄ appears (identical with the Eg. *wḏb*), that is, "to delimit." In Brunner's view, the passage in Coptic may be understood in the light of the verse in *The Instruction of Ptaḥḥotep.* It is true that in the latter source the verb *sni* appears and not *wḏb*, which is parallel to ⲟⲩⲱⲧⲃ̄ , but he claims that the two words ⲟⲩⲱⲧⲃ̄ and ⲥⲉⲓⲛⲉ , that is, *sni* in Egyptian, are synonyms in Coptic.

12. Thus also in *Seḥetep-ib-Ra* 8,5 (and other mss.) — "Do not go beyond my example (*m sni ḳd.i*)"; TC — "Copy my example (*sni r ḳd.i*)." Although the two verses (7,6 and 8,5) are identical, Brunner translates each of them differently: 7, 6 — "*Ahmt mein Wesen nach*"; 8,5 — "*Geht nicht an meinen Wesen vorbei*" (*AW* 182).

13. For this meaning of *thi* ("to err"), see *To Merikare* 52; *The Eloquent Peasant* B1 281; *The Man Who Was Tired of Life* 11, and cf. the Hebrew equivalent *šgh* (hiph‘il) (Prov. 28,10; wisdom Ps. 119,10) which belongs to the wisdom terminology; cf. Weinfeld, *Deuteronomy*, 278; Hurvitz, *Wisdom Language*, 111.

14. Cf. *Wb.* V 320.

15. Cf. "Hesitate before a foe (*rḳ3*), bend before a transgressor (*n thw*)" — *Amenemope* 5, 12; and also *The Eloquent Peasant* B1 236.

16. *mḏd w3.t/mṯn* belongs to the language of the king's court beginning with

the Old Kingdom. In the 11th Dynasty's writings it appears in synonymous parallelism with the term "sure-footed" (Polotsky par. 5B); and in the texts of the Middle and New Kingdoms the officials extensively employ *mḏd w3.t/mṯn* to demonstrate their obedience and devotion to the king (e.g., *Urk.* IV 898,15; Blumenthal 341; Janssen I pp. 70-71). The hieroglyph designating *mḏd* is not uniform (see Janssen ibid.). Nevertheless, we concur with the view (of Janssen II pp. 103-104 and cf. Vogelsang, *Kommentar zu den Klagen des Bauern*, 163) that the description here is of a winepress, since the hieroglyph which signifies *šsp.w*, the god of pressing wine and oil, is identical to some of the hieroglyphs accompanying *mḏd* (see *Wb.* IV 534, 13 and Janssen I p.70, Bc 13, 14). Thus one may conclude that the primary sense of *mḏd* was "press," "squeeze," and when used as an epithet it means a man who submits (lit. "is pressed") to the will of another person. This interpretation of the hieroglyph *mḏd* is not accepted by Gardiner who sees in it the drawing of a "warp stretched between two uprights" and therefore assumes that *mḏd* means "to make straight" (Gr A23,24 n. 1).

17. Cf. also *The Instruction of Ptaḥḥotep* 273-274: "About him who rebuffs petitioners, men say: 'Why does he reject (*thi*) them?'" On the same subject *Rekhmire* 11: "Do not pass over (*m wni*) a petitioner before you have attended to his pleas."

18. See *Wb.* V 319-320 esp. 319,20-320,4.

19. Thus according to Griffith's translation. But according to Brunner, Lichtheim and Lange, it is "Do not shout against one who attacked you."

20. See Gr A14*.

21. See also *Insinger* 35,3; and cf. ibid. 34,17.

22. See below, pp. 92-93.

23. Cf. *BDB*: *'zb* 737, 2a; *swr* 693, 1; *nṭh* 640, 3. This collocation is characteristic of wisdom literature: in Proverbs, Job and the wisdom Psalms (34,15; 37,27) 11 times; in prophecy it appears only once (Isa. 59,15).

24. Cf. the combination *šgh* + *m^e*, which in meaning parallels *swr* + *m^e* but occurs only once in Prov. 19,27 (and 3 times in wisdom Ps. 119, 10,21,118); see *BDB* 993 and Hurvitz, *Wisdom Language*, 110-111.

25. Cf. Y. Kaufmann, *The Book of Judges*, 131-132; C.F. Burney, *The Book of Judges*, 106-109; *KBL* 779.

26. The synonymous phrase *swr min derek* regularly appears in the Deuteronomic literature, often associated with a religious background, and its meaning is "to turn away" from God; see Weinfeld, *Deuteronomy*, 339; cf. *Anii* 3,4.

27. The combination *'qš* + *derek* or *'ōrah* appears five times in Proverbs. Cf. the synonymous expression *n^{e}lôz* + *derek/ma'gāl* (Prov. 14,2; 2,15).

28. The application of the sapiential word pair *tm* —*'qš* was investigated by W. Brueggemann, "A Neglected Sapiental Word Pair," *ZAW* 89(1977), 234-258.

29. See n. 16.

30. Cf. also *pls* + *ma'gāl*, *'ōraḥ*, *nātîb* in the sense of "to straighten," "to smooth" (Prov. 4,26; 5,6, 21; wisdom Ps. 78,50); *hlk* + *b^{e}derek* (Prov. 1,15; 2, 20; etc.); *hlk* + *'ōraḥ* (ibid. 8,20); *'aššēr b^{e}derek* (ibid. 4,14; 9,6; 23,19); *sll* + *derek*, *'ōraḥ* (ibid. 15,19; Job 19,12).

31. We found one term parallel in meaning in *Anastasi* III 4,3 where the young

scribe is told: "Do not be lazy! Write! Do not feel disgust! (*ft*)."

32. See *BDB* 610.

33. It is worth mentioning another verb in this connection, namely, *'bh* ("be willing"). Even though it appears only twice in Proverbs (1,25,30) and does not belong directly to the semantic subject under discussion, it again indicates that the early educators recognized that obligation was not enough to lead to study, but that learning also depended on the willingness of the pupil.

34. Rössler, 287, par. 7, compares it with the Semitic (Akka., Ugar., Syr. and Heb.) root *yšb* (*sitzen*).

35. *Wb.* I 357.

36. Our interpretation accords with that given by Perry, *The Eloquent Peasant*, 534. Another view is held by Assmann (*Ma'at*, 60-69), who assumes that this verse relates to the lack of a conscience on the part of the lazy man who habitually forgets the events of the past.

37. Thus Glanville in 70 nn. 82,83; but Lichtheim (*LEWL*) translates *ẖsy* with "slack" and Thissen "*schwach*," "*müde*."

38. In Proverbs it appears 15 times, in Qoheleth once.

39. We find an approach similar to that of Proverbs in *The Instruction of Ankhsheshonqy*, but there the verb is *ẖsy*, not *wsf*. The words of Qoheleth (10,18), citing the popular saying "Through sloth (*'ăṣaltayim*) the floor sinks in, and through indolence (*šiplût yādayim*) the house leaks," are close to the admonition of *The Eloquent Peasant*, in that they intimate the indolence of the country's leaders, to whom the preceding verses (B1 16, 17) refer.

40. Once more in Jer. 48,10; cf. *BDB* 941.

41. Cf. *Wb.* I 357,3. The antonym of the adjective *'āṣēl*, *ḥārûṣ*, appears only in Proverbs (collocated with *yād* or *nepeš* — 10,4; 12,24; 13,4). *ḥārûṣ* usually appears in connection with accumulation of property diligently and honestly, (cf. ibid. 21,5). In the Egyptian corpus of this research we have found no lexeme identical in meaning to *ḥārûṣ*. *iḳr* has a similar sense when it is combined with a noun, for example, *iḳr m ḏb'.w.f*, that is, "diligent (lit. "excellent") with his fingers." See *GM* 3, 9ff.; *GM* 4, 41ff.

42. *Wb.* III 473-474; in Copt. [S] ⲥⲱϩ; p ⲥⲱϩ— "to be deaf."

43. *sẖy* is often synonymous with the phrase "he who does not hear (*sḏm*)" (*Koller* 2,5; *Anastasi* I 6,5-6; IV 2,7), or in proximity with the root *sḏm* (*The Eloquent Peasant* B1 113, 188); *sẖy* also appears in synonymous parallelism with "blind" (*The Eloquent Peasant*, ibid.).

44. *Wb.* I 151. *idi* appears regularly in the Literature of the Dead and in medical texts of the Middle Kingdom.

45. Following Helck, our reading is *sḏm ḥr idw*, that is, "when the hearer is deaf" (*Neferti* 38).

46. See *LEM* 131. According to *Wb.* V 470, 2, the subject is a defective ear.

47. Cf. this phrase with the following expressions bearing the opposite meaning: "the instruction enters the ear" (*'ḳ r msḏr.t*), "to fill the ear" (*mḥ m msḏr*), i.e., "to pay attention," "to be vigilant."

48. See above, p. 79.

49. Cf. below, p. 168.

50. The figurative use of "deaf" appears in Psalms and prophecy. Being among people who seek to take his life, the pious man makes the following comparison: "I am like a deaf man, I do not hear, like a dumb man who does not open his mouth" (Ps. 38,14). Elsewhere the psalmist describes the wicked man as "a deaf adder that stops up (*ya'ṭēm*) her ear" (58,5). The phraseology used by Deutero-Isaiah to describe the obstinate people is closer to the Egyptian: "...the people who are blind, yet have eyes, who are deaf, yet have ears" (43,8); "Hear, you deaf, and look you blind that you may see. Who is blind but my servant, or deaf as my messenger that I send?... He sees many things, but does not observe them; his ears are open but he does not hear" (42,8-20; cf. the opposite situation in the future, in Isa. 29,18). As in Egyptian, the metaphor of deafness indicates the refusal to listen and to obey. But while in the Egyptian school literature deafness is a reaction to the teacher's instruction, in Biblical prophecy and in Psalms its object is the words of God. The linguistic usages found in this context in the Bible and some of which are close to the Egyptian parallels are: (a) Parallelism: *ḥērēš* appears in synonymous (or in complementary) parallelism with *'iwwēr* ("blind") (Isa. 29,18; 42,18, 19, cf. *sẖy*), and in antithetic parallelism with *šm'* ("hear") (Ps. 38,14; Isa. 29,18; etc.; cf. *sẖy, idw*); (b) The verb *ḥrš* is collocated with the noun *'ōzen* (see Mic. 7,16; Isa. 35,5; 43,8 and cf. in Egyptian *msḏr.t dnrg*); (c) In Proverbs phrases appear that are comstructed with a verb (*'ṭm*, *kbd*, etc.), followed by the object *'ōzen*. These terms parallel semantically the terms signifying "deafness" in Egyptian and in non-wisdom sources in the Bible (see below).

51. Cf. ⲧⲁϫⲟ, in Copt.; see Meeks I, 76, *Wb.* I 241 and *ÄgHWb* 31. Devaux (*ZÄS* 61, 110-111) asserts that the Copt. form derived from *'ḏ3* is ⲟϫⲓ [B] and not ⲟϫ, ⲱϫ [S], which derives from *iṯ3* — "steal."

52. See Blackmann, *JEA* 22, 44. The adjective *'ḏ3* means "to be guilty" in a legal context and it does not belong to the semantic field under review. Its antonym is *p3 m3'.tw* — "the innocent"; see *Wb.* I 241, 7; *Anastasi* II 6, 7; *Bologna* 1094 2,6-7; etc.

53. "Abomination to god" are: lying speech and hypocrisy (*Amenemope* 13, 15-16; 14,2-3), writing false testimony (ibid. 15,20-21), and falsification of weights and measures (ibid. 18,23-19,1).

54. Collocations of interest for comparison with the Bible are: man of deceit, liar — *rmt 'ḏ* (Dem.); false matter, speech — *mdy 'ḏ3*, *mt.t* (*n*) *'ḏ* (Dem.); perjury — *'nḫy n 'ḏ3*; *'rḳ 'ḏ* (Dem.); false testimony — *mty n mdy n s'ḏ3*; a deceitful act — *sp n 'ḏ3*.

55. Calice No. 886 suggests that *grg* may be connected with the Arab. *qrq*, "to cheat."

56. In the sense of "to utter lying words," *grg* usually serves as a direct object of the verb "say" — *ḏd* (e.g., *The Man Who Was Tired of Life* 98; *Admonitions* 13, 2; *Peasant* B1 132-133; 160; cf. "lying speech" *tp.t r3 gry.t* — *Urk.* IV 1180, 7).

57. The image of a gardner and a garden appears in this context in the Bible too. Proverbs 11,18 speaks of the sower of righteousness whose reward is truth, while the wicked man who sows falsehood has falsehood as his wages; cf. Job 8, 16-17.

58. It is hard to translate the term *m3'.t*. Scholarship commonly equates it

with the Hebrew *ṣedāqâ* and translates it with "truth," "justice." For further discussion of this term, see pp. 107, 268—270.

59. See Brunner, "Gerechtigkeit."

60. See Klopfenstein's exhaustive monograph on *šeqer* in the Bible: *Die Lüge nach dem A.T.*

61. The term *'ēd beliyya'al* is explicable against the background of the story of Naboth's vineyard, which sheds light on its *Sitz im Leben*. *beliyya'al* men testify falsely against Naboth and bring about his death (1 Kgs. 21,10,13); cf. Klopfenstein, *Die Lüge*, 23-36;272.

62. See Bühlmann, *Von rechten Reden*, 137-167.

63. See Klopfenstein, *Die Lüge*, 171ff.

64. Cf. *'akzāb*, i.e., water that disappoints, causes despair because it dries up — Jer. 15,18; and *tōḥaltô nikzābâ*, i.e., "hope in him is in vain" (Job 41,1).

65. Once the phrase *'ēd kezābîm* appears in antithetic parallelism with *'îš šômēa'* (Prov. 21, 28).

66. The homonymous noun *remiyyâ* bearing the sense of "slackness" appears 3 times in Prov.: see p. 91 above.

67. The organ that serves as the instrument of deception is the mouth. In this context appear the collocations "mouth," "lips," "tongue" + *mirmâ*. These are especially common in Psalms; cf. Ps. 10,7; 50,19; 52,6; etc.

68. See also Amos 8,5; Hos. 12,8; Mic. 6,11.

69. Cf. p. 95 above.

70. For a comprehensive discussion of the term *kḥš* in the Bible see Klopfenstein, *Die Lüge*, 254-310.

71. Cf. also *The Man Who Was Tired of Life*, who complains about the unreliability of his friends (103-130).

72. In the "abomination laws" in Deuteronomy the following deeds relating to the religious-cultic context are forbidden: craving for the graven images of the peoples of Canaan, burning of sons in the fire, offering of blemished animals as sacrifices, miscellaneous practices of sorcery and witchcraft, transvestism, sacrifices financed by earnings through prostitution or by wages of a dog, making a statue or a mask, remarrying one's previously divorced wife after she had meanwhile been another's. Only once is a social wrong mentioned: falsification of weights and measures (25, 13-16), but it seems that we have here a citation of a wisdom passage (Prov. 20,10,23; 11,1); on this matter see Weinfeld, *Deuteronomy*, 267ff.

73. See Brunner, "Gerechtigkeit." The terms belonging to the semantic field of falsehood, refer both to relations between man and his fellow men and between man and God. Included in the latter category are assertions by a pious Egyptian that he has brought to the god an offering of justice (*mȝ'.t*) and that there is no falsehood in his heart (*ÄHG* 71, 74; 214, 105-106); and in Biblical wisdom we read of the "deceit" (*rmh*) of men towards God (Job 13,7; 27,4) and the "denial" (*kḥš*) of God (Prov. 30,9; Job 31,28). Cf. Klopfenstein, *Die Lüge*, 264ff.

74. Other stylistic devices of interest are the following: (1) *'wn* appears in synonymous parallelism with *ḥnt* — "greed" (*Ptaḥḥotep* 316-317; *Peasant* B1 291) and *ḏw.t* — "evil" (*Ptaḥḥotep* 299-300; cf. ibid. 309); (2) in antithetic parallelism with *mȝ'.t* — "truth" (*Ptaḥḥotep* 312 # 315; cf. also ibid. 91,97; *Peasant* B2 110),

and *sfn* — "be kindly," "kindness" (*Ptaḥḥotep* 318-319; *Peasant* B1 117); (3) in *Ptaḥḥotep* L2 91, *'wn ib* of P 91 is replaced by *ḫm ḫ.t* ("fool").

75. A. de Buck, *Egyptian Readingbook*, 117,15ff.

76. Cf. Fecht, *Der Habgierige*, and also Assmann, *Ma'at*, 85-89, whose discussion agreės with ours.

77. The words of the sage in *Ptaḥḥotep* 315 are understandable in light of the "Confession of the Dead." As stated above, covetousness is one of the negative traits in which the deceased confesses he had no part. Hence, we learn that according to the Egyptian concept someone who is guilty of covetousness does not reach the next world. In the words of Ptaḥḥotep, he is "without a tomb." In Fecht's view (*Der Habgierige*, 44) the last reference relates to the conventional Egyptian belief that a man's property ensures performance of the ritual of the dead and so assures life in the next world. The author of *Ptaḥḥotep* comes out against this concept, arguing that only a man possessing ethical values can "achieve the grave," i.e., reach the beyond.

78. In the Greek Period *'f'* signifies crocodile; see *Wb.* I 182, 13.

79. Cf. Qoh. 2,18-19, 21,26; 6,2; Ps. 49,11; etc.

80. *3f'* stands in synonymous parallelism with the terms "oppress" — *'3g* (*Amenemope* 6,14), "evildoers" — *isf.ty.w* (*Sallier* I 8,10); and in antithetic parallelism with "restraint" — *d3r ib* (*Kagemni* I 4) and "generous man" — *wstn* (*Insinger* 15,10-11,21).

81. Sometimes with metathesis *snk* (*Amenemope* 7,14; 18,8).

82. In the Late Period *ḥnty* serves as an epithet for enemy, especially the god Seth, in the image of a crocodile; see *Wb.* III 121,14.

83. *'wh* appears in Prov., Job and Qoh. 15 times out of ca. 50 times in the Bible. In BS it is mentioned 3 times.

84. Cf. passages in the Pentateuch and Psalms noting the "craving" of the people in the wilderness for the foods of Egypt (Num. 11,4,5; Ps. 106,14; 78,20ff.).

85. See also n. 79 above.

86. Prov. 4 times and Job once, out of 15 times in the Bible; BS 4 times.

87. This basic meaning of *ḥmd* is preserved in expressions such as in Gen. 3,6: "So when the woman saw that the tree was good for food and that it was a delight to the eyes, and that the tree was to be desired (*neḥmād*) to make one wise"; and in the expression "pleasing (*maḥmad*) to the eye" (1 Kgs. 20,6; Ezek. 24,16, 21,25; etc); see Wallis, *TDOT* IV, 454. Cf. also BS 40,22 (Gr.).

88. The intention is desire in thought only, for the deed is stated in the words "You shall not commit adultery (*lō' tin'āp*)."

89. So Volten's translation. Lichtheim has "water monster" and similarly *Wb.* IV 177,2, according to which *snk* is the primeval waters that the god subdued. Helck, Faulkner, Gardiner have "the greed of the water." In our opinion there is a connection between *snk*, "crocodile," and *skn*, "to be greedy." In the Egyptian world greed is associated with the crocodile, as shown in by the preceding analysis (cf. Faulkner 234, 251, *Wb.* III 318). We do not accept Redford's view ("The Sea," 843) that *snk* derives from the root *snk*, "darkness."

90. Vestiges of this myth are also found in the poorly preserved *Astarte Papyrus* which was apparently composed during the 18th Dynasty. For the

restorations of this story, in which the sea god appears in conflict with the other gods of the Egyptian pantheon, see A.H. Gardiner, in *Griffith Studies*, 74-85; J.A. Wilson, *ANET* 17-18; E.F. Wente, in W.K. Simpson (ed.), *The Literature*, 133-136; A. H. Sayce, *JEA* 19 (1933), 56-59; R. Stadelmann, *LÄ* I, 509-511 and the extensive bibliography there. For the preservation of this myth in the medical texts of the New Kingdom Period, which hint at the struggle of the god Seth against the sea and for a possible iconographic illustration of this struggle, see G. Posener, *Annuaire de l'Institut de Philologie et d'Histoire Orientales et Slaves* 13 (1953), 461-478, and A.H. Gardiner, *JEA* 19 (1933), 98.

91. See O. Kaiser, *Die mythische Bedeutung des Meers in Ägypten, Ugarit und Israel* (Berlin 1959); for the myth about God's war against the sea in the Bible, see U. Cassuto, "The Israelite Epic," in *Biblical and Canaanite Literatures* (Jerusalem 1972), 62-90; S.E. Loewenstamm, in *Comparative Studies in Biblical and Ancient Orient Literature* (*AOAT* 204) (Neukirchen-Vluyn 1980), 91-92; 346-361; 465-470; and T.L. Fenton, "Variant Approaches." See also A. Malamat, in *Studies in Bible Dedicated to the Memory of U. Cassuto* (Jerusalem 1987), 184-188 (Hebrew); and idem *Mari and the Early Israelite Experience* (Oxford 1989), 107-112, J. Day, *God's Conflict*, and N. Wyatt, *UF* 17 (1985), 375-381.

92. See Cassuto, "The Israelite Epic," 82ff; and Fenton, ibid. 351ff.

93. Nebuchadnezzar is depicted here as an insatiable monster, a voracious crocodile that sucks up the delicacies of the land, these being the Temple treasures and the leaders of the nation. Cf. W. Rudolph, *Jeremia* (Tübingen 1968), 312. In addition to the passages cited above, the crocodile is mentioned in the story of the creation — Gen. 1,21; set against a clearly Egyptian background are the transformation of the staffs of Aaron and Moses into crocodiles — Exod. 7,9-10, and the description of the Leviathan as a crocodile — Job 41; see below, pp. 142—143.

94. Wallis (*TDOT* IV, 453) suggests the following Eg. parallels for *ḥmd*: *ḥḥy* ("look for"), *mri* ("love, want"), *wḫ3* ("seek"); but these terms, in my view, do not match the supposed parallels inthe Bible, at least not in wisdom literature.

95. *Wb.* III 366.

96. In the Coptic Version ϩⲙⲙⲉ replaces the root *ḥmm* in the Bible (Job 6,17; 31,20; 37,17); see Crum 677; and Rössler, 297 par. 22.

97. See *Wb.* IV 468ff.; cf. *šmw* — "summer," *Wb.* IV 480.

98. Calice No. 285.

99. Posener, *Deir el Médineh*, II, pl. 71-73.

100. This collocation occurs 3 times in our sample: see *Hier. Ostr.* I, pl. 7,5.

101. A hint of this basic meaning of *t3w* is preserved in the image found in *The Instruction to Merikare*. There we read in a passage dealing with the suppression of rebellion: "Suppress the multitude, prevent its heat (*t3*)" (27).

102. In *The Instruction of Ptaḥḥotep t3* collocates with *ib* and *ẖ.t* (352;378). In *The Instruction of Amenemope* it is collocated with *r3*, and is always accompanied by the definite article and by the determinative of a snake and a bound man (5,10; 12,16).

103. Cf. also *r3 t3* # *hrw ḳi* ("quiet-natured") in *The Autobiography of Anhurmose*, pl. 25, l. 35 (Ockinga, *El-Mashayikh*).

104. For the counsel to avoid strife in Egyptian wisdom literature (*Instruction by a Man for His Son*, *Anii*, *Ankhsheshonqy*) and parallels in Mesopotamian wisdom, see *LEWL* 13-18.

105. *Wb*. IV 557,13-558,1.

106. *To Merikare* (colophon P) 147; *Instruction by a Man for His Son* XVIII 5; *Amenemope* 22,20; 21,10.

107. Cf. the expression *iry ṯṯt* — "a partner to a quarrel" (*Amenemope* 22, 20).

108. Further references: *Amenemope* 5,10; 12,10; 13,1.

109. *Wb*. II 456.

110. In the Coptic Version, ϣⲱⲛⲧ replaces the expressions *midyānîm* ("contention") (Prov. 21,9) and *ḥāmās* ("violence") (Prov. 3, 31); see Crum 572.

111. Mentioned in *Urk*. IV 137,14; 613,1, etc; See *Wb*. IV 520,3-5; cf. also *Instruction by a Man for His Son* VIII 6.

112. Also appears as a noun meaning "offense," "invective," but this usage is not present in our sample.

113. Thus translate by Lichtheim and Gardiner (*Admonitions* 45) but not by *Wb*.III 383, 13, which regards this as a plural adjective.

114. For a semantic discussion of the term *'np* — *'ap* in Hebrew — see Bergmann, *TDOT* I, 348 ff.

115. For this fire-shooting snake see *nsr* — *Wb*. II 335, 8; *nsr.t*, ibid. 336, 5; *ḫ.tj*, *ḫ.t.t*, ibid. III 218, 14-15; *t3.w*, ibid. V 229, 19; and also M. Görg, *BN* 8 (1979), 11-13.

116. Grapow, *Die bildlichen Ausdrücke*, 96; *LÄ* I, 350-351; ibid. V, 649, 909, and also G. Posener, *Annuaire de l'Institut de Philologie et d'Histoire Orientales et Slaves* 13 (1953), 475, and bibliography there.

117. See also *Wb*. II 340, 16; 336, 5.

118. In one instance the antonym of "hot-mouthed," i.e., the "silent man", is likened to a crocodile in its silence (ex. 7); perhaps on account of the mistaken belief, repeated in Greek literature, that the crocodile has no tongue; see Hopfner, *Der Tierkult*, 125.

119. See Grapow, *Die bildlichen Ausdrücke*, 95-96 and *LÄ* III, 794.

120. See *RÄR* 392-394, *LÄ* III 796, Hopfner, *Die Tierkult*, 131-136 and *Wb*. IV 520, 6.

121. See *RÄR* 702-715 and *LÄ* V, 909.

122. See *RÄR* 715; and also *ḫnn.w* — *Wb*. III 383, 11, 12; *nšni* — *Wb*. II 340, 15 and ibid. 341, 20.

123. For the connection between king and lion see *LÄ* III, 1086-7; on the king as Sekhmet see Blumenthal, 97-98, 102, Grapow, *Die bildlichen Ausdrücke*, 73-96, and for the fury of the latter see *Wb*. II 340, 18; 341, 21.

124. H.G. Blersch deals with the difference between the synonyms *šmm*, *srf* and *t3w* (in the Egyptian medical texts) in *Medizinhistorisches Journal* 8/1(1973), 35-51.

125. See *LÄ* II, 206.

126. We have counted ca. 10 examples. Apart from the examples given in the discussion below, see also *Neferti* 49; *Admonitions* 11, 13; *Kheti* XXIII B-C.

127. In the later wisdom instruction the *rmṯ swg*, who is eager for a quarrel, is described as an igniter of fire (*Insinger* 13, 16-17).

128. Cf. also the expressions "cool-tempered man" (*ḳb*); "cool-bellied man" (*ḳb ẖ.t*), etc. (see below, pp. 163—164) with their antonyms — "hot-tempered" (*tȝ*); "hot-bellied" (*tȝ ẖ.t*). In these examples the interplay of motifs of heat and cold, water and fire is evident. *ḳbb* means "to cool" (determinative of water flowing and a water pot), while *srf* means "heat," "flame." A similar play appears in chapter 4 of *Amenemope*, where the hot-tempered man (*šmm*) meets his end in a double punishment — in water and fire, water described here indirectly by the words "raft" (*mḫrw*) and "float" (*mḥw*), both of which are accompanied by the determinative of water; cf. also *Sallier* I 8, 5-6, in which the god Thoth is likened to a well of water that the hot-tempered man does not find and to a date tree in whose fruit are stones containing water; see below, pp. 160ff.

129. See Borghouts, "The 'hot one.'"

130. For a discussion of these terms see the section dealing with "heart," Chap. 7 below.

131. For a discussion of *Pap. Anastasi* V 7,5-8,1 see Fischer Elfert, "Dein Heisser."

132. Our view on this matter is similar to that of Borghouts ("The 'hot one'") but differs from that of Gilula (review of Grumach, 506).

133. Also in other places where synonyms of *šmm* or its antonym *grw* are mentioned, there is a religious context, e.g., *Ostracon Deir el Medineh* 1265, *Admonitions of an Egyptian Sage* 5, 3, and *Amenemope* 7, 7-9, which speaks of the "silent ones in the temple." But *šmm* and *grw* are not contrasted in these passages.

134. *ḥēmâ* appears 9 times in Proverbs, 4 times in Job and 3 times in the wisdom Psalms (twice in BS), out of 118 times in the Bible.

135. The term *ḥēmâ* is also mentioned also in Job 19, 29; 36, 18; in one instance in Job (6,4) it means "venom" (cf. the venom of animals in Ps. 58, 5 and 140, 4).

136. Cf. the following collocations in Egyptian: *ḫsf nšni* — "repress a quarrel"; *ḫsf srf* — "subdue a fire"; *'ḫm ḫ.t* — "extinguish a fire"; *ḳbb fnḏ* — "cool of anger"; *dr srf* — "subdue fire."

137. Cf. McKane, *Proverbs*, 404-405; *TDOT* V, 176.

138. See *Thesaurus* III, 29 and *TDOT* IV, 46ff.

139. *BDB* 267-268; *KBL* 250.

140. The term *zēdîm* appears in Psalms 8 times out of 13 times in the Bible. On *zēdîm* in a religious context see also n. 171 below.

141. *zwd* is used in the wisdom literature in: the collocation *'ebrat zādôn* (Prov. 21,24); synonymous parallelism: *zēd* || *rā'* (BS 12,4); *zēdîm* || *haššōgîm mimmiṣwōtèkā* (wisdom Ps. 119, 21); *zādôn* || *'azzût 'ap* (BS 10,18); antithetic parallelism: *zēd* # *māk* (i.e., modest, BS 12, 5); *zādôn* # *ṣᵉnû'îm* (Prov. 11,2).

142. *mādôn* appears in Prov. 18 times out of 22 times in the Bible.

143. Cf. the expression *ḫbw ṯṯṯ* "start a quarrel" (*Amenemope* 5,10; see *Wb.* V 413, 9). For an expression of the contrary idea, calming of a dispute, the following collocations are used: *štq mādôn* (Prov. 26,20); *yṣ' mādôn* (22,10). For their parallels in Egyptian see n. 136 above.

144. See Gemser, "The *rib*," 120ff.

145. For the legal connotation of the stem *ryb* in the Bible, see ibid., 122ff.

146. Cf. the call of the Egyptian sage to keep away from and avoid the company of the "hot-tempered" man (*Amenemope* 5,16; 11,13; 15,13; *Anii* 5, 7). *rîb* is in synonymous parallelism with *mādôn* (see under *mādôn*) and in antithetic parallelism with *šalwâ* (Prov. 17,1).

147. Cf. the meaning of the cognates of *z'm* in Syr. "scold," and in Arab. "speak angrily": *TDOT* IV,107.

148. *z'm* appears in Prov. 3 times, in the wisdom Ps. once, and in BS 5 times.

149. *TDOT* I, 351.

150. See pp. 145ff. below.

151. Six times in Prov., 4 times in Qoh., 4 times in Job; the total here is about half of all the appearances of the noun *ka'as* in the Bible. In the wisdom Psalms and BS *k's* is present as a verb (Ps. 106, 29; 112, 10; BS 3, 16).

152. See Prov. 12,16; 21,19; 27,3; Qoh. 7,9; Job 5,2.

153. We did not find in the Egyptian terminology presented above an equivalent for the Hebrew *k's*, i.e., a term expressing the idea of anger in association with pain and grief.

154. The children of Israel provoke the anger of God with their "vanities" (i.e., false gods), the "work of their hands," their "idols," etc. — Deut. 32,21; 2 Kgs. 22,17; Jer. 32,30; etc.; cf. wisdom Ps. 106,28.

155. The root *'br* appears 38 times in the Bible, out of which 14 are to be found in the wisdom literature: Prov. 8 times, Job twice, Ps. 78 four times and BS twice.

156. If the idea presented above is correct, the closest Egyptian term to *mit'abbēr* is *thw* — the violent, unruly man who "deviates" from the path.

157. In this usage *'br* appears 29 times in the Bible and it is parallel to the following terms: *'ap*, *ḥărôn 'ap*, *za'am*.

158. In Prov. 11,4, the phrase refers to the day of death mentioned there in verse 7; see Oesterley, *Proverbs*, 82 and also Toy, *Proverbs*, 221. McKane, *Proverbs*, 436, takes a different view, arguing that *yôm 'ebrâ* refers to the Day of God (cf. Zeph. 1,15, 18).

159. In this usage *z'p* approximates the Egyptian *šnṯ* and *nšni*, which are also associated with the rage of animals.

160. Cf. Oesterley, *Proverbs*, 136; McKane, *Proverbs*, 494. A similar picture of *nirgān* appears in BS 11, 31.

161. See McKane, *Proverbs*, 519; BDB 529-530.

162. See pp. 291ff. below.

163. Cf. *TDOT* I, 353/J.

164. A loose connection between *lḫ*, one of the Egyptian types of the stupid man, and anger may be present in *Insinger* 13,14-15, where the harm done through transgressions of the *lḫ* is compared to the destruction wrought by the crocodile in his anger (see p. 126 above, ex. 9).

165. Cf. also Job 10,16, where God is compared to a lion in his passion to hunt the enemy. Further on in the next verse the anger of God is referred to: "And increase your (God's) vexation against me" (ibid. 17).

166. See H. Gunkel, *Schöpfung und Chaos*, 48ff., and recently Day, *God's*

Conflict, 62ff. We know from classical sources that the description of the hunt of the Leviathan in Job 40 parallels, at least partially, the method of hunting the crocodile in Eygpt; see Hopfner, *Der Tierkult*, 131. It is interesting to compare the passage in Job with the image of Rahab, the mythical monster, enemy of God (Job 9,13; 26,12; Ps. 89,11), which also appears in parallelism with *tannîn* (Isa. 51,9). The word Rahab derives from the Semitic (Akka., Arab. or Syr., see *EMiqr* VII 329; *BDB* 923; *KBL* 875) and its literal meaning is probably "storm," "arrogance." Worthy of note is the fact that Egypt is called Rahab in Isa. 30,7; Ps. 87,4.

167. An image close to the Egyptian one is found in BS 3, 30: "Water will extinguish blazing fire," but the subject appearing in the second part of the verse — "thus righteousness will atone for sin" — is a wholly different one.

168. For examples of the use of this image in the Mesopotamian wisdom see Bryce, *A Legacy of Wisdom*, 223 n.23.

169. Drioton ("Aménémopé," 254ff.) finds in *The Instruction of Amenemope* Semitisms recognizable in the grammar, the syntax and the vocabulary. Kevin ("Amen-em-opt,"115ff.) holds a similar view; for a contrary opinion see Bryce, below.

170. Drioton, "Aménémopé," 264, translates: "A haughty man, swollen with arrogance and who busies himself with an abundance of insolence (*zādôn*), is called a *zēd*."

171. The plural adjective appears often in the wisdom Psalms (119, 21,51,69, etc. and 19,14). The *zēdîm* transgress against the Law of God and are enemies and oppressors of the pious man in Psalms (cf. 86, 14). In later prophecy they are evildoers who spurn the words of the prophets (Isa. 13,11; Jer. 43,2; Mal. 3,15,19; etc.)

172. Cf. Oesterley, *Proverbs*, 100-101; Toy, *Proverbs*, 267. The collocation *rîb zēdîm* appears once, in BS (11,9).

173. Humbert, *Recherches*, 74.

174. See, e.g., Williams, "Semitic Original," 104; Bryce, *A Legacy of Wisdom*, 66-69.

175. cf. Introduction above, p. 3.

176. Bryce, *A Legacy of Wisdom*, 67-71, 90, 120-124, 132, 228 n.3.

177. Ibid., 67.

178. For a detailed treatment of this subject, see pp. 160ff. below.

179. Following are some remarks on Bryce's analysis of *'îš ḥēmâ* which reflects the difficulties inherent in his theory. First, with regard to the adaptive stage, the verb *r'h*: the use of the verb *r'h* in hithpa'el in the Bible to express the idea of "befriend" is not unusual (see examples in *BDB* 945), and there is no call to look for any Egyptian influence in this verbal form. Concerning *šqṭ* in Prov. 15,18, furthermore, Bryce fails to see the use of the stem *štq*, which is an exact equivalent of the Egyptian terms *gr*, *sgr*. *štq* also appears in reference to "strife": "And when there is no slanderer strife (*mādôn*) is quietened (*yištōq*)" (Prov. 26, 20). It seems to us that both Prov. 15,18 and 26,20 express a truth connected with human conduct in general and do not necessarily reflect the "Egyptian model."

Second, it is hard to attribute the phrases *qᵉṣar rûaḥ*, *'erek 'appayim* and *mōšēl bᵉrûḥô* mentioned in Prov. 14,29 and 16,32 to the assimilative stage. In both verses the central Egyptian motif is missing and in its stead the Hebrew text contains a new idea. In 14,29 *q[e]ṣar rûaḥ* and *'erek 'appayim* are the symbols of foolishness and of wisdom, while *'erek 'appayim* and *mōšēl b[e]rûḥô* in 16,32 concern the capture of a city and heroism in war, but again, unlike the Egyptian, do not involve the motif of strife. At most, these terms may be linked to the integrative stage.

180. See pp. 137—138 above.

181. See p. 122 above.

182. For a discussion of *'erek 'appayim* see p. 171 below.

183. For a discussion of these terms see pp. 171—172 below.

184. The verbal use (*qṣr rûaḥ m[e]*) and the nominal use (*qōṣer rûaḥ*) appear in other books of the Bible (e.g., Job 21,4; Exod. 6,9).

CHAPTER FOUR

1. ϭⲱ means "stop," "desist"; see Crum 803/b.

2. Is there a connection with *gr*, "fish" (*Wb.* V 180,12), i.e., "silent like a fish"?

3. "Heart" here has the sense of "mind"; cf. pp. 300 below.

4. See Volten's translation of *To Merikare*, 110.

5. The god Amon is "the lord of the silence," "who loves the silent," "the protector of the silent" —— see *SAL* 24, nn. 34, 35; cf. "lord of silence" (*nb sgr*) p. 152 below.

6. The term *sgȝ* appears in the New Kingdom (*Wb.* IV 320, 7,8). Its primary meaning is "muteness," "silence," through surprise and confusion. It is connected to the verb *sgȝ* (ibid. 320, 5), "to be surprised" (Copt. ⲥⲓϭⲉ). According to *Wb.* (ibid. 7), *s.t sgȝ* refers in *Anastasi* III 1,2 to the realm of the dead. But Caminos' suggestion (*LEM* 71) that *s.t sgȝ* should be seen as a variant of *s.t sgr* and translated here with "the palace" suits the context better.

7. Cf. also *Khakheperre-sonb*, recto 12.

8. *Wb.* IV 324; Erichsen 470.

9. E.g., Zech. 1,11 and Judg. 3,30; see Crum 389; cf. the Egyptian "Becalmer of the two lands," *Wb.* IV 324, 7.

10. See also *Ptaḥḥotep* 604; Janssen I p. 108, Ff 1,2; etc.

11. *ḳb* and *ḳbḥ* interchange and from the Middle Kingdom on they are indistinguishable: see *Wb.* V 22,5. *sḳbb*, the causative form, appears once in our corpus, in the sense of "make cool" (*Urk.* IV 918, 8).

12. In the Coptic Version ⲕⲃⲟ replaces the Hebrew root *qwr*, e.g., Prov. 25,25; see Crum 100.

13. For the meaning of *fnḏ* here see p. 122 above.

14. Since the beginning of the verse is missing, the translation is uncertain; for a different translation see Brunner *AW* 191.

15. The verb *ḳb* stands in synonymous parallelism with *hrw* (Janssen I p. 35, Ba 3); in antithetic parallelism with *štm* (*Instruction by a Man for His Son* XVIII 5); the collocation *ḳb fnḏ.w* stands in antithetic parallelism with *nšni* (*Seḥetep-ib-Ra* St 3,5).

16. Gardiner translates "speak coolly (?)" (*Anastasi* I 9*); for a different translation see Fischer-Elfert, *Die satirische Streitschrift*, 59, 61/b.

17. See *Sallier* I 8, 11; *Anastasi* III 4, 8; *Wb.* II 496, 6.

18. See Job 26,12; 37, 17 in Crum 704.

19. Owing to the common use of the noun "heart" (*ib*) as the subject of *hrw* (i.e., "contented heart"), the drawing of a heart is used as the determinative of *hrw* beginning with the New Kingdom; from then on it is difficult to distinguish between cases where the heart is the subject of the verb, and where it signifies a determinative only.

20. Cf. the passage in *Instruction by a Man for His Son* in which *hrw* is contrasted with *ḫ3ḫ r3*, "one who is hasty in speech" (XIV 3-4), and also the phrases "an utterance... that is calmness for the heart" *hrw* (*ḥr*) *ḥ3.ty* — *Lansing* 15,3 and *Anastasi* III 1,3; "speech that pleases the heart," *ḏd hr.t ib* — *Mentuhotep* 11; to matters of speech, but not pertaining to the semantic field under consideration, belongs the formula "He with whose sayings/ utterances etc., one is pleased (*hrw*)," which is common in the king's court writings in reference to the high official and the leader. The subjects of the contentment may be the king, the citizens, etc. (*Urk.* IV 411,2; 938, 10; 1011, 7; 1183, 12; etc.; Janssen I p. 28, Ak 8, and cf. ibid. 2,3,5,11); sometimes the gods are content with the graceful utterances of the scribe (*Anastasi* III 4,8).

21. Without *sg3* and *sḳb*, which appear once in our corpus.

22. E. Brunner-Traut, "Weiterleben der ägyptischen Lebenslehren," 173-216.

23. Confirmation that garrulousness is deemed a sin in ancient Egypt is found in the "Confession of the Dead," in which the deceased declares: "I was not a *'š3 ḫrw* ("chatterer") in speech" (Budge, *The Book of the Dead*, 370 [chap. 125, 33]).

24. On this matter see Faulkner, in O. Firchow (ed.), *Aegyptologische Studien*, 84-88, and for the meaning of the saying and its mythological background see Posener, "Amenemope 22, 9-10."

25. For a discussion of these phrases see Chap. 7, sections "mouth," "belly," "heart."

26. See p. 161 below.

27. Cf. Posener (n. 24 above).

28. Cf. *The Eloquent Peasant* B1 26-27, *Urk.* IV 1031, 9, and see Assmann, *Ma'at*, 138-139.

29. The ambivalent attitude to speech and silence in Egyptian literature from the Old Kingdom up to the New Kingdom Period has been treated in detail by Lanczkowski, "Reden und Schweigen," 186-196; in his view the "ideal of silence" arose in a political setting, as freedom of speech constitutes a political threat. Silence was then provided with human and theological grounds and it became an ideal.

30. For *šmm* see above, Chapter 3.

31. For a comprehensive discussion of this chapter see Posener, "Le chapitre IV d'Aménémopé," 129-135; Perdue, *Wisdom and Cult*, 54-58; Kevin, "The Wisdom of Amen-m-opt," 149 ff; Anthes, "Die Funktion des vierten Kapitels," 9-18; and lately Israeli, "Chapter Four of Amenemope," 464-484.

32. Various interpretations have been offered for the tree-growing places — *ḫnty* with respect to *šmm* and *tḥn.t* with respect to *grw m3'*. Here two suggestions are given that seem most suitable as regards context and orthography. For other

proposals see the bibliography in n. 31, especially the review by Israeli, 474 ff. Particularly interesting for purposes of comparison with the Bible is Kevin's suggestion. Kevin amends *ḫnty* to *ḥn.t*, "a channel" (a mishearing by the scribe), and finds here the influence of the image of "streams of water" appearing in Psalms 1,3; this suggestion will be rejected by those who assume that the Egyptian composition predates the Hebrew Psalm. Israeli suggests distinguishing between "a tree growing in a place into which water may be easily channelled" and "a tree which grows in a place where there is no access to channelled water," op. cit., 483. This proposal is as good as any other conjecture. But when Israeli seeks to elucidate other terms in chapter 4 of *Amenemope* in light of her novel explanation (such as *pḫ*, *mḫrm*), the explanation, despite its originality, is not as convincing.

33. Burial not in one's place of birth is considered a serious disgrace in Egypt; cf. the fate of Sinuhe (B 190ff). A similar concept was held by the Hebrews: Joseph makes his brothers swear that "you shall carry my bones from here" (Gen. 50,25); cf. also the story of the carrying of Jacob's body from Egypt for burial in Canaan (ibid. 4ff.).

34. Cf. Israeli (n. 31 above), 473; Borghouts, "The 'Hot One,'" 24-25.

35. Fischer-Elfert, "Dein Heisser," 83, and Perdue (n. 31 above).

36. Cf. Chap. 3 above, p. 130.

37. The comparison of wisdom to a "fountain of water" is present also in Proverbs: "The teaching of the wise is a fountain of life" (13,14); "The fountain of wisdom is a gushing stream" (18,4; cf. 16,22). Wisdom interchanges with the "fear of God" and "righteousness" which are also "a fountain of life" (10,11; cf. 25, 26).

38. In the Bible the image of God as a "fountain of living waters" appears often (Jer. 2,13; 17,13; Ps. 36,10; the opposite — Jer. 15, 18).

39. Cf. the expression *sgr ḳ3 ḫrw*, "to silence the loud of voice" (Janssen I p. 108, Fe 1), and also "there is not raising of voice (*n ḳ3 ḫrw*) in the house of the lord of silence (*nb sgr*)" (*Urk.* IV 1031, 9).

40. *Urk.* IV 1181, 14; Janssen I p. 35 Ba, 5, 7.

41. *Urk.* IV 970, 15; Blumenthal G3,36; Janssen ibid. Ba 6; *Instruction by a Man for His Son* XIV 5, and also in *Urk.* IV 1930, 18 (see n. 64 below).

42. *Ptaḥḥotep* 323; Janssen ibid. Ba 2.

43. Otto p. 67, No. 73, 4-5; Jansen-Winkeln II 3, 4, 12.

44. Otto No. 70, 8.

45. See *Admonitions of an Egyptian Sage* 11,13; and also Grapow, *Die bildlichen Ausdrücke*, 51.

46. *šnty* # *ḳb ẖ.t* (*Ptaḥḥotep* 323); *ḳ3 srf* # *ḳbb srf* (for a discussion of these terms see Blumenthal 302-303); *ḳ3/šd ḫrw* # *ḳb m3ʿ/ḏd/nmt.t* (Otto pp. 67-68).

47. Janssen I p. 35, Ba 3 (as a verb).

48. Among the attributes of the "ideal scribe" — Hatnub, in Janssen, ibid. 2.

49. Ibid. 6.

50. Cf. the synonymous adjective *hr ḳi*, "quiet natured," in *The Autobiography of Anhurmose*, pl. 25, l. 35 where it is opposed to *r3 t3*, the "hot-mouthed man," Ockinga, *El Mashayikh*. For references to *hrw ib*, see, e.g., *Urk.* IV 63, 13; Janssen I p. 28, Ak 14-18, etc; see *Wb.* II 497,14; cf. also the expression *hrw s.t ib* (calm-tempered), Janssen I p. 28, Ak 13 (already in the 6th Dynasty); and also the

phrase *hrw ḥr ib*, usually present in *Urk.* IV as an attribute of the high official (1016, 12; etc.).

51. Janssen I p. 29, Ak 19-23; 25-31.

52. *hrw ib* stands in parallelism with: *mnḫ ṯsw* (ibid. p. 28, Ak 18); *d3r srf* (ibid. 15); *šw m pri.t ib* (ibid. 17).

53. Cf. "sealed of lips," that is, regarding palace affairs in the inscriptions of the 10th Dynasty (*Urk.* IV 63,14).

54. See p. 154 above.

55. *hrw nmt.t*||*mdd w3.t/mtn* — Janssen I p. 29, Ak 19, 22, 23, 25, 29; ||*mn ṯb.t*, ibid. 22, 23, 28, 29; ||*iḳr s.t ns*, ibid. 26.

56. In this context the following phrase occurring in the biographies of the 22nd-23rd Dynasties is instructive: "I am a silent man (*grw*) since I came from the belly. As one who has good character I came (into the world) as a child" (Jansen-Winkeln I B28, 1; B29, 1).

57. The scribe who copied *The Instruction to Merikare* — see colophon, ibid.

58. See n. 62 below.

59. See Hermisson, *Studien zur Israelitischen Spruchweisheit*, 72-73; Humphreys, in *Isr. Wisd.*, 179-180; Skaldny, *Die ältesten Spruchsammlungen*, 44-45. For the contrary view, see Brunner, *Erziehung*, 119-123.

60. See Brunner, ibid. 45, 56, 119-123.

61. Brunner-Traut, (n. 22 above).

62. See Assmann, *SAL* 11ff.; idem "Die 'Loyalistische Lehre'" 1ff.; and *Ma'at*, 259. The believer presents himself now as "lowly" and as "poor," subject to distress — see *ÄHG* 148 B,15: "You are Amon, lord of the silent, who comes to the voice of the poor," and ibid. 169, 2 where Amun is "the protector of the silent man, the rescuer of the poor"; see also Brunner, "Die religiöse Wertung der Armut," 330-331, and Gunn, "The Religion of the Poor," 83 ff. A similar way of representation in the "style of the poor" and description of God as "protector of the poor" is found in the Biblical psalmody, e.g., Ps. 35,10; 40, 18; 140,13: Kaufmann, *The Religion* II, 681-687.

63. The colophon is preserved in *Pap. Petersburg* 1116a, which does not predate the 18th Dynasty.

64. Also, in *Urk.* IV 1930, 17 (W. Helck, *Urkunden der 18. Dynastie*), not included in the corpus of this research, appears *grw m3'* (in synonymous parallelism to *ḳb srf*) in a religious context. Here we are dealing with an offering stele from the time of Amenhotep III in honor of Renenutet, the goddess of fertility and harvest.

65. For references see n. 43 above.

66. On the *Ma'at* see pp. 96—97, 107 above.

67. Cf. n. 62 above.

68. It is not clear if we are dealing with separate roots or different words deriving from the same root: see *TDOT* III, 262-263.

69. *BDB* 198-199, *KBL* 213-214.

70. Proverbs twice, Job 5 times, wisdom Psalm once, out of 22 times in the Bible.

71. Cf. Toy, *Proverbs*, 29; like *šqṭ*, *šlw* also serves to describe the land in times of peace (cf. Eg. *sgrḥ*) (1 Chr. 4,40).

72. Also in the Greek Version of BS 1,23.

73. For *qeṣar rûaḥ* see pp. 148–149 above.

74. Already pointed out by Grollenberg in *RB* 59 (1952), 42-43.

75. For elucidation of this verse see the commentaries to Proverbs: Oesterley, 230; Toy, 471; McKane, 590; etc.

76. The Eg. *snḏ*, i.e., "modest," "humble," appears as a synonym for *grw* and *hrw* (see *Kagemni* I 1) and as the antonym of *sḫm*, "violent man" (*Urk.* IV 1092,14 *Rekhmire*; *Admonitions of an Egyptian Sage,* 11, 13).

77. Cf. *šepālîm* in Job 5,11.

78. The adjective *ʿānāw* belongs to the vocabulary of the Psalms, in which it refers to the righteous, the pious man.

79. In Ps. 141,3 the pious man begs God to watch over (*nṣr*) "the door of his lips"; and in wisdom Ps. 34,14 *nṣr* is accompanied by the objects *lāšôn* and *śepātayim*, but here the phrase concerns a prohibition against speaking falsely and not a command to guard against talking too much.

80. A comprehensive study of speech and silence in Proverbs was published by Bühlmann, *Von rechten Reden und Schweigen.* For our subject see ibid. 214ff. and cf. McKane's later article in *SAT*, esp. 174-185. The Babylonian teacher also recommends silence and warns the pupil against excessive speech: see Dürr, *Das Erziehungswesen*, 86-87.

81. Cf. *Amenemope* 22,13ff.

82. Cf. Job 40,4: "I lay my hand on my mouth"; the meaning of the phrase is "to keep silent" and the action described by it is identical to the determinative accompanying most of the Egyptian lexemes belonging to the semantic field of silence. Couroyer ("Mettre sa main," 197-209) has shown that the phrase "lay hand on mouth" is Egyptian. Cf. *The Instruction of Kheti* XXIV B-C: "When you enter and the householder ... then sit and lay a hand on your mouth" (i.e., be silent); cf. also Faulkner, *The Ancient Egyptian Pyramid Texts* §254.

83. Cf. Oesterley, *Proverbs*, 280; for other interpretations see Toy, *Proverbs*, 537 and the suggestions made by McKane, *Proverbs*, 664ff and Bühlmann (n. 80 above), 221ff.

84. See Perdue, *Wisdom and Cult*, 180-187.

85. Gressmann, *Die neugefundene Lehre des Amen-em-ope*, 284.

86. The mention of "the wicked men's judgement" in Ps. 1, regarded by scholarship as belief in the world to come which inflitrated into Judaism under Hellenistic influence, has caused most researchers to regard Ps. 1 as a late psalm dating to the period of the Second Temple. But Gressmann, and following him Blackman ("The Psalms," 195), hold that the motif here is clearly Egyptian, namely, the Egyptian Judgement of the Dead, and that therefore the psalm is early. In our view the topic is a request addressed to God which recurs in Psalms. It comes from the pious man, the righteous, who asks God to take revenge against his enemies, the wicked. Whether this theme should be associated with the Day of Judgement of prophetic literature as Kaufmann (*The Religion* II, 676-677) suggested, or not, is open to discussion; it should not, however, be seen as a foreign implant of an early Egyptian belief or as a late Hellenistic concept.

87. Blackman, "The Psalms," 195.

88. Cf. *Sallier* I 3,6: "Apply yourself to writing by day, whilst you read by night" (‖ *Chester Beatty* V recto 5,5-6 ‖ *Turin* C 1,3-4; see also *Lansing* 2,1).

89. The image in Jeremiah is indeed closer to the Egyptian sources than the description in Psalms. "The hot-tempered" is connected in the Egyptian literature with the motif of lack of water, drought, desert: In *Ostracon Deir el Médineh* 1265 II4, the heart of the hot-tempered man is compared to a "lone tree in a desert" and in *Ostracon Leipzig* 8, 4-5 he is cursed that he will perish in the summer's heat; and according to one explanation the *šmm* in *Amenemope* chapter 4 is like a tree which has no access to channeled water (see Israeli, [n.32 above]), just like the "shrub in the desert" in Jeremiah, which "shall dwell in the parched places of the wilderness in an uninhabited salt land" (Jer. 17,6).

90. Contrary to Gressmann's view (n. 85 above) that the descriptions of the "heated" and "silent man" in *Amenemope* chapter 4 are "*rein profan.*"

91. Kevin ("The Wisdom of Amen-m-opt") holds that *Amenemope* was influenced by the Bible. He goes even further and states that chapter 4 was translated directly from the Hebrew Ps. 1; Drioton is of a like opinion ("Sur la sagesse d'Aménémopé"). Williams ("The Alleged Semitic Original"), followed by Anthes ("Die Funktion"), opposes this view, insisting on the authenticity of the passage in *Amenemope*.

92. See pp. 165—167 above. The "fool" and the "wise man," as representing positive and negative human types in Hebrew, serve the same purpose in the Egyptian wisdom literature (*ḫm*, *wḫ3* # *rḫ*). This pair is later replaced by the "wicked man" and the "man of God" (*s3be* # *rmt n nṯr*); see pp. 258 ff. below.

93. In the Bible this motif involves a religious setting and appears in the Psalms and in prophecy: see Kaufmann, *The Religion*, II, 685 n.68; and also Crenshaw, *SAIW* 485-486.

CHAPTER FIVE

1. The collocation *ḫm ḫ.t*, identical in meaning, is rare in our sample.

2. "Not to know" things, people, events, etc.; e.g., *Khakheperre-sonb* recto 7; *Anastasi* I 14,7; etc.; a formula repeated in the writings of the 18th Dynasty and referring to the king and high official is: "There is nothing that (he) does not know" (*Urk.* IV 449,16; 1071,9).

3. On the political level, enemies who do not recognize Egypt and its king are termed *ḫmw Kmt* (see Blumenthal, p. 239 and *Wb.* III 278,13), as are rebels against the king who do not recognize his authority (Blumenthal, ibid.). On the religious level *ḫm* means "to ignore god" (*Admonitions* 8,7).

4. The supposition that *rmt ḫm* in Demotic derives from *ḫm*, "fool" in Egyptian, on which Lexa's translation is based (sometimes rendering *rmt ḫm* as "*l'imbecile*," "*stupide*" [Lexa, *Pap. Insinger* II,91]), is doubtful; translation is based on the assumption that the Demotic expression derives from the homonymic lexeme *ḫm33* (*Wb.* III 281,13), i.e., "become thin," "meager," which is ϩⲏⲙ / ϣⲏⲙ in Coptic and therefore *rmt ḫm* means "inferior man" (see Černý 252 and also Erichsen 359-360; *LEWL* 58, 174).

5. *wḫ3* || *ḫm* — *The Peasant* B1 218, 219, etc; *wḫ3* # *rḫ* — *Ptaḥḥotep* 573, 574: *Admonitions* 6,13; etc.

6. *Admonitions* 6,13: "The sage says 'yes' the fool (*wḫ3*) says 'no.' He who does not know (*iw.ty rḫ.f*) this is pleasing in his eyes"; according to Gardiner (*Admonitions*, 52) three people are spoken of here: "(1) the man who knows and admits the fact... (2) the ignorant man who denies it, and (3) the man who does not know of it and is indifferent to its truth or falsehood." But Gardiner prefers the alternative version of this passage, as given in *Amenemhet* IV B-C, i.e., to read "*ḥr ntt n rḫ.f*" (instead of "*iw.ty rḫ.f*") and to take this as a dependent clause relating to the *wḫ3*, namely, "the ignorant man says no because he does not know it; it is fair in his eyes." Since the latter interpretation suits the image of the *wḫ3* better, we have followed it in our discussion above.

7. The *wḫ3* is described as one who complains against the trial in the next world (*To Merikare* 56).

8. Crum 714; *Wb.* III 27,15.

9. The Coptic Version has ⲁⲧϩⲏⲧ for the following terms in the Bible: *k^esîl* (Qoh. 4,17; 7,6,9); *siklût* (ibid. 2,13); *'iwwelet* (Prov. 14,8); *nābāl*, *n^ebālâ* (Ps. 74,18; Deut. 22,21).

10. Brunner (*Erziehung*, 112) holds that *iw.ty ḥ3.ty* is a man without talent from birth who is incapable of learning; but this view has no support in the sources presented in our sample.

11. In the opinion of Volten (*Ani*, 167-168) *ḫn* is linked to the term *ḫnw*, "child," hence its primary meaning is "be childish," "be without understanding, like a child."

12. Thus according to Volten's translation, ibid. For other interpretations see Lichtheim, *Literature* II,145 and Brunner, *AW* 213. *ḫn* parallels *iw.ty ḥ3.ty* in *Israel Stele*, line 12.

13. Černý, *JEA* 15, 243ff.; for references in *Pap.* 10052 in the British Museum see ibid. 251 n.50.

14. See also T.E. Peet, *The Great Tomb Robberies* I, 145-146 n. 32, where *p3 i3wt š3š3* appears, translated by Peet as "doddering old man."

15. Erichsen 263.

16. In Coptic the term has a different meaning, "hypocrite." See Crum 148 and Westendorf 81.

17. *lḫ* also appears in the feminine form *t3 lḫ.t*, "foolish woman" (*Ankhsheshonqy* 18,9).

18. *lḫ* is found in antithetic parallelism with: # "wise man" (*rmt rḫ* — many times, e.g., *Ankhsheshonqy* 6,14; 21,7,8; etc.); # "good man" (*rmt nfr* — *Insinger* 2,19); # "man of god," "pious man" (*rmt nṯr* — ibid. 28,3); and juxtaposed to "learned man" (*sb3* — *Ankhsheshonqy* 5,10).

19. Erichsen 417.

20. *swg*‖*lḫ*, in e.g., *Ankhsheshonqy* 13,6,7; *Insinger* 10,4,5; 12,4,5; 13,11,12.

21. Cf. the term *swg3* — "*unmündiges Kind*," (*Wb.* IV 76,9) which is *swg* in Demotic (Erichsen 417), and also *Metternich Stele* 196,170, "a *swg* child (*nḫn*) without a father" (according to Gardiner, *Anastasi* I, 13* n.4). Cf. also G.R. Hughes, "The Cruel Father," *Studies in the Honour of J.A. Wilson* (Chicago 1969), 47, who defines the *swg* as "incompetent, needing the care of parent or guardian."

22. ⲥⲟϭ replaces the stems *nbl*, in e.g., Isa. 32,5; Deut. 32,6 (*nābāl*); Isa. 32,6

(n^e*bālâ*); and *b'r*, in e.g., Jer. 10,14 (*nib'ar*); Isa. 19,11 (*nib'ārâ* ['*ēṣâ*]); Ps 94,8 (*bō'ărîm*); see Crum 388.

23. Once in the combination *swg h3.ty*, "foolish in his heart, his mind" — *Pap. Louvre* 2380, line 5, in *Studies in Honor of G.R. Hughes*, 263ff.

24. Glanville, *The Instruction of 'Onchsheshonqy*, 70-71 n. 90. The translation given for *Ankhsheshonqy* 19,8 in our discussion accords with Lichtheim's, *Literature* III, 174. Another possible translation of this verse is: "If a stupid man repents he becomes a wise man" — thus Lichtheim in her revised translation of the work in *LEWL* 84; and also Brunner, *AW* 283, line 299 and Thissen, *Anchscheschonqi*, 45. According to this translation also the *swg* is corrigible, *pace* Glanville, above.

25. Gardiner (n. 21 above) gives another example from *Karnak* 52,17, where the *swg* is said to be senseless as goose.

26. "To slay" — this translation, following Erichsen 398, who renders *ḫtb* as "kill," is not conclusive. *ḫtb* may also mean "thrash" (see Lichtheim, *Literature* III, 215 n.43 and idem *LEWL* 211) or "*schlagen*" (see Brunner, *AW* 319).

27. It is found once as a noun —"stupidity" (in *Insinger* 10,18).

28. Some find the early meaning of *ḫn* — "quarrelsome man" — in the later instruction also; see the translation in Brunner's *AW*, of *Ankhsheshonqy* 23,12 and of *Insinger* 4,11: *ḫn* is "*Unruhestifter.*"

29. Brunner, *Erziehung*, 114-116; also idem "Zentralbegriffe," 414-415.

30. These determinatives are: a hand holding a stick accompanied by the sign of two crossed sticks, which signifies breakage, damage (Gr Z9); a sparrow and legs walking backwards, signifying turning back (Gr D55); see also *Wb.* V 160-161.

31. *'iqqēš* — Ps. 18,27; *'iqq^ešût peh* — Prov. 4,24; *'ăqalqallôt* — Judg. 5,6; *tahpukôt* — Prov. 6,14; *nālôz* (# *yšr*) — Prov. 14,2; see Crum 836.

32. *Hier. Ostr.* I, pl. 1,4; discussed by Volten, *Ani*, 143, Brunner, *Erziehung*, 114-116 and idem *AW* 468 n. 353; for translation see ibid. 216 line 10 and Lichtheim, *LEWL* 7. Cf. this passage to *Anii* 9, 14-15 — *idḥw s nbt r inw*, where the same idea is expressed, i.e., "every man is led by his nature."

33. See pp. 34ff. above.

34. Cf. also *The Instruction of Anii* 10,13,14 — "crooked stick (*gwš.w*)" # "straight stick (*mtr.w*)."

35. The root *'qš* is characteristic but is not exclusive to Biblical wisdom. The adjective *'iqqēš* is found in Prov. (7 times); the nominal form is also present in Prov. (twice) as is the verb (twice), which also appears in Job (once). As an adjective *'iqqēš* is also found in Deut. 32,5, in a passage bearing a wisdom imprint.

36. Only once is *'iqqēš* identified with k^e*sîl* — in Prov. 19,1: "Better is a poor man (*rāš*) who walks in his integrity than a man who is perverse in speech (*'iqqēš ś^epātāyw*) and is a fool (k^e*sîl*)"; but the k^e*sîl* is replaced in the parallel verse 28,6 by *'āšîr*, which apparently is the correct version as *rāš* and *'āšîr* are a pair in parallelism of members.

37. The stem *'qš* appears in the following collocations: *'iqq^ešût peh* (|| *l^ezût ś^epātayim*) — Prov. 4,24; 6,12; cf. the words of Wisdom in 8,8; *'iqqēš ś^epātāyw* — ibid. 19,1; *'iqqēš lēb* — 11,20; 17,20 (|| *nehcppāk bilšônô*); *'orḥōtêhem 'iqq^ešîm* (|| *n^elôzîm b^ema'g^elôtām*) — 2,15; cf. 22,5; for a discussion of the combination *'iqqēš* + *derek* and its synonyms see above, p. 87.

38. In the Bible the roots *yšr* and *tmm* serve as antonyms of *'qš*; *yšr* outside the wisdom literature and *tmm* in the wisdom books, see Isa. 42,16; Mic. 3,9; Prov. 19,1; 10,9; 11,20; 28,6,18, and Job 9,20.

39. On the relation between the terms *sǝbe* and *lḥ* see pp. 259—261 below.

40. For a discussion of this subject see Chapter 6.

41. *ḥăsar lēb* stands in synonymous parallelism with: *petî*, *'ěwîl* (BS) and in antithetic parallelism with *nābôn*, *'îš tᵉbûnâ/ôt*.

42. This etymology of *pth* is accepted by most of the scholars who identify the Hebrew stem with the Aramaic root *ptj/'* meaning "to be open, wide" and argue that this sense is also preserved in the expression *pōteh śᵉpatāyw*, "one who opens wide his lips", in Prov. 20,19 (cf. 24,28). Others, however, reject this assumption and link *pth* with the Arabic *fatā(w)*, "be a young man," "in prime of life" (see *TWAT* VI 822-823 and *BDB* 834; *KBL* 786). In any case, the verb *pth* is not characteristic of the sage's vocabulary.

43. *petî* stands in synonymous parallelism with *kᵉsîlîm* as well (Prov.), *lēṣîm* (Prov.), *'ěwîl* (BS). In Ezekiel 45,20 *petî* is synonymous with *šōgeh*, i.e., one who sins through ignorance. On this see Whybray, *The Intellectual*, 137.

44. For *petî* in the wisdom Pss. see discussion by Hurvitz, *Wisdom Language*, 51-52.

45. In Psalms *kᵉsîl* appears also in 92,7 and 94,8, which in Whybray's view are psalms with wisdom features; see above, Corpus, n. 17.

46. See *TDOT* IV 372, *BDB* 492.

47. Prov. 17,10 — "A rebuke enters (lit. descends) into a man of understanding (*mēbîn*) more than a hundred stripes into a stupid man (*kᵉsîl*)" — does not contradict this view. It is not said here that lashes are ineffective in improving the *kᵉsîl*, but rather is his wild nature compared with the obedient nature of the *mēbîn*; this counters the opinion of Mandry, *There is No God*, 16,20.

48. Cf. Ps. 32,9, where the influence of Prov. 26,3 is evident, and *The Instruction of Anii* 9,17-10,7, which compares the education of a youth to the taming of an animal (ox, lion, horse, dog, camel [?], goose).

49. See Fox's interpretation of these verses in *Qohelet*, 227-229.

50. On *mit'abbēr* there: see pp. 138—139 above.

51. Various solutions have been put forward for the contradiction between verses 4 and 5 in Prov. 26: see commentaries to Proverbs. Rotenberg's proposal ("To the Meaning of *'iwwelet*") is the least acceptable; in his view the word *'iwwelet* has two meanings in Proverbs, as a feminine adjective — "stupid woman" — and as abstract noun — "stupidity"; in 26,4 *'iwwelet* is the stupid woman, i.e., "do not answer him roughly like his stupid wife"; in 25,5 *'iwwelet* is his stupidity, i.e., "answer him in a manner necessitated by his stupidity."

52. See Gordis, *Koheleth*, 246-248; Perdue, *Cult and Wisdom*, 180ff.

53. So also Gordis, Barton and others in their commentaries to Qoheleth.

54. See *BDB* 17; Kahana, *Proverbs*, 3, but this etymology of *'wl* is not accepted by other scholars; cf. Cazelles, *TDOT* I, 137ff., and *KBL* 19, present additional suggestions, and n. 56 below.

55. Whybray, *The Intellectual*, 134 assumes that the two passages in the prophecy — Isa. 19,11; Jer. 4,22 — also belong to the wisdom tradition.

56. Cazelles, *TDOT* I, 138-139 compares the Hebrew *'ěwîl śᵉpātayim* with the

Egyptian *'šȝ rȝ/ḫrw* (lit. "rich in mouth" or "words"), i.e., garrulous. The proximity between the two terms is evident, since the Egyptian idiom is sometimes compounded with *ḥry*, i.e., "leader"; while *'ĕwîl* derives from the root *'wl* — "first," "strong," — and so "the princes of Zoan" are described in Isa. 9,11 as foolish (*'ĕwîlîm*). In this light, Cazelles believes that *'ĕwîl śᵉpātayim* was applied as a scornful epithet to the babbler of the wisdom school and presupposes a connection with international wisdom. But this opinion has several vulnerable points: (1) the expression *'šȝ rȝ/ḫrw* is not attached specifically to the figure of the leader in Egypt; and (2) the etymology of *'ĕwîl* is not clear, and not all scholars will accept the one offered by Cazelles above.

57. In the Masoretic text *'iwwelet* is written, but it should be read *'ĕwîl*, which fits with *lēṣ* in the second part of the verse; see McKane, *Proverbs*, 399.

58. *'iwwelet* appears only twice outside the wisdom literature, being found in the psalms of lamentation, where the believer presents himself as one with sin and transgression, defined as *'iwwelet* (Ps. 38,6; 69,6).

59. See p. 215 and n. 85 below.

60. Nouns: *lāṣôn*, Prov. 1,22; *mᵉlîṣâ*, ibid. 1,6; see pp. 329—330 below. Adjective: *mēlîṣ*, Job 33,23; 16,20; verb: *yālîṣ* (qal, future), 3 times in Prov.; the adjective *lēṣ* is also found in Isa. 29,20, which according to Whybray, *The Intellectual*, 147, belongs to the wisdom tradition.

61. See *BDB* 539, *KBL* 481 and also Richardson, "Some Notes on 'Liz'," 163.

62. Cf. McKane, *Proverbs*, 464.

63. See Toy's interpretation, *Proverbs*, 408. *'ebrâ* may also be understood from the phrase *'abar 'al* — "overflow," "excess," that is, an "excess of insolence." On this and other interpretations see *BDB* 720; McKane, *Proverbs*, 550ff.

64. *šᵉbāṭîm* should not be read for *šᵉpātîm* (as do Scott, Gemser, Toy and others).

65. Cf. the use of the verb *b'r*, which does not belong to wisdom terminology; in Isa. 19,11 the wise counsellors of Pharaoh are *'ĕwîlîm* and give "stupid (*nib'ārâ*) counsel"; in a religious context *b'r* denotes non-recognition of God (on the part of the people, e.g., Jer. 10,21; or the idol worshippers — Jer. 10,8; etc.).

66. See Whybray, *The Intellectual*, 130.

67. Cf. *KBL* 589; *KBL*³ 626; *BDB* 614; and see on this problem Roth, "*nbl*," 394-409, who on the basis of the usage in Akkadian and examination of the different meanings of the root *nbl* in the Bible, distinguishes between two groups, the noun *nᵉbēlâ* and the verb *nābal* (qal), and the noun *nᵉbālâ* and the adjective *nābāl*. Roth states that the basic meaning of *nābāl* is "outcast from the community," an "ostracized member of society," and *nᵉbālâ* means "sacrilege"; see also J.J. Paul Jouön, *Biblica* 5 (1924), 357-361; A. Coquot, *Revue d'histoire des Religions*, 155 (1959), 1-16, and recently the thorough discussion of J. Marböck in *TWAT* V, 171-185.

68. *nādîb* is polysemic in Biblical Hebrew and signifies both character — generous, noble man — and status — a member of the higher class, princely in rank (see *BDB* 622). It seems to us that the second meaning of *nadîb* fits Prov. 17,7 (cf. McKane, *Proverbs*, 507). This is not the view of *BDB* 622, *KBL* 597 or Bühlmann, *Von rechten Reden*, 142, who believe that the first sense applies here.

69. Cf. the interpretations of Oesterley, *Proverbs*, 278; Toy, *Proverbs*, 533. Coquot (n. 67 above), 4, has a different explanation: the *nābāl* will never be able to satisfy his appetite for possessions. Roth ("*nbl*," 403-404) interprets the verse in light of a custom that he believes to have existed in tribal-nomadic society, the custom being that "anyone who did not belong to a family or tribe who was 'without a name'... was left in the desert without food and consequently soon died"; hence the *nābāl* was one without bread as he had been expelled.

70. See also here, pp. 137—138 above and p. 286 below.

71. Read *yōšer* instead of *yeter* in parallelism with *šeqer* in the second part of the verse (see commentaries to Proverbs).

72. In Whybray's view (*The Intellectual*, 148) these passages also belong to the wisdom tradition.

73. As distinct from *śekel*, "understanding," which has a different etymology; see Kedar, *Biblische Semantik*, 133. The verb *skl*, i.e., "be foolish," does not appear in the Biblical wisdom books.

74. Mandry, *There is No God*, 83.

75. Cf. *Ankhsheshonqy* 5, 9-10, which is remarkably similar to the above passage in Qoheleth; see also the words of Agur, Prov. 30, 21-23. In the above passages a stylistic device common in the Biblical wisdom literature appears, namely, the use of contrasts to highlight the absurdity of the current state of affairs. This is also characteristic of the Egyptian speculative wisdom: see, e.g., *Admonitions* 7,6ff.; *Neferti* 54-57. For more details see my article "Egyptian 'Prophetic' Writings and Biblical Wisdom Literature," 87-88.

76. In prophecy *skl* denotes lack of knowledge of God; the people are *sākāl* owing to their ignorance of God (Jer. 4,22; 5,21).

77. See *TDOT* III, 412, *BDB* 237-239.

78. *hôlēlôt* is the plural participle form used for an abstract noun, see Ginsburg (*Qoheleth*, 64) and others.

79. In the view of Gordis, *Koheleth*, 216, the word "shows a semantic progression from 'revelry,' to 'sin' and then to 'folly.'" He translates "madness," and so also *BDB* 239. But Barton and Scott in their commentaries to Proverbs translate it as "foolishness," "folly," as does Ginsburg, who renders "*'iwwelet*" in Hebrew.

80. On the antecedence of the second and fifth collections in Proverbs see Skaldny, *Die ältesten Spruchsammlungen*, and McKane, *Proverbs*, 14-18. As for the first collection in Proverbs, its link with the Egyptian sources, attesting to the antecedence of at least part of the material in it, has long since been proven by Whybray, *Wisdom in Proverbs*, and Kayatz, *Studien zu Proverbien* 1-9.

81. See Whybray, *Wisdom in Proverbs*, 51; Mandry, *There Is No God*, 69; Scott, "Wise and Foolish," 146.

82. Licht, "*K^e^sîl*," 222.

83. See pp. 258ff. below.

84. See pp. 267ff. below.

85. The pointing *ḥakmôt* of the Masoretic text is incorrect. It should be read as in 9,1 *ḥokmôt* conforming it to the abstract noun *'iwwelet*, which appears in the second part of the verse, and the verb in 3rd fem. sing., *bān^e^tâ*; see *BDB* 315; Toy, *Proverbs*, 285-286.

86. See pp. 268—270ff. below.

87. Some linguists, e.g., O. Jespersen, are of the opinion that: "The more advanced a language is, the more developed is its power of expressing abstract or general ideas" (*Language*, 429; cf. Ullmann, *The Principles of Semantics*, 95). However, the fact that the present corpus does not contain abstract nouns relating to the subject of foolishness in Egyptian can not lead to the inadequate conclusion that the latter is an "unadvanced" language. Abstract nouns can very well be found in other semantic fields, e.g., the Eg. *m3ʿ.t* and *si3*; after all, every language expresses "ein Denken über die Welt nur innerhalb der eigenen Sprachwelt (Glottozentrismus)" (H. Wein, in *Sprach und Wissenschaft* [Göttingen 1960], 17. For a rejection of the view above, see also J. Barr, *The Semantics*, 30ff.

CHAPTER SIX

1. Crum 541; Erichsen 252.

2. See Assmann, *SAL* 18; and also Zandee, "Das Alte Testament," 148-149.

3. See *Wb.* II 446,8; *ZÄS* 47, pl. I 1,5; and also *TDOT* V, 455.

4. Compare this Egyptian expression with the transliteration of the parallel Semitic term in *Pap. Anastasi* I 17,7-8 —— *ṯpr ydʿ*, in Heb. *sôpēr yôdēaʿ** ("skilled scribe"). The original Hebrew term was most probably modified here to fit the Egyptian structure, in which the root *ydʿ* serves as an attributive to the noun. In Hebrew the object usually follows *ydʿ*; cf. *yôdēaʿ sēper* (Isa. 29,11-12) and the combinations *yōdēaʿ naggēn*, *yōdēaʿ ṣayid*, etc. —— *BDB* 394/4B; see also Gardiner, *Pap. Anastasi* I, 19* n. 18.

5. Cf. the plural form: *sš.w rḫyt* (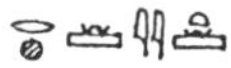) "the learned scribes" (*Chester Beatty* IV, pl. 18 verso 2,5; see also p. 218 above). The grammatical and orthographical form of the two rolled papyri in *rḫyt* is difficult. Brunner's view that the original form was *sš.w rḫ iḫ.t* should be accepted: see Brunner, "Die 'Weisen,'" 30.

6. On magic in the wisdom writings see H. Brunner, *Antaios* 3 (1962), 534-543.

7. The ability to predict is one of the sage's faculties; thus, Neferti, "the wise man," prophesies before the king Snefru and in *Pap. Chester Beatty* IV the "wise" scribes are said to "foretell the future," (pl. 19 verso 3,7-8).

8. Cf. the tomb inscription of the prince Si-Renpowet, where he presents himself as follows: "coming out of the womb, as one that knows (*rḫ*) and understands (*wḥʿ ib*)": Gardiner, "Inscriptions from the Tomb of Si-Renpowet," 135-136, pl. viii.

9. The different types of fool are termed here "fool" in accordance with the parallel pair "wise man —— fool" in the Bible.

10. In addition to the references above the traditional conception is expressed also in: *Pap. Chester Beatty* IV pl. 20 verso 6,6; *Mentuhotep* 5; *Ptaḥḥotep* 54; *Urk.* IV 368,1; etc.

11. See Gardiner, *JEA* 39 (1959), 16; and Janssen II p. 49.

12. On this image see pp. 65-66 above.

13. Kayatz, in *Studien*, 42, states: "Der Begriff Weisheit (*sꜣꜣ.t*) spielt... keine besondere Rolle" in the Egyptian instruction. But she enumerates only two appearances of the term, while in our sample the root *sꜣꜣ* appears 22 times, eight of them being in the literary genre of instruction.

14. In *The Instruction of Ptaḥḥotep sꜣꜣ* of *Pap. Prisse* 41 is replaced by *sꜣrw* in mss. L2 and C; *sꜣꜣ* and *rḫ* interchange with each other in the expressions *sꜣꜣ sbḳ* or *rḫ sbḳ*, which mean "wise in understanding."

15. The term is reconstructed in this way by Gardiner and, following him, Lichtheim, *Literature* I, 99, 107 n.2; Helck (*To Merikare* 17) completes it differently, and reads *imḏr*, "defensive wall."

16. In view of this sole reference we find it difficult to accept Perdue's opinion that the scribe in Egyptian is addressed as *sꜣꜣ* and therefore *sꜣ.t* is "scribal wisdom": Perdue, *Wisdom and Cult*, 65 n.7.

17. See Gr T12. It is difficult to determine the link between this determinative and the meaning of the term.

18. Of the 28 occurrences of this term in our corpus, eight belong to the didactic and pessimistic wisdom (*Ptaḥḥotep*, *Amenemope*, *Seḥetep-ib-Ra*, *Admonitions of an Egyptian Sage*, and *The Eloquent Peasant*).

19. For the discussion of the personified image of *siꜣ* in association with *ḥokmôt* in Proverbs, see p. 268 below.

20. Cf. *Wb.* IV 31,2; and Gardiner, "Some Personifications," 51.

21. For more examples see Gardiner, ibid. 50-52, and Kalugila, *The Wise King*, 21ff.

22. Calice, No. 716 compares the Eg. term with the Akka. *ummânu*, "*Werkmeister*," *'ômmān* in Heb.

23. Cf. *Urk.* IV 970, 1-3: Intef "distinguishes between fool (*wḫꜣ*) and wise man (*rḫ*)/ values the talented (*ḥmww*)/ turns his back on the stupid man (*ḫm*)"; and see also *Ptaḥḥotep* 51-59. Sometimes *ḥmww* is accompanied by the preposition *m* + object, e.g., *ḥmww m wp ḫꜣi.t*, "qualified to diagnose illness" (Janssen I p. 29, Al 2).

24. Gardiner, *Ancient Egyptian Onomastica*, I 66.

25. See *TDOT* V, 454.

26. Akka. *idû*, Ugar. *yd'*, etc. The Semitic root *yd'* also appears in *Anastasi* I 17,8: see n.4 above, and also *TDOT* V, 449. According to Rössler (mentioned in *TDOT* ibid.), *rḫ* in Eg. is the regular phonological equivalent of Hamito-Semitic *yd'*.

27. In non-wisdom texts God is said to "know" the "heart" of men (Ps. 139,23; 2 Chr. 6,30), and to "know" them "by name" (Exod. 33,12); cf. the Egyptian usage.

28. See Chap. 9, n. 46.

29. Cf. *Thesaurus* II, 317. For the variety of interpretations of the nature of the knowledge that comes from eating the fruit of this tree, see *TDOT* V, 464-465.

30. See ibid. 468ff.

31. See *BDB* 395/1C.

32. Cf. Dan. 1,20; and see *BDB* 395/2A and also Di Lella, *Daniel*, *AB* 129.

33. Cf. *TDOT* V, 467. The collocation *'îš da'at*, which is parallel in structure to *rmt rḫ* in Demotic, occurs once (Prov. 24,5).

34. The root *ḥkm* appears 318 times in the Bible, 196 times in the wisdom books.

35. Scholars are divided over the grammatical form of *ḥokmôt*. Some regard it as an abstract plural (*BDB* 315), others as a feminine singular form with the ending *wt* instead of *t* (*Thesaurus* III, 145; see also *TDOT* IV, 371). The latter opinion is based on Albright's interpretation, which sees here a Hebrew transliteration of the Canaanite form *ḥukmatu*, the name of the goddess of wisdom: Albright, "Some Canaanite-Phoenician sources," 8.

36. See Chap. 5, n. 85.

37. The expressions *rdi rḫ* and *rdi šs3* in Egyptian parallel the Hebrew pi'el form meaning "make wise," e.g., "I shall cause you to be versed in (*in di.i šs3.tn*) the plan of the god" (Lefebvre 116,4). The sense "be wise," "become wise," rendered in Hebrew in qal, appears once in our corpus in *Urk.* IV: "I have become wise (*ss33.kwi*) in the wisdom (*m s3r.t*) of the gods" (160,6).

38. Other collocations in which *ḥākām* stands in construct state are: *dibrê ḥăkāmîm*, "the words of the wise" (Prov. 1,6; Qoh. 9,17; etc.); *lešôn, śiptê, 'ozen / ḥăkāmîm*, "tongue, lips, ear of the wise" (Prov. 12,18; 14,3; 18,15; etc.); *lēb ḥākām*, "heart of a wise man" (Qoh. 8,5); cf. *ḥăkām lēb/lēbab*, "one wise of heart" (Prov. 10,8; 16,21; Job 9,4; etc.), whose antonym is *ḥăsar lēb*, "one without heart," i.e., "the fool" (Prov. 7,7; etc.).

39. The following discussion centers on a textual analysis of the passages in which *ḥākām* appears in the Biblical wisdom literature. On the nature of this term in the Bible, whether it is a general attribute or a professional label, etc., see Appendix C below.

40. For a discussion of this expression see p. 320 below.

41. This concept is also reflected in the following sources: concerning El, the head of the Canaanite pantheon, it is said, "Art great indeed, O El, and wise, / Thy beard's gray hair instructs thee" (II AB, V 64-66, trans. H.L. Ginsberg, *ANET* 133); the wise Aḥiqar is similarly portrayed as an old man (line 17); see also wisdom Ps. 105,22, BS 25,4-6 (Gr.) and Ezek. 27,9. "Elder" and "wise man" interchange in the parallel verses Jer. 18,18 and Ezek. 7,26. Old age in the last example denotes longevity and has no connection with the political institution of elders, as is claimed by Kalugila, *The Wise King*, 79; McKenzie, "The Elders," 527; and lately van Leeuwen, "The Sage in the Prophetic Literature," 304; see also Lang, *Die weisheitliche Lehrrede*, 46.

42. In Proverbs 9 there is a contrast between the abstract nouns *ḥokmôt* and *kesîlût*, which has no equivalent in the Egyptian sources. On the contrast between *ḥākām* and *kesîl* see also pp. 258ff. below.

43. The eloquence of the wise man finds expression in several ways: in the form and content of the words spoken — "The mind of the wise makes his speech judicious and increases learning on his lips" (Prov. 16,23; cf. 15,2); "The words of the wise man's mouth win favor" (Qoh. 10,12; cf. Prov. 13,14); in the right timing of the speech — knowing when to keep silent is one of the qualities of the wise man (Prov. 17,28; Job 13,5; cf. Qoh. 9,17).

44. Wisdom stands in antithetic parallelism with *'iwwelet* (Prov. 14,1) and with *hôlēlôt weśiklût* (Qoh. 1,17).

45. "Hearing" in this context concerns the ability to try a case, which is one of the functions of the ruler; see p. 57 above.

46. On the god Re' as creator of the world by means of his wisdom see p. 225 above. Thoth, the god of scribes, is deemed the "god of wisdom" par excellence in Egypt, but other Egyptian gods are also conceived as possessors of wisdom: see Kalugila, *The Wise King*, 12-15. In the Ugaritic texts the adjective "wise" is attached to El, the head of the pantheon: Cazelles, "La Sagesse," 37; Kalugila, ibid. 62 ff. In Mesopotamia several gods are considered gods of wisdom, among them Enki, who created the world and granted divine wisdom to mankind; see Perdue, *Wisdom and Cult*, 89; Kalugila, ibid. 39 ff. On the wisdom of the Hebrew God revealed in the creation see also Jer. 10,12 || 51,15; Ps. 104,24.

47. This sense is also revealed in the substantive *bayin* "interval, space between" and in the preposition *bên*, "between"; cf. *BDB* 106-107; *KBL* 120-122; *TDOT* II, 99, and see also there for cognates in other Semitic languages (Arab., Ugar., etc.).

48. See Whybray, *The Intellectual Tradition*, 126-127.

49. See also Prov. 23,1: "When you sit down to eat with a ruler, observe carefully (*bîn tābîn*) what is before you." In light of the parallel in *The Instruction of Amenemope* 23,17, *bîn tābîn* should be rendered "look at," "watch."

50. *nābôn* also is juxtaposed to *da'at* and stands in antithetic parallelism with *k^esîl, lēṣ, ḥăsar lēb, sākāl* (the last term in Jer. 4,22).

51. The perception underlying this collocation is that the heart is the seat of wisdom. An identical idea is reflected in the Egyptian phrases *wḥ' ib, ḥmww ib*, and in the image of the *si3* residing in the heart; cf. also pp. 299ff. below.

52. Outside the wisdom literature *nābôn* refers to additional areas: expertise in matters of justice and administration (Solomon has a "*nābôn* heart," which helps him to dispense justice — 1 Kgs. 3; Moses appoints judges over the people who are "wise and *n^ebōnîm*" — Deut. 1,13ff.); counseling (the advisers of Hezekiah are wise and *n^ebônîm* — Isa. 29,14); interpreting dreams (Joseph — Gen. 41,39); the knowledge of God (the people obeying the Law is a "wise and *nābôn* people" — Deut. 4,6).

53. Duesberg and Fransen, *Les scribes inspirés*, 188.

54. Perhaps an additional faculty of the *mēbîn*, namely, counseling in political matters, is alluded to here; cf. the function of Jonathan, the uncle of David, who is "counselor" and "man of understanding" (*'îš mēbîn*) (1 Chr. 27,32); in any event, the meaning of the second part of the verse in Prov. 28,2 is uncertain; for other interpretations see Toy, *Proverbs*, 495; McKane, *Proverbs*, 630-631.

55. Cf. Duesberg and Fransen (n. 53 above), p. 188.

56. In the opinion of Whybray, *The Intellectual Tradition*, 142-145, all the appearences of *bînâ* outside the wisdom books show a wisdom influence or denote passages with wisdom features.

57. According to McKane, *Proverbs*, 292, who believes that several stages may be discerned in the development of Hebrew wisdom, Prov. 3,5 reflects the second stage, i.e., the "nationalizing of the Instruction." *bînâ*, which has a positive connotation at the first stage, assumes a negative connotation at the second stage becoming "*hubris*, which is incompatible with trust in God." Cf. ibid. 368.

58. Cf. *śkl*, "to understand" in Aram. — *BDB* 968, *KBL*[3] 1238. For the use of the root in Akka. see *BDB* ibid.

59. Whybray, *The Intellectual Tradition*, 137, believes that Deut. 32,29 and Jer. 9,23 also belong to the wisdom tradition. The root *śkl* appears frequently in Daniel (ten times).

60. The meaning of *maśkîl*, which appears as the title of 13 Psalms (32, 42, 44, etc.), is subject to debate; but all agree that the term points to a connection between the Psalmic literature and wisdom. See Barucq, *L'expression*, 45; Mowinckel, *The Psalms*, II, 94; Blenkinsopp, "The Sage, the Scribe", 311-312; and commentaries to Psalms.

61. *śekel ṭôb* is found only once outside the wisdom books, see Hurvitz, *Wisdom Language*, 94-96. Couroyer, "A propos de Luc" assumes that the Hebrew phrase derived from the Egyptian *spd ḥr*, which means "*intelligence aiguisée*" and appearing in tombstone formulations. He relies mainly on the fact that *spd ḥr* appears in these inscriptions together with *ḥs.t* — which is the Eg. equivalent of the Heb. *ḥēn* — exactly as *śekel ṭôb* is juxtaposed with *ḥēn* in Prov. 3,4; 13,15. But Couroyer ignores the ambivalence of the Hebrew expression, which refers to physical appearance as well as to human intelligence. Also, the references he cites are not convincing since *spd ḥr* is enumerated here among other values — life, health, prosperity, love, favor — which the believer wishes to be granted him by the gods; from this context it is difficult to conclude that *spd ḥr* indeed means intelligence. However, it is clear that Prov. 13,15 is based on an ancient formulation, parallels of which are to be found not only in the Egyptian sources but also in the Phoenician tomb inscriptions as demonstrated by Hurvitz, *Wisdom Language*, 95.

62. In Arab. *'rm* means "be ill natured," see *BDB* 791; *KBL* 737; the verb is found also in Aram. and Syr. — *KBL*[3] 839; *TWAT* VI, 387.

63. In the view of Whybray, (n. 59 above), 148, Gen. 3,1 belongs to the wisdom tradition. For the connection between the serpent and wisdom see lately *TWAT* VI, 389 and there additional bibliography.

64. McKane, *Proverbs*, 563. Duesberg and Fransen (n. 53 above), 190 define *'ormâ* as an intuitive response rather than intelligence. This view is difficult to accept because *'ormâ*, according to Proverbs, is not a natural virtue but a faculty acquired by learning: *'ormâ* serves as teaching matter for the *petî* (Prov. 1,4).

65. In light of the definition of the *'ārûm* as one who "conceals knowledge," Cazelles ("Les débuts," 35 n. 2) conjectures that the Egyptian equivalent of the *'ārûm* is the *grw*, the silent man. This sense of laconic behavior fits Prov. 12,16; 22,3; 1 Sam. 23,22; and also, perhaps, Gen. 3,1, where the serpent, at least today a silent creature, is deemed *'ārûm*. But since the meaning "to be silent" does not suit the remaining passages where the term *'ārûm* appears it is difficult to accept this view. It is particularly unapt in clarifying Ps 83,4. Cf. Cazelles' interpretation ibid. with that of Briggs, *Psalms*, 220. For another proposal of Cazelles ("Les débuts," 37), that *spd* in Egyptian be regarded as the equivalent of *'ārûm*, see p. 281, n. 12.

66. Syr. *zam*, "whisper"; Arab. *zamzama*, "murmur," "hum"; see *TDOT* IV, 87; *KBL*[3] 262. The discussion does not treat the qal form of the verb, *zāmam*, or the noun, *zimmâ*, which are not characteristic of the wisdom vocabulary (*zamam* twice in Prov.; 13 times in other books; *zimmâ* three times in Prov., twice in Job

and 28 times in other books). Duesberg and Fransen, *Les scribes inspirés*, 192, on the other hand, relate these forms of *zmm* also to the sapiential vocabulary.

67. McKane (*Proverbs*, 17) holds that the ambivalent meaning of *m^{e}zimmâ* is connected with different stages in the development of wisdom. At the early stage "*m^{e}zimmâ* is an intellectual virtue," as reflected in Prov. 8,12b and 14,17b; but at the later stage, reflected in Prov. 12,2b, *m^{e}zimmâ* is pejorative. Toy (*Proverbs*, 242), ascribes the difference in sense to a difference in authorship for Prov. chaps. 1-9 and Prov. chaps. 10-24.

68. This etymology is maintained by *BDB* 444, but other scholars contend that the noun *tûšiyyâ* derives not from the root *'š'* (Arab.) "to assist," "to support," but from *yēš*, "being," "substance," (Akka. *išû*, "to have"). See Grimm, "*tûšiyyâ*," 42, *PWM* 80 n.4, and *KBL*^{3} 1579.

69. Some translations given are "wisdom," "insight," "power," "success," "skill," etc.; see the commentaries of Toy, Scott and McKane on Proverbs, and also Genung, "*tûšiyyâ*," 114. Grimm ("*tûšiyyâ*," 35) opposes this approach and asserts that at the basis of every mention of the word *tûšiyyâ* lies a single meaning, and this is "prop" or "support." But when explaining the different verses he follows the others and interprets it as "help," "success," "power," etc.

70. For this interpretation of Job 30,22 see Grimm, ibid. 36.

71. Some translate "might," "strength" also in Prov. 8,14 and Job 26,3.

72. Outside the wisdom literature *tûšiyyâ* refers also to advanced agricultural techniques, given to man by God — Isa. 28,29.

73. In the present framework the discussion is restricted to the nominal form of the root *kšr*, which is of interest for the subject under review. *kšr* is found in verbal form too, in Qoheleth (10,10; 11,6), Psalms, and Esther.

74. See Loader, *Polar Structures*, 91.

75. Cf. Prov. 6,6; 26,12; Qoh. 2,13; 4,1; etc.

76. See n. 57 above.

77. Dan. 8,15; 9,22-23.

78. Keel, "Eine Diskussion," 225 ff.; Lichtheim, "Observations on Pap. Insinger," 283 ff. and also idem *LEWL* 45-48; 118-122, 165; recently also Brunner, *AW* 298-299. For an investigation of the relevant Biblical related material see below.

79. A brief comparison between the Hebrew and the Egyptian material was recently made by Lichtheim (*LEWL*), but there the orientation is a different one, i.e., to outline the place and unique nature of the Demotic wisdom in its international context.

80. Lichtheim, "Observations on Pap. Insinger," 291; cf. idem *LEWL* 45.

81. See ibid. 118ff., esp. 121.

82. See *To Merikare* 26,49; *Sehetep-ib-Ra* 6,4 and *Neferti* 62, which speak of a rebel against the monarchy; and also *To Merikare* 110, 134, where the *sbi* is portrayed as a rebel against god.

83. Crum 231.

84. Skaldny, *Die ältesten Spruchsammlungen in Israel*.

85. Hermisson, *Studien zur israelitischen Spruchweisheit*, 73-76.

86. McKane, *Proverbs*, 14-18; Loader, *Polar Structures*, 117-123; Mandry, *There is No God*, 85ff.

87. Conrad, "Die innere Gliederung," 67-76.

88. Scott, "Wise and Foolish," 146-165; his important observation is that out of 145 contrasts in Proverbs 10-15 only in two examples is "the righteous man" linked with wisdom (10,31; 11,9) and only once does he appear in contrast to "the fool," *'ĕwîl* (10,21).

89. Kovacs, "Is There Class-Ethic," 173-189; see esp. 181-182 and 189 n. 40.

90. The contrast of righteous man — wicked man appears in the second collection 33 times (principally in chaps. 10-11: 14 times) in the fifth collection nine times, in the third and fourth collections five times and in the first collection three times.

91. The analysis focuses on verses in which both roots *rš'*, *ṣdq* are present (in contrast or in juxtaposition), while verses containing only one member of the pair are not dealt with.

92. *ṣaddîq* appears two other times in parallelism with *ḥākām*, though not in a didactic setting: in Prov. 11,30 where the parallelism between *ḥākām* and *ṣaddîq* is difficult, since we expect a term opposed to *ṣaddîq* in the second part of the verse (and indeed, the Septuagint here reads *ḥāmās* for *ḥākām*); and in 23,24 where the parallelism *ṣaddîq*||*ḥākām* is presented in a family setting. According to Hurvitz, *Wisdom Language*, 77-80, the identification of the righteous with the wise man (like that of the wicked man with fool) is a typical wisdom concept.

93. See Mandry, *There is no God*, 84-85; Loader, *Polar Structures*, 46ff. The abstract nouns *ṣedeq* and *reša'* are also found once in contrast in Qoheleth (3,16), but here they always refer to matters of judgement and justice (cf. ibid. 5,7).

94. It is remarkable that in BS the contrast between *ṣaddîq* and *rāšā'* is marginal and appears only twice (12, 2,3; 13,17 — not in parallelism).

95. This meaning is based on the Akka. *ummânu*, i.e., "skill in some craft"; cf. Prov. 3,19; another rendering is *'āmôn*, i.e., "little child." See Scott, *Proverbs*, 72; Fohrer, "Sophia," 78, and Kayatz, *Studien*, 93, who translates "*Liebling*."

96. Donner, "Prov. Sal. 8," 16.

97. For a discussion of the phenomenon of hypostasis in Egypt and in other cultures, see Gardiner, "Some Personifications," 43-54; 83-95; "Personifications," in Hastings, *Encyclopaedia of Religion and Ethics*, IX 787-803; Ringgern, *Word and Wisdom*, 9-88; E. Hornung, *Der Eine und die Vielen*, 65-74; Guglielmi, "Personification"; the most comprehensive investigation of the relevant Egyptian material was published recently by J. Baines, *Fecundity Figures, Egyptian Personfication and the Iconology of a Genre* (Warminster-Chicago 1983); for further references to preceding bibliography see ibid. 7-16.

98. Albright, "The Goddess of Life," 258-294.

99. Albright, ibid., speaks of the influence of the Canaanite goddess of wisdom, who appears nowhere in the Canaanite literature and whose existence he reconstructs in light of the following: Canaanite words and grammar present in Proverbs 1-9; the Heb. word *ḥokmôt* which in his view is the name of the goddess of wisdom; and the personification of wisdom in *The Story of Aḥiqar* (lines 94-95), which in his opinion is of Canaanite origin. But Albright's proposal is difficult to accept for the questions it raises: (a) The form *ḥokmôt* does not provide adequate proof for the existence of a Canaanite goddess, and the term may be explained in other ways (see n. 35 above); (b) The idea that Canaanite wisdom exerted an

influence on Proverbs is not well based; recent studies attest to the limited scope of this wisdom: see Khanjian, "Wisdom in Ras Shamra," and Thompson, *The Form and Function*, 54-57. (Even the most recent articles by M. Fisher published in *SIANE* [67-80; 109-118] arguing for the existence of wisdom literature and sages in Ugarit do not change this picture, since his major arguments do not hold up under scrutiny).

Other scholars identify "Dame Wisdom" with Isis-Sophia, who appears in the Hellenistic period as the goddess of wisdom. But these sources postdate Proverbs 1-9. At most it may be assumed, as does Conzelmann, "Die Mutter der Weisheit," 225-234, that Ben Sira (24,3-6) is influenced by Isis hymns. The latter opinion is rejected by Sanders, *Ben Sira*, 45-50, who believes that the passage in BS is of a "Judaic character." See also Lang, "Frau Weisheit," 152-154, and Ringgern, *Word and Wisdom*, 128 ff.

100. Boström, *Proverbiastudien*; see also Whybray, *Wisdom in Proverbs*, 72-104, who holds that several elements in the description of Widsom in Prov. 1-9 (e.g., Wisdom as an precious object, as builder of a house of seven pillars, and the image of Wisdom as a bride) arise from the combination of the writer's imagination and features taken from the mythology of the goddess Ishtar.

101. Kayatz, *Studien*; Donner ("Prov. Sal. 8") also believes that the image of Wisdom in Prov. 8 was affected by the concept of the Egyptian Ma'at, albeit indirectly: the influence transpired by way of *The Story of Aḥiqar*, in which, too, personification of Wisdom is found and which acquired its final form at the Jewish settlement at Elephantine in Egypt. The passage in *Aḥiqar* on which Donner bases his argument is partially erased (lines 94-95):

94. Whose wisdom fails ...
From heaven the people are favored;
Wisdom is of the gods
95. Indeed, she is precious to the gods;
Her kingdom is et[er]nal
She has been established in heaven;
Yea, the Holy Lord has exalted her.

Cf. Cowley, *Aramaic Papyri* 223; *ANET* 428/B; Lindenberger, *Ahiqar*, 65-70.

102. Kayats's position raises several difficulties: (a) Kayats assumes that the Hebrew writers were versed not only in the Egyptian wisdom literature but also in other literary genres (such as the *Coffin Texts*); (b) despite the features common to Wisdom and Ma'at there are some important differences: Ma'at, unlike Wisdom, does not appear as a goddess who delivers a speech. In the Egyptian wisdom literature Ma'at usually is present as an abstract noun. (Even in passages where it appears as a personified figure in the wisdom literature, the figure remains pale and of secondary significance and cannot be compared to the vivid description of Dame Wisdom in the first collection in Proverbs. Cf. *Ptaḥḥotep* 88ff.: "Great is Ma'at, lasting in effect"; *Khakheperre-sonb* recto 11: "Ma'at is cast out, falsehood is in the counsel-room"; also *To Merikare* 34; *The Eloquent Peasant* B1 182); (c) Ma'at and Wisdom are indeed central concepts in the Egyptian and the Hebrew wisdom literature respectively, but they are not identical. Ma'at signifies the harmonious order that has reigned over the universe since creation and to which gods and kings

are subject. It is otherwise with Wisdom, who is the representative and messenger of God but not an absolutely independent force like Ma'at. It is significant that the most up-to-date investigation of the various aspects of Ma'at, published recently by Assmann, does not contain any details proving the identification of Dame Wisdom with Ma'at.

103. For the thesis that the personification of Wisdom mirrors a social reality in which women occupied a special status and played certain roles in the Israelite familial setting as well as in the public arena see, most recently, Camp, "The Female Sage," 190-202; Camp, however, agrees that "there are almost certainly adumbrations of ancient N.E. goddesses at work here" (ibid. 191).

104. A similar position is maintained by Bonnard, "De sagesse."

105. The theory of "development by stages" of the Hebrew wisdom is accepted by most scholars; on this see p. 41 above, especially n. 49.

106. See above, p. 42.

107. See Lindblom, "Wisdom in the O.T. Prophets," 192-203. He is opposed by Whybray, *The Intellectual Tradition*, 15-54, and "The Sage," 133-139, who believes that the wise men are not a professional class but people possessing the virtue of wisdom. Whybray's view is accepted with reservation by Crenshaw, *Ecclesiastes*, 34 n. 16.

108. See von Rad, *Wisdom in Israel*, 20-23; Perdue, *Wisdom and Cult*, 140-142; Fohrer, "Sophia," 69; McKane, *PWM* 40-41; van Leeuwen, "The Sage in the Prophetic Literature," esp. 301-306.

109. Kovacs, "Is There Class-Ethic," 173-189; Ceresko, "The Sage in the Psalms," 219-230; Frymer-Kensky, "The Sage in the Pentateuch," 281; Oesterley, *Proverbs*, lxviii-lxxiii; Morgan, *Wisdom*, 102, 141.

110. Lemaire, "The Sage in School and Temple," esp. 174, 180-181; Crenshaw, "The Sage in Proverbs," 212.

111. For the meaning of the term "elders" in this verse, see n. 41 above.

112. Cf. nn. 107, 109 above.

113. In the Bible only information on the scribes of the Judean kings' court has survived (2 Sam. 8,17; 20,25; 1 Kgs. 4,3; 1 Chr. 18,16; etc.). The non-preservation of the title in Israel is apparently incidental. For the role of the scribe in Israel see de Vaux, *RB* 48 (1939), 394-405; Cody, *RB* 72 (1965), 381-393; Mettinger, *Solomonic State Officials*, 19ff., 25ff., 42ff., and most recently H. Nier, *TWAT* V, 921-929 and additional bibliography there.

114. Jer. 8,8 is a difficult locus and various interpretations have been proposed. In our view, *laššeqer* should be understood as "in vain" rather than "falsely"; cf. Kaufmann, *The Religion of Israel*, III, 453 n.54; Weinfeld, *Deuteronomy*, 160 n.8. For other interpretations see ibid. 158ff.; Kalugila, *The Wise King*, 82; McKane, *PWM* 40, 103-104 and R.P. Carroll, *The Book of Jeremiah*, 228-229.

115. For this shift in the significance of the term *sôpēr* see *TWAT* V, 927-928.

116. Cf. lately Sweet, "The Sage in Mesopotamian Palaces," esp. 103-107; Perdue, *Wisdom and Cult*, 93-95; Whybray, *The Intellectual Tradition*, 15-16.

117. Cf. the most recent investigations of Frymer-Kensky (n. 109 above), 281; Lemaire (n. 110 above), 180-181 and Blenkinsopp, "The Sage, the Scribe," 307-315.

CHAPTER SEVEN

1. See *Wb.* II 154; Erichsen 180. A shorter version of the following discussion dealing with the ear has been published in my article "The *Sitz im Leben* of the Book of Proverbs," 113-116.

2. The term *idn* (*Wb.* I 154), whose origin is apparently Semitic (see M. Gilula, *JEA* 61 [1975], 251), does not occur in our corpus.

3. The function of the ear as an organ of obedience is very evident in the Elohistic law in Exodus 21,5ff. The ear of the Hebrew slave who rejects freedom is placed against the doorpost of his master's house and pierced through as a sign of his belonging to that house. Cf. S.R. Driver, *Exodus*, *CB*, (Cambridge 1953), 211.

4. The title refers to the function of the king's representative in receiving the supplications of the people; see *Wb.* I 205,3.

5. Drioton ("Sur la sagesse d'Aménémopé," 261) argues that the expression "give ear" in *Amenemope* 3,9 is borrowed from Semitic. However, his view cannot be accepted since the term is common in Late Egyptian; see Williams, "The Alleged Semitic Original," 103.

6. See Driver and Gray, *Job*, 116.

7. Cf. *TDOT* IV, 367-368. In our sample the Egyptian expression *wb3 m sḏm(t)*, which is parallel to Hebrew and Akkadian applications, occurs only once (*Instruction by a Man for His Son* II 3).

8. The passages above, cited from Deutero-Isaiah, recall features that are characteristic of Mesopotamian school life. For linguistic contact between these passages and Sumerian school writings see the following examples: The Father of the "House of Tablets" addresses a pupil and says to him: "Now I am going to speak to you, open your ears" (Gadd, *Teachers and Students in the Oldest Schools*, 17). In a composition portraying a quarrel between two schoolboys, one of them is described as vilifying the other in the following terms: "You sophomore, cover, cover your ears... Why do you say close, close my ears" (Kramer, *The Sumerians*, 242).

9. See Calice No. 61; Vycichl, "Grundlagen," 395 No. 55; and also Cohen No. 436; *Wb.* II 320; Rössler, pars. 29,34.

10. The verb *šsr*, "to express," and the noun *šsr* "utterance," are also derived from the root *šsr*; see *Wb.* IV 547-548.

11. The tongue as an instrument of speech appears in Egyptian in parallelism with and in proximity to terms signifying "speaking," "saying": *md.t*, *mdy*, *ṯs*, *ḏd*, *r3*, *tp.t r3*, *sp.ty* ("lips"); and in combination: *s.t ns*, "place of the tongue," i.e., speech; *skm ns*, "grey tongue," i.e., a tongue skilled in speech (Polotsky par. 63), and *spd ns* — see the discussion that follows. In Biblical wisdom "tongue" appears in this context in parallelism with *śāpâ*, "lip" (Prov. 12,19; Job 27,4; etc.) and *peh*, "mouth," (Prov. 10,31; 15,2; etc).

12. Cf. *spd r3* and *spd ḏbʿ.w*, meaning "skilled in speech, fingers." It is difficult to accept Cazelles' view (*SPOA* 37) that *spd* is the equivalent of *ʿārûm* in the Bible — the Semitic etymology of *ʿārûm* (see *BDB* 791 and *KBL* 737) is remote from the sense of the Egyptian ideogram depicting *spd*, which is a thorn, something sharp (Gr M44).

13. Eloquent speech (without the use of "tongue") is also compared to milk in the Egyptian autobiography, Jansen-Winkeln I A7,e,4; A12,c,5-6.

14. In Egyptian the root *ḥḏ* (v. and n.) serves to express the sense of "harm" contained in speech (see *Anii* 2,8; *Amenemope* 10,21; *Anastasi* I 28,2); the opposite sense, "be safe," "guard," is expressed by *wḏ3* (see *Anii* 2,8; *Amenemope* 10,21; 11,15).

15. A "speedy tongue," condemned by the Egyptian sage, is present in the Bible in a positive sense. The Hebrew scribe takes pride that his tongue is like "the pen of a speedy scribe," that is, his tongue is as fast as the pen of a dextrous scribe (Ps. 45,2; cf. Ezra 7,6); for an interpretation of the expression *sôpēr māhîr*, "speedy scribe," in the Bible in light of extra-Biblical material, see Rainey, "The Soldier Scribe," 58-60.

16. On the relation of the collocation *nṣr* + *lāšôn* to the Hebrew wisdom terminology see Hurvitz, *Wisdom Language*, 64-67.

17. Cf. Bühlmann, *Von rechten Reden*, 279 ff.

18. A comprehensive study on this subject was conducted by S. Herrmann, "Steuerruder, Waage, Herz und Zunge," 105-116. Brunner, *HH* 396-401, also deals with it. Herrmann showed that the tongue and the heart play a part in the Egyptian cosmogony. According to the creation tradition of Heliopolis the heart and the tongue are symbols of the god Atum, who through them created the world. The creation was accomplished by the tongue expressing the thoughts of the heart, i.e., the world was created by means of divine fiats (cf. Genesis 1). Ptah, the creator god of Memphis, borrowed these symbols from Atum and became "the heart and tongue of the gods." The god Horus emerged from Ptah's heart and the god of wisdom, Thoth, from his tongue. The special relationship between the heart and the tongue and their mastery over the other bodily parts are expressed in the theology of Memphis in the following words: "The sight of the eyes, the hearing of the ears, and the smelling of the air by the nose, they report to the heart. It is this which causes every completed (thought) to come forth, and it is the tongue which announces what the heart thinks" (*ANET* 5, lines 53ff.). Thus, the role of the bodily parts is to transmit information to the heart, which weighs the matter up, decides, and commands. These commands are expressed by the tongue (cf. Kayatz, *Proverbien* 1-9, 43-47).

On the other hand, the heart and the tongue are connected with belief in the next world: In the Judgment of the Dead the heart is weighed on the scales against the symbol of the goddess Ma'at, while the tongue is represented there indirectly by means of the god of wisdom, Thoth, whose task it is to register the results of the weighing.

19. The title given to the high official, "the tongue of the king, his guidance in the Two Lands" (*Anastasi* III 1,4), may be understood against the background of this image, that is, he is the guide and advisor of the king in matters of rule and government; cf. "speaking tongue of him who is in the palace, the heart of the lord of the palace" (Intef — *Urk.* IV 968,7-8).

These two traditions, the tongue of man as the plummet of the scales and the tongue as rudder of the ship of life, merged. The traces of this convergence may be found in *The Eloquent Peasant* B1 91-92; cf. also B1 267-269.

20. Cf. also *Amenemope* 19,11ff; 22,5-8 || 23,8-11; *Anii* 8,9-10.

21. See *BDB* 804-805, López, *TWAT* VI, 522-538, and *Wb.* II 389-392. In Akka. *pû*, Ugar. *p*; to the Copt. [SBA] ⲣⲟ, [F] ⲗⲁ, cf., Akka. *lu'u*, which according to Rössler, pars. 28,34, is equivalent to the Hebrew *lōa'*.

22. Cf. *dibrê pî* (Prov. 18,4; Qoh. 10,12); *'imrê peh* (e.g., Prov. 4,5; 5,7; 7,24; Job 8,2); *māšāl b^e pî* (Prov. 26,7,9; see also wisdom Ps. 78,2 and Job 15,13).

23. See Janssen II, pp. 50-51. Once the combination *spd r3* appears in reference to the pupil's ability to read: "*spd r3* (at) reading," (*Lansing* 3,1).

24. For possibility of an Egyptian source for the Hebrew expression "to put the hand on the mouth," i.e., be silent (Job 21,5; 29,9; 40,4; Mic. 7,16) see Couroyer, "Maitre sa main," 197-209.

25. Cf. also the phrase "A unique mouth that speaks when (other) mouths are silent" — Jansen-Winkeln I A6,e,12; II 3,6,13 and similarly ibid. I A12, c,5-6, II 3,6,15.

26. See *Wb.* II 390,1; Vergote, *Joseph*, 99-102; Grinz, *The Book of Genesis*, 118; cf. also Yahuda, *The Accuracy of the Bible*, 95-97.

27. For the primary meaning of *k^e bad peh*, *k^e bad lāšôn* as a physical defect, speech impediment, relating to medical terminology see: J.H. Tigay, "'Heavy of Mouth' and 'Heavy of Tongue,' on Moses' Speech Difficulty," *BASOR* 23(1978), 57-67.

28. Bühlmann, *Von rechten Reden*, 289ff.

29. The term *peh* commonly appears in a negative connotation in the Biblical wisdom. The collocations that are found in this context are similar to those presented respecting the term *lāšôn* — *pî r^e šā'îm*, *pî tahpukôt*, *pî zārôt*, *pî k^e sîl*, *pî 'ĕwîl*; *peh ḥālāq*, *'iqq^e šût peh*.

30. Bühlmann (n. 28 above), 183 ff.

31. The phrase *pṣh peh*, which bears the same meaning, appears once (Job 35,16).

32. Cf. *Wb.* III 356,3-6; see, e.g., Prov. 13,25; Job 20,15.

33. Cf. *Wb.* ibid. 8; see, e.g., Job 3,11; 10,18; 31,15; Jer. 1,5; and, metaphorically, Job 15,35. In this context the expression *pri m ḫ.t* (lit. "come out of the belly"), i.e., "to be born," is common (cf. *Wb.* ibid,10; Meeks II 292-293). This parallels the Hebrew *p^e rî beṭen* (lit. "fruit of the belly"), i.e., "son" (cf. Gen. 30,2; Ps. 132,11; etc.).

34. Cf. *Wb.* ibid. 357,2-4; and see the discussion below. The *Wb.* translates *ḫ.t* as "*Leib.*" In the direct parallelism between *The Instruction of Amenemope* (3, 9-10) and Prov. 22,18, the Hebrew writer "translated" the Egyptian *hnw n ḫ.t* using the term *beṭen* ("belly"). In the present study we have followed him, rendering *ḫ.t* as the Hebrew *beṭen*. Scholars are divided on the translation of *ḫ.t*. While the *Wb.* reads "*Leib*," Lichtheim sometimes translates it as "belly" and sometimes "body." In the translation edited by Simpson, "body," "soul" and "insides" appear. In Lange's *Das Weisheitbuch des Amenemope* and Brunner's *AW*, "*Leib*," "*Inneres*," etc., are used.

35. See section on *lēb* below. Besides "heart," the word "intestines" (*mē'ayim*) at times plays the same role (Jer. 4,19; Job 30,27); as does "liver" (*kabēd*), which interchanges with "heart" in Lam. 1,20; 2,11.

36. Ten times in wisdom books and once in a Psalm with wisdom features.

37. The comparison of a speech or a saying to honey appears also in Prov. 16,24; 24,13-14 and Cant. 4,11; cf. p. 281 above.

38. But this verse can be explained differently as referring to the act of kneeling in sorrow (as in Ps. 44,26), and *beṭen* here is used in the literal sense, i.e., a part of the body, parallel to *nepeš*, "neck," see *TDOT* II 96.

39. E.g., *The Eloquent Peasant* B1 275-276; *Amenemope* 3,13-14; *Urk.* IV 1198,12-13.

40. Some explain *ẖ.t* here not as "belly" but as "body"; thus *hnw n ẖ.t* is rendered "the casket of the body," referring to the chest whose ribs are compared to a casket in which the heart lies (see n.47). But even if the above interpretation is accepted, this does not preclude the assumption that the Hebrew writer understood *ẖ.t* to mean "belly" since the Eg. term is polysemic and means both *Leib* and digestive organ (|| intestines).

41. This according to *Pap. Boulaq* IV. A different version is found in *Pap. Deir el Médineh* I recto 5,2-6: "As for the belly of a man, it is wider than a granary, deeper than a deep pool, a man's field-hedge, which is impossible to encompass, and the heart is the guard (of the belly)"; cf. also the description of the "heated man" in *Ostracon Deir el Médineh* 1265, col. II 7.

42. Heb. *mitlahămîm* derives from Arab. *lhm*, "to swallow". See Kahana, *Proverbs*, 84 and McKane, *Proverbs*, 519-520.

43. This is Kahana's interpretation, ibid. For a different interpretation see McKane, ibid. 547. With the Biblical description compares the Egyptian one of god Anubis as "he who opens bellies and knows what they contain" (19th-Dynasty tomb inscription from Thebes, according to *Wb.* III 357, 3).

44. This is the Septuagint rendering; for a different interpretation see McKane, ibid. 540.

45. Thus in *The Instruction of Amennakht* 12, the wish is expressed that the scribe's apprentice might become familiar with the books of the House of Life (the school): "Be like a casket of books" (*ḫpr mi hni n sš.w*). In *Urk.* IV 1015,17, the official is "the king's casket, containing the counsel of the Two Lands." Cf. Grapow, *Die bildlichen Ausdrücke*, 166-167. As to the affinity between the expression "casket of the belly" in *Amenemope* and *ḥadrê bāṭen* in Proverbs, Drioton ("Sur la sagesse d'Aménémopé," 261) has argued that "casket of the belly" is foreign to the Egyptian concept. He considers the term to be a translation of the Semitic *ḥadrê bāṭen*, basing his premise on the fact that the determinative of *hn* in *Amenemope* is the drawing of a house (Gr O1), which shows that a room is indicated. But the drawing of a room as a determinative of *hn* has been found in other Egyptian sources as well, where no Semitic influence can be assumed (see *Wb.* II 491,18). The above analysis has demonstrated that the metaphor of the "belly" as the heart's residence was common in Egyptian thought. One should therefore join Couroyer ("Amenemope," 394-400), who contests Drioton's view stating that the above description concurs with "the anatomical and psychological concepts of the Egyptians"; a similar opinion was expressed by Williams, "The Alleged Semitic Original," 103.

46. Some support for the premise that the Egyptians regarded the belly as the residence of the heart may be found in the Egyptian term for stomach, *r3 (n) ib*, i.e., "the opening of the heart" (see Lefebvre, *Tableau*, pars. 39,34).

47. Thus in a letter from Golenisheff's collection 1,11; cf. also *Edfu* I 272: "Your heart is steady in its casket" (according to *Wb.* II 492,2). Some scholars assume that *hnw* in these two sources refers to the "chest" (Caminos, *A Tale of Woe*, 19-20; Lefebvre, *Tableau*, par. 24, who adduces this premise in addition to the rendering of "*estomac*"). Nevertheless, the meaning of "belly" still appears to be more apposite in view of the references mentioned above.

48. Cf. to the description of fear of the enemy in Ps. 22,15: "...My heart has turned to wax and it is melted in *my intestines.*"

49. The "authentic" Hebrew equivalent is probably *qîrôt lēb*, "the walls of the heart," (Jer. 4,19).

50. A description of building a house recurs in Proverbs, e.g., the grandiose abode of Wisdom in 9,1ff.; and ibid. 14,1; 24,3,4,27; Qoh. 10,18. On the other hand, nothing has so far come up in archaeological excavations that could throw light on the structure of schools existing in pre-exilic Israel. Therefore, if such an institution existed, it would presumably have been a part of the temple or of the palace complex; it could hardly be credited with the technical standards and the means available to the Egyptian scribe; cf. Mettinger, *Solomonic State Officials*, 140ff.

51. *lb* in Heb., Arab., Akka.; see Vycichl, "Grundlagen," 390-391, No. 38,39; *Wb.* I 59-60; Rössler 314; Calice No. 6.

52. Thus Piankoff, *Le "coeur."* Bonnet (*RÄR* 296 ff.), and Brunner ("Herz," *LÄ* II, 1158ff.) find it difficult to accept Piankoff's conclusion.

53. *Wb.* III 27.

54. See Loewenstamm, "*Lēb*," *EMiqr* IV, 413.

55. The term appears 598 times in the Bible; of these, 141 references are in Proverbs and Qoheleth and 51 in didactic passages in Deuteronomy. Cf. Wolff, *Anthropologie*, 78.

56. See n. 18 above.

57. See Brunner, *Das Herz als Sitz*, 140-141.

58. The *kꜣ* and the "heart" interchange in variants of the mss.: see *Ptaḥḥotep* 186 (L2,P) and Spiegelberg, "Das Herz," 35-37.

59. For attempts to explain the differences in meaning of the terms *rûaḥ*, *nepeš*, *lēb* see: Pedersen, *Israel*, I, 99-109; Schmidt, "Anthropologische Begriffe," 374 ff.; Wolff, *Anthropologie*, 77-78.

60. See the studies of Brunner, "Das Herz im ägyptischen Glauben," 81-106; idem *LÄ* II, 1158-1168; Bonnet, *RÄR* 296-298; Herrmann, "Das steinharte Herz," 77-107; Piankoff, "Le 'Coeur' dans les textes égyptiens," Long, in *Hommages à François Daumas* (Montpellier 1986), 483-494; Wolff, *Anthropologie*, 68-95; Pedersen (n. 59 above); Loewenstamm (n. 54 above), 412-415; Baumgartel, "*Lev*," 606-607.

61. The expression *iꜥ ib* is polysemic; for its different meanings see A. Moret, *Recueil de Travaux*, 14 (1893), 120-123.

62. Cf. Heb. *lēb mēbîn* to Eg. *ib wḥꜥ*, namely, a heart that explains (see p. 64). The phrase *pᵉtôr libbô* (BS 50,27), i.e., "solution of his heart," is identical in meaning.

63. See Briggs, *Psalms*, *ICC* (Edinburgh 1906), II, 144.

64. G. Barkay, "The Priestly Benediction on the Ketep Hinnom Plaques," *Cathedra* 52 (1989), 71-76 (Hebrew).

65. Cf. Deut. 6,8; 11,18; Jer. 31,32, which speak of writing the Law of God on the heart and binding it on the hands and forehead; and see McKay ("Man's Love for God," 430-431) for wisdom features in these passages. On the possibility that "write them on the tablet of your heart" (Prov. 3,3; 7,3) relates to the Egyptian custom of carrying the writing tablets on the chest (heart), being tied by a cord around the neck for the purposes of memorization and repetition, see Couroyer, "La tablette du coeur," esp. 427-428.

66. See Assmann, "Fest des Augenblicks," 79-80.

67. See Otto No. 46 || Lefebvre 58,16; 127,3; other references to *šms ib* in the late autobiography are: Jansen-Winkeln I A10, e,5-6 (*Neb-neteru*, 22nd Dynasty); Otto No. 57 || Brugsch, *Thesaurus*, 926 (*Ta-im-hotep*, ca. 50-30 B.C.). The expression is also present in the songs known as the "Intef," or "Make Merry" or "Harper's Songs" which appear in tombs from the Middle and New Kingdom (see Lichtheim, *Literature* I, 194-197; idem "The Songs of the Harpers"; Wente, "Egyptian 'Make Merry' Song."

68. In research various proposals have been made as to the interpretation of *šms ib*: from the hedonistic interpretation of love of pleasure and enjoyment of life (Kees, *ZÄS* 74 [1938], 82-85; Lichtheim, *Literature* III, 24 n. 16) or a call to an active life without a hedonistic tone (Assmann, "Fest des Augenblicks," 79), to the opposite sense, following one's own conscience, fulfilling of duty (Otto, p. 39; Piankoff, *Le "coeur"*; Lorton, *JARCE* 7 [1968], 41-51; ibid. 8 [1969-70], 55-56; ibid. 12 [1975] 24,29; *Wb.* IV 483, 11); there are some who add a third interpretation — serving someone else's desire (Brunner, *LÄ* II 1161; Lorton *JARCE* 7 [1968], 51-54; ibid. 8 [1969-70], 55-57). Some scholars, and this is our view also, hold that all these meanings are applicable, that is, the meaning of *šms ib* changes according to its context.

69. This is the opinion of Humbert, *Recherches*, 107ff.; Galling, "Kohelet." See also Corpus, n. 13 above.

70. On the interchange ability of "character" and "heart" see also Lichtheim, "Demotic Proverbs," 127-128.

71. *Wb.* V 469,4.

72. Ibid. IV 246, 15-17.

73. Herrmann, "Das steinharte Herz"; see also Brunner, "Das Herz in ägyptischen Glauben," 96ff., and Budge, *Egyptian Magic*, 29-35.

74. A distinction should be made between a negative (Exod. and Ezek.) and a positive connotation of *ḥzq lēb*. In the latter case *ḥzq lēb* means "to gain strength," "to take courage," e.g., Jos. 11,20; Ps. 31,25.

75. Since the passage in Ezekiel does not belong to the wisdom literature and since the idiom *lēb 'eben* does not relate to its vocabulary either, the present discussion does not deal with this issue, which is extensively treated in my article "On the Concept of Heart," 209-211.

76. See Humbert, *Recherches*, 98-99.

77. Lichtheim, "Observations on Pap. Insinger," 293-300; Otto, pp. 37 ff.; Görg, *Gott-Köning-Reden*, 87 n. 253.

78. See n. 18 above. The mark of the Memphitic theology is still considerable in the school writings of the Ramesside Period (*Anastasi* IV 5,1-2).

79. Our rendering differs from that of Lorton, *JARCE* 7 (1968), 42, who reads here, "Follow your conscience." Cf. Lichtheim's translation in *Literature* I, 66 and her remark on Lorton's view, ibid. 77 n. 22.

80. See Couroyer, "*Amenemope* I 9," 394-400; Drioton, "Sur la sagesse," 260.

81. This according to *Pap. BM* 10474 whose version is: "The heart of man is the nose of god." Another version appears in *Turin Tablet*, reading "gift" instead of "nose."

82. See Assmann, "Weisheit, Loyalismus," 18ff.

83. See Gordis, *Koheleth*, 231-232, for interpretation of this verse.

84. Von Rad, "Die Nehemia Denkschrift," 183-185, finds an Egyptian influence in these verses since he believes that the idea of individuals being directed by God is not "popular" in Israel; but this view is unacceptable since a direct contact between the believer and God is a basic component of Judaism, cf. Otto, p. 42.

85. These formulas are characteristic of the Deuteronomist school — Deut. 29,18; Jer. 16,12; 23,17. The opposite is: "to walk before God/to follow God with all the heart"; see Weinfeld, *Deuteronomy*, 334, 340.

86. For a discussion of the meaning of these terms in Proverbs and their link to the Egyptian motif of the heart's weight in the Judgment of the Dead see my article "Egyptian Idioms and Imprints," 476-478, and recently also Griffiths, "The Idea of Posthumous Judgement," 189-191.

87. Cf. comments in the same spirit in Görg, *Gott-König-Reden*, 85-87.

CHAPTER EIGHT

1. Six times in the Biblical wisdom books (5 times in Prov., once in Job); 3 times in BS (6,25; 35,16; 37,17).

2. See Scott, *Proverbs*, 36; Duesberg and Fransen, *Les scribes inspiré*, 189.

3. Driver and Gray, *Job*, 319.

4. See similar description, Job 38,35; Ps. 97,4.

5. This is also the opinion of Lichtheim, who compares the Heb. *taḥbulôt* to the Eg. *ḥmy*, steering, in *Pap. Insinger*, *LEWL* 137.

6. Cf. the description in Isa. 33,13.

7. See Gemser, *Sprüche Salomos*, 14; McKane, *Proverbs*, 266; Oesterley, *Proverbs*, 4; Toy, *Proverbs*, 8; Zimmerli, *Zur Struktur*, 183; *SPOA* 125; *BDB* 287.

8. The relationship existing in Hebrew between the profession of sea-captain and wisdom also exists in Egyptian. The "captain," *sḫry* in Egyptian, is a *nisbe* adjective derived from the noun *sḫr*, advice, plan. The latter term is also used to signify instruction and words of wisdom (see pp. 42ff. above).

9. See Y. Hoffmann, *The Prophecies against Foreign Nations in the Bible* (Tel Aviv 1977), 140 (Heb.).

10. See *EMiqr* V, 612.

11. Collections I, III exhibit contact with the Egyptian sources: Collection III (chaps. 22,17-24,22) contains, as is well known, a direct parallel with *The*

Instruction of Amenemope; for collection I (chaps. 1-9) see Kayatz, *Studien zur Proverbien* 1-9; as to collection II (chaps. 10,1-22,16) it includes maxims dealing with the king and dating from the period of the United Monarchy.

12. One finds support for the assumption that this verse (37,12) belongs to the original material of the book in that it repeats things said in the earlier strata; cf. God's answer to Job (28,35). For the dating of Job and its composition see *EMiqr* I, 253-254.

13. Brunner, "Die 'Weisen', 32; also idem *Erziehung*, 130, and recently "Zentralbegriffe."

14. The noun is derived from the verb *ṯs* ("to tie knots"); Copt. [S]: ϫⲱⲥ ; see *Wb.* V 396. The use of *ṯs* is varied: It can mean instruction by a father to his son (*Ptaḥḥotep* above; *Chester Beatty* IV pl. 19 verso 3,7), order to officials (in the *Kemit*; *Kheti* II D; *Urk.* IV 1089,7 [an appointment of a vizier]), words of "prophecy" (*Khakheperre-sonb*, above; *Neferti*, above) or love songs (Luft, "Zur Einleitung," 108). Owing to the varied use of *ṯs*, it is hard to determine its exact meaning. However, it seems that the unifying feature in most of the references of *ṯs* and that which separates it from the other terms for wisdom sayings is that it refers to a traditional, conventional saying. This sense is obvious in the opening of *Khakheperre-sonb*, who wishes to depart from the routine of traditional wisdom handed down from father to son, saying, "Had I... *ṯs.w* that are strange; novel untried words, free of repetition; not transmitted *ṯs.w*..." (recto 2); we find the opposite approach in *Chester Beatty* IV: "The teaching is good, it has no weariness, when a son answers with the *ṯs.w* of his father" (pl. 20 verso 6,7-8). Against this background it is possible to understand the passage in *Khakheperre-sonb* (verso 5) describing the bad situation in the land: "There is no one who loves getting knowledge, a man loves only his *ṯs*," that is, people are not keen on innovations, they adhere to hoary sayings and adages that they have long known. *ṯs* is therefore an ancient, traditional saying, passed down from former generations. This may be the reason why it has become difficult to understand and requires an explanation, as may be gathered from the verbs that accompany it, namely, *wḥʿ*, "to release, understand" (see discussion below) and *wšb*, "to reply, respond" (*Neferti* 13). The *ṯs* may be transmitted both orally from father to son (as in the two examples given above: *Khakheperre-sonb* recto 2; *Chester Beatty* IV pl. 20 verso 6,7-8), and in writing, as a proverb written in a book (see *Wb.* V 403,14): thus, it is said in *Chester Beatty* IV that what the sages say "is found as *ṯs(w)*, written in their books" (Pl. 19 verso 3,7); in *Ptaḥḥotep* (292) and in the speeches of *The Eloquent Peasant* (B2 107) maxims termed "*ṯs*" are quoted; "*ṯs*" is a citation from *The Instruction of Djedefhor*, mentioned in *Anastasi* I (11,1) (see also *Kheti* II D). (Additional appearances of *ṯs* are in: *Ptaḥḥotep* 511; *Amenemope*, 19,7 [unclear]; *Amennakht* 1; *Kheti* III B; *Lansing* 14,10; *Chester Beatty* IV pl. 20 verso 6,13; *Instruction by a Man for His Son* XVI 1 [unclear], XVIII 7; *Urk.* IV 47,12; 419,8; 435,2; Otto No. 3 || *KCG* 42213 p. 35 l.3 || Jansen-Winkeln I A7, e,2-3; II 3,6,8; idem I A10,d,13; II 3,6,7).

15. In the view of Ockinga, "The Burden," 91,93, the goal of the Egyptian priest does not center on novelties in the literary sphere but in expressing a new message in order to correct the poor state of affairs.

16. See *Wb.* I 348-349. It is interesting to compare the Eg. expression with the

Aramaic expression in Dan. 5,12: *mᵉšārē' qiṭrîn*, i.e., "one who looses knots," which, along with *mᵉpaššēr ḥelmîn* ("interpreter of dreams") and *'aḥăwāyat 'ăḥîdān* ("explainer of riddles"), is one of Daniels' titles. From the context one can assume that the image "opening the knots" indicates, as in Egyptian, the solution of obscure sayings, and concretely explaining dreams and riddles. However, some scholars interpret the Aramaic expression in Daniel with the actual tying of knots for a magic purpose; see H.P. Müller, "Lösen von Zauberknoten (?)," *VT* 20 (1970), 474 n.3.

17. Additional references to *wḥꜥ*: *Ptaḥḥotep* 366; *Khakheperre-sonb* verso 1, *Instruction by a Man for His Son* II 6; *Lansing* 2,9; *Onomasticon*, Title; *Urk.* IV 47,12; 969,14; etc.

18. Perhaps the *Sitz im Leben* of these proverbs was the verbal dispute between the rivals that preceded warfare, as in the battle between David and Goliath (1 Sam. 17,43-47); or in the battle between Sinuhe and the man of Retenu (*The Story of Sinuhe* B 109-110). These disputes could also be between representatives of the rivals: cf. the agents of Hezekiah, King of Judah, and Ravshake, the messenger of the Assyrian king (2 Kgs. 18,17ff. || Isa. 36).

19. In the New Kingdom the form *mdw* is supplanted by *md.t* (and during the 21st Dynasty by *mdty*): *Wb.* II 180; in Demotic *mt(t)*: Erichsen 184; in Coptic [S] ; the two latter forms function as a nominal prefex to nouns and adjectives which become abstract feminine nouns.

20. See *Wb.* above and also Lesko I 256. The term is written by means of an ideogram meaning walking stick (Gr S43; Faulkner 122) and by the determinative of a man with his hand to his mouth, indicating an action involving the mouth.

21. In this sample *mdw* appears in the instructions from *To Merikare* to the Demotic instructions (49 times), in the "loyalist" instruction (once), the pessimistic literature (16 times), the school writings (7 times), the king's court inscriptions (20 times) and the late autobiography (3 times).

22. See Davies, *The Tomb of Rekh-mi-re*, 81 n. 16; cf. *Urk.* IV 971,2; etc.

23. Cf. *Anii* 9,9,15,16; *Anastasi* III 1,3; *Urk.* IV 122,16; 510,14; Jansen-Winkeln I A13,1,4; II 3,6,14.

24. Another meaning of *mdw* when referring to a spoken word is a "legal claim." The complaints of the Peasant are so termed (B1 72, 234; B2 118; cf. *Urk.* IV 1090,10 — *Rekhmire*); and see Shupak, "A New Source," 12 and n. 46.

25. Cf. "the speech of men of former times (*md.t imy.w ḥ3.t*)," *Khakheperre-sonb* recto 3.

26. Cf. *Amenemope* 4,1; *Seḥetep-ib-Ra* 7,6; *Urk.* IV 1185,1.

27. See *Wb.* II 180,13; 181,3, Lesko I 256-257 and Caminos, *LEM* 227; and also *Anastasi* I 1,1; V 6,1-2; 15,7; *Urk.* IV 1223,13; etc.

28. The etymology of the word *dābār* is not clear, but the root appears in Phoenician, Punic and Aramaic, see *TDOT* III 94ff.

29. See ibid. 103ff. and *BDB* 182-184.

30. See Prov. 1,6; 22,17; cf. 24,23; Qoh. 9,17; 12,11; in Egyptian the collocation "words of wise men (*md.w rḫ.w iḫ.t*)" appears once in *Admonitions* 2,14.

31. In the wisdom literature *dābār* refers to the wisdom of human beings — the teacher or the father. Only once in the teaching of Agur does *dābār* relate to

the words of God: "Every word of God is pure... Add not to his words..." (Prov. 30,5) Most scholars maintain that "his words" refers here to *tôrâ*. Oesterley, *Proverbs*, 270-271, believes that "his words" in Prov. 30,5 denotes the third part of the Canon, i.e., the Writings that was at this time in the process of being created; cf. also Toy's interpretation, *Proverbs*, 523. Fichtner, who disputes this, identifies "his words" with the sayings of the sages; cf. p. 41 above.

32. Like *ṯs*, *r3* sometimes bears the sense of a popular folk saying (*Mentuhotep* 15); and at times in the sense of a father's rebuke to his son (*Amennakht* 6); see also *Urk.* IV 1223,1 || 118,13.

33. The expression *s.t r3*, meaning "speech" (lit. "the seat of the mouth"), is rare in our corpus (twice only, in *Urk.* IV and the autobiography). *tp.t/tp(y) r3*, first appears in use in the Old Kingdom and means "speech," "utterance," lit. "beginning of the mouth" (*Wb.* V 287). *tp.t r3* belongs to the terminology of the king's court inscriptions and the autobiography. In this framework the expression refers to: (1) speech of men (common in the titulary of the officials of the 18th Dynasty, "with whose sayings the Lord of the Two Lands is satisfied," Otto No. 75 || *ZÄS* 62, 86ff., l.3; *Urk.* IV 411,2; 993,8); (2) order of the king (Blumenthal, p. 403); (3) word of the god, the divine fiat (*Wb.* V 287,9, cf. *Urk.* IV 165, 13-15; 974,9).

34. See *BDB* 826.

35. Another regular collocation is *p^e rî beṭen* (lit. "fruit of womb"), meaning "offspring," which appears in Egyptian as *pri m ẖ.t*; see Chap. 7, n. 33.

36. Cf. "Death and life are in the power of the tongue and those who love it will eat its fruits" (Prov. 18,21), where *p^e rî* comes in proximity to tongue; cf. also the collocation "the fruit of the arrogant heart" (Isa. 10,12), meaning "insolent speech"; see *BDB* 826.

37. *Wb.* I 523,18. *pri n/m r3* stands in synonymous parallelism with "speech", *md.t* (*Neferti* in the discussion above) or *ḏd* (*Urk.* IV 546,9). The phrase is not characteristic of the wisdom instructions. In our sample it appears in the king's court phraseology (6 times), the school writings (twice), and the pessimistic wisdom texts (*Neferti* 50).

38. *Wb.* I 530ff.; Copt. ⲉϭⲣⲁ ; in Calice's view the Egyptian *pr.t* is analogous with the Hebrew *p^e rî* and belongs to the group of Egyptian words whose provenance is Semitic; see Calice No. 38 and cf. *KBL* 778.

39. For additional references see *Wb.* I 523,18.

40. The following opinion is conjectural: It is also possible that the Hebrew phrase is the outcome of an independent linguistic development and that the analogy between it and the Egyptian expression is purely incidental.

41. The collocation *môṣā' peh/ś^e pātayim*, with meaning identical to that of *p^e rî peh*, is found outside Proverbs; but unlike *p^e rî peh* it always concerns the religious sphere and not the secular (the words of God, Ps. 89,35; Deut. 8,3; the words of the messenger of God, the prophet, Jer. 17,16; the vow of the believer, Deut. 23,24).

42. Kedar-Kopfstein, "*pārāh/p^e rî*," has reservations about the possibility that the basic meaning of *p^e rî peh* is "what emerges from the mouth," and not a reference to fruit, since the Hebrew phrase always involves verbs of "eating" and "being sated" and nouns denoting "produce," "crops." But if it is assumed that

the phrase was adapted from Egyptian, the problem may be solved by tracing these elements back to an adaptation of the Egyptian material to the Hebrew framework by the Biblical scribe.

43. In respect of subject matter cf. Ps. 51, 17,18; 69, 31,32; and Psalms of Solomon 15,3. See also W.R. Harper, *Hosea*, *ICC* (Edinburgh 1973), 411-412, and J. Licht, *The Rule Scroll*, (Jerusalem 1965), 189 (Heb.).

44. Licht, ibid. Licht's interpretation underlies the translation of the passage cited below; cf. *pᵉrî tᵉhillâ* (1QS 10,8) and *pᵉrî qôdeš* (ibid. 22); see: Licht, ibid., 220,211 and also Kedar- Kopfstein (n. 42 above), 752.

45. In this corpus *ḫn* appears in the instructions from the New Kingdom: *Anii*, *Amenemope* (4 times), the "loyalist" instruction (twice), the pessimistic literature (4 times), the school writings (4 times), the royal inscriptions (twice).

46. See *Wb.* III 287.

47. Cf. *Neferti* 49: "Speech falls (*ḫn.w md.t*) on the heart like fire" (according to Helck's reading, and also Lichtheim, *Literature* I, 142; not so *Wb.* III 289,8, which reads *ḫn n md.t*, i.e., "maxim"). Other meanings of *ḫn* are "affair," "matter" (see *Wb.* III 289) and "complaint" (e.g., *The Eloquent Peasant* B1 280; *Instructions by a Man for His Son* IX 9), and see Shupak, "A New Source," 12.

48. Brunner conjectures that the Egyptians used *ḫnw* to signify *Bildrede*, see *LÄ* I, 807. But the references he cites on 811 n.6, do not bear this out.

49. My interpretation of these references differs from that of Perry (*A Critical Study of The Eloquent Peasant*, 146, 157-158), who explains *ḫn n md.t* as "complaint, official protest rather than 'proverb,'" and also Ockinga, "The Burden," 89-90, Faulkner 196, and others. On this see my article "A New Source," n.47.

50. *nfr* + *md.t* occurs in the instructions (only in *Ptaḥḥotep*, 5 times), the pessimistic literature (3 times), the royal inscriptions (once) and in the autobiography (once). *nfr md.t* stands in parallelism with *wȝḥ ib* (tolerant man) and *nfr sḏm* (good of hearing).

51. Stock, "*nṯr nfr*."

52. Janssen I pp. 122-123; II pp. 166-167; Polotsky, par. 65.

53. Edel, par. 43; Janssen I ibid. Hc 20,22, 26, 31, 39, 40, 41, etc.; in parallelism with *biȝ iḳr* ("excellent character"), Otto No. 28 || *MDAIK* 12, 114 l. 16.

54. *mnḫ* is collocated also with the noun *wšb.t*, "answer" (*Anastasi* V 15, 1).

55. *mnḫ* + *ḏd* occurs in the instructions (4 times), the school texts (5 times), *Urk.* IV (once), and autobiography (twice).

56. *ʿm m sḫr.w* "to know the plans," appears also in *Lansing* 13B,9. Posener renders this expression differently: "to know scripts and professions" (*Amennakht*, n.0). Also regarding "in order to state the excellent," Posener's interpretation differs from the one presented above since he understands "excellent" as referring to "the literary value of the work."

57. Otto No. 28 || *MDAIK* 12, 114 l. 18 ; see also *Urk.* IV 419,8; 1198, 15; Janssen I p.5, G 57,58; pp.22-23, Aa 42,46,52; and also ibid., p. 125, Hc 73,76 and p. 6, G 61, 62.

58. The combination *s.t ns* is identical in meaning to *ns* (see Janssen II p. 38). When *s.t* stands before a bodily organ it stresses its "effectivity," see Gardiner, *PSBA* 34 (1912), 261; Janssen ibid. p. 17.

59. Janssen I p. 5, G 42,44-46; idem II pp. 17-18, 38.

60. Cf. pp. 329—330 below.

61. Cf. Nel, *The Structure*, 7-8; Polk, "Paradigms," 565; Beyse, "*māšāl*," 72.

62. In our corpus there are only a few parallels to the sophisticated literary forms termed *māšāl* in Post-Biblical Hebrew, viz., allegory (a metahpor expanded into a folk tale), parable (a moral folktale), and fable (a story whose heroes are taken from the animal and plant world). (For explanation and examples of these genres see M. Haran, "*Māšāl*," 548-549; Nel, *The Structure*, 9-10; and Polk, "Paradigms," 564-573.) These literary forms, however, are not rare in non-wisdom literature both in Israel and Egypt. A use of allegory is found in *The Dispute of a Man with His Ba*, see p. 329 and n. 68 below. J.G. Griffiths (*JEA* 53 [1967], 79-102) in his comprehensive study on "Allegory in Greece and Egypt" actually includes within this term all literary forms listed above: "In its original Greek sense allegory implies that an author proclaims a meaning other than the one which is instantly apparent" (89). In any event, Griffiths succeeded in showing that the device of allegory originated in Egypt and that such works as *The Blinding of Truth*, *The Lion and the Mouse*, or *The Disputation between the Body and the Head* contain a rich allegorical tradition. It is particularly instructive to compare fables in the Bible (e.g., Judg. 9,8ff.; 2 Kgs. 14,9) with these Egyptian folk legends, whose theme is personification of bodily parts and the animal and plant world and which flourished in the literature of the New Kingdom and in Demotic, and also found expression in the art of the period; see Brunner-Traut, *Altägyptische Tiergeschichte*.

63. A further example of the use of *ḫn n md.t* in the sense of "wisdom saying" finds *Wb.* III 289,8 in *Neferti* 49. His rendering accords with ms. C 25224. The context, however, makes it difficult to decide whether *ḫn n md.t* bears this sense here. It is possible therefore also to follow ms. DeM 1189, which reads *ḫnw md.t* and to take *ḫn* as a verb, not a noun.

64. "The opponent" is the rival in love or the patron of the woman. A further example of the use of *ṯs* in the sense of "proverb" is possibly *Amenemope* 19,7, but the passage is not clear.

65. In *Wb.* VI, which includes a German-Egyptian lexicon, the terms *Fabel*, *Gleichnis* do not appear; *ḫn n md.t* is given for *Sprichwort*. For criteria to distinguish these proverbs even when the text does not indicate that they are such, see Gunn, "Some Middle Egyptian Proverbs" and recently Lichtheim, "Demotic Proverbs."

66. See Gilula, *The Wisdom of Amen-m-ope*, 30-31, 33-37, who compares this to a similar feature in the Biblical wisdom.

67. Lichtheim, "Demotic Proverbs." For additional proverbs see *The Eloquent Peasant* B1 146; *Amenemope* 24, 6-7.

68. Griffiths (n. 62 above), 94-95; Goedicke, *The Report about the Dispute of a Man and His Ba*, 45ff., 130ff. For the use of the stylistic devices of allegory and metaphor in Egyptian literature in general see ibid. 15 and nn. 69, 70; see also Brunner's study, "Bildliche Ausdrücke," with many examples.

69. A distinction should be made between the use of the term *māšāl* independently, relating to literary pattern, and its meaning in the collocation "to be *l^{e}māšāl w^{e}lišnînâ*" and in variants of this expression; see *BDB* 605/2.

70. In the wisdom literature *māšāl* appears in: Prov. 1,1,6; 10,1; 25,1; 26, 7,9;

Job 13,12; 27,1; 29,1; Qoh. 12,9; Ps. 49,5; 78,2; BS 3,29; 6, 35; 44,5; 47,17; 50,27 (*môšel*) (39,2-3 [Gr.]). In other books: Num. 1, Sam., 1 Kgs., Isa., Ezek., Mic., Hab.

71. Also in BS 47,17.

72. In Num., Judg., 1 Kgs., 2 Chr., Ezek., Dan. In the apocryphal wisdom literature BS 8,8; 47,17; (39,3 [Gr.] and the Wisdom of Solomon 8,8 [Gr.]).

73. For a discussion on *taḥbulôt* and *dᵉbarîm*, the latter being combined with *ḥăkamîm* only in the wisdom literature (4 times), see pp. 313—317, 320 above. *'ămārîm* (as distinct from the derivatives *'ōmer*, *'imrâ*, which do not belong to the wisdom vocabulary) appears 40 times in Prov., Job and the wisdom Psalms. In the rest of the Bible its occurrence is limited to 12 times. See the discussion below, pp. 331—332.

74. Selected studies referring to these terms — *māšāl*: Eissfeld, *Der Maschal in A.T.*; Schmidt, *Studium zur Stilistik*; Fontaine, *Traditional Sayings in the O.T.*; Haran, "*Māšāl*"; Johnson, "Mashal"; Beyse, "māšāl"; Thompson, *The Form and Function*, esp. 9-95. *mᵉlîṣâ*: Richardson, "Some Notes"; Canney, "The Hebrew *mēlîṣ*." *ḥîdâ*: Torcszyner, "The Riddle"; idem (Tur Sinai) "*Ḥîdâ*"; Müller, "Der Begriff 'Rätsel'"; Hamp, "*Chîdāh*"; Crenshaw, *SAT* 96-111; idem *Samson* (Atlanta 1978), 99-120; for the interesting suggestion that the proverbs of parallel couplet which predominate in Prov. resulted from the "proverb-riddle" containing one stich which was answered by corresponding line, see Thompson, ibid. 75-76, 92-93.

75. E.g., *'imrê nō'am* (# *maḥšᵉbôt rā'*): Prov. 15,26; 16,24; *'imrê dā'at*: ibid. 23,12; 19, 27; *'imrê bînâ*: ibid. 1,2; *'imrê* + *ṣedeq*, *'ĕmet*, *nᵉkōḥîm*, *yōšer*: ibid. 8,8; 22,21; Job 6,25; etc.

76. The chief difficulty in this verse is the cryptic *'ōpen*, which is repeated in BS 36,5 and 50,27. Various interpretations have been proposed; some suggest "manner" or "circumstance," namely, he who speaks at the right time (*BDB*, Gemser, Toy, etc.); others explain it through the word "wheel" which applies to one part of the verse. Thus the term refers to a certain type of proverb in which the two halves of the verse balance (McKane, *Proverbs*, 584); Barucq and others also speak of a special sort of proverb. The last explanation fits well BS 50,27: "Wise instruction and *'ōpānîm* proverbs of Simeon, the son of Jeshua."

77. There is no need to amend *ṭēṭîb* to *ṭēṭîp* (as do *BH* and Gemser); see Bühlmann, *Von rechten Reden*, 53-55.

78. *ḥēn* is mentioned 13 times in Prov. (in parallelism with *yōpî* — Prov. 31,30; cf. 5, 19; 11,16; etc.).

79. See *Wb.* II 378; and ibid. 379,4 for more references.

80. See *Wb.* I 137; Calice No. 396.

81. See Bühlmann (n. 77 above), 42-45.

82. See Brunner, *Erziehung*, 101-102.

83. For additional references in the Egyptian sources see Brunner, ibid.; Bühlmann (n. 77 above), 38-85; Lanczkowski, "Reden und Schweigen."

84. See Corpus, p. 26, and bibliography there, and also Brunner, *Erziehung*, 102 and idem *AW* 368-369.

CHAPTER NINE

1. Cf. Ullendorff, "Thought Categories," 273-275, 286-287.

2. Adjectives 13-21 belong to the sapiential vocabulary only when qualifying a human being.

3. This expression, mentioned in Chap. 7, p. 310 above, is treated extensively in my article "Egyptian Idioms," 476-478.

4. A further group of equivalent terms in Hebrew and Egyptian wisdom vocabulary may be appended to the list given above, but the usage of these terms is not restricted to wisdom literature, e.g., *sb3*, *sb3y.t* — *ysr*, *mûsār*; *mtr* — *ykḥ* (hiph'il), *tôkaḥat*; *tp rd* — *tôrâ*, *miṣwâ*; *sḏm ib* — *lēb šōmēa'*; *dns/sḫm* + *ib* — *kbd/qšh/ḥzq* + *lēb*.

5. Terminology obviously does not furnish the sole criterion for determining the existence of a connection between Hebrew and Egyptian wisdom compositions. The comparative study of terminology is based on the assumption that the contact between the two wisdom traditions also took place both on a formal level and on the level of content and ideas. This subject is beyond the scope of this research, but occasionally parallels emerged that are adequate to illustrate this side of the inter-literary contact. The history of comparative research in this field is reviewed in the Introduction; see pp. 1-4 above.

6. Two of the terms exclusive to the Biblical wisdom terminology, *'āṣēl* and *ḥārûṣ*, which recur frequently in the second collection of Proverbs (12 out of 19 references), also corroborate the assumption that this collection constituted part of the syllabus in the Israelite educational framework. What is more, *wsf*, the Egyptian equivalent of the Hebrew *'āṣēl*, is common in the Egyptian school writings (see p. 350 below).

7. *ba'ar* and *k^esîl* occur only in the wisdom books and in psalms with wisdom features (according to Whybray, Ps. 92 and 94).

8. The verb *rgn* appears an identical number of times within and outside the wisdom books, but the participle form *nirgān* is exclusive to Prov. (cf. p. 140 above).

9. *mēbîn* is found an identical number of times within and outside the wisdom books.

10. *nṣr* as a component in collocation which bears the sense of "restraint" appears only once outside the wisdom literature in Ps. 141,3 where "lips" serve as object.

11. Most of these terms have equivalents or parallels in the Egyptian wisdom lexicon. See the list of words belonging to the Egyptian wisdom terminology below.

12. On the criterion of "cumulative testimony" see Hurvitz, *Wisdom Language*, 27. Whybray, *The Intellectual Tradition*, 142-149, uses this criterion to determine that the following words are exclusive to the wisdom literature: *ba'ar*, *k^esîl*, *lēṣ*, *sākāl*, *bînâ*, *'ārûm*, *leqaḥ*, *nābôn*, *tûšiyyâ*. To this list Hurvitz (ibid. passim) adds the following collocations: *ṣpn* + object; *nṣr* + object; *y^ešar/tām derek*, *śēkel ṭôb*, *swr m^era'*. The wisdom terminology given by Hurvitz contains more words and collocations, but these have not been dealt with, since they have no link with the Egyptian material.

13. In parentheses the analogies in Biblical wisdom language appear, which do not always constitute equivalents in the full sense of the Egyptian term but approximate it on the level of subject matter. To distinguish between these analogies and real equivalents the latter are marked with an asterisk.

14. *grw* is replaced by *ḳb*, "cold-tempered," in the school writings and the autobiographies and by *ḳb* and *hrw*, "calm," in the royal inscriptions.

15. The following terms belong to the semantic field of "restraint" in the Biblical wisdom: *'erek 'appayim*, *qar rûaḥ*, *nṣr/šmr + peh*, *lāšôn*, *lēb*; see pp. 171–173 above.

16. See Chap. 4, n. 29 above.

17. This view does not contradict the fact that during the New Kingdom pupils of humble origin are to be found in the schools for scribes, and that among the readers of the Egyptian instructions were also peasants (*Ankhsheshonqy*) and common folk (*Instruction by a Man for His Son*); see Brunner, *Erziehung*, 118, and idem *LÄ* III, 965.

18. See Skaldny, *Die ältesten Spruchsammlungen*. Skaldny specifies 4 collections in Proverbs, each addressing a different group: 10-15 is addressed to young people; 17-22,16 is an instruction for officials in the king's service; 25-27 is directed to the common people, peasants; 28-29 is applied to the governing class (the "sovereign's mirror"); see also McKane, *Proverbs*, 9, and Hermisson, *Studien*, 123ff.

19. At the same time, it should be noted that the adjective *fleissig* does not appear at all in the German-Egyptian dictionary of *Wb*. VI.

20. Although scholars are divided over the etymology of *ḥîdâ*, all agree that the root is Semitic; see Hamp, *TDOT* VI, 320ff; Müller, "Der Begriff 'Rätsel,'" 483-486. On the custom of sages' engaging in posing riddles in the ancient Near Eastern court, see ibid., 482, and cf.: 1 Esdras 3,1-5,3; Josephus, *Antiquities*, 8,5.

21. Cf. p. 77 above.

22. The "negative connotation," which predominates in the Egyptian wisdom phraseology, finds its expression in the following details, which have arisen in the course of our investigation: (a) The theme of the behavior of the negative human type is expressed with verbal richness and variety. The positive type, by contrast, is qualified by a limited number of terms (cf. Chap. 3 with Chap. 4). (b) Six terms in Egyptian wisdom belong to the semantic field of "silence," "calmness"; this is less than half the number of terms covering the opposite semantic field of "hot temper," "anger" and "strife" (cf. Chap. 4, pp. 150ff. with Chap. 3, pp. 116ff.). (c) To these one may add the fact that there is no equivalent in Egyptian wisdom vocabulary to *ḥārûṣ* ("diligent"), a term characteristic of Hebrew wisdom; and on the other hand the image of "deafness" in Egyptian has no parallel in Biblical wisdom.

23. The Egyptian *ḏ'r* is close in meaning to the Hebrew *ḥqr* and *bqš*, but it appears only twice in regard to a typical wisdom activity: in an inscription of the 18th Dynasty's architect and in *The Complaints of Khakheperre-sonb* (see p. 71 above). Specially relevant to the Biblical verses are the words of Khakheperre-sonb, who voices his desire to be part of this group of creative people and to possess the ability "to investigate speech (*ḏ'r ḫnw*)." But according to his personal confession, this is unfortunately beyond his powers.

24. See p. 267 above.

25. See p. 127 above.

26. See pp. 123—124 above.

27. See Chap. 7, pp. 284—285 and n. 18 there. On the connection between the heart and the Egyptian Judgement of the Dead see my article "Egyptian Idioms," 476-478. The Egyptian motif is evoked in the collocation *tōkēn libbôt* in Proverbs (21,2; 24,12 and cf. 16,2) and is reflected even more clearly in the image of the balance in Job 31,6: "Let he (God) weigh me in just balance."

28. See pp. 40—42, 270—272 above.

29. As shown by Assmann; cf. p. 42 above. Fox (in "Aspects" and in *The Book of Qoheleth* [dissertation]) challenges the accepted opinion regarding the gradual development of Hebrew wisdom, giving the following arguments: (1) There is no development from utilitarianism to religiousness in Egyptian wisdom, for Ankhsheshonqy, who came after Amenemope, was far less "religious" than his forerunner. (2) Even if there were such a development in Egyptian wisdom, the Biblical sages were not influenced by it as they accepted the Egyptian wisdom as a monolithic entity. Fox's belief is that Hebrew wisdom was ethical-moral from the beginning. His premise regarding the lack of affinity in the development of Hebrew and Egyptian wisdom may be correct, but his arguments are not immune to criticism: (1) It is true that Ankhsheshonqy was less "religious" than Amenemope, who preceded him, but he was an exception in the entire complex of Egyptian instructions owing to his close ties with the contemporary international wisdom which left its mark on his work. (For the influence of Greek wisdom on *Ankhsheshonqy* see Walcot, "Hesiod," 215ff., and also Lichtheim, *LEWL* 13-22 who discusses the impact of other wisdom traditions as well, specially that of *The Story of Aḥiqar*. (2) Fox's assertion that Israelite sages considered Egyptian wisdom as one monolithic whole is not incontrovertible for we know of the existence of ties between Egypt and Israel throughout and after the pre-exilic era (there was a Jewish diaspora in Egypt in the days of Jeremiah and there were Jewish military colonies during the Persian era). Morgan holds a view similar to Fox's. In his *Wisdom in the O.T.*, 60, 144-145, 152, and his "Wisdom and the Prophets," 221, Morgan rejects the thesis of gradual development of Hebrew wisdom from "secular" to "religious," believing that it was religious from the start.

30. See Chap. 6, pp. 258—267 above.

31. See, e.g., *The Psalmist*, ed. Simpson, particularly ibid. 196-197.

32. Alleged evidence for the existence of a school structure found at Kuntilat Ajrud is proposed by A. Lemaire, *Les écoles et la formation de la Bible dans l'ancien Israël*. *OBO* 39 (1981) 30, 32, 52-53. However, this is the only evidence of its kind and is of questionable validity. The excavators believe that the site was a center of worship, and that the empty room surrounded by benches, which according to Lemaire was a classroom, functioned as a location for collecting and storing the gifts and offerings of the faithful. See Z. Meshel, *Kuntilat Ajrud: A Holy Site from the Period of the Monarchy on the Sinai Border* (Israel Museum) (Jerusalem, 1978) and idem *Kadmoniot*, 9 (1977), 119-124(Heb.).

33. H. J. Hermisson, *Studien*, 113-136, has set out all circumstantial evidence in support of the existence of schools in Israel. See also L. Dürr, *Das Erziehungswesen*, 106ff.; T.N. D. Mettinger, *Solomonic State Officials*, 143ff; J. P.

J. Olivier, "Schools and Wisdom Literature," *JNSL* 4 (1975), 49-60; Crenshaw, "Education," 607-610; Lemaire (n. 32 above) and lately idem "The Sage in School and Temple." The most comprehensive work to date on the subject of education and schools in ancient Egypt is the monograph of H. Brunner, *Altägyptische Erziehung* and idem "L'éducation en ancienne Égypte," in *Histoire mondiale de l'éducation*, eds. G. Mialaret and J. Vial (Paris 1981), 65-86; see also E. Otto, "Bildung und Ausbildung," 41-48, and recently my article, "The Sitz im Leben," 104-106, where an earlier version of part of the following discussion was published.

34. See Lemaire, (above) and also B. Lang, "Schule und Unterricht." In view of the limited scope of the epigraphical evidence, it seems that this view must await further findings before it can be confirmed; cf. Crenshaw, "Education," 605-607.

35. For an extensive discussion of these terms see the preceding chapters and my article (n. 33 above), 106-116.

36. But *sbꜣ* as a verb and an adjective (participle) appears 13 times in the instructions as compared with 4 times in the school literature.

37. See Mettinger (n. 33 above), 25ff.; Williams, "People Come Out," 235; R. de Vaux, "Titres et fonctionnaires égyptiens à la cour de David et de Salomon," *RB* 48 (1939), 394ff.; I. Begrich, "Sōfer und Mazkir," *ZAW* 58 (1940-1), 1ff. and Crenshaw, "Education," 610.

38. See Lambdin, "Egyptian Loan Words," 149; Williams, ibid. 238-239.

39. For the view that all the education in ancient Israel took place in a private setting, the teachers being the fathers or master craftsmen, see F. W. Colka, "Die Israelitische Weisheitsschule oder 'Des Kaisers neuer Kleider,'" *VT* 33 (1983), 257-270; on the location of family and tribe as possible life-setting for wisdom, cf. most recently Fontaine, "The Sage in Family and Tribe," and the up-to-date bibliography there.

40. See p. 43 above, and n. 62 there; see also the acts of the *ḥărtummîm* (synonymous with *ḥăkāmîm*) in Pharaoh's court in the stories of Joseph and Moses (Gen. 41,8,24; Exod. 7,11; 8,3,14,15; 9,11) and the reference to "Pharaoh's counsellors" in Isa. 19,11; cf. these Biblical passages with the sorcery performed by the three *ḥry-tp* priests before the king in *Pap. Westcar* and the appearance of the sage Neferti before the king Snefru in *The Prophecies of Neferti*, 26. The royal court was the center for learning and wisdom activity in ancient Mesopotamia as well, see Sweet, "The Sage in Mesopotamian Palaces."

41. This is the view of von Rad, *Wisdom in Israel*, 17; Mettinger, (n. 33 above); Lang, *Die weisheitliche Lehrrede*, 36-40; Morgan, *Wisdom in the O.T.*, 142; idem "Wisdom and the Prophets," 222-224; and others.

42. Many studies on the influence of Biblical wisdom tradition on other literary genres have been published recently; see bibliography in Whybray, *The Intellectual Tradition*, 1 n. 1; Murphy, "Hebrew Wisdom," 27-28; and Morgan, *Wisdom in the O.T.*, passim. For the sapiential influence on the prophets also see Thompson, *The Form and Function*, 103-110.

43. Murphy and Carm, "Wisdom — Theses and Hypotheses," 39-40; Murphy, "The Forms of O.T.," 3-4.

44. Crenshaw, "Method in Determining," 129ff.; idem *OT Wisdom*, 39-41; cf. pp. 6—7 above.

45. Crenshaw, ibid., 133-136; Morgan, "Wisdom and the Prophets," 214.

46. Whybray, (n. 42 above), 154, offers a list of Biblical passages outside the wisdom books in which he discerns the imprint of an "intellectual tradition." He finds influence of the wisdom tradition at work in the story of Joseph; the story of the Fall of Man in Gen. 2-3; the Succession Narrative in 2 Sam. 9-10 and 1 Kgs. 1ff.; the book of Esther, Deuteronomy, Isa. 1-39, and so on. To this, Morgan, (n. 45 above) 229ff., adds a list of prophetic texts in which scholars have found evidence of the presence of the wisdom tradition. See also Murphy, (n. 42 above). Obviously, each passage must be examined on its own merits, and hasty and extravagant conclusions should be avoided. Thus, the recent argument that the passages showing wisdom influence are "model tales," written for the purpose of explaining and demonstrating the didactic ideology of the "wisdom movement," is questionable; see Hermisson, *Studien*, 126ff.; Scott, *The Way*, 87ff.; Crenshaw, "Education," 601-605.

47. Williams, (n. 37 above). This view that the Solomonic court was the life-setting of the composition of Proverbs first suggested by von Rad (*O.T. Theology* I, 48-56) has been dismissed in research (see, e.g., Scott, "Solomon and the Beginnings of Wisdom"; Whybray, "Wisdom Literature in the Reigns of David and Solomon." But, it has, at least in part, been reassessed in recent investigations: see, e.g., Thompson, *The Form and Function*, 81-83; Crenshaw, "The Sage in Proverbs," and especially the most instructive survey published by Brueggemann — "The Social Significance of Solomon as a Patron of Wisdom" — who, pursuing the social transformation that took place in the Solomonic era, comes to the conclusion that "... it is sociologically probable that Solomon was a patron of wisdom that was at once emancipatory and ideological" (ibid. 131).

48. Cf. Lang, (n. 41 above), 36-40, 101-102; Hermisson, *Studien*, 113ff.; Kayatz, *Studien zu Proverbien*, 135ff.; Scott, *The Way*, 13ff.; idem *PWM* 23ff.; Murphy, *Wisdom Literature*, 53; Lemaire, "The Sage in School," 171-175; and others. Hebrew wisdom, of course, was inspired not only by universal but also by local wisdom, deriving from a tribal or a nomadic society. Fontaine (*Traditional Sayings* and idem "The Sage in Family and Tribe") has recently proved the existence of a local wisdom in Israel from the times of the Judges and the El Amarna Period; cf. Lang, ibid. 40ff.; Whybray (n. 42 above), 2ff. and idem "Wisdom Literature in the Reign of David and Solomon," esp. 22-25; Morgan, *Wisdom in the O.T.*, 138ff., idem "Wisdom and the Prophets," 217-218, 224-225.

SELECT BIBLIOGRAPHY

For publications and studies dealing with the Egyptian sources see also Corpus pp. 12-30 above. Works cited completely in the footnotes are not listed here.

Alberston R.G., "Job and Ancient Near Eastern Wisdom Literature," *Scripture in Context* II*: More Essays on the Comparative Method*, eds. W.W. Hallo, J.C. Moyer, and L.G. Perdue (Indiana 1983), 213-230.

Albertz R., "The Sage and the Pious Wisdom in the Book of Job: The Friends' Perspective," *SIANE* 243-261.

Albright W.F., "The Goddess of Life and Wisdom," *AJSL* 36 (1919-1920), 258-294.

—— "Some Canaanite-Phoenician Sources of Hebrew Wisdom," *SVT* 3 (1955), 1-15.

Aling C.F., *Egypt and Bible History: From Earliest Times to 1000 B.C.* (Michigan 1984²).

Alster B., *The Instructions of Šuruppak, Mesopotamia,* vol. II (Copenhagen 1974).

Alt A., "Die Weisheit Salomos," *ThLZ* 76 (1951), 139-144.

Altbauer M., "Semantic Changes," *Lešonenu La'am* 9 (1958), 35-69 (Hebrew).

Altmüller H., "Bemerkungen zu Kapital 13 der Lehre des Amenemope (Am. 15,19-16,14)," *Fontes Atque Pontes, Eine Festgabe für H. Brunner*, *ÄAT* 5 (1983), 1-17.

Anthes R., *Lebensregeln und Lebensweisheit der Alten Ägypter, Der Alte Orient* 32/2 (Leipzig 1933).

—— "The Legal Aspect of the Instruction of Amenemhet," *JNES* 16 (1957), 176-190.

—— "A Further Remark on the Introduction to the Instruction of Amenenhet," *JNES* 17 (1958), 208-209.

—— "Die Funktion des vierten Kapitels in der Lehre des Amenemope," *Archaeologie und A.T., Festschrift für K. Galling*, eds. A. Kuschke and E. Kutsch (Tübingen 1970), 9-18.

—— "Zur Echtheit der Lehre des Amenemhet," *FaL* 41-84.

Arzt M., "The Teacher in Talmud and Midrash," *M.M. Kaplan Jubilee Volume* (New York 1953), 35-47.

Assmann J., "Weisheit, Loyalismus und Frömmigkeit," *SAL* 11-72.

—— "Fest des Augenblicks, Verheissung der Dauer, die Kontroverse der ägyptischen Harfnerlieder," *FaL* 53-84.

—— "Die 'Loyalistische Lehre' Echnatons," *SAK* 8 (1980), 1-32.

—— "Königsdogma und Heilserwartung. Politische und kultische Chaosbeschreibung in ägyptischen Texten," *Apocalypticism in the Mediterranean World and the Near East* (Tübingen 1983), 345-377.

—— *Ma'at, Gerechtigkeit und Unsterblichkeit im Alten Ägypten* (Munich 1990).

Bains J., "Literacy and Ancient Egyptian Society," *Man* (N.S.) 18 (1983), 572-599.

Bains J., and Eyre C.J., "Four Notes on Literacy," *GM* 61 (1983), 65-96.

Barr J., *Comparative Philology and the Text of the O.T.* (Oxford 1968).

—— *Biblical Words for Time, Studies in Biblical Theology* 33 (London 1969), 11-20, 159-169, 184-188.

—— *The Semantics of Biblical Language* (Oxford 1975[4]).

Barta W., "Das Gespräch des Ipuwer mit dem Schöpfergott," *SAK* 1 (1974), 19-33.

—— "Die Erste Zwischenzeit im Spiegel der pessimistischen Literature," *JEOL* 24 (1975-76), 50-61.

—— "Das Schulbuch Kemit," *ZÄS* 105 (1978), 6-14.

—— "Der anonyme Gott der Lebenslehren," *ZÄS* 103 (1976), 79-89.

Barton G.A., *Ecclesiastes, ICC* (1908).

Barucq A., *L'expression de la louange divine et de la prière dans la Bible et en Egypte, Bibliothèque d'Étude* 33 (Cairo 1962).

—— *Le Livre des Proverbes, Sources Bibliques* (Paris 1964).

—— Une veine de spiritualité sacerdotale et sapientielle dans l'Egypte ancienne," in *A la rencontre de Dieu; Mémorial Albert Gélin*, ed. idem, Bibliothèque de la Faculté Catholique de Théologie de Lyon (Paris 1961), 193-202.

Baumann A., "*dāmāh*," *TDOT* III, 260-265.

Baumgärtel, "Lēb, lēbâb in the O.T.," *Theological Dictionary of the N.T.*, ed. G. Kittel, trans. & ed. G.W. Bromiley (Michigan 1968[3]), III, 606-607.

Baumgartner W., *Israelitische und altorientalische Weisheit* (Tübingen 1933).

—— "The Wisdom Literature," *The O.T. and Modern Study*, ed. H.H. Rowley (Oxford 1967), 210-237.

Beckerath J. von, "Ostrakon München ÄS 396," *SAK* 10 (1983), 63-69.

Bergant D., *What are They Saying about Wisdom Literature* (New York 1984).

Bergmann J., and Botterweck G.J., "*yāda‘*," *TDOT* V, 448-481.

Bergmann J., and Johnson E., "*'ānāph*," *TDOT* I, 348-360.

Bergmann J., Lutzmann H., and Schmidt W.H., "*dābhar*," *TDOT* III, 84-125.

Bergmann J., Haldar H., Ringgren H., and Koch K., "*derekh*," *TDOT* III, 270-293.

Bergmeier R., "Zum Ausdruck ‘עצת רשעים’ im Ps. 1,1; Hi 10,3; 21,16; 22,18," *ZAW* 79 (1967), 229-232.

Berlev O.D., "The Data of the Eloquent Peasant," *Form und Mass: Festschrift für G. Fecht*, eds. J. Osing, and G. Dreyer, *ÄAT* 12 (1987).

Beyse K.M., "*ḥmm*," *TDOT* IV, 473-477.

—— "*māšāl*," *TWAT* IV, 69-73.

Birch S., "The Praise of Learning," *Records of the Past*, vol. III, 145-146.

Bissing W., *Altägyptische Lebensweisheit* (Zurich 1955).

Bjorkmann G., *Kings at Karnak* (Uppsala 1971), 16-25.

Blackman A.M., and Peet T.E., "Pap. Lansing — A Translation with Notes," *JEA* 11 (1925), 284-297.

—— "The Psalms in the Light of Egyptian Research," *The Psalmist*, ed. D.C. Simpson (Oxford 1929), 177-197.

Blank S.H., "Wisdom," *The Interpreters Dictionary of the Bible* IV, 852-861.

Blenkinsopp, J. "The Sage, the Scribe and the Scribalism in the Chronicler's Work," *SIANE* 307-315.

Bloomfield L., *Language* (London 1970).

Blumenthal E., "Eine neue Handschrift der Lehre eines Mannes für seinen Sohn (Pap. Berlin 14374)," *Festschrift zum 150 jährigen Bestehen des Berliner ägyptischen Museums* (Berlin 1974), 55-66.

Boer P.A.H. de, "The Counsellor," *SVT* 3 (1955), 42-71.

Böhling A., "In der Übersetzung des Koptischen Neuen Testaments," *Fontes Atque Pontes, Eine Festgabe für H. Brunner, ÄAT* 5 (1983), 47-61.

Bonnard P.E., "De la sagesse personnifiée dans l'Ancien Testament à la sagesse en personne dans le Nouveau," *SAT* 117-149.

Borghouts J.F., "The 'hot one' (*p3 šmw*) in Ostracon Deir el Médineh 1265," *GM* 38 (1980), 21-28.

Boström G., *Proverbiastudien: Die Weisheit und das fremde Weib in Spr. 1-9* (Lund 1935).

Breasted J.H., *Development of Religion and Thought in Ancient Egypt* (Philadelphia 1972[4]).

—— *The Dawn of Conscience* (London 1933).

Brekelmans C., "Wisdom Influence in Deuteronomy," *SAT* 28-38.

Brunner H., "Die Weisheitliteratur," *HO* 90-110.

—— "Das hörende Herz," *ThLZ* 11 (1954), 697-700; also *HH* 3-9.

—— "Die Lehre vom Königserbe in frühen Mittleren Reich," *Ägyptologische Studien, Festschrift H. Grapow* (Berlin 1955), 4-11; also *HH* 273-280.

—— "Das Herz als Sitz des Lebensgeheimnisses," *Archiv für Orientforschung* 17 (1956), 140-141; also *HH* 6-7.

—— "Eine neue Entlehnung aus der Lehre des Djedefhor," *MDAIK* 14 (1957), 17-19; also *HH* 45-47.

—— *Altägyptische Erziehung* (Wiesbaden 1957).

—— "Gerechtigkeit als Fundament des Thrones," *VT* 8 (1958), 426-428; also *HH* 393-395.

—— "Ptahhotep bei den koptischen Mönchen," *ZÄS* 86 (1961), 145-147; also *HH* 417-420.

—— "Der Gottesvater als Erzieher des Kronprinzen," *ZAW* 86 (1961), 90-100; also *HH* 70-81.

—— "Die religiöse Wertung der Armut im Alten Ägypten," *Saeculum* 12 (1961), 319-344; also *HH* 189-214.

—— "Der freie Wille Gottes in der ägyptischen Weisheit," *SPOA*, 103-117; also *HH* 85-102.

—— "Ein weiteres Djedefhor Zitat," *MDAIK* 19 (1963), 53; also *HH* 48.

—— "Das Herz im ägyptischen Glauben," *Das Herz im Umkreis des Glaubens* (Biberach 1965), 81-106; also *HH* 8-41.

—— "Die 'Weisen', Ihre 'Lehren' und 'Prophezeiungen' in altägyptischer Sicht," *ZÄS* 93 (1966), 29-35; also *HH* 59-65.

—— "Zitate aus Lebenslehren," *SAL* 105-171.

—— "'Eure Rede sei ja ja, nein nein' im Ägyptischen," *Festschrift S. Schott* (Wiesbaden 1968), 7-12; also *HH* 396-401.

—— (trans.) "Ägyptische Texte" in *Religionsgeschichtliches Textbuch zum Alten Testament, Grundrisse zum A.T.*, ed. W. Beyerlin, (Göttingen 1975), Vol. I, 29-93..

—— "Bildische Ausdrücke und Übertragungen," *LÄ* I, 805-811 .

—— "Herz," *LÄ* II, 1158-1168.

—— "Lehren," *LÄ* III, 964-991.

—— "Literature," *LÄ* III, 1067-1072.

—— "Vita brevis, ars longa," *ZÄS* 107 (1980), 42-45; also *HH* 66-69.

—— Review of G.E. Bryce, "A Legacy of Egypt," *WdO* 11 (1981), 148-150.

—— "Zentralbegriffe ägyptischer und israelitischer Weisheitslehren," *Saeculum* 35 (1984), 185-199; also *HH* 402-416.

Brunner-Traut E., "Der Lebensmüde und sein Ba," *ZÄS* 94 (1967), 6-15.

—— "Weiterleben der ägyptischen Lebenslehren in den koptischen Apophthegmata am Beispiel des Schweigens," *SAL*, 173-216.

—— *Altägyptische Tiergeschichte und Fabel* (Darmstadt 1974).

—— "Krokodil," *LÄ* III, 791-801.

—— *Lebensweisheit der Alten Ägypter* (Freiburg 1986).
—— "Mädchenbildung und Gesellschaftliche Stellung der Frau im alten Ägypten," *Der weite Schulweg der Mädchen*, eds. J.G.P. von Hohenzollern, and M. Liedtke (Bad Heilbrunn 1990).
Bryce G.E., "Another Wisdom 'Book' in Proverbs," *JBL* 91 (1972),145-157.
—— "Omen-Wisdom in Ancient Israel," *JBL* 74 (1975), 19-37.
—— *A Legacy of Wisdom. The Egyptian Contribution to the Wisdom of Israel* (London 1979).
Buccellati G., "Wisdom and Not: The Case of Mesopotamia," *JAOS* 101/1 (1981), 35-47.
Buck A. de, "The Instruction of Amenemmes," *Mél. Masp.* I/2, 847-852.
Budge E.A.W., *The Book of the Dead* (London 1898).
—— *Egyptian Magic* (New York 1971^2).
—— *The Teaching of Amen-em-apt, Son of Kanekht* (London 1924).
Bühlmann W., *Von rechten Reden und Schweigen, OBO* 12 (1976).
Burkard G., *Textkritische Untersuchungen zu ägyptischen Weisheitslehren des alten und mittleren Reiches, Ägyptologische Abhandlungen* 34 (Wiesbaden 1977).
Cadbury H.J., "Egyptian Influence in the Book of Proverbs," *Journal of Religion* 9 (1929), 99-108.
Camp C.V., *Wisdom and the Feminine in the Book of Proverbs* (Sheffield 1985).
—— "The Female Sage in Ancient Israel and in the Biblical Wisdom Literature," *SIANE* 190-202.
Canney M.A., "The Hebrew *mēlîṣ*," *AJSL* 40 (1923-1924), 135-137.
Caquot A., "Sur une désignation vétéro-testamentaire de l'insensé," *Revue d'Histoire des Religions* 155 (1959), 1-16.
—— "Israelite Perceptions of Wisdom and Strength in the Light of the Ras Shamra Texts," *Isr. Wisd.* 25-33.
Cassuto U., *Biblical and Canaanite Literatures, Studies on the Bible and Ancient Orient* I (Jerusalem 1972) (Hebrew).
Castellino G.R., "Qohelet and His Wisdom," *CBQ* 30 (1968), 15-28.
Cazelles H., "*'evil*," *TDOT* I, 137-140.
—— "*hll*," *TDOT* III, 411-413.

—— "Les débuts de la Sagesse en Israël," *SPOA* 27-40.

Ceresko A.R., "The Sage in the Psalms," *SIANE* 217-230.

Černý J., *Paper and Books in Ancient Egypt* (London 1947).

Clère J.J. "'Dns Mhwt' des autobiographies égyptiennes," *JEA* 35 (1949), 41-42.

Cohen M., *Essai comparatif sur le vocabulaire et phonétique du chamito-sémitique, Bibliothèque de l'École des Hautes Études* 248 (Paris 1948).

Conrad J., "Die innere Gliederung der Proverbien," *ZAW* 79 (1967), 67-76.

Conzelmann H., "Die Mutter der Weisheit," *Zeit und Geschichte: Dankesgabe an R. Bultmann*, ed. E. Dinkler (Tübingen), 225-234.

Couroyer B., "Le chemin de vie en Egypte et en Israël," *RB* 56 (1949), 412-432.

—— "L'idéal sapientiel en Egypte et en Israël," *RB* 57 (1950), 174-179.

—— "Mettre sa main sur sa bouche en Egypte et dans la Bible," *RB* 67 (1960), 197-209.

—— "Amenemope I 9; III 13: Egypte ou Israël?" *RB* 68 (1961), 394-400.

—— "L'origine égyptienne de la Sagesse d'Amememopé," *RB* 70 (1963), 208-224.

—— "Un égyptianisme dans Ben Sira 4, 11," *RB* 82 (1975), 206-217.

—— "A propos de Luc, II, 52," *RB* 86 (1979), 92-101.

—— "La tablette du coeur," *RB* 90 (1983), 416-434.

Cowley A., *Aramaic Papyri of the 5th Century B.C.* (*The Story of Aḥiḳar*) (Oxford 1923).

Crenshaw J.L., "Method in Determining Wisdom Influence upon 'Historical' Literature," *JBL* 88 (1969), 129-142; also *SAIW* 481-494.

—— "Questions, dictions et épreuves impossibles," *SAT* 96-111.

—— *Old Testament Wisdom: An Introduction* (Atlanta 1981).

—— "Education in Ancient Israel," *JBL* 104 (1985), 601-615.

—— *Ecclesiastes, A Commentary, OTL* (Philadelphia 1987).

—— "The Sage in Proverbs,"*SIANE* 205-216.

Dahood M.J., "Canaanite Phoenician Influence in Qoheleth," *Biblica* 33 (1952), 191-221.

—— *Proverbs and Northwest Semitic Philology* (Roma 1963).

Davies N., *The Tomb of Rekh-mi-Re at Thebes* (New York 1973), 79-94.
Day J., *God's Conflict with the Dragon and the Sea: Echoes of Canaanite Myth in the Old Testament* (Cambridge 1985).
Derchain P., "Intelligenz als Karriere (Neferti 10-11)," *GM* 3 (1972), 9-14.
Donald T., "The Semantic Field of 'Folly' in Proverbs, Job, Psalms and Ecclesiastes," *VT* 13 (1963), 285-292.
—— "The Semantic Field of Rich and Poor in the Wisdom Literature of Hebrew and Accadian, *Oriens Antiquus* 3 (1964), 27-41.
Donner H., "Die religiongeschichtlichen Ursprünge von Prov. Sal. 8," *ZÄS* 82 (1970), 8-18.
Drioton E., "Sur la Sagesse d'Aménémopé," *Mélanges bibliques rédigés en l'honneur de A. Robert* (1957), 254-280.
—— "Le désert du Sinaï couvert par une forêt impénétrable," *Rd'E* 12 (1960), 90-91.
Driver S.R., and Gray G.B., *Job, ICC* (Edinburgh 1931).
—— "Problems in the Hebrew Text of Proverbs," *Biblica* 32 (1951), 173-197.
Drubbel A., "Le conflit entre la sagesse profane et la sagesse religieuse," *Biblica* 17 (1936), 45-70, 393-406.
Duesberg H., and Fransen I., *Les scribes inspirés* (Paris 1966).
Dürr L., *Die Wertung des Lebens im A.T. und im Alten Orient* (Münster 1926), 1-20.
—— *Das Erziehungswesen im Alten Testament und im Alten Orient* (Leipzig 1932).
Eissfeldt O., *Der Maschal im A.T., BZAW* 24 (Giessen 1913).
—— *The Old Testament — Introduction* (Oxford 1966).
Ellenbogen M., *Foreign Words in the O.T., Their Origin and Etymology* (London 1962).
Emerton J.A., "Notes and Studies," *JTS* 20 (1969), 202-221.
—— *Wisdom, Tradition and Interpretation*, ed. G.W. Anderson (Oxford 1979), 214-237.
Engnell I., "'Knowledge' and 'Life' in the creation story," *SVT* 3 (1955), 103-119.
Erman A., *Life in Ancient Egypt* (New York 1971²).

—— "Eine ägyptische Quelle der 'Sprüche Salomos,'" *Sitzungsberichte der Preussischen Akademie der Wissenschaft* 15 (1924), 86-93.

—— *Die ägyptischen Schülerhandschriften, Abhandlungen der Preussischen Akademie der Wissenschaften, Philologisch-Historische Klasse* 2 (Berlin 1925).

—— *The Ancient Egyptians*, ed. M.A. Blackman (New York 1966).

Fabry H.J., "*ḥbl*," *TDOT* IV, 172-179.

Faulkner R.O., "The Installation of the Vizier," *JEA* 41 (1955), 21-28.

—— "Some Notes on the 'Teaching of Amenemmes I to his Son,'" *Griffith Studies* (London 1932), 69-72.

—— "The Man Who Was Tired of Life," *JEA* 42 (1956), 21-40.

—— "Notes on 'The Admonitions of an Egyptian Sage'," *JEA* 50 (1964), 24-36.

—— "The Admonitions of an Egyptian Sage," *JEA* 51 (1965), 53-62.

Fecht G., *Der Habgierige und die Maat* (Gluckstadt 1958).

—— *Der Vorwurf an Gott in den "Mannworten des Ipu-wer"* (*Pap. Leiden* I 344 *recto*, 11, 11-13,8; 15,13-17,3) (Heidelberg 1972).

—— "Schicksalsgöttinnen und Könige in der Lehre eines Mannes für seinen Sohn," *ZÄS* 105 (1978), 14-42.

Federn W., "Notes on the Instruction to Kagemni," *JEA* 36 (1950), 48-56.

Fenton T.L., "Variant Approaches to the Theomachy Myth in Biblical Writing, in *Studies in the Bible and the Ancient Near East* (*Fs. S.E. Loewenstamm*), eds. I. Avishur and Y. Blau (Jerusalem 1978), 337-381 (Hebrew).

Ficher H.G., "A Didactic Text of the Late Middle Kingdom," *JEA* 68 (1982), 45-50.

—— "'Dein Heisser' in P. Anastasi V 7,5-8,1 und seine Beziehung zur Lehre des Amenemope, Kap. 2-4," *WdO* 14 (1983), 83-90.

—— "Ich bin das Schiff—Du bist das Ruder," *SAK* 11 (1984), 335-345.

—— *Literarische Ostraka der Ramessidenzeit in Übersetzung* (Wiesbaden 1986), 8-12.

Fichtner J., *Die altorientalische Weisheit in ihrer israelitisch-jüdischen Ausprägung*, *BZAW* 62 (1933).

—— "Isaiah among the Wise," *SAIW* 429-438.

Fohrer G., "Sophia," *SAIW* 63-83.

Fontaine C.R., *Traditional Sayings in the O.T.* (Sheffield 1982).

Foster J.L., "Thought Couplets in Khety's Hymn to the Inundation," *JNES* 34 (1975), 1-29.

—— *Thought Couplets and Clause Sequences in a Literary Text — The Maxims of Ptaḥ-Ḥotep* (Canada 1977).

—— "The Conclusion to the Testament of Ammenemes King of Egypt," *JEA* 67 (1981), 36-47.

—— "Texts of the Egyptian Composition, 'The Instruction of a Man for His Son' in the Oriental Institute Museum," *JNES* 45 (1986), 197-211.

Fôti L., "The History in the Prophecies of Neferti: Relationship between the Egyptian Wisdom and Prophecy Literatures," *Studia Aegyptica* 2 (1976), 3-18.

Fox M.V., "Aspects of the Religion of the Book of Proverbs," *HUCA* 39 (1968), 55-69.

—— "Two Decades of Research in Egyptian Wisdom Literature," *ZÄS* 107 (1980), 120-135.

—— *The Book of Qoheleth and His Relation to the Wisdom School*, Ph.D. diss., The Hebrew University of Jerusalem (Jerusalem 1982) (Hebrew).

—— "Qohelet," *EMiqr* VII, 70-83 (Hebrew).

—— "LXX Proverbs 3:28 and Ancient Egyptian Wisdom," *Hebrew Annual Review* 8 (1984), 63-69.

—— "Egyptian Onomastica and Biblical Wisdom, *VT* 36 (1986), 302-310.

—— *Qohelet and His Contradictions* (Sheffield 1989).

Frankfort H., *Ancient Egyptian Religion* (New York 1948).

Freedman D.N., Lundbom J.R., and Botterweck G.J., "*ḥārâ*," *TDOT* V, 171-176.

Frymer-Kensky T., "The Sage in the Pentateuch: Soundings," *SIANE*, 275-287.

Gaál, E. von, "Ein neues Ostrakon zur 'Lehre eines Mannes für seinen Sohn,'" *MDAIK* 40 (1984), 13-25; pls. 1-5.

Gadd C.J., *Teachers and Students in the Oldest Schools* (London 1956).

Galling K., "Kohelet Studien," *ZAW* 50 (1932), 276-299.

Gardiner A.H., "Inscriptions from the Tomb of Si-Renpowet," *ZÄS* 45 (1908), 123-140.

—— *Egyptian Hieratic Texts; Series 1, Literary Texts of the New Kingdom, 1; The Pap. Anastasi 1 and the Pap. Koller* (Leipzig 1911).

—— "New Literary Works from Ancient Egypt," *JEA* 1 (1914), 20-35.

—— "Some Personifications," *PSBA* 38 (1916), 43-54.

—— "The Eloquent Peasant," *JEA* 9 (1923), 5-23.

—— "The Teaching of Amenophis, The Son of Kanakht, Pap. B.M. 10474," *JEA* 13 (1927), 191-231.

—— "The House of Life," *JEA* 24 (1938), 157-170.

—— "The Earliest Manuscripts of the Instruction of Amennmhet I," *Mél. Masp.* I, 479-496.

—— *Hieratic Papyri in the British Museum Third Series, Chester Beatty, Gift 1*, vol. 1, Text (London 1935).

—— "Kagemni once again," *JEA* 38 (1951), 109-110.

—— "A Didactic Passage Re-examined (*Ani* III 3-9)," *JEA* 45 (1954), 12-15.

—— "A New Moralizing Text," *WZKM* 54 (1957), 43-45.

Gaspar R.V.W., "Social Ideas in the Wisdom Literature of the O.T.," *Studies in Sacred Theology, Second Series* 8 (1947), 108-165.

Gemser B., *Sprüche Salomos, HAT* (Tübingen 1937).

—— "The *rîb*- or Controversy Pattern in Hebrew Mentality," *SVT* 3 (1960), 120-137.

—— "The Instructions of *'Onchsheshonqy* and Biblical Wisdom Literature," *SVT* 7 (1960), 103-128.

—— *Adhuc Loquitor* (Leiden 1968), 138-149.

Genung J.F., "Meaning and Usage of the Term תושיה," *JBL* 30 (1911), 114-122.

Gese H., "Die Krisis der Weisheit bei Koheleth," *SPOA*, 139-151.

—— *Lehre und Wirklichkeit in der alten Weisheit* (Tübingen 1958).

Gilula M., *The Wisdom of Amenemope and Its Relation to the Book of*

Proverbs , M.A. thesis, The Hebrew University of Jerusalem (Jerusalem 1963) (Hebrew).

—— Review of I. Grumach, *Untersuchungen zur Lebenslehre des Amenemope*, *JAOS* 98 (1978), 503-507.

Ginsburg C.D., *Qoheleth* (Tel Aviv 1961) (Hebrew).

Glanville S.R.K., ed., *The Legacy of Egypt* (Oxford 1963).

Goedicke H., "Zur Einleitungformal didaktischer Texte (*Ptaḥḥotep* Maxim 32)," *ZÄS* 86 (1961), 147-149.

—— "A Neglected Wisdom Text," *JEA* 48 (1962), 25-35.

—— Review of G. Fecht, *Der Habgierige und die Maat, JARCE* 5 (1966), 130-133.

—— "Die Lehre eines Mannes für seinen Sohn," *ZÄS* 94 (1967), 62-71.

—— "The Beginning of the Instruction of King Amenmhet," *JARCE* 7 (1968), 15-21.

Gordis R.,"The Social Background of Wisdom Literature," *HUCA* 18 (1943-44), 77-118.

—— "The Original Language of Qoheleth," *JQR* 37 (1946-1947), 67-84.

—— *Koheleth, The Man and His World. A Study of Ecclesiastes* (New York 1968⁴).

—— "The Significance of the Paradise Myth," in *The Word and the Book*, ed. idem (New York 1976), 75-83.

Gordon E.I., *Sumerian Proverbs* (New York 1968).

Görg M., *Gott-König Reden in Israel und Ägypten, Beitrage zur Wissenschaft von Alten und Neuen Testament* (Stuttgart-Berlin-Cologne-Mainz 1975).

—— "Komparatistische Untersuchungen an ägyptischer und israelitischer Literature," *FaL* 197-215.

Grapow H., *Die bildlichen Ausdrücke des Ägyptischen* (Leipzig 1924).

—— *Wie die alten Ägypter sich anredeten, wie Sie sich grüssten und wie Sie miteinander sprachen* (Berlin 1960²).

—— "Die Einleitung der Lehre des Königs Amenmhet," *ZÄS* 79 (1954), 77-79.

—— "Beiträge zur Untersuchung des Stils ägyptischer Lieder," *ZÄS* 79 (1954), 17-27.

Gray J., "The Book of Job in the Context of Near Eastern Literature," *ZAW* 82 (1970) 251-269.

Gressmann H., "Die neuegefundene Lehre des Amen-em-ope und die vorexilische Spruchdichtung Israels," *ZAW* 42 (1924), 272-296.

—— *Israels Spruchweisheit im Zusammenhang der Weltliterature, Kunst und Altertum, Alte Kulturen im Lichte neuer Forschung,* vol. 6 (Berlin 1925).

Grieshammer R., "Altes Testament," *LÄ* I, 163-166.

—— "Feuer," *LÄ* II, 205-206.

Griffith F.Ll., "Stela of Mentuhetep Son of Hepy," *PSBA* 18 (1896), 195-204.

—— "The Teaching of Amenophis, the son of Kanakht, Pap. B.M. 10474," *JEA* 13 (1927), 191-231.

Griffiths G., "The Idea of Posthumous Judgement in Israel and Egypt," *Fontes Atque Pontes, Ein Festgabe für H. Brunner, ÄAT* 5 (1983), 186-204.

Grimm J., "The Meaning and Etymology of the Word תּוּשִׁיָּה in the O.T.," *JAOS* 22 (1901), 35-44.

Grinz Y.M., "The Proverbs of *'Aluqa,*" *Tarbiz* 28 (1959), 135-137 (Hebrew).

—— *Proverbs, Introductory Chapters* (Jerusalem 1968[3]) (Hebrew).

—— *From the Ancient Egyptian Literature* (Jerusalem 1975) (Hebrew).

—— "Solomon's Proverbs," *Biblical Studies* (Jerusalem 1979), 79-105 (Hebrew).

—— *The Book of Genesis* (Jerusalem 1983) (Hebrew).

Grollenberg L., "A propos de Prov. 8,6 et 17,27," *RB* 59 (1952), 40-43.

Gugulielmi W., "Personifikation," *LÄ* IV, 978-987.

Gunkel H., "Ägyptische Parallelen zum Alten Testament," *ZDMG* 63 (1909), 531-539.

Gunn B., "Some Middle Egyptian Proverbs," *JEA* 12 (1926), 282-284.

—— "Notes on Amenemes 1," *JEA* 27 (1941), 1-6.

—— "The Religion of the Poor in Ancient Egypt," *JEA* 3 (1917), 81-94.

Hamp V., "*chîdhāh,*" *TDOT* IV, 320-323.

Haran M., "*Māšāl*," *EMiqr* V, 548-553 (Hebrew).
—— "Scribal Workmanship in Biblical Times: The Scrolls and the Writing Implements," *Tarbiz* 50 (1980-81), 65-87 (Hebrew).
—— "On the Diffusion of Literacy and Schools in Ancient Israel," *SVT* 40 (1988), 81-95.
Hartom A.S., *Ben Sira* (Tel Aviv 1963) (Hebrew).
Hastings J., ed., *Encyclopaedia of Religion and Ethics* (New York 1955), vol. 9: "Personification" (Egyptian — A.H. Gardiner; Greek — E.A. Gardner; Roman — J.B. Carter; Semitic — W.H. Bennett), 787-803.
Hatch E., and Redpath H.A., *A Concordance to the Septuagint and Other Greek Versions of the Old Testament*, 2 vols. (Graz 1954 [1897]).
Heaton E.W., *Solomon's New Men* (London 1974).
Helck W. "Eine kleine Textverbesserung (Amenmhet)," *JEOL* 19 (1965-1966), 464-467.
—— *Die Beziehungen Ägyptens zu Vorderasien im 3. und 2. Jahrtausend v. Chr.*, *Ägyptologische Abhandlungen* 5 (Wiesbaden 1971).
Hermann A., Review of S. Herrmann, *Untersuchungen zur Überlieferungsgestalt mitteläygptischer Literaturewerke*, *OLZ* 5/6, (1959), 252-263.
—— "Das steinharte Herz," *JAC* 4 (1961), 77-107.
Hermisson H.J., *Studien zur israelitischen Spruchweisheit*, Wissenschaftliche Monographien zum Alten und Neuen Testament (Neukirchen-Vluyn 1968).
Herrmann S., "Prophetie in Israel und Ägypten," *SVT* 9 (1963), 47-65.
—— "Steuerruder, Waage, Herz und Zunge in ägyptischen Bildreden," *ZÄS* 79 (1963), 106-115.
Hodge C.T., "Egyptian and Survival," *Hamito-Semitica*, 171-189.
—— "Evidence for Egyptian Phonology, *Studies Presented to H.J. Polotsky*, ed. D.W. Young (East Gloucester, Mass. 1981), 401-413.
Holladay W.L., *A Concise Hebrew and Aramaic Lexicon of the Old Testament* (Leiden 1988[10]).
Hopfner T., *Der Tierkult der alten Ägypter* (Vienna 1913), 125-136.
Hornung E., Brack A., "Apophis," *LÄ* I, 350-352.
Hughes G.R., "The Blunders of an Inept Scribe," *Studies in Philology in*

Honour of R.I. Williams, eds. G.E. Kadish and G.E. Freeman (Toronto 1982), 51-67.

Humbert P., *Recherches sur les sources égyptiennes de la littérature sapientiale d'Israël* (Neuchâtel 1929).

Humphreys W.L., "The Motif of the Wise Courtier in the Book of Proverbs," *Isr. Wisd.*, 177-190.

Hurvitz A., *The Transition Period in Biblical Hebrew. A Study in Post-Biblical Hebrew and its Implications for the Dating of Psalms* (Jerusalem 1972) (Hebrew).

—— "The Date of the Prose Tale of Job: Linguistically Reconsidered," *HTR* 67 (1974), 17-34.

—— "Wisdom Vocabulary in the Hebrew Psalter: A Contribution to the Study of 'Wisdom Psalms,'" *VT* 38 (1988), 41-51.

—— *Wisdom Language in Biblical Psalmody* (Jerusalem 1991).

Israeli S., "Chapter Four of Amenemope," *Studies in Egyptology, Presented to M. Lichtheim*, ed. S. Israelit-Groll (Jerusalem 1990), vol. I, 464-484.

Johnson A.R., "Mashal," *SVT* 3 (1955), 162-169.

—— *The Vitality of the Individual in the Thought of Ancient Israel* (Cardiff 1964), 75-87.

Junge F., "Die Welt der Klagen," *Fragen an die altägyptische Literature, E. Otto Gedenkschrift*, eds. J. Assmann, E. Peucht, and R. Grieshammer (Wiesbaden 1977), 275-284.

Kadish G.E., "British Museum Writing Board 5645: The Complaints of Kha-heper-Reʿ-senebu," *JEA* 59 (1973), 77-90.

Kahana A., *The Book of Proverbs* (Tel Aviv 1889) (Hebrew).

—— *The Book of Qoheleth* (Tel Aviv 1890) (Hebrew).

—— *The Book of Job* (Tel Aviv 1963²) (Hebrew).

—— *The Apocrypha*, I, II (Jerusalem 1970) (Hebrew).

Kalugila L., *The Wise King, Studies in Royal Wisdom as Divine Revelation in the O.T. and Its Environment* (Stockholm 1980).

Kaplony P., "Eine neue Weisheitslehre aus dem alten Reich," *Orientalia* 37 (1968), 1-62.

—— "Der Schreiber, das Gotteswort und die Papyruspflanze," *ZÄS* 110 (1983), 143-173.

Kaplony-Heckel U., "Schüler und Schulwesen in der ägyptischen Spätzeit," *SAK* 1 (1974), 227-243.

Kaufmann Y., *The Religion of Israel*, II (Tel Aviv-Jerusalem 1964[6]) (Hebrew).

Kayatz C., *Studien zu Proverbien 1-9, Wissenschaftliche Monographie zum Alten und Neuen Testament* 22 (Neukirchen-Vluyn 1966).

Kedar B., *Biblische Semantik* (Stuttgart 1981).

Kedar-Kopfstein B., "*pārāh-p^{e}rî*," *TWAT* VI, 740-752.

Keel O., *Die Weisheit Spielt vor Gott* (Freiburg 1974).

—— *The Symbolism of the Biblical World* (New York 1978).

—— "Eine Diskussion um die Bedeutung polarer Begriffspaare in den Lebenslehren," *SAL* 225-234.

Kevin R.O., "The Wisdom of Amen-em-opt and Its Possible Dependence upon the Hebrew Book of Proverbs," *JSOR* 14/4 (1930), 115-153.

Khanjian J., "Wisdom in Ras Shamra Parallels 2," *An. Or.* 50 (1975), 371-400.

Kitchen K.A., "Proverbs and Wisdom Books of the Ancient Near East: The Factual History of Literary Form," *Tyndale Bulletin* 28 (1977/78), 69-114.

—— "The Basic Literary Forms and Formulations of Ancient Instructional Writings in Egypt and Western Asia," *SAL* 235-282.

—— "Egypt and Israel during the First Millennium B.C.," *Congress Volume Jerusalem 1986*, ed. J.A. Emerton, *SVT* 40 (1988), 107-123.

Klopfenstein M.A., *Die Lüge nach dem A.T.* (Zurich-Frankfurt 1964).

Kovacs B.W., "Is there class-ethic in Proverbs?" *Essays in O.T. Ethics*, eds. J.L. Crenshaw, and J.T. Willis (New York 1974), 173-189.

Kramer S.N., "Man and his God," *SVT* 3 (1955), 170-182.

—— *Schooldays — A Sumerian Composition Relating to the Education of a Scribe* (Philadelphia 1950).

—— *The Sumerians* (Chicago 1983).

Kuentz C., "Deux versions d'un panégyrique royal," *Griffith Studies*, 97-110.

Kuntz K., "The Canonical Wisdom Psalms of Ancient Israel," *Rhetorical*

Criticism. Essay in honour of J. Muilenburg, eds. J.L. Jackson, and M. Kessler (Pittsburgh 1974), 186-222.

Lalouette C., *La littérature égyptienne* (Paris 1981).

Lanczkowski G., "Zur ägyptischen Religionsgeschichte des Mittleren Reiches," *Zeitschrift für Religion und Geistesgeschichte* 6 (1954), 1-18.

—— "Reden und Schweigen im ägyptischen Verständnis vornehmlich des Mittleren Reiches," *Deutsche Akademie der Wissenschaften zu Berlin, Institut für Orientforschung* 29 (1955), 186-196.

—— *Altägyptischer Prophetismus, Ägyptologische Abhandlungen* 4 (Wiesbaden 1960).

Lambdin T.O., "Egyptian Loan Words in the O.T.," *JAOS* 73 (1953), 145-155.

Lambert W.G., *Babylonian Wisdom Literature* (Oxford 1960).

Landau R., *Chapters in Hebrew Semantics*, Bar Ilan University (Ramat Gan 1974) (Hebrew).

Lang B., *Weisheitliche Lehrrede, Stuttgarter Bibel Studien 54* (Stuttgart 1972).

—— *Frau Weisheit* (Düsseldorf 1975).

—— "Schule und Unterricht im alten Israel, *SAT* 186-201.

Leclant J., "Sagesses de l'Egypte Ancienne," *SPOA* 5-26.

Lefebvre G., "Egyptiens et Hébreux," *RB* 31 (1922), 481-488.

—— *Tableau des parties du corps humain mentionnées par les égyptiens* (Cairo 1952).

Lemaire A., *Les écoles et la formation de la Bible dans l'ancien Israël*, *OBO* 39(1981).

—— "The Sage in School and Temple," *SIANE* 165-181.

Lesko L.H., "Some Comments on Ancient Egyptian Literacy and Literati," *Studies in Egyptology Presented to M. Lichtheim*, ed. S. Israelit-Groll (Jerusalem 1990), vol. II, 656-667.

Leeuwen R.C. van, "The Sage in the Prophetic Literature," *SIANE* 295-306.

Lexa F., "L'Enseignement de *Ptaḥḥotep*, chapitre 6," *Archiv Orientalni* 7 (1935), 200-207.

Licht J., "*K^{e}sîl*," *EMiqr* IV, 221-222 (Hebrew).

—— *The Rule Scroll: A Scroll from the Wilderness of Judaea 1QS, 1QSa, 1QSb* (Jerusalem 1965) (Hebrew).

Lichtheim M., "The Songs of the Harpers," *JNES* 4 (1945), 178-211.

—— *Ancient Egyptian Literature*, 3 vols. (Berkeley-Los Angeles-London 1973- 1980).

—— "Observations on Pap. Insinger," *SAL* 283-305.

—— "Demotic Proverbs," *Grammata Demotika, Festschrift für E. Luddekens* (Würzburg 1984), 125-140.

Lindblom J., "Wisdom in the O.T. Prophets," *SVT* 3 (1955), 192-203.

Lindenberger J.M., *The Aramaic Proverbs of Ahiqar* (Baltimore-London 1983).

Lipiński E., "Ancient Types of Wisdom Literature in Biblical Narrative," *Isac Leo Seeligmann Volume, Essays on the Bible and the Ancient World*, eds. A. Rofé and Y. Zakovitch, vol.III (Jerusalem 1983), 39-55..

Loader J.A., *Polar Structures in the Book of Qohelet* (Berlin-New York 1979).

Loewenstamm S.E., "*Lēb*," *EMiqr* IV, 412-415 (Hebrew).

Lopez F.G., "*paeh*," *TWAT* VI, 522-538.

Lopez J., "L'auteur de l'Enseignement pour Mérikarê," *Rd'E* 25 (1983), 178-191.

Loprieno-Behlmer H., "Weiterleben von Motiven," *LÄ* VI, 1204-1209.

Loretz O., *Qohelet und der Alte Orient* (Freiburg 1964).

Lorton D., "A Note on the Expression *šms-ib*," *JARCE* 7 (1968), 41-54; 8 (1969/1970), 55-57.

—— *The Juridical Terminology of International Relations in Egyptian Texts through the 18th Dyn.* (Baltimore 1974).

—— "The Expression 'Iri Hrw Nfr'," *JARCE* 12 (1975), 23-31.

Luft U., "Zur Einleitung der Liebesgedichte auf Pap. Chester Beatty 1, XVI, 9ff.," *ZÄS* 99 (1973), 108-116.

Lundbom J., and Freedman D.N., "*beṭen*," *TDOT* II, 94-99.

Luyten J., "Psalms 73 and Wisdom," *SAT* 59-81.

Lyons J., *Semantics*, vol. I (Cambridge 1977), 230-335.

Mace A.B., "The Influence of Egypt on Hebrew Literature," *AAA* 9 (1922), 21-23.

Malinine M., Un fragment de l'enseignment d'Amenemhet I, *BIFAO* 34 (1934), 63-74.

Mandelkern S., *Veteris Testamenti Concordantia* (Tel Aviv 1965[6]).

Mandry S.A., *There is No God! A Study on the Fool in the O.T. Particularly in Proverbs and Qoheleth* (Roma 1972).

Martin K., "Uräus," *LÄ* VI, 864-868.

Mayer G., "*'āvāh*," *TDOT* I, 134-137.

—— "*ykḥ*", ibid. VI, 64-71..

McKane W., *Proverbs, OTL* (London 1970).

—— "Functions of Language and Objectives of Discourse according to Prov., 10-30," *SAT* 166-185.

McKay J.W., "Man's Love for God in Deuteronomy and the Father-Teacher, Son-Pupil Relationship," *VT* 22 (1972), 426-435.

McKenzie J.L., "The Elders in the O.T.," *Biblica* 40 (1959), 522-540.

Meltzer E.S., Review of Aling C.F., *Egypt and Bible History; From Earliest Times to 1000 B.C.*, *JSSEA* 12 (1982), 189-192.

Mettinger, T.N.D., *Solomonic State Officials* (Lund-Gleerup 1971).

Meyer E., *Die Israeliten und ihre Nachbarstämme* (Halle a.S. 1906), 446-455.

Misch G., *Geschichte der Autobiographie* (Bern-Frankfurt 1949-1950).

Montet P., *Everyday Life in Egypt*, trans. M. Hyslop, and M.S. Drower (London 1958).

—— *L'Egypte et la Bible, Cahiers d'Archéologie Biblique* 11 (Neuchâtel 1959).

Morenz S., "Ägyptische und davidische Königsliteratur," *ZÄS* 79 (1954), 73-74.

—— "Ägyptologische Beiträge," *SPOA* 63-71.

—— "Eine weitere Spur der Weisheit Amenemopes in der Bibel," *ZÄS* 84 (1959), 79-80.

Morenz S., and Müller D., *Untersuchungen zur Rolle des Schicksals in der ägyptischen Religion* (Berlin 1960).

Morgan D.F., "Wisdom and the Prophets," *Studia Biblica* 1978, ed. E.A. Livingstone (Sheffield 1979), 209-244.

—— *Wisdom in the O.T. Traditions* (Atlanta 1981).

Mosis R., "*pth*," *TWAT* VI, 820-831.

Mowinckel S., "Psalms and Wisdom," *SVT* 3 (1960), 205-224.

Müller D., "Grabausstattung und Totengericht in der Lehre für König Merikare," *ZÄS* 94 (1967), 117-124.

Müller H.P., "Der Begriff 'Rätsel' im A.T.," *VT* 20 (1970), 465-489.

—— "Die weisheitliche Lehrerzählung im A.T. und seiner Umwelt," *WdO* 9 (1977), 77-98.

Müller H.P., Krause M., "*chākham*," *TDOT* IV, 364-385.

Murphy R.E., "A Consideration of the Classification 'Wisdom Psalms'," *SVT* 9 (1963), 156-167.

—— "The Sage in Ecclesiastes and Qoheleth the Sage," *SIANE* 263-271.

Murphy R.E., Carm O., "Wisdom — Theses and Hypotheses," in *Isr. Wisd.*, 35-42.

—— "Hebrew Wisdom," *JAOS* 101/1 (1981), 21-34.

—— *Wisdom Literature, The Forms of the O.T. Literature*, vol. 13 (Michigan 1981).

Nel P., "The Concept of 'Father' in the Wisdom Literature of the Ancient Near East," *JNSL* 5 (1977), 53-66.

—— *The Structure and Ethos of the Wisdom Admonitions in Proverbs* (Berlin-New York 1982).

Niditch S., and Doran R., "The Success Story of the Wise Courtier: A Formal Approach," *JBL* 96/2 (1977), 179-193.

Nir R., *Semantics of Modern Hebrew* (Tel Aviv 1979) (Hebrew).

Noth M., and Thomas D.W., eds., *Wisdom in Israel and the Ancient Near East*, *SVT* 3 (1955).

Ockinga B., "The Burden of Kha'kheperrē'sonbu," *JEA* 69 (1983), 88-95.

Ockinga B.G., Yahya al-Masri, *Two Ramesside Tombs at El Mashayikh*, Part I (Sidney 1988).

Oesterley W.O.E., "The Teaching of Amen-em-ope and the O.T.," *ZAW* 45 (1927), 9-24.

—— *The Book of Proverbs with Introduction and Notes*, *WC* (London 1929).

—— *The Wisdom of Egypt and the O.T., in the Light of the Newly Discovered Teaching of Amen-em-ope* (London 1931²).

Otto E., "Die beide vogelgestaltigen Seelenvorstellungen der Ägypter," *ZÄS* 77 (1942), 78-91.

—— "Bildung und Ausbildung im alten Ägypten," *ZÄS* 81 (1956), 41-48.

Otzen B., "O.T. Wisdom Literature and Dualistic Thinking in Late Judaism," *SVT* 28 (1974), 146-157.

Pedersen J., *Israel, Its Life and Culture*, 4 vols.(Oxford 1973[6]).

Peet T.E., *A Comparative Study of the Literature of Egypt, Palestine and Mesopotamia* (London 1931).

Perdue L.G., "The Riddles of Psalm 49," *JBL* 93(1974), 533-542.

—— *Wisdom and Cult* (Montana 1977).

—— "The Testament of David and Egyptian Royal Instructions," *Scripture in Context II, More Essays on the Comparative Method*, eds. W.W. Hallo, J.C. Moyer, and L.G. Perdue (Indiana 1983), 79-86.

Pezin M., "Fragment de sagesse démotique (P. inv. Sorbonne 1260)," *Enchoria* 11 (1982), 59-61.

Pfeiffer R.H., "Edomic Wisdom," *ZAW* 44 (1926), 13-25.

Piankoff A., *Le "coeur" dans les textes égyptiens* (Paris 1930).

Polk T., "Paradigms, Parables and *Mĕšālîm*: On Reading the *Māšāl* in Scripture," *CBQ* 45 (1988), 564-583.

Polotsky H.J., *Collected Papers* (Jerusalem 1971), 21-27; 43-51; 71-96; 319-338.

Pope M.H., *Job*, *AB*, 1965.

Porter B., "The Structure and Theme of the Solomon Narrative (1 Kings 3-11)," *HUCA* 38 (1967), 93-128.

Posener G., "Section finale d'une sagesse inconnue," *RdE* 7 (1950), 71-84.

—— "Les richesses inconnues de la littérature égyptienne," *RdE* 6 (1951), 27-48.

—— "Ostraca inédits du Musée de Turin," *RdE* 8(1951), 171-189.

—— *Catalogue des ostraca hiératiques littéraires de Deir El-Médineh* II (Cairo 1951-1972), pls. 1-25, 67, 71-73.

—— "Aménémope 21,3 et *bjȝjt* au sens d'oracle," *ZÄS* 90 (1963), 98-102.

—— "L'Expression *bjȝ.t ʿȝ.t* (Ani VI, 12)," *RdE* 16 (1964).

—— "Aménémope 22,9-10 et l'infirmité du crocodile," *Festschrift für S. Schott*, ed. W. Helck (Wiesbaden 1968), 106-111.

—— "Le chapitre 4 d'Aménémope," *ZÄS* 99 (1973), 129-135.

—— "Pour la reconstitution de l'Enseignement d'un homme à son fils," *Rd'E* 36 (1985), 115-119.

Rabin C., "Biblical Semantics: Is it possible?" *Beth Mikra* 7/2 (1962), 17-27 (Hebrew).

Rad G. von, "Josephsgeschichte und ältere Chokma," *SVT* 1 (1953), 120-127.

—— "Hiob 38 und die altägyptische Weisheit," *SVT* 1 (1955), 293-294.

—— "Die Nehemia Denkschrift," *ZAW* 34 (1965), 183-185.

—— *Wisdom in Israel* (London 1972).

—— *Old Testament Theology*, 2 vols. (London 1975).

Rainey A.F., "The Soldier Scribe in Pap. Anastasi I," *JNES* 26 (1967), 58-60.

—— "The Scribe at Ugarit: His Position and Influence," *Proceedings of the Israel Academy of Sciences and Humanities* 3 (1969), 126-146.

Rankin O.S., *Israel's Wisdom Literature* (Edinburgh 1936).

Ranston H., *The O.T. Wisdom Books and Their Teaching* (London 1930).

Redford D.B., *A Study of the Biblical Story of Joseph* (Genesis 37-50) (Leiden 1970).

—— "The Relations Between Egypt and Israel from El-Amarna to the Babylonian Conquest," *Biblical Archaeology Today, Proceedings of the International Congress on Biblical Archeology, Jerusalem, April 1984* (Jerusalem 1985), 192-205.

—— *Egypt and Canaan in the New Kingdom*, *Beer Sheva* 4 (1990), 1-121.

Reider J., "Etymological Studies in Biblical Hebrew," *VT* 2 (1952), 113-130.

Richardson A., ed., *A Theological Word-Book of the Bible* (New York 1960), 144-146.

Richardson H.N., "Some Notes on 'Liz' and Its Derivatives," *VT* 5 (1955), 163-179.

Ringgren H., "*bîn*," *TDOT* II, 99-107.

—— "*b'r*," *TDOT* II, 201-205.

—— *Word and Wisdom, Studies in the Hypostatization of Divine Qualities and Functions in the Ancient Near East* (Uppsala 1947).

Ritner R.K., Review of H.J. Thissen, *Die Lehre des Anchscheschonqi*, *Bibliotheca Orientalis* 44 (1987), 641-646.

Römheld D., *Wege der Weisheit* (Berlin-New York 1989).

Rössler-Köhler U., "*Löwe*," *LÄ* III, 1080-1090.

Rotenberg M., "On the Meaning of *'iwwelet* in Prov.," *Lešonenu* 25 (1960), 201 (Hebrew).

Roth W.M.W., "*nbl*," *VT* 10 (1960), 394-409.

—— *Numerical Sayings in the O.T.*, *SVT* 13 (1965).

Rubins E., "Wisdom from Egypt and Greece," *DE* 1 (1985), 35-41.

Ruffle J., "The Teaching of Amenemope and Its Connection with the Book of Proverbs," *Tyndale Bulletin* 28 (1977), 29-68.

Ruppert L., *Die Josephserzählung der Genesis* (Munich 1965).

—— "*yā'aṣ*," *TDOT* VI, 156-185.

Sanders J.A., "Wisdom at Qumran," *Isr. Wisd.* 277-285.

Sanders J.T., *Ben Sira and Demotic Wisdom*, *SBL* 28 (Chico 1983).

Sawyer J.F.A., "Root-Meaning in Hebrew," *JSS* 12 (1967), 37-50.

—— *Semantics in Biblical Research* (London 1972).

—— "The Historical Description of the Hebrew Root *Yš'*," *Hamito-Semitica*. 75-84.

Scharff A., "Der historische Abschnitt der Lehre für König Merikarê," *Sitzungsberichte der Bayerischen Akademie der Wissenschaften zu München* 8 (1936).

Schlott A., *Schrift und Schreiber im alten Ägypten* (Munich 1989).

Schmid H.H., *Wesen und Geschichte der Weisheit*, *BZAW* 101 (1966).

Schmidt J., *Studien zur Stilistik der Alttestamentlichen Spruchliterature*, *AA* 13/1 (1936).

Schmidt W., "Anthropologische Begriffe im A.T.," *Evangelische Theologie* 24 (1964), 374-388.

Schunck K.D., "*chēmāh*," *TDOT* IV, 462-465.

Scott R.B.Y., *Proverbs, Ecclesiastes*, *AB* (1965).

—— "Solomon and the Beginnings of Wisdom in Israel," *SVT* 3 (1955), 262-279.

—— *The Way of Wisdom in the O.T.* (New York 1971).

—— "Wise and Foolish, Righteous and Wicked," *SVT* 23 (1972), 146-165.

Segal M.Z., *The Complete Book of BS* (Jerusalem 1958²) (Hebrew).

—— "*Ben Sira'*," *EMiqr* II, 162-169 (Hebrew).

Seibert P., *Die Charakteristik*, vol. I, *Ägyptologische Abhandlungen* 17 (Wiesbaden 1967), 68-84; 87-89; 99-189.

Seters J. van, "A Date for the 'Admonitions' in the Second Intermediate Period," *JEA* 50 (1964), 13-23.

Sethe K., *Die Einsetzung des Veziers unter der 18 Dyn.* (Leipzig 1909).

Seybold K., "*gāmal*," *TDOT* III, 23-33.

Shirun-Grumach I., "Remarks on the Goddess Maat," in *Pharaonic Egypt, The Bible and Christianity*, ed. S. Israelit-Groll (Jerusalem 1985), 173-20.

—— "Bemerkungen zu Rythmus, Form und Inhalt in der Weisheit," *SAL* 317-352.

Shisha-Halevy A., "Coptic Translations," *Bible Translation, An Introduction*, ed. C. Rabin, *The Biblical Encyclopaedia Library*, general editor S. Aḥituv (Jerusalem 1984), 129-134 (Hebrew).

—— "*A propos* of a New Edition of the Instructions for King Merikarē," *Orientalia* 49 (1980), 195-198.

Shupak N., "Some Idioms Connected with the Concept of 'Heart' in Egypt and the Bible," in *Pharaonic Egypt*, ed. S. Israelit-Groll (Jerusalem 1983), 202-212.

—— "Egyptian idioms and imprints in Biblical Wisdom," *Tarbiz* 54 (1985), 479-483 (Hebrew).

—— "The *Sitz im Leben* of the Book of Proverbs in the Light of a Comparison of Biblical and Egyptian Wisdom Literature," *RB* 94 (1987), 98-119.

—— "Comparative Aspects of Biblical and Ancient Egyptian Wisdom," *Bulletin of the Israeli Academic Center in Cairo* 11 (1989), 4-11.

—— "Egyptian 'Prophecy' and Biblical Prophecy: Did the Phenomenon of Prophecy, in the Biblical Sense Exist in Ancient Egypt?," *JEOL* 31(1989-1990), 5-40.

—— "Egyptian 'Prophetic' Writings and Biblical Wisdom Literature," *BN* 54 (1990), 81-102.

—— "A New Source for the Study of the Judiciary and Law of Ancient Egypt — 'The Tale of The Eloquent Peasant'," *JNES* 51/1 (1991), 1-18.

Simpson D.C., "The Hebrew Book of Proverbs and the Teaching of Amenophis," *JEA* 12 (1926), 232-235.

Simpson W.K., ed., *The Literature of Ancient Egypt* (New Haven-London 1972).

Skaldny U., *Die ältesten Spruchsammlungen in Israel* (Göttingen 1962).

Smith G.R., "The Story of 'Onchsheshonqy," *Serapis* 6 (1980), 133-155.

Smith M.J., "Weisheit, demotische," *LÄ* VI, 1192-1204.

Smith W.S., "The Relationships between Egyptian Ideas and O.T. Thought," *JBR* 19 (1951), 12-15.

Snaith J.G., *Ecclesiasticus, The Cambridge Bible Commentary* (Cambridge 1974).

Spiegel J., *Das Werden der altägyptischen Hochkultur* (Heidelberg 1953), §§654-707.

Spiegelberg W., "Das Herz als zweites Wesen des Menschen," *ZÄS* 66 (1931), 35-37.

Stevenson W.B., *The Poem of Job* (London 1947), 21-29, 73-76.

Stock H., *'Nṯr Nfr' — Der Gute Gott?* (Hidelsheim 1951).

Stork L., "Ohr," *LÄ* IV, 559-561.

—— "Schlange," *LÄ* V, 644-652.

Story C.I.K., "The Book of Proverbs and Northwest Semitic Literature," *JBL* 64 (1945), 319-337.

Sweet, R.F.G. "The Sage in Mesopotamian Palaces and Royal Courts," *SIANE* 99-107.

Tait W.J., Review of H.J. Thissen, *Die Lehre des Anchscheschonqi* (P.B.M. 10508), *Enchoria* 15 (1987), 233-235.

Talmon S., "Wisdom in the Book of Esther," *VT* 13 (1963), 419-455.

Terrien S., "Job as a Sage," *SIANE* 231-242.

Thissen H.J., Review of M. Lichtheim, *Late Egyptian Wisdom Literature in the International Context*, *Enchoria* 13 (1985), 189-197.

Thomas D.W. "Additional Notes on the Root 'Yada'' in Hebrew," *JTS* 15 (1964), 54-57.
Torczyner H., "The Riddle in the Bible," *HUCA* 1 (1924), 125-149.
Torrey C.C., "The Question of the Original Language of Qoheleth," *JQR* 39 (1948), 151-160.
Toy C.H., *Proverbs, ICC* (1977).
Trumper V.L., *The Mirror of Egypt in the O.T.* (London 1931).
Tur Sinai N.H., *The Book of Job*, 2 vols. (Jerusalem 1901).
—— *Solomon's Proverbs* (Tel Aviv 1907).
—— "Hiob," *EMiqr* I, 241-257 (Hebrew).
—— "*Ḥākām, Ḥokmâ*," *EMiqr* III, 127-133 (Hebrew).
—— "*Ḥîdâ*," *EMiqr* III, 108-111 (Hebrew).
Ullendorff E., "Thought Categories in the Hebrew Bible," *Studies in Rationalism, in Memory of L. Roth*, ed. R. Loewe (London 1966), 275-288.
Ullmanm S., *The Principles of Semantics* (Oxford 1967).
—— *Semantics, An Introduction to the Science of Meaning* (Oxford 1972).
Velde te H., "Seth," *LÄ* V, 908-911.
Vergote J., "La notion de Dieu dans les livres de sagesse égyptiens," *SPOA* 159-190.
—— *Joseph en Egypte: Genèse chap. 37-50 à la lumière des études égyptologiques récentes* (Louvain 1959).
Vernus P., "Littérature et autobiographie, les inscriptions de S3-Mwt surnommé Kyky," *Rd'E* 30 (1978), 115-146.
—— "La date du *Paysan Eloquent*," in *Studies in Egyptology presented to M. Lichtheim*, ed. S. Israelit-Groll (Jerusalem 1990), vol. II, 1033-1047.
Vittmann G., "Zum Verständnis der Weihformel (*irjnf m mnw.f*)," *WZKM* 69 (1971), 21-32.
Volten A., "Der Begriff der Maat in den ägyptischen Weisheitstexten," *SPOA* 73-101.
Vycichl W., "Grundlagen der ägyptische-semitischen Wortvergleichung," *MDAIK* 16 (1958), 367-405.

—— "Studien der ägyptisch-semitischen Wortvergleichung," *ZÄS* 84 (1959), 70-74.

—— "Egyptian and the Other Hamito-Semitic Languages," *Hamito-Semitica* 201-212.

Wagner S., "*'amār*," *TDOT* I, 328-345.

—— "*naṣar*," *TWAT* V, 577-587.

Walcot P., "Hesiod and the Instructions of 'Onchsheshonqy," *JNES* 21 (1962), 215-219..

Walle B. van de, La transmission des textes littéraires égyptiens (Brussels 1948).

—— "Le thème de la satire des métiers dans la littérature égyptienne," *Chronique d'Egypte* 22 (1947), 50-72.

Wallis G., "*chāmadh*," *TDOT* IV, 452-461.

Weinfeld M., "The Dependence of Deuteronomy upon the Wisdom Literature," *Y. Kaufmann Jubilee Volume: Studies in Bible and Jewish Religion, Dedicated to Y. Kaufmann on the Occasion of His 70th Birthday*, ed. M. Haran (Jerusalem 1960), 89-108.

—— *Deuteronomy and the Deuteronomic School* (Oxford 1972).

Wente E.F., "Egyptian 'Make Merry' Song Reconsidered," *JNES* 21 (1962), 118-128.

Westendorf W., "Die Qualitäten des Weisen Neferti" *GM* 4 (1973), 41-44.

Westermann C., "Die Begriffe für Fragen und Suchen in A.T.," *Forschung an A.T.*, vol. II (Munich 1974), 162-190.

—— "Die Menschen als Ebenbilder Pharaos," *GM* 46 (1981), 33-42.

Whybray R.N., *Wisdom in Proverbs, Studies in Biblical Theology* 45 (London 1965).

—— *The Intellectual Tradition in the O.T.* (Berlin-New York 1974).

—— "Yahweh-sayings and Their Contexts in Proverbs 10,1-22,16," *SAT* 153-165.

—— "Wisdom Literature in the Reigns of David and Solomon," *Studies in the Period of David and Solomon and Other Essays*, ed. T. Ishida (Tokyo 1982), 13-26.

—— *Ecclesiastes, New Century Bible Commentary* (London 1989).

—— "The Sage in the Israelite Royal Court," *SIANE* 133-139.

Williams J.G., *Those who Ponder Proverbs: Aphoristic Thinking and Biblical Literature* (Sheffield-Almond 1981).

Williams R.J., "The Alleged Semitic Original of the Wisdom of Amenemope," *JEA* 47 (1961), 100-106.

—— "Reflections on the Lebensmüde," *JEA* 48 (1962), 49-56.

—— "Scribal Training in Ancient Egypt," *JAOS* 92 (1972), 214-221.

—— "A People Come Out of Egypt," *SVT* 28 (1975), 231-252.

—— "The Sages of Ancient Egypt in the Light of Recent Scholarship," *JAOS* 101/1 (1981), 1-19.

—— "Ägypten und Israel," *Theologische Realenzyklopädie* I, 492-505.

—— "Some Egyptianisms in the Old Testament," *Studies in Honour of J.A. Wilson* (Chicago 1969), 93-98.

Wolff H.W., *Anthropologie des A.T.* (Munich 1973), 68-113.

Würthwein E., "Die Weisheit Ägyptens und das A.T.," *Schriften der Philipps-Universität* (Marburg 1960), 3-17.

Yahuda A.S., *The Accuracy of the Bible* (Kingswood 1934).

Yeivin S., "The High Place at Gibeon," *Revue de l'Histoire Juive en Egypte* 1 (1947), 143-147.

Zandee J., "Das Alte Testament im Lichte des Ägyptologie," *Vruchten van de Uithof* (Utrecht 1974), 145-157.

—— "Egyptological Commentary on the O.T.," *Travels in the World of the O.T., Studies Presented to M.A. Beek*, ed. H.G.H. van Vos (Assen 1974), 269-281.

Zarfati G., *Hebrew Semantics* (Jerusalem 1978) (Hebrew).

Zimmerli W., "Zur Struktur der alttestamentlichen Weisheit," *ZAW* 10 (1933), 177-204.

—— "Ort und Grenze der Weisheit im Rahmen der alttestamentlichen Theologie," *SPOA* 121-137.

TERMS INDEX

HEBREW

EGYPTIAN

COPTIC

ARAMAIC

UGARITIC

AKKADIAN

ARABIC

GREEK

SOURCES INDEX

BIBLE AND APOCRYPHA

EGYPTIAN TEXTS

Instruction by a Man for His Son

AKKADIAN TEXTS

WEST SEMITIC TEXTS

QUMRAN

CLASSICAL TEXTS

---

* Only when used as a reference source.

ORBIS BIBLICUS ET ORIENTALIS

Bd. 1 OTTO RICKENBACHER: *Weisheitsperikopen bei Ben Sira.* X–214–15* Seiten. 1973. Vergriffen.

Bd. 2 FRANZ SCHNIDER: *Jesus der Prophet.* 298 Seiten. 1973. Vergriffen.

Bd. 3 PAUL ZINGG: *Das Wachsen der Kirche.* Beiträge zur Frage der lukanischen Redaktion und Theologie. 345 Seiten. 1974. Vergriffen.

Bd. 4 KARL JAROŠ: *Die Stellung des Elohisten zur kanaanäischen Religion.* 294 Seiten, 12 Abbildungen. 1982. 2. verbesserte und überarbeitete Auflage.

Bd. 5 OTHMAR KEEL: *Wirkmächtige Siegeszeichen im Alten Testament.* Ikonographische Studien zu Jos 8, 18–26; Ex 17, 8–13; 2 Kön 13, 14–19 und 1 Kön 22, 11. 232 Seiten, 78 Abbildungen. 1974. Vergriffen.

Bd. 6 VITUS HUONDER: *Israel Sohn Gottes.* Zur Deutung eines alttestamentlichen Themas in der jüdischen Exegese des Mittelalters. 231 Seiten. 1975.

Bd. 7 RAINER SCHMITT: *Exodus und Passa. Ihr Zusammenhang im Alten Testament.* 124 Seiten. 1982. 2. neubearbeitete Auflage.

Bd. 8 ADRIAN SCHENKER: *Hexaplarische Psalmenbruchstücke.* Die hexaplarischen Psalmenfragmente der Handschriften Vaticanus graecus 752 und Canonicianus graecus 62. Einleitung, Ausgabe, Erläuterung. XXVIII–446 Seiten. 1975.

Bd. 9 BEAT ZUBER: *Vier Studien zu den Ursprüngen Israels.* Die Sinaifrage und Probleme der Volks- und Traditionsbildung. 152 Seiten. 1976. Vergriffen.

Bd. 10 EDUARDO ARENS: *The ΗΛΘΟΝ-Sayings in the Synoptic Tradition.* A Historico-critical Investigation. 370 Seiten. 1976.

Bd. 11 KARL JAROŠ: *Sichem.* Eine archäologische und religionsgeschichtliche Studie, mit besonderer Berücksichtigung von Jos 24. 280 Seiten, 193 Abbildungen. 1976.

Bd. 11a KARL JAROŠ/BRIGITTE DECKERT: *Studien zur Sichem-Area.* 81 Seiten, 23 Abbildungen. 1977.

Bd. 12 WALTER BÜHLMANN: *Vom rechten Reden und Schweigen.* Studien zu Proverbien 10–31. 371 Seiten. 1976. Vergriffen.

Bd. 13 IVO MEYER: *Jeremia und die falschen Propheten.* 155 Seiten. 1977. Vergriffen.

Bd. 14 OTHMAR KEEL: *Vögel als Boten.* Studien zu Ps 68, 12–14, Gen 8, 6–12, Koh 10, 20 und dem Aussenden von Botenvögeln in Ägypten. – Mit einem Beitrag von Urs Winter zu Ps 56, 1 und zur Ikonographie der Göttin mit der Taube. 164 Seiten, 44 Abbildungen. 1977. Vergriffen.

Bd. 15 MARIE-LOUISE GUBLER: *Die frühesten Deutungen des Todes Jesu.* Eine motivgeschichtliche Darstellung aufgrund der neueren exegetischen Forschung. XVI–424 Seiten. 1977. Vergriffen.

Bd. 16 JEAN ZUMSTEIN: *La condition du croyant dans l'Evangile selon Matthieu.* 467 pages. 1977. Epuisé.

Bd. 17 FRANZ SCHNIDER: *Die verlorenen Söhne.* Strukturanalytische und historisch-kritische Untersuchungen zu Lk 15. 105 Seiten. 1977.

Bd. 18 HEINRICH VALENTIN: *Aaron.* Eine Studie zur vor-priesterschriftlichen Aaron-Überlieferung. VIII–441 Seiten. 1978.

Bd. 19 MASSÉO CALOZ: *Etude sur la LXX origénienne du Psautier.* Les relations entre les leçons des Psaumes du Manuscrit Coislin 44, les Fragments des Hexaples et le texte du Psautier Gallican. 480 pages. 1978.

Bd. 20 RAPHAEL GIVEON: *The Impact of Egypt on Canaan.* Iconographical and Related Studies. 156 Seiten, 73 Abbildungen. 1978.

Bd. 21 DOMINIQUE BARTHÉLEMY: *Etudes d'histoire du texte de l'Ancien Testament.* XXV–419 pages. 1978. Epuisé.

Bd. 22/1 CESLAS SPICQ: *Notes de Lexicographie néo-testamentaire.* Tome I: p. 1–524. 1978. Epuisé.

Bd. 22/2 CESLAS SPICQ: *Notes de Lexicographie néo-testamentaire.* Tome II: p. 525–980. 1978. Epuisé.

Bd. 22/3 CESLAS SPICQ: *Notes de Lexicographie néo-testamentaire.* Supplément. 698 pages. 1982.

Bd. 23 BRIAN M. NOLAN: *The Royal Son of God.* The Christology of Matthew 1–2 in the Setting of the Gospel. 282 Seiten. 1979. Out of print.

Bd. 24 KLAUS KIESOW: *Exodustexte im Jesajabuch.* Literarkritische und motivgeschichtliche Analysen. 221 Seiten. 1979. Vergriffen.

Bd. 25/1 MICHAEL LATTKE: *Die Oden Salomos in ihrer Bedeutung für Neues Testament und Gnosis.* Band I. Ausführliche Handschriftenbeschreibung. Edition mit deutscher Parallel-Übersetzung. Hermeneutischer Anhang zur gnostischen Interpretation der Oden Salomos in der Pistis Sophia. XI–237 Seiten. 1979.

Bd. 25/1a MICHAEL LATTKE: *Die Oden Salomos in ihrer Bedeutung für Neues Testament und Gnosis.* Band Ia. Der syrische Text der Edition in Estrangela Faksimile des griechischen Papyrus Bodmer XI. 68 Seiten. 1980.

Bd. 25/2 MICHAEL LATTKE: *Die Oden Salomos in ihrer Bedeutung für Neues Testament und Gnosis.* Band II. Vollständige Wortkonkordanz zur handschriftlichen, griechischen, koptischen, lateinischen und syrischen Überlieferung der Oden Salomos. Mit einem Faksimile des Kodex N. XVI–201 Seiten. 1979.

Bd. 25/3 MICHAEL LATTKE: *Die Oden Salomos in ihrer Bedeutung für Neues Testament und Gnosis.* Band III. XXXIV–478 Seiten. 1986.

Bd. 26 MAX KÜCHLER: *Frühjüdische Weisheitstraditionen.* Zum Fortgang weisheitlichen Denkens im Bereich des frühjüdischen Jahweglaubens. 703 Seiten. 1979. Vergriffen.

Bd. 27 JOSEF M. OESCH: *Petucha und Setuma.* Untersuchungen zu einer überlieferten Gliederung im hebräischen Text des Alten Testaments. XX–392–37* Seiten. 1979.

Bd. 28 ERIK HORNUNG/OTHMAR KEEL (Herausgeber): *Studien zu altägyptischen Lebenslehren.* 394 Seiten. 1979.

Bd. 29 HERMANN ALEXANDER SCHLÖGL: *Der Gott Tatenen.* Nach Texten und Bildern des Neuen Reiches. 216 Seiten, 14 Abbildungen. 1980.

Bd. 30 JOHANN JAKOB STAMM: *Beiträge zur Hebräischen und Altorientalischen Namenkunde.* XVI–264 Seiten. 1980.

Bd. 31 HELMUT UTZSCHNEIDER: *Hosea - Prophet vor dem Ende.* Zum Verhältnis von Geschichte und Institution in der alttestamentlichen Prophetie. 260 Seiten. 1980.

Bd. 32 PETER WEIMAR: *Die Berufung des Mose.* Literaturwissenschaftliche Analyse von Exodus 2, 23–5, 5. 402 Seiten. 1980.

Bd. 33 OTHMAR KEEL: *Das Böcklein in der Milch seiner Mutter und Verwandtes.* Im Lichte eines altorientalischen Bildmotivs. 163 Seiten, 141 Abbildungen. 1980.

Bd. 34 PIERRE AUFFRET: *Hymnes d'Egypte et d'Israël.* Etudes de structures littéraires. 316 pages, 1 illustration. 1981.

Bd. 35 ARIE VAN DER KOOIJ: *Die alten Textzeugen des Jesajabuches.* Ein Beitrag zur Textgeschichte des Alten Testaments. 388 Seiten. 1981.

Bd. 36 CARMEL McCARTHY: *The Tiqqune Sopherim and Other Theological Corrections in the Masoretic Text of the Old Testament.* 280 Seiten. 1981.

Bd. 37 BARBARA L. BEGELSBACHER-FISCHER: *Untersuchungen zur Götterwelt des Alten Reiches im Spiegel der Privatgräber der IV. und V. Dynastie.* 336 Seiten. 1981.

Bd. 38 MÉLANGES DOMINIQUE BARTHÉLEMY. *Etudes bibliques offertes à l'occasion de son 60e anniversaire.* Edités par Pierre Casetti, Othmar Keel et Adrian Schenker. 724 pages, 31 illustrations. 1981.

Bd. 39 ANDRÉ LEMAIRE: *Les écoles et la formation de la Bible dans l'ancien Israël.* 142 pages, 14 illustrations. 1981.

Bd. 40 JOSEPH HENNINGER: *Arabica Sacra.* Aufsätze zur Religionsgeschichte Arabiens und seiner Randgebiete. Contributions à l'histoire religieuse de l'Arabie et de ses régions limitrophes. 347 Seiten. 1981.

Bd. 41 DANIEL VON ALLMEN: *La famille de Dieu.* La symbolique familiale dans le paulinisme. LXVII–330 pages, 27 planches. 1981.

Bd. 42 ADRIAN SCHENKER: *Der Mächtige im Schmelzofen des Mitleids.* Eine Interpretation von 2 Sam 24. 92 Seiten. 1982.

Bd. 43 PAUL DESELAERS: *Das Buch Tobit.* Studien zu seiner Entstehung, Komposition und Theologie. 532 Seiten + Übersetzung 16 Seiten. 1982.

Bd. 44 PIERRE CASETTI: *Gibt es ein Leben vor dem Tod?* Eine Auslegung von Psalm 49. 315 Seiten. 1982.

Bd. 45 FRANK-LOTHAR HOSSFELD: *Der Dekalog.* Seine späten Fassungen, die originale Komposition und seine Vorstufen. 308 Seiten. 1982. Vergriffen.

Bd. 46 ERIK HORNUNG: *Der ägyptische Mythos von der Himmelskuh.* Eine Ätiologie des Unvollkommenen. Unter Mitarbeit von Andreas Brodbeck, Hermann Schlögl und Elisabeth Staehelin und mit einem Beitrag von Gerhard Fecht. XII–129 Seiten, 10 Abbildungen. 1991. 2. ergänzte Auflage.

Bd. 47 PIERRE CHERIX: *Le Concept de Notre Grande Puissance (CG VI, 4).* Texte, remarques philologiques, traduction et notes. XIV–95 pages. 1982.

Bd. 48 JAN ASSMANN/WALTER BURKERT/FRITZ STOLZ: *Funktionen und Leistungen des Mythos.* Drei altorientalische Beispiele. 118 Seiten, 17 Abbildungen. 1982. Vergriffen.

Bd. 49 PIERRE AUFFRET: *La sagesse a bâti sa maison.* Etudes de structures littéraires dans l'Ancien Testament et spécialement dans les psaumes. 580 pages. 1982.

Bd. 50/1 DOMINIQUE BARTHÉLEMY: *Critique textuelle de l'Ancien Testament.* 1. Josué, Juges, Ruth, Samuel, Rois, Chroniques, Esdras, Néhémie, Esther. Rapport final du Comité pour l'analyse textuelle de l'Ancien Testament hébreu institué par l'Alliance Biblique Universelle, établi en coopération avec Alexander R. Hulst †, Norbert Lohfink, William D. McHardy, H. Peter Rüger, coéditeur, James A. Sanders, coéditeur. 812 pages. 1982.

Bd. 50/2 DOMINIQUE BARTHÉLEMY: *Critique textuelle de l'Ancien Testament.* 2. Isaïe, Jérémie, Lamentations. Rapport final du Comité pour l'analyse textuelle de l'Ancien Testament hébreu institué par l'Alliance Biblique Universelle, établi en coopération avec Alexander R. Hulst †, Norbert Lohfink, William D. McHardy, H. Peter Rüger, coéditeur, James A. Sanders, coéditeur. 1112 pages. 1986.

Bd. 50/3 DOMINIQUE BARTHÉLEMY: *Critique textuelle de l'Ancien Testament.* Tome 3. Ézéchiel, Daniel et les 12 Prophètes. Rapport final du Comité pour l'analyse textuelle de l'Ancien Testament hébreu institué par l'Alliance Biblique Universelle, établi en coopération avec Alexander R. Hulst†, Norbert Lohfink, William D. McHardy, H. Peter Rüger†, coéditeur, James A. Sanders, coéditeur. 1424 pages. 1992.

Bd. 51 JAN ASSMANN: *Re und Amun.* Die Krise des polytheistischen Weltbilds im Ägypten der 18.–20. Dynastie. XII–309 Seiten. 1983. Vergriffen.

Bd. 52 MIRIAM LICHTHEIM: *Late Egyptian Wisdom Literature in the International Context.* A Study of Demotic Instructions. X–240 Seiten. 1983.

Bd. 53 URS WINTER: *Frau und Göttin.* Exegetische und ikonographische Studien zum weiblichen Gottesbild im Alten Israel und in dessen Umwelt. XVIII–928 Seiten, 520 Abbildungen. 1987. 2. Auflage. Mit einem Nachwort zur 2. Auflage.

Bd. 54 PAUL MAIBERGER: *Topographische und historische Untersuchungen zum Sinaiproblem.* Worauf beruht die Identifizierung des Ǧabal Mūsā mit dem Sinai? 189 Seiten, 13 Tafeln. 1984.

Bd. 55 PETER FREI/KLAUS KOCH: *Reichsidee und Reichsorganisation im Perserreich.* 119 Seiten, 17 Abbildungen. 1984. Vergriffen. Neuauflage in Vorbereitung.

Bd. 56 HANS-PETER MÜLLER: *Vergleich und Metapher im Hohenlied.* 59 Seiten. 1984.

Bd. 57 STEPHEN PISANO: *Additions or Omissions in the Books of Samuel.* The Significant Pluses and Minuses in the Massoretic, LXX and Qumran Texts. XIV–295 Seiten. 1984.

Bd. 58 ODO CAMPONOVO: *Königtum, Königsherrschaft und Reich Gottes in den Frühjüdischen Schriften.* XVI–492 Seiten. 1984.

Bd. 59 JAMES KARL HOFFMEIER: *Sacred in the Vocabulary of Ancient Egypt.* The Term *ḎSR,* with Special Reference to Dynasties I–XX. XXIV–281 Seiten, 24 Figures. 1985.

Bd. 60 CHRISTIAN HERRMANN: *Formen für ägyptische Fayencen.* Katalog der Sammlung des Biblischen Instituts der Universität Freiburg Schweiz und einer Privatsammlung. XXVIII-199 Seiten. Mit zahlreichen Abbildungen im Text und 30 Tafeln. 1985.

Bd. 61 HELMUT ENGEL: *Die Susanna-Erzählung.* Einleitung, Übersetzung und Kommentar zum Septuaginta-Text und zur Theodition-Bearbeitung. 205 Seiten + Anhang 11 Seiten. 1985.

Bd. 62 ERNST KUTSCH: *Die chronologischen Daten des Ezechielbuches.* 82 Seiten. 1985.

Bd. 63 MANFRED HUTTER: *Altorientalische Vorstellungen von der Unterwelt.* Literar- und religionsgeschichtliche Überlegungen zu «Nergal und Ereškigal». VIII–187 Seiten. 1985.

Bd. 64 HELGA WEIPPERT/KLAUS SEYBOLD/MANFRED WEIPPERT: *Beiträge zur prophetischen Bildsprache in Israel und Assyrien.* IX–93 Seiten. 1985.

Bd. 65 ABDEL-AZIZ FAHMY SADEK: *Contribution à l'étude de l'Amdouat.* Les variantes tardives du Livre de l'Amdouat dans les papyrus du Musée du Caire. XVI–400 pages, 175 illustrations. 1985.

Bd. 66 HANS-PETER STÄHLI: *Solare Elemente im Jahweglauben des Alten Testamentes.* X–60 Seiten. 1985.

Bd. 67 OTHMAR KEEL / SILVIA SCHROER: *Studien zu den Stempelsiegeln aus Palästina/Israel.* Band I. 115 Seiten, 103 Abbildungen. 1985.

Bd. 68 WALTER BEYERLIN: *Weisheitliche Vergewisserung mit Bezug auf den Zionskult.* Studien zum 125. Psalm. 96 Seiten. 1985.

Bd. 69 RAPHAEL VENTURA: *Living in a City of the Dead.* A Selection of Topographical and Administrative Terms in the Documents of the Theban Necropolis. XII–232 Seiten. 1986.

Bd. 70 CLEMENS LOCHER: *Die Ehre einer Frau in Israel.* Exegetische und rechtsvergleichende Studien zu Dtn 22, 13–21. XVIII–464 Seiten. 1986.

Bd. 71 HANS-PETER MATHYS: *Liebe deinen Nächsten wie dich selbst.* Untersuchungen zum alttestamentlichen Gebot der Nächstenliebe (Lev 19,18). XII–204 Seiten. 1990. 2. verbesserte Auflage.

Bd. 72 FRIEDRICH ABITZ: *Ramses III. in den Gräbern seiner Söhne.* 156 Seiten, 31 Abbildungen. 1986.

Bd. 73 DOMINIQUE BARTHÉLEMY/DAVID W. GOODING/JOHAN LUST/EMANUEL TOV: *The Story of David and Goliath.* 160 Seiten. 1986.

Bd. 74 SILVIA SCHROER: *In Israel gab es Bilder.* Nachrichten von darstellender Kunst im Alten Testament. XVI–553 Seiten, 146 Abbildungen. 1987.

Bd. 75 ALAN R. SCHULMAN: *Ceremonial Execution and Public Rewards.* Some Historical Scenes on New Kingdom Private Stelae. 296 Seiten, 41 Abbildungen. 1987.

Bd. 76 JOŽE KRAŠOVEC: *La justice (Ṣdq) de Dieu dans la Bible hébraïque et l'interprétation juive et chrétienne.* 456 pages. 1988.

Bd. 77 HELMUT UTZSCHNEIDER: *Das Heiligtum und das Gesetz.* Studien zur Bedeutung der sinaitischen Heiligtumstexte (Ez 25–40; Lev 8–9). XIV–326 Seiten. 1988.

Bd. 78 BERNARD GOSSE: *Isaie 13,1-14,23.* Dans la tradition littéraire du livre d'Isaïe et dans la tradition des oracles contre les nations. 308 pages. 1988.

Bd. 79 INKE W. SCHUMACHER: *Der Gott Sopdu - Der Herr der Fremdländer.* XVI–364 Seiten, 6 Abbildungen. 1988.

Bd. 80 HELLMUT BRUNNER: *Das hörende Herz.* Kleine Schriften zur Religions- und Geistesgeschichte Ägyptens. Herausgegeben von Wolfgang Röllig. 449 Seiten, 55 Abbildungen. 1988.

Bd. 81 WALTER BEYERLIN: *Bleilot, Brecheisen oder was sonst?* Revision einer Amos-Vision. 68 Seiten. 1988.

Bd. 82 MANFRED HUTTER: *Behexung, Entsühnung und Heilung.* Das Ritual der Tunnawiya für ein Königspaar aus mittelhethitischer Zeit (KBo XXI 1 – KUB IX 34 – KBo XXI 6). 186 Seiten. 1988.

Bd. 83 RAPHAEL GIVEON: *Scarabs from Recent Excavations in Israel.* 114 Seiten. Mit zahlreichen Abbildungen im Text und 9 Tafeln. 1988.

Bd. 84 MIRIAM LICHTHEIM: *Ancient Egyptian Autobiographies chiefly of the Middle Kingdom.* A Study and an Anthology. 200 Seiten, 10 Seiten Abbildungen. 1988.

Bd. 85 ECKART OTTO: *Rechtsgeschichte der Redaktionen im Kodex Ešnunna und im «Bundesbuch».* Eine redaktionsgeschichtliche und rechtsvergleichende Studie zu altbabylonischen und altisraelitischen Rechtsüberlieferungen. 220 Seiten. 1989.

Bd. 86 ANDRZEJ NIWIŃSKI: *Studies on the Illustrated Theban Funerary Papyri of the 11th and 10th Centuries B.C.* 488 Seiten, 80 Seiten Tafeln. 1989.

Bd. 87 URSULA SEIDL: *Die babylonischen Kudurru-Reliefs.* Symbole mesopotamischer Gottheiten. 236 Seiten, 33 Tafeln und 2 Tabellen. 1989.

Bd. 88 OTHMAR KEEL/HILDI KEEL-LEU/SILVIA SCHROER: *Studien zu den Stempelsiegeln aus Palästina/Israel.* Band II. 364 Seiten, 652 Abbildungen. 1989.

Bd. 89 FRIEDRICH ABITZ: *Baugeschichte und Dekoration des Grabes Ramses' VI.* 202 Seiten, 39 Abbildungen. 1989.

Bd. 90 JOSEPH HENNINGER SVD: *Arabica varia.* Aufsätze zur Kulturgeschichte Arabiens und seiner Randgebiete. Contributions à l'histoire culturelle de l'Arabie et de ses régions limitrophes. 504 Seiten. 1989.

Bd. 91 GEORG FISCHER: *Jahwe unser Gott.* Sprache, Aufbau und Erzähltechnik in der Berufung des Mose (Ex. 3–4). 276 Seiten. 1989.

Bd. 92 MARK A. O'BRIEN: *The Deuteronomistic History Hypothesis:* A Reassessment. 340 Seiten. 1989.

Bd. 93 WALTER BEYERLIN: *Reflexe der Amosvisionen im Jeremiabuch.* 120 Seiten. 1989.

Bd. 94 ENZO CORTESE: *Josua 13–21.* Ein priesterschriftlicher Abschnitt im deuteronomistischen Geschichtswerk. 136 Seiten. 1990.

Bd. 95 ERIK HORNUNG (Herausgeber): *Zum Bild Ägyptens im Mittelalter und in der Renaissance. Comment se représente-t-on l'Egypte au Moyen Age et à la Renaissance.* 268 Seiten. 1990.

Bd. 96 ANDRÉ WIESE: *Zum Bild des Königs auf ägyptischen Siegelamuletten.* 264 Seiten. Mit zahlreichen Abbildungen im Text und 32 Tafeln. 1990.

Bd. 97 WOLFGANG ZWICKEL: *Räucherkult und Räuchergeräte.* Exegetische und archäologische Studien zum Räucheropfer im Alten Testament. 372 Seiten. Mit zahlreichen Abbildungen im Text. 1990.

Bd. 98 AARON SCHART: *Mose und Israel im Konflikt.* Eine redaktionsgeschichtliche Studie zu den Wüstenerzählungen. 296 Seiten. 1990.

Bd. 99 THOMAS RÖMER: *Israels Väter.* Untersuchungen zur Väterthematik im Deuteronomium und in der deuteronomistischen Tradition. 664 Seiten. 1990.

Bd. 100 OTHMAR KEEL/MENAKHEM SHUVAL/CHRISTOPH UEHLINGER: *Studien zu den Stempelsiegeln aus Palästina/Israel.* Band III. Die Frühe Eisenzeit. Ein Workshop. XIV–456 Seiten. Mit zahlreichen Abbildungen im Text und 22 Tafeln. 1990.

Bd. 101 CHRISTOPH UEHLINGER: *Weltreich und «eine Rede».* Eine neue Deutung der sogenannten Turmbauerzählung (Gen 11,1–9). XVI–654 Seiten. 1990.

Bd. 102 BENJAMIN SASS: *Studia Alphabetica.* On the Origin and Early History of the Northwest Semitic, South Semitic and Greek Alphabets. X–120 Seiten. 16 Seiten Abbildungen. 2 Tabellen. 1991.

Bd. 103 ADRIAN SCHENKER: *Text und Sinn im Alten Testament.* Textgeschichtliche und bibeltheologische Studien. VIII–312 Seiten. 1991.

Bd. 104 DANIEL BODI: *The Book of Ezekiel and the Poem of Erra.* IV–332 Seiten. 1991.

Bd. 105 YUICHI OSUMI: *Die Kompositionsgeschichte des Bundesbuches Exodus 20,22b–23,33.* XII–284 Seiten. 1991.

Bd. 106 RUDOLF WERNER: *Kleine Einführung ins Hieroglyphen-Luwische.* XII–112 Seiten. 1991.

Bd. 107 THOMAS STAUBLI: *Das Image der Nomaden im Alten Israel und in der Ikonographie seiner sesshaften Nachbarn.* XII–408 Seiten. 145 Abb. und 3 Falttafeln. 1991.

Bd. 108 MOSHÉ ANBAR: *Les tribus amurrites de Mari.* VIII–256 Seiten. 1991.

Bd. 109 GÉRARD J. NORTON/STEPHEN PISANO (eds.): *Tradition of the Text.* Studies offered to Dominique Barthélemy in Celebration of his 70th Birthday. 336 Seiten. 1991.

Bd. 110 HILDI KEEL-LEU: *Vorderasiatische Stempelsiegel.* Die Sammlung des Biblischen Instituts der Universität Freiburg Schweiz. 180 Seiten. 24 Tafeln. 1991.

Bd. 111 NORBERT LOHFINK: *Die Väter Israels im Deuteronomium.* Mit einer Stellungnahme von Thomas Römer. 152 Seiten. 1991.

Bd. 112 EDMUND HERMSEN: *Die zwei Wege des Jenseits.* Das altägyptische Zweiwegebuch und seine Topographie. XII–282 Seiten, 1 mehrfarbige und 19 Schwarz-weiss-Abbildungen. 1992.

Bd. 113 CHARLES MAYSTRE: *Les grands prêtres de Ptah de Memphis.* XIV–474 pages, 2 planches. 1992.

Bd. 114 THOMAS SCHNEIDER: *Asiatische Personennamen in ägyptischen Quellen des Neuen Reiches.* 480 Seiten. 1992.

Bd. 115 ECKHARD VON NORDHEIM: *Die Selbstbehauptung Israels in der Welt des Alten Orients.* Religionsgeschichtlicher Vergleich anhand von Gen 15/22/28, dem Aufenthalt Israels in Ägypten, 2 Sam 7, 1 Kön 19 und Psalm 104. 240 Seiten. 1992.

Bd. 116 DONALD M. MATTHEWS: *The Kassite Glyptic of Nippur.* 208 Seiten. 210 Abbildungen. 1992.

Bd. 117 FIONA V. RICHARDS: *Scarab Seals from a Middle to Late Bronze Age Tomb at Pella in Jordan.* XII–152 Seiten, 16 Tafeln. 1992.

Bd. 118 YOHANAN GOLDMAN: *Prophétie et royauté au retour de l'exil. Les origines littéraires de la forme massorétique du livre de Jérémie.* XIV–270 pages. 1992.

Bd. 119 THOMAS M. KRAPF: *Die Priesterschrift und die vorexilische Zeit. Yehezkel Kaufmanns vernachlässigter Beitrag zur Geschichte der biblischen Religion.* XX-364 Seiten. 1992.

Bd. 120 MIRIAM LICHTHEIM: *Maat in Egyptian Autobiographies and Related Studies.* 236 Seiten, 8 Tafeln. 1992.

Bd. 121 ULRICH HÜBNER: *Spiele und Spielzeug im antiken Palästina.* 256 Seiten. 58 Abbildungen. 1992.

Bd. 122 OTHMAR KEEL: *Das Recht der Bilder, gesehen zu werden. Drei Fallstudien zur Methode der Interpretation altorientalischer Bilder.* 332 Seiten, 286 Abbildungen. 1992.

Bd. 123 WOLFGANG ZWICKEL (Hrsg.): *Biblische Welten. Festschrift für Martin Metzger zu seinem 65. Geburtstag.* 268 Seiten, 19 Abbildungen. 1993.

Bd. 124 AHMED FERJAOUI: *Recherches sur les relations entre l'Orient phénicien et Carthage.* 528 pages, 57 planches. 1993.

Bd. 125 BENJAMIN SASS/CHRISTOPH UEHLINGER (eds.): *Studies in the Iconography of Northwest Semitic Inscribed Seals. Proceedings of a symposium held in Fribourg on April 17-20, 1991.* 368 pages, 532 illustrations. 1993.

Bd. 126 RÜDIGER BARTELMUS/THOMAS KRÜGER/HELMUT UTZSCHNEIDER (Hrsg.): *Konsequente Traditionsgeschichte. Festschrift für Klaus Baltzer zum 65. Geburtstag.* 418 Seiten. 1993.

Bd. 127 ASKOLD I. IVANTCHIK: *Les Cimmériens au Proche-Orient.* 336 pages. 1993.

Bd. 128 JENS VOß: *Die Menora. Gestalt und Funktion des Leuchters im Tempel zu Jerusalem.* 124 Seiten. 1993.

Bd. 129 BERND JANOWSKI/KLAUS KOCH/GERNOT WILHELM (Hrsg.): *Religionsgeschichtliche Beziehungen zwischen Kleinasien, Nordsyrien und dem Alten Testament. Internationales Symposion Hamburg 17.–21. März 1990.* 572 Seiten. 1993.

Bd. 130 NILI SHUPAK: *Where can Wisdom be found?* The Sage's Language in the Bible and in Ancient Egyptian Literature. XXXII–516 pages. 1993.

Sonderband PASCAL ATTINGER: *Eléments de linguistique sumérienne. La construction de* du_{11}*/e/di «dire».* 816 pages. 1993.

UNIVERSITÄTSVERLAG FREIBURG SCHWEIZ

English Summary

In the comparative study of Egyptian and Biblical literature emphasis has been laid on content and ideas, while the formal and terminological aspects have been neglected. The present work deals with the semantics of terminology in Biblical wisdom literature as compared to that of the Egyptians and centers, therefore, on a somewhat abandoned aspect of the comparative research of the Biblical and Egyptian writings. The work has three primary objectives: (a) to draw up a glossary of Egyptian wisdom terms, a task as yet not undertaken elsewhere; (b) to elucidate the semantics of these terms; (c) to clarify the Biblical wisdom terms in relation to their Egyptian parallels. The fresh comparative inquiry into Hebrew and Egyptian wisdom vocabulary sheds light on some general problems intrinsic to Biblical wisdom, e.g.: Does the Hebrew sage *(ḥākām)* signify a function or a quality? Did Hebrew wisdom evolve from a secular to a religious stage? What was the Sitz im Leben of Biblical wisdom?